Response Times

OXFORD PSYCHOLOGY SERIES

EDITORS
DONALD E. BROADBENT
JAMES L. McGAUGH
NICHOLAS J. MACKINTOSH
MICHAEL I. POSNER
ENDEL TULVING
LAWRENCE WEISKRANTZ

RESPONSE TIMES

Their Role in Inferring
Elementary Mental Organization

R. DUNCAN LUCE

Victor S. Thomas Professor of Psychology
Harvard University

OXFORD PSYCHOLOGY SERIES NO. 8

OXFORD UNIVERSITY PRESS   *NEW YORK*
CLARENDON PRESS   *OXFORD*
1986

Oxford University Press

Oxford   New York   Toronto
Delhi   Bombay   Calcutta   Madras   Karachi
Petaling Jaya   Singapore   Hong Kong   Tokyo
Nairobi   Dar es Salaam   Cape Town
Melbourne   Auckland

and associated companies in
Beirut   Berlin   Ibadan   Nicosia

Library of Congress Cataloging-in-Publication Data
Luce, R. Duncan (Robert Duncan)
  Response times: their role in inferring elementary mental organization.
  (Oxford psychology series; no. 8)
  Bibliography: p.
  Includes indexes.
  1. Reaction-time—Mathematical models. 2. Psychology, Experimental.
I. Title. II. Series. [DNLM: 1. Mental Processes.
2. Models, Theoretical. 3. Reaction Time. BF 317 L935r]
BF317.L83   1986   153.4   85-15396
ISBN 0-19-503642-5

Printed in Northern Ireland
at the Universities Press, Belfast
Bound at the University Printing House, Oxford
by David Stanford, Printer to the University

Printing (last digit): 9 8 7 6 5 4 3 2 1

Dedicated to Those of My Ph.D. Students
Who Have Contributed to Our Understanding
of Response Times:

Stephen L. Burbeck

Robert T. Ollman

Joan Gay Snodgrass

Saul Sternberg

Brian A. Wandell

Preface

For almost as long as I have been doing research, response times have struck me as a fascinating, albeit tricky, source of information about how the mind is organized. Whenever I teach mathematical psychology or psychophysics, I include a dose of response times along with the repeated admonition that we surely do not understand a choice process very thoroughly until we can account for the time required for it to be carried out. When I came to Harvard in 1976 I offered, for the first time, a seminar-course on the subject (in style more a course, in size more a seminar), first with David Green and later alone. It was only then that I felt a need for a more systematic mastery of the field, and in academic 80–81 when I had a sabbatical leave, the Guggenheim Foundation agreed to support my self-education and the beginnings of this book.

Gradually, with much rewriting and reorganization as I came better to know those parts of the area I had previously slighted, the book has evolved. It has been four years in the making, slowed considerably by two facts: that I was department chairman during three of those years and that I have maintained an active research program, with Louis Narens, in axiomatic measurement theory.

My attempt is a critical, but even-handed, treatment of the major themes of how response times play a role in out thinking about the mind. I am quite aware of my tendency, apparently not wholly idiosyncratic, to be more protective of and sensitive to the nuances of those topics in whose birth and nurturing I have participated. I can only hope that the reader will discount my biases accordingly.

One bias, not easily overlooked since it pervades the book, is my preference for hypotheses formulated as explicit mathematical models and for developing their logical implications for experiments. That fact necessarily raises questions of mathematical prerequisites and about the general mathematical level of the book. Let me try to answer that explicitly. I assume familiarity with elementary calculus and with elementary probability theory, both of which are used freely as needed. Chapter 1 attempts to outline all of the probability ideas that are used, and I believe that with some diligence on the part of the reader, it should suffice for all but small parts of Chapters 3 and 4, much of Chapters 8 and 9, the first part of Chapter 11, and all of Appendix A. Within the rest of the book, there are extensive empirical sections that demand nothing beyond logarithms, power functions, and the like. This least mathematical material includes all of Chapters 2 and 6, a good deal of Chapter 10, and parts of Chapters 11 and 12. So, put another way, the book really lives at three different mathematical levels, and the reader can expect to learn something additional at each level.

The work has benefited greatly from the contributions of others. Most important is what my students, both in seminar and doing Ph.D. dissertations, have taught me. As the book has developed, some students and professional colleagues have been exposed to early drafts and have provided feedback. Especially important were two sources of comments. One was the incisive and accurate marginal notes of Donald Laming who, more often than I like to admit, rooted out errors in my text and took reasoned exception to my views. I have gratefully corrected the errors, but my views have not always proved equally responsive. The other was a series of seminars conducted at the Bell Telephone Laboratories in Murray Hill, N.J., under the auspices of Saul Sternberg. His enormous erudition and analytical ability have led to marked improvements in both coverage and interpretation. Beyond his comments, those of several who participated in the seminar were of immense value to me and deserve explicit mention: George W. Furnas, James C. Johnson, Ronald Knoll, Thomas K. Landauer, Robert Ollman, Steven E. Poltrock, and C. E. Wright. Others who have provided detailed and useful written comments on parts of the earlier manuscript are F. Gregory Ashby, John Baird, Thomas Hanna, Stephen Link, David H. Krantz, A. A. J. Marley, James Townsend, John Tukey, and Elke Weber. Nobody has actually seen the book whole, for it has been in flux until the final weeks of revisions. And certainly no one but me is culpable for its remaining weaknesses, but I can assure the reader that its failures would have been more severe without the help of all these people, whom I thank.

At a practical level, the Guggenheim Foundation along with Harvard University financed the beginning, sabbatical year. After that there was no direct support of the project, but the National Science Foundation and Harvard University have, for other reasons, placed some secretarial help at my disposal that has been useful. Most important, both institutions have contributed to my having microcomputers on which many chapters have been drafted and all of the revisions have been made. During the final two months of revisions, I have been on leave from Harvard at the AT & T Bell Laboratories in Murray Hill, N.J., and some of my time has been devoted to this book. A. F. Smith and R. M. Nosofsky programmed and ran a number of computations for me, Ellen Rak photographed figures from articles, Annemarie Wrenn drafted original figures, and Sandra Susse and Zoe Forbes did the bulk of the typing before I had word processing. They all receive my thanks.

Those on whom the writing has impinged personally and whose patience has no doubt been strained as I have hunched over my IBM PC are my daughter, Aurora, and my close friend Carolyn Scheer. Their good cheer has been appreciated.

Now, I only hope that you find our efforts worthwhile.

Cambridge, Mass.   R.D.L.
November 1984

Contents

Part III. MATCHING PARADIGMS 423

11. Memory Scanning, Visual Search, and Same-Difference Designs 425

12. Processing Stages and Strategies 456

1

Representing Response Times
as Random Variables

1.1 THE STUDY OF RESPONSE TIMES

1.1.1 Why?

Response time is psychology's ubiquitous dependent variable. No matter what task a subject is asked to do in an experiment, its completion always takes time. That obvious fact is not, however, necessarily interesting, and until relatively recently psychologists have not typically recorded response times. Should response times be ignored or do they tell us things we should like to know?

The notion that response times might reveal information about mental activity is old. For example, in 1868 F. C. Donders suggested that one could infer the time taken up by a particular hypothetical mental stage by subjecting the subject to two procedures that differed only in whether that stage is used. Joseph Jastrow, in an 1890 volume entitled *The Time Relations of Mental Phenomena*, stated more generally one major argument for examining response times. If the processing of information by the mind is highly structured, as most psychologists believe, then different paths through that structure will entail different time courses, and those differences will be reflected in the response times. Thus, perhaps, one can infer back from the pattern of response times obtained under different experimental conditions to the structures involved. To the extent this is possible, response times are valuable. My aim is to survey what we know about the feasibility of that strategy.

Let me admit at the outset that there are reasons to be skeptical of the enterprise. Consider the task of inferring the architecture of a computer from measurements of its performance times using different programs and different inputs. This certainly would be difficult, especially if one lacked the technology of modern electronics to help carry out the measurements. At best, one would expect to learn something about the gross organization of the computer, but it seems unlikely that the fine details would succumb to such an attack.

So, as psychologists, we can hope at best to learn something about overall organization and very little if anything about the details. That presumably will develop only as we look, in some fashion or another, inside the "black box." This means using physiological observations, which traditionally have taken either of three approaches—two of which are largely restricted to animals and the third is better suited to human subjects. In ablation studies entire regions of the brain are destroyed in an attempt to gain some understanding of the role of that region. In single unit studies, the electrical activity of the individual neurons is observed. In the third tradition non-intrusive electrical scalp measurements are taken. Recently these methods have become far more powerful through the use of computer techniques to make inferences about average electrical activity in different regions. Although physiological results to some degree inform model building, they usually are secondary to questions of fitting the models to behavioral data; such physiological data will not loom large in this book.

From the first attempts to use response times until the growth of modern cognitive psychology beginning, say, in the mid 1950s, response times were largely the focus of specialists and were not usually recorded by others. The specialists, who tended to come from the tradition of psychophysics, were mostly interested in the limits of human performance; they spoke of studying "reaction" times.* The term was appropriate—they asked how long it took a subject to react to a signal onset (or offset) under various conditions of observation. A prime reason reaction times were a matter for specialists was the sheer technical difficulty of carrying out the measurements with the equipment of the time. It is difficult, although not impossible, to measure times of a few hundred milliseconds to an accuracy of a few milliseconds with pre-World War II technology. The past 35 years have seen electronic developments that have made such observations, if not easy, at least highly feasible.

The other major change, which also took place after World War II, was the striking shift from a strongly behaviorist-operational orientation to a cognitive one. The idea of postulating an internal mental structure that, on the one hand, has properties about which we can make inferences from external observations and, on the other hand, provides a compact theoretical summary of what we know, has passed from being an anathema to being the mainstream orientation at many major centers of psychology. Ease of measurement and philosophical adjustment has led to very extensive use of response times as a crucial dependent variable.

1.1.2   How?

In practice, the use of response times to infer something about how we process information is a good example of the interplay of experimental

---

* Although the current literature does not attempt to make a distinction, I shall distinguish between reaction and response times. In my usage, response time is the generic term and reaction time refers only to experiments in which response time is made a major focus of attention for the subject. The experimenter may request the subject to respond as fast as possible, or to maintain the response times in a certain temporal interval, and so on. I may be the only person who attempts the distinction. For example, the recent volume by Welford (1980) that covers many of the same topics as I do is titled *Reaction Times*, and that usage is characteristic of much of the cognitive literature. Nevertheless, I feel that the distinction should be made until we are more sure than we are now that it does not matter.

design, measurement technology, and mathematical theorizing. All three are essential to the enterprise. Without precision of measurement, one cannot possibly answer some of the detailed questions raised by theory. Without clever experimental designs, one cannot drive the subject to exaggerate some aspect of the workings of his or her brain so that we have a chance to observe it relatively uncontaminated by other factors normally more dominant. And without the mathematical working out of the consequences of our hypotheses about mental organization, we cannot bring the data to bear on these hypotheses.

I do not treat the three horses of this troika equally. Little is said about the techniques of measurement despite the fact it is absolutely essential they be of sufficient quality to get the millisecond accuracy found in most of the data discussed. I shall simply take for granted that it can be done. Questions of calibration of equipment, of reliability, and all of the host of things a good experimenter must spend endless hours perfecting are simply ignored. Somewhat more attention is devoted to experimental design at the conceptual level. I make no attempt to discuss in detail all of the precautions a good experimenter must take to avoid pitfalls of various sorts. Rather, the focus is on the underlying idea of various experiments—the ways in which the experimenter was attempting to force the subjects to reveal one or another aspect of their mental processing. That focus will be very apparent in some of the chapters. Other chapters are largely concerned with working out the consequences of various ideas we have about the mental processing involved. These chapters, especially 8, 9, and 12, are relatively mathematical in nature.

The approach of the theoretical chapters is traditional in two respects. First, they take well-formulated hypotheses about what might be going on and attempt to discover what these say about things that can be observed—choices that are made and times to make them. The aim of these deductions is, of course, to compare them with data, to see ways in which subjects behave as the theory predicts and ways in which they don't. That is quite typical of any development of a mathematical theory of an empirical phenomenon. Second, the mathematics used is itself traditional, being basically 19th century analysis applied in this century to probability.

During the four years I was writing this book, the microcomputer revolution became a reality, which raises the question: does one any longer need to carry out mathematical analyses of models such as those described here? Although in late 1984 I know of no microcomputer software for the major response-time models, I am confident that within a few years such programs will be available at a relatively low price. Anyone with a modest amount of computer skill will be able to carry out simulations of processes that now require some mathematical training to analyze, and so the fitting of models to bodies of data should become appreciably simpler than it has been. To the degree that we have carried out mathematical analysis in the past primarily to estimate parameters and evaluate fits to data, the computer approach may well be easier and faster—though subject to the vagaries of numerical and statistical approaches. To the degree that we find the analysis useful in understanding the structure of the model and in arriving at experimental designs that take advantage of that structure, the mathematics will continue to be useful. Judging by what has happened in the other sciences, the computer will add to our ability to understand the theoretical underpinnings of what we observe—it already has—and it will complement, not replace, the mathematics. For example, computer simulations will turn up regularities that suggest mathematical results to be proved about the model; but without proofs we cannot be sure what is structural and what is an accident of our numerical explorations.

1.1.3   Organization

The primary mathematical device of the book is to treat response times as observations of a random variable and to use the mathematics of stochastic processes to understand something about the processes giving rise to the distributions of these random variables. The remainder of this chapter is devoted to some elementary properties of this representation.

The major ideas we shall need are few. The first is how to encode the information that describes the random variable. The most common coding is in terms of its distribution or density function, which we shall always assume exists. A mathematically, although not subjectively, equivalent representation is in terms of the hazard function. Since many texts on probability theory say little about that representation and since I find it exceedingly useful, I devote considerable space to it. It is the essential tool whenever one is concerned with races between several independent processes, and it also conveys important information that is difficult to see in a density function. Since it is equally true that the density function conveys important information not easily seen in the hazard function, I urge that both be routinely presented.

The second idea is the concept of independence of several random variables. Without this assumption we often do not know how to proceed, and for that reason we must invoke it with caution since ease of computation is not a sufficient reason to assume independence. The third is the idea of summary statistics about a random variable such as its mean, variance, skewness, and the like. The fourth is how to study the distribution of a sum of two independent random variables by means of generating functions that transform an apparently difficult integral into a simple product. And the fifth introduces the idea of random variable models in time, called stochastic processes. Some of the fundamental concepts that will be mentioned from time to time are described in Section 1.5.

These major tools, which are essential to understanding the book, will carry us through Chapter 7. After that additional mathematical knowledge becomes necessary for Chapters 8, 9, and 12. This knowledge is developed in two ways. Some of the classical limit theorems for both serial and parallel systems are developed in Appendix A. And certain specific stochastic processes for response times are developed in the later chapters, drawing upon results in Appendix A as needed or developed in context. In some cases where I deem the mathematical development too complex for the use to which I plan to put the model, I reference another source for a proof.

The book breaks into three main parts, each of which brings forward some basic difficulties in the task of inferring mental structure from observed behavior. The first part, called "Detection Paradigms" and encompassing Chapters 2 to 5, is devoted to so-called simple reaction times—experiments in which only one type of reaction signal is presented and the subject is usually required to respond as rapidly as possible. The major difficulties are three. First, what one observes is not only the time to carry out the mental processes involved in apprehending the signal, but also all of the times it takes to move information about the nervous system and to effect a response. These are often a major fraction of the observed time, and serve only to mask the decision process, which is the subject of all the models considered. This difficulty first comes up in Chapter 2, which is largely an empirical chapter, and it is dealt with explicitly in Chapter 3. Second, the subject can vary how responsive he or she will be, which creates difficulties in understanding the data. Again we see evidence of this in the data of Chapter 2, and Chapter 4 is devoted to models that attempt to capture what is going on in this simplest of cases. The theme of subject-controlled tradeoffs will recur throughout the book. The third difficulty arises only when we try to mimic more accurately the normal environment which, of course, is not partitioned into trials. In that case, signals may arrive so close together in time that the processing of one may still be under way when the next signal arrives and demands attention. This possibility raises a question of interaction that is considered in some detail in Chapter 5, and reappears again in later chapters in the guise of sequential effects.

The second major part, called "Identification Paradigms" and encompassing Chapters 6 to 10, concerns the absolute identification design in which one of a fixed set of signals is presented on each trial and the subject attempts to identify which one, often under the instruction to react as quickly as possible. Two of the difficulties seen with simple reactions appear even more sharply. The first takes the form of a major tradeoff between accuracy of responding and response times. This phenomenon, once it is recognized and studied, becomes a powerful tool in selecting among models. Despite that fact, it is not widely used, in large part because its study greatly increases the expense of data collection. Some experimenters (those of psychophysical bent) focus mostly on discrimination with little regard to response times, and others (of a cognitive bent) focus mostly on response times with little interest in errors. Both groups argue that if the variable they choose to ignore is held fixed, then variation in the other dependent variable provides all the information needed. The difficulty in both cases is in achieving such constancy. The second major problem is the existence of pronounced sequential effects in the data: the response on any trial is affected not only by the signal presented, but also by the particular pattern of preceding signals and responses. This makes very difficult the task of estimating properties of the response random variable. These sequential effects are of such magnitude that one may be misled if they are ignored; but dealing with them is complex and expensive, in part because they are still far from well understood. All of this is taken up for the identification of one of two signals in Chapter 6, and the three subsequent chapters are devoted to various classes of (mostly) two-stimulus, two-response models for these phenomena. The mathematical developments in Chapters 8 and 9 go somewhat beyond elementary random variables, which was all we needed earlier. Chapter 10 treats identification experiments with more than two signals. To some extent it is a continuation of the preceding chapters, except that the theoretical work is somewhat different and less complete.

The third and last part of the book is titled "Search and Matching Paradigms" and consists of Chapters 11 and 12. Chapter 11 takes up three classes of closely related experiments called memory scanning, visual search, and matching. In each case more than two stimuli are involved but rather fewer responses, often only two, are permitted. Thus, some categorization of the stimuli is effected by the subject. Here the models are more strictly cognitive in character than anything treated previously. The central issue that arises is how to infer uniquely the nature of the underlying cognitive structure. We will encounter several cases of data that seem to have a natural interpretation in terms of a particular model of mental structure, but were later shown to be equally well accounted for by a different structure—one that entails a quite contradictory conceptualization of what the mind is doing. This can be described as a question of identifiability of underlying structures. Chapter 12 presents some mathematical theorems designed to clarify the issues. This chapter, like Chapters 8 and 9, is mathematically somewhat more complex than the rest of the book.

When we are done, I will not attempt to sum up where we are. Suffice it to say now that the task of inferring mental structure from observable responses and response times is plagued with a number of inherent difficulties we know only partially how to overcome. A consensus has yet to develop as to which structure is involved in any of the main types of experiments; there are many partial successes, but no class of models has swept the field. The book is perforce a progress report of a field, not an attempt at a definitive statement.

I should also make clear that the focus of the book is on response-time methods and theories, and I shall select from among all studies in which response time is a dependent variable those that, in my opinion, best illustrate the points being made. This means that numerous studies will not be referenced even if they have made heavy use of response times and have been influential in their own areas. Perhaps the most notable example of such a study is Posner's (1978) extensive use of what he calls chronometric methods to illuminate cognitive theory. Other examples can be found in the later chapters of Welford (1980) and in Blumenthal (1977), who used the times associated with behavior as a major organizing principle.

Much more serious is the total omission of one conceptually important topic—operant psychology. As is well known, the behaviorism of B. F. Skinner is completely entwined with a particular experimental procedure he invented. In contrast with most of the rest of psychology during the 1930s, 1940s, and 1950s, these experimental techniques, mostly with animals, were totally wrapped up with time. Such experiments do not have trials, but rather probabilistic time patterns of reinforcement—called schedules of reinforcement—and the major dependent variable is rate of responding. Momentary rate, when one is observing only punctate events such as pecks by a pigeon or bar presses by a rat, is nothing more than the reciprocal of the time interval between two such events. The use of cumulative records summarizing the data was feasible with relatively crude recording techniques because Skinner and his school evolved an experimental procedure in which the relevant events could be measured in seconds rather than milliseconds. Nonetheless, the dependent measure is pure response times; in the original studies there was little else to observe. In recent years, some operant psychologists have shifted their attention to choice paradigms, but the early studies really focused on rate of responding as a function of properties of the schedule of reinforcement.

So I had to decide whether to include any of this work in this book. Until the past few years there has been little communication, aside from rather bitter philosophical attacks, between the operant and cognitive camps, and there is little tradition for putting their work together. That, in fact, is an excellent argument for including it here. Two reasons led me to decide otherwise. The less attractive, although probably more compelling, reason is my limited familiarity with the operant literature and the enormous amount of time it would have taken to master it to the point where I would have had some chance of getting it right. The more attractive rationalization is the fact that the limited amount of formal theory that has been developed—limited, in part, because Skinner adamantly opposed such theory (Skinner, 1950)—does not attempt to formulate a theory of mental structure.

Let us turn now to our major mathematical device, the concept of a random variable. Section 1.2 is a prerequisite for Chapter 2 and Sections 1.3 to 1.5 for the later chapters.

1.2 RANDOM VARIABLES

The intuitions behind the concept of a *random variable* are nicely caught in those two words. It is a numerical quantity associated with a system that is to be observed; it is a *variable* reflecting an aspect of elements of that system. Even though the system is prepared in the same way before two observations, it may turn out that the observed values are not the same; there is an element of chance or *randomness* in its observed values. Response time is prototypic. It is clearly a (dependent) variable of the system composed of a human being in a particular experimental context, and it varies somewhat haphazardly from observation to observation, even though the two observations are made under as nearly identical conditions as we know how to achieve. Of course, we may also systematically vary aspects of the system—for example, signal intensity (Section 2.3)—in which case there will be a family of random variables, one for each different intensity.

Because there is a decided distinction between a random variable and its value when it is observed, we must follow some convention to distinguish the two. The one I shall follow is to use boldface type for the random variable and regular type, usually lower case, for its value—for example, **T** and *t* or **X** and *x*, in which case we write **T** = *t* to say the observed value of the random variable **T** was *t*. In order to make distinctions among random variables without changing the generic symbol, they are sometimes ornamented with subscripts, superscripts, or primes.

1.2.1   *Distribution and Density Functions*

To say that **T** is the random variable denoting a particular person's response time in a particular experiment with particular parameters really tells us nothing except how to go about observing values of it. Not until we know, first, how it depends on experimental parameters and, second, what the nature of the randomness is do we begin to understand **T** as a unitary concept. Our concern now is with the second part—the description of randomness. That has to do with probability, and it is generally agreed that a complete probabilistic description of **T** for a single observation (or for a series of independent observations, see Section 1.3.3) is the probability that, for each real number *t*, **T** is less than or equal to *t*. We may denote each of these probabilities as $\Pr(\mathbf{T} \leq t)$; this description is, in general, an infinite collection of numbers. If we suppress the name of the random variable, **T**, and think of this as a function of *t*, then it is customary to use the function notation

$$F(t) = \Pr(\mathbf{T} \leq t). \tag{1.1}$$

F is called the (cumulative) *distribution function* of the random variable *T*. If we are dealing with more than one random variable, as will often occur, we must distinguish the distribution functions in some way. Three conventions are common: different symbols such as *F* and *G*, subscripting the same symbol by an index such as F_1, F_2, F_3, or subscripting the same symbol by the names of the random variables such $F_\mathbf{T}$, $F_\mathbf{X}$. I use all three conventions at one time or another.

For a function to be a distribution function, it need only satisfy three properties:

1. Monotonicity: if $t \le t'$, then $F(t) \le F(t')$.

2. $\lim\limits_{t \to -\infty} F(t) = 0$.

3. $\lim\limits_{t \to \infty} F(t) = 1$.

The first follows from the fact that probability is nonnegative and additive over disjoint sets:

$$
\begin{aligned}
F(t') &= \Pr(\mathbf{T} \le t') \\
&= \Pr[(\mathbf{T} \le t) \cup (t < \mathbf{T} \le t')] \\
&= \Pr(\mathbf{T} \le t) + \Pr(t < \mathbf{T} \le t') \\
&\ge \Pr(\mathbf{T} \le t) \\
&= F(t).
\end{aligned}
$$

Statement 2 follows from the fact that $\mathbf{T} \le -\infty$ is impossible (probability $= 0$) and statement 3 from the fact that $\mathbf{T} < \infty$ is certain (probability $= 1$).

If a distribution function is differentiable except at discrete points, we denote its derivative by

$$ f(t) = dF(t)/dt = F'(t), \tag{1.2} $$

and refer to it as the *density function* of the random variable; it is immaterial what value is assigned f at those discrete points where f is not differentiable. Of course, we may also write the relation between the distribution and density functions as

$$ F(t) = \int_{-\infty}^{t} f(x)\, dx. \tag{1.3} $$

In the other extreme case where the random variable only assumes a discrete set of values—possibly not the case for physical time, but certainly the case for our observations of time—we alter the symbolism. Suppose $\mathbf{T}$ is a discrete random variable with at most countably many values $\{t_i\}$, where $t_i < t_j$ if and only if $i < j$, and let f_k be the probability that $\mathbf{T}$ takes on the value t_k, where

$$ \sum_{k=-\infty}^{\infty} f_k = 1. $$

The corresponding distribution function is

$$ F(t_k) = \sum_{i=-\infty}^{k} f_i. $$

Often p_i is used instead of f_i for discrete distributions.

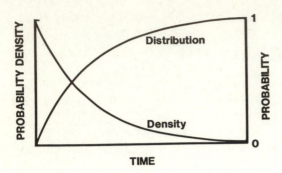

FIG. 1.1 An exponential density function and its corresponding distribution function.

Most of this book will deal with continuous rather than discrete random variables, but there will be exceptions.

An important example of a distribution function that is continuous except at 0 is the *exponential*:

$$F(t) = \begin{cases} 1 - e^{-\lambda t}, & t \geq 0, \lambda > 0 \\ 0, & t < 0. \end{cases} \tag{1.4}$$

It is immediate that the density is

$$f(t) = \begin{cases} \lambda e^{-\lambda t}, & t > 0 \\ 0, & t < 0. \end{cases} \tag{1.5}$$

It is usual to define $f(0) = \lambda$. This density and its distribution function are shown in Figure 1.1.

Suppose $\mathbf{T}$ is a random variable with distribution function F. For *any* monotonic strictly increasing function φ, $\varphi(\mathbf{T})$ is also a random variable and its distribution function G is related to F as follows:

$$G(y) = \Pr[\varphi(\mathbf{T}) \leq y]$$
$$= \Pr[\mathbf{T} \leq \varphi^{-1}(y)]$$
$$= F[\varphi^{-1}(y)].$$

where the inverse of φ, φ^{-1}, exists because φ is monotonic. Recall that the inverse of a function, when it exists, undoes what the function does—that is, $\varphi^{-1}[\varphi(x)] = x = \varphi[\varphi^{-1}(x)]$. For example, suppose $\mathbf{T}$ has an exponential distribution and that φ is the natural logarithm. Then $\ln \mathbf{T}$ has the distribution function

$$G(y) = 1 - \exp(-\lambda \ln^{-1} y)$$
$$= 1 - \exp(-\lambda e^{y}).$$

*1.2.2 A Somewhat More General Treatment of Random Variables

Probability is a way to describe the outcomes of observations of nature. An opportunity to observe an outcome is called an "experiment" by probabilists. Their usage of this term is neither inconsistent with nor the same as its usage by psychologists. An experiment, in this sense, has various possible outcomes, a listing of which is called the *sample space* or *population*, depending upon the particular application in question. An element of the sample space is one of the possible observations, exactly one of which will occur. Put another way, the elements constitute a mutually exclusive and exhaustive listing of the possible outcomes. Mathematically, the sample space is nothing more nor less than a set Ω. It may be finite or infinite. It is usually not numerical.

Often we do not care about the precise outcome, but merely whether it is of one type or another. For example, in roulette, the possible outcomes are some 37 or 38 slots into one of which the ball falls. They are both numbered and painted red, black, or white. The precise outcome is characterized by giving the number of the slot the ball ends in, but if you have bet on red, it is enough that you know whether the outcome was red or not, not the exact slot. For a finite or countably infinite sample space, any collection of outcomes is called an *event*. For most other sample spaces—for example, Euclidean spaces—one must be more selective because there is no way to assign probabilities to all conceivable events in a way that is suitably continuous. To bypass that problem, one considers a family $\mathscr{F}$ of subsets with the following properties, where A and A_i are subsets of Ω:

   (i) Ω is in $\mathscr{F}$.

   (ii) If A is in $\mathscr{F}$, then its complement $\sim A = \Omega - A$ is in $\mathscr{F}$.

   (iii) If a sequence A_i is in $\mathscr{F}$, $i = 1, 2, \ldots$, then $\bigcup_{i=1}^{\infty} A_i$ is in $\mathscr{F}$.

Such a family is called a *σ-algebra* of sets. Its members are called *events*. Note that $(\varnothing, \Omega)$, where $\varnothing$ is the null set, is a σ-algebra; it is the *trivial* one. Often one elects to work with the smallest σ-algebra that contains a particular set of events. One important example has as its sample space the unit interval $[0, 1]$. The smallest σ-algebra that includes all of the subintervals of $[0, 1]$—that is, all intervals $[a, b]$ such that $0 \leq a < b \leq 1$—is often used, and these sets are called the *Borel sets*.

A probability measure is an assignment of numbers between 0 and 1 to a σ-algebra that satisfies several very simple properties. Formally, $\langle \Omega, \mathscr{F}, P \rangle$ is a *probability space* if Ω is a set, $\mathscr{F}$ is a σ-algebra of subsets of Ω, and P is a

---

* Sections marked by an asterisk are not essential for understanding the remainder of the book.

real valued function on $\mathscr{F}$ such that for all A and A_i in $\mathscr{F}$, $i = 1, 2, \ldots$:

1. $P(\Omega) = 1$,
2. $P(A) \geq 0$,
3. If $A_i \cap A_j = 0$, $i \neq j$, then

$$P\left(\bigcup_{i=1}^{\infty} A_i\right) = \sum_{i=1}^{\infty} P(A_i).$$

Note that if $A \cap B = \varnothing$, it follows that $P(A \cup B) = P(A) + P(B)$ since we can form the infinite sequence A, B, $\varnothing$, $\varnothing$, ... and the conclusion follows from property 3.

Within this framework, the notion of a random variable is easily defined: it is a function $\mathbf{X}$ from Ω into the real numbers. Any function? Just about, provided we are able to discuss the distribution function, $\Pr(\mathbf{X} \leq x)$. That is to say, we must be able to talk about the probability of all of the outcomes to which the associated values do not exceed x. This is the set

$$\{\omega \mid \omega \text{ in } \Omega \text{ and } \mathbf{X}(\omega) \leq x\},$$

Thus for the corresponding probability to exist, it is necessary and sufficient that, for each x, this set be in $\mathscr{F}$.

Formally, given a probability space $\langle \Omega, \mathscr{F}, P \rangle$, a function $\mathbf{X} : \Omega$ into the real numbers is a *random variable* if and only if for every real number x the set $\{\omega \mid \omega \text{ in } \Omega \text{ and } \mathbf{X}(\omega) \leq x\}$ is in $\mathscr{F}$. The *distribution function* of $\mathbf{X}$ is

$$F(x) = P(\{\omega \mid \omega \text{ in } \Omega \text{ and } \mathbf{X}(\omega) \leq x\}).$$

Note that from this perspective, a random variable is itself neither random nor a variable; it is a mathematical function that quite deterministically maps the sample space into the real numbers. What is random is the observation of a sample point that through the function is encoded as a number.

Sometimes, although not in this book, a representation more general than a number is needed; the most common example is a random vector of real numbers.

If the basic structure is the probability space, why do we bother with the apparently extraneous baggage of random variables? There are two reasons. First, the observation—an element of the sample space—often tells us far more than we care to concern ourselves. For example, if a physician is concerned about the impact of weight on heart attacks, the appropriate sample space is, perforce, a set of people (such as the United States population) from which a sample of observations is made according to some probabilistic measure. Obviously, the concern is not about each individual per se, but only about that person's weight, gender, and heart attack history. Once the units of measurement are specified, weight is a random variable. Gender and having a heart attack do not appear to be random variables, but any descriptive categorization can be made into a random variable by identifying the categories with integers—for example, males $= 0$ and females $= 1$.

Second, by restating a problem into the real numbers, one can sometimes bring to bear the powerful mathematical techniques of analysis—calculus, differential equations, functional equations, transform theory, and the like. It is curious that this rich body of material, developed mostly for classical physics, which hardly mentions probability, is made available by the simple device of random variables for the study of non-deterministic processes. However, considerable skill must be employed in order for the power of the techniques to lead to meaningful results.

In some cases, random variables are the natural concept to work with, as in reaction time. Often the thing one is observing is a random variable, not the underlying probability space, which can be rather abstract and difficult to characterize. In other cases, random variables seem artificial, as when a heart attack is coded 1. There is some art in making these arbitrary choices, for one choice will lead to a simple formulation, another to a complex one.

1.2.3 Hazard Functions

Consider waiting for something to occur—a bus to arrive, a subject to respond, a light to fail, or the next commercial air crash to occur. One can, of course, describe the "waiting time"—the time from the last event to the next one—by its density or distribution function, but that is not the natural way one thinks about it as the process unfolds in time. Rather, if the event has not yet occurred, one senses there is some tendency for it to occur in the next instant of time. One thinks of the tendency as either staying constant, or increasing, or decreasing as the time increases since the wait began. Death is a process whose tendency undoubtedly increases with age after a certain age; the data are unequivocal. Some people seem to believe there is an increased tendency for an air crash to occur immediately following one, and they avoid flying for several weeks thereafter; the data do not justify that belief.

What is it that we are talking about when we speak of the tendency for an event to occur? The most obvious answer—the density function itself—is surely wrong. The death example makes that clear. A simple example illustrates how we should reason. Suppose an event must occur at one of three times $t_1 < t_2 < t_3$ and that the probabilities are equally likely—that is, $p_1 = p_2 = p_3 = \frac{1}{3}$. Does that mean the tendency has a constant value of $\frac{1}{3}$? It surely is $\frac{1}{3}$ just prior to t_1, but what if the event fails to occur at t_1 and one approaches time t_2? Is the tendency still $\frac{1}{3}$? We know that the event must now occur at either t_2 or t_3, since t_1 has been ruled out, and since the two times were equally likely before we started, it is hardly reasonable to assume this has been altered just because the event did not occur at t_1. So, it must be that the tendency is now $\frac{1}{2}$. What we have done is to renormalize the probabilities that remain so that the shape of the remaining distribution is unchanged, but the probability still sums to 1 (certainty). The renormalization factor is $1 - \frac{1}{3} = \frac{2}{3}$, and so the two renormalized values are equal

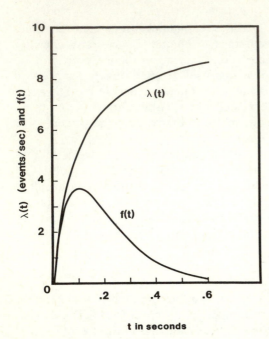

FIG. 1.2 A gamma density function and its corresponding hazard function.

$(\frac{1}{3})/(\frac{2}{3}) = \frac{1}{2}$. If the event fails to occur at time t_2, then just prior to t_3 the tendency has grown to 1—the event must occur at t_3. Again, it is just a matter of renormalizing $\frac{1}{3}$ by the factor $1 - \frac{2}{3} = \frac{1}{3}$.

Generalizing to an arbitrary density, the tendency for the event to occur at time t is the density renormalized by the probability that the event failed to occur prior to t—that is, $1 - F(t)$. So it is defined as

$$\lambda(t) = \frac{f(t)}{1 - F(t)}, \tag{1.6}$$

for all t for which $F(t) < 1$. An illustration of the relation between f and λ is shown in Figure 1.2. This important quantity for the study of temporal processes goes under various names in the literature including: hazard function, conditional density function, intensity function, force of mortality, failure rate function, instantaneous failure rate, and very likely many other names of which I am unaware. I will refer to it as the *hazard function*. Useful treatments of hazard function are found in Barlow and Proschan (1965, 1975), Gross and Clark (1975), and Singpurwalla and Wong (1983).

Observe that

$$\lambda(t) = \frac{f(t)}{1 - F(t)}$$

$$= \frac{dF(t)/dt}{1 - F(t)}$$

$$= -\frac{d}{dt} \ln[1 - F(t)]. \tag{1.7}$$

The quantity $\ln[1-F(t)]$ is known as the *log survivor function*, and temporal data are often summarized by plotting $\ln[1-F(t)]$ versus t, in which case the negative of the slope is the hazard function.

Integrating Eq. 1.7,

$$F(t) = 1 - \exp\left[-\int_{-\infty}^{t} \lambda(x)\,dx\right],\tag{1.8}$$

and so

$$f(t) = \lambda(t)\exp\left[-\int_{-\infty}^{t} \lambda(x)\,dx\right].\tag{1.9}$$

Thus, we can pass from the density to the hazard function by Eq. 1.6 or the other way by Eq. 1.9.

We can answer a basic question: what random variable has a constant tendency to occur for $t>0$? Setting

$$\lambda(t) = \begin{cases} 0 & \text{for} \quad t<0 \\ \lambda & \text{for} \quad t\geq 0 \end{cases}$$

in Eq. 1.9 we see that the answer is Eq. 1.5, the exponential density. This may come as a bit of a surprise since, after all, the largest value of the exponential density is at 0—instantaneous repetition—which must tend to produce clustering if the process is repeated in time. This is, indeed, the case, as can either be seen, as in Figure 1.3, or heard if such a process is made audible in time—it seems to sputter. To neither the eye nor the ear does it seem uniform in time, but that is an illusion, confusing what one sees or hears with the underlying rate of these events. The tendency for the event to occur is constant. Such a process is called *Poisson*—more of it in Chapters 4 and 9. It is the basic concept of constant randomness in time—that is, the unbounded, ordered analogue of a uniform density on a finite, unordered interval.

As it is by no means obvious how qualitative features of λ correspond to those of f, it is useful to study the relationship. We concentrate on conditions for which λ is strictly increasing or strictly decreasing. Recall that a

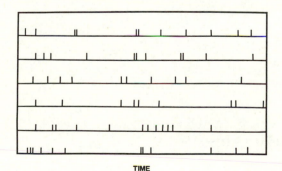

TIME

FIG. 1.3 A sample of events generated by a Poisson process. Each line continues the line immediately above it.

function g is *convex (concave)* if for every $s < t$ and α with $0 \leq \alpha \leq 1$,

$$\alpha g(s) + (1-\alpha)g(t) > (<)g[\alpha s + (1-\alpha)t].$$

If g is differentiable, convexity (concavity) is the same as dg/dt increasing (decreasing) with t.

Theorem 1.1. *If f is a differentiable density function such that $f(t) \to 0$ as $F(t) \to 1$ and $\ln f(t)$ is convex (concave), then the hazard function of f is increasing (decreasing).*

Proof.   Since $-\ln f(t)$ is convex and differentiable,

$$g(t) = -\frac{d}{dt} \ln f(t) = -\frac{f'(t)}{f(t)}$$

is increasing. Observe

$$\frac{\int_t^\infty g(x)f(x)\,dx}{\int_t^\infty f(x)\,dx} = \frac{-\int_t^\infty \frac{f'(x)}{f(x)}f(x)\,dx}{\int_t^\infty f(x)\,dx}$$

$$= \frac{f(t)}{1-F(t)}.$$

Taking the derivative with respect to t yields, for the left side,

$$f(t)\int_t^\infty [g(x)-g(t)]f(x)\,dx \Big/ \left[\int_t^\infty f(x)\,dx\right]^2,$$

which is positive since g is increasing and so for $x > t$, $g(x)-g(t) > 0$. Thus, the hazard function is increasing. ∎

This useful result is due to Thomas (1971), who also gave a necessary and sufficient condition that is sometimes of greater value, although more difficult to use. Glaser (1980) has provided sufficient conditions on a density function for a hazard function to be either increasing, decreasing, increasing and then decreasing, or decreasing and then increasing.

As an example of the use of Theorem 1.1, consider the Gaussian (also called the normal) density:

$$f(t) = \frac{1}{(2\pi)^{1/2}\sigma} \exp[-(t-\mu)^2/2\sigma^2],$$

then

$$-\ln f(t) = \tfrac{1}{2}\ln 2\pi + \ln \sigma + (t-\mu)^2/2\sigma^2.$$

Taking the derivative,

$$-\frac{d}{dt}\ln f(t) = (t-\mu)/\sigma^2,$$

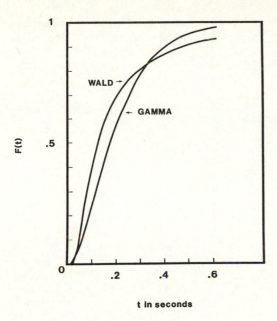

FIG. 1.4 Gamma and Wald distribution functions for two random variables having the same mean and variance. These distribution functions will arise in Chapters 4 and 8; also see Appendix B.

which is an increasing function of t. Therefore, the hazard function of the Gaussian, which does not have a simple mathematical form, is increasing.

Bloxom (1984) noted that in the region where the density function has a positive slope, the hazard function is increasing. To show this, differentiate the definition of a hazard function (Eq. 1.7):

$$\lambda'(t) = \frac{f'(t)}{1 - F(t)} + \lambda(t)^2.$$

Since $\lambda(t)^2 > 0$, if $f'(t) > 0$, then necessarily $\lambda'(t) > 0$. The converse is not true.

1.2.4 On Contemplating Distributions

As we have just seen, there are several different, but mathematically equivalent, ways to present the information about a distribution function: F, $f = F'$, $\ln(1 - F)$, and the negative of its derivative $\lambda = f/(1 - F)$. In principle, we may present the data as estimates of any of these functions and it should not matter which we use. In practice, it matters a great deal, although that fact does not seem to have been as widely recognized by psychologists as it might be.

Let me summarize my experience working with distributions. From a plot of F one can easily read off the mean and standard deviation (for precise definitions see Section 1.3.4) and with some practice one can sense skewness, but beyond that all distribution functions look vaguely alike and one cannot extract and describe easily other salient features. Figure 1.4 provides

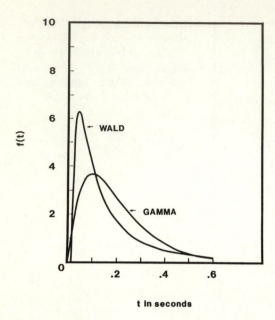

FIG. 1.5 Density functions corresponding to the distribution functions of Figure 1.4.

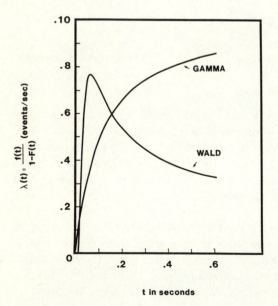

FIG. 1.6 Log survivor functions corresponding to the distribution and density functions of Figures 1.4 and 1.5.

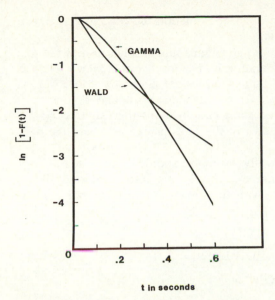

FIG. 1.7 Hazard functions corresponding to the distribution, density, and log survivor functions of Figures 1.4, 1.5, and 1.6.

examples of two theoretically important distribution functions—the gamma and the Wald (see Chapter 4)—with the same mean and standard deviation (Section 1.3.4). All that one can extract from F is seen at least as easily in the plot of f, although empirical estimates of it tend to be more ragged than those of F, especially if the sample is smaller than 1000 observations. The f's corresponding to Figure 1.4 are shown in Figure 1.5. The main failing of this plot is in knowing what is happening in the tails of the distribution, especially the right tail for reaction-time data.

The tail is much amplified by replotting the data as $\ln(1-F)$. If there are enough data so that the magnification is moderately stable, one is able to see quite clearly features of the data that are hardly noticeable in plots of f, as is illustrated in Figure 1.6, which shows this version of the same pair of distributions. Note, however, that it is very difficult to sense either the central tendency or the variability of the distribution from this plot. If one is good at mental differentiation, which most of us aren't, then one can read off the hazard function as the negative of the slope. For large t it is moderately easy to do, but it is quite difficult to see what is going on for values of t less than the mean or median. So we turn to the hazard function itself which is shown in Figure 1.7. To my mind it is one of the most revealing plots because it displays what is going on locally without favoring either short or long times, and it can be strikingly different for f's that seem little different. For example, it is easy to characterize the major difference between the gamma and Wald: the former has an increasing hazard function with decreasing slope and the latter has a peaked hazard function that appears to asymptote to a constant value. Needless to say, it is virtually impossible to see from a glance at a hazard function the central tendency or variability of the random variable.

There are difficulties in estimating the hazard function because of the fact that as t becomes large the denominator $1 - F$ approaches 0, which tends to produce wild fluctuations. Again, large samples are necessary. Moreover, as we shall see in Chapter 4, there is an estimation scheme that is very satisfactory in that it maintains constant variability of the estimates at the expense of reducing the detail shown in the plot in regions where the data are sparse.

The upshot of all this is that, ideally, estimates should be provided of both the density and the hazard function, and if only one is to be plotted, then I would favour the hazard function with the mean and variance being given numerically.

1.3 SEVERAL RANDOM VARIABLES

1.3.1 *Joint and Conditional Distributions*

Consider two continuous random variables defined for the same experiment. For example, if the experiment involves selecting people at random from some population, let $\mathbf{X}$ be the individual's height in centimeters and $\mathbf{Y}$, the weight in grams. Each of these random variables has its own distribution function

$$F(x) = \Pr(\mathbf{X} \le x) \qquad \text{and} \qquad G(y) = \Pr(\mathbf{Y} \le y). \tag{1.10}$$

Moreover, there is a joint distribution function characterizing the probability of simultaneously finding $\mathbf{X} \le x$ and $\mathbf{Y} \le y$,

$$H(x, y) = \Pr(\mathbf{X} \le x \text{ and } \mathbf{Y} \le y). \tag{1.11}$$

It is plausible that there is some relation between height and weight, so that $H(x, y)$ is not in general known just by knowing $F(x)$ and $G(y)$ separately. Going from $H(x, y)$ to $F(x)$ and $G(y)$ is simple. I write it both in terms of distribution and, when they exist, density functions:

$$H(x, y) = \int_{-\infty}^{x} \int_{-\infty}^{y} h(u, v) \, du \, dv, \tag{1.12}$$

$$F(x) = H(x, \infty) = \int_{-\infty}^{x} f(u) \, du, \tag{1.13}$$

$$G(y) = H(\infty, y) = \int_{-\infty}^{y} g(v) \, dv, \tag{1.14}$$

where

$$f(u) = \int_{-\infty}^{\infty} h(u, v) \, dv \qquad \text{and} \qquad g(v) = \int_{-\infty}^{\infty} h(u, v) \, du.$$

$F(x)$ and $G(y)$ are known as the *marginal distributions* of the joint distribution $H(x, y)$; similarly, $f(u)$ and $g(u)$ are the *marginal densities* of the joint density $h(u, v)$.

Often it is useful to consider the distribution of one random variable while holding fixed the value of the other one. The distribution of the one may well vary with the value of the other. For example, we all know that the distribution of weights for people 180 centimeters tall is quite different from those 165 centimeters tall.

Consider the density $h(u, v)$ renormalized by the variable being held fixed:

$$f(u \mid v) = h(u, v)/g(v), \tag{1.15a}$$

$$g(v \mid u) = h(u, v)/f(u). \tag{1.15b}$$

These are the conditional density functions for $\mathbf{X}$ conditional on $\mathbf{Y} = v$ and for $\mathbf{Y}$ conditional on $\mathbf{X} = u$, respectively. The corresponding conditional cumulative distributions are

$$F(x \mid \mathbf{Y} = v) = \int_{-\infty}^{x} f(u \mid v)\, du$$

$$= \int_{-\infty}^{x} \frac{h(u, v)}{g(v)}\, du, \tag{1.16}$$

$$G(y \mid \mathbf{X} = u) = \int_{-\infty}^{y} g(v \mid u)\, dv$$

$$= \int_{-\infty}^{y} \frac{h(u, v)}{g(u)}\, dv, \tag{1.17}$$

$$H(x, y) = \int_{-\infty}^{x} \int_{-\infty}^{y} h(u, v)\, du\, dv$$

$$= \int_{-\infty}^{x} G(y \mid \mathbf{X} = u) f(u)\, du$$

$$= \int_{-\infty}^{y} F(x \mid \mathbf{Y} = v) g(v)\, dv. \tag{1.18}$$

1.3.2 Bayes' Theorem

Often in probability situations one knows something theoretical about how one random variable depends upon another, but is only able to observe something about the converse dependency. This can be important in making systematic inferences using observations and theory. The very simple result that describes how this is done is attributed to Rev. Thomas Bayes (1702–1761).

The terminology usually used is hypothesis and data, with the theory telling how the data relate probabilistically to the hypotheses, and the experiment presumably allowing us to infer the probabilities of the hypotheses given the observed data. Let the random variable **H** represent the hypotheses, where they have been numbered from 1 to n and are defined in such a way that one and only one can obtain. In the case of a continuum of hypotheses, **H** is taken to be a continuous random variable. Let **D** be the random variable representing the possible outcomes of the experiment to be performed. It may be discrete or continuous. One supposes that theories yield the conditional probability density functions $f(d \mid i) = \Pr(\mathbf{D} = d \mid \mathbf{H} = i)$, and the point of running the experiment is to infer $g(i \mid d) = \Pr(\mathbf{H} = i \mid \mathbf{D} = d)$.

Perhaps the simplest way to state and prove the result is in terms of relative density functions:

$$\frac{g(i \mid d)}{g(j \mid d)} = \frac{f(d \mid i)g(i)}{f(d \mid j)g(j)}. \tag{1.19}$$

This is known as the "odds" formulation of Bayes' Theorem. The ratio $g(i)/g(j)$ on the right is the *prior odds* of hypothesis i to hypothesis j, whereas the ratio $g(i \mid d)/g(j \mid d)$ on the left is the *posterior*—after the experiment—*odds* of hypothesis i to j. The middle ratio $f(d \mid i)/f(d \mid j)$ is called the *likelihood ratio* of the datum d under hypotheses i and j.

Although the result is useful, the proof is trivial. For each conditional density simply substitute its definition in terms of the joint density (Eq. 1.15), and Eq. 1.19 is seen to be an identity.

The result can be cast in another form. If we sum (or integrate as the case may be) over all hypotheses j in the denominator, then the left denominator is $\sum_j g(j \mid d) = 1$, and so Eq. 1.19 yields

$$g(i \mid d) = \frac{f(d \mid i)g(i)}{\sum_j f(d \mid j)g(j)}. \tag{1.20}$$

Equation 1.20 implies 1.19 since when the ratio $g(i \mid d)/g(j \mid d)$ is formed the denominator on the right of Eq. 1.20 cancels out.

In most presentations, Bayes' Theorem is formulated directly in terms of the underlying probability space and not in terms of random variables. The two formulations are, in fact, equivalent in the sense that either can be derived from the other. In practice, most applications involve the random variable version.

1.3.3   Independence

Intuitively, two random variables are independent if knowing the value of one tells nothing whatsoever about the value of the other. Stated in terms of densities, **X** is *independent* of **Y** if

$$f(u \mid v) = f(u).$$

By Eq. 1.12, we see this is equivalent to

$$h(u, v) = f(u)g(v), \tag{1.21}$$

which is the usual definition of independence. It also makes clear that the concept is symmetric: if $\mathbf{X}$ is independent of $\mathbf{Y}$, then $\mathbf{Y}$ is also independent of $\mathbf{X}$.

Substituting Eq. 1.21 into Eqs. 1.16 and 1.17, for all y,

$$F(x \mid \mathbf{Y} = y) = \int_{-\infty}^{x} \frac{h(u, y)}{g(y)} \, du$$

$$= \int_{-\infty}^{x} f(u) \, du$$

$$= F(x), \tag{1.22a}$$

and similarly for all x,

$$G(y \mid \mathbf{X} = x) = G(y). \tag{1.22b}$$

Substituting them in Eq. 1.18 yields

$$H(x, y) = \int_{-\infty}^{x} G(y \mid \mathbf{X} = u)f(u) \, du$$

$$= \int_{-\infty}^{x} G(y)f(u) \, du$$

$$= F(x)G(y). \tag{1.23}$$

Equations 1.22 and 1.23 are equally good definitions of independence.

A very basic result about independent random variables, one that is often used, is:

Theorem 1.2.   *If $\mathbf{X}$ and $\mathbf{Y}$ are independent random variables and φ and ψ are (measurable) functions such that $\varphi(\mathbf{X})$ and $\psi(\mathbf{Y})$ are random variables, then $\varphi(\mathbf{X})$ and $\psi(\mathbf{Y})$ are also independent.*

The proof is a routine use of the definitions; see Brunk (1975, p. 104).

Throughout the book, we will be repeatedly concerned with structures assumed to be composed of various separate subprocesses that are organized either in series, so that each subprocess begins only when the preceding one is completed, or in parallel, so that all subprocesses begin at the same time. Moreover, it is assumed that the times to complete the subprocesses are independent in the sense of Eqs. 1.21 and 1.23. In the serial case, we will be interested in the random variable $\mathbf{T}_1 + \mathbf{T}_2 + \cdots + \mathbf{T}_n$, where the $\mathbf{T}_i$ are the independent random variables associated with the subprocesses. In the parallel case, there are two obvious quantities to be interested in—the time until the first subprocess is completed and the time until the last one is completed. The former is of interest when the completion of any one triggers a response, the latter when all must be completed for a response to occur. In analyzing these problems, various techniques and concepts are helpful. It turns out that for the fastest of a set of independent random variables, the notion of a hazard function is just what is needed.

Theorem 1.3. *If* $\mathbf{T}_1, \mathbf{T}_2, \ldots, \mathbf{T}_n$ *are independent random variables with hazard functions* $\lambda_1(t), \lambda_2(t), \ldots, \lambda_n(t)$, *respectively, then the random variable* $\mathbf{T} = \min(\mathbf{T}_1, \mathbf{T}_2, \ldots, \mathbf{T}_n)$ *has the hazard function*

$$\lambda(t) = \sum_{k=1}^{n} \lambda_k(t).$$

Proof. Let F be the distribution function of $\mathbf{T}$ and F_k of $\mathbf{T}_k$. The probability that $\mathbf{T}$ has not occurred by time t is, by independence,

$$1 - F(t) = \prod_{k=1}^{n} [1 - F_k(t)].$$

Differentiating,

$$f(t) = \sum_{k=1}^{n} \frac{f_k(t)}{[1 - F_k(t)]} \prod_{j=1}^{n} [1 - F_j(t)]$$

$$= \sum_{k=1}^{n} \lambda_k(t)[1 - F(t)].$$

Therefore,

$$\lambda(t) = \frac{f(t)}{1 - F(t)} = \sum_{k=1}^{n} \lambda_k(t). \qquad \blacksquare$$

Thus, for example, if the crashes of airline k are Poisson (exponential time between crashes) with constant parameter λ_k, then the crashes of all airlines are Poisson with parameter $\sum \lambda_k$.

It is rather more difficult to say things about the hazard functions of sums of independent random variables. One result of importance is the following:

Theorem 1.4. *Suppose* $\mathbf{X}$ *and* $\mathbf{Y}$ *are independent random variables and* $\mathbf{Z} = \mathbf{X} + \mathbf{Y}$. *Let their hazard functions be* $\lambda_{\mathbf{X}}$, $\lambda_{\mathbf{Y}}$, *and* $\lambda_{\mathbf{Z}}$.

(i) *If* $\lambda_{\mathbf{Y}}$ *is nondecreasing, then* $\lambda_{\mathbf{X}} \geq \lambda_{\mathbf{Z}}$ (Ashby, 1982).
(ii) *If* $\lambda_{\mathbf{X}}$ *and* $\lambda_{\mathbf{Y}}$ *are both nondecreasing, then* $\lambda_{\mathbf{Z}}$ *is nondecreasing* (Barlow, Marshall, & Proschan, 1963).

Proof. (i) Let f and F be the density and distribution functions, then since $\mathbf{Z} = \mathbf{X} + \mathbf{Y}$ and $\mathbf{X}$ and $\mathbf{Y}$ are independent,

$$\int_0^t [1 - F_{\mathbf{X}}(t - x)]f_{\mathbf{Y}}(x)\, dx = F_{\mathbf{Y}}(t) - F_{\mathbf{Z}}(t).$$

Therefore, the following is an identity:

$$\lambda_X(t) = \int_0^t \lambda_X(t)[1 - F_X(t-x)]f_Y(x)\,dx/[F_Y(t) - F_Z(t)].$$

Using the fact that λ_X is nondecreasing and the definition of the hazard function,

$$\lambda_X(t) \geq \int_0^t \lambda_X(t-x)[1 - F_X(t-x)]f_Y(x)\,dx/[F_Y(t) - F_Z(t)]$$

$$= \int_0^t f_X(t-x)f_Y(x)\,dx/[F_Y(t) - F_Z(t)]$$

$$= f_Z(t)/[F_Y(t) - F_Z(t)]$$

$$\geq f_Z(t)[1 - F_Z(t)] \qquad (\text{because } F_Y(t) \leq 1)$$

$$= \lambda_Z(t).$$

(ii) See Barlow & Proschan (1975, p. 100). ∎

For example, if X is exponential and Y is Gaussian—which as we shall see in Section 3.2.1 often gives a good fit to simple reaction times—the hazard function of Z is increasing.

1.3.4 Expectation and Variance

For many purposes one does not need complete information about a distribution; some sort of summary quantity suffices. From a purely theoretical point of view, quantities based on what is called the mathematical expectation have generally proved most satisfying, but considerable care must be taken in trying to estimate these quantities from data. More of that later.

If X and Y are random variables with the joint density function h, and K is any function defined over the joint range of X and Y, then the *expected value* of K is defined to be

$$E[K(X, Y)] = \int_{-\infty}^{\infty} \int_{-\infty}^{\infty} K(x, y)h(x, y)\,dx\,dy. \tag{1.24}$$

In particular, the expected value of X^k is defined to be

$$\mu^k = E(X^k) = \int_{-\infty}^{\infty} x^k f(x)\,dx. \tag{1.25}$$

This is called the *raw moment of order k*. When $k = 1$, we simply write μ_X and call it the *mean*.

The *covariance* of X and Y is

$$\text{cov}(X, Y) = E[(X - \mu_X)(Y - \mu_X)]. \tag{1.26}$$

The *variance* of $\mathbf{X}$ is

$$V(\mathbf{X}) = \text{cov}(\mathbf{X}, \mathbf{X}) = E[(\mathbf{X} - \mu_{\mathbf{X}})^2]. \tag{1.27}$$

The following captures most of the general properties that we shall need.

Theorem 1.5. *If $\mathbf{X}$ and $\mathbf{Y}$ are random variables and a and b are numbers, then*:

    (i) $E(a) = a$.
    (ii) $E(a\mathbf{X} + b\mathbf{Y}) = aE(\mathbf{X}) + bE(\mathbf{X})$.
    (iii) *If $\mathbf{X}$ and $\mathbf{Y}$ are independent, then* $E(\mathbf{XY}) = E(\mathbf{X})E(\mathbf{Y})$.
    (iv) $\text{cov}(\mathbf{X}, \mathbf{Y}) = E(\mathbf{XY}) - E(\mathbf{X})E(\mathbf{Y})$.
    (v) *If $\mathbf{X}$ and $\mathbf{Y}$ are independent, then* $\text{cov}(\mathbf{X}, \mathbf{Y}) = 0$.
    (vi) $V(\mathbf{X}) = E(\mathbf{X}^2) - E(\mathbf{X})^2$.
    (vii) $V(a) = 0$.
    (viii) $V(\mathbf{X} + a) = V(\mathbf{X})$
    (ix) $V(a\mathbf{X}) = a^2 V(\mathbf{X})$.
    (x) $V(\mathbf{X} + \mathbf{Y}) = V(\mathbf{X}) + V(\mathbf{Y}) + 2\,\text{cov}(\mathbf{X}, \mathbf{Y})$.

These results are easily proved; see Brunk (1975, Ch. 5).

1.3.5 Random Samples

The intuitive idea of a random sample is this: Suppose a random variable is defined on a population from which we plan to draw a sequence of random instances and then, as each case is drawn, we record the value of the random variable assigned to that instance. These values are said to be the observations. Moreover, the plan for generating the sample is such that each element of the population is equally likely to be selected on each drawing. This means not only that the same probability structure is involved in each drawing, but that the drawings are independent of each other. Since a fixed random variable is involved, one can think of each drawing as an independent realization of that random variable. So summarizing, a *random sample* is a sequence of random variables $\mathbf{X}_1, \mathbf{X}_2, \ldots, \mathbf{X}_n$ that are identically distributed; that is, for some distribution function F,

$$\Pr(\mathbf{X}_i \leq x) = F(x), \quad i = 1, 2, \ldots, n,$$

and for each $i, j = 1, \ldots, n$, $i \neq j$, $\mathbf{X}_i$ and $\mathbf{X}_j$ are independent.

Typically when we run an experiment—say, a reaction-time one—we attempt to arrange a sequence of trials that are as nearly identical as we know how to make them and at the same time, by temporal spacing among other things, as independent as possible. We then record values of a random variable—for example, reaction time—on each trial. Having been very careful about the experimental conditions, we frequently assume that the sequence of observations of the empirical random variables form a random sample. Sometimes we make partial attempts to verify either the identity of the distributions or the independence of the random variables or both. The former is usually done by searching for temporal trends in the data, which cannot exist if the same distribution function is involved, and the latter by searching for signs of sequential dependencies, usually between successive observations. The standard method for establishing sequential dependencies is to partition the data according to some portion of the immediate past history of the sample, and then to see if the estimated distribution (often, in practice, just the mean) is independent of that history. Fairly extensive use of this will be found in Section 6.4. Despite the fact that when sequential dependencies have been looked for they have usually been found, most experimenters ignore them and hope for the best.

Suppose $\mathbf{X}_1, \mathbf{X}_2, \ldots, \mathbf{X}_n$ is a random sample with distribution function F, mean μ, and standard deviation σ. The *sample mean* is defined to be

$$\bar{\mathbf{X}} = (1/n) \sum_{i=1}^{n} \mathbf{X}_i. \tag{1.28}$$

Observe that $\bar{\mathbf{X}}$ is a random variable. By Theorem 1.5(ii),

$$E(\bar{\mathbf{X}}) = E\left[(1/n) \sum_{i=1}^{n} \mathbf{X}_i \right]$$

$$= (1/n) \sum_{i=1}^{n} E(\mathbf{X}_i)$$

$$= (1/n) \sum_{i=1}^{n} \mu$$

$$= \mu. \tag{1.29}$$

Thus, the expected value of the sample mean is actually the mean of the random variable. Because the sample mean is a statistic (combination of observations) that provides some information about the mean, we call it an *estimator* of the mean. Whenever we have a function $\hat{\theta}(\mathbf{X}_1, \ldots, \mathbf{X}_n)$ of the observations that we have reason to believe bears on some property θ of the underlying distribution function, we call $\hat{\theta}$ an estimator of that property θ. And if it turns out that

$$E[\hat{\theta}(\mathbf{X}_1, \ldots, \mathbf{X}_n)] = \theta, \tag{1.30}$$

we say that $\hat{\theta}$ is an *unbiased estimator* of θ. So, Eq. 1.29 establishes that the sample mean is an unbiased estimator of the mean.

Consider the sample variance, also a random variable,

$$\mathbf{S}^2 = (1/n) \sum_{i=1}^{n} (\mathbf{X}_i - \bar{\mathbf{X}})^2 \tag{1.31}$$

We compute $E(\mathbf{S}^2)$ to see whether or not it is an unbiased estimator of σ^2, which we might anticipate it to be. Using Theorem 1.5(ii),

$$E(\mathbf{S}^2) = E\left[(1/n) \sum_{i=1}^{n} (\mathbf{X}_i^2 - 2\mathbf{X}_i\bar{\mathbf{X}} + \bar{\mathbf{X}}^2)\right]$$

$$= (1/n) \sum_{i=1}^{n} E(\mathbf{X}_i^2) - E(\bar{\mathbf{X}})^2. \tag{1.32}$$

By Theorem 1.5(vi),

$$E(\mathbf{X}_i^2) = V(\mathbf{X}_i) + E(\mathbf{X}_i)^2 = \sigma^2 + \mu^2, \tag{1.33}$$

and also using Theorem 1.5(ix),

$$E(\bar{\mathbf{X}}^2) = V(\bar{\mathbf{X}}) + E(\bar{\mathbf{X}})^2$$

$$= (1/n^2) \sum_{i=1}^{n} V(\mathbf{X}_i) + \mu^2$$

$$= \sigma^2/n + \mu^2. \tag{1.34}$$

Substituting Eqs. 1.33 and 1.34 into Eq. 1.32.

$$E(\mathbf{S}^2) = \frac{n-1}{n}\sigma^2. \tag{1.35}$$

And so the sample variance is not, in fact, an unbiased estimator of the variance, but as is obvious from Eq. 1.35, $n\mathbf{S}^2/(n-1)$ is.

Observe that the variance of the sample mean is, by Eq. 1.34,

$$E[(\bar{\mathbf{X}} - \mu)^2] = E(\bar{\mathbf{X}}^2) - \mu^2$$

$$= \mu^2/n. \tag{1.36}$$

This means that the standard deviation of the sample mean about the true mean diminishes in proportion to $1/\sqrt{n}$, where n is the sample size. It is this very slow reduction in the error of estimates with sample size that is the bane of all experimental work. In Appendix A we will derive the limiting form of the distribution

$$\frac{\bar{\mathbf{X}} - \mu}{\sigma/\sqrt{n}}.$$

Although unbiasedness is a nice property for an estimator to have, it is not really as important as another, consistency. We say that an estimator $\hat{\theta}$ is a *consistent estimator* of θ if for each choice of $\epsilon > 0$,

$$\lim_{n \to \infty} \Pr[|\hat{\theta}(\mathbf{X}_1, \ldots, \mathbf{X}_n) - \theta| < \epsilon] = 1.$$

This simply means that as the sample size becomes large, the probability that the estimate of θ deviates appreciably from θ is vanishingly small. That property is essential if we are to have any motive for collecting samples of data and computing θ.

Theorem 1.6. *Suppose* $\mathbf{X}_1, \ldots, \mathbf{X}_n$ *is a random sample. The sample moment* $(1/n) \sum_{i=1}^{n} \mathbf{X}_i^k$ *is a consistent estimator of* $E(\mathbf{X}^k)$ *provided that* $E(\mathbf{X}^k)$ *exists.*

A proof may be found in Brunk (1975, p. 163).

In a random sample of size n, the *sample distribution* $\mathbf{F}_n(x)$ is the fraction of the $\mathbf{X}_i$'s with $\mathbf{X}_i \leq x$. This is a random variable. It is the quantity one plots when attempting to estimate the underlying distribution function. The reason that the sample distribution of a random sample can be viewed as an estimator of the distribution is that it exhibits the following property, which is known as convergence in quadratic mean:

Theorem 1.7. *Suppose* $\mathbf{X}_1, \ldots, \mathbf{X}_n$ *is a random sample with distribution function F. If* $\mathbf{F}_n$ *is the sample distribution, then*

$$\lim_{n \to \infty} E[(\mathbf{F}_n(x) - F(x))^2] = 0.$$

This property implies that $\mathbf{F}_n(x)$ is a consistent estimator of $F(x)$, for all x. For a proof, see Parzen (1960, p. 423).

We frequently use the sample mean, variance, and distribution as estimators of the corresponding population property.

1.3.6 Random Samples of Random Size

On occasion, one finds oneself dealing with a random sample whose size is itself a random variable (of course, integer valued) that is independent of the random variable being observed. The sum of such a sample is of the form

$$\mathbf{S}_\mathbf{N} = \sum_{k=1}^{\mathbf{N}} \mathbf{X}_k. \tag{1.37}$$

Because $\mathbf{N}$ is independent of the $\mathbf{X}_k$, it follows that

$$\Pr(\mathbf{S}_\mathbf{N} = s) = \sum_{n=1}^{\mathbf{N}} \Pr(\mathbf{N} = n) \Pr\left(\sum_{k=1}^{n} \mathbf{X}_k = s\right).$$

Using this and Eqs. 1.29 and 1.36 we may calculate expressions for the mean and variance of $\mathbf{S}_\mathbf{N}$:

$$E(\mathbf{S}_\mathbf{N}) = \int_{-\infty}^{\infty} s \Pr(\mathbf{S}_\mathbf{N} = s) \, ds$$

$$= \sum_{n=1}^{\infty} \Pr(\mathbf{N} = n) \int_{-\infty}^{\infty} s \Pr\left(\sum_{k=1}^{n} \mathbf{X}_k = s\right) ds$$

$$= \sum_{n=1}^{\infty} \Pr(\mathbf{N} = n) n\mu$$

$$= \mu E(\mathbf{N}), \tag{1.38}$$

$$V(\mathbf{S_N}) = \int_{-\infty}^{\infty} [s - \mu E(\mathbf{N})]^2 \Pr(\mathbf{S_N} = s)\, ds$$

$$= \sum_{n=1}^{\infty} \Pr(\mathbf{N} = n) \int_{-\infty}^{\infty} [s - \mu n + \mu n - \mu E(\mathbf{N})]^2 \Pr\left(\sum_{k=1}^{n} \mathbf{X}_k = s\right) ds$$

$$= \sum_{n=1}^{\infty} \Pr(\mathbf{N} = n) \int_{-\infty}^{\infty} \left\{(s - \mu n)^2 + 2(s - \mu n)[\mu n - \mu E(\mathbf{N})]\right.$$

$$\left. + [\mu n - \mu E(\mathbf{N})]^2\right\} P\left(\sum_{k=1}^{n} \mathbf{X}_k = s\right) ds$$

$$= E(\mathbf{N})\sigma^2 + V(\mathbf{N})\mu^2. \tag{1.39}$$

1.4   GENERATING FUNCTIONS

This section introduces several related mathematical tools that are useful when dealing with sums of independent random variables. Sums of random variables arise in serial models that postulate distinct, successive stages of processing. The most recurrent model of this type, which is dealt with more fully in Chapter 3, supposes the observed response time is the sum of two processes: a decision process that arises when the central nervous system operates upon the internal representation of the input signal, and everything else—sensory transduction time, transit times, the time for the muscles to react, and any time other than the decision time. Moreover, in one part of cognitive psychology it is assumed that the decision time results from distinct stages of information processing, and one model assumes they are in series; this is dealt with in Chapters 11 and 12.

1.4.1   *Convolution*

Consider the simple serial model just mentioned:

$$\mathbf{T} = \mathbf{D} + \mathbf{R}, \tag{1.40}$$

where $\mathbf{T}$ is the observed time, $\mathbf{D}$ the decision latency, and $\mathbf{R}$ the residual latency. All three are random variables. In a sense, this model lacks any content since for any decision latency we choose to assume, one can define $\mathbf{R} = \mathbf{T} - \mathbf{D}$. However, matters are not nearly so trivial if we are willing to assume that the structure of the organism is such that $\mathbf{D}$ and $\mathbf{R}$ are independent random variables and that we know something of the structure of one or the other. Independence is a strong assumption which in particular applications requires justification or testing or both. But for the purposes of this section we simply assume independence. On that assumption we will learn how to calculate the distribution of $\mathbf{T}$ from that of $\mathbf{D}$ and $\mathbf{R}$. Let these three distributions be denoted, respectively, F, $F_\mathbf{D}$, and $F_\mathbf{R}$. Assume further that the densities, f, $f_\mathbf{D}$, and $f_\mathbf{R}$ exist.

Consider the various ways that the observed time is t. For that to happen, **D** must assume some value x, where $0 \le x \le t$, and **R** must assume the value $t - x$. Or, if we consider the event $\{\mathbf{T} \le t\}$, then we need to consider the joint event of $\{\mathbf{D} = x\}$ and $\{\mathbf{R} \le t - x\}$. Invoking the independence of **D** and **R**,

$$\Pr(\mathbf{D} = x \text{ and } \mathbf{R} \le t - x) = \Pr(\mathbf{D} = x)\,\Pr(\mathbf{R} \le t - x)$$

$$= f_{\mathbf{D}}(x) F_{\mathbf{R}}(t - x).$$

Now, to calculate the probability of $\{\mathbf{T} \le t\}$ requires that we integrate over all possible values of x, which in the case of latencies are necessarily nonnegative:

$$F(t) = \Pr(T \le t)$$

$$= \int_0^t \Pr(\mathbf{D} = x \text{ and } \mathbf{R} \le t - x)\,dx$$

$$= \int_0^t f_{\mathbf{D}}(x) F_{\mathbf{R}}(t - x)\,dx.$$

Differentiating with respect to t to get the density yields

$$f(t) = \int_0^t f_{\mathbf{D}}(x) f_{\mathbf{R}}(t - x)\,dx. \tag{1.41}$$

This expression is known as the *convolution* of the densities $f_{\mathbf{D}}$ and $f_{\mathbf{R}}$. If we were dealing with random variables that could be both positive and negative, then the limits of integration would have to be adjusted accordingly; but mostly in this book we will deal only with nonnegative random variables. The major exception is when a latency is approximated by the Gaussian distribution.

It is easy to see that we could have run the argument through just as well with **R** fixed at y and $\mathbf{D} = t - y$, which is equivalent to the change of variable $y = t - x$ in Eq. 1.41, to get the equivalent form

$$f(t) = \int_0^t f_{\mathbf{D}}(t - y) f_{\mathbf{R}}(y)\,dy.$$

So convolution is a symmetric concept.

For some purposes it is not too difficult to deal with the convolution equation directly provided that the integral can be explicitly evaluated. There are, however, several important problems for which Eq. 1.41 is really quite formidable. One of these is a situation where one knows or can estimate f and, say, $f_{\mathbf{R}}$, and the question is to calculate $f_{\mathbf{D}}$. Our first major tool, discussed in this section, is designed to solve that problem; it is one or another of a class of integral transforms that convert convolutions into multiplication.

A second important problem, which is made manageable by this tool, is the question of what happens when we add up a large number of independent, identically distributed random variables. The origin of this question lies not in reaction times, but in the statistical theory of random sampling. Recall a random sample is, by definition (Section 1.3.5), a sequence of independent, identically distributed random variables, $\mathbf{X}_1, \mathbf{X}_2, \ldots, \mathbf{X}_n$—it is what we observe when the same random variable is used for independent repetitions of the same experiment. A statistic often computed for a random sample is the sample mean,

$$\bar{\mathbf{X}}_n = (1/n) \sum_{k=1}^{n} \mathbf{X}_k.$$

And the question is: how does this random variable behave as n becomes large? Assuming that both the mean μ and variance σ^2 of the $\mathbf{X}_k$ exist, we showed in Eqs. 1.29 and 1.36 that

$$E(\bar{\mathbf{X}}_n) = \mu \qquad \text{and} \qquad V(\bar{\mathbf{X}}_n) = \sigma^2/n.$$

So we see that as n becomes large, the mean stays fixed but the variance becomes vanishingly small. This, of course, makes it really quite difficult to see what happens to the shape of the distribution of $\bar{\mathbf{X}}_n$. For this reason, it is desirable to normalize $\bar{\mathbf{X}}_n$ in such a way that both the mean and the variance do not change with n. One way to do so is to study the random variable

$$\bar{\mathbf{X}}_n^* = \frac{\bar{\mathbf{X}}_n - \mu}{\sigma/\sqrt{n}}, \tag{1.42}$$

which has $E(\bar{\mathbf{X}}_n^*) = 0$ and $V(\bar{\mathbf{X}}_n^*) = 1$. So the question is what can one say about the distribution of $\bar{\mathbf{X}}_n^*$ as n becomes large. Appendix A.1.1 states formally the famed Central Limit Theorem—namely, that quite independent of the distribution of the $\mathbf{X}_k$ the distribution of $\bar{\mathbf{X}}_n^*$ approaches the Gaussian distribution with mean 0 and standard deviation 1. The proof of this quite remarkable result—also given in Appendix A.1.1—uses integral operator methods.

1.4.2 The Moment Generating Function

Integral transforms of certain types are important for us because of three very simple observations and one that is not so simple. The first is the fact that the exponential function, which is a measurable function, converts sums to products. So if $\mathbf{X}$ and $\mathbf{Y}$ are random variables and θ is any real number, then $e^{\theta \mathbf{X}}$ and $e^{\theta \mathbf{Y}}$ are also random variables and

$$e^{\theta(\mathbf{X}+\mathbf{Y})} = e^{\theta \mathbf{X}} e^{\theta \mathbf{Y}}. \tag{1.43}$$

The second is the fact that, according to Theorem 1.2, if $\mathbf{X}$ and $\mathbf{Y}$ are independent, so too are $e^{\theta \mathbf{X}}$ and $e^{\theta \mathbf{Y}}$. This together with Theorem 1.5(iii) leads to the third point—namely, that if $\mathbf{X}$ and $\mathbf{Y}$ are independent, then

$$E[e^{\theta(\mathbf{X}+\mathbf{Y})}] = E(\theta^{s\mathbf{X}})E(\theta^{s\mathbf{Y}}). \tag{1.44}$$

This suggests the following definition: for all θ for which the right side is defined,

$$\mathcal{M}_{\mathbf{X}}(\theta) = E(e^{\theta\mathbf{X}}) \tag{1.45}$$

is called the *moment generating function* and abbreviated mgf. The last and not so obvious fact is that the mgf contains almost exactly the same information as the distribution function. It is perfectly obvious that if we know the density function $f_{\mathbf{X}}$, then we can compute

$$\mathcal{M}_{\mathbf{X}}(\theta) = \int_{-\infty}^{\infty} e^{\theta x} f_{\mathbf{X}}(x)\, dx.$$

What is far less obvious is that knowing $\mathcal{M}_{\mathbf{X}}(\theta)$ we can compute $f_{\mathbf{X}}(x)$. We formulate this precisely, but do not give its proof as it is somewhat difficult (see Feller, 1966, especially Sections 5 and 6 of Chapter VII).

Theorem 1.8. *Suppose* $\mathbf{X}$ *and* $\mathbf{Y}$ *are two random variables with distributions* $F_{\mathbf{X}}$ *and* $F_{\mathbf{Y}}$ *and moment generating functions* $\mathcal{M}_{\mathbf{X}}$ *and* $\mathcal{M}_{\mathbf{Y}}$ *defined for all* $\theta < \theta_0$. *Then,* $\mathcal{M}_{\mathbf{X}} = \mathcal{M}_{\mathbf{Y}}$ *if and only if* $F_{\mathbf{X}} = F_{\mathbf{Y}}$. *Moreover, if the density functions exist and are continuous, this holds if and only if* $f_{\mathbf{X}} = f_{\mathbf{Y}}$.

Thus, in principle, we lose nothing by working with mgf's, and we see by Eq. 1.44 that the convolution of densities is converted into simple multiplication when we work with the corresponding mgf's: if $\mathbf{X}$ and $\mathbf{Y}$ are independent,

$$\mathcal{M}_{\mathbf{X}+\mathbf{Y}}(\theta) = \mathcal{M}_{\mathbf{X}}(\theta)\mathcal{M}_{\mathbf{Y}}(\theta). \tag{1.46}$$

The reason for the name "moment generating function" can be seen in either of two equivalent ways. From the fact that the exponential has the power series expansion

$$e^x = 1 + x + x^2/2! + x^3/3! + \cdots$$

it follows that

$$\mathcal{M}_{\mathbf{X}}(\theta) = E(e^{\theta\mathbf{X}})$$

$$= E\left[\sum_{k=0}^{\infty} \frac{(\theta\mathbf{X})^k}{k!}\right]$$

$$= \sum_{k=0}^{\infty} \theta^k E(\mathbf{X}^k)/k!$$

proving that $\mathcal{M}_{\mathbf{X}}$ has a power series expansion in which the coefficient of the kth term is the kth raw moment divided by $k!$. We say that $\mathcal{M}_{\mathbf{X}}$ generates $E(\mathbf{X}^k)/k!$.

Another way of approaching it is to calculate the derivative of the mgf:

$$\frac{d\mathcal{M}_{\mathbf{X}}(\theta)}{d\theta} = \frac{dE(e^{\theta\mathbf{X}})}{d\theta}$$

$$= E\left[\frac{de^{\theta\mathbf{X}}}{d\theta}\right]$$

$$= E(\mathbf{X}e^{\theta\mathbf{X}}).$$

By induction,

$$\frac{d^{n}\mathcal{M}_{\mathbf{X}}(\theta)}{d\theta^{n}} = E(\mathbf{X}^{n}e^{\theta\mathbf{X}}).$$

Evaluating this at $\theta = 0$ we see that

$$\frac{d^{n}\mathcal{M}_{\mathbf{X}}(0)}{d\theta^{n}} = E(\mathbf{X}^{n}). \tag{1.47}$$

which is the nth raw moment. So knowing the mgf provides a very simple way to calculate the moments. This is not a minor gain since one can often develop an expression for the mgf without knowing an explicit formula for the distribution function.

A useful property is the relation between the mgf of $\mathbf{X}$ and a linear transformation of it, $a\mathbf{X} + b$:

$$\mathcal{M}_{a\mathbf{X}+b}(\theta) = E[e^{\theta(a\mathbf{X}+b)}]$$

$$= E(e^{\theta b}e^{\theta a\mathbf{X}})$$

$$= e^{\theta b}\mathcal{M}_{\mathbf{X}}(a\theta). \tag{1.48}$$

In the mathematical and physical science literature the transform $\int_{0}^{\infty} e^{-ux}f(x)\,dx$, where u is a complex number is widely used for functions defined on the positive real numbers. It is called the *LaPlace transform*. Thus, the mgf of a positive random variable is the special case where u is a real number and the sign is changed. This transform is not as convenient to compute numerically as the characteristic function, which is essentially the same as the Fourier transform; it is discussed in Section 1.4.4.

1.4.3 Three Examples: Exponential, Gaussian, and Ex-Gaussian

The mgf of the exponential density $\lambda e^{-\lambda x}$ is

$$\mathcal{M}_{\mathbf{X}}(\theta) = \int_{0}^{\infty} e^{\theta x}e^{-x}\,dx$$

$$= \lambda/(\lambda - \theta). \tag{1.49}$$

It is easy to show by induction that

$$\frac{d^{n}\mathcal{M}_{\mathbf{X}}(\theta)}{d\theta^{n}} = \frac{n!\lambda}{(\lambda - \theta)^{n+1}},$$

and so the raw moments are

$$E(\mathbf{X}^n) = n!/\lambda^n.$$

For the Gaussian density $(1/\sqrt{2\pi}) \exp(-\frac{1}{2}x^2)$, the mgf is

$$\mathscr{M}_{\mathbf{X}}(\theta) = \int_{-\infty}^{\infty} e^{\theta x}(1/\sqrt{2\pi}) \exp(-\tfrac{1}{2}x^2)\, dx$$

$$= (1/\sqrt{2\pi}) \int_{-\infty}^{\infty} \exp[-\tfrac{1}{2}(x^2 - 2x\theta + \theta^2) + \tfrac{1}{2}\theta^2]\, dx$$

$$= \exp(\tfrac{1}{2}\theta^2)(1/\sqrt{2\pi}) \int_{-\infty}^{\infty} \exp[-\tfrac{1}{2}(x - \theta)^2]\, dx$$

$$= \exp(\tfrac{1}{2}\theta^2).$$

So, using Eq. 1.48, the mgf of the general Gaussian density $(1/\sqrt{2\pi}) \exp[-\frac{1}{2}(x - \mu)^2/\sigma]$ is easily seen to be

$$\mathscr{M}_{\mathbf{X}}(\theta) = \exp(\mu\theta + \tfrac{1}{2}\sigma^2\theta^2). \qquad (1.50)$$

From this and Eq. 1.47 we show that the mean is μ and variance is σ^2:

$$\frac{d\mathscr{M}_{\mathbf{X}}(\theta)}{d\theta} = (\mu + \sigma^2\theta) \exp(\mu\theta + \tfrac{1}{2}\sigma^2\theta^2),$$

and so

$$\frac{d\mathscr{M}_{\mathbf{X}}(0)}{ds} = E(\mathbf{X}) = \mu.$$

Taking the second derivative,

$$\frac{d^2\mathscr{M}_{\mathbf{X}}(\theta)}{d\theta^2} = [\sigma^2 + (\mu + \sigma^2\theta)^2] \exp(\mu\theta + \tfrac{1}{2}\sigma^2\theta^2),$$

and so

$$\frac{d^2\mathscr{M}_{\mathbf{X}}(0)}{d\theta^2} = \sigma^2 + \mu^2.$$

As will be shown in Section 3.2.1, there are some vaguely plausible reasons and some rather striking empirical reasons for supposing that simple reaction times can be well approximated as the sum of two independent random variables, one of which is Gaussian and the other exponential. Burbeck and Luce (1982) called this distribution the *ex-Gaussian*. Its mgf is the product of Eqs. 1.49 and 1.50, which is not the mgf of a known distribution. However, it is not difficult to calculate the convolution of its density function (see Eq. 1.41, but note that the lower limit of integration must be $-\infty$ because the Gaussian is not necessarily positive):

$$f_{\mathbf{T}}(t) = \int_{-\infty}^{t} (1/\sqrt{2\pi}) \exp[-\tfrac{1}{2}(x-\mu)^2/\sigma^2]\lambda \exp[-\lambda(t-x)]\,dx$$

$$= (\lambda/\sigma\sqrt{2\pi})e^{-\lambda t}\int_{-\infty}^{t} \exp[-\tfrac{1}{2}(x-\mu/\sigma^2+\lambda x]\,dx$$

$$= (\lambda/\sigma\sqrt{2\pi})\exp(\mu\lambda+\tfrac{1}{2}\lambda^2\sigma^2)e^{-\lambda t}\int_{-\infty}^{(t-\mu-\lambda\sigma^2)/\sigma} \exp(-\tfrac{1}{2}y^2)\,dy$$

$$= (\lambda/\sigma)\exp(\mu\lambda+\tfrac{1}{2}\lambda^2\sigma^2)e^{-\lambda t}\Phi[(t-\mu-\lambda\sigma^2)/\sigma].$$

where Φ is the unit Gaussian distribution.

The mean and variance follow from those of the exponential and Gaussian:

$$E(T) = \mu + 1/\lambda,$$
$$V(T) = \sigma^2 + 1/\lambda^2.$$

From the fact that the hazard function of the Gaussian is increasing (Section 1.2.3) and that of the exponential is constant, Theorem 1.4(ii) establishes that the hazard function of the ex-Gaussian is increasing.

1.4.4   The Characteristic Function

The formal definition of the *characteristic function* (cf) of a random variable $\mathbf{X}$ is little different from that of a mgf:

$$\mathscr{C}_{\mathbf{X}}(\omega) = E(e^{i\omega\mathbf{X}}), \quad \text{where } \omega \text{ is real and } i = \sqrt{-1}. \tag{1.51}$$

The difference is that the argument is the pure imaginary $i\omega$ rather than the pure real θ. For this reason it is very closely related to the Fourier integral transform

$$(1/\sqrt{2\pi})\int_{-\infty}^{\infty} e^{-i\omega x}f(x)\,dx, \tag{1.52}$$

differing by a factor of $\sqrt{2\pi}$ and with ω replaced by $-\omega$.

For theoretical purposes it matters not at all whether we use the mgf or the cf because both, being special cases of $E(e^{z\mathbf{X}})$, turn convolutions into products. There are extensive tables of both transforms and their inverses; see, for example, Erdelyi, Magnus, Oberhettinger, and Tricomi (1954). However, beyond that, the cf has several general advantages. First, the theory of Fourier transforms is very well developed; see, for example, Bracewell (1965), Brigham (1974), and Titchmarsh (1948). Second, as compared with LaPlace transforms, it is defined for any random variable, not just for positive ones. (In discussing reaction time, this is of little import.) And third, there is a standard computer program—called the Fast

Fourier Transform (FFT)—that, by taking advantage of a nice symmetry property of the Fourier transform, manages to make the calculation of transforms and their inverses completely feasible with commonly available computers. For a general discussion of the FFT see Brigham (1974), and for its application to reaction-time data see Green (1971).

Because of the fact that $i^2 = -1$, there is a slightly different relation between the moments and the derivative of the cf:

$$d^n \mathscr{C}_{\mathbf{X}}(0)/d\omega^n = i^n E(\mathbf{X}^n).$$

(1.53)

One lovely property of the characteristic function transform is the fact that the cf of $d^n f(x)/dx^n$ is simply $(-i\omega)^n \mathscr{C}(\omega)$, where $\mathscr{C}(\omega)$ is the cf of f. This makes the analysis of linear differential equations with constant coefficients quite simple and systematic; it will play a role in Sections 4.3.2 and 9.2.1.

1.4.5   Cumulants

Often it is easier to compute the derivative of the logarithm of the cf or of the mgf rather than of those functions themselves. Both logarithms have been called *cumulant generating functions*. The quantities

$$\kappa_r(\mathbf{X}) = \left(\frac{1}{i^r}\right) \frac{d^r \log \mathscr{C}_{\mathbf{X}}(0)}{d\omega^r}$$

$$= \frac{d^r \log \mathscr{M}_{\mathbf{X}}(0)}{ds^r},$$

(1.54)

if they exist, are called the *cumulants* of $\mathbf{X}$. Their use in reaction-time data was first discussed by Taylor (1965) and has been exploited in a few empirical papers.

Their nicest feature is that they are all additive across sums of independent random variables. For suppose $\mathbf{X}_k, k = 1, 2, \ldots,$ form a sequence of independent random variables and $\mathbf{S}_n = \sum_{k=1}^{n} \mathbf{X}_k$, then since

$$\mathscr{C}_{\mathbf{S}_n}(\omega) = \prod_{k=1}^{n} \mathscr{C}_{\mathbf{X}_k}(\omega),$$

we see that by taking logarithms,

$$\log \mathscr{C}_{\mathbf{S}_n}(\omega) = \sum_{k=1}^{n} \log \mathscr{C}_{\mathbf{X}_k}(\omega),$$

whence

$$\kappa_r(\mathbf{S}_n) = \sum_{k=1}^{n} \kappa_r(\mathbf{X}_k).$$

(1.55)

The relation between the lower order cumulants and moments is readily established. If one sets $\kappa(\omega) = \log \mathscr{C}(\omega)$, then by computing derivatives of $\mathscr{C}(\omega) = \exp \kappa(\omega)$, we obtain

$$
\begin{aligned}
E(\mathbf{X}) &= \kappa_1, \\
E(\mathbf{X}^2) &= \kappa_2 + \kappa_1^2, \\
E(\mathbf{X}^3) &= \kappa_3 + 3\kappa_2\kappa_1 + \kappa_1^3, \\
E(\mathbf{X}^4) &= \kappa_4 + 4\kappa_3\kappa_1 + 3\kappa_2^2 + 3\kappa_2\kappa_1^2 + \kappa_1^4.
\end{aligned}
\tag{1.56}
$$

Equally well, by evaluating the derivative of

$$
\exp[\log \mathscr{C}_{\mathbf{X}}(\omega) - i\omega E(\mathbf{X})],
$$

it is easy to show that

$$
\begin{aligned}
E\{[\mathbf{X} - E(\mathbf{X})]^2\} &= \kappa_2, \\
E\{[\mathbf{X} - E(\mathbf{X})]^3\} &= \kappa_3, \\
E\{[\mathbf{X} - E(\mathbf{X})]^4\} &= \kappa_4 + 3\kappa_2^2.
\end{aligned}
\tag{1.57}
$$

The dimensionless quantities

$$
\gamma_1 = \frac{\kappa_3}{\kappa_2^{3/2}} = \frac{E\{[\mathbf{X} - E(\mathbf{X})]^3\}}{E\{[\mathbf{X} - E(\mathbf{X})]^2\}^{3/2}},
\tag{1.58}
$$

$$
\gamma_2 = \frac{\kappa_4}{\kappa_2^2} = \frac{E\{[\mathbf{X} - E(\mathbf{X})]^4\}}{E\{[\mathbf{X} - E(\mathbf{X})]^2\}^2} - 3,
\tag{1.59}
$$

are known as the *skew* and *kurtosis*, respectively. They will be used in evaluating models in Section 8.5.1.

1.4.6 Discrete Generating Functions

A slightly different theory is developed for the case of discrete random variables that assume values only in the integers $0, 1, 2, \ldots$, which occurs whenever we count the number of occurrences of something. Suppose $\mathbf{X}$ and $\mathbf{Y}$ are two such random variables with

$$
\Pr(\mathbf{X} = k) = f_k \qquad \text{and} \qquad \Pr(\mathbf{Y} = k) = g_k,
$$

where $\sum_{k=0}^{\infty} f_k = \sum_{k=0}^{\infty} g_k = 1$. Then, $\mathbf{Z} = \mathbf{X} + \mathbf{Y}$ is another random variable with integer values, and if $\mathbf{X}$ and $\mathbf{Y}$ are independent, an argument parallel to that for the continuous case yields

$$
\begin{aligned}
\Pr(\mathbf{Z} = k) &= \sum_{j=0}^{k} \Pr(\mathbf{X} = j) P(\mathbf{Y} = k - j) \\
&= \sum_{j=0}^{k} f_j g_{k-j},
\end{aligned}
\tag{1.60}
$$

which is the convolution equation for this discrete case.

The simplest operator technique to use is to define the *generating function* of the random variable **X**:

$$\mathscr{G}_{\mathbf{X}}(z) = \sum_{k=0}^{\infty} f_k z^k = E(z^{\mathbf{X}}), \tag{1.61}$$

which amounts to replacing $e^{i\omega}$ by z in the cf. The name generating function is used in the probability and mathematical literature; in engineering it is called the *z-transform*, and it has been studied extensively, usually in the form

$$\sum_{k=-\infty}^{\infty} f_k z^{-k},$$

where z is a complex number (Jury, 1964; Rabiner & Gold, 1975; and Tretter, 1978).

Again, the generating function has the happy property of converting convolution into multiplication: if **X** and **Y** are independent integer-valued random variables, then

$$\mathscr{G}_{\mathbf{X}+\mathbf{Y}}(z) = \mathscr{G}_{\mathbf{X}}(z)\mathscr{G}_{\mathbf{Y}}(z). \tag{1.62}$$

The proof involves substituting Eq. 1.61 into the expression for the convolution, Eq. 1.60, and then collecting like terms. We will use these transforms and Eq. 1.62 in formulating the models of Section 8.1.

Note that to compute moments, the evaluation is done at $z = 1$. For example,

$$\frac{d\mathscr{G}(z)}{dz} = \sum_{k=0}^{\infty} k f_k z^{k-1},$$

and so

$$\frac{d\mathscr{G}(1)}{dz} = \sum_{k=0}^{\infty} k f_k = E(\mathbf{X}). \tag{1.63}$$

Similarly,

$$E(\mathbf{X}^2) = \frac{d^2\mathscr{G}(1)}{dz^2} + E(\mathbf{X}) \tag{1.64}$$

because

$$\frac{d^2\mathscr{G}(z)}{dz^2} = \sum_{k=1}^{\infty} k(k-1) f_k z^{k-2}$$

$$= z^{-2} \sum_{k=1}^{\infty} k^2 f_k z^k - \sum_{k=1}^{\infty} k f_k z^k.$$

1.4.7 Three Examples: Binomial, Poisson, and Geometric

The *binomial distribution*—the probability of k 1's occurring in n independent observations of a $0, 1$ random variable with a probability p of 1 occurring at each observation—is well known to be

$$\binom{n}{k} p^k (1-p)^{n-k}.$$

Its generating function is

$$\sum_{k=0}^{n} \binom{n}{k} (pz)^k (1-p)^{n-k} = (1-p+pz)^n.$$

This illustrates the result about convolutions going into multiplication since the generating function of a single observation is $1-p+pz$. Using Eqs. 1.63 and 1.64, the binomial mean and variance are:

$$E(\mathbf{X}) = \frac{d[(1-p+pz)^n]}{dz}\bigg|_{z=1}$$

$$= np, \tag{1.65}$$

$$V(\mathbf{X}) = \frac{d^2[(1-p+pz)^n]}{dz^2}\bigg|_{z=1} + E(\mathbf{X}) - E(\mathbf{X})^2$$

$$= np(1-p). \tag{1.66}$$

The *Poisson distribution* is of the form $\lambda^k e^{-\lambda}/k!$, $k = 0, 1, 2, \ldots$, and has the generating function

$$\sum_{k=0}^{\infty} \frac{e^{-\lambda}(\lambda z)^k}{k!} = e^{-\lambda(1-z)}.$$

Thus, by Eq. 1.62, if $\mathbf{X}$ is Poisson with parameter λ and $\mathbf{Y}$ is Poisson with parameter μ and $\mathbf{X}$ and $\mathbf{Y}$ are independent, then $\mathbf{X}+\mathbf{Y}$ has the generating function

$$e^{-\lambda(1-z)} e^{-\mu(1-z)} = e^{-(\lambda+\mu)(1-z)},$$

and so $\mathbf{X}+\mathbf{Y}$ is Poisson with parameter $\lambda + \mu$. The Poisson distribution arises naturally from the Poisson process as the distribution of the number of events in a fixed time. If the intensity parameter of the process is μ and the time duration is Δ, then $\lambda = \mu\Delta$.

The Poisson mean and variance are given by

$$E(\mathbf{X}) = \frac{de^{-\lambda(1-z)}}{dz}\bigg|_{z=1}$$

$$= \lambda. \tag{1.67}$$

$$V(X) = \lambda^2 + \lambda - \lambda^2$$

$$= \lambda. \tag{1.68}$$

The *geometric distribution*—the discrete analogue of the exponential—is

$p(1-p)^k$, $k = 0, 1, \dots$. Its generating function is

$$p \sum_{k=0}^{\infty} (1-p)^k z^k = \frac{p}{1-(1-p)z},$$

which is similar to the mgf of the exponential, Eq. 1.49. The mean and variance are given by

$$E(\mathbf{X}) = \frac{p(1-p)}{[1-(1-p)z]^2}\bigg|_{z=1}$$

$$= \frac{1-p}{p}, \tag{1.69}$$

$$V(\mathbf{X}) = \frac{2p(1-p)^2}{[1-(1-p)z]^3}\bigg|_{z=1} + \frac{1-p}{p} - \left[\frac{1-p}{p}\right]^2$$

$$= \frac{1-p}{p^2}. \tag{1.70}$$

1.5   ELEMENTARY CONCEPTS OF STOCHASTIC PROCESSES

1.5.1   *Basic Definitions*

Suppose T is a set of real numbers—called an index set—and suppose, for each t in T, $\mathbf{X}(t)$ is a random variable. The collection $\{\mathbf{X}(t)\}_{t \in T}$ is called a *stochastic process*. Intuitively, one may think of T as a set of times (or of spatial locations in some interpretations) and $\mathbf{X}(t)$ is the observation made at time t. Two introductory references to the subject are Karlin and Taylor (1975) and Parzen (1962).

The simplest case of a stochastic process is, of course, when all of the random variables are independent of each other. In that case, the process is completely characterized by each of the individual distribution functions

$$F(x, t) = \Pr[\mathbf{X}(t) < x].$$

But, in general, processes that unfold in time do not exhibit such an extreme degree of independence. Usually if s is near t, the observations $\mathbf{X}(s)$ and $\mathbf{X}(t)$ are related in some manner. Often they are positively correlated, but not always. For example, in a pulse train on a neural fiber, if a pulse has occurred at some location on the fiber at time t and if s is less than $\frac{1}{2}$ msec later, there is virtually no chance of another pulse occurring at the same location at time s.

In cases such as these, a description of the process entails either knowing or being able to compute from some known probabilities the probability of anything that might occur to one to ask about the process. That is to say, given any integer n and any sequence of times $t_1 < t_2 < \cdots < t_n$, where each t_i is in T, and any numbers $x_1, x_2, \dots, x_n$, we must be able, in principle at least, to calculate

$$\Pr[\{\mathbf{X}(t_1) < x_1\} \,\&\, \{\mathbf{X}(t_2) < x_2\} \,\&\, \cdots \,\&\, \{\mathbf{X}(t_n) < x_n\}].$$

Given the infinity of numbers involved, this is feasible only if the process is so constrained that a relatively few (empirically estimated) numbers or distribution functions determine all of the rest.

Before turning to a description of some of the major constraints that have been studied and that appear to lead to useful models of response times, we need to introduce a little terminology. If the index set is a real interval—often $(-\infty, \infty)$ or $[0, \infty)$—the process is said to be one in *continuous time*. If, on the other hand, T is some subset of the integers, finite or infinite, then it is said to be a process in *discrete time*. In the latter case, we replace the typical index t by a symbol usually reserved for an integer, such as i, j, or n, and we write the random variables as, for example, $\mathbf{X}_i$, $i = 1, 2, \ldots$. Models of both types arise in the study of response times. Continuous-time models occur in Chapter 9 and discrete-time ones in the remainder of Chapters 7 to 12.

If the range of values of all of the random variables in the process forms a set that is finite or countable, then the process is called *discrete state*. If the range forms a real interval, then the process is called *continuous state*. One very important type of discrete state process, called a *counting process*, arises whenever a single type of discrete event occurs in time—such as neural pulses or accidents or births—and the random variable $\mathbf{X}(t)$ is simply the number of events that have occurred by time t. When dealing with a counting process it is common to change the notation from $\mathbf{X}(t)$ to $\mathbf{N}(t)$ in order to remind ourselves that the random variable is integer valued. Note that $\mathbf{N}(t)$ is an increasing function of t.

It is handy to abbreviate an event of the form

$$\{[\mathbf{X}(t_1) = x_1] \,\&\, [\mathbf{X}(t_2) = x_2] \,\&\, \cdots \,\&\, [\mathbf{X}(t_n) = x_n]\}$$

by

$$\{\mathbf{X}(t_i) = x_i, i = 1, \ldots, n\},$$

and in that notation conditional probability takes the form

$$\Pr[\mathbf{X}(t_n) = x_n \mid \mathbf{X}(t_i) = x_i, i = 1, \ldots, n-1)]$$
$$= \frac{\Pr[\mathbf{X}(t_i) = x_i, i = 1, \ldots, n]}{\Pr[\mathbf{X}(t_i) = x_i, i = 1, \ldots, n-1]}. \quad (1.71)$$

1.5.2 Some Important Constraints

Five major types of constraints concern us; they all capture some form of independence in the process. The first we are already familiar with from Section 1.3.3—namely, independence of the defining random variables. For a discrete-time process $\{X_i\}$, *independence* is equivalent to: for each integer

n and each sequence of real numbers $\{x_i\}$, $i = 1, \ldots, n$,

$$\Pr(\mathbf{X}_n = x_n \mid \mathbf{X}_i = x_i, i = 1, \ldots, n-1) = \Pr(\mathbf{X}_n = x_n), \qquad (1.72)$$

which simply states that knowledge of the earlier states of the process in no way affects the probability distribution of the current state. An example of such a discrete-time, independent process is a random sample (Section 1.3.5). For continuous-time processes, exactly the analogous property can be stated, but these processes do not tend to be of much use because they are so chaotic they cannot be realized in the physical world.

A rather more useful concept in the continuous-time context is that of *independent increments* in the sense that for each choice of $t_0 < t_1 < \cdots < t_n$ in T, the increments $\mathbf{X}(t_i) - \mathbf{X}(t_{i-1})$, $i = 1, \ldots, n$, are all independent random variables.

A third major notion is, perhaps, the least amount of dependence that one can envisage. It says that knowledge of the entire past of the process is of no greater use in predicting the future than knowledge of the present state of the process. Put another way, the prediction of where a process will go from the present state is not improved by knowing how it got to where it is. Such processes have the most primitive memory imaginable. Formally we say that a process exhibits the *Markovian property* or forms a *Markov process* if for each $t_1 < t_2 < \cdots < t_n$ in T and each sequence $\{x_i\}$, $i = 1, 2, \ldots, n$,

$$\Pr[\mathbf{X}(t_n) = x_n \mid \mathbf{X}(t_i) = x_i, i = 1, \ldots, n-1]$$

$$= \Pr[\mathbf{X}(t_n) = x_n \mid \mathbf{X}(t_{n-1}) = x_{n-1}]. \quad (1.73)$$

Although the Markov property is quite restrictive, it is nonetheless useful in modeling, in part because such processes are very well understood and in part because a problem that does not seem to be Markovian can sometimes be reformulated into an equivalent one that is.

A fourth important concept concerns temporal invariance. The idea is that the process is, in an important sense, independent of time: no matter when one chooses to look at it, the process looks probabilistically the same as at any other instant in time. Formally, the process $\{\mathbf{X}(t)\}$ is said to be *stationary* if for each sequence $\{t_i\}$ in T, each real sequence $\{x_i\}$, and each number h such that all $t_i + h$ are in T,

$$\Pr[\mathbf{X}(t_i + h) = x_i, i = 1, \ldots, n]$$

$$= \Pr[\mathbf{X}(t_i) = x_i, i = 1, \ldots, n]. \quad (1.74)$$

Consider a process that is discrete in time and has finitely many (discrete) states, whose values may, with no loss of generality, be denoted $1, 2, \ldots, m$. Suppose further that it is stationary and Markovian. Then its probability structure is completely captured by the m^2 numbers that tell how it passes from one state to another at the next instant of time:

$$P_{ij} = \Pr(\mathbf{X}_2 = j \mid \mathbf{X}_1 = i) = \Pr(\mathbf{X}_{k+1} = j \mid \mathbf{X}_k = i). \quad (1.75)$$

Such processes are called (discrete-time, finite-state) *Markov chains*; they are very well understood. Elementary references are Kemeny and Snell (1960) and Isaacson and Madsen (1976).

For processes with independent increments it is really too demanding also to ask that it be stationary; however, it is by no means unreasonable to ask whether the process is time invariant to the degree that the increments themselves are stationary. We say that a process has *stationary increments* if the distribution of $\mathbf{X}(t+h) - \mathbf{X}(t)$ is solely a function of h, not of t. This is the fifth major concept.

An example of a process with both independent and stationary increments, one which is also Markovian, is the *random walk on the line* defined as a discrete-time process in which the state at time i is obtained from that at time $i-1$ simply by adding an independent random variable $\mathbf{Z}_i$, where the $\mathbf{Z}_i$ are independent and identically distributed. Thus, the process is characterized by the recursion

$$\mathbf{X}_i = \mathbf{X}_{i-1} + \mathbf{Z}_i, \tag{1.76}$$

where the $\{\mathbf{Z}_i\}$ are independent and identically distributed: that is, they form a random sample of the so-called steps of the process. Such a process is Markovian since by its recursive definition,

$$\Pr(\mathbf{X}_n = x_n \mid \mathbf{X}_i = x_i, i = 1, \ldots, n-1) = \Pr(\mathbf{X}_{n-1} + \mathbf{Z}_n = x_n \mid \mathbf{X}_{n-1} = x_{n-1})$$
$$= \Pr(\mathbf{Z}_n = x_n - x_{n-1} \mid \mathbf{X}_{n-1} = x_{n-1}).$$

By induction on Eq. 1.76,

$$\mathbf{X}_{i+h} - \mathbf{X}_i = \mathbf{Z}_{i+h} + \mathbf{Z}_{i+h-1} + \cdots + \mathbf{Z}_{i+1}.$$

Since the $\mathbf{Z}_i$'s are independent and identically distributed, we see that these increments are identically distributed, and this distribution depends only upon the distribution of $\mathbf{Z}_i$ and on h, but not on i.

The term "random walk" arises from the interpretation of $\mathbf{X}_i$ as the location of a creature and $\mathbf{Z}_i$ as its next random step, which is said to the left if $\mathbf{Z}_i < 0$ and to the right if $\mathbf{Z}_i > 0$. We investigate certain random walks in Sections 8.2 and 8.3.

I turn next to the last restriction to be taken up in this section. It concerns a counting process $\{\mathbf{N}(t)\}$. Often it is useful to view a counting process in a complementary and equivalent way by recording the times at which each count occurs. Let $\mathbf{T}_n$ denote the first value of t such that $\mathbf{N}(t) = n$; that is, $\mathbf{T}_n$ has the following two properties:

(i) $\mathbf{N}(\mathbf{T}_n) = n$.
(ii) If $t < \mathbf{T}_n$, then $\mathbf{N}(t) < n$.

Observe that

$$\Pr[\mathbf{N}(t) \leq n] = \Pr[(\mathbf{T}_n) \geq t]. \tag{1.77}$$

Let $\mathbf{U}_n = \mathbf{T}_n - \mathbf{T}_{n-1}$, which is the time between the occurrence of the

TABLE 1.1. Relations among elementary concepts about stochastic processes

General concepts	Discrete-time concepts	Continuous-time concepts
Independence	+ identically distributed = random sample	—
Independent increments ⎫ Stationary increments ⎬ Markov ⎭	Example: random walk	+ counting + ident. dist. = renewal;˙ renewal + exponential = Poisson
Markov ⎫ Stationary ⎬ Finite state ⎭	(Discrete-time, finite-state) Markov chain	⎱ Continuous-time ⎰ Markov chain

$(n-1)$st and nth event and is called an *interarrival time*, abbreviated IAT. Such a counting process is called a *renewal process* when the IATs are independent random variables that are identically distributed. The reason for the name is that as each event occurs the process renews itself. The prototypic example is the replacement of burned out light bulbs in a socket, where the new bulbs are drawn of a population of statistically identical bulbs.

A *Poisson process* is a renewal process in which the common distribution of the IATs is exponential (Section 1.2.3). Since the hazard rate of an exponential is constant and since all of the exponentials are the same, this means that a Poisson process is characterized by a constant hazard rate throughout. We will study some properties of renewal processes and Poisson ones in a number of places, in particular Sections 3.2.4, 4.4, 9.2.4, and 9.3.

A summary of the several terms mentioned and some of the interconnections is outlined in Table 1.1.

I
DETECTION PARADIGMS

2

Simple Reaction Times: Basic Data

2.1 THE PROBLEM

How fast can one detect the occurrence of a signal without, however, necessarily identifying it among several possibilities? Put another way, how rapidly can a person initiate a simple, preprogrammed response to a simple triggering signal? That question motivates what is known as the simple reaction-time experiment and the theories designed to explain the data. Oddly, it is a far trickier question to formulate precisely and to answer than it first seems. At least four major subquestions are involved: What in the environment constitutes a signal? What is the temporal organization of signal occurrences? How does a person indicate that a signal has been detected? How do we know (or attempt to manipulate) the state of preparedness and attention of the person responding?

Consider a familiar example—albeit, one that is more complicated than just the detection of a single type of signal, but one that sets the general stage for both simple and choice reaction-time studies. You are driving at night under slightly misty conditions on a relatively lonely country road. The visual display is continually fluctuating, occasionally causing you to suspect that something is on the road but then turning out to have been only a darker swirl in the mist. Sooner or later, however, such a perturbation persists and suddenly you move your foot from the gas pedal to the brake, and as you slow down and veer you recognize what it is—a disabled and unlighted vehicle, a person in dark clothes walking, a deer, or whatever. This is a typical situation in which some changes in the environment must be detected and responded to as rapidly as possible—one for which we can discuss these four questions: What are reaction signals? What is their temporal pattern? How does one react? What role does level of attention play?

In this, as in most other realistic examples, signals involve a complex of changes in the environment that over some relatively short time—from tens of milliseconds to hundreds of milliseconds or even seconds—become increasingly more pronounced and unambiguous. The changes are such that one can usually detect the existence of something before one can identify it. Moreover, natural fluctuations in a "noisy" background, such as mist, are sometimes signal-like and may very well initiate the braking response that is then aborted once it becomes clear the apparent detection is false. These occurrences are known as false alarms.

What is a reasonable experimental abstraction of such signals? First, it seems easiest to study just one type of signal—although later we must also consider multiple types—and to have the signals vary in the single most relevant dimension for detection—namely, intensity. Typically, then, experimental signals are lights or sounds that involve a change in intensity—it may be either an increase or decrease. Second, if the signal is to mimic many natural situations it should increase gradually in intensity at least until the subject responds and perhaps longer in order to provide information feedback telling when it was really there. In fact, most experimental signals are not of this character, but rather involve changes that are nearly discontinuous; we return to this in Section 2.2.1.

What of the temporal pattern of the signals? In the natural environment they usually occur haphazardly in time and, more often than not, without warning that they are about to occur. An exception to the latter case is when either an oncoming car signals danger ahead or the operator of a disabled vehicle places some sort of warning marker on the road. But, in general, the driver must assume that there will be no warning, and signals must be detected as they arise. In an experiment, the haphazard occurrence of signals must be controlled by some sort of well-specified random process. Perhaps the most natural one to consider is the Poisson process, the one with the constant hazard function in which the time since the last occurrence provides no information whatsoever about the occurrence of the next event. Obviously, one may choose to deviate from this if one wishes to study the impact on reaction times of changes in the hazard function governing signal presentations, but the most natural baseline condition is pure temporal randomness.

Next, consider the responses of, for example, a driver. Of the complex of actions available, the most salient for present purposes is the movement of the foot to the brake. In setting speed limits and designing roads, response times are crucial, and road designers need to know them, at least crudely, for moderate to poor drivers. But from the point of view of a psychologist, that time is far too crude since it takes a basic time constant of the person—namely, how rapidly the information can be processed and a response to it be activated—and confounds it with the time to complete a rather lengthy motor response—lifting the foot from the gas pedal, moving it some 6 to 10 cm to the brake, and depressing the brake perhaps 10 cm. Since the one is an inherent limitation of the organism and the other can be greatly influenced by the design of the vehicle, they need to be separated as much as possible. So it is common in the experimental abstraction to design response procedures—usually response keys—so that as little time as possible is actually absorbed in the execution of the response. Very little excursion of either the finger or the key is acceptable. Even so, one finds substantial differences in the times reported by different laboratories, suggesting that this normally ignored variable may be under poorer control than is desirable.

Closely related to key design is the question of the force exerted in making the response. This, too, is a ubiquitous dependent variable, one that may very well be correlated with response time. It is much less often recorded than response time, and it is far less completely studied (see, however, Angel, 1973). I shall ignore this variable in this book.

Finally, there is the question of the state of the person at the time of a response. We all know that our performance varies with our state of health, the time since the last meal, the time since and the nature of one's last rest, drugs ingested, emotional state, how long one has been driving, and how recently there has been a reminder of the dangers involved—a near miss, seeing the aftermath of an accident, or a warning by a passenger. The experimenter can, depending upon his or her concerns, treat the state of attention, or preparedness as it is often called, either as a variable to be studied or a parameter to be controlled as much as possible. In either case, problems exist. Even when we study the effects of state of preparation, we usually manipulate it in just one way—say, by drugs or by the length of time that close attention has been required—and the experimenter hopes to control or randomize all other ways it may be affected. In practice we have precious little actual control over what subjects do and experience outside the laboratory, and so we must to a large extent rely on their cooperation in telling us when something is wrong, be it illness, malaise, hangover, tension, and so on. Much of the art of running a good reaction-time experiment centers on gaining the cooperation of subjects in admitting deviations from optimal attentional states and in maintaining a high level of attention when actually running in the experiment. It is a major variable and, by comparison with our sophisticated stimulus control, it is largely out of control.

2.2 THE SIMPLE REACTION-TIME PARADIGM

What we have just described—a single type of intensity change occurring randomly in time with the subject free to respond in some standard way at any time—is known in the literature as a *free-response* or *vigilance* design. The former is probably the more general term since vigilance designs, having been motivated by military sonar and radar watches, usually involve relatively infrequent signal presentations over relatively long experimental sessions. Chapter 5 is devoted to these studies. Here we shall consider certain further restrictions that lead to what is called the *simple reaction-time paradigm*.

2.2.1 Reaction Signals

The first restriction is that almost all studies have been conducted using reaction signals that are ramped on rapidly, usually achieving maximum intensity in something on the order of 25 msec. That peak intensity is maintained until either a fixed time has passed, usually not more than 500 msec, or until the subject has responded, after which it is ramped back to baseline, again rather rapidly. The ramping is not made more rapid because that leads to energy splatter—that is, substantial amounts of energy at frequencies different from the base frequency of the signal—which in audition is heard as a click at signal onset.

It is very rare, indeed, to find studies in which the signal is ramped on relatively slowly and is permitted to increase steadily until it is unambiguously present. Presumably the reason for studying signals with rapid onsets is to uncover the inherent temporal limitations of the human being. Nonetheless, in my opinion, it is important for us to gain better understanding of the very common situation of steady signal growth, such as occurs in driving. It is true that gradually ramped signals are much more difficult to study theoretically since the signal cannot be described as a simple shift in the value of a parameter, but this type of signal is much too prevalent in ordinary experience to ignore it for that reason.

Although most published studies use signals of fixed duration, which probably does not really matter for moderate to very intense signals, it has recently been realized that for weak signals a response terminated design may sometimes be more appropriate (see Chapter 4). However, for reasons that will become apparent in Section 2.2.2, it is not really very feasible to use response terminated, constant intensity signals in a free-response design.

2.2.2   Trials and Reaction Time

A second restriction arises because of the following problem in free-response designs. If one uses a Poisson schedule to control signal onset, then signals often occur very close to one another and, since they necessarily are of finite duration, they may overlap. This situation arises because the inter-onset times are exponentially distributed, which for any $\tau > 0$ makes the interval $(0, \tau)$ more likely to contain the signal than any other interval of length τ. Although this property may seem counterintuitive, it is inherent in processes that are uniformly random in time. Three problems result. First, what should the experimenter do when the presentation schedule dictates overlapping signals? Second, what should the subject be instructed to do and what is it possible for him or her actually to do when a second signal begins before the response has been completed to an earlier signal? And third, when analyzing data, how should the experimenter assign responses to two or more signals that are very close together?

These difficulties can be viewed either as a defect of the free-response design, which then should be modified, or as something inherent in the real world, which must therefore be confronted. After all, an occasional rapid succession of emergencies may be a characteristic of real life that should be retained in our experiments. In such situations everything seems to be (and indeed is) going wrong at once. But if one is trying to disentangle the factors that underly fast responding, it is probably wise initially to avoid this particular complication. One way to do so is to forego the Poisson schedule of signals at least to the following extent. Hold the hazard function of the schedule constant until the process orders a signal to be presented, then drop it to zero until the response occurs, at which point reset it at the previous constant level until the next signal occurs, drop it to zero, and so on. This not only prohibits signals from overlapping, but prevents a second one from intervening between a signal and the response to it.

Such a hazard function also has the feature of defining an unambiguous *trial* during which exactly one signal and one response occur. The onset of the next trial is the completion of the current response, and the time from that response to the onset of the next signal—the *response-stimulus interval*—is exponentially distributed. The time from the signal onset to the response is called the *reaction time* (or response time when the subject has not been instructed to pay attention to time and is unaware that they are being recorded), and it is denoted **T**, where the boldface reflects the fact that we shall treat the observed time as a random variable.

2.2.3 Warning Signals and Foreperiods

Subjects find the pace of such an experiment rather breathless, and it appears difficult for them to maintain a high level of attention at all times. For this and other reasons—such as providing explicit information feedback about the subject's performance on a trial-by-trial basis—it is quite common to modify further the hazard function governing signal presentations so that it goes to zero at signal onset and remains there for some period of time after the response. In that case, it is usual to introduce a stimulus—called the *warning signal*—to alert the subject to the fact that the hazard function has shifted from zero back to its other level and that, therefore, it is time to attend to the reaction signal. It is usual for the warning signal to be moderately intense, and often it is in a modality different from the reaction signal; in most cases we discuss, one is visual and the other auditory. Some experimenters question the use of different modalities on grounds that this necessarily divides attention between the two.

The interval **S** from the change in the hazard function until the onset of the reaction signal is called the *foreperiod*. Depending on the experimental design, **S** may be constant or a random variable. Various relations are possible between the warning signal and the change in the hazard function, perhaps the most common being that the offset of the warning signal coincides with the change in the hazard function. As it seems to take some time for the subject to return to a high level of attention, I prefer a warning signal that in some sense provides a countdown to this change. This can be done in a number of ways. One is to introduce a sequence of, say, five brief signals spaced regularly in time, and change the hazard function at the offset of the last one. Another is to use a continuous sweep, similar to the second hand of a clock, whose crossing of a particular line marks the start of a trial.

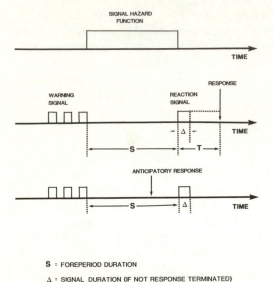

S = FOREPERIOD DURATION

Δ = SIGNAL DURATION (IF NOT RESPONSE TERMINATED)

T = REACTION TIME

FIG. 2.1 The temporal structure of a typical response-time experiment. The top line shows the hazard function governing the—in this case, exponential—foreperiod random variable, which selects the time of signal onset. The second line shows the events that occur on a reaction trial. The warning signal is, in this example, three brief signals with the foreperiod beginning at the termination of the third warning signal. The foreperiod ends with the presentation of the signal, which is of some duration Δ, after which the response occurs. The third line shows the events that occur on an anticipation trial, which is the same as line two except that the response precedes signal onset.

Figure 2.1 summarizes the temporal structure of a typical trial in a simple reaction-time experiment.

2.2.4   Random Foreperiods

More must be said about the distribution of foreperiods. Because of the way we have arrived at the design—abstracting from a natural detection problem—we have been led to the exponential distribution. This distribution has the property—which many consider a virtue in this context—of there being nothing in the developing situation that tells the subject when to expect the reaction signal. The time that has elapsed since the warning signal is completely unhelpful, and so no gain results from doing anything beyond attending to the reaction signal and then responding as rapidly as possible. I find this property a highly compelling reason for using a Poisson schedule unless we wish to manipulate attention by means of the elapsed time. The argument against using it is the fact that some very long times may occur, and the subject may be unable to sustain attention for so long. As we shall see in Section 2.4.3, data can be brought to bear on this question.

Either because of this attention argument or because of a misunderstanding about hazard functions, many studies have been run using all sorts of variable, but non-exponential, foreperiod distributions. Perhaps the most common one is to select a fixed and usually small number of times and to make them equally likely—a uniform distribution over a discrete set. Possibly those electing to use this distribution believed it to lead to (approximate) uniformity in time, but as we know from Section 1.2.3 that is not true.

I will cover some, although by no means all, of the effects of foreperiod distribution on behavior in Section 2.4.

2.2.5 Constant Foreperiods and Catch Trials

In addition to the variable foreperiod designs, there is one constant foreperiod design widely used by some experimenters who believe it leads to better estimates of the minimum time to react. It uses a fixed, relatively brief foreperiod. This has the advantage that the time a subject has to attend carefully is both short and constant from trial-to-trial, whereas in the variable foreperiod design the times vary, and one fears that either attention may flag or expectation may grow on those trials when the foreperiod is particularly long. The drawback to any fixed foreperiod design is that it invites the subject to base his or her response not exclusively on the reaction signal, but on an estimate of the time from the warning signal to the reaction signal, which can be done with adequate accuracy (see Section 2.4). If that happens, the estimated reaction time is in danger of being spurious and misleading.

To suppress timing from the warning signal, the reaction signal can simply be withheld on a certain proportion (usually not more than a quarter) of the trials. These are called *catch trials*. Such a procedure was called the c method in Donders's (1868, 1969) classification of procedures, and today it sometimes goes under the name, Go, No-Go. The occurrence of many responses on the catch trials—*false alarms*—is taken as evidence of the subject's failure to wait for the reaction signal before responding. Feedback to this effect is used to modify the subject's behavior until the number of false alarms on the catch trials is low. Some experimenters (e.g., Kohfeld, Santee, & Wallace, 1981) only accept experimental runs, usually in the range of 25 to 100 trials, for which there are no false alarms on the catch trials and discard all other data. Such a selection procedure, which obviously is nonrandom, capitalizes on chance in a way that many fear is misleading and distorting. This whole topic of false alarms bears considerably more discussion.

2.2.6 Anticipations and False Alarms

Not every time you start to brake a car do you actually find an obstacle imbedded in the mist. In any complex background there are accidental configurations that can be mistaken for signals, and false alarms are inherent whenever there is pressure for rapid responding. It is reasonably clear from everyday experience that we have some sort of subjective criteria for responding that we may adjust so as either to increase or to decrease the tendency to emit false alarms, and that this is likely to be at the expense of also altering the speed with which one responds to signals. If you don't brake until you are absolutely sure there is an obstacle, your stops are either more sudden or more catastrophic than those of a person who makes an occasional false movement to the brake. In many situations there appears to be some sort of tradeoff between the reaction time to signals and the false alarm rate. This is our first example of a speed-accuracy tradeoff (see Section 2.5).

In the literature, especially that part using variable foreperiods, any response that occurs prior to the onset of a signal is called an *anticipation* (see Figure 2.1). Presumably that word was chosen because these were thought to be responses triggered by the warning signal, not by the reaction signal, in which case the term tends to prejudge matters. For even if the subject avoids time estimates, "anticipations" that are really false alarms are to be expected unless a very strict criterion is established for responding. Indeed, once the possibility of false alarms is accepted, we realize that some of the responses subsequent to signal onset must also be due to something— misinterpreted as a signal—that actually occurred prior to signal onset. It is, of course, completely futile using only behavioral data to isolate, other than statistically, which responses are actually false alarms and which are true reactions. Such isolation may become possible with physiological observations, but that is for the future.

Thus in the Go, No-Go design one must also consider the possibility that the false alarms on catch trials are just that, not evidence of time estimation. Furthermore, the fact that some false alarms do occur on catch trials without there being any anticipations is not, by itself, completely convincing evidence that the false alarms on catch trials are due to time estimation. The role of time estimation may be not to initiate responses, but on the contrary to suppress the false alarms that would otherwise occur during the probable duration of the foreperiod. Such a mechanism would artificially suggest that the true false alarm rate is zero. If that is so and if the experimenter induces the subject to establish a criterion so stiff that no responses occur on catch trials, then reaction times may be forced to be longer than they otherwise would be. That tradeoff is our next topic.

2.2.7 Speed-Accuracy Tradeoff

In the simple reaction-time design we face a very common problem in psychology: the existence of a tradeoff between dependent variables, in this case false alarms and reaction time. The only sensible long-range strategy is, in my opinion, to study the tradeoff, as is done for example in the error tradeoff described by the ROC curve of the theory of signal detectability (Green & Swets, 1974, Chapter 2), and to devise some summary statistic to describe it. However, as its study tends to be expensive in experimental time and in some designs is not really feasible,* experimenters often follow another path. They attempt through instructions, information feedback, and data selection to hold one of the dependent variables, in this case the false alarm rate, to some low constant value. In general, there are reasons to doubt the actual success of the practice. Kohfeld et al. (1981) only accepted runs with no false alarms. But as there were only 8 catch trials in a run of 32, an error-free run says very little about the actual probability of false alarms; for example, if the true probability of a false alarm is .25, the chance of a perfect run is about .1. So one has little confidence that the procedure is effective at holding the false alarm rate at a constant value, let alone a very low one.

Despite these problems, much of the data presented below either arose from procedures similar to the ones described or the false alarm rate was not dealt with explicitly in the report of the experiment. Just how serious an omission this may have been has to be considered case-by-case in an attempt to judge whether the results are misleading.

2.2.8   Information Feedback and Payoffs

When speed of response is of interest, it is advisable to provide the subject with some information feedback and reinforcement. Practice varies considerably. At a minimum, the subject is told at the end of a block of trials something about the quality of the performance—the mean time to respond, and either the number of anticipations or, in the case of catch trials, the number of false alarms. In some designs, the subject is provided with trial-by-trial feedback, which may include the actual reaction time measured as closely as a millisecond or as crudely as (i) whether it was before or after some assigned deadline, or (ii) whether the response was an anticipation or, in a Go, No-Go design, a false alarm, or (iii) whether it fell in some band of times. Usually when trial-by-trial feedback is used, some form of payoff is also involved that punishes anticipations and false alarms and rewards fast responses. As there is no single agreed upon procedure, whenever feedback and payoffs appear to have played a crucial role, I will indicate what feedback was involved. It should be emphasized that any payoff scheme—be it money or instructions or repetitions of "unsatisfactory" blocks of trials— establishes for the subject a value concerning the tradeoff between errors and speed, and it is to be assumed that were the experimenter to change the payoff schedule, the subject would alter his or her behavior.

---

* For example, in the Go, No-Go design, allowing the false alarm rate to increase raises the specter of responses to the warning signal and generates a statistical problem of how to correct for them.

2.3 EFFECT OF SIGNAL PROPERTIES ON REACTION TIME

2.3.1 *Intensity and the Mean Time*

Intuition does not reveal a great deal about the impact of signal intensity upon reaction time. Often when it is important to respond rapidly, signals simply grow steadily in intensity, and so it is difficult to conclude anything about the impact of different intensities. For those signals that do change discontinuously from one level to another, we are mostly aware of our startle response. But do you startle faster to the unexpected discharge of a nearby gun or to the slight rustle of a person who has, without warning, come into your room?

   Still, we know enough to reason our way to a plausible guess. Suppose we approach the problem of detecting a signal by subdividing time into a sequence of intervals of length τ, perhaps in the region from 10 to 50 msec. Let us think of each time segment as an opportunity to decide whether or not the signal is there. Let $p(I, \tau)$ denote the probability that a signal of intensity I presented during time τ would be detected. If—and this is a major "if"—each of these time segments can be considered independent, then the probability that the nth segment of signal is the first one to be detected is

$$p(I, \tau)[1 - p(I, \tau)]^{n-1}.$$

Equation 1.69 provides us with the mean of this geometric distribution, whence the expected time of detection is

$$\tau[1 - p(I, \tau)]/p(I, \tau).$$

Since, as is well known, the probability $p(I, \tau)$ of detecting a signal of fixed duration τ is an increasing function of intensity I, the mean time to respond is a decreasing function of intensity. Of course, the model just outlined is suspect—it makes sense only if information is absorbed in independent time quanta. Nonetheless, it strongly suggests we may find a very simple relation between the time to respond to a signal of sufficiently long duration and the probability of responding to one of the same intensity but of fixed duration.

   Although Cattell and Berger (Cattell, 1886a) demonstrated a decreasing reaction time with intensity, it was Piéron (1914, 1920) who suggested that mean reaction time to light intensity follows a very simple law,[*] namely,

$$E(\mathbf{T}) = r_0 + kI^{-\beta}, \tag{2.1}$$

where $E(\mathbf{T})$ is the expected reaction time, and r_0, k, and β are parameters.[†]

---

[*] Other empirical laws have been fit to such data. For example, Bartlett and Macleod (1954) use $E(T) = r_0 + k/\log(I/I_0)$.

[†] The same functional form relating the force of the response to signal intensity was found by Angel (1973) to fit the data for visual, auditory, and shock signals.

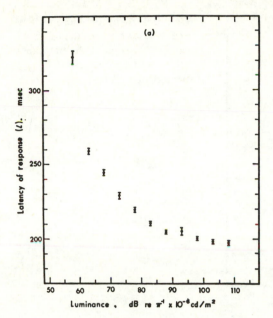

FIG. 2.2 Mean reaction times to a visual signal versus signal intensity in logarithmic scale (dB, with the reference level equal to 10^{-10} Lambert). [Figure 2a of Mansfield (1973); copyright 1973; reprinted by permission.]

The quantity r_0 is often given an interpretation, but we will postpone doing that. It has been variously called the "nonsensory factor" (Scharf, 1978), the "irreducible minimum" (Woodworth & Schlosberg, 1954), or the "mean residue" (Green & Luce, 1971). Typical modern data from Mansfield (1973) are shown in Figure 2.2 for a dark adapted observer with light flashes of 30 msec duration and a foreperiod that "varied irregularly" with a mean 3.31 sec. For monochromatic lights and adapting fields of either the same or different colors, which are used in the study of the Stiles' color mechanisms, the results are appreciably more complex and probably cannot be fit by a law as simple as Piéron's (Mollon & Krauskopf, 1973).

Observe that if Eq. 2.1 is correct, then a plot of the function $\log[E(\mathbf{T}) - r_0]$ versus $\log I$ should be linear,

$$\log[E(\mathbf{T}) - r_0] = \log k - \beta \log I, \tag{2.2}$$

and its slope is an estimate of β, a quantity it turns out that is of some interest. The problem in developing this plot is that one must estimate r_0. In Figure 2.2, r_0 is the value to which the curve becomes asymptotic as I becomes very large. It could be anywhere from 185 to 200 msec. To get a more precise estimate, we could try various values of r_0 in the log-log plot. The trouble is that the curve in this plot is very nearly straight for any choice of r_0 in this interval, but the estimated value of β is much affected by that choice. So there is an estimation problem of some delicacy. Two methods have been used, neither of which is terribly good, and both have been

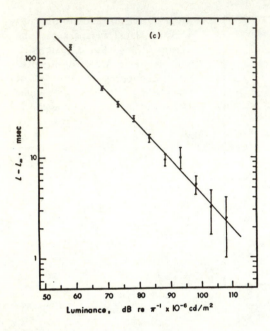

FIG. 2.3 A fit of Piéron's law $E(\mathbf{T}) = r_0 + k\mathbf{I}^{-\beta}$ to the data of Figure 2.2 [Figure 2b of Mansfield (1973); copyright 1973; reprinted by permission.]

superceded by more optimal methods available due to modern computing power.

Mansfield simply chose a number of plausible values for r_0, and for each calculated the best fitting linear regression* of $\log(\mathrm{MRT} - r_0)$ versus $\log I$. He then selected the value of r_0 yielding the largest value of the correlation between the data and predicted values. The correlation was a rather peaked function, with the estimated value of β depending very much on the choice of r_0. It varied by a factor of 2 over a 5 msec change. The resulting plot of the "best fitting" r_0 and β is shown in Figure 2.3.

Kohfeld et al. (1981) suggested another approach. If one takes the derivative of Eq. 2.1 and then the logarithm of the absolute value, the linear regression

$$\log\left[\frac{dE(\mathbf{T})}{dI}\right] = \log k\beta - (\beta + 1)\log I \qquad (2.3)$$

is entirely free of r_0. From this k and β can be estimated and once these are known r_0 can be estimated as the value of $\mathrm{MRT} - k\mathbf{I}^{-\beta}$. This technique is applied in Figure 2.4 to a variety of data obtained by varying the intensity of a 1000-Hz tone in fixed foreperiod designs with catch trials. Two things are

---

* Beginning here and throughout the rest of the book, I will distinguish between a theoretical expectation of a response time, $E(\mathbf{T})$, and the sample mean, which I will denote MRT. Likewise, I will distinguish the theoretical variance $V(\mathbf{T})$ and the sample variance, VRT, of the response times.

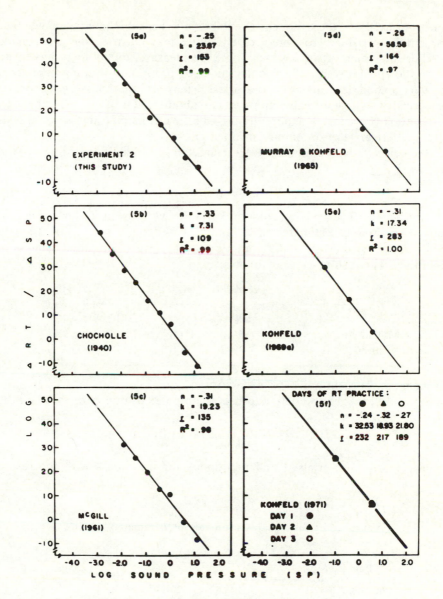

FIG. 2.4 A fit of Piéron's law to MRT versus signal intensity in dB for several auditory studies using 1000-Hz tones. Experiment 2 (this study) refers to Kohfeld (1981). [Figure 5 of Kohfeld et al. (1981); copyright 1981; reprinted by permission.]

noteworthy. First, the exponent β exhibits a remarkable invariance whereas r_0 is quite variable across studies. The latter may illustrate the point made earlier that some of the response time we measure undoubtedly has to do with the apparatus, not the people, and such properties of equipment seem to vary a good deal among laboratories. It may also be that r_0 varies among subjects; we do not really know much about it. Or it may be that the estimation procedure is inherently unstable, which is plausible since it rests on the derivative of an empirical function.

To compare the methods, I had simulated* "data" according to the function

$$\mathbf{T} = 100 + 200I^{-.2} + \boldsymbol{\epsilon},$$

where ϵ was a Gaussian random variable with mean 0 and standard deviation 5 msec. Estimates of r_0 and β based on a sample of 10 with intensities spaced every 10 dB from 10 to 110 dB were computed using both methods. The results were as follows:

	r_0	$\sigma(r_0)$	β	$\sigma(\beta)$
True	100		.200	
Mansfield	84.6	10.8	.106	.043
Kohfeld et al.	79.8	10.0	.135	.052

Both methods seem quite unsatisfactory.

It would probably be better to use a computer to minimize the quantity

$$\sum_{j=1}^{n} [\mathrm{MRT}_j - r_0 - k(I_j)^{-\beta}]^2,$$

where j runs over trials. I had this done† for these data with the results

TABLE 2.1. Least-squares estimates of parameters of Piéron's law

Data source		r_0(msec)	k	β	SS/n
Chocholle	Obs. 1	123.8	261.4	.552	118.8
	Obs. 2	123.8	267.8	.535	118.9
	Obs. 3	147.4	252.8	.628	187.0
Kohfeld		159.8	217.0	.153	15.7
Mansfield		194.6	64.88	.343	34.2
McGill		110.0	215.6	.094	18.2
Murray & Kohfeld		168.3	577.2	.141	51.6

* A. F. Smith carried out the computation.
† R. M. Nosofsky carried out these calculations.

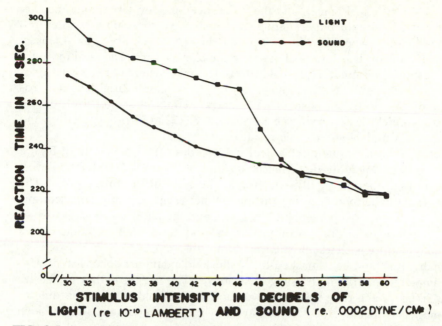

FIG. 2.5 A comparison of MRT versus signal intensity in dB for light and sound collected in the same laboratory. The auditory signals were 1000-Hz tones and the visual ones were a large, diffuse area of white light. The sample size is 60 reactions per point. [Figure 3 of Kohfeld (1971); copyright 1971; reprinted by permission.]

shown in Table 2.1. These estimates are strikingly different from those obtained by Kohfeld et al. in Figure 2.4. Clearly, more attention must be paid to how the estimates are carried out since it affects the value of r_0 by tens of milliseconds and, more important, β by factors of 2 or 3.

With the exception of panel *d* of Figure 2.4, all of the auditory mean residues are substantially faster than Mansfield's for light; however, there were many differences of procedure. The only direct comparison, keeping everything the same except whether light or sound intensity is the reaction signal, is reported by Kohfeld (1971) and is shown in Figure 2.5. Several important facts emerge. First, for signals that are a comparable, but large, amount above threshold there seems to be no difference whatsoever in the reaction time to light or sound; however, auditory reaction times of 220 msec at 60 dB seem rather slow compared to other laboratories, and one cannot be certain that visual and auditory reaction times will be the same in those laboratories. Indeed, it is commonly said that minimal visual reaction times are of the order of 180 msec and auditory ones 140 msec (Woodworth & Schlosberg, 1954, Chapter 2).

Elliott (1968) suggested that the difference between audition and vision might be due to the use of quite small visual fields. He ran a study with a wide field (80° visual angle), and the difference between visual and auditory times was 24 msec (in Experiment 2, the means over five subjects were 168 and 144 msec), whereas with a small field the difference was 40 msec. However, it is unclear how well matched the signals were. The auditory ones were response terminated, 80-dB, 1000-Hz tones, whereas the visual ones were described only as "instantaneous, brief, extremely bright light" produced by an electronic flashgun. We know neither the intensity nor the duration, which, as we shall see in Section 2.3.3, are both necessary and important in understanding this result.

Second, Piéron's equation 2.1 clearly does not fit the visual data of Figure 2.5. This does not contradict Mansfield's data in Figure 2.2 since the lowest intensity used there is 60 dB, which is to the right of the break point. The break is thought to reflect the distinction between photopic and scotopic vision, the former being mediated by cones and the latter by rods. Below 46 dB the light activates only scotopic vision, and above that photopic comes into play and their characteristics are quite different.

Finally, it should be remarked that Mansfield's data are inconsistent with the simple geometric model suggested above. The reason is that all flashes were 30 msec, and they were also well above threshold. Thus, according to the model we could expect to see at most a 30-msec change in the mean reaction times, whereas over 100 msec occurs. Of course, the model is easily saved by assuming that the time associated with each subdecision is not τ, the observation period, but $\tau + \mathbf{X}$, where $\mathbf{X}$ is either the time required for processing or the duration of the flash in iconic memory (after image) or some mix of the two.

2.3.2 Intensity and the Standard Deviation of Time

Intensity affects not only the mean reaction time, but also the variability of the reaction times. In fact, the mean and the standard deviation covary over much of the range in an extremely simple way, as shown in Figure 2.6 for Chocholle's (1940) data in which both intensity and frequency were manipulated. To a good approximation—surprisingly good for empirical data—the estimate of the coefficient of variation (= the ratio of the standard deviation to the mean) as a function of MRT is a constant, slightly less than .1. Green and Luce (1971), using response terminated 1000-Hz tones in low level noise, exponential foreperiods with several mean values, and varying both intensity and the false alarm rate (see Section 2.5), found the pattern shown in Figure 2.7. For reaction times up to 500 msec, the pattern is similar to Chocholle's, although the coefficient of variation is somewhat larger, .2, which may reflect a difference between the random and fixed foreperiod designs. But when weaker signals are used, reaction times are measured in seconds and the coefficient of variation is more nearly 1. Some clarification of the change from .2 to 1 can be found in Chapter 4.

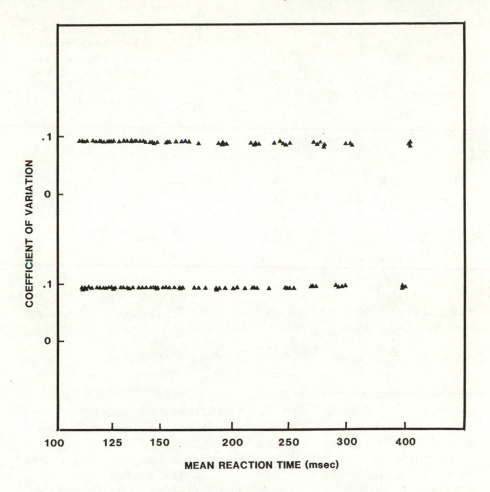

FIG. 2.6 Coefficient of variation (=standard deviation/mean) of simple reaction times to a 1000-Hz pure tone (1000 Hz) versus MRT. This figure was prepared from data tables in Chocholle (1940).

2.3.3 Duration and the Mean Time

A second signal variable we can manipulate, provided the signals are of fixed duration rather than response terminated, is their duration Δ. A large number of visual studies were summarized by Teichner and Krebs (1972). One plot of the data is MRT against the total stimulus energy, as shown in Figure 2.8. The smooth curves, which they faired in by eye, represent the authors' estimate of the fastest mean reaction time for that level of energy. Later Mansfield (1973) carried out a more comprehensive study using light flashes with durations between .3 and 300 msec and intensities from 53 to 108 dB. His highly regular results are shown in Figure 2.9. It is quite clear

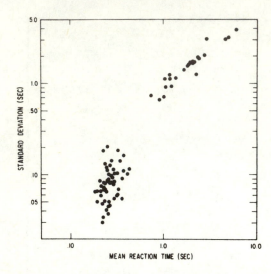

FIG. 2.7 Standard deviation versus MRT for simple reaction times to a 1000-Hz pure tone. [Figure 15 of Green and Luce (1971); copyright 1971; reprinted by permission.]

that at about 12.8 msec the process undergoes a decided change. In fact, the descriptive equation is

$$\text{MRT} = r_0 + \begin{cases} k_1(I\Delta)^{-\beta}, & \Delta < 12.8 \text{ msec} \\ k_2 I^{-\beta}, & \Delta \geq 12.8 \text{ msec.} \end{cases} \tag{2.4}$$

This equation says that for very brief flashes the mean reaction time is a function of signal energy—that is, $I\Delta$—whereas for longer ones it is a function just of intensity, I, independent of duration, Δ. The same exponent $\beta = .33$ fits both regions.

Many fewer data have been collected for the auditory system. The only study of which I am aware is Raab (1962). The warning signal was a 750-msec 1000-Hz tone, there were three equally likely foreperiods, and the signal was band limited noise (100–7000 Hz) of one of six possible durations from 2 to 100 msec. Only two intensity levels, 40 and 60 dB, were used. The data are shown in Figure 2.10, and they appear to exhibit a structure similar to that of vision in that energy is the relevant variable up to some duration and intensity is relevant after that; however, there is some suggestion that the break point may be a function of intensity, which is certainly not true for the visual data of Figure 2.9. A parametric study comparable to Mansfield's needs to be carried out in order to see clearly the pattern.

Not all studies find MRT to be decreasing or constant with signal duration. For example, Gregg and Brogden (1950) used a visual warning signal, a fixed foreperiod of 1750 msec, and a 71-dB auditory signal. They employed a design in which different groups of subjects were run both at one signal duration and under a response terminated condition. They found that MRT grew from 194.3 msec for a 100-msec signal to 224.3 with a

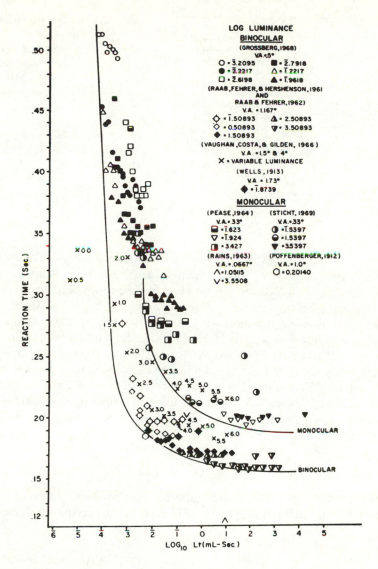

FIG. 2.8 Summary of data for MRT versus signal energy (= intensity ×duration) for visual signals. [Figure 8 of Teichner and Krebs (1972); copyright 1972; reprinted with permission.]

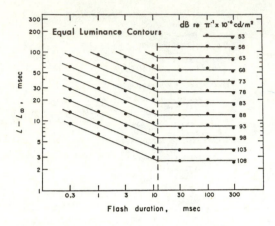

FIG. 2.9 MRT−r_0 (denoted $L-L_\infty$) versus signal duration with signal intensity as a parameter for light flashes. Note that for durations >12 msec, MRT depends only on intensity; whereas for durations <12 msec, MRT depends on signal energy. [Figure 7 of Mansfield (1973); copyright 1973; reprinted by permission.]

2400-msec signal, whereas the response terminated signals were at approximately 200 msec, with very little variability among groups. More recently, Kelling and Halpern (1983) found an even more pronounced increase with what they called taste "flashes." For salt, the increase was from about 480 msec at 100-msec duration to 550 msec at 1000-msec duration; for saccharin the increase was from 900 to 1200 msec. The only "explanation" offered, quoted from Brebner and Welford (1980, p. 3), is that when given the opportunity subjects elect to take larger samples than are really necessary to respond. This statement is surely consistent with Gregg and Brogden's data, and it is something to be kept in mind in designing simple reaction-time experiments, but the phenomenon can hardly be said to be understood.

2.3.4 Subjective Intensity and the Mean Time

Chocholle (1940) in his classic study reported reaction times to tones both as a function of intensity and frequency. If one takes into account judgments of

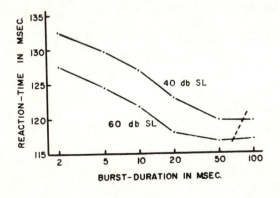

FIG. 2.10 MRT versus signal duration with signal intensity as a parameter for 100–7000 Hz band of noise [Figure 1 of Raab (1962); copyright 1962; reprinted by permission.]

equal loudness, which also depend upon both intensity and frequency, his data showed reaction time to be a decreasing function of subjective loudness. Somewhat later, S. S. Stevens in a long series of papers (see his posthumous 1975 book for a summary and list of publications) argued that subjective intensity grows as a power function of signal intensity. That together with Piéron's Eq. 2.1 suggests mean reaction time might be a linear function of subjective intensity to some power. Indeed, the visual data suggest that that power may be 1, since the exponents for both loudness and reaction time as a function of intensity appear to be in the neighborhood of .3. (Note that this assumes sound intensity measured in amplitude, not power units, where the exponent is about .67.)

Pure tone data favoring this hypothesis can be found in Pfingst, Hienz, Kimm, and Miller (1975). They obtained equal loudness contours in the usual way, and reaction times as a function of signal intensity and frequency (using a variable foreperiod, the release of a key as the response, punishment of anticipations by 7-sec delays, and information feedback about responses less than 100 msec). From the reaction-time data, they constructed equal latency curves that is, intensity-frequency pairs having the same reaction time. The two types of data—loudness and latency contours—are shown for one subject in Figure 2.11 and the correspondence is striking.

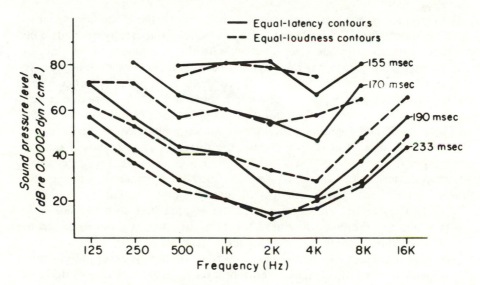

FIG. 2.11 For pure tones, equal loudness and equal latency (MRT) curves for one subject. Each curve gives a locus of intensity-frequency pairs that were judged by this subject to be equally loud or that produced the same MRT in a simple reaction-time experiment. Thirty observations were collected at each intensity spaced at 2 dB over a 20 dB range, a psychometric function was fit to the data, and the threshold was defined to be the intensity value corresponding to 75% correct responses. [Figure 5 of Pfinfst et al. (1975); copyright 1975; reprinted by permission.]

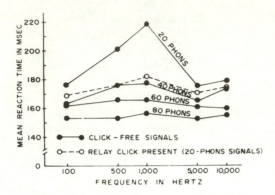

FIG. 2.12 For pure tones, MRT versus frequency for several levels of loudness (measured in phons). There are 576 observations per point. If MRT depended only on loudness, these curves should be horizontal. [Figure 3 of Kohfeld et al. (1981a); copyright 1981; reprinted by permission.]

However, some of the discrepancies are as large as 10 dB, which is a difference that usually cannot be ignored in well-run auditory studies. From the information provided (the sample sizes are unclear), I cannot tell if these discrepancies can reasonably be attributed to chance. The authors also report equal-latency contours for monkeys, and they closely resemble the human data. Pfingst, Hienz, and Miller (1975) explored the reaction times at threshold more fully.

Unfortunately, matters may not be as neat as these studies suggest. Kohfield et al. (1981) pointed out that Chocholle's study really needed to be replicated because he had been unable, with the equipment of his day, to eliminate a click accompanying signal onset, and he was obliged to ask sugjects to ignore it. So using the appropriate contemporary procedures, they first developed equal loudness contours and then carried out the reaction-time experiment. Reaction time as a function of loudness is shown in Figure 2.12, and apparently loudness alone does not account for the mean reaction time data; note, however, that the discrepancy rests mostly on one data point (20 phons, 1000 Hz). To test their hypothesis that the clicks had affected Chocholle's data, they purposely introduced clicks into the lowest loudness level, instructing subjects to ignore them; the flat curve shown resulted. These data should, however, be approached with considerable caution because the equal loudness contours they report differ as much as 30 dB from those usually reported in the literature.

Another argument against the idea that reaction time is determined solely by subjective intensity is indirect, but compelling. Raab (1962) pointed out that his data, shown in Figure 2.10, are inconsistent with that hypothesis because the break from energy to intensity control of loudness occurs at much larger durations (shown by dashed lines on the figure) than the break controlling reaction time. A comparable study does not appear to exist for vision; however, we may draw the same conclusion indirectly. Figure 2.13 shows curves of equal brightness drawn from two sources. Just as we saw for the latency data, brightness grows with energy for short durations and with intensity for longer ones. The only problem is that the transition point varies from about 12 msec for the most intense signals to 200 msec for the moderate ones, whereas the transition for reaction time is independent of intensity (see Figure 2.9). So reaction time cannot be a function just of brightness.

2.4   EFFECT OF FOREPERIOD ON REACTION TIME

The literature on foreperiod effects on reaction time, which is sizable and complex, is well covered by the survey papers of Teichner (1954) and Niemi and Näätänen (1981). I shall only report selected parts of it here.

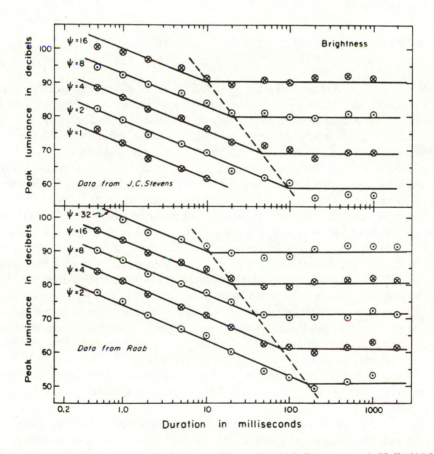

FIG. 2.13 Curves of equal brightness from data of Stevens and Hall (1966) and Raab (1962b) in the coordinates of luminance in dB and signal duration in log scale. [Figure 5 of Stevens and Hall (1966); copyright 1966; reprinted by permission.]

2.4.1   Constant Foreperiods

By a constant foreperiod design, one means that the experiment is run in
blocks of trials, usually from 25 to 100 trials per block, and during each
block the value of the foreperiod is constant. The basic result is simple: the
larger the constant foreperiod duration, the larger the MRT. For example,
Klemmer (1956) used a click as a warning signal and a "clearly visible" neon
light of 20-msec duration as a reaction signal; he found:

Foreperiod	250	425	825	(msec)
MRT	209	252	269	(msec)

Karlin (1959), using the same 250-Hz tone both as the warning signal and as
the reaction signal, ran signals of 100 msec at 33 dB and of 30 msec at
49 dB; he found:

Foreperiod	500	1000	2000	3500	(msec)
MRT at 33 dB	221	256	271	280	(msec)
MRT at 49 dB	178	205	234	234	(msec)

Why does this happen? Basically, three ideas have been suggested. The
first supposes that the subject becomes more uncertain as to when the signal
will occur the longer it is necessary to wait for it to occur. The evidence for
increasing uncertainty with time are data on time estimates (Woodrow,
1930, 1933, with no feedback, and Snodgrass, Luce, and Galanter, 1967,
with feedback) that show the coefficient of variation is roughly constant,
about .1 for time estimates in the range of 0.5 to 5 sec (however, see Section
2.5.3 for more refined data on time estimates less than 500 msec). These
increasingly variable estimates of foreperiod duration could impact reaction
times in at least two ways. If the capacity to attend to the signal is limited
and if time estimation is used to determine when to apply full attention to
the task, then the longer the foreperiod the more likely it is that less than
full attention is actually involved when the signal is presented. Alternatively,
if the time estimate is used in an attempt to anticipate the signal onset and
to initiate the motor response before the reaction signal has actually
occurred, then the increasing variability of the estimates entails an increasing number of anticipations. Since the occurrence of an appreciable number
of false alarms is more-or-less explicitly punished, the subject has little
option but to reduce the percentage of anticipations by increasing the time
estimate to something greater than the foreperiod, thereby increasing the
observed MRT.

The second idea is that the subject establishes some sort of criterion
concerning the amount of evidence about the signal necessary to initiate a
response. In order to be fast, the criterion must be lax so that marginal
evidence is sufficient for a response, and that tends to generate some false
alarms. Obviously, for a fixed criterion, any increase in the foreperiod
duration must lead on the average to an increase in the number of false

alarms. Since that is unacceptable, the criterion must be made increasingly more stringent, thereby slowing down the observed reaction times.

And the third idea is that the quality of information available is affected by the subject's attention, and that attention cannot be sustained at its maximum possible level for prolonged periods of time. Exactly what "attention" is differs from theory to theory. In some it is a parameter that is identified with the concept of capacity to process the information; in others it is equated with some notion of sample size of information available for processing by the brain. However it is modeled, "attention" is reflected in the quality of discrimination that the subject is able to sustain, and it is quite different from the criterion shifts. These two notions—sensitivity and response bias—have been major features of the static theory of signal detectability (Green & Swets, 1966, 1974), and they will reappear throughout this book.

A general discussion of these issues can be found in Näätänen and Merisalo (1977).

Sometimes it is ambiguous which of the mechanisms we have just discussed underlies the data we observe. Other times, the evidence is clearer. For example, the data from exponential foreperiods shed some light on these alternatives since the phenomenon of increased MRT with mean foreperiod duration occurs when time estimates are actually useless. Moreover, additional data involving false alarms support the idea of either a changing response criterion or a shift in sensitivity. Further analysis is required to select between these two. Despite the fact that time estimation can sometimes be avoided, one must be very wary of subjects using them in any design, such as a constant foreperiod one, in which such estimates may prove beneficial.

2.4.2 Equally Likely Foreperiods

Because the constant foreperiod design leads to results that can be interpreted in terms either of time estimation or criterion shifts or both, various authors have suggested that time estimation can be suppressed by using variable foreperiods. Suppose that on each trial, the foreperiod duration S is selected from among the distinct times, $s_1 < s_2 < \cdots < s_k$. The argument for suppression of time estimation is that there is no point in estimating any particular value of s_j, $j < k$, because responses at or near any of these times will simply lead to too many anticipations, and there is no point in time estimating s_k because that time, being the longest, is too imprecisely estimated to be of much value; one is simply better off using the reaction signal on all trials.

The major empirical finding obtained for small k (2 to 5) and equally likely distribution of foreperiods is that the MRT decreases monotonically with actual foreperiod duration (Aiken & Lichtenstein, 1964a,b; Annett,

1969; Davis, 1959; Drazin, 1969; Klemmer, 1956, Näätänen, 1967; Nickerson, 1965a; Rubinstein, 1964). As was noted in Section 1.2.3, a uniform distribution on a finite number of times has a hazard function that increases with time. Stilitz (1972) systematically studied the effect of manipulating the conditional probability of signal occurrence; he clearly established that MRT is a monotonic decreasing function of that conditional probability.

If one assumes that the procedure has successfully suppressed the use of time estimation to anticipate the signal, then the data imply that subjects shift their criterion for evidence that a signal has been presented toward greater laxness as the wait increases. However, as Ollman and Billington (1972) pointed out, it is by no means certain that equally likely use of a few foreperiods has in fact suppressed time estimation. They assume that on some proportion P of the trials, the subject establishes a deadline D, which is assumed to be a random variable with the distribution function G. If the deadline occurs before a response has arisen from the signal, then the subject initiates an anticipatory response. If, however, the signal occurs first, then it controls the response according to a random variable T with the same distribution function H no matter when the signal occurs. When the signal occurs at time s_j and a deadline is established, the observed response time, measured from signal onset, is the $\min(D - s_j, T)$, and when no deadline is established it is just T. Assuming that the random variables D and T are independent, the distribution function F_j of observed response times when the signal occurs at time s_j must satisfy

$$1 - F_j(t) = P[1 - G(t - s_j)][1 - H(t)] + (1 - P)[1 - H(t)]$$
$$= [1 - PG(t - s_j)][1 - H(t)]. \tag{2.5}$$

The first term arises when the deadline is being used, and in that case no response has occurred by time t if and only if neither the deadline has passed, which has probability $1 - G(t - s_j)$, nor the reaction has occurred, which has probability $1 - H(t)$. The second term arises when no deadline is being used, and so the subject responds only to the signal. If, in addition, catch trials are introduced on which the subject is not supposed to respond and are terminated by the experimenter at some time L, when the subject does fail to respond, then the distribution of responses on catch trials (CT) is entirely determined by the deadlines,

$$F_{CT}(t) = \begin{cases} PG(t), & 0 \le t < L \\ 1, & t = L. \end{cases} \tag{2.6}$$

Substituting Eq. 2.6 in Eq. 2.5 and solving for H,

$$H(t) = 1 - \frac{1 - F_j(t)}{1 - F_{CT}(t - s_j)}, \quad t < L. \tag{2.7}$$

Kornblum (1973a) discussed exactly the same model except he assumed $P = 1$; he interpreted the deadline as a case of time estimation.

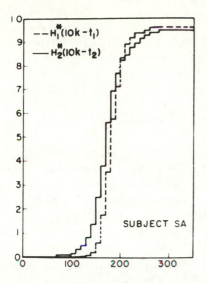

FIG. 2.14 For an experiment with two foreperiods, t_1 and t_2, a comparison of H_1 and H_2, estimated by Eq. 2.7, for one of three subjects run. The data for the other two are similar. According to the dead-line model $H_1 = H_2$. [Figure 8 of Ollman and Billington (1972); copyright 1972; reprinted by permission.]

The key test of the model is that the right side of Eq. 2.7, which involves two terms that each vary with the actual foreperiod duration, is predicted to be independent of foreperiod duration. This experiment was performed with two foreperiods and the computation of Eq. 2.7 carried out (with some statistical refinements I will not go into) with the results shown in Figure 2.14. The two estimates in each case agree sufficiently well that Ollman and Billington were unwilling to accept the assumption that equally likely foreperiods have completely eliminated the time estimation. No statistical test was made for agreement, and there is some reason to think they may differ significantly in the tails.

Because of this argument and because even if estimation is suppressed there is ample reason to believe that the response criterion changes with the changing hazard function, this type of variable foreperiod seems most unsatisfactory.

There are other data about variable, but non-exponential, foreperiods that are worth noting. First, sequential effects due to the foreperiod on the preceding trial may exist; Karlin (1959) reported them, but Näätänen (1970) did not find them. Second, an interaction between foreperiod duration and intensity may exist (see Section 2.4.4), although with non-exponential foreperiods one suspects that this may result from a complex interplay of conditional probability, intensity, and criterion.

2.4.3 Exponentially Distributed Foreperiods

Both from the point of view of criterion (or expectancy) arguments and from that of time estimation, the most appropriate variable foreperiod design is one with a constant hazard function governing signal presentations—an exponential distribution of foreperiods (Thomas, 1967). Because the hazard function is constant, the time elapsed since the warning signal does not affect at all the momentary tendency for the reaction signal to appear. And because the reaction signal can occur at any time, it is very difficult to see how the subject can make any successful use of time estimates. As we shall see, it is relatively easy to check whether systematic time estimates are being used.

The primary reason some experimenters resist using exponential foreperiods is the possibility of some very long waits. They argue that subjects cannot sustain their attention or their patience for more than a few seconds, and that therefore such foreperiods do not achieve the constancy of performance that is a priori appropriate to them. As we shall see in Figure 2.20, there is some empirical evidence to suggest that subjects are able to maintain a constant rate of anticipation for as long as nine seconds.

The literature includes three versions of exponential or, as they are often called, non-aging distributions of foreperiods. The first, no longer used because of the widespread availability of adequate online computers, employs some exponential physical process, such as radioactive decay, to trigger the signal onset. The second involves a time quantized, geometric approximation to the exponential in which each integral multiple of some time interval δ is a possible foreperiod, and it occurs with a fixed probability p provided the signal has not been activated earlier. And the third involves a probability quantized approximation in which boundaries $b_1, b_2, \ldots, b_j, \ldots$ are chosen so that the area in each subinterval,

$$\int_{b_j}^{b_{j+1}} e^{-t}\, dt = \exp(-b_j) - \exp(-b_{j+1})$$

is the same small value (less than 1%). The foreperiods are placed at the mean of each interval

$$s_j = \int_{b_j}^{b_{j+1}} te^{-t}\, dt,$$

and they occur equally often.

As with the fixed foreperiod, the result is that MRT increases with mean foreperiod. Nickerson and Burnham (1969), using a tone as the warning signal, a red light as the reaction signal, and a 25-msec time quantized geometric distribution, found a MRT of 270 msec at a mean foreperiod of 0.25 sec growing to 450 msec at a mean of 32 sec. Green and Luce (1971), using a sequence of five "countdown" lights as a warning signal, a 1000-Hz, 54-dB, response terminated tone as a reaction signal, and a probability quantized exponential distribution with 256 different foreperiods, found a growth from 205 msec at a 0.5-sec mean wait to 290 at 16-sec mean wait.

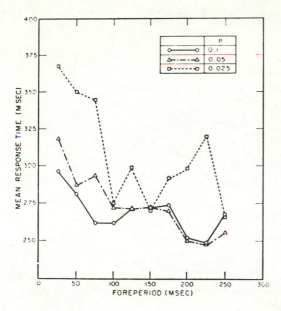

FIG. 2.15 MRT versus the actual foreperiod duration for a 800-Hz, 70-dB warning signal and reactions to the onset of red neon light signals. The foreperiods were partitioned into 10 intervals and the MRT for those foreperiods calculated and plotted against the mean of the corresponding interval. The samples varied from 14 at a foreperiod of 250 msec and $p = 0.025$ to 80 with a foreperiod of 25 msec and $p = 0.1$. [Figure 2 of Nickerson and Burnham (1969); copyright 1969; reprinted by permission.]

Näätänen (1971), using no explicit warning signal, a 1000-Hz, 95-dB, 500-msec reaction signal, and a 1-sec time quantized geometric distribution, found a growth from 204 msec at a mean of 5 sec to 230 msec at a mean of 40 sec, which is rather more shallow than either of the other two studies.

The next natural question to ask is whether this growth has to do with actual waits involved or with the average wait of the condition or both. Put another way, any particular wait, say 2 sec, can occur under any exponential schedule; does the MRT depend only on that value itself or on the mean wait or both? At least some of the data have been analyzed in this way in each of the three papers; that is, for each mean wait, the MRT is plotted as a function of the actual waits in Figures 2.15 to 2.18. The overall result is that the major factor is the mean wait, but in addition there is some sort of interaction that is none too consistent over the studies. For very brief waits (250 msec), MRT decreases with the actual wait (Figure 2.15). This is thought to reflect what has sometimes been called refractoriness: a subject's inability to achieve full readiness immediately after the warning signal. Näätänen (1971), using a uniform distribution of foreperiods, found the same thing. For longer waits, Figures 2.16 and 2.17 are in some disagreement. The former suggests that MRT is independent of the actual wait for the short ones (.5, 1, and 2) and increases for the longer times (4, 8, and 16 sec); whereas, the latter exhibits a statistically significant rise for a mean wait of 5 sec and is flat for the longer mean waits (10, 20, and 40 sec).

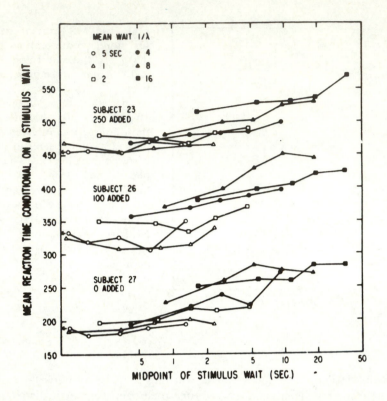

FIG. 2.16 MRT versus the actual foreperiod duration for low intensity pure tone signals. The sample sizes vary from 120 on the left to 50 on the right. [Figure 17 of Green and Luce (1971); copyright 1971; reprinted by permission.]

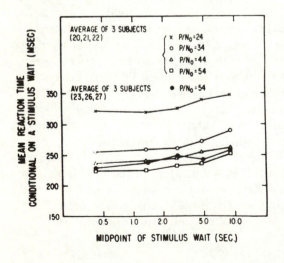

FIG. 2.17 MRT versus the actual foreperiod duration for pure tone signals of various intensities (in dB relative to background noise level). The sample sizes are about 500 observations per point. [Figure 18 of Green and Luce (1971); copyright 1971; reprinted by permission.]

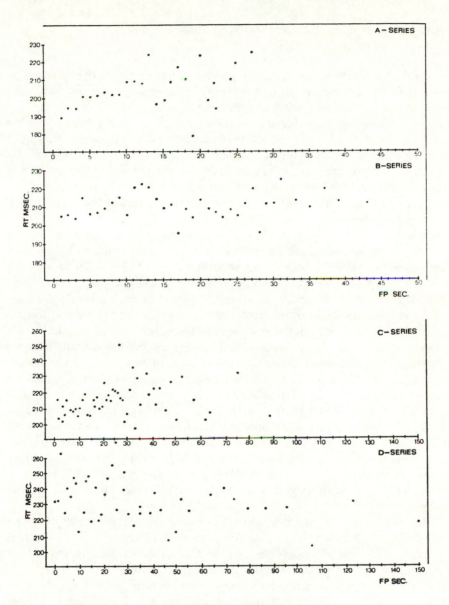

FIG. 2.18 MRT versus actual foreperiod duration for reactions to a 95-dB, 1000-Hz, 500-msec pure tone. The four conditions are mean foreperiod waits of 5, 10, 20, and 40 sec, *A* to *D* respectively, with sample sizes of 2304 for *A* and each successive one halved. In each plot, the sample size drops exponentially from left to right. [Figure 1 of Näätänen (1971); copyright 1971; reprinted by permission.]

2.4.4   Interaction of Foreperiod, Intensity, and Presentation Probability

Since the late 1960s a number of investigators have studied the question as to whether the effects on MRT of foreperiod duration, signal intensity, and the proportion of catch trials are independent of each other or if they interact. According to a line of reasoning due to S. Sternberg, which we will examine in some detail in Sections 3.3.4 and 12.4.1, if the processing of information goes on in a series of discrete stages, each of which must be completed before the next is begun, then interaction is evidence that the experimental variables affect the same stage. Lack of interaction is less easy to interpret. Here I shall limit my attention to the empirical literature, which is moderately confusing.

Niemi (1979) and Sanders (1975, 1977) reviewed the literature on the interaction of intensity and foreperiod. At that time (and including new experiments of these authors) there appeared to be evidence for an interaction of, at least, randomized foreperiods and weak auditory signals (see, especially, Kellas, Baumeister, & Wilcox, 1969). The interaction diminishes and, perhaps, vanishes for relatively intense signals. In the visual domain there was no evidence for an interaction. However, Niemi and Lehtonen (1981) argued that the existing visual data may be inadequate because sufficiently low intensities had not been studied, mainly because the stimuli used were of such a small visual angle that insufficient energy would be present to detect the signal at low intensities. And, indeed, they found this to be the case in what amounted to a visual replication of Kellas et al. (1969) with large visual fields and low intensities. Interestingly, when the experiment is run with constant foreperiods at two different levels, no interaction was found in the visual case and only a slight one with auditory signals. Niemi and Valitalo (1980) showed a similar lack of effect of signal intensity for lights with a small visual angle, but a distinct effect with a larger angle.

The possibility of an interaction between signal probability (= 1 − probability of a catch trial) and foreperiod duration seems moderately plausible since each appears to involve the subject's having to restrain responses triggered independently of the signal. Gordon (1967) reported that MRT decreased with increasing presentation probability, but as Näätänen (1972) pointed out the procedure was odd. In order to hold constant both the sample of signals presented and the total experimental time, the time between trials was varied inversely with presentation probability. Näätänen modified the procedure so that for each presentation probability <1, the experimental run was divided into blocks that interleaved blocks of probability 1 trials in such a way as to maintain constant the total number of signal presentations. He found MRT to grow linearly with the proportion of catch trials, increasing from between 20 and 34 msec, depending on the foreperiod, over the range from no catch trials to 75% catch trials. This, except for the linearity, agreed with Gordon's results.

Buckolz and Rogers (1980) expressed skepticism that this lack of interaction can be true and they suggested that perhaps it was due to a floor effect—admitting, however, there was no evidence in the data for that. In any event, they ran a design which, in addition to manipulating foreperiods and presentation probability, included a condition, called "mediation," in which the subjects count while waiting for the signal to occur. With no mediation, they replicated Näätänen's finding of no foreperiod effect, but not the linearity of MRT with proportion of catch trials. With mediation, an interaction was demonstrated. Exactly what to make of this, especially since the foreperiods were not exponentially distributed, is not clear to me. And I find their discussion of the result unpersuasive.

2.5 SPEED-ACCURACY TRADEOFF

2.5.1 The Phenomenon in Simple Reactions

From what we have seen, it is plausible that the change in MRT with mean foreperiod wait is due to a shift in the subject's response criterion for the evidence needed to trigger a response—a change that is aimed at holding the frequency of false alarms (anticipations) constant. This is an example of a speed-accuracy tradeoff at work in which both false alarm rate and MRT are varying in order to maintain the near constancy of the total number of false alarms. As can be seen in Figure 2.19, if the fraction of false alarms (with a fixed mean foreperiod of 10 sec and signal-to-noise power of 10 dB) is systematically varied over a large range, there is a strong covariation of MRT as would be expected if the criterion were being varied. Explicit models of this character will be developed, first in Section 2.5.2 and more fully in Chapter 4; for now, they are informal intuitions. There is also strong evidence that the criterion becomes less stringent with the actual wait, especially for the stricter (low false alarm frequency) values.

The only study of which I am aware in which the time course of false alarms itself has been examined is Burbeck and Luce (1982). In this study the subject was required to detect the off-set of a barely detectable pure tone in noise. The warning signal was a countdown sequence of lights and the foreperiod distribution was exponential with a mean wait of 3 sec. Figure 2.20 shows the log survivor function for three different subjects each responding to a different frequency. The false alarm rate (slope) is moderately constant from about 750 msec to about 9 sec, at which point the rate increases. This is the opposite of the effect seen earlier, which suggests that there may be strategy differences among subjects and/or laboratories.

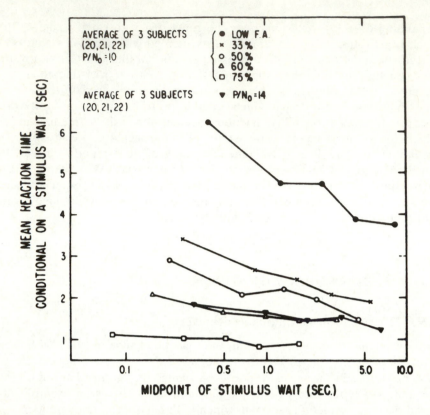

FIG. 2.19 MRT versus actual foreperiod duration for low intensity pure tones with the subject under instructions to produce various proportions of anticipatory responses. The curves are based on from 600 to 1500 responses. [Figure 19 of Green and Luce (1971); copyright 1971; reprinted by permission.]

2.5.2   *A Representation of Criterion Effects*

As I noted earlier, it is often difficult to decide whether a phenomenon such as a speed-accuracy tradeoff is due to the subject's altering how to interpret information about the signal or to an actual change in the quality of information. This is the distinction between bias and sensitivity changes. A major factor affecting sensitivity is, of course, signal intensity, but it may also be affected by states of the subject that can be lumped together as attention. For the present section I will assume that the speed-accuracy tradeoff is a result of bias changes, for which we develop a simple model.

Consider a model of the following character. The physical stimulation undergoes some sort of transduction into an internal representation in the nervous system; it is, of course, a representation that unfolds in time. The brain in some way operates on this information in its attempt to arrive at an

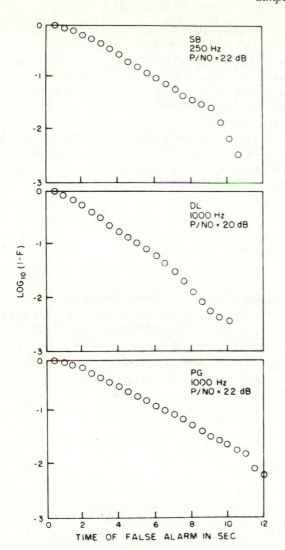

FIG. 2.20 Log survivor function for the anticipations (false alarms) in a simple reaction-time experiment involving low intensity pure tones and an exponential foreperiod distribution. From top to bottom, the sample sizes were 277, 547, and 501. [Figure 4 of Burbeck and Luce (1981); copyright 1981; reprinted by permission.]

"understanding" of what is transpiring outside the body. For stimulation that is substantially steady except for a change of a single aspect, which we call the signal, the brain need only search for some change in the representation that corresponds to the onset of the signal. However, this is made difficult by the fact that there are spontaneous changes in the representation—originating either in the stimulation itself or in the transduction of it or, most likely, both—that may appear the same as the start of the change due to a signal. These false changes may trigger a response because the subject is attempting to respond rapidly, and so must arrive at a decision before all of the information that will ultimately become available actually is available. It seems clear, then, that the brain is in a situation where information is accumulating at some presumably constant average rate, but it varies in quality, and the brain must establish a response criterion that effects a compromise between the level of accuracy and the speed of response. Before we are done, we shall see a number of specific variants of this general idea. At the moment, the plan is to formulate what must be the simplest possible version of it for mean reaction times.

Let us assume that the mean rate of information accumulation is A units of information per unit of time when the signal is present. We assume that only certain experimental factors affect A; in particular, we assume that A grows with signal intensity. If the system examines the process for τ units of time, then the average total accumulation of information is $A\tau$. If the subject establishes a criterion C for the number of units of information required for a response to be initiated, then on average the observation time τ required to achieve C units satisfies

$$C = A\tau. \tag{2.8}$$

Of course, the value for C is also affected by experimental factors, but we shall assume that they are different factors from those that affect A, such as the length of the foreperiod, payoffs, and the like. The observed MRT is assumed to be composed of the sum of two times, the observation time τ and other times, such as the time for the signal information to get to the brain from the periphery and the time for an order to respond to get from the brain to the periphery, which we call the mean residue r_0. So,

$$E(\mathbf{T}) = r_0 + \tau. \tag{2.9}$$

Solving for τ in Eq. 2.8 and substituting in Eq. 2.9 we obtain the simple model

$$E(\mathbf{T}) = r_0 + C/A. \tag{2.10}$$

Since the only thing observed is an estimate of $E(\mathbf{T})$, MRT, this model may seem a trifle pointless. But it is not for the following reason. If the three parameters are really all independent, then by varying the factors that influence each separately we quickly generate more equations than there are unknowns. For example, suppose an experiment is run in which there are three intensity levels, and corresponding to each there is some rate A_i, $i = 1, 2, 3$. Similarly, suppose there are four levels of something that affect the criterion resulting in C_j, $j = 1, 2, 3, 4$. And suppose that we do nothing to affect r_0. Then, there are 12 experimental conditions with eight parameters. In general, if there are m experimental conditions that affect A and n independent ones that affect C, then there are $m + n + 1$ parameters to account for mn MRTs:

$$E(\mathbf{T}_{ij}) = r_0 + C_j/A_i, \quad i = 1, \ldots, m, \quad j = 1, \ldots, n. \tag{2.11}$$

There is a very simple graphical display of this model in which information is plotted versus time. The criteria C_j are lines of constant information,

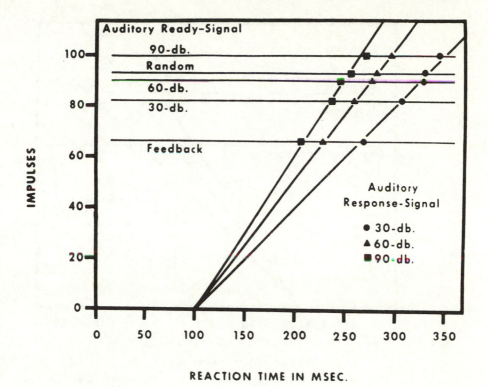

REACTION TIME IN MSEC.

FIG. 2.21 MRT to pure tones at three levels of intensity and five conditions involving the warning signal and feedback. Each data point is based on 30 observations. The ordinate is hypothetical and is adjusted to account for the data as well as possible by a linear fan from a common point r_0, with slopes corresponding to signal intensity, and five horizontal lines, with levels corresponding to hypothetical criteria (Eq. 2.11). [Figure 1 of Kohfeld (1969); copyright 1969; reprinted by permission.]

and the accumulation rates are lines fanning out from r with constant slope A_i, as seen in Figure 2.21. This model for reaction time is due to Grice (1968). The data shown are from Kohfeld (1969); they involve variations in the reaction signal and feedback conditions to affect the criterion. A similar plot based on practice effects is shown in Figure 2.22. Anderson (1974, 1981, 1982) has discussed similar models in other contexts.

To estimate the parameters used in a plot such as Figures 2.21 and 2.22, Grice and Kohfeld proceeded as follows. Observe from Eq. 2.11, we have the two averages

$$\frac{1}{m}\sum_{i=1}^{m} E(\mathbf{T}_{ij}) - r_0 = C_j \frac{1}{m}\sum_{i=1}^{m}\frac{1}{A_i}, \qquad (2.12)$$

$$\frac{1}{n}\sum_{j=1}^{n} E(\mathbf{T}_{ij}) - r_0 = \frac{1}{nA_i}\sum_{j=1}^{n} C_j. \qquad (2.13)$$

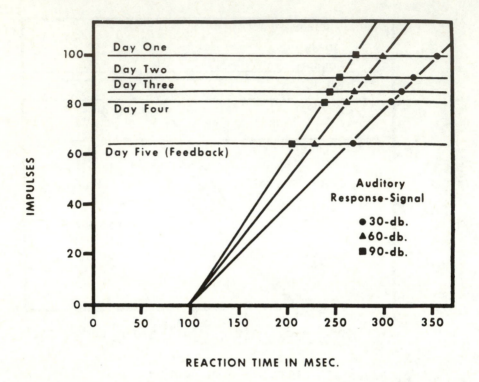

REACTION TIME IN MSEC.

FIG. 2.22 This plot is constructed in the same way as Figure 2.21 except that the horizontal conditions are amount of experience in the experiment. [Figure 2 of Kohfeld (1969); copyright 1969; reprinted by permission.]

They take a shrewd guess that $r_0 = 100$ msec, and for the condition yielding the slowest average in Eq. 2.12, call it $j = n$, they arbitrarily set $C_n = 100$. This then determines $(1/m) \sum (1/A_i)$, and so the data determine all of the other C_j. With these as fixed values, then for each signal intensity i they do a linear regression of MRT_{ij} against C_j with the requirement that for $C = 0$, $E(\mathbf{T}) = r_0$.

A slightly better procedure, in my opinion, would be as follows: for each value of r_0, determine the C_j as described. With the C_j known, use Eq. 2.13 to determine A_i. Since these estimates all depend to some extent on the arbitrary choice of r_0, choose r_0 so as to minimize the squared deviations of the predictions

$$\sum_{i=1}^{m} \sum_{j=1}^{n} (\mathrm{MRT}_{ij} - r_0 - C_j/A_i)^2.$$

Observe that Eq. 2.11 predicts that any independent manipulation of the criterion C and the rate of accumulation A will evidence itself as an interaction in the response times since

$$E(\mathbf{T}_{ij}) - E(\mathbf{T}_{i'j}) = C_j[(1/A_i) - (1/A_{i'})]$$

depends upon the value of C_j and

$$E(\mathbf{T}_{ij}) - E(\mathbf{T}_{ij'}) = (C_j - C_{j'})/A_i$$

depends upon the value of A_i. The prediction in no way depends upon how A_i depends on the experimental condition i or how C_j depends on the experimental condition j so long as they are not constant functions.

In a very insightful review of the literature, Nissen (1977) examined the adequacy of Grice's model for both simple and choice reaction times (see Section 6.4.3 for some discussion of the choice data). She noted that a variety of simple reaction-time studies with auditory signals exhibited the predicted interaction (the references can be found in her paper), but for vision it was far less clear that the model is correct. Thrane (1960b) found only a slight interaction when visual intensity was run in mixed (i.e., random selection among intensities) and blocked (a single intensity at a time) conditions. The blocked conditions presumably invite different criteria for the intensities, whereas the mixed condition requires a single, compromise criterion. In (1960a) she found no interaction of intensity with either practice or individual differences in speed. Sanders (1975) reported no interaction between intensity and mixed and blocked trials. One possible criticism of these studies was a somewhat limited range of intensities, and so Grice, Nullmeyer, and Schnizlein (1979) carried out another mixed-blocked intensity study in which the brightnesses differed by 25.3 dB. The sample sizes were large—in each condition, 20 subjects and 240 trials per subject. An analysis of variance showed no evidence of an interaction. So it appears that Eq. 2.11 is not a correct description of the visual data, but it may be for auditory simple reaction times.

2.5.3   Payoffs and Reaction Time

Up to now, the designs have involved urging the subjects to respond as rapidly as possible, but without making too many anticipations or false alarms on catch trials. The feedback and reprimands, if any, were provided after blocks of trials. This technique is to be contrasted with two other extremes. In the one, the response time (definitely not reaction time) is observed unbeknownst to the subjects and no mention is made to them about response times. In the other, subjects are differentially rewarded according to their reaction times, and this is almost always accompanied by performance feedback on a trial-by-trial basis. It is the topic of this section.

In general, a temporal payoff scheme is some function that assigns to each possible reaction time some form of payoff, often money with human subjects; usually the function is defined in terms of deviations from signal

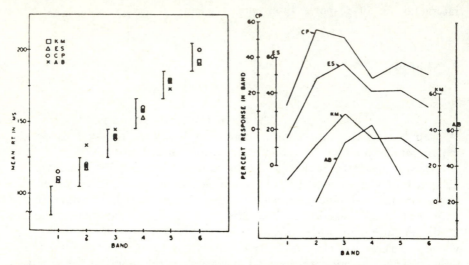

FIG. 2.23 For a 1000-Hz pure tone, simple reaction-time experiment with payoff for responses falling within a specified temporal band (20 msec wide), MRT and probability of the response falling within the band versus band location (equally spaced from 95 to 195 msec). Each point is based on 500 observations except for subject *AB*, band 2, which is 190. [Figure 1 of Snodgrass et al. (1967); copyright 1967; reprinted by permission.]

onset, independent of foreperiod duration. Often anticipations and presumed anticipations (such as responses within 100 msec of the signal onset) are fined, and some positive but declining function of times later than the anticipation boundary rewards fast reactions. A special example of this, called a band payoff, involves the same positive payoff in a narrow (5 to 50 msec) band of times and fines elsewhere. Snodgrass, Luce, and Galanter (1967) varied a 20-msec band from a center at 95 msec to a center at 195 msec using a fixed foreperiod of 2 sec and a brief, 1000-Mz reaction tone. Figure 2.23 shows both MRT and percentage of responses as a function of band location. They used percentage of responses in the band as a measure of variability rather than standard deviation because their data included a substantial number of slow responses—the distribution of RTs appeared to be high tailed as compared with a Gaussian, gamma, or other distributions with an exponential decay in the tail. When that is the case, the estimated standard deviation is a very unstable estimate of the true one, and one is well advised to use some measure that is quite insensitive to the actual values observed at the tails of the distribution. The standard deviation can be grossly overestimated when the data include unusually slow (or fast) responses.

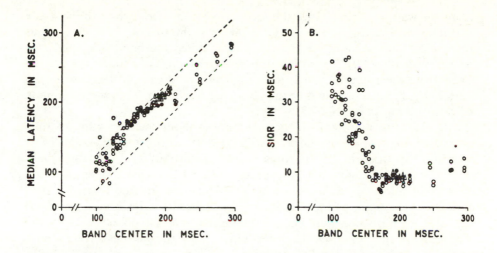

FIG. 2.24 For a visual simple-reaction time experiment with monkeys and temporal reinforcement within a 50-msec band, MRT and semi-interquartile range versus band location. Upper and lower edges of the band are shown as dashed lines. The foreperiods were 1 sec (open circles), 2 sec (triangles), or variable (closed circles). Each data point comes from a block of 100 trials. [Figure 1 of Saslow (1972); copyright 1972; reprinted by permission.]

It is clear that these subjects were able to track the band quite closely, but each subject appears to have an optimal location for the band in the sense that the proportion of correct responses is maximized. Snodgrass (1969) replicated and extended this work and found the same results. Among other things, she used both fixed and variable foreperiods, but that seemed to have little impact on the band performance.

One happy feature of this technique is that it is readily used with animals. Saslow (1968, 1972) ran comparable studies using monkeys, a one-second foreperiod, a light reaction signal, and food rewards. Her data, reported in terms of medians and semi-interquartile ranges, are shown in Figure 2.24. These results are obviously similar to those of human subjects, and the optimal band of 200 ± 20 msec is approximately the same MRT for light flashes as is reported for human beings. We will return later (Chapter 4) to the distributions found in these studies.

What should one make of these results? Snodgrass et al. argued as follows. If the coefficient of variation of time estimates is at least as great as that for reaction times—and they provided data to suggest that it is for times in excess of 500 msec—then when the band is centered at their true MRT—assuming such exists—it is to the subject's advantage to react to the signal. When, however, the band is less than that, reactions to the signal are mostly too slow, and so it becomes advantageous to attempt to time estimate from the warning signal. Since the foreperiod is long compared to the MRT (a factor of at least 5 in these experiments), this results in a precipitous increase in the variability of the responses. When the band is located at a time slower than MRT, then it becomes advantageous to time estimate the band from the reaction signal, and this leads to a gradual increase in the variability. And so the band having the least variability gives some estimate of the true reaction time.

All of this is fine provided the assumption about the variability of time estimates is correct. Kristofferson (1976, 1984), Hopkins (1984), and Hopkins and Kristofferson (1980), whose work on distributions of reaction times will be treated in Chapter 4, have presented data that cast serious doubt on that assumption for at least the region 200 msec greater than the time thought to correspond to true reactions. In a word, they have shown subjects are able to introduce pure delays in this region that do not add to the variability of the responses. Their technique is as follows: one second after a warning signal they present an auditory "reaction" signal (10-msec, 68-dB, 1000-Hz tone). Following the fixed period to be estimated another identical pulse occurs that provides information feedback about the accuracy of the estimate. Times to be estimated were run in blocks of trials, and over blocks they were varied throughout the range 150 to 900 msec. The major new wrinkle as far as time estimates are concerned is the feedback pulse; however, that is exactly the role played by the reaction signal for the time estimates occurring in a reaction-time experiment.

They found two important things. First, the response variability does not change substantially over the region between 300 and 500 msec. Second it is unusually small—a standard deviation of 7 msec in the 1980 paper. The slightly more variable 1976 data are shown in Figure 2.25. (Note that variance, not standard deviation, is plotted.) This constancy means that we cannot really count on there being a well-defined minimum in the variance of reaction times, as Snodgrass et al. had argued. In fact, their times ranged from 100 to 200 msec, which is a range where Kristofferson's data show a decreasing variance. His results suggest that we should maintain a very cautious stance about using the band method to determine "true" reaction times.

2.6   THE RESPONSE AND REACTION TIME

It will surprise no one that the exact nature of the response may affect the observed reaction times. There are, however, at least three layers of complexity to that remark, the last of which is not obvious.

At the first level, the experimenter has the option of selecting among response modes. The three most common ones are vocal responses, finger motions, and eye blinks. Not only does each have its own characteristic

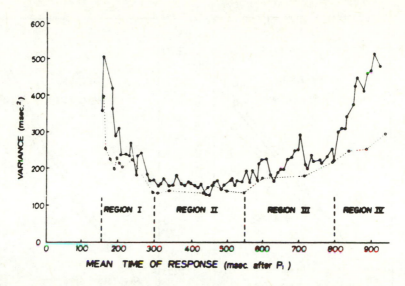

FIG. 2.25 Variance of time estimates of a single subject versus the time to be estimated for times less than one sec. The filled circles and solid line is a descending series with 300 observations per point; the open ones and dotted line is an ascending series with 900 or more observations per point. The indicated regions have no experimental significance. [Figure 5 of Kristofferson (1976); copyright 1976; reprinted by permission.]

reaction time, but there are interactions with other aspects of the experimental design that often determine which response mode must be used. I am not aware of any systematic, parametric study of the time characteristics of the several possible response modes, although there is a certain amount of laboratory lore.

Second, whatever motor response is used, the exact nature of the mechanical device the person manipulates affects the times recorded. Considerable effort has gone into developing devices and response procedures, especially in conjunction with finger manipulated keys, aimed at minimizing both the mean and variance of the extraneous times added to the observed reaction time. There appears to be a significant difference between activating and releasing a response key; however, it is possible that this is due primarily to different amounts of experience with the two. We mostly depress keys (e.g., when using a typewriter). The release of an accelerator is an exception. Similarly, there has been a long development of voice keys, aimed at picking up as rapidly as possible the onset of a vocal response, but, at the same time, maintaining a low frequency of false alarms. I will not go into these technical matters here, but anyone planning to run reaction-time experiments must devote much attention and effort to these mechanical problems.

The third level, which has only recently begun to be studied, is less

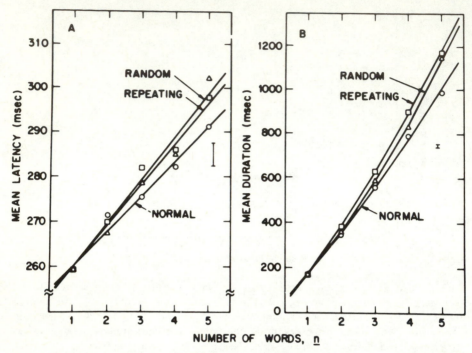

FIG. 2.26 MRT to the initiation of an oral response and the duration of the response versus number of words to be spoken by the subject. The sequences of words were of three types: normal speech, random sequences of words, and the same word repeated. The data, averaged over four subjects, represent 100 observations per point. [Figure 2 of Sternberg et al. (1978); copyright 1978; reprinted by permission.]

obvious. The experimenter may consider having the signal initiate not a single discrete response, such as tapping a single key, but rather a whole preplanned sequence, such as typing or writing a word.* In our driving example, it is hardly adequate for the operator to indicate by some slight gesture, say an eye blink, awareness of an obstacle in the road. Rather, he or she must set into motion a complex, although highly overlearned, series of actions that ultimately lead to the braking of the car. Sternberg, Monsell, Knoll, and Wright (1978) posed the question: does the length of the response sequence in any way affect the time it takes to get it started?

Their typical experimental procedure involves an auditory countdown warning signal, a fixed foreperiod with 15–20% catch trials, a brief flash as the reaction signal, and a response consisting of *n* distinct, preplanned items, where *n* runs from 1 through as many as 6. A variety of responses have been used, including: oral recitation of a consecutive sequence of natural

*The entire volume 54, 1983, of *Acta Psychologica* is given over to papers from an International Workshop on Motor Aspects of Handwriting.

numbers, such as either 2, 3, and 4 or 4 and 5; oral recitation of a sequence of days of the week in their natural order (Tuesday, Wednesday), or random order (Tuesday, Sunday, Friday, Saturday), or simply repeated (Monday, Monday, Monday); words of either one or two syllables; words and pronounceable non-words (in Sternberg, Wright, Knoll, & Monsell, 1980, where a slightly different procedure was used); and, with professional typists, lists of letters to be typed that varied according to whether all the typing used one hand or whether it alternated between two.

The results are uniform: the reaction time to the onset of the response grows with the number of distinct items in the list at a rate of approximately 10 msec per item, with the MRT for one item at about 260 msec for the procedure used in the first study and about 165 msec for that of the second study. The results are not affected to any appreciable degree by the several variations: natural versus random versus repeated order; word length in syllables; or the meaningfulness of words. A sample data plot is shown in Figure 2.26. The typing data, while qualitatively somewhat similar, are a bit different in detail, as can be seen in Figure 2.27.

There is considerably more material in these papers, including a theory as

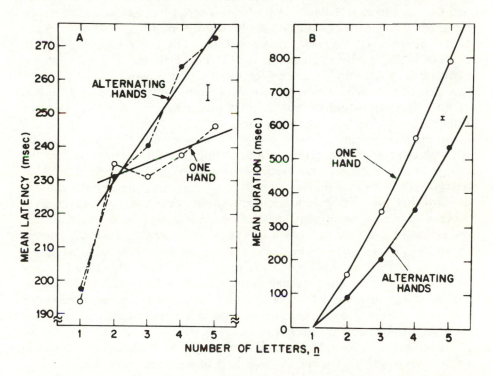

FIG. 2.27 This figure is similar to Figure 2.26 except that the response is typing the words. The four subjects were skilled typists. There are 200 observations per point. [Figure 5 of Sternberg et al. (1978); copyright 1978; reprinted by permission.]

to what may be producing these and related results about the time taken to complete the entire sequence. For our purposes here, it is sufficient to realize that complex, preprogrammed response sequences are somewhat slower to initiate than less complex ones.

There are numerous other aspects of the response topography that affect response-time results. Earlier we mentioned the amount of force exerted or required by the response key. Another aspect is the response itself—voice, key press, eye blink. Still another that will arise in choice reactions is the correspondence between the response alternatives and the possible signals.

2.7   WHAT FACES A MODEL BUILDER?

The first thing that simple reaction-time data seem to suggest is that the observed reaction times are, at a minimum, the sum of two quite different times. One of these has to do with decision processes, invoked by the central nervous system, aimed at deciding when a signal has been presented. The other has to do with the time it takes signals to be transduced and transmitted to the brain and the time it takes orders issued by the brain to activate the muscles leading to responses. These processes may, in fact, be quite complex and may also be affected by the stimulus conditions. Since these are believed by many to be entirely different processes, we will attempt to decompose them and deal with them separately. Since the focus of this book is entirely on models for the decision process, I shall view the other times as a nuisance, as noise to be gotten around. Chapter 3 focuses on this issue. It should be realized that others find the motor and/or the transit times at least equally interesting.

On the assumption that we can in some sense isolate the decision times, then we can turn to the question of modeling them. The first aspect of the models is a postulate about the nature of the recoding in the peripheral nervous system of the stimulus information, effected by the transducer—eye or ear—and the second is a postulate about the nature of the decision process that acts upon that recoded information. We know from our discussion so far that the decision process can quickly become complex, involving strategies based in some way on estimates as well as direct reactions to the signal. Our models must try to keep these alternatives explicit, and some of our experiments must attempt to isolate one strategy at a time, if at all possible. Once the two aspects of the model are stated—the encoding and the decision mechanism—we face some purely mathematical and statistical problems, such as the derivation of the distributions of reaction times predicted by the model, working out methods for estimating parameters of the model, and devising tests of goodness of fit. The development of decision models of this character begins in Chapter 4 and runs throughout the rest of the book, growing more complex as we attempt to understand more complex experiments.

Typically, models in this area, as in much of psychology, include a number of free parameters that are used to fit the model to data. Often they seem to have a natural interpretation that suggests which experimental variables—either stimulus ones such as intensity or duration, or motivational ones such as foreperiod distribution or payoffs—we might expect to affect the parameters. Sometimes we find moderately simple empirical relations between the parameters and experimental variables without, however, suggesting any real understanding of the connection. In the long run we must search for deeper theories for the connections between the physics of the stimulation and the nature of the transduction and for the relation between non-sensory experimental variables and the nature of the decision process, but there is comparatively little of that in this book.

3
Decomposition into Decision and Residual Latencies

3.1 INDEPENDENT, ADDITIVE STAGE LATENCIES

It is widely, although by no means universally, believed that the total observed reaction time is the sum of a number of successive times. This idea dates to Donders' (1868) classic paper, if not earlier. The times involved include, at least, the following: (1) the time required for the physical signal to be transduced from physical energy into the neural spike trains, which appear to be the information code of the nervous system; (2) the transit time for such pulses to pass from the output of the transducer to that part of the brain where the information arriving on the entire fiber bundle (the optic and auditory nerves being the most thoroughly studied) is processed and interpreted—the *decision center*; (3) the time required for that processing and for an order to be issued to the relevant muscle group—the *decision latency*; (4) the transit time between the issuing of an order and its arrival at the muscle group that effects a response; and (5) the time for the muscles to complete the response. Any one of these stages may be subdivided further. For example, Chapters 11 and 12 will focus on additive and other decompositions of the decision stage.

The evidence for such a serial conception is largely anatomical and a priori, although in principle it can be tested in some detail if one knows of manipulations that affect each component time individually (see Sections 3.3 and 12.4). Doubts about it are easily raised. Since transducers such as the eye and ear encode the information both in time—for example, changes in auditory intensity cause changes in spike rate on individual fibers—and over groups of parallel fibers—for example, changes in auditory intensity also affect which fibers are firing above or below their background rates—it is quite conceivable that the decision process may begin before the transmission is complete, thereby creating some overlap of processes, contrary to the serial hypothesis. Nonetheless, in the absence of conclusive evidence one way or the other, researchers often assume that response time is the sum of these separate times.

For many purposes, including those of this chapter, it is useful to lump all delays save the decision latency* into one time, which can be called the

---

* Although there does not seem to be an agreed upon distinction between "latency" and "time" or "duration," I shall try to follow the convention of referring to unobserved, hypothetical times as latencies.

residual latency It is almost certainly a random variable, although as we shall see some authors have argued that its variance is really quite small. The term "residual" makes clear that our interest is in the decision process, not in the transduction, transit, and motor times. Much of the rest of the book is an attempt to understand the distribution of decision latencies, and from that point of view the residual latency is a nuisance factor, serving only to muddy our view of the decision latency. Of course, other scientists are primarily interested in parts of the residual time and from their point of view the decision latency may be a nuisance. For example, Marteniuk and MacKenzie (1980) review results on motor organization. The purpose of this chapter is to consider the extent to which we can bypass the residual latency. The situation is rather less satisfactory than one might wish.

If we denote by $\mathbf{R}$ the residual latency, by $\mathbf{D}$ the decision latency, and by $\mathbf{T}$ the observed overall reaction time, then according to the assumption of additivity these three random variables are related as

$$\mathbf{T} = \mathbf{R} + \mathbf{D}. \tag{3.1}$$

This assumption of additivity has been much debated and is not easy to resolve even physiologically because there are no known electrical events unambiguously separating successive stages. Attempts to trace electrical activity through the system yield some evidence in favor of a somewhat serial organization, but it does not foreclose a degree of overlap. For example, the input of sensory information presumably spans at least the duration of the signal, and almost certainly the decision mechanism begins to process information as soon as it begins to arrive, which for sufficiently long signals—say more than 50 msec—means before the signal is terminated. The motor response system may well be brought to some state of readiness long before the final order to execute a response is issued. For some purposes (see Section 3.3) physiological events can be used to define an observable time that is clearly a subset of another, unobservable time of interest. For example, the electromyogram (EMG) of the responding muscle allows us to determine when electrical activity is first activated on the motor neuron that leads to a response, and surely that time occurs after the initiation of the motor process. So the time from that event to the response is a portion of the entire motor time, and that, in turn, is a portion of the residual $\mathbf{R}$.

The second assumption is that $\mathbf{R}$ and $\mathbf{D}$ are independent random variables. As far as I am aware, there is no direct way to test this hypothesis until one has a way to measure $\mathbf{R}$ and $\mathbf{D}$ separately on each trial—that is, until we have physiological markers for the end of one stage and the beginning of another. The nearest thing that we do have is the possibility of physiological measurements such as the EMG, which introduces a partition somewhat different from the $\mathbf{R}$ and $\mathbf{D}$ partition. To be precise, we have a partition $\mathbf{T} = \mathbf{R}' + \mathbf{D}'$, where $\mathbf{R}'$ is the time between the beginning of EMG activity and the completed response and $\mathbf{D}' = \mathbf{T} - \mathbf{R}'$. Necessarily, $\mathbf{R}' \leq \mathbf{R}$ and

$\mathbf{D}' \geq \mathbf{D}$. Aside from technical difficulties of measurement, it is unclear what conclusions to draw about $\mathbf{R}$ and $\mathbf{D}$ from measurements about $\mathbf{R}'$ and $\mathbf{D}'$. In particular, if $\mathbf{R}'$ and $\mathbf{D}'$ are found not to be independent, as Grayson (1983) reports, that could very well be due to nonindependence of $\mathbf{R}'$ and $\mathbf{R} - \mathbf{R}'$, which includes some of the motor time, rather than having anything to do with lack of independence of $\mathbf{R}$ and $\mathbf{D}$. Even if evidence for the independence of $\mathbf{R}'$ and $\mathbf{D}'$ were forthcoming, one could not necessarily infer that $\mathbf{R}$ and $\mathbf{D}$ are independent.

Given our present incomplete state of knowledge about the physiological processes involved, additivity and independence must both be treated as hypotheses whose usefulness will have to be evaluated by where they lead us. Accepting them, we know from Section 1.4.1 that the densities of the three random variables are related by the convolution equation

$$f_{\mathbf{T}}(t) = \int_0^t f_{\mathbf{R}}(x) f_{\mathbf{D}}(t-x) \, dx, \tag{3.2}$$

and the corresponding characteristic functions satisfy

$$\mathscr{C}_{\mathbf{T}}(\omega) = \mathscr{C}_{\mathbf{R}}(\omega) \mathscr{C}_{\mathbf{D}}(\omega). \tag{3.3}$$

(Of course, the same holds for the moment generating function, but in practice most authors have used the characteristic function because of the availability of programs for the Fast Fourier Transform. For discrete random variables, Eq. 3.2 is replaced by a sum and Eq. 3.3 by a similar expression, Eq. 1.61, for the generating function.)

Although the conversion of convolutions into simple multiplication of functions has been known to mathematicians and physicists since the last century, its relevance to reaction time was apparently first noted explicitly by Christie and Luce (1956). Little development of this idea occurred until about 1970 when the computations involved became sufficiently cheap to warrant collecting the large amounts of data needed to estimate characteristic functions with any accuracy.

The major problem in estimating the characteristic function of an empirical distribution arises from inadequate specification of the tails of the distribution. As a result, it is often wise not to consider Eq. 3.3 as such, but only its implications for the lower moments of the distribution. We know from Theorem 1.5 that additivity alone (Eq. 3.1) implies $E(\mathbf{T}) = E(\mathbf{R}) + E(\mathbf{D})$, and that adding independence yields $V(\mathbf{T}) = V(\mathbf{R}) + V(\mathbf{D})$ and the countable set of corresponding equations for the higher cumulants (Eq. 1.54). Even if we do not have enough data to use Eq. 3.3, it is often possible to carry out analogous calculations for these weaker constraints on mean and variance.

The remainder of the chapter describes several different attempts to make use of Eq. 3.3. It is apparent that, as it stands, nothing is possible: $\mathscr{C}_{\mathbf{T}}$ is known, but nothing is known about $\mathscr{C}_{\mathbf{R}}$ and $\mathscr{C}_{\mathbf{D}}$, and so if there is any additive, independent decomposition of $\mathbf{T}$, there is a continuum of possible decompositions. This result follows from $\mathbf{T} = \mathbf{R} + \mathbf{D} = (\mathbf{R} + \mathbf{X}) + (\mathbf{D} - \mathbf{X})$, where $\mathbf{X}$ is required to have the properties that $\mathbf{X}$ is independent of $\mathbf{R}$ and $\mathbf{D}$, $\mathbf{X} \geq 0$, and $\mathbf{D} - \mathbf{X} \geq 0$. Some further knowledge (or, to be candid, guesses) will have to be injected into the situation before anything can be concluded. Each subsection differs in exactly what else is assumed. Historically, the development has tended from the more specific to the less specific, and I find it convenient to follow that order.

3.2 SPECIFIC ASSUMPTIONS

3.2.1 *One Variable Gaussian, the Other Exponential*

Because the right tail of many empirical reaction-time densities is fairly long—which makes the density function distinctly skewed—a number of authors have conjectured that one of the times involved is exponential. McGill (1963) cited data of Greenbaum (1963) in which the right tail seemed to be exponential; he postulated that this tail reflects an exponential residual distribution. It is not completely clear why he assumed the tail to reflect the residual rather than the decision process; later physiological results suggest otherwise. Transit times are variable, but not enormously so. Meijers and Eijkman (1974) summarized physiological data about the motor system and a model for it. Their summary suggests that very little variability is involved in the overall process—less than in its various components, the reduction being achieved by feedback mechanisms. This does not rule out the possibility of these times being exponential, but it does suggest that the unusually long observed response times are due to something else. A possible reason for attributing the tail to the residue is the fact Greenbaum's data exhibited no impact of signal-to-noise ratio on the tail. However, care must be taken in interpreting this result because the signal onset was very slow—a rise time of 120 msec—and so in effect all signals went through a weak signal phase. Later studies, such as those discussed shortly in this section and in Sections 3.2.2 to 3.2.4, while continuing to confirm the approximate exponential nature of the tail, have found that signal intensity affects the exponential parameter. In those studies, signal onset was rapid. As a result, exactly the opposite attribution has been made—namely, that the tail of the observed distribution probably results from the decision process, not the residual one.

Another assumption we might make is that the decision process has an exponential latency (later we will weaken this to be asymptotically exponential) in which case we need only decide what to assume for the residual. Hohle (1965) suggested that the central limit theorem be invoked on the grounds that the residual latency is the sum of a number of terms (such as transduction, various neural synapses, and so on) of comparable variability, in which case the distribution should be approximately Gaussian (Theorem

A.1). The argument is suspect because the number of terms in the sum may very well be rather small, and so an asymptotic argument is not very accurate. Moreover, we shall see data in Section 3.2.3, which makes the assumption doubtful; nonetheless, we pursue it because the resulting model is surprisingly accurate.

So, we assume the residual density is Gaussian:

$$f_{\mathbf{R}}(t) = (1/\sigma\sqrt{2\pi}) \exp[-(t-\mu)2/2\sigma^2].$$

(Of course, this assumption cannot be strictly correct since $\mathbf{R}$ must be a positive random variable, whereas a Gaussian variable is defined from $-\infty$ to $+\infty$. However, as an approximation, it is satisfactory provided that $\mu > 3\sigma$, in which case the chance of a negative value is less than 0.14%.) And we assume the decision latency is distributed as an exponential:

$$f_{\mathbf{D}}(t) = \lambda e^{-\lambda t}.$$

In Section 1.4.3 we derived the convolution of these two densities, the ex-Gaussian,

$$f_{\mathbf{T}}(t) = (\lambda/\sigma) \exp(\mu\lambda + \tfrac{1}{2}\lambda^2\sigma^2)e^{-\lambda t}\Phi[(t-\mu-\lambda\sigma^2)/\sigma], \tag{3.4}$$

where Φ is the unit Gaussian with zero mean. Note that from our assumptions and what we know about the Gaussian and the exponential,

$$E(\mathbf{T}) = \mu + 1/\lambda,$$

$$V(\mathbf{T}) = \sigma^2 + 1/\lambda^2.$$

Hohle's procedure for fitting the ex-Gaussian, Eq. 3.4, to data was as follows. For the empirical distribution function, he found the nine times that partitioned it exactly into 10 equal sized groups. He then adjusted the three parameters of the distribution so as to minimize χ^2 for the predictions of the areas defined by the nine boundary points. As there are 9 independent areas and 3 parameters, there are 6 degrees of freedom and so the expected value of χ^2 is 6.

The experiment involved the onset of lights as a warning signal, four foreperiods of durations 1.60, 3.20, 4.65, and 6.13 sec, and a 60-dB 1000-Hz reaction signal. Both the warning signal and reaction signal were response terminated. The foreperiods were run both individually in blocks and together, where they were equally likely to occur. There were four subjects. Thus, summing over conditions, the total expected value of χ^2 is $4 \times 8 \times 6 = 192$; the observed sum was 172.17. The fits are remarkably good. A sample of the distribution functions is shown in Figure 3.1. Figure 3.2 shows the estimates of μ and λ as a function of the foreperiod durations. It appears that λ is somewhat less dependent on foreperiod duration than is μ. Hohle argued as follows: if the impact of the foreperiod duration is to alter muscle tension, and so the residual time, and if μ but not λ is affected by foreperiod, which is perhaps suggested by the data but certainly is not

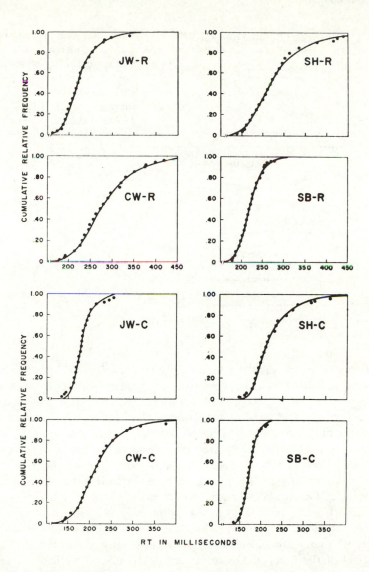

FIG. 3.1 Empirical distribution functions of simple reaction times to pure tones (1000-Hz, 60-dB SPL) with either four equally likely foreperiods (condition *R*) or a constant foreperiod (condition *C*). In all cases, the responses to the 1.60-sec foreperiod are shown. There are 100 observations per distribution. The fitted curves are the ex-Gaussian distribution. [Figure 1 of Hohle (1965); copyright 1965; reprinted by permission.]

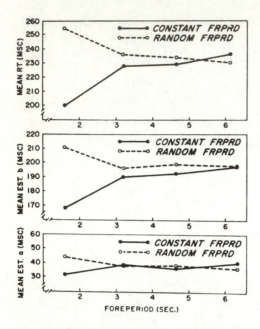

FIG. 3.2 MRT and the estimated constants of the ex-Gaussian (in my notation, $\mu = b$ and $\lambda = a$) versus the actual foreperiod wait for the experiment of Figure 3.1. [Figure 2 of Hohle (1965); copyright 1965; reprinted by permission.]

strictly true of them, then the Gaussian distributed variable is the residual. This argument is not conclusive for at least three reasons. First, the constancy of λ as a function of foreperiod duration is not convincing. Second, because the hazard function of the signal onset increases with duration, it may very well be that the decision criterion changes, in which case the decision latency is affected by foreperiod duration. Third, suppose $\mathbf{T} = \mathbf{G} + \mathbf{E}$, where $\mathbf{G}$ is a Gaussian random variable with mean g and $\mathbf{E}$ is exponential. For any g_1, $0 < g_1 < g$, there exist independent Gaussian random variables $\mathbf{G}_1$ and $\mathbf{G}_2$ such that the mean of $\mathbf{G}_1$ is g_1 and $\mathbf{G} = \mathbf{G}_1 + \mathbf{G}_2$. If we set $\mathbf{D} = \mathbf{E} + \mathbf{G}_2$, then $\mathbf{T} = \mathbf{G}_1 + \mathbf{D}$, where $\mathbf{G}_1$ is Gaussian and $\mathbf{D}$ is ex-Gaussian. The data are equally consistent with such a decomposition, as well as infinitely many others including decompositions of the exponential, and the impact of the foreperiod can be attributed just as well to the Gaussian component of the decision latency as to the residual. In Section 3.3 we shall return to this question of attribution in a far more general context. And in Section 4.1.3 we provide data that are distinctly inconsistent with the ex-Gaussian distribution.

Given how well the ex-Gaussian accounted for Hohle's data, its lack of use with other bodies of data, is really rather surprising. To my knowledge, the only other authors to use it are Ratcliff and Murdock (1976) and Ratcliff (1978). In his dissertation, Link (1968) used the convolution of a gamma with a truncated Gaussian. The two former papers found the ex-Gaussian to fit well (see Figure 3.3), and Ratcliff used it as an economical way to summarize data in studying memory (see Section 11.4.4). Hockley (1984) used it in comparing memory and visual searches, and he showed that experimental manipulations affected the three parameters differently (see Section 11.1.2).

3.2.2 *One Variable Bounded, the Other Exponential in the Tail*

Considering the sources of the times entering into the residue— transduction, transit, and muscle action—it seems moderately plausible that

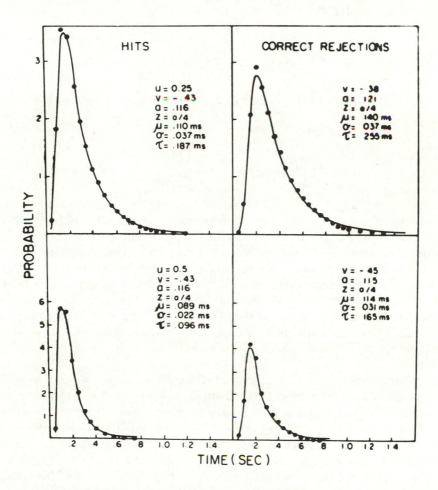

FIG. 3.3 Histograms of simple reaction times to visual signals fitted by the ex-Gaussian density function. The parameters of the legend are μ, σ, and τ for the ex-Gaussian fit to the data (where τ is the exponential parameter), and u, v, a, and z are parameters of a diffusion model, to be discussed in Sections 9.2.1 to 9.2.2, that was then fit to the ex-Gaussian. I was unable to deduce the sample sizes involved. [Figure 7 of Ratcliff (1978); copyright 1978; reprinted by permission.]

there is some absolute bound τ_1, on the random variable **R**; that is,

$$f_{\mathbf{R}}(t) = 0 \quad \text{for} \quad t > \tau_1. \tag{3.5}$$

For a number of theories about the decision process, it turns out that for sufficiently large times the distribution of decision latencies is approximately exponential; that is, for some τ_2,

$$f_{\mathbf{D}}(t) = k e^{-\eta t} \quad \text{for} \quad t > \tau_2. \tag{3.6}$$

We will see a number of examples of such theories, one in Section 3.2.4 and several in Chapter 4.

Using Eqs. 3.5 and 3.6 in Eq. 3.2, we see that for $t > \tau = \tau_1 + \tau_2$,

$$
\begin{aligned}
f_{\mathbf{T}}(t) &= \int_0^\tau f_{\mathbf{R}}(x) f_{\mathbf{D}}(t-x)\, \mathrm{d}x + \int_\tau^t f_{\mathbf{R}}(x) f_{\mathbf{D}}(t-x)\, dx \\
&= \int_0^\tau f_{\mathbf{R}}(x) k e^{-\eta t}\, dx + 0 \\
&= A e^{-\eta t}, \quad t > \tau
\end{aligned}
\tag{3.7}
$$

where

$$A = k \int_0^\tau f_{\mathbf{R}}(x) e^{\eta x}\, dx \qquad \text{and} \qquad \tau = \tau_1 + \tau_2.$$

Not only does Eq. 3.7 tell us that the right tail of the observed reaction-time distribution is exponential, a prediction that is moderately easily checked, but it also provides a way of estimating the parameter η that, of course, must arise from the parameters of the model underlying the theory of the decision process. If we are able to use Eq. 3.7 to provide a complete estimation of the parameters of the decision model, which may or may not be possible depending upon the exact details of the decision model (see Section 3.2.4 for an example), then we can calculate η and from the data estimate $\mathscr{C}_{\mathbf{T}}(\omega)$, whence from Eq. 3.3 we have an estimate of $\mathscr{C}_{\mathbf{R}}(\omega) = \mathscr{C}_{\mathbf{T}}(\omega)/\mathscr{C}_{\mathbf{D}}(\omega)$. Inverting this Fourier transform, we obtain an estimate of $f_{\mathbf{R}}(t)$.

Of what interest is that? For one thing, if it turns out not to be a legitimate density function—and there is nothing in the procedure for calculating it that forces it to be one—then we know something is wrong with one or more of our assumptions: either the quality of the estimate of $\mathscr{C}_{\mathbf{T}}(\omega)$ is not really adequate, or the decision and residual latencies fail to be additive and independent, or the residual times are not bounded, or the theory of the decision process is basically wrong. Section 3.2.4 illustrates a use of this method, which does indeed lead to an impossible density function. Were we able to develop a theory leading to legitimate density functions, then by manipulating the decision stage, say by varying the response criterion, we should recover the same residual density independent of the manipulation (for another use of this idea, see Section 3.3). This procedure, to my knowledge, has not been attempted.

The ideas just reported first appeared in McGill (1963), where he assumed that both processes are exponential, the one with a much larger parameter than the other, which, in effect, makes the process with the larger parameter bounded relative to the other one. Luce and Green (1970) and Green and Luce (1971) provided the formulation given here.

3.2.3 One Variable Gamma

Ashby and Townsend (1980) considered, among other things, the case of $\mathbf{T} = \mathbf{X} + \mathbf{Y}$, where $\mathbf{X}$ and $\mathbf{Y}$ are independent, $\mathbf{Y}$ is gamma distributed, the densities of $\mathbf{T}$ and $\mathbf{X}$ exist and are denoted f and g, respectively, and the derivative of f exists. For the special case where $\mathbf{Y}$ is exponential, with parameter λ, they observe that

$$\lambda = g(t)/[G(t) - F(t)].$$

This result follows from the fact that the *mgf* of $\mathbf{Y}$ is $\lambda/(\lambda - s)$ (Eq. 1.49), and so $(\lambda - s)\mathcal{M}_{\mathbf{T}}(s) = \lambda \mathcal{M}_{\mathbf{X}}(s)$. But $-s\mathcal{M}_{\mathbf{T}}(s)$ is the *mgf* of f', and so we have

$$\int_0^\infty e^{-st}[\lambda f(t) + f'(t)]\, dt = \lambda \int_0^\infty e^{-st} g(t)\, dt.$$

Since this must hold for every s for which the integrals are defined, it follows that

$$\lambda f(t) + f'(t) = \lambda g(t).$$

Integrating from $-\infty$ to t and solving yields the result. An application of this is discussed briefly below. To my knowledge, this method has not been applied to the issues of this chapter because we do not, in practice, have direct evidence for the distribution G.

For a gamma distribution of order n, rather than an exponential, they show by analogous methods that

$$\lambda = [E(\mathbf{T}) - E(\mathbf{X})]/[V(\mathbf{T}) - V(\mathbf{X})],$$
$$n = [E(\mathbf{T}) - E(\mathbf{X})]^2/[V(\mathbf{T}) - V(\mathbf{X})].$$

3.2.4 Responding to the First Spike: A Successful Analysis of an Unsuccessful Model

In order to illustrate in detail the ideas just discussed, we work through what must be just about the simplest model of the decision latency one can think of (Luce & Green, 1970; Green & Luce, 1971). It will demonstrate two things: the method is adequate to reject an incorrect model, and matters get mathematically messy rather easily.

Consider a response terminated design with an exponential distribution of foreperiods $\mathbf{S}$, where $E(\mathbf{S}) = 1/\lambda$. Suppose the information available to the decision center is a single spike train, which prior to signal onset is Poisson with (noise) intensity parameter ν and at signal onset changes instantaneously to $\mu > \nu$.

The instantaneous change is an idealization, as perhaps is the constancy of μ (see Section 4.3.1). Suppose that the decision rule is to respond to the first spike that occurs following the warning signal. For this to make any sense at all, the parameter ν of the noise process must be under the subject's control so that the rate of anticipations can be controlled as the experimenter alters the distribution of foreperiods. The independent residual **R** is assumed to be a bounded random variable, with bound τ and density $f_{\mathbf{R}}$.

Once we become as specific as this, we see that there are really three times to be observed in the experiment: the distribution of anticipations, the distribution of responses after signal onset (reaction times), and the distribution of signal onsets given that an anticipation has not occurred (as we shall see, because of the conditioning on no anticipation, this density is not just $\lambda e^{-\lambda t}$ and, of course, it is not independent of the others). Each of these distributions provides us with some information about the underlying Poisson processes describing the noise and the signal-plus-noise.

Consider first the anticipation density—the density of response times conditional on the signal onset following the response:

$$f_A(t) = \Pr(\mathbf{T} = t \mid \mathbf{S} > \mathbf{T})$$
$$= \Pr(\mathbf{T} = t \ \& \ \mathbf{S} > t)/\Pr(\mathbf{S} > \mathbf{T}).$$

The numerator is just the convolution of a noise induced spike with the residual delay, but subject to the statistically independent condition that the signal does not occur during the time 0 to t, which has probability $e^{-\lambda t}$:

$$\Pr(\mathbf{T} = t \ \& \ \mathbf{S} > t) = e^{-\lambda t} \int_0^t \nu e^{-\nu x} f_{\mathbf{R}}(t - x) \, dx$$

$$= \nu e^{-(\nu + \lambda)t} \int_0^t e^{\nu y} f_{\mathbf{R}}(y) \, dy.$$

The denominator is simply the integral of this quantity over all t,

$$\Pr(\mathbf{S} > \mathbf{T}) = \int_0^\infty \Pr(\mathbf{T} = t \ \& \ \mathbf{S} > t) \, dt$$

$$= \int_0^\infty \nu e^{-(\nu + \lambda)t} \int_0^t e^{\nu y} f_{\mathbf{R}}(y) \, dy \, dt.$$

Integrating by parts,

$$\Pr(\mathbf{S} > \mathbf{T}) = -\frac{\nu}{\nu + \lambda} e^{-(\nu + \lambda)t} \int_0^t e^{\nu y} f_{\mathbf{R}}(y) \, dy \ \Big|_0^\infty$$

$$+ \frac{\nu}{\nu + \lambda} \int_0^\infty e^{-\lambda t} f_{\mathbf{R}}(t) \, dt$$

$$= \frac{\nu}{\nu + \lambda} R_{-\lambda},$$

where we introduce the abbreviation

$$R_\alpha = \int_0^\infty e^{\alpha t} f_{\mathbf{R}}(t) \, dt = \int_0^\tau e^{\alpha t} f_{\mathbf{R}}(t) \, dt, \tag{3.8}$$

which is just the moment generating function of $\mathbf{R}$. Putting it all together,

$$f_A(t) = \frac{\nu + \lambda}{R_{-\lambda}} e^{-(\nu+\lambda)t} \int_0^t e^{\nu y} f_{\mathbf{R}}(y) \, dy \tag{3.9a}$$

$$= \frac{R_\nu}{R_{-\lambda}} (\nu + \lambda) e^{-(\nu+\lambda)t} \quad \text{if} \quad t > \tau. \tag{3.9b}$$

The characteristic function follows from Eq. 3.9a by an integration of parts,

$$\mathscr{C}_{A(\omega)} = \frac{\nu + \lambda}{(\nu + \lambda - i\omega)R_{-\lambda}} \mathscr{C}_{-\lambda\mathbf{R}}(\omega), \tag{3.10}$$

where $\mathscr{C}_{-\lambda\mathbf{R}}(\omega)$ is the characteristic function of $e^{-\lambda t} f_{\mathbf{R}}(t)$.

The calculations for the other two densities are exactly analogous, and I will not go through them:

$$f_{RT}(t) = \Pr(\mathbf{T} - \mathbf{S} = t \mid \mathbf{S} \le \mathbf{T})$$

$$= \frac{\lambda \nu e^{\lambda t} \int_t^\infty e^{-\lambda x} f_{\mathbf{R}}(x) \, dx + \lambda \mu e^{-\mu t} \int_0^t e^{\mu x} f_{\mathbf{R}}(x) \, dx}{\nu(1 - R_{-\lambda}) + \lambda} \tag{3.11a}$$

$$= \frac{\lambda R_\mu}{\nu(1 - R_{-\lambda}) + \lambda} \mu e^{-\mu t}, \quad t \ge \tau, \tag{3.11b}$$

$$\mathscr{C}_{RT}(\omega) = \frac{\lambda}{\nu(1 - R_{-\lambda}) + \lambda} \left[\frac{\nu R_{-\lambda}}{\lambda + i\omega} + \left(\frac{\nu}{\lambda + i\omega} + \frac{\mu}{\mu - i\omega} \right) \mathscr{C}_{\mathbf{R}}(\omega) \right] \tag{3.12}$$

$$f_S(t) = \Pr(\mathbf{S} = t \mid \mathbf{S} \le \mathbf{T})$$

$$= \frac{\lambda(\nu + \lambda)}{\nu(1 - R_{-\lambda}) + \lambda} \left[e^{-(\nu+\lambda)t} \int_0^t e^{\nu x} f_{\mathbf{R}}(x) \, dx + e^{-\lambda t} \int_t^\infty f_{\mathbf{R}}(x) \, dx \right] \tag{3.13a}$$

$$= \frac{\lambda R_\nu}{\nu(1 - R_{-\lambda}) + \lambda} (\nu + \lambda) e^{-(\nu+\lambda)t}, \quad t \ge \tau,$$

$$\mathscr{C}_S(\omega) = \frac{\lambda(\nu + \lambda)}{\nu(1 - R_{-\lambda}) + \lambda} \left[1 - \frac{\nu}{\nu + \lambda - i\omega} \mathscr{C}_{-\lambda\mathbf{R}}(\omega) \right].$$

Luce and Green's data analysis proceeded as follows. Using simple reaction-time data from very strong signals, τ was selected to be a value that exceeds any observed reaction time. That is a reasonable bound if it is assumed that the residue is not affected by signal intensity, but that assumption may be false (see Section 3.3.2). Since for $t > \tau$ the tails of all the distributions are predicted to be exponential, the reciprocal of the mean of the tail less τ is the maximum likelihood estimate of the empirial time constant. To check the adequacy of the exponential fit, they subdivided time into a number of equal probability intervals, and used χ^2 to check the adequacy of the fit. J. W. Tukey (personal communication) has questioned this choice, suggesting that it may not be as sensitive to deviations from the exponential as the use of equal time intervals.

If the fits are found to be acceptable, then the time constants estimated from the empirical histograms corresponding to f_A and f_S are used to estimate $\nu + \lambda$. Since λ is experimenter determined, it estimates ν. The time constant from f_{RT} is used to estimate μ. The areas under the three tails, Eqs. 3.9b, 3.11b, 3.13b, also depend on R_ν, R_μ, and $R_{-\lambda}$. Since the other parameters are known, these three constants may be solved for. With the constants known and with an empirical estimate of $\mathscr{C}_{RT}$, using the Fast Fourier Transform (FFT, see Section 1.4.4) on the smoothed empirical histogram, we may solve for $\mathscr{C}_{\mathbf{R}}$ from Eq. 3.12. That can then be inverted by the inverse FFT to obtain an estimate of $f_{\mathbf{R}}$.

The empirical study run by Luce and Green (1970) was auditory with the following features. The warning signal was a countdown sequence of lights, $\lambda = 0.22 \sec^{-1}$, background noise was 50-dB spectrum level, and the signal was the onset of a 1000-Hz tone that was response terminated. Information feedback involved lights corresponding to the intervals <0, 0–300, 300–400, 400–500, >500 msec, where 0 is located at signal onset. The corresponding payoffs were -1, 5, 3, 1, -1 points, which were converted to a money reward. Six signal levels were run between $10 \log(P/N) = 11.5$ and 24.5 dB. Approximately 5000 observations were obtained in each condition for each observer.

Using $\tau = 0.5 \sec$, a very conservative choice, exponentials were fit to the tails; Figure 3.4 shows the resulting distributions, and there is a suggestion of some deviation from the exponential. We will return to this deviation in Chapter 4 because, although not large, it probably is significant not only in the statistical sense but also substantively. Accepting the fit as satisfactory, Figure 3.5 shows the growth of μ/ν with intensity. It is a power function of intensity relative to a threshold of about 14.5 dB with an exponent of 1.6. Obviously, such a rapid growth cannot continue for long without far exceeding the spike rates that are observed in physiological studies.

An attempt was made in this study to vary the response criterion, but as the results were not very clear that part was repeated in Green and Luce (1971) with 40-dB noise, 20-dB signal, $= 0.25 \sec^{-1}$, and a sample size of over 10,000. In different runs, the three observers were instructed to maintain anticipation rates of .01, .33, .50, .60, and .75. The fit of the exponential to the tails of some of the anticipation densities are shown in Figure 3.6. Again, there is some deviation, but it seems relatively satisfactory. The covariation of the estimated Poisson rates are shown in Figure 3.7; it appears that these data are described as satisfying $\mu = \nu + \rho$, where ρ is a constant (presumably dependent upon intensity) and ν varies with the

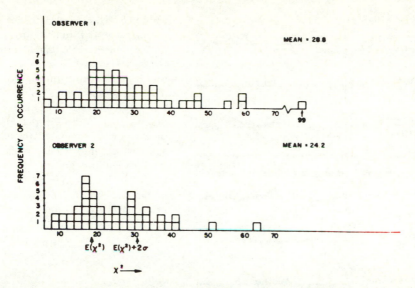

FIG. 3.4 Distribution of chi-square fits of exponential densities to the tails (>500 msec) of simple reaction-time distributions to weak pure tone signals in noise. Each chi square is based on at least 100 observations. The expected value and the upper two standard deviation point is shown. [Figure 5 of Luce and Green (1970); copyright 1970; reprinted by permission.]

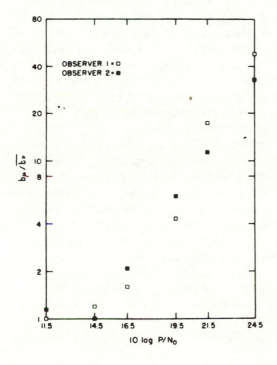

FIG. 3.5 For the simple Poisson detection model described in the text, the ratio of the estimated Poisson intensity parameters for signal in noise (μ) and for noise alone (ν) versus signal intensity in dB. [Figure 9 of Luce and Green (1970); copyright 1970; reprinted by permission.]

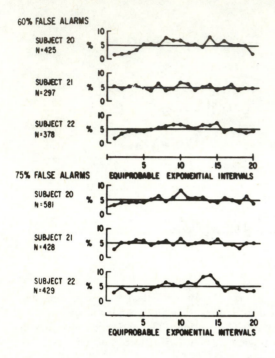

60% FALSE ALARMS

SUBJECT 20
N = 425

SUBJECT 21
N = 297

SUBJECT 22
N = 378

EQUIPROBABLE EXPONENTIAL INTERVALS

75% FALSE ALARMS

SUBJECT 20
N = 581

SUBJECT 21
N = 428

SUBJECT 22
N = 429

EQUIPROBABLE EXPONENTIAL INTERVALS

FIG. 3.6 Examples of the fit of the exponential density to the tails (>500 msec) of anticipatory responses in the detection of a low intensity pure tone in noise. The sample sizes are shown on the figure. From the observed mean time, the exponential parameter was estimated, the density divided into 20 intervals of 0.05 probability, and the proportion of responses in each interval is shown. [Figure 2 of Green and Luce (1971); copyright 1971; reprinted by permission.]

subject's criterion. I noted earlier that variation of ν with criterion is essential in this model. Note that by Theorem 1.3 this is what one would expect if the noise and signal processes are independent and exponential and a response is initiated by whichever event occurs first. Green and Luce used an averaging process to smooth the data, calculated the FFT, factored out the FFT of the estimated decision time, and inverted the result to yield an estimate of f_R. This procedure was followed for both subjects on the data involving the lowest anticipation rate. One such estimate is shown in Figure 3.8; the other observer was essentially the same.

The resulting function is unsatisfactory in two respects. First, it is not a density function because of the negative excursion between 400 and 600 msec. Assuming everything else about the model is satisfactory except the decision model, the negative excursion means that the distribution from that model does not drop sufficiently rapidly just to the right of its peak value to account for the corresponding drop in the data. The only freedom is for the drop off to be encorporated into the residue, but what is needed to fit the data results in the violation of the density requirement. This consequence suggests that a somewhat unusual hazard function is needed in the decision model. Second, the mean of the positive mode is about 300 msec, which is greater by at least 100 msec than the mean of reaction times to strong signals and that, of course, must be greater than the mean of residue. The conclusion is that one, or more, of the assumptions is wrong. Since the

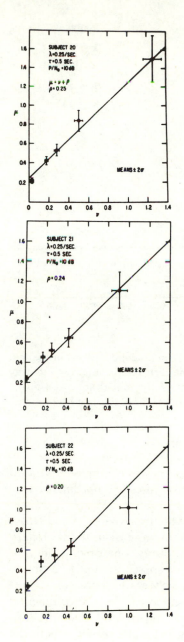

FIG. 3.7 For simple reaction times to a low intensity pure tone in noise, and with instructions to achieve various proportions of anticipatory responses, estimates of signal (μ) and noise (ν) parameters of the Poisson model described in the text. The line fit to the data is $\mu = \nu + \rho$, and the estimated values of ρ are shown. The sample sizes are as in Figure 3.6. [Figure 3 of Green and Luce (1971); copyright 1971; reprinted by permission.]

111

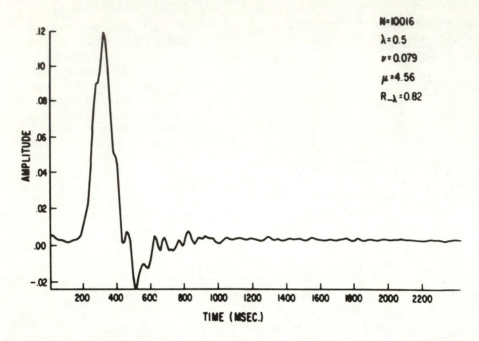

FIG. 3.8 Estimated residual "density" after the Poisson model described in the text has been deconvolved from the simple reaction-time distribution to a low intensity pure tone in noise. The estimated parameter values of the model are given in the legend [Figure 14 of Green and Luce (1971); copyright 1971; reprinted by permission.]

evidence is that over 100 msec of the decision latency has been incorporated in the residual, the natural conclusion is that responses are not initiated by the first spike to occur following the warning signal.

Since it is known from physiological observations (Kiang, 1965; Rose, Brugge, Anderson, & Hind, 1967) that spike rate, at least in the periphery of the auditory system, increases with signal intensity, one obvious idea to pursue is that subjects accumulate more than one spike, attempt to estimate the rate, and respond when the estimated rate appears to increase. Models of this character have been developed with some success for choice reaction times where the time of the signal onset is known (see Section 9.3); however, it seems to be quite difficult to get usable results when the foreperiod is random. Perhaps the simplest model of this character is to suppose that the interval between each successive pair of spikes is compared with a criterion, and the first time it is less than the criterion (evidence of a higher rate) a response is initiated. That model was examined by Luce and Green (1972) in some detail and some theoretical results were obtained, but they are not sufficiently full to permit a detailed analysis of the sort we have just reported for the single spike model. Further discussion of it will be given in Section 4.3.5.

3.2.5   Spline Approximations

In the examples presented so far, we have reduced the degrees of freedom associated with either the distribution of decision latencies or with the residue, or with both, by making some sort of more-or-less theoretically motivated assumptions. Another approach is to be totally atheoretical and consider a class of simple functions, completely described by a few parameters, that are, nonetheless, sufficiently flexible to fit any data we are likely to encounter. One currently popular example is the class of functions known as *splines*: the independent variable is partitioned into K segments and the function is approximated in each segment by a polynomial of order n but subject to the constraint that the function and a certain number of its derivatives are continuous at the boundaries. For a general reference to this class of functions, see de Boor (1978).

Bloxom (1979, 1984, 1985) applied this method to the decomposition problem we have been discussing using cubic splines ($n = 3$) in which the function and its first two derivatives are required to be continuous. Moreover, he added a constraint that is not usual in the spline literature—namely, that the splines describing the densities of **R** and of **D** shall actually be density functions that are unimodal. In the 1979 paper he developed a procedure for the case where one component was assumed to be known and the other is approximated by a cubic spline. The parameters of the spline are chosen by numerical approximation so as to minimize the squared deviations between the observed and predicted convolutions. In the 1985 paper, he approximated both components, the known and the unknown, by cubic splines, and he developed various estimation procedures, including maximum likelihood, for estimating all parameters. The method is subject to various constraints on the possible general types of hazard functions. A general summary of the results is given in Bloxom (1984).

So far as I know, these methods have not in fact been applied to any response-time data. Bloxom (1979) did carry out simulations in which both components were gamma distributed (Eq. A.5 of Appendix A) with shape parameters (n) of 1, 2, 5, and 10 for the unobserved component and of 2, 3, 6, 11, and 20 for the observed ones. Sample sizes of 100 and, in selected cases, of 300 were used to generate "data" from convolutions of the gammas, from which the parameters of the unobserved component were estimated. The fits are shown in Figure 3.9, and at least for the larger sample sizes they are tolerably good. It seems clear, however, that to answer subtle distributional questions this way, it is essential to have much larger sample sizes, in which case the advantages of this over smoothing and using FFT are not apparent to me.

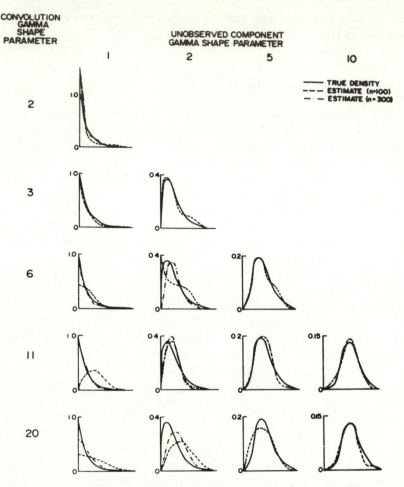

FIG. 3.9 Data were simulated from the convolution of two gamma distributions, one of which is assumed to be known (or observed) and the other (unobserved) is to be estimated. The unobserved one was approximated by a cubic spline. Shown is this approximation to the gamma actually used as a function of the shape parameters of the known and "unknown" distributions; in several cases the sample size used was varied. [Figure 2 of Bloxom (1979); copyright 1979; reprinted by permission.]

3.3   MANIPULATION OF STAGES

3.3.1   *Negligible Decision Latencies to Strong Signals*

From the fact that MRT is slow for weak signals and quite fast for intense ones (Section 2.3.1), it is plausible that the decision center is acting on information that accumulates slowly when the signals are weak and a great deal faster when they are intense. It has occurred to several authors—Luce and Green (1972, p. 21) mentioned it explicitly—that perhaps the decision latency to an intense signal is, relative to the decision latency to a very weak signal, negligible. If so, then the observed *RT* distribution to the intense signal is a slightly biased estimate of the residual distribution, in which case it is easy to estimate the distribution of the decision latency to weak signals. Let s and w denote strong and weak signals, then our assumptions are that **R** does not vary with intensity and **D** is approximately a spike at 0, so

$$\mathscr{C}_\mathbf{T}(\omega \mid s) = \mathscr{C}_\mathbf{D}(\omega \mid s)\mathscr{C}_\mathbf{R}(\omega)$$
$$\cong \mathscr{C}_\mathbf{R}(\omega).$$

Substituting,

$$\mathscr{C}_\mathbf{T}(\omega \mid w) = \mathscr{C}_\mathbf{D}(\omega \mid w)\mathscr{C}_\mathbf{R}(\omega)$$
$$\cong \mathscr{C}_\mathbf{D}(\omega \mid w)\mathscr{C}_\mathbf{T}(\omega \mid s).$$

Thus, inverting $\mathscr{C}_\mathbf{T}(\omega \mid w)/\mathscr{C}_\mathbf{T}(\omega \mid s)$ yields an estimate of $f_\mathbf{D}$ for the weak signal.

An example of carrying out this procedure, due to Burbeck (1979), is shown in Figure 3.10. Later, in Section 4.4, I will present a theoretical analysis of these inferred decision latencies.

A more extensive use of the approach is found in Kohfeld, Santee, and Wallace (1981) where they used discrete generating functions (z-transforms) rather than Fourier transforms. The reason was that Fourier transforms did not yield clear results, whereas z-transforms did. I do not understand why

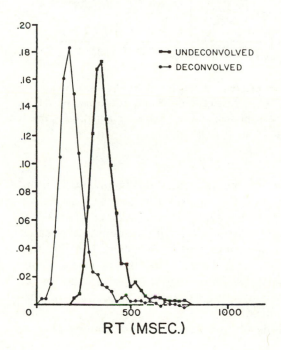

FIG. 3.10 Histograms of observed simple reaction times to the offset of a pure tone, low intensity signal, and the resulting density function obtained by deconvolving from it the distribution of reaction times to an intense noise signal. The two empirical distributions were each based on 1474 observations. Assuming that the latter approximates the residual distribution, the deconvolved distribution is an estimate of the decision time. [Figure 12a of Burbeck (1979); reprinted by permission.]

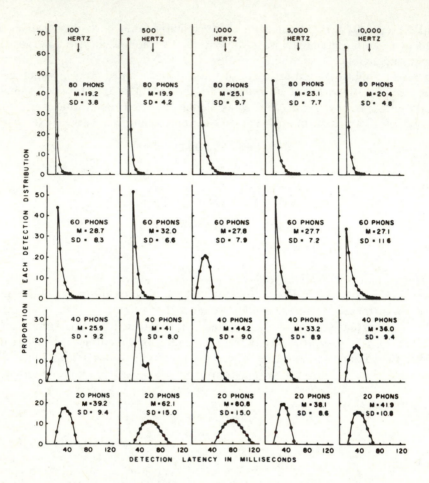

FIG. 3.11 A deconvolution similar to that of Figure 3.10, but using discrete generating functions. Each distribution was based on 288 observations. The signals were pure tones that varied in loudness (phons) and frequency. [Figure 3 of Kohfeld et al. (1981); copyright 1981; reprinted by permission.]

they had success with the one and not the other method. In any event, using the method just outlined, the reaction-time distribution to a 110-dB, 1000-Hz tone (unspecified duration) was deconvolved from a series of distributions obtained using a Go, No-Go procedure, with response terminated signals at a number of different intensities and frequencies. The resulting distributions are shown in Figure 3.11. These distributions when reconvolved with the same intense signal distribution gave a good account of the data; the fact that it is not a perfect account may reflect approximations that are made in the deconvolving procedure.

I know of two major criticisms of this approach. One is the lack of empirical evidence to support the assumption that the decision latency to a strong signal is negligible. Indeed, there are reasons to be very suspicious of that assumption. For one, the distributions found in the literature of reactions to intense signals are not very similar. For example, Snodgrass, Luce, and Galanter (1967) and Snodgrass (1969) studied reaction times to quite intense clicks, which involve exceedingly large intensities at all frequencies for very brief times, yet the tails of these distributions were quite long as can be seen in Figure 4.1 below. By contrast, Burbeck's distribution to response-terminated noise and Kohfeld et al.'s to a very intense pure tone seem to be tightly bounded on the right and to be relatively symmetric, as seen in Figure 3.12. I do not know what causes the very long times in the click data, and no one has yet compared the several classes of intense signals on the same subjects in the same laboratory. Quite obviously, however, Figures 4.1 and 3.12 cannot both be good estimates of the residual unless there are substantial differences in subjects or laboratories, or both, which I doubt is the explanation.

A better assumption, perhaps, than a negligible mean decision time is that the variance of the decision latency is negligible. The main evidence for this is indirect—namely, the very low variance of responses found by Kristofferson and his colleagues (see Section 2.5.3). If we assume that the decision latency to a strong signal is a fixed value d with no variability, then we see

$$\mathscr{C}_{\mathbf{T}}(\omega \mid s) = e^{i\omega d}\mathscr{C}_{\mathbf{R}}(\omega),$$

whence

$$\mathscr{C}_{\mathbf{D}}(\omega \mid w) = e^{i\omega d}\mathscr{C}_{\mathbf{T}}(\omega \mid w)/\mathscr{C}_{\mathbf{T}}(\omega \mid s).$$

To use this equation, which has not yet been done, it is necessary to estimate the value d. One way to proceed is to explore the distributions obtained for various choices of d and to see how sensitive the estimate is to its choice.

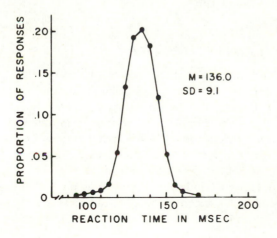

M = 136.0
SD = 9.1

FIG. 3.12 Histogram of simple reaction times to an intense (110-phon, 1000-Hz) tone. The sample size was 288. [Figure 2 of Kohfeld et al. (1981); copyright 1981; reprinted by permission.]

3.3.2   Is the Residual Latency Affected by Signal Intensity?

The second criticism about using response times to very intense signals as an estimate of the residual distribution is that, in fact, the residual may not be independent of signal intensity. Should it be the case that intensity affects the residual, then we clearly are not justified in using the procedure just outlined in Section 3.3.1.

Consider the very conservative definition of the onset of motor activity in terms of a significant change in the electromyogram (EMG), and let $\mathbf{R}'$ be the time from that change until the response occurs. The assumption is that if $\mathbf{R}'$ exhibits a dependence upon signal intensity, then the chances are that $\mathbf{R}$ will be affected also, which it will be unless the effects on $\mathbf{R}'$ and $\mathbf{R} - \mathbf{R}'$ are equal and opposite—an unlikely possibility.

Bartlett (1963) measured MRT and EMG for two levels of light stimuli differing by 19 dB, and he found a small—2 msec—effect in a total $\mathbf{R}'$ of about 50–60 msec. The change in MRT was about 10 msec in an overall time of 160 msec. The effect, while statistically significant, is certainly slight in absolute terms. Costa, Vaughn, and Gilden (1965) did a comparable experiment using click signals at 10, 30, and 90 dB relative to threshold. The mean change in $\mathbf{R}'$, averaged over three subjects, was 7.5 msec on values of $\mathbf{R}'$ ranging over subjects from 42 to 76 msec for the 10-dB signal. This effect was decidedly significant ($p < 0.001$). Grayson (1983) pointed out that both analyses of variance involved a misestimated error term; the more accurate analysis would have increased the significance level. He has collected new data of his own and subjected them to careful statistical analysis, finding statistically significant but comparatively small effects. Moreover, the nature of the effects cannot easily be summarized since they varied from subject to subject.

It, therefore, appears that signal intensity does have some ill-understood impact on the residual. Thus, we are forced to conclude that the method described in Section 3.3.1 is unsatisfactory in that the residue to intense signals is not the same as that to weaker ones.

3.3.3   Is the Residual Latency Affected by Foreperiod Duration?

The other major independent variable, the distribution of foreperiods, is widely believed to affect the decision latency $\mathbf{D}$ through shifts in the subject's criterion to respond. Of course, the possibility exists that it may also affect some part of the residual, presumably the motor, component. Weiss (1965) and Botwinnick and Thompson (1966) carried out similar experiments aimed at deciding this question. Weiss used quasi-randomized foreperiods of durations 1, 2, 3, and 4 sec. For each duration, each of 24 subjects was run three trials under two conditions. One involved normal instructions and the other included shock incentive against excessively long reaction times. Botwinnick and Thompson used foreperiods of $\frac{1}{2}$, 3, 6, and

15 sec, ran 54 subjects, and used both blocked and randomized foreperiod conditions. Both studies reached the conclusion that foreperiod does not affect R', which makes it somewhat plausible that foreperiod does not affect R.

Grayson (1983) was critical of both analyses of variance in that within-cell observations were collapsed into a single number, thereby excluding the possibility of showing that foreperiod wait may affect $\mathbf{R}'$, but in different ways for different subjects. Again, he found statistically significant, but small effects. In this case, the impact of foreperiod on $\mathbf{T}$ was considerably larger and in the opposite direction to that on $\mathbf{R}'$. So the conclusion remains uncertain, but a reasonable working hypothesis is that foreperiod duration probably does not much affect the residue latency.

3.3.4   Independent Manipulation of the Stages

I shall describe here a very special case of a procedure, developed by Sternberg (1969a), which is described more fully in Section 12.4. We do not need to get into the full nuances of the method for present purposes.

Suppose that we have one experimental manipulation we believe affects only the decision latency and another manipulation we believe affects only the residual latency. Consider an experiment in which each manipulation, call them i and j, respectively, takes on at least two values, call them 1, 2, when manipulation ij is applied to the subject. Our assumption is that i but not j affects the residual latency and j but not i affects the decision latency, so

$$\mathbf{T}_{ij} = \mathbf{D}_i + \mathbf{R}_j, \tag{3.15}$$

or in characteristic function form

$$\mathscr{C}_{\mathbf{T}_{ij}} = \mathscr{C}_{\mathbf{D}_i} \mathscr{C}_{\mathbf{R}_j}. \tag{3.16}$$

As Ashby and Townsend (1980) observed,

$$\begin{aligned}
\mathscr{C}_{\mathbf{T}_{11}} \mathscr{C}_{\mathbf{T}_{22}} &= \mathscr{C}_{\mathbf{D}_1} \mathscr{C}_{\mathbf{R}_1} \mathscr{C}_{\mathbf{D}_2} \mathscr{C}_{\mathbf{R}_2} \\
&= \mathscr{C}_{\mathbf{D}_1} \mathscr{C}_{\mathbf{R}_2} \mathscr{C}_{\mathbf{D}_2} \mathscr{C}_{\mathbf{R}_1} \\
&= \mathscr{C}_{\mathbf{T}_{12}} \mathscr{C}_{\mathbf{T}_{21}} \tag{3.17}
\end{aligned}$$

is a testable empirical consequence of three assumptions: additivity, independence, and the ability to influence the two factors selectively and independently. Note, there are two distinct uses of the word "independence," namely of the random variables in any one experimental condition and of the factors. As Grayson (1983) discussed in detail, there are many ways in which one could be misled if Eq. 3.17 seems sustained in the data. It is easy to show by example cases where each of the assumptions is false, but Eq. 3.17 follows. He also raised questions about the statistical test to apply to such data, and developed a suitable one.

To my knowledge, only one attempt has been made to apply this idea to the residual and decision latencies, and it is doubtful if the stage manipulations were suitable. Schnizlein (1980) performed a simple reaction-time experiment with two equally likely foreperiods (.5 and 1 sec), a .5-sec visual warning signal, and a 1000-Hz pure tone reaction signal. He separated the data according to the two foreperiods, and treated that as a manipulation affecting the residual. In addition, he varied signal intensity from 56 to 96 dB in 10-dB steps, and treated that as a second manipulation affecting just the decision latency. The intensity manipulation was as follows. There were three sets of three intensities each, adjacent sets having two intensities in common. During any one run, only those intensities from a single set were used, and their presentation was randomized.

Contrary to Schnizlein's assumption, the limited data discussed above suggest that signal intensity affects both the decision latency and to a lesser degree the residual latency (Section 3.3.2) and the foreperiod affects the decision latency and quite possibly does not affect the residual latency (Section 3.3.3)—just the opposite of his assumptions.

So far as I can tell, the only reliable manipulation of the residual time would be to change the response mode, say using a key press versus a voice response. Since it is possible that intensity may affect both stages, it probably would be best to use criterion changes (whose variation can be checked by observing the frequency of false alarms or anticipations) to manipulate the decision stage but not the residual. To my knowledge, this study has not been performed.

A special case of Eqs. 3.16 and 3.17 should be mentioned explicitly. Consider varying only the treatment that affects the decision latency, holding fixed the one affecting the residual. Then,

$$\mathscr{C}_{T_{ij}}/\mathscr{C}_{T_{kj}} = \mathscr{C}_{D_i}/\mathscr{C}_{D_k} \tag{3.18}$$

is an equation linking observables to the decision latencies (Christie & Luce, 1956). The residue has disappeared completely. Thus, if one has a theory describing the distribution of decision latencies—Chapter 4 includes a number—as an explicit function of n parameters, then Eq. 3.18 relates an observable function to an explicit function of $2n$ parameters, n for the manipulation i and n for k. (Sometimes interpretations of the parameters will lead us to postulate that certain ones are unaffected by the manipulation.) Thus, one need only estimate the parameters and evaluate the goodness of fit. The problem seems reasonably sharply defined, and one might very well expect to find a detailed treatment of it in the statistical literature, but that seems not to be so. The problem is to formulate a satisfactory criterion for goodness-of-fit to the ratio of two characteristic functions; once a criterion is agreed upon, then numerical methods can be used to search for the set of parameters that minimize that criterion.

In the long run, this is probably the most satisfactory approach since it does not entail any special assumptions about the residue, save that one knows of a manipulation that affects the decision latency and not the residue. Manipulation of the response criterion, which we know from Chapter 2 to be empirically effective, seems the safest choice.

3.4 CONCLUSIONS

Most psychologists are interested primarily in the decision latencies as a possible avenue to some understanding of the organization of the mind, and they view the residual latency as a source of "noise" that serves only to blur the random variable of interest. This is the reason for trying one way or another to "subtract" it from the reaction time. All of the methods to do so entail knowing something about one process or the other—either the form of both distributions, or the fact the residue is bounded and the decision latency is exponential in the tail, or that the decision latency is negligible for intense signals, or some manipulation that affects one but not the other latency. With the possible exception of the latter technique, which has not yet been much pursued, none of these assumptions seems to be based on very secure knowledge. As a result we are not in a very satisfactory situation.

The one bright light is the possibility of finding a manipulation that affects the decision latency without affecting the residual. Some psychologists appear to be willing to assume signal intensity is such a variable, but the limited physiological data available make that assumption suspect. To my mind, manipulation of the decision criterion by instructions is the most promising way to affect just the decision latency. Assuming such a manipulation, there are two additional problems. One, for which we may hope to receive aid from the statistical community, is a suitable measure of goodness of fit for data in the form of the ratio of two characteristic functions. The other, which will be our topic throughout the book, is theories for the decision process.

4
Distributions of Simple Decision Latencies

4.1 EMPIRICAL DISTRIBUTIONS

Many mathematical distributions have been suggested to describe the decision latency for simple reactions. Some of these are ad hoc—suggested primarily because they exhibit the skewed form that seems typical of reaction-time distributions and must, therefore, be a characteristic of the decision latency if the residual is symmetrical and has a comparatively small variance. A summary of these distribution functions along with some of their salient properties—mean, variance, moment generating function, and hazard function—is presented in Appendix B.2. Other distributions arise from rather explicit models, more-or-less plausible in nature, for the decision process itself (Sections 4.2 to 4.4 and Appendix B.1). I have attempted to group these suggestions according to the general strategy of the rationalization that is provided, lumping together those that seem to me basically similar. There is no uniquely compelling way to do this. In addition, some data are presented at the outset and are referred to when appropriate in an attempt to exclude some of the suggestions.

Perhaps the most striking fact to emerge from the chapter is that while many distributions appear to the eye to be in gross qualitative correspondence with the data, virtually none exhibit the appropriate characteristics to fit the data obtained using weak signals. This consequence is demonstrated not by looking at the distributions directly, but at their hazard functions. As this conclusion is based primarily on one body of data, but with much collateral evidence, one must be reserved in drawing conclusions about the adequacy of any particular distribution, although not, I think, in concluding that hazard functions are by far the most effective way to compare data of this type to theoretical decision process.

4.1.1 Estimating Hazard Functions

When we turn to data—which I present separately for reaction signals that are well above their detection threshold and for those that are within a few dB of threshold—we find that not many distributions have been presented in the literature and, until recently, hardly any hazard functions have been published. In some cases, drawings of the estimated density functions were presented in enough detail that I have been able to estimate f and from that to calculate an estimate of λ.* For these cases, I report both estimates. The hazard function, like the density, has units of time^{-1}, and so its numerical value is changed by that choice of unit. It is usual to use sec for density functions, and I shall do the same for the hazard function. This places its numerical values roughly in the range from 1 to 100 events sec^{-1}, which is convenient.

Some mention must be made of the difficulties encountered in estimating hazard functions. First, the most obvious procedure of estimating f and F from the data histogram and then computing $f/(1-F)$—which is what I am forced to do when only plots of f or F are available—is notoriously unstable (Rice & Rosenblatt, 1976). The problem arises mostly in the right tail where the ratio being estimated comes close to $0/0$. Clearly, the larger the sample size, the better off one is in using this procedure. When the raw data are available, at least two other, better procedures exist. The whole issue of estimation is discussed in detail by Gross and Clark (1975) and Singpurwalla and Wong (1983). Moreover, several of the well-known statistical packages include estimation programs for the hazard function: BMDP (Dixon et al., 1981), SPSS (SPSSx User's Guide, 1983), and SAS (SUGI Supplemental Library User's Guide, 1983). To my knowledge, none includes the method called random smoothing, due to Miller and Singpurwalla (1977). This method in essence divides time into invervals that have roughly equal sample sizes and so maintains the quality of the estimate over all values.

Their idea is to allow the density of observed reaction times determine the width of the intervals used in smoothing the data. Let $\mathbf{Z}(i)$, $i = 1, \ldots, n$, be the order statistic; that is, the times are rank ordered and $\mathbf{Z}(i)$ is the time having the ith rank. Let $\mathbf{Z}(0) = 0$. Then, the estimate of the hazard rate for the ith interval is

$$\hat{\lambda}(i) = \frac{j}{\displaystyle\sum_{k=i-j+1}^{i} \mathbf{S}(k)}, \quad j < i < n, \tag{4.1}$$

where j is a parameter to be chosen to give the degree of smoothing desired and

$$\mathbf{S}(k) = (n - k + 1)[\mathbf{Z}(k) - \mathbf{Z}(k-1)]. \tag{4.2}$$

For the first $j - 1$ intervals, one sets $j = i$.

Another approach, described in various variants by Bloxom (1979, 1983, 1984a, b), uses quadradic spline approximations (see Section 3.2.5) to the density function. Moreover, as he goes into in detail, the splines can be constrained in various, a priori ways, for example, so as to yield a density

---

* The bin width used in the presentation of the density function has also been used when constructing the hazard function estimate. If f_i is the estimated probability of a response in bin i, and the width is δ_i, then the estimated hazard value for that bin is $\lambda_i = \dfrac{f_i}{\delta_i \sum_{j \geq i} f_j}$.

function and to require the hazard function to be increasing or decreasing, or increasing followed by decreasing. To my knowledge, this method has yet actually to be used with reaction-time data.

A second problem, of course, is that the observed distributions include the unwanted residual latency. As we know from Theorem 1.4, relatively little can be said about the hazard functions of additive components from information about the distribution of the sum. If, as we have some reason to believe, the variance of the residual is small, then the hazard function of the decision latency and of the observed response times do not differ greatly. Alternatively, if one is willing to assume that the impact of intensity on the residual is small, then one can deconvolve the response times to an intense signal from the response times to weak signals as an estimate of the decision latency for the latter (Section 3.3). I illustrate the use of the deconvolution procedure in Section 4.1.3.

A third problem that affects any interpretation of the observed response times is the possibility that they result from a mixture of two or more quite distinct processes. For example, if the subject is either paying attention or not and if response time differs appreciably in the two attention states, as seems most reasonable, then our observations are a mixture of the two distributions, each weighted by the probability of the corresponding state of attention. As far as I know, little theoretical work has been done on this difficulty in the context of simple reaction times, although there is a substantial literature about mixtures for choice reaction times (Chapter 7). In Section 4.1.3 an empirical procedure for "purifying" simple reaction-time data is described.

4.1.2 Signals Well Above Threshold

The few studies of intense signals that have collected enough data to provide distributional information are all auditory. The first of these was Snodgrass, Luce, and Galanter (1967), who presented estimates of two of the density functions; however, the drawings are not adequate for me to estimate the hazard function. It was observed that these distributions to a 30-dB pure tone were extremely peaked functions with what appeared to be outliers on the right tail. Several classes of distributions were fitted to the data, and the best fit was by an ad hoc distribution called the double monomial, which is composed of two power functions back-to-back:

$$f(t) = \frac{(\delta+1)(\epsilon-1)}{(\delta+\epsilon)t_0} \begin{cases} (t/t_0)\delta, & 0 \le t \le t_0 \\ (t/t_0)-\epsilon, & t_0 \le t. \end{cases} \tag{4.3}$$

There was no justification for doing this except that it seemed to have about the correct qualitative properties. It is not difficult to compute its hazard function (Item 9, Appendix B) and to show that it increases as t goes from 0 to t_0, reaching a peak there, after which it decreases to 0 as $1/t$. The fact that the double monomial exhibited some of the characteristics of the distribution hint that the empirical hazard function, were we able to compute it, would also be a peaked function.

Snodgrass (1969) continued this work using a loud click as stimulus. Her manipulations included three foreperiod conditions: (1) a fixed foreperiod, (2) two not very different foreperiods that were equally likely, and (3) two quite different ones that were equally likely. Also, there were five different payoff bands, running from appreciably faster than the usual reaction time to somewhat slower. She presented some of the data in log survivor form, which is reproduced in Figure 4.1. In each case, the maximum proportion of responses in the band occurred for band 3, 110–129 msec. These are thought to be relatively pure reactions, and the others probably entail additional mechanisms, possibly involving time estimation, which introduce additional delays. The theoretical curves are the double monomial, based on maximum likelihood estimates of the parameters. It should be noted that for the optimal band, the data fall off at least as fast as the double monomial, which means their hazard function is descending to 0 as fast as or faster than $1/t$.

Kohfeld, Santee, and Wallace (1981), in deconvolving reaction times to intense signals from those to weak signals, also present the distribution of one subject to the intense signal (110 phons at 1000 Hz, 288 observations). I have estimated the hazard function from their plot, and both are shown in Figure 4.2. Here we see that the hazard function is indeed very peaked.

Burbeck and Luce (1982) also deconvolved the distribution arising from an intense signal—exponential foreperiod, offset of a 70-dB spectrum noise, and about 600 observations—from those arising from signals near threshold. They did not report these distributions, but Figure 4.3 shows them together with their hazard functions for two subjects. The pattern is different in that the hazard function does not return to 0 and the mean times are over 20 msec longer than those for clicks and tones. These data are discussed further in Section 4.4.2.

In his dissertation, Schnizlein (1980) reported the distributions obtained from six subjects reacting to five 1000-Hz tones ranging in intensity from 56 to 96 dB in 10-dB steps. These intensities were run in groups of three adjacent ones with random presentations within a group. The warning signal was a light and there were two equally likely foreperiods of 500 and 1000 msec. Separating the data by foreperiod, there were 18 distributions for each subject, each based upon 360 observations. They were reported as the order statistics corresponding to every .05 change—that is, as the time, to the nearest msec, where the 5% changes occur in the empirical frequency distribution. There was considerable evidence that the distributions to the longer foreperiod were contaminated by time estimates, and I do not think one can rule out the possibility of contamination of the shorter ones too. In any event, Schnizlein focussed his attention only on the nine distributions arising from the short foreperiod. Figure 4.4 shows the estimated hazard functions for several cases; they are typical. The right tail of the distribution

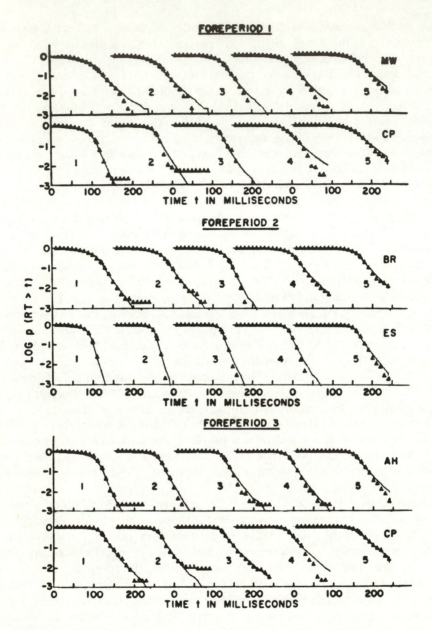

FIG. 4.1 Log survivor functions of simple reactions to a loud click as a function of reinforced band location (see Figure 2.23) and foreperiod condition (see text). The smooth curves are fitted double monomial distributions (Eq. 4.3). The sample sizes were 600 per distribution. [Figure 10 of Snodgrass (1969); copyright 1969; reprinted by permission.]

126

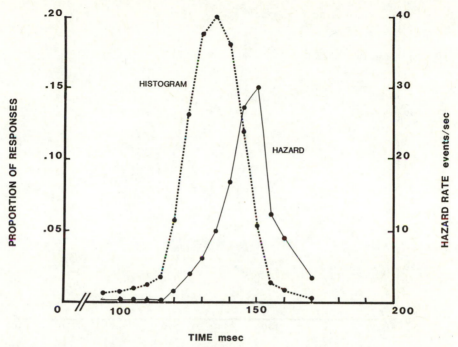

FIG. 4.2 Estimated hazard function for the histogram of simple reaction times to an intense tone shown in Figure 3.12. The sample size was 288.

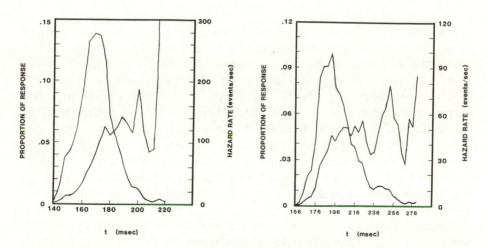

FIG. 4.3 Histogram and estimated hazard function for simple reaction times to an intense noise signal. The sample size was about 600. These data were reported in Burbeck (1979).

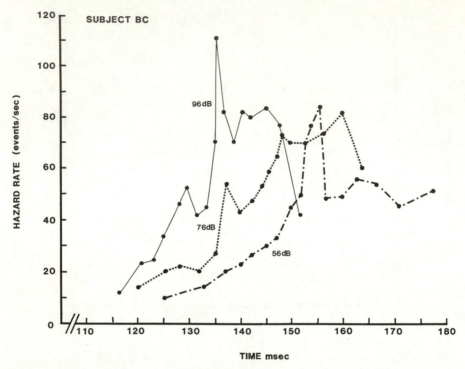

FIG. 4.4 Estimated hazard functions for simple reaction times to pure tones at the intensity levels shown calculated (see text for the method) from data of Schnizlein (1980). The sample size in each case was 360.

is not as precisely specified as one might wish, and so it is somewhat unclear as to how that part of the hazard function is behaving. To gain some idea of where the maximum of the hazard function is located, I grouped the latter half of the hazard function into three groups and averaged them: (1) $p = .50$, .55, .60, .65, (2) $p = .70$, 75, .80, and (3) $p = .85$, .90 (the uneven grouping favors the maximum appearing in group 3). The number of cases where the maximum appears in each group are shown in Table 4.1. The pattern is as it was for the click and pure tone data, and it serves as our summary of all the data except that to noise: to an intense signal, the hazard function is peaked, decaying toward zero for sufficiently long times. For more moderate signals, this tendency toward peakedness is less pronounced, and as we shall see for very weak signals it disappears.

Miller (1982) raised the question whether the detection of two signals simultaneously presented in different modalities can be viewed as a statistical race between the two separate detection processes. There is, within the cognitive domain, a sizable literature on this in connection with attentional issues, some of which, but by no means all, will be taken up in Chapters 11

TABLE 4.1. Estimated location of maximum of hazard function in Schnizlein (1980) data. The entries are numbers of cases

	Location of maximum		
Intensity group	1	2	3
High	4	$11\frac{1}{2}$	$2\frac{1}{2}$
Medium	1	12	6
Low	1	8	9

and 12. He reviewed it in detail. I report one experiment here, rather than later, because it is possible from the relatively raw data provided in this case to estimate the hazard functions for the case of two simultaneous signals and for the average distribution function of the individual signals separately.

The experiment involved on each trial one of four possible presentations: either a 780-Hz, 150-msec bell on a microcomputer or an asterisk on the video screen of the computer, or both, or neither. The subject was simply to respond as rapidly as possible. There were several different experiments, which I do not go into, but one involved four trained subjects who each received 640 presentations of each condition. I have estimated the hazard functions for these subjects for both the simultaneous case and for the average of the single presentation (he did not present these data separately). Figure 4.5 presents these for two subjects, *DF* and *EH* (the others are similar), and we see that the functions are increasing, reaching the levels we would expect from previous data. Note, however, that the rise is a great deal slower for these stimuli; I suspect the slow rise is due mostly to the relatively poor quality of the stimulus materials.

The substance of Miller's paper is that the performance in the simultaneous case is better than can be expected from the race model. For example, if one chooses to assume that the two processes are independent, then one merely doubles the hazard function for the average stimulus to get the prediction of the race model, and clearly that falls short by a considerable amount of the observed hazard function for the simultaneous condition. Miller draws the same conclusion without making the independence assumption by the following observation. Suppose the random variable associated with signal type s_i is $\mathbf{T}_i$ and $\mathbf{T} = \min(\mathbf{T}_1, \mathbf{T}_2)$ is the race model. Then,

$$
\begin{aligned}
F(t) &= \Pr(\mathbf{T} \leq t \mid s_1 \ \& \ s_2) \\
&= \Pr(\mathbf{T}_1 \leq t \mid s_1) + \Pr(\mathbf{T}_2 \leq t \mid s_2) \\
&\quad - \Pr(\mathbf{T}_1 \leq t \ \& \ \mathbf{T}_2 \leq t \mid s_1 \ \& \ s_2) \\
&\leq F_1(t) + F_2(t).
\end{aligned}
$$

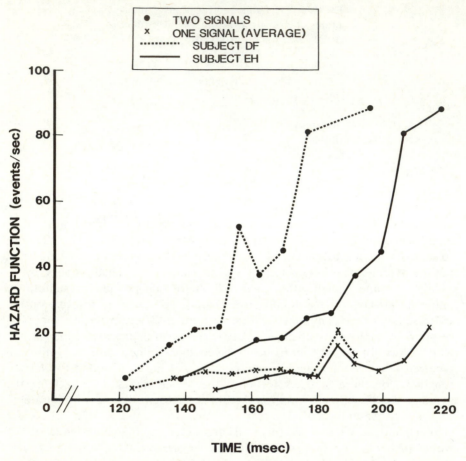

FIG. 4.5 Estimated hazard functions for two of four subjects reported by Miller (1982). In the two signal case, the reaction signal was the simultaneous presentation of a tone and a visual stimulus. In the one signal case, only the sum of the two distribution functions was provided, so the estimate is from the average single signal. The sample size in each case is 640.

Note that this equation does not entail the assumption that T_1 and T_2 are statistically independent. His data clearly reject this inequality, and so he concluded that the race model, which he called the separate-activation model, does not hold. He favours, instead, a coactivation model in which the sensory information is combined before a decision is reached.

The argument as stated is incomplete in two ways. First, a kind of independence, albeit not statistical independence, is implicit—namely,

$$\Pr(\mathbf{T}_i \le t \mid s_1 \ \& \ s_2) = \Pr(\mathbf{T}_i \le t \mid s_i).$$

This is not obviously true, and it is difficult to know how to verify it. However, the only hope for reversing the conclusion about the failure of the race model would be to replace the equality with >, which is tantamount to saying that the presence of the one signal facilitates the detection of the other even if it is irrelevant. So far as I know, that experiment has not been performed. Second, the argument given about the nature of the race really applies not to the overall response times but to the decision times. Suppose, therefore, that a residual time **R**, independent of **T**, is added to it, then (omitting the conditioning stimuli)

$$\Pr(\mathbf{T}+\mathbf{R}\leq t) = \int_0^t \Pr(\mathbf{R}=r)\,\Pr(\mathbf{T}\leq t-r)\,dr$$

$$\leq \int_0^t \Pr(\mathbf{R}=r)[\Pr(\mathbf{T}_1\leq t-r)+\Pr(\mathbf{T}_2\leq t-r)]\,dr$$

$$= \Pr(\mathbf{T}_1+\mathbf{R}\leq t)+\Pr(\mathbf{T}_2+\mathbf{R}\leq t),$$

which is the same inequality. So the existence of an independent residual does not affect the argument.

4.1.3   Signals Near Threshold

Probably the first study of reaction times to signals that are barely detectable and for which sufficient data were collected to look at distributional questions for individual subjects, was Luce and Green (1970). We used a light as a warning signal, an exponential foreperiod with a mean of 5 sec, and as a reaction signal the onset of a 1000-Hz tone ranging from 11.5 to 24.5 dB above a 50-dB spectrum level white noise. The reaction signal was response terminated. Over 10,000 observations went into each distribution. Because the main interest was in the tails of these distributions, we unfortunately did not publish all of the distributional data; however, the tails were approximately exponential, which suggests a hazard function that asymptotes to a nonzero constant. In Green and Luce (1971) a similar study was reported in which we used: five countdown lights as a warning signal, a mean exponential foreperiod of 4-sec, 40-dB spectrum loud noise, and a 1000-Hz reaction tone at 10 dB E/N_0. In discussing Fourier transform methods, we provided complete plots for two subjects with the curves smoothed by a Hamming procedure.[*] For these plots, I have estimated the hazard functions and both are shown in Figure 4.6. Note that these hazard functions are appreciably different from those obtained using signals well above threshold; they do not return to zero, but seem to be relatively constant for long times, which means (as we had concluded from a direct fitting to the tails) that the tails are exponential or approximately so.

---

[*] Without going into detail, such a smoothing procedure amounts to convolving the empirical function with a smoothing distribution; it necessarily increases the variance of the data.

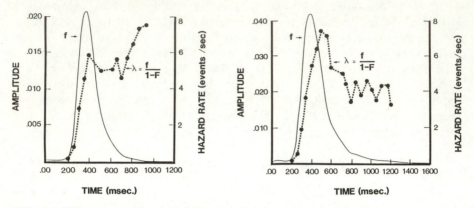

FIG. 4.6 Histogram and estimated hazard function for simple reaction times to a low intensity pure tone in noise (see text). The sample sizes were over 10,000. [Adapted by permission from Figures 11 and 13 of Green and Luce (1971).]

An unpublished experiment by R. Shannon, similar to the above but with the offset of a tone as the signal, yielded the data shown in $\ln(1-F)$ form in Figure 4.7. The distinct bend attracted our attention because it was not predicted by any of the models we were then looking at—ones that we will call level detection models below. Burbeck (1979) then took up the problem (see Burbeck and Luce [1982] for a published summary of a portion of his dissertation) and explored the data using a hazard function analysis. In these experiments the warning signal was three successive light flashes followed by an exponential foreperiod with a mean of 3 sec at the end of which a pure tone in low level background noise was terminated. Three frequencies—250, 1000, and 4000 Hz—were run at two intensities, 2 dB apart, near threshold on three subjects. The original sample size in each condition ranged from 776 to 2441, but the data analysis procedure to be described reduced these to the range of 242 (subject *DG* at 250 Hz, softer tone) to 1353 (subject *DL*, louder tone).

There were two major considerations in the data analysis that are discussed in detail in Burbeck and Luce (1982). First, there is considerable danger in data collected over a long period of time that some of the subject's parameters may vary. This can have severe consequences for the hazard function. For example, suppose the behavior for a fixed set of parameters is described as an exponential, so the hazard function is constant; but suppose further that the exponential parameter over experimental runs is distributed as a gamma, then the resulting mixture distribution has a hazard function that decreases as $1/t$. To reduce this problem, Burbeck eliminated any data block (depending on the condition, a block consisted of between 75 and 100 trials) that deviated by more than a certain amount from the mean of all of the data. He referred to this as censoring the data.

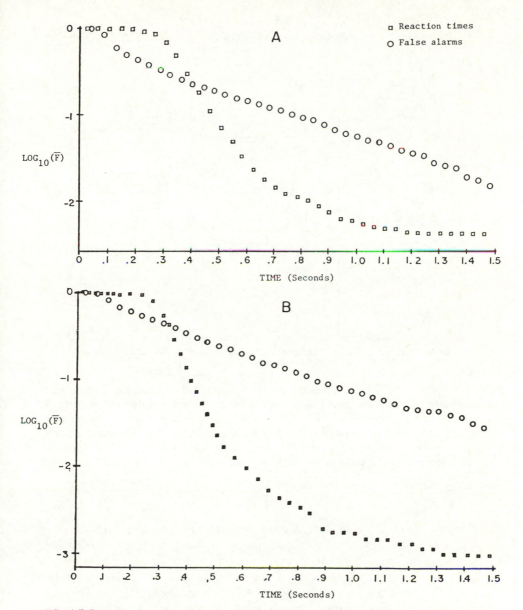

FIG. 4.7 Log survivor functions for simple reaction times to low intensity, response terminated pure tones in noise. The time scale for false alarms has been compressed by a factor of ten to show that the tails of the false alarm distribution are well approximated by exponentials at least as far out as 15 seconds. Thus the data point at one second represents false alarms at ten seconds. The sample size is not available. (These are unpublished data of R. Shannon reported in Burbeck, personal communication; reprinted by permission.)

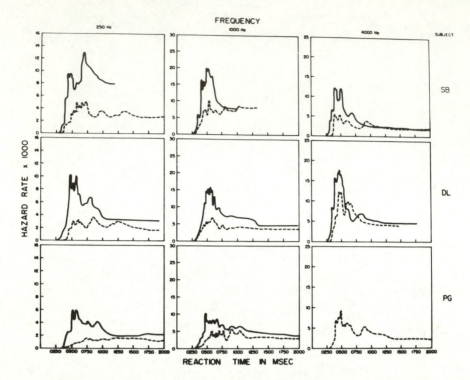

FIG. 4.8 Estimated hazard functions for the deconvolved (see text and Figure 3.10) distribution of simple reaction times to the offset of a low intensity tone in noise. In each case, the upper curve is for a signal 2 dB greater than that of the lower curve. The rows are different subjects; the columns are different signal frequencies. The sample size ranged from 242 to 1353 depending upon the amount of censoring involved (see text). [Figure 4 of Burbeck and Luce (1982); copyright 1982; reprinted by permission.]

Second, there is a problem of how best to estimate a hazard function since, quite obviously, the data get sparce in the tail of the distribution. Burbeck used the distribution free method of Miller and Singpurwalla (1977), which was stated in Eqs. 4.1 and 4.2 of Section 4.1.1. The estimated hazard functions are shown in Figure 4.8. We see here exactly the same pattern as in the onset data of Green and Luce: the hazard function rises to a peak and either stays approximately constant at that level or it drops a bit before becoming constant. The magnitude of the peak is greater for the more intense signal, and in that case there is always a drop from the peak before the exponential tail begins. To verify that the hazard function really does become constant, Burbeck and Luce used a test proposed by Gnedenko, Belyayev, and Soloyev (1969). Suppose there are n events in the section of the tail of the distribution to be tested; order these events and split them into a lower and upper group of sizes r_1 and r_2, $n = r_1 + r_2$. With **S** defined by Eq. 4.2, the test statistic is

$$\mathbf{Q}(r_1, r_2) = \frac{\sum\limits_{k=1}^{r_1} \mathbf{S}(k)/r_1}{\sum\limits_{k=r_1+1}^{n} \mathbf{S}(k)/r_2}, \tag{4.4}$$

which is distributed as an F with $2r_1$ and $2r_2$ degrees of freedom under the null hypothesis of a constant hazard function. In all cases, a time could be chosen so that at the .05 level the null hypothesis of a constant hazard value from that point on was not rejected.

Green and Smith (1982), in a study much like that of Burbeck and Luce, concluded, on the contrary, that there is no evidence for a peak in the hazard function and, hence, as we shall see in Section 4.4 no evidence for the existence of a change detector. In their experiment the signal was the onset of a 1000-Hz tone of fixed duration, either 50 or 1000 msec. The warning signal was a countdown of five equally spaced events, and the foreperiod was exponentially distributed with a mean of 10 sec. Information feedback was provided, but no great emphasis was placed upon speed of responding and some attempt was made to hold down anticipations. Three signal intensities were used in randomized fashion for each duration, the choice adjusted in each case to be within a few dB of threshold. A total of 2984, 1198, and 1817 trials were run for subjects *DS*, *DT*, and *PN*, respectively. The resulting density and hazard functions (the latter estimated from estimates of f and $1-F$) are shown in Figures 4.9 and 4.10. (Note that in both types of plot, the scales of the ordinates differ by a factor of 2 for the two durations.

The question arises of reconciling these data with those of Burbeck and Luce. There are, of course, some differences in the design that may be relevant: tone onset versus offset, fixed duration versus response terminated (although in practice a 1000-msec signal is little different from a response terminated one), little emphasis on speed of responding versus considerable emphasis, and somewhat different signal intensities. Let me explore the latter. Table 4.2 presents a comparison of the intensities relative to the noise background and with the approximate peak values of the hazard function in units of number of events per sec. Note that for the one common value of intensity used for the 1000 msec and response terminated signal, the rates are substantially identical, suggesting some degree of comparability. Observe in Figure 4.7 that for the 20-dB, 1000-Hz tone Burbeck and Luce also report no peak. It arises only at 2 dB higher level. So I suspect that Green and Smith simply did not use a sufficiently intense signal to see the peakedness reported by Burbeck and Luce. Smith (personal communication) feels that the lack of time pressure may also have mattered.

For the 50-msec signal, the intensity levels are sufficiently high for a peak

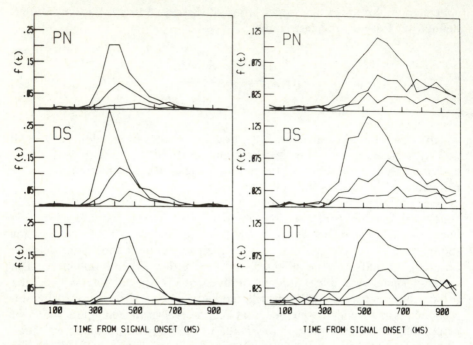

FIG. 4.9 Histograms for simple reaction times to low intensity pure tones in noise. The rows correspond to subjects; the left column is for a signal of 50 msec duration and the right for 1000 msec duration; and the three curves in each panel correspond to the intensities shown in Table 4.1. Reading down over subjects, the sample sizes were approximately 605, 995, and 399. [Figure 5 of Green and Smith (1982); copyright 1982; reprinted by permission.]

TABLE 4.2. Comparison of peak values of the hazard function (in events/sec) for 1000-Hz tones of Burbeck and Luce (1981) and Green and Smith (1982)

Signal intensity (dB)	Signal duration		
	Response terminated	1000 msec	50 msec
28			10
25			3
22	15		1
20	5	5	
17		1	
14		$\frac{1}{2}$	

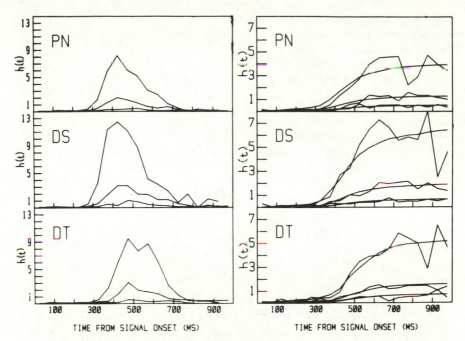

FIG. 4.10 Estimated hazard functions corresponding to the data shown in Figure 4.9. [Figure 6 of Green and Smith (1982); copyright 1982; reprinted by permission.]

to appear, but the apparent peak in the data probably has as much to do with the brief duration as anything else. What is noticeable, however, is that the rate of rise for these more intense cases is very different from that for the 1000-msec signals. For example, the 28-dB, 50-msec signal exhibits a slope of roughly 100 events sec^{-2}, whereas that for the most intense 1000-msec signal has a slope smaller by a factor of at least 5. We notice in Figure 4.7 that for the 1000-Hz signal the initial rise when there is a peak is substantially faster than when there is no peak, which seems quite consistent with the pattern of the 50-msec data. So, my tentative conclusion is that there is no real inconsistency between these two experiments. This does not appear to be Green and Smith's conclusion.

Wandell, Ahumada, and Welsh (1984) reported a visual study designed to test a theory we discuss in Section 4.3.1. The reaction signals were a 1.1-deg spot of 670-nm light on a 10.8-deg background field of 580 nm and 8.68 log quanta $deg^{-2} sec^{-1}$ intensity. The test flashes lasted either 10 or 500 msec. Four intensities were used for each duration; at 10 msec they spanned about 3 dB and at 500 msec about 4 dB. The intensities were within a few decibels of threshold. The warning signal was a tone and the foreperiods were exponentially distributed with a mean of 400 msec, but truncated at 1200 msec. Any response prior to 100 msec after signal onset

FIG. 4.11 Histograms of simple reaction times to 10-msec visual flashes at the intensities shown. Each distribution is based on from 800 to 1000 observations. The smooth curves are cubic spline approximations. [Figure 3 of Wandell et al. (1984); copyright 1984; reprinted by permission.]

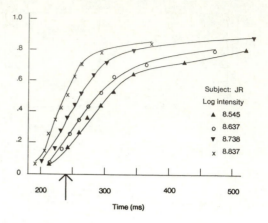

was regarded as an anticipation and removed from the data analysis. The only distribution functions presented were for the 10-msec flash, and they are shown in Figure 4.11. The continuous curves are cubic splines. From the smooth curves I have estimated* the hazard functions shown in Figure 4.12. They resemble those for weak auditory signals in that they are peaked and asymptote to an approximately constant value. The value of the asymptote, which is comparable to those from audition, appears to be independent of the intensity. That apparent fact should be treated with considerable caution for several reasons: the sample sizes were not large, the range of intensities is only 3 dB, and with such a brief signal the hazard function in the tails may well be at the noise level.

In evaluating models for simple reaction times, I shall focus greatly on their ability to produce hazard functions that are capable of mimicking the patterns we have seen: (1) for sufficiently long signals very near threshold, the hazard function rises to an asymptote; (2) at somewhat greater intensities it rises more rapidly to a peak and then declines to an asymptote well above the noise level of the process; and (3) at very high intensities it rises rapidly to a much higher peak and, except for auditory noise signals, it then falls off sharply. These qualitative features, if correct, are by themselves, without any estimation of model parameters and evaluation of goodness of fit, sufficient to reject many of the classical theories and most of the ad hoc distributional suggestions.

---

* Wandell et al. (1984, p. 648) remarked that this may well be unsatisfactory because the estimated distribution function, while consistent, is a biased estimator. This means that the estimate of the hazard function is particularly suspect at the two extremes; however, my conclusions are based on its shape in the mid range.

4.2   DISCRETE-TIME, INFORMATION-ACCUMULATION DETECTORS

4.2.1   The General Schema

The literature on decision latencies is dominated by models of a common type. These mechanisms are not especially sensitive to signal onset or offset, but they become more sensitive to the change the longer the signal remains present. They have the common feature that information about the signal accumulates steadily until some condition is satisfied, at which point a decision is made based on the information then available. I am using the term "information" informally, not in the technical sense of information theory. As I use the term here, it amounts to nothing more or less than changes in the nervous system that can be employed in making discriminations. I attempt in this and the following section to describe these models in a broad, qualitative fashion, much as John (1967) did at an earlier time, in order that their conceptual similarities and differences may be understood. In addition, I shall cite precisely the distributional conclusions that are known for the simple reaction-time paradigm, but in some cases their formal development is best postponed until Part II on identification paradigms. There are two reasons for this delay. First, it is necessary to know something about several classes of stochastic (=probabilistic in time; see Section 1.5)

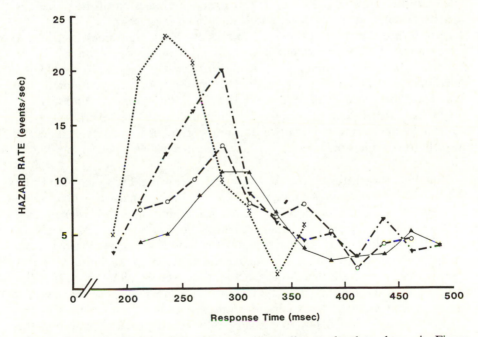

FIG. 4.12 Estimated hazard functions corresponding to the data shown in Figure 4.11. The points are coded in the same way.

processes in order to work them out, and we have yet to take up that mathematics. And second, the proofs are not really simpler for the simple reaction time case than for the choice one, and so we might just as well develop them in the more general context.

It is important to realize that the models arising from choice contexts all assume that the normal function of such accumulation detectors is not signal detection but signal identification. As a matter of fact, in applying the models to choice situations, detection is usually taken for granted. The experiments often involve an intense signal in another modality to mark the time of signal onset, and that marker signal is detected by some sort of detector in its modality. In the special context of simple reactions to weak signals, these identification mechanisms may possibly be invoked to detect the presence of a signal that has gone unnoticed by the mechanism that usually detects change of intensity in that modality.

The general conceptual schema is this. At all times, the nervous system is assumed to be accumulating information about the level of stimulation. The accumulation is very slow when no signal is present and more rapid when there is one, the rate being a monotonic function of signal intensity. At some point, the decision mechanism judges that enough information has accumulated in order to make a judgment about the nature of the stimulation. In the choice context, that judgment concerns which of several signals was presented, and it is made on the basis of the information that has accumulated. In the simple reaction context, the mere termination of the process is usually tantamount to a decision that the signal is present.

Specific models differ in three major aspects. First, what does it mean for information to accumulate and how is that accumulation to be modeled? Second, what is the stopping rule? And third, what is the basis for making a decision once information collection has ceased? As was just noted, the third question is usually degenerate in the simple reaction case, and so I will not discuss it here except incidentally. Because there are several plausible alternative answers to the first two questions, there are a variety of different models to consider, only some of which have been developed in considerable detail.

Roughly, the distinctions run along the following lines. In all of the models the information is thought of as something numerical, whose value and sign tell the central decision center something about the signal. One distinction is whether information changes continuously or discretely in time: is it analogous to reading a meter or does it arrive at discrete times much as the price of a stock recorded on a daily basis? Technically, is it a continuous or discrete-time stochastic process (see Section 1.5)? The discrete case treats the sensory system a bit like a movie camera that takes a series of still photographs at discrete times. Despite some interest in the problem, it has turned out to be very difficult to prove or disprove the existence of some such time quanta (Allport, 1968; Stroud, 1965).

Nevertheless, such models are common, and I have used this mathematical distinction to make the major cut between this section and the next, the present one being devoted to the discrete-time case and Section 4.3 to the continuous one.

In the discrete-time case, it is convenient to distinguish between those models where the increments in information are binary from those in which they are more general random variables. The next two subsections are devoted to binary models, and Sections 4.2.4 and 5 to variable ones. In the continuous time case, three distinctions may be made: continuous and deterministic growth, continuous and stochastic growth, and binary accumulation. These are broken down into Sections 4.3.1–4.3.2, 4.3.3, and 4.3.4–4.3.6.

Given that information is accumulative, the third distinction concerns the conditions under which the brain stops accumulating information and makes a response. In general, there seem to be three possibilities for stopping: when the aggregate information exceeds a criterion or when a certain amount of time has elapsed or when some sort of statistical condition is fulfilled, such as when a fixed sample size is achieved or the likelihood ratio of the two hypotheses exceeds a criterion. As we shall see, under certain assumptions about the accumulation process, some of the distinctions among stopping rules vanish.

Since one of the goals is to give a rational account for the distribution of decision latencies, it is essential to provide a plausible mechanism that leads to variability. As I write, there is very little work on mechanisms that might underlie variability in any of the stopping rules—criterion, time, or sample size. Rather, the focus has been entirely on mechanisms for the accumulation of information, and either that is inherently stochastic or the criterion is assumed to be a random variable with some ad hoc distribution.

4.2.2   Binary Sampling and Fixed Criterion: Recruitment Model

Working in the spirit of stimulus sampling theory (Estes, 1950), LaBerge (1962) formulated what he called recruitment theory which, among other things, provided a distributional theory for simple reaction times. The general idea is that the stimulus is represented internally in terms of a set of "elements" and it is characterized by the proportion of them that are distinguished from the others—"conditioned" was the term used. It is assumed that the decision center samples one element at random, notes whether or not it is conditioned, replaces it, and at the next discrete-time interval repeats the process. This continues until a fixed number k of conditioned elements have been "recruited." In this model, k is the criterion for a response. If the proportion of conditioned elements is p, then it is a standard combinatorial problem to calculate the probability that in m

trials exactly k conditioned elements will be sampled; it is

$$\frac{(m-1)!}{(k-1)!(m-k)!} p^k(1-p)^{m-k},$$

which is known as the negative binomial distribution. Put in cumulative form, it can be shown to be equivalent to the incomplete beta function

$$Ip(k, m-k+1) = \frac{(m-1)!}{(k-1)!(m-k)!} \int_0^p x^{k-1}(1-x)^{m-k} \, dx,$$

which is tabulated (Pearson, 1932) or can be readily programmed. Assuming a residual $\mathbf{R}$ and a physical time τ for each discrete step, the response latency is given by

$$\mathbf{T} = \mathbf{M}\tau + \mathbf{R},$$

where $\mathbf{M}$ is the number of trials needed to recruit k conditioned elements.

Figure 4.13 presents several examples of the density and hazard functions of this model. Clearly, it is not adequate since the hazard function is always increasing. Another way to see this result is to note that the continuous-time analogue of selecting with a fixed probability is the Poisson process, and so the distribution of times to the kth event is the gamma which as we know (Section A.1.5) has an increasing hazard function.

Schnizlein (1980) fit this model to his data which, it will be recalled, involved five intensities run in three groups of three adjacent ones, resulting in a total of nine distributions. The parameters were five values of p, corresponding to the intensities, three values of k corresponding to the groups, one value of $r_0 = E(\mathbf{R})$, and τ, for a total of nine since the time scale is arbitrary. The distributions were divided into 20 intervals of equal probability, so the total degrees of freedom were $9 \times 19 - 9 = 162$, which is the expected value of χ^2. The observed values (over subjects) lay between 204 and 330, all significantly different from the model.

*4.2.3 Binary Events at Almost Periodic Times

For some purposes, mainly the analysis of neural pulse trains or patterns of heart beats but not reaction times, it is reasonable to suppose that one is dealing with a point process that is basically periodic but subject to minor perturbations. For example, this will happen when there is a purely periodic driving force—for example, the amplitude passes a threshold—that initiates a process of variable duration that leads to an observable event—for example, a neural pulse on an auditory nerve fiber. If we denote the period of the driving mechanism by τ, the random delay by $\mathbf{S}$, and the time between successive observable events by $\mathbf{T}$, the situation is as diagrammed in Figure

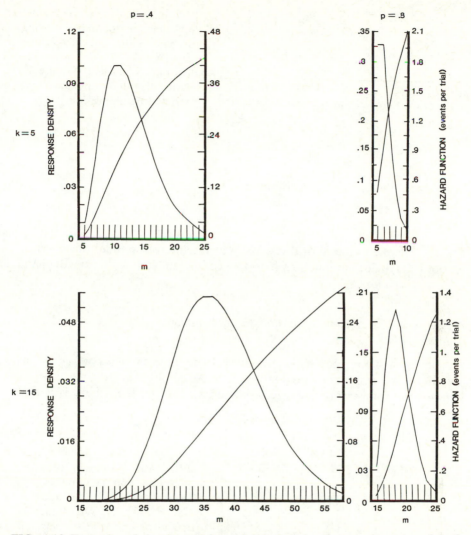

FIG. 4.13 Examples of density and hazard functions for the recruitment model of LaBerge (1962) for the parameter values shown.

4.14. McGill (1962), using a mgf argument, showed that if **S** is distributed according to the (improper) exponential $\mu e^{-\mu s}$, $0 \leq s \leq \tau$, then **T** is distributed according to

$$f(t) = \begin{cases} [\mu\alpha/(1-\alpha)]\sinh \mu t, & t \leq \tau \\ [(1-\alpha)/2\alpha]\mu e^{-\mu t}, & t > \tau \end{cases}$$

where $\alpha = e^{\mu\tau}$. When $\mu\tau$ is large—that is, the perturbation is small on the average relative to the period—then α is small and the density of $t - \tau$

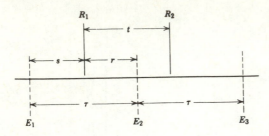

FIG. 4.14 Scheme of the model involving a periodic driving mechanism E_i with observable responses R_i delayed by a random time **S** (see text). [Figure 10 of McGill (1963); copyright 1963; reprinted by permission.]

approaches the LaPlace distribution:

$$f(t-\tau) = (\mu/2)\exp(-\mu|t-\tau|).$$

Figure 4.15 shows the fit of this density to the interpulse times observed on an optic nerve fiber of limulus when the eye is stimulated with a steady light.

4.2.4 Variable Accumulation and Fixed Criterion: Random Walk Model

Instead of assuming a simple binary variable at each observation, let us assume that a continuous random variable $\mathbf{X}_n$ is observed at time n. If $\mathbf{A}_n$ denotes the total information accumulated by time n, then there is a very

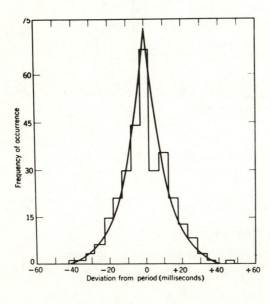

FIG. 4.15 Histogram of interpulse times on the optic nerve of light stimulated limulus fitted by the density derived from the model described in the text and Figure 4.14. [Figure 9 of McGill (1963); copyright 1963; reprinted by permission.]

simple relation between its values on successive time units; namely,

$$\mathbf{A}_n = \mathbf{A}_{n-1} + \mathbf{X}_n = \sum_{k=1}^{n} \mathbf{X}_k,$$

where we assume $\mathbf{X}_n$ is a random variable independent of $\mathbf{A}_{n-1}$ and the distribution of $\mathbf{X}_n$ does not depend on n. So $\mathbf{A}_n$ is the total information accumulated and $\mathbf{X}_n$ is the increment added at time n.

Consider the three possible stopping rules. First, we note that the constant time and the constant sample size rules are identical. Since it is widely believed that the decision latency is not constant—although, because we cannot reliably partition the reaction time into the decision and residue latencies, we have provided no direct evidence for that supposition—no one has bothered to study the random walk model with a fixed number of steps. Of course, one could make the number of steps a random variable, but then its distribution and so that of the reaction-time distribution would be ad hoc. Since the goal is to rationalize that distribution, one turns to the only remaining alternative, a fixed criterion on the amount of information. So the decision rule is that the subject selects a value for C—which may be affected in some unknown way by many factors including payoffs—and the rule is to stop collecting information on the first n for which $\mathbf{A}_n \geq C$.

To my knowledge, no one has worked out this model for the case where the information increment $\mathbf{X}_k$ has one nontrivial distribution during the foreperiod and a different one following signal onset, which is of course the case of interest. The case for which a result is known involves three assumptions. First, contrary to the evidence on anticipations, it assumes that $\mathbf{X}_k = 0$ prior to signal onset. Second, it assumes that the distribution of $\mathbf{X}_k$ is Gaussian with mean $\mu > 0$ and standard deviation σ. And third, it assumes that μ is small relative to C (see Section 8.2.2 for a precise formulation of this assumption). Under those assumptions, the density of decision latencies—number of steps n—will be shown in Section 8.2.5 to satisfy

$$(\alpha/2\pi n^3)^{1/2} \exp[-\alpha(n-\beta)^2/2\mu^2 n], \tag{4.5}$$

where $\alpha = (C/\sigma)^2$ and $\beta = C/\mu$. By a limiting process one can replace n by continuous time t. Or better, one can set up the process in the first place as a continuous-time, Markov process—technically a diffusion process—as Emerson (1970) did (care must be taken with this paper as there are several misprints in the equations). The continuous version of Eq. 4.5 is called the Wald density because it was first derived by Wald (1947); it is also called the inverse Gaussian because there exists an inverse relationship between the cumulative generating functions (log of the mgf) for these two classes of distributions. The mean is β and the variance is β^3/α. Observe that we expect β to be affected by signal intensity through its effect on μ and for both α and β to be affected by motivational variables via C.

To gain some understanding of the shape of the hazard function, we observe that if f denotes the Wald density with a continuous variable t

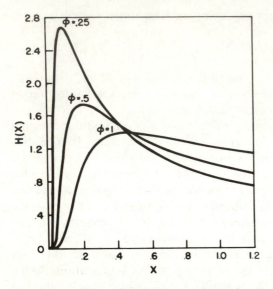

FIG. 4.16 Examples of the hazard function for the Wald distribution for several values of the parameter ϕ, which is the ratio of the boundary of the random walk divided by the mean step size (see Section 8.2.5). [Figure 6 of Burbeck and Luce (1982); copyright 1982; reprinted by permission.]

replacing n and λ denotes its hazard function, then

$$\lim_{t \to 0} \lambda(t) = \lim_{t \to 0} \frac{f(t)}{1 - F(t)} = f(0) = 0,$$

$$\lim_{t \to \infty} \lambda(t) = \lim_{t \to \infty} \frac{f(t)}{1 - F(t)}$$

$$= -\lim_{t \to 0} f'(t)/f(t)$$

$$= -\lim_{t \to \infty} \frac{d \ln f(t)}{dt}$$

$$= -\lim_{t \to \infty} \frac{d}{dt} [\tfrac{1}{2} \ln(\alpha/2\pi) - (3/2) \ln t - \alpha(t - \beta)^2/2\beta^2 t)]$$

$$= \lim_{t \to \infty} [(3/2t) + (\alpha/2\beta^2)(t - \beta)(t + \beta)/t^2]$$

$$= \alpha/2\beta^2$$

$$= \tfrac{1}{2}(\mu/\sigma)^2.$$

Moreover, it can be shown that the hazard function has a maximum different from the asymptote, and so it is peaked and has a nonzero asymptote; see Figure 4.16 for examples. These are exactly the correct qualitative properties to fit the empirical hazard functions shown in Figures 4.6, 4.8, and 4.12.

So, to evaluate it as a possible theory, it is necessary to fit the Wald density to the data. Burbeck and Luce (1982) did just this on data from which the strong signal distribution was deconvolved in an attempt to get rid of the residual time. The parameters were selected numerically so as to minimize χ^2. In general, the fits were not satisfactory. Figure 4.17 provides an example of a success and of a failure. The conclusion is that the classic random walk model with a Gaussian distribution of steps is not adequate to account for these data despite the fact that its hazard function is qualitatively correct. Perhaps some modification of the Gaussian distribution assumption of that model would alter the hazard function enough to deal with these data, or perhaps if we had a more satisfactory way to estimate the distribution of residual times the fit would be improved.

Schnizlein (1980) also fit this model to his data, and it was distinctly inferior to either recruitment theory or to the model discussed in Section 4.3.2.

4.2.5 *Variable Accumulation and Fixed Probability Boundary*

As in Section 4.2.4, suppose that $\mathbf{X}_k$ are independent and distributed according to one density, f_0, prior to signal onset and a different one, f_1, after signal onset. Moreover, suppose that the distribution of signal onsets is geometric with parameter p; this is the discrete analogue of the exponential foreperiod. Now, instead of comparing $\mathbf{A}_n = \sum \mathbf{X}_k$ with a criterion, as in the random walk model, suppose that the subject uses all of the information available—namely, that the onset is geometric with parameter p and the observed values are $\mathbf{X}_1, \mathbf{X}_2, \dots, \mathbf{X}_n$—in order to estimate the probability $\mathbf{P}_n$ that the signal onset has occurred. Assume then that the decision rule is to

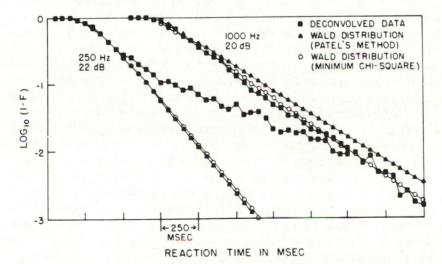

FIG. 4.17 Fit of the Wald log survivor function to the deconvolved data shown in Figure 4.8. [Figure 7 of Burbeck and Luce (1982); copyright 1982; reprinted by permission.]

establish a criterion P and to respond to the first n when $\mathbf{P}_n \geq P$. This model was first proposed and studied in Chapter 3 of Rapoport, Stein, and Burkheimer (1979).

In order to understand this process, it is necessary to develop information about the distribution of $\mathbf{P}_n$. Suppose that the probability of the signal occurring before trial $n-1$ is $\mathbf{P}_{n-1}$ and that this fails to trigger a response. Before any information is examined on trial n, we know on the basis of the geometric pattern of onsets that $\mathbf{P}_{n-1}$ has been increased to

$$\mathbf{P}^*_{n-1} = \mathbf{P}_{n-1} + (1 - \mathbf{P}_{n-1})p.$$

This, then, is the prior probability that the observation $\mathbf{X}_{n-1}$ is distributed according to f_1, and $1 - \mathbf{P}^*_{n-1}$ is the probability that the distribution is f_0; hence, the prior density that $\mathbf{X}_{n-1} = x$ is

$$\mathbf{P}^*_{n-1} f_1(x) + (1 - \mathbf{P}^*_{n-1}) f_0(x).$$

According to Bayes Theorem (Section 1.3.2; Brunk, 1975, p. 36), which systematically combines prior probabilities and the results of data to arrive at a posterior probability, in this case the posterior probability of a signal onset given $\mathbf{X} = x$ is

$$\mathbf{P}_n = \frac{\mathbf{P}^*_{n-1} f_1(x)}{\mathbf{P}^*_{n-1} f_1(x) + (1 - \mathbf{P}^*_{n-1}) f_0(x)}$$

$$= \frac{[\mathbf{P}_{n-1} + (1 - \mathbf{P}_{n-1})p] f_1(x)}{[\mathbf{P}_{n-1} + (1 - \mathbf{P}_{n-1})p] f_1(x) + (1 - \mathbf{P}_{n-1})(1 - p) f_0(x)}.$$

At this point Rapoport et al. proceed by approximating the process in the following way. They assume that the probability levels form a discrete set, which means in practice that the actual $\mathbf{P}_n$'s are rounded to the nearest acceptable value. This casts the problem in the form of a Markov chain with an absorbing state, and they then apply known theorems about Markov chains (Section 1.5) to derive an expression for the distribution of times to absorption—that is, to the initiation of a response. That result is presented on pp. 52–54 of their monograph; I do not reproduce it here.

Rapoport et al. derive from their approximation the asymptotic forms for the three observable distributions: the anticipations, the reactions following signal onset, and the signal onsets when the response follows the onset. As was the case in the model discussed in Section 3.2.4, all of these tails are exponential and the time constants for the first and third are identical. Of course, this is not a very strong test of the model, and one would like to know the entire hazard function. Because of the complexity of the equations, one is forced to numerical solutions. Rapoport et al. show in their Figure 3.7 (p. 57) the reaction-time distributions generated by the model for three levels of the criterion. Reading the numbers from the graph, I have computed the hazard functions, which are shown in Figure 4.18 (the last few values in the tails are omitted because they are quite unstable as a result both of the small sample size and of my errors in reading the graphs).

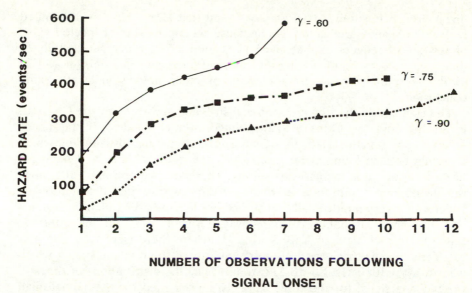

FIG. 4.18 Hazard functions for the model of Rapoport et al. (1979) in which responding is triggered by a probability criterion γ. These functions were estimated from simulations of the response-time distributions shown in Figure 3.7 of Rapoport et al. (1979). I was unable to infer the sample size used in the simulations.

Obviously, these hazard functions do not exhibit the peaked character found in the data for weak signals.

4.3   CONTINUOUS-TIME, INFORMATION-ACCUMULATION DETECTORS

4.3.1   *Deterministic Accumulation and Variable Criterion*

Grice (1968) proposed a model in which information accumulates continuously and deterministically, responses occur whenever the accumulated information exceeds a criterion, and the criterion varies from trial to trial. All other models of information accumulation postulate randomness in the accumulation process itself and usually none in the criterion; but, as Grice argued, it seems quite unrealistic to suppose that people are able to maintain a constant criterion over prolonged periods of time. However, given what is known physiologically, it is equally unrealistic to suppose that sensory information is deterministic. Presumably chance plays a role in both places, but there are few effective models of that character (an example is given in Section 9.2.5).

   Let $A(t)$ denote the deterministic accumulation function—the numerical measure at time t of evidence favoring the presence of a signal—and let $\mathbf{C}$ be the criterion. The response is initiated at time $\mathbf{T}$ for which $A(\mathbf{T}) = \mathbf{C}$, where $\mathbf{C}$ is a random variable, but $A(t)$ is not. Initially, Grice assumed a linear growth function $A(t) = \alpha t$, $\alpha > 0$, and that $\mathbf{C}$ is Gaussian distributed with mean μ and variance σ^2. Under these assumptions, the expected value of this model reduces to that given in Section 2.5.2, which successfully fit data generated by manipulating the rate and criterion separately; however, at the level of expectations a number of other models yield the same conclusion.

The assumption that the criterion is distributed according to the Gaussian is ad hoc and, as Grice (1972) pointed out, coupled with the linear accumulation function leads to a Gaussian reaction-time distribution, which is wrong both in being symmetric, which the data are not, and having a hazard function that increases to infinity. There are two options: either alter the distribution assumption to whatever the reaction-time distribution is, which is not very intellectually satisfying, or alter the accumulation assumption in some reasonably satisfying way. Grice (1972) did the latter as follows. He took data of LaBerge (1971) where there were four different catch trial signals that varied in their similarity to the reaction signal, which was always a 1000-Hz, 80-dB SPL tone. Using the distributions of times to the reaction signal for the three subjects, he searched for the Thurstonian scale that would render all of the distributions Gaussian with a common variance (Thurstone, 1927b, Case V), and he found this scale to be well approximated by

$$A(t) = \alpha[1 - e^{-\beta(t - r_0)}], \quad t \geq r_0, \tag{4.6}$$

where r_0 is the mean residual time.

It should be noticed that Eq. 4.6 leads to a model for the means different from that given in Section 2.5.2 and apparently no one has checked to see if the nonlinear model fits those data as well as the linear one.

Another important fact about Eq. 4.6 is that it satisfies the differential equation:

$$A'(t) = dA(t)/dt = -\beta[A(t) - \alpha], \quad t \geq r_0, \tag{4.7}$$

which simply says that the rate of accumulation varies linearly with the difference between the amount of information and a fixed level α, increasing when $A(t) < \alpha$ and decreasing when $A(t) > \alpha$. Thus, for sufficiently large amounts of information, the model embodies a diminishing rate-of-return concept. It or something much like it play a role in the cascade model of the next subsection and in the model of Section 9.2.5.

Assuming that the criterion is distributed according to a Gaussian, we see that for an arbitrary growth function $A(t)$,

$$f(t) = \Pr[\mathbf{C} = A(t)]$$
$$= -(1/\sqrt{2\pi}) \exp\{-\tfrac{1}{2}[A(t) - \mu]^2/\sigma^2\} A'(t)/\sigma$$
$$= [\beta/(2\pi)^{1/2}\sigma][A(t) - \mu] \exp\{-\tfrac{1}{2}[A(t) - \mu]^2/\sigma^2\} \tag{4.8}$$

is the density of the reaction times. Assuming that Eq. 4.6 holds, we have an explicit model for the density involving four parameters: r_0, μ, β, and σ. So far as I can tell, it is not possible to get an explicit formula for the hazard function, but one can compute a closely related quantity from Eqs 4.6 to 4.8,

$$-\frac{f'(t)}{f(t)} = \frac{d \ln f(t)}{dt}$$

$$= \beta + \frac{[A(t) - \mu]A'(t)}{\sigma^2}$$

$$= \beta + \frac{[A(t) - \mu][A(t) - \alpha]}{\sigma^2}.$$

Since as $t \to \infty$, $\lim \lambda(t) = -\lim(f'/f)$ and clearly $\lim A(t) = \alpha$, we see that the asymptotic value of λ is β. Moreover, we know (Theorem 1.1) that the hazard function is increasing or decreasing as $-f'/f$, which we can determine by calculating the slope of $-(A - \mu)(A - \alpha)$:

$$-\frac{d(A - \mu)(A - \alpha)}{dt} = -A'(2A - \mu - \alpha) = \beta(A - \alpha)(2A - \mu - \alpha).$$

This quantity is negative, and so the hazard function is decreasing, if and only if either $\frac{1}{2}(\mu + \alpha) < A < \alpha$ or $\alpha < A < \frac{1}{2}(\mu + \alpha)$. The former condition, which implies $\mu < \alpha$, holds if and only if $t > t_0 = r_0 + [\ln 2/(1 - \mu/\alpha)]/\beta$. So, in this case, the hazard function increases until t_0, after which it decreases. The latter condition, which implies $\alpha < \mu$, leads to the contradiction $e^{-\beta(t-r)} < 0$, and so for $\alpha < \mu$ the hazard function can only increase.

Thus, for $\alpha > \mu$ this hazard function is peaked and asymptotes on the right to β, which agrees qualitatively with the data of Section 4.1.3 provided we assume that as intensity increases both β decreases and $\alpha\beta$ increases. The former follows from the fact that the asymptote decreases with intensity. The latter follows from the fact that for small β, $A(t) = \alpha\beta(t - r)$ and from the plots of Section 2.5.2, which demonstrate that $\alpha\beta$ must increase with intensity.

The question, then, is just how well does this model fit the data. As we do not have analytical expressions for any of the usual statistics of the data, it is necessary to undertake some numerical search for the parameters. Schnizlein (1980) did so, minimizing χ^2 for his data. Schnizlein assumed that α is controlled by intensity, μ and σ by the grouping, and that β is constant, which ended up with 12 free parameters. Since the distributions were partitioned into 20 intervals of equal probability, there are $9 \times 19 - 12 = 159$ df. The observed values of χ^2 ranged from 208 to 654, evidencing some degree of failure to fit the data. This failure may be due in part to an incorrect identification of the factors that influence the parameters. We have just seen that β and possibly α are affected by signal intensity, whereas he assumed that β was not.

At the present time it is uncertain how well Eqs. 4.6 and 4.8 will account for simple reaction-time distributions, but it appears to be a highly viable model that deserves more attention.

4.3.2   *Deterministic, Aggregated Accumulation: Cascade Model*

As was discussed at length in Chapter 3 and as will recur in Chapters 11 and 12, many of us like to think of mental processes as being carried out in stages. Moreover, we typically think of the activity in a stage as beginning only when the stages feeding it have completed their activity. That tends to be the dominant view—perhaps it is more a matter of mathematical and modeling convenience than a deep conviction. McClelland (1979) challenged this view and showed that one can develop a model of activation in which each stage operates on inputs from the previous stages in a continuous manner. He termed such a process a *cascade*.

Let us think of the mental organization as being in levels, such that a unit at level n is fed by inputs from and only from level $n-1$. At each level there are several units, each of which is thought of as a linear integrator of the sort Grice had postulated (Section 4.3.1). Let a_{nk} refer to unit k of level n, where $k = 1, 2, \ldots, N(n)$, and let $a(t)_{nk}$ denote the amount that unit k is activated at time t. The inputs from one level to the next are weighted—perhaps just 0, 1, but not necessarily—so that $w_{nkk'}$ is the weight assigned the link from k' at level $n-1$ to k at level n. We let W_n denote the matrix of weights connecting level $n-1$ to level n, and

$$A_n(t) = (a_{n1}(t), \ldots, a_{nN(n)}(t))$$

the vector of activation at level n. The basic assumption governing the process is that the rate of change of activation at level n tends to decay in proportion to its level and to be augumented by the inputs received from the previous level:

$$A'_n(t) = \beta_n[A_{n-1}(t)W_n - A_n(t)], \tag{4.9}$$

where β_n is a decay constant for level n.

This is a system of linear differential equations with constant coefficients, and its solution is well understood. One way to proceed is with generating function arguments. In particular, if we let

$$\mathscr{A}(s) = \int_0^\infty e^{-st}A(t)\,dt$$

be the LaPlace transform of $A(t)$ and use the fact that the transform of $A'(t)$ is given by

$$\mathscr{A}'(s) = s\mathscr{A}(s) - A(0),$$

then Eq. 4.9 is equivalent to

$$s\mathscr{A}_n(s) - A_n(0) = \beta_n[\mathscr{A}_{n-1}(s)W_n - \mathscr{A}_n(s)]. \tag{4.10}$$

Using standard techniques, the solution to this difference equation is

$$\mathcal{A}_n(s) = \mathcal{A}_0(s) \prod_{k=1}^{n} [\beta_k/(s+\beta_k)] \prod_{k=1}^{n} W_k. \qquad (4.11)$$

Assuming that we are dealing with response terminated signals, that signal onset defines time 0, that there is only one unit at stage 0, and that

$$A_0(t) = \begin{cases} 0 & \text{for } t \leq 0 \\ A_0 & \text{for } t > 0 \end{cases}$$

then $\mathcal{A}_0(s) = A_0/s$. Substitute this into Eq. 4.11, and then consider its solution. It can be shown rather easily that if all the β_k terms are distinct, then the key term of the restricted Eq. 4.11 can be rewritten as a sum:

$$\frac{1}{s} \prod_{k=1}^{n} \frac{\beta_k}{s+\beta_k} = \frac{1}{s} - \sum_{k=1}^{n} B_k \frac{1}{s+\beta_k},$$

where

$$B_k = \prod_{j \neq k}^{n} \frac{\beta_j}{\beta_j - \beta_k}.$$

Recall that the transform of $e^{-\beta t}$ is $1/(s+\beta)$, and so using the fact that the transform of a sum is the sum of the transforms, we see

$$A_n(t) = A_0 \prod_{j=1}^{n} W_j \left[1 - \sum_{k=1}^{n} B_k e^{-\beta_k t} \right]. \qquad (4.12)$$

McClelland called this the *cascade equation*.

As he pointed out, the dynamic part of Eq. 4.12 is what McGill (1963) referred to as the generalized-gamma distribution. The gamma function arises as the sum of independent, identically distributed exponentials; the generalized gamma eliminates the restriction that the exponentials be identically distributed.

Since the accumulation model is a generalization of Grice's, which we already know does a moderately satisfactory job in dealing with at least some reaction-time data, its generality is not really needed at this point. It will be applied, however, to problem of speed-accuracy tradeoff in two choice situations (Section 6.4.3).

The model just described, leading to Eq. 4.12, is deterministic. To make it noisy, and so result in variable response times, one can proceed in the following ad hoc fashion. Let

$$\mathbf{A}_n(t) = \mathbf{A}E_n(t) + \mathbf{B},$$

where

$$E_n(t) = 1 - \sum_k B_k e^{-\beta_k t},$$

and $\mathbf{A}$ and $\mathbf{B}$ are Gaussian random variables with means of a and 0 and variances of σ_k^2 and 1, respectively. The response-time model is then effected by assuming a response occurs whenever $\mathbf{A}_n(t)$ exceeds a fixed criterion C; that is,

$$\Pr(\mathbf{T} < t) = \Pr[\mathbf{A}_n(t) > C].$$

Since $\mathbf{A}_n(t) - C$ is Gaussian with mean $C - aE_n(t)$ and variance $1 + \sigma_k^2$ and since as $t \to \infty$, $E_n(t) \to 1$, we see that

$$\Pr(\mathbf{T} < t) = 1 - \Phi\{(C - a)/[1 + \sigma_k^2]^{1/2}, 1\} < 1.$$

This means that there is a finite chance, not necessarily negligible, that no response occurs. This fact, which was first pointed out by Ashby (1982b), does not accord with any data.

Assuming, however, that the subject invokes some sort of deadline for responding, Ashby continued to study this model, but with it conditioned so that a response must occur. Using the resulting, somewhat complex analytic expressions, he calculated the mean and variance for several different values of the parameters. His general conclusion from these numbers, which I do not reproduce here, was that the pattern of covariation of standard deviation and mean was quite different from the data in Section 2.3.2—the model predicts too slow a growth of the standard deviation with the mean.

One likely reason for the difficulties of this random generalization of the cascade model is that the randomness is brought in as an afterthought. Section 4.3.3 presents a more deeply stochastic version of the simpler Grice model, and Chapters 8 and 9 will present various versions of the random walk model in which the randomness is inherent to the process.

4.3.3 Stochastic Accumulation: Linear, Dynamic, Stochastic Model

The differential equation approach to information accumulation has been generalized in at least two distinct ways to cases where the accumulation is not deterministic. In the one case, which we take up here, the process is exactly the same as in Grice's model (Eq. 4.7) except the derivative is assumed to be perturbed by additive random noise. In the other case, taken up in Section 9.2.5, the rate of change is assumed to be proportional to $e^{-\theta \mathbf{A}(t)}$, not to $\mathbf{A}(t)$, and again is perturbed by additive noise. In that case, a more complex threshold model is also assumed.

The present model can be written as follows:

$$d\mathbf{A}(t) = -\beta[\mathbf{A}(t) - \alpha S(t)] + d\mathbf{w}(t), \qquad \mathbf{A}(0) = \mathbf{A}_0, \qquad (4.13)$$

where $S(t)$ represents the signal strength. The term $d\mathbf{w}(t)$ represents the noise, which technically is taken to be a diffusion (also called Wiener) process, which will be discussed in some detail in Section 9.2.1. It can be thought of as a continuous process that at any instant is distributed as a Gaussian random variable with zero mean and variance proportional to elapsed time. In the case of a rapid onset of a response terminated signal, we may take $S(t) = 0$ for $t < 0$ and $S(t) = 1$ for $t \geq 0$. It is assumed that the initial condition $\mathbf{A}_0$ is a Gaussian random variable with mean μ_0 and variance σ_0^2.

A response is assumed to occur whenever a criterion is exceeded, and in general the criterion is assumed to be a random variable.

The model in this form, which is called a *linear, dynamic, stochastic model*, is due to Pacut (1977, 1978, 1980, 1982; Pacut & Tych, 1982). His 1977 paper lists a variety of earlier models due to Hull (1943), Spence (1954), and Grice (1968, 1971), which he compares mathematically with his. In the 1978 paper, he showed that the general solution to Eq. 4.13 is of the form

$$\mathbf{A}(t) = \alpha + e^{-\beta t}\left[\mathbf{A}_0 - \alpha/t + \int_0^t e^{\beta x}\, d\mathbf{w}(x)\right].$$

As he remarked in his 1982 paper, this solution is far too complex to apply at present to reaction-time data. Rather, what he has done is to work out a number of special cases in which just one of the three possible sources of randomness is included. He concluded that the best of these special cases is exactly the one that Grice had postulated, and which we have already seen has properties appropriate to at least some reaction-time data. Pacut (1982) successfully applied the model to escape latency data and Pacut and Tych (1982) applied the same ideas to avoidance learning.

4.3.4 Binary Accumulation and Fixed Criterion: Counting Processes

Another way in which information about the signal might be encoded is as the occurrence of events, whose only relevant property is their occurrence, but whose rate is affected by signal intensity. The electrical pulses that pass along a nerve fiber are thought to be of this character. The passage of automobiles over a trip wire can, from the point of view of traffic rate, also be thought of in this way. It is obvious from the automobile example—and it is also true of the neural one—that events do not occur at regularly prescribed times similar to the quantized steps of the random walk models. Rather, their occurrence is irregular. Since all that is involved in such processes is the number of events $\mathbf{N}(t)$ that have occurred by time t, they are reasonably called *counting processes*. If one makes the added two assumptions that the times between successive events are independent and identically distributed random variables, then they are called *renewal processes* (see Section 1.5). The Poisson process is the renewal process in which the common distribution is exponential. We shall discuss more general renewal processes in Section 9.3.

If as in some of the earlier continuous accumulation models the brain establishes a criterion in terms of $\mathbf{N}(t)$ at which the collection of information is stopped, then the only thing to be observed is the time at which the pre-assigned count is achieved. This, of course, means that the sample size on which the rate is estimated is constant, independent of the value of that rate and so independent of signal intensity. Because that time is the random variable of interest, these are called *timing models* (Luce & Green, 1972) or *clocking models* (Uttal & Krissoff, 1968). In this case we are dealing with sums of independent, identically distributed random variables or, if we assume information accumulates over a number of independent but statistically identical channels, with the maximum of independent, identically distributed random variables. These two probabilistic structures are discussed in Appendix A, leading in the case of sums to the Gaussian, whose hazard function is strictly increasing, and in the case of maxima to three possibilities. The first is the double exponential or extreme value type I (Item 3 of Appendix B) with a hazard function increasing to ∞. The second is known as extreme value type II (Item 4) with a peaked hazard function decreasing to 0. And the third is Weibull or extreme value type III (Item 5) with a hazard function either increasing to ∞ or decreasing to 0. So within the context of simple reaction times, the timing models yield nothing fully satisfactory, although as we shall see in Section 9.3 they do offer some interesting conclusions in the choice context.

As with Grice's continuous model and the random walk model, another stopping rule is conceivable—namely, to fix the total time of observation. This is what one usually does in estimating a pulse rate or in carrying out a traffic count, although it has the disadvantage of having a highly variable sample size, and so a highly variable quality of the estimate, when the rate varies over a large range. Since the time is fixed and the observed random variable is the count, these are called *counting models* (McGill, 1963). Everything said earlier about a fixed time stopping rule applies here without change.

4.3.5 *Binary Decisions with Separable Hazard Functions*

Maloney and Wandell (1984) developed a theory for simple reaction times in visual detection. Their model is based on the detection of events in a Poisson information process governed by a hazard function that depends upon the intensity I and is denoted $\lambda(I, t)$. Suppose further that a change in the intensity introduces a change in the level of the hazard function but not in its form; that is, for $k > 0$

$$\lambda(kI, t) = \varphi(k)\lambda(I, t), \tag{4.14}$$

where φ is an unknown, increasing function. Such a hazard function may be termed *separable*. They derive Eq. 4.14 from somewhat more basic assumptions about the visual system, using a property they call the "stability hypothesis." It should be noted that the data of Section 4.1.3, in particular those of Wandell et al. (1984) shown in Figure 4.11, do not exhibit separability since no multiplicative constant carries one hazard function into another. For other data (e.g., Figure 4.7) the discrepancy is even more pronounced in that an increase of intensity changes the form from an increasing function to a peaked one. In any event, under the assumption of separability we see, by using Eq. 4.14 three times, that for k, $k' > 0$,

$$\lambda(kk'I) = \varphi(k)\lambda(k'I, t)$$
$$= \varphi(k)\varphi(k')\lambda(I, t)$$
$$= \varphi(kk')\lambda(I, t),$$

whence $\varphi(kk') = \varphi(k)\varphi(k')$. It is well known (Aczél, 1966, p. 39) that the only increasing solution to this functional equation is $\varphi(x) = x^\beta$, $\beta > 0$. If we write

$$\Lambda(I, t) = \int_0^t \lambda(I, x)\, dx,$$

then substituting, we obtain

$$\Lambda(I, t) = I^\beta \Lambda(t),$$

where $\Lambda(t) = \Lambda(1, t)$. Using the relation between the hazard function and the distribution function (Eq. 1.9), we have

$$F(I, t) = 1 - \exp[-I^\beta \Lambda(t)]. \qquad (4.15)$$

In terms of the variable I, with t held fixed, this is the Weibull distribution (Appendix B.1, item 5), which as is shown in Appendix A (Theorem A.5) arises as one of the limiting forms of the maximum of independent, identically distributed random variables.

In order to bypass estimating time hazard functions, which as I noted earlier they felt to be risky, and yet to have some check on the model, Wandell et al. (1984) noted that Eq. 4.15 is equivalent to

$$\log\{-\ln[1 - F(I, t)]\} = \beta \log I + \log \Lambda(t).$$

So, for each value of t, the left side is predicted to grow linearly with signal intensity measured in decibels. Their experiment to test this prediction was described in Section 4.1.3. The plot for one subject using the 500-msec signal is shown in Figure 4.19. They interpret this as support for Eq. 4.15. Considering the narrowness of the range, I am not persuaded. In both duration conditions and for both subjects, they find β is about 2.

From Eq. 4.15 we can immediately write down the relation between $E(\mathbf{T})$ and I:

$$E(\mathbf{T}) = \int_0^\infty tf(I, t)\, dt$$

$$= \int_0^\infty [1 - F(I, t)]\, dt$$

$$= \int_0^\infty \exp[-I^\beta \Lambda(t)]\, dt.$$

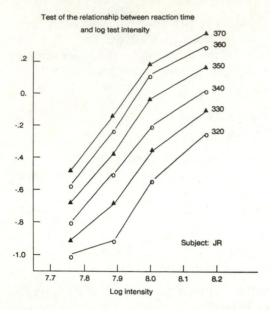

Test of the relationship between reaction time
and log test intensity

Subject: JR

Log intensity

FIG. 4.19 Logarithm of the log survivor function versus intensity in dB for the response times to a faint flash of light. The parameter is response time. According to the model of Eq. 4.15, these curves should be linear with the same slope. [Figure 5, Wandell et al. (1984); copyright 1984; reprinted by permission.]

For a specific choice of $\Lambda(t)$, this can be evaluated either analytically or numerically. For example, with $\Lambda(t) = \lambda t$, which of course is a mighty poor approximation to the data of Figure 4.11, it is easy to verify that $E(\mathbf{T}) = r_0 + 1/\lambda I^\beta$, which is Piéron's law; however, the estimate of $\beta = 2$ is far larger than the constants reported in Table 2.1 for this law. No one has investigated Eq. 4.15 carefully for more realistic assumptions for the temporal hazard function.

4.3.6   Binary Increments and Decrements and Fixed Criterion: Difference of Counting Processes

The following variant of a counting process, due to McGill (1963), is a type of random walk where the jumps occur at irregular times. Suppose the decision center is able not only to monitor the counting process that is affected by the signal—let $\mathbf{N}(t)$ denote the count at time t on that process—but also a counting process that reflects the (presumably) internal noise level of the typical, relevant nerve fibers—let $\mathbf{I}(t)$ denote the count at time t on the internal noise process. So long as no signal is present and assuming that there is no external noise, the process $\mathbf{N}$ is assumed to be statistically identical to $\mathbf{I}$. Thus, $E[\mathbf{N}(t) - \mathbf{I}(t)] = E[\mathbf{N}(t)] - E(\mathbf{I}(t)] = 0$. If the two counting processes are renewal ones, then it can be shown that the variance of $\mathbf{N}(t) - \mathbf{I}(t)$ grows in proportion to t. When a signal is present, we assume that $\mathbf{N}$ is increased relative to $\mathbf{I}$ and that $E[\mathbf{N}(t) - \mathbf{I}(t)]$ grows with t. Thus, if a criterion is established for a sufficient difference to indicate the presence of a signal, we should be able to derive (under some assumptions about **N** and **I**) the distribution of times at which the signal is detected. In fact, it is the diffusion process of Section 4.2.4 that leads to the Wald distribution, and so we have already dealt with it.

4.4   RACE BETWEEN LEVEL AND CHANGE DETECTORS

4.4.1   *Change and Level Detectors*

Ample physiological evidence suggests the existence of two quite distinct mechanisms, both of which may have something to do with signal detection. One type of neural cell, called *transient,* is active immediately following a change in signal intensity, but otherwise remains quiescent. A second type, called *sustained,* is more-or-less steadily active when the signal is present, but otherwise is inactive. Direct physiological evidence exists for such cells both in vision and audition: see Abeles and Goldstein (1972), Cleland et al. (1971), Enroth-Cugell and Robson (1966), Gerstein, Butler, and Erulkar (1968), Kiang, Watanabe, Thomas, and Clark (1965), Kulikowski and Tolhurst (1973), Marrocco (1976), Moller (1969), Pfeiffer (1966), and Tolhurst (1975b).

In addition, there is a limited amount of psychophysical evidence suggesting functional units (often called channels in vision) of this general type; they might be cells or networks of cells. In order to distinguish clearly between physiologically observed cells and hypothetical units proposed to account for behavioral data, I will use the terms "transient" and "sustained" only for cells and "change" and "level" detectors for the more speculative units. A change detector is, in effect, a differentiator operating on the sensory flow of information. It is not difficult to construct a change detector from a comparative simple network of electrical components having properties typical of neural cells.

MacMillan (1971, 1973) interpreted some auditory detection and recognition in terms of change and level detectors, as do Ahumada, Marken, and Sandusky (1975). But the clearest behavioral data, by far, are certain simple reaction-time data. Tolhurst (1975b) did a visual study involving sinusoidal gratings that were relatively difficult to detect. A tone served as the warning signal for a random, but nonexponential foreperiod, following which a sinusoid grating of low contrast was presented. There were catch trials. The subject, Tolhurst, responded whenever he became aware of the signal. Two major variables were manipulated. First, the onsets and offsets of the signal were either abrupt or ramped over a 300-msec period, the idea being that a change detector can only respond to the abrupt changes and not to the slow ramps. Second, other evidence had suggested that low spatial frequencies activate the transient cells whereas high frequencies activate the sustained ones, so data were collected at 0.2c/deg and at 3.5c/deg. The several conditions that were run are apparent in Figures 4.20 to 4.22. Note the clear

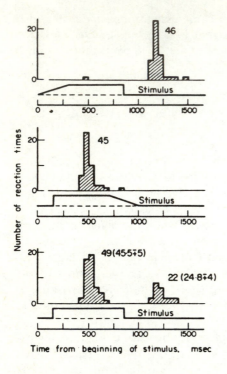

FIG. 4.20 Histograms of simple reaction times to low contrast gratings of 0.2 c/deg under the three temporal patterns of signal intensity shown. The sample size can be inferred from the figure. [Figure 1 of Tolhurst (1975a); copyright 1975; reprinted by permission.]

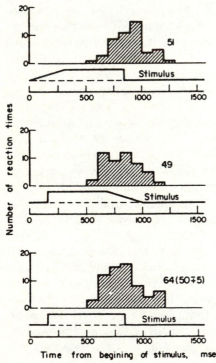

FIG. 4.21 This figure is similar to Figure 4.20, but with an abrupt signal onset and three durations. [Figure 3 of Tolhurst (1975a); copyright 1975; reprinted by permission.]

160

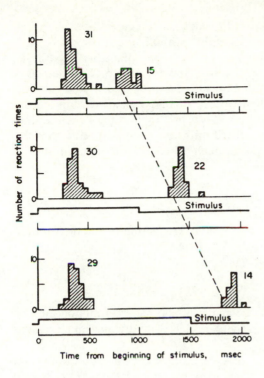

FIG. 4.22 This figure is similar to Figure 4.20, but with a grating of 3.5 c/deg. [Figure 4 of Tolhurst (1975a); copyright 1975; reprinted by permission.]

evidence in Figures 4.18 and 4.19 that at low frequency the abrupt change initiates a response and the ramp does not, whereas at high frequency the abrupt changes are ignored and only the sustained level matters. Additional data supporting this point of view are found in Breitmeyer (1975), and a parametric study of mean reaction time as a function of the spatial frequency and contrast of gratings was carried out by Harwerth and Levi (1978). Although they continued to find evidence for these two types of detectors, the pattern of shifting between them was complex. Parker (1980) and Parker and Salzen (1977) found additional complexities including evidence for reaction-time changes with spatial frequency within one type of channel.

In the auditory domain no one has yet discovered a signal parameter, comparable to spatial frequency, that delineates psychophysically the two classes of cells so sharply.* Therefore, it is necessary to approach the problem somewhat less directly.

---

* J. W. Tukey (personal communication) has suggested that frequency modulation might be suitable.

On the assumption that there are two types of detectors, both of which may be activated with appropriately complex stimuli, the question is: how does the system go about generating a response? One plausible hypothesis, which we explore in this section, is that whichever detector first detects a signal triggers a response. If a system responds when the first of several random processes is completed, then we are involved in a *race* among the processes. Suppose that in general there are n processes, that $\mathbf{T}_k$ is the time to complete the kth process and its distribution function is F_k, and that the detectors are statistically independent of each other, then the distribution of times to complete the race is given by

$$\Pr[\min(\mathbf{T}_1, \mathbf{T}_2, \ldots, \mathbf{T}_n) \leq t] = 1 - \prod_{k=1}^{n} [1 - F_k(t)]. \qquad (4.16)$$

If $\lambda_k(t)$ are the hazard functions of the $\mathbf{T}_k$ and $\lambda(t)$ is that of the distribution of Eq. 4.16, then we know by Theorem 1.3 that

$$\lambda(t) = \sum_{k=1}^{n} \lambda_k(t). \qquad (4.17)$$

Thus, it is very simple to study the behavior of the hazard function, and so the distribution function, of race models involving independent subprocesses.

The literature includes a number of race models that are different from the one I am about to describe. Two examples are Ollman (1973) and Logan, Cowan, and Davis (1984).

Burbeck (1979) and Burbeck and Luce (1982) pointed out that if a signal activates both classes of detectors, if neither totally overwhelms the other, and if there is a race between them, then we should see a characteristic pattern in the reaction-time distribution. This pattern is most easily understood by looking at the hazard functions. Motivated by the data shown in Sections 4.1.2 and 4.1.3, they assumed that a change detector is characterized by a hazard function that rises from its constant noise level when no signal is present to a peak shortly after signal onset, after which it soon again returns to the noise level. By contrast, a level detector rises rather more slowly from the noise level to some constant value that is sustained so long as the signal is present. Specific models yielding these two shapes are discussed shortly. Figure 4.23 exhibits these two hazard function patterns separately as well as giving their sums and the corresponding log survivor function. Observe that this hazard function has the pattern shown in the data of Figures 4.5, 4.7, and 4.11. The question to be dealt with below is whether plausible specific models can account for these data in detail.

The theoretical literature on level detectors, per se, is rather sparse, most of the effort having gone into models in which decisions are based upon an accumulation of information over time (Sections 4.2 and 4.3). Basically both level and change detectors are devices with an absolute minimum of

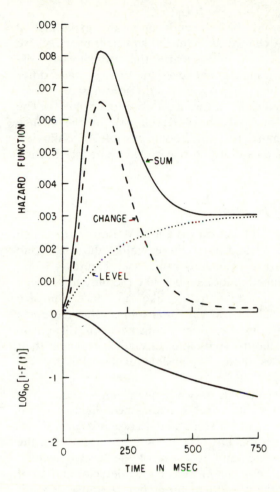

FIG. 4.23 Illustration of the hazard and log survivor functions that arise from a race of two systems, thought to be change and level detectors, with the hazard functions shown. [Figure 1 of Burbeck and Luce (1982); copyright 1982; reprinted by permission.]

memory, whereas the accumulator models have substantial memories of a sort. It is possible, however, that an accumulator process normally designed to identify signals can serve the function of a level detector.

Two kinds of ideas for level and change detectors have received limited attention. In both, the sensory input is assumed to be transduced into a spike train whose firing rate is an increasing function of signal intensity; in fact, we shall suppose that these are Poisson processes in which the hazard function has one constant value ν before the signal onset and another value μ after the signal onset. In the first class of models, we assume that the decision mechanism acts on the resulting pulse train in the way a naive statistician would; I make no attempt to state how this behavior could come about physiologically. A level detector is assumed to keep updating its estimate of the current firing rate, and it initiates a response whenever that estimate exceeds a fixed criterion that depends upon the experimental conditions (see Section 4.4.3). A change detector has sufficient memory also to retain the preceding estimate, and it compares this estimate with the current estimate and initiates a response whenever the two estimates differ sufficiently in the appropriate direction. Again, a criterion must be established for what constitutes a sufficient difference (see Section 4.4.4). The other class of models, which has only been developed for the change detector, attempts to be far more realistic about possible physiological mechanisms, and it has been fitted carefully to one body of data (see Section 4.4.5).

4.4.2   The Hazard Function for Noise

As we saw in Figure 4.3, the hazard function for a loud noise rises to a high value (about 60–100 events sec^{-1}) and stays there, unlike those for loud clicks and pure tones that return to near zero values (see Figures 4.1 and 4.2). In form, the noise hazard function looks much like the pure tone, weak signal functions of Figures 4.5 and 4.7—that is, like our conception of a level detector shown in Figure 4.21. However, in absolute value there is a substantial difference, with the noise functions being between 10 and 40 times higher than the near threshold signals and, of course, reaching their maximum at an earlier time. Is there a plausible explanation for the difference?

One untested possibility is that there is only a single change detector but many level detectors located at various frequencies—most likely one for each critical band of frequencies, of which something between 20 and 30 are estimated to exist in human beings (Scharf, 1970). Thus, for a pure tone the race is between the change detector and just one of the level detectors; whereas, for a noise signal the race is among the change detector and all of the level detectors activated by the noise, which number of course depends upon its bandwidth. It is easy to see that the sum of the n (nearly) identical hazard functions of the level detectors itself looks like the hazard function of a level detector, but with a magnitude n times as large as for a pure tone of the same intensity. This means that for wide band noise the level should be 20 to 30 times the height of the comparable pure tone data, which is about where the asymptote is. The height of the single change detector component does not change as one goes from a pure tone to wide band noise, it only increases the rise time of the apparent level detector.

This explanation needs to be tested. For one thing, why there should be only one change detector rather than one for each critical band is not obvious, but that assumption is necessary in order to avoid having a peaked hazard function for noise. Presumably the change detector somehow operates on something corresponding to the temporal waveform of the signal rather than on a decomposition of the waveform into frequencies, as in the critical bands. Obviously, reaction times should be obtained with the same subject for various bandwidths and for multiple bands of noise and their hazard functions estimated to see if they behave as predicted. Moreover, as J. Johnson (personal communication) suggested, if this hypothesis is correct, then an auditory signal composed of one frequency for a short period and then shifted to an appreciably different frequency, but without a change of intensity, should activate the change detector just once and not at each frequency separately. That prediction should be easy to check.

4.4.3   Level Detection as Comparison of an Estimated Local Rate with a Criterion

One general idea for a level detector was outlined earlier. A criterion C is established (under the influence of the payoffs and instructions) and the rate of firing is continually estimated from local samples of data, compared with C, and a response is initiated whenever the estimated rate exceeds C (assuming signal onset involves an increase in intensity). There are a number of ways to carry out the local estimate, including counting and timing, but all lead to substantially the same result. I consider several specific examples.

First, suppose time is quantized into intervals of duration δ, and the number of pulses $\mathbf{N}_n$ in the nth interval is counted as that interval is completed. The local estimate of the rate is $\boldsymbol{\mu}_n = \mathbf{N}_n/\delta$. Assume for simplicity that both noise and signal generate Poisson processes. Obviously, during any interval for which the Poisson rate is constant, $\mathbf{N}_n$ has some distribution (called the Poisson) and so does $\boldsymbol{\mu}_n$; thus, there is some fixed probability (independent of n so long as the Poisson rate is constant), call it p, that $\boldsymbol{\mu}_n \geq C$. This is the well-known geometric process; it is the discrete analogue of the exponential, and both have constant hazard functions—the one in discrete time and the other in continuous time. So this level detector can be described as a geometric process with parameter p_ν up to the interval at which the signal change occurs, a second geometric process with parameter p_μ until a response occurs. During the time between the two geometric processes, there is some sort of smooth transition from p_ν to p_μ.

An alternative way to estimate a local firing rate is to observe the interarrival times (**IAT**) between successive pulses, which under the Poisson assumption has an expected value of $1/\nu$ prior to the signal onset and $1/\mu$ following it. The decision criterion is to respond whenever $\mathbf{IAT} \leq C$. The mathematics of such a decision process is more complex than that for counting in fixed time intervals, but certain approximate results are possible. For example, consider the time t from the first spike to occur after the signal onset until the response. Let $g(t)$ denote that distribution. For a response to occur at $t > C$, it is necessary that at least one spike occur in the interval (C, t). If no spike occurs, there would be no response, and if it had occurred in $(0, C)$, the response would have occurred then, contrary to assumption. Let x be the time of the first intermediate spike; at that point, we can think of the process as beginning anew, but with time $t - x$ to the response, so

$$g(t) = \int_C^t \mu e^{-\mu x} g(t - x)\, dx$$

$$= \mu e^{-\mu t} \int_0^{t-C} e^{\mu y} g(y)\, dy.$$

If we assume C is small—with firing rates on the order of 10 to 100 per sec, C must be less than .1—and if we expand the integral in a Taylor's series and retain only the linear term in C, then we get

$$e^{\mu t} g(t) = \mu \int_0^t e^{\mu y} g(y)\, dy - \mu C e^{\mu t} g(t).$$

Differentiate this with respect to t, cancel $e^{\mu t}$, and collect terms,

$$g'(t) = \frac{\mu^2 C}{1 + \mu C}\, g(t),$$

which is well known to have the exponential as its solution with the parameter $\mu^2 C/(1 + \mu C)$. So, once again, this sort of local level detector has a hazard rate with one constant value up to signal onset, at which point it increases and eventually settles down to another constant value. The exact nature of the transition is not understood except that it is monotonic increasing.

Obviously, this last model can be generalized so as to base the local estimate of the rate upon k successive IATs, which of course are gamma distributed (Appendix A.1.5). Nothing is known of the properties of this model, but on intuitive grounds one expects qualitatively the same sort of transition from one constant level to another, but the transition should be slower the larger the value of k.

Rapoport, Stein, and Burkheimer (1979) examined the following model. Time is discrete, and an event occurs at one of these times according to a fixed geometric distribution. Observations $\mathbf{X}_n$ are obtained at each instance of time; they are independent and before the event they are distributed according to one distribution and after the event according to another one. This obviously is a generalization of the counting situation just described. In Chapter 5 of their monograph they study the decision rule that a response is initiated whenever there have been k successive observations that exceed a fixed criterion. The counting model was the case where $k = 1$ and $\mathbf{X}_n$ has a Poisson distribution. They provide exact formulas for the response distribution, but as they are very complex and none too revealing I will forego reproducing them. To gain some idea of the performance of such a system, they report several simulations of the process. Reading the numbers from the graphs of the distributions of response times following the event (signal onset), I computed the hazard functions. As one would anticipate, the process has the character of all level detectors: a monotonic transition between two constant levels.

A further generalization, which they do not study, would be to respond when j out of the last k observations met the criterion. They do study (Chapter 4) the case where the system responds whenever a total of k observations meet the criterion, but that really is an accumulation model of the recruitment type discussed in Section 4.2.2.

Still another idea, due to Kingman (1963), is for time to be partitioned according to a fixed Poisson process. The sensory process is a counting process, not necessarily Poisson, and a criterion N is established so that whenever the sensory count between two successive Poisson events exceeds N, a response is initiated.

While different in detail, all such processes end up with a hazard function that rises gradually from one constant level to another when the signal is a sudden change to a constant value.

4.4.4 Change Detection as Comparison of Two Estimated Local Rates

Using either the counting method or timing method for estimating rates, if the system has sufficient memory to retain successive estimates, μ_n and μ_{n-1}, then a decision rule that is plausible is to respond whenever $\mu_n - \mu_{n-1} \geq C$ or, alternatively, when $\mu_n/\mu_{n-1} \geq C$. In principle, one should be able to work out the hazard functions for either of these rules, but in fact nothing yet exists. In order to get some idea as to the actual performance of such a change detector, I had simulated* a process in which the rate estimate is based on k successive IATs and the ratio decision rule is used. The results are summarized in Figure 4.24. There are two curves on each plot. Those to the left of the origin are the hazard function of the ratio mechanism when it is applied to a Poisson process with a mean rate of 5 spikes per sec. Those to the right of the origin result when Poisson noise is decreased discontinuously from either 20 or 50 spikes per sec to 5 spikes per sec and the change is controlled by an exponential distribution with a mean of 3 sec. The mechanism used $k = 2$ (samples of two IATs for each estimate μ_n) and a criterion C of $\frac{1}{5}$. Such a mechanism clearly gives results of the correct character and order of magnitude.

4.4.5 Change Detection as Neural Post Inhibitory Rebound

Although the simple-minded statistical models of detectors are indeed simple to state, they are not always as tractable as one might like and they are not particularly reasonable from a physiological point of view. By that I mean that simple networks of units having known neural properties do not

---

* A. F. Smith carried them out.

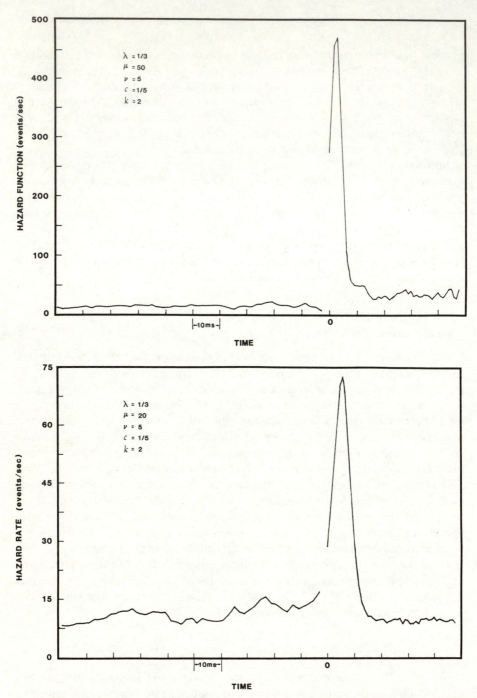

FIG. 4.24a, b Hazard functions estimated from simulations of a decision rule in which a Poisson rate is estimated from two successive samples of k interarrival times and their ratio is compared with a criterion C. The foreperiod is exponential with parameter λ, and the two Poisson rates are ν before the signal onset and μ after onset.

168

result in either counting or timing behavior as such. Both processes require a means of counting, of timing, and of dividing. This lack of realism led Burbeck (1979, 1985) to suggest an explicit neural model for change detection; it is an adaptation of one first suggested by Perkel (1974) in another context.

Assume that a neural spike train, which encodes the sensory information, impinges upon a decision neuron, which is characterized by three functions of time. The first is its membrane potential, $p(t)$. The second is its threshold, $\theta(t)$, which serves to control when the decision neuron emits a spike namely, when $p(t) \geq \theta(t)$, and that in turn initiates a response. And the third is a rebound variable, $q(t)$, which functions in the following ways. Whenever a sensory spike arrives, the rebound variable is incremented; otherwise it decays exponentially. It plays a role of memory in the process by increasing the likelihood of a spike output (and so a response) both by increasing the membrane potential and decreasing the threshold.

Assuming that all of the changes are linear, we write down the three equations for what happens when no spike occurs:

$$p' = -\alpha(p - p_\infty) + \alpha\eta q,$$
$$\theta' = \beta(\theta - \theta_\infty) - \beta(1 - \eta)q,$$
$$q' = -\sigma q,$$

where α, β, and σ are time constants of the three processes, $0 \leq \eta \leq 1$, and p_∞ and θ_∞ are the equilibrium levels of p and θ. [These equations are closely similar to, but more complex than, the accumulation model postulated by Grice (Section 4.3.1).] The solutions to these simultaneous equations are easily written down, but there is no reason to give them here.

The impact of a sensory spike arriving at time t can be expressed directly in terms of increments on p and q: for small $\delta > 0$,

$$p(t + \delta) = p(t - \delta) + \Delta p[p(t - \delta) - p_R],$$
$$q(t + \delta) = p(t - \delta) + \Delta q[q_R - q(t - \delta)],$$

where Δp, Δq, p_R, and q_R are parameters. There are a total of 10 free parameters in the equations as written, but it is natural to assume that

$$\theta_\infty = p_R + q_R,$$

reducing the total to 9.

To apply the model to data, Burbeck proceeded as follows. First, he attempted to reduce the number of free parameters by taking into account various facts known from other sources. Second, he attempted to deconvolve the residual distribution in order to reveal the decision distribution. And third, since the data are for weak signals, he took into account that a level detector might be working in parallel with the change detector. I take each up separately.

Since the variables have explicit physiological meanings, those parameters having to do with equilibrium behavior can be estimated directly from physiological observations. Burbeck selected the following values from the literature: $p_\infty = -70$ mv, $\theta_\infty = -60$ mv, $p_R = -75$ mv, $q_R = \theta_\infty - p_R = 15$ mv. Moreover, he assumed that θ is not directly affected by q—that is, $\eta = 1$. This renders θ independent of the rest of the system and, for large t, θ approaches θ_∞ independent of the value of β, and so it need not be estimated. These assumptions leave one with α, σ, Δp, and Δq to be estimated.

As we have seen in Chapter 3, no clearly satisfactory method exists to rid ourselves of the residual times. Among the questionable alternatives, Burbeck opted to approximate the residual distribution by the reaction-time distribution to an intense signal and to deconvolve it from the distribution of reaction times to the weak signals of interest. There is the distinct possibility that too much is removed in this way, but aside from a displacement it should have limited impact on the form of the hazard function.

But working with weak signals and assuming a race model, we know that the level detector will play a role. As we have seen, none of the models led to an explicit usable formula for the hazard function, and yet all were roughly of the same character—namely, a gradual rise at signal onset from one constant value to another. Burbeck selected the cumulative exponential as a reasonable approximation to this type of growth:

$$a[1 - e^{-(t - t_0)/\tau}],$$

where a and τ are two free parameters and t_0 is the time of the signal change. This increases to six the number of free parameters.

The sensory spike trains were assumed to be Poisson, with parameter ν when the signal is present and μ when it is absent. On the basis of physiological data, he set $\nu = 10$ spikes/sec; the actual value does not matter greatly since to a good first approximation the model is only sensitive to μ/ν.

Note that the numbers of free parameters do not increase in proportion to the number of experimental conditions run. If the signal intensity is changed, we anticipate that μ and a will change, but all of the other parameters will remain fixed. So Burbeck proceeded as follows. He ran three conditions: signal offset to noise from both 23 dB and 25 dB and signal offset from 25 dB to 23 dB. The first two sets of data were used to estimate all of the parameters, and these were used to make a parameter-free prediction of the third condition. The technique was an exploration of presumably relevant regions of the parameter space using a computer simulation of the model; it was very time consuming and it is by no means clear that optimal results were attained. In any event, Figure 4.25 shows the fit of the model to the three sets of data. It is obvious, and was confirmed statistically, that significant discrepancies exist, but also that it is clearly capturing much of the phenomenon.

One would expect some relation between the estimates of μ and a since both reflect the Poisson spike rate in the two types of detectors. Figure 4.26 shows the relation, and it is strikingly linear.

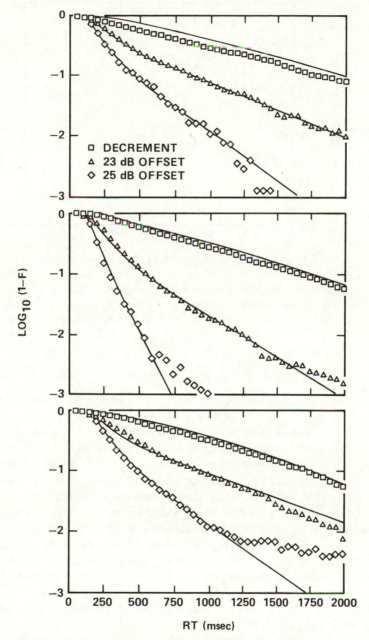

FIG. 4.25 Fit of the physiologically based model (PIR) discussed in text to a sample of simple reaction time data. [Figure of Burbeck (1985); copyright 1985; reprinted by permission.]

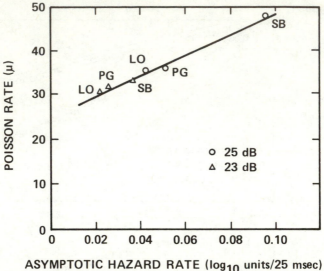

FIG. 4.26 Estimated Poisson rate parameter from the PIR model (see text) as function of the estimate asymptotic value of the hazard function for simple reaction times. [Figure of Burbeck (1985); copyright 1985; reprinted by permission.]

4.4.6   *Why Two Types of Detector?*

Because the distinction between change and level detectors has only recently been clearly drawn and shown to be relevant to reaction time, most papers are not explicit about the type of detector intended. On the one hand, since most of the models have been confronted by data from relatively intense signals, one could interpret them to be models for a change detector. But, equally well, they may be models for a level or some other type of detector that were simply fit to the wrong data because the author was unaware of the possible distinction. On the other hand, internal evidence in some of the models, such as those described in Sections 4.2 and 4.3, suggest they were definitely not intended as change detectors. Many models derive from ideas about choice reaction time, where it is not enough for the subject to become aware of a change in stimulation, but he or she must accumulate sufficient information about the signal in order to identify it among several possibilities. To do that surely requires the use of processes that continue to carry information about the signal throughout the period of its presentation. This raises the possibility that a level detector is nothing other than an adaptation of a mechanism normally used to recognize signals. It is brought into play as a detection mechanism when either the intensity change is so small or the change is so gradual that the usual change detector is rendered inoperable.

If this be true, two things follow. First, we must be quite careful in the data we use to test either kind of model, since otherwise the other type of detector is likely to have an impact. If our interest is in level detectors, then we probably should be using low intensity, slowly ramped signals. The major difficulty with that advice is that the models are either silent as to what happens with a changing signal or, if not silent, difficult to analyze. Second, since most of the modeling appears to have been driven by considerations not at all suited to change detectors, we lack really adequate models for them. This is ironic since at intensities well above threshold only these, if they exist, are relevant.

4.5 CONCLUSIONS

It is easy to give a qualitative summary of the data for simple reaction-time distributions to auditory signals: for intense pure tones and clicks, but not intense noise, the hazard function for the reaction time begins some 100 to 150 msec after signal onset to rise rapidly from its noise level, reaches a peak, and falls rapidly at approximately the same rate ending at the noise level. As signal intensity is reduced, the height of the peak is reduced, as one would expect; but at the same time for signals of sufficient duration (>500 msec) the right side of the hazard function no longer drops to the initial noise level, but rather becomes constant at some higher value. At sufficiently low levels, the peak disappears and so the function rises monotonically to its asymptotic value.

For vision, less seems to be known about simple reaction-time distributions. For weak monochromatic signals, the behavior seems similar to that to pure tones. I know of no distributional data comparing intense signals to weak signals for monochromatic light nor of any whatsoever for white light, the analogue of auditory noise.

Of the traditional theories of information accumulation, only two have the appropriate qualitative features: the variable criterion model with a nonlinear deterministic accumulation function (and, of course, its several generalizations) and the Wald distribution arising from the random walk model. A more careful fit of the Wald model to tone data showed it to be inadequate. The possibility remains that if we were able to estimate the residue better and deconvolve it and/or alter the assumption that the steps in the random walk are normally distributed, then that model would be adequate. The one attempt to fit the Grice model, which was fairly successful, suffered from an incorrect reduction of the parameter space.

A different account was given in terms of a race between two types of detectors—called change and level—that are postulated to have hazard functions corresponding, respectively, to what one sees for the most intense and for the least intense, but detectable, signals. The psychophysical evidence for this distinction is moderately direct in vision, but less direct in audition; the physiological evidence is direct in both domains. What we now need is considerably more work on theories for the two types of detector. The physiologically motivated theory of Burbeck for a change detector is complex and has many free parameters. The statistical one of comparing interarrival times locally has not yet led to analytic solutions. The same is true for the local version of a level detector. And finally, a number of the information accumulation models have hazard functions similar to those we have postulated for a level detector.

One major reason for trying to arrive at the precise nature of the reaction-time distribution is to be able to gain some understanding of how the various experimental manipulations reported in Chapter 2 impact the basic parameters of the model. Had we a well-accepted theory of the relevant decision process(es), then at this point we could look into how the parameters of the process vary with those manipulations, thus bringing some closure to Chapter 2. In addition, we could anticipate the evolution of theories for those relations and some account about how they relate to functions found in other parts of psychophysics. However, this is not yet the case, and our story ends here awaiting further understanding of the mechanisms that give rise to change and level detection.

5

Detection of Signals Presented
at Irregular Times

5.1 INTRODUCTION

All of the experiments discussed to this point and all to follow in later
chapters were conducted in highly structured, trial designs. Although this
strategy is most convenient for the experimenter, it is after all really quite
unlike any ordinary situation encountered by the subject. One can therefore
wonder if the experiments are so atypical as to mislead us seriously about
the subject's normal behavior. The purpose of the present chapter is to
explore the extremely limited literature that exists on designs in which there
is little or no experimenter-imposed time structure on signal presentations.
This leads one, however, into a special problem that has mostly been studied
in the context of trial designs, and that is treated in Section 5.4.

The simplest case to consider is the one in which there is only one type of
signal, as in any simple reaction-time experiment, that is presented randomly in time at some constant rate. The subject has a single response, such
as a key to press, and is free to respond whenever the signal is thought to
occur. Judging by our discussion in Section 1.2.3, presenting signals randomly in time should mean presentation according to a Poisson process—
that is, with a constant hazard function—and so the time between successive
signal presentations is distributed exponentially. The data from such an
experiment consist of two time series: the one recording the times at which
signals are presented, and the other recording the times at which the subject
responds.

Although such a design is quite reasonable as an idealization of the
subject's natural environment, it encounters two quite serious difficulties
that have greatly limited its use. The first is that under an exponential
interstimulus interval the most probable time between signals is zero, which
of course is impossible to realize since signals must be of some duration in
order to be detected. So the experimenter cannot avoid deviating somewhat
from the strict Poisson process whenever a very short interstimulus time
arises. But even if that can be dealt with in a satisfactory manner—for
example, by dropping the hazard function of signal presentations to zero for
the duration of the signal plus a short additional time in order to make the
signals distinct—there is still a concern. The subject's response to a signal
may well differ when that signal is isolated from other signals as compared

to when it is immediately preceded by one whose processing is still under-way. As we shall see, this is quite a serious matter.

The second difficulty is that there is no sure way to establish correspon-dences between the response-time series and the signal one. Which re-sponses go with which signals? Sometimes it is obvious that a response cannot possibly have been due to any experimental signal because none has occurred for some seconds before the response; but in other cases matters are not as clear. Examples are a signal 700 msec before the response and two signals one 500 msec and the other 150 msec before the response. In the former case, was that response actually due to that signal, or was the signal missed and the response technically a false alarm in the sense that it was initiated by noise? In the second case, was the response a slow one to the first signal, perhaps slowed additionally by the interference of the second one, or was the first signal missed or ignored and the response actually a fast one to the second signal? The fact is that we really do not know how to answer such questions unequivocally, and one is forced to explore various models of what is going on.

The structure of the chapter is this: In Section 5.2 I examine briefly the earliest literature, which goes under the name of *vigilance*, in which the signals occur quite infrequently. One of the primary concerns is the manner in which performance deteriorates with the duration of the "watch." That term arises because this work, which began during World War II, was largely motivated by military applications having to do with radar and sonar watches. The fact that the signal rate is very low largely eliminates the problem of two signals being very close together and so that difficulty can be ignored; but the problem of associating responses to signals remains. In Section 5.3 I take up experiments that resemble typical simple reaction-time ones in that the signal rate is relatively high; here, of course, the question of signals close together is an issue, and several attempts to deal with the two problems are outlined. Section 5.4 is devoted exclusively to studies aimed at discovering the impact that the processing of one signal has on the proces-sing of a second signal when the second occurs very shortly after the first. Unlike the earlier experiments of the chapter, these are trial designs.

5.2   VIGILANCE AT LOW SIGNAL RATES

The major concern in the vigilance literature is with the factors that lead to the decreased performance observed when the events to be detected occur sporadically and infrequently. The basic fact is quite simply that observers detect more signals early in a watch than they do toward the end of it. To bring this into the laboratory, two major types of design have been used. One is in fact a trial design, not unlike those we have already studied, except that the probability of a signal occurring on a trial is exceedingly low. Perhaps the most famous version of this design is the clock experiment of N.

H. Mackworth (1950) in which a clock hand jumped once per second through a circle divided into 100 equal intervals. A signal was a jump of two intervals rather than one. The signal to non-signal ratio was 1:150 and the watch lasted two hours. The detection rate fell from 85% in the first half hour to 73% during the rest of the watch. Because this is actually a trial design, the methods we have previously discussed can be applied.

It is, however, obvious that one can run closely analogous experiments in which the usual analysis is not applicable. An example is any design in which a signal, such as a brief duration tone, occurs every now and then without any indication of possible times of occurrence. Such a study was run by Broadbent and Gregory (1963) as part of an effort to disentangle the sources of decay in performance. They asked whether the loss is due to reduced sensory sensitivity or to some change in the tendency to make a detection response. They reported two experiments: a visual one that was a trial design and an auditory one that was trial free. In the latter the signals were 1-sec, 1000-Hz tone bursts that were 5 dB above absolute threshold. The watch was 45 min long, with (unknown to the subject) the same temporal pattern of presentations during each 15 min subinterval. In one condition a total of 18 signals occurred and the times between them varied from 25 to 299 sec. In the other, 72 signals were spaced from 4 to 153 sec. The subjects gave confidence ratings on a four-point scale. The authors wished to analyze the data in terms of the concepts of signal detection theory—sensitivity and response bias. There was little difficulty in doing this for the trial design since one could clearly identify both signal and non-signal trials, but in the auditory experiment nothing corresponded directly to non-signal trials. Their solution was to suppose that the subject covertly divides time into intervals, comparable in size to the duration of the signals, and so renders the situation into a series of Yes-No detection trials. This permitted them to calculate a false alarm rate. Using the confidence ratings they constructed an ROC curve in the usual way, and so calculated the measures d' of sensitivity and β of response bias. Their finding was that performance deteriorated from the first third to the last third of the watch because β increased whereas d' did not change significantly. This conclusion had considerable impact on theorizing about the cause of the diminished performance. For a detailed summary of these and numerous other studies about vigilance, see Davies and Parasuraman (1982), Davies and Tune (1969), Mackie (1977), J. F. Mackworth (1969, 1970), and Stroh (1971).

Although efforts have been made to show that selection of the time interval in this analysis little affects the conclusions, there clearly is something terribly artificial about introducing it. We have no reason whatsoever to suppose that subjects actually reduce ordinary detection tasks—either in life or in the laboratory—into a series of discrete judgments, and there are surely reasons to think otherwise. The signals that one constantly contends with come in all sizes, magnitudes, and durations with no prior indication about the type with which one will have to deal, and so it is difficult to imagine how an appropriate unit of time can be chosen. Such an assumption appears to be more a matter of convenience for data analysis than a serious theory about detection behavior. It probably results from the general discomfort psychologists have evidenced about dealing with probabilities in continuous time—that is, data as time series and models that are continuous stochastic processes. As we shall see, the study of such processes is not without its complications; nonetheless, that seems to be the natural formulation of experiments in which signals occur at irregular, perhaps random, times.

5.3   VIGILANCE AT HIGH SIGNAL RATES

5.3.1   *Pseudo-Random Presentations and Pseudo-Hazard Functions*

To my knowledge, the first experiment in which weak signals were presented at irregular times but at a relatively high rate was Egan, Greenberg, and Schulman (1961). They spoke of the method as "free responding," but I am more inclined to emphasize the irregularity of the signal presentations than that of the responses. The temporal structure of the design consisted of inter-stimulus intervals of 3.5, 5.5, 7.5, 8, 8.5, 9, 9.5, 10, 10.5, 11, 11.5, 13.5, and 15.5 sec, which were selected according to a uniform distribution. As we know (Section 1.2.3) this means a rising hazard rate governing the time of the next presentation. In their second experiment the signals were 1000-Hz pure tones in a background of noise with signal-to-noise ratios of 9, 11, and 13 dB. Responses, which the subject was free to make at any time a signal was thought to have occurred, were recorded only to an accuracy of 133.3 msec. Each of four subjects was run under three instructions about the criterion to use: strict, medium, and lax.

The procedure of data analysis was, first, to eliminate all interstimulus intervals (ISIs) of 3.5 and 5.5 sec, and then to estimate the density of stimulus-response times conditional on neither a response nor a signal intervening. To be quite explicit, what they did was partition time into 133.3-msec bins, and then they counted the total number of responses whose time since the preceding signal fell into each bin. Of course, this count excludes all ISIs shorter than that bin, which makes the estimated distribution conditional on no signal intervening, and by the very way the estimate is constructed it deals with the first response following the signal. Thus, it is a kind of hazard function, unusual in its conditioning on no intervening signal. The type of result this leads to is shown in Figure 5.1. We see three major features: The response pseudo-hazard function exhibits a sharp peak at about 1 sec, which appears to have been caused by the signal, after which there is a long, flatish tail that resembles a Poisson process of false alarms. Both the height of the peak and the level of the false alarm rate increases with the laxness of the criterion, and the height of the peak increases systematically with signal strength.

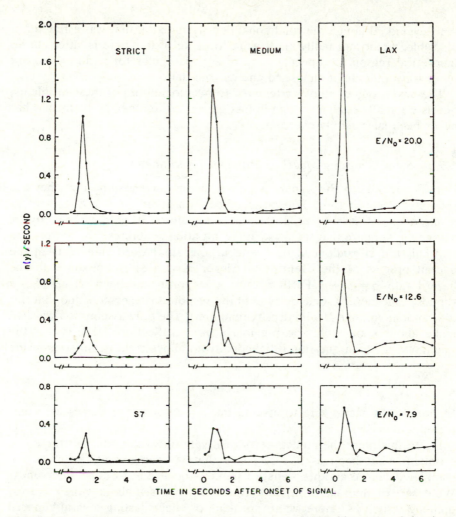

FIG. 5.1 For a free-response, auditory detection experiment, histogram of the times between a signal and the next response conditional on no intervening signal. The distribution of times between signals was equally likely on 13 values. There were from 240 to 640 observations per condition for each subject. This is one of four subjects run. [Figure 12 of Egan et al. (1961); copyright 1961; reprinted by permission.]

To my mind, the approach taken in this experiment and its analysis is in the correct direction in that it does not attempt an artificial partitioning into trials. It has, however, two drawbacks. First, the fact that the signals are not really random in time is worrisome since, as in the simple reaction-time experiment, this may induce the subject to modify his or her response strategy as a function of the time that has elapsed since the last response.

And second, although the conditional density function that was estimated is plausible, we do not really know what to make of it. There is, after all, no theoretical reason to expect it to have any particular form, and there are other ways one might choose to analyze the data.

The next group of studies attempted to overcome both of these problems; but as we shall see their design in fact generated another problem that has never been successfully overcome.

5.3.2   Signal Queuing Model for Random Presentations

Consider idealizing the signals as points in time and assume that they are presented according to a Poisson schedule with hazard rate λ. Suppose that when a signal is presented the subject detects it with probability q. Moreover, suppose that the noise in the situation generates false alarms and that this too is random in time with a constant hazard rate ν. Then the overall process of the events that trigger responses is Poisson with the hazard rate $\eta = q\lambda + \nu$. Further, once a response has been triggered, we suppose that there is some delay until the response is executed, and that this is a random variable **R** with density function r. The only assumption we shall make about r, one that was previously used in Section 3.2.2, is that the random variable in question is bounded from above; that is, for some value τ,

$$r(t) = 0 \quad \text{for all} \quad t > \tau. \tag{5.1}$$

In practice, it seems safe to assume that all response processes are completed within 2 sec.

Up to this point the model seems relatively unexceptional, but there is a problem: what happens if a response that is triggered at time t is not completed before another signal or pseudo-signal due to noise intervenes? What sort of interaction arises between the two signals and their corresponding responses? Here we are speaking of effects lasting several hundred milliseconds, and so they are not simple stimulus masking effects that are measured in tens of milliseconds. Such interaction is a serious matter when signal events follow a Poisson schedule because it is not uncommon for two to occur close together. Obviously, it is an empirical matter to uncover the nature of the interaction, and one can follow either of two strategies. The most obvious strategy—and, it turns out, the most successful—is to isolate experimentally the problem of responding to two signals as a function of the inter-stimulus time and to study it in isolation. This procedure I discuss in the next section. The other alternative is to make guesses as to what might happen, selecting them in part so that the mathematics of the theory can be developed, and deriving predictions about what is to be expected in the data. This is what Luce (1966), Green and Luce (1967), and Luce and Green (1970) attempted, and I recount these developments briefly.

In the first two papers listed, they postulated a lock-out model in which any signal that occurred during the completion of a response process was simply ignored, or locked out. This assumption—invoked in classical models of certain Geiger counters—coupled with the previous assumptions, makes it possible to derive a number of unconditional and conditional density functions. In the 1970 paper they also considered three other models. One, called response suppression, assumed that each signal event—either a signal detected or noise event perceived as a signal—initiates a response process, and a new process suppresses an ongoing one. A second was again a lock-out model, but with the more realistic assumption that the signals are of short but non-negligible duration. And the third was queuing model in which each signal initiates a response process provided that none is under way, and when one is underway the signal is stored in a queue until the response mechanism is free, at which point it initiates the process. The last model is of interest since it is one of the major proposals that has evolved from empirical studies of responses to pairs of signals presented in close succession. This topic is discussed in the next section. I therefore present here the queuing model for random signal presentations.

Consider, first, just the density between two responses, call it f_1. This is the sum of two terms, one arising if there is a signal in the queue and the other if there is none. When a signal is in the queue, the density of responses is just $r(t)$. If not, the density is simply the convolution of the density of the stimulus event, which is exponential with parameter η, and the response density r. The queuing assumption is implicit since while a second stimulus event can occur in the interval between the first signal and its response, we do not set up a race between the two response processes as leading to the next response. Let ρ = probability that a signal is in the queue. If $\eta E(\mathbf{R}) < 1$, then it can be shown that, asymptotically, $\rho = \eta E(\mathbf{R})$ (Cox & Smith, 1961, p. 53). Thus we see,

$$f_1(t) = \rho r(t) + (1-p)\int_0^t \eta e^{-\eta(t-x)} r(x)\, dx$$

$$= \rho r(t) + (1-\rho)\eta e^{-\eta t} \int_0^t e^{\eta x} r(x)\, dx. \tag{5.2}$$

Observe that by invoking the boundedness of the response process, Eq. 5.1, we obtain

$$f_1(t) = (1-\rho)\eta e^{-\eta t} R_\eta, \quad \text{for all} \quad t > \tau, \tag{5.3}$$

where we have defined the quantity

$$R_\eta = \int_0^\tau e^{\eta x} r(x)\, dx. \tag{5.4}$$

So, by Eq. 5.3, the tail of this distribution beyond time τ is predicted to be exponential with the time constant η, which provides one way to estimate η. Another observable quantity is the probability of a response occurring within time τ of the previous response, which is given by integrating Eq. 5.3:

$$1 - (1 - \rho)R_\eta e^{-\eta\tau}. \tag{5.5}$$

A second observable density is of the interresponse times conditional on there being no signal within the time between the two responses; call this $f_2(t)$. Note that by the conditioning, the second response must have been initiated either by a signal in the queue or, if none exists, then by a noise event. Place the first of the two responses at the origin and let $\mathbf{X}_S$ and $\mathbf{X}_R$ denote the random variables representing the time until the next signal and the next response, respectively. Keeping in mind that the signals are governed by a Poisson process, and so occur quite independently of the response processes, we see that

$$\begin{aligned}
f_2(t) &= \Pr(\mathbf{X}_R = t \mid \mathbf{X}_S > \mathbf{X}_R) \\
&= \Pr(\mathbf{X}_R = t \ \& \ \mathbf{X}_S > t)/\Pr(\mathbf{X}_S > \mathbf{X}_R) \\
&= \Pr(\mathbf{X}_R = t)\Pr(\mathbf{X}_S > t)/\Pr(\mathbf{X}_S > \mathbf{X}_R). \tag{5.6}
\end{aligned}$$

We evaluate each of the three terms:

$$\begin{aligned}
\Pr(\mathbf{X}_R = t) &= \rho r(t) + (1 - \rho)\int_0^t \nu e^{-\nu(t-x)} r(x)\, dx \\
&= (1 - \rho)\nu e^{-\nu t} R, \text{ if } t > \tau,
\end{aligned}$$

where R_ν is defined by Eq. 5.4 with ν substituted for η.

$$\Pr(\mathbf{X}_S > t) = e^{-\lambda t},$$

$$\Pr(\mathbf{X}_S > \mathbf{X}_R) = \int_0^\infty \Pr(\mathbf{X}_R = t)\Pr(\mathbf{X}_S > t)\, dt.$$

Substituting the two preceding expressions, simplifying, and integrating by parts yields

$$\Pr(\mathbf{X}_S > \mathbf{X}_R) = (\nu + \rho\lambda)R_{-\lambda}/(\nu + \lambda).$$

Substituting these three expressions in Eq. 5.6 yields as the tail of the distribution

$$f_2(t) = (1 - \rho)\nu(\nu + \lambda)e^{-(\nu+\lambda)t}R_\nu/(\nu + \rho\lambda)R_{-\lambda}, \text{ for } t > \tau. \tag{5.7}$$

Integrating this from τ to ∞ and subtracting from 1 yields the probability of an IRT with no intervening signal and not longer than τ:

$$1 - (1 - \rho)\nu e^{-(\nu+\lambda)\nu}R_\nu/(\nu + \rho\lambda)R_{-\lambda}. \tag{5.8}$$

Without going into the mathematical details, one can derive several other distributions. For example, the density of times from a signal to the next response conditional on there being no observable event—either signal or response—in the τ sec before the signal can be shown to satisfy

$$f_3(t) = (1 - q)\eta e^{-\eta t}R_\eta/R_\nu, \text{ for } t > \tau. \tag{5.9}$$

And the corresponding probability of such times being less than τ is

$$1-(1-q)e^{-\eta\tau}R_\eta/R_\nu. \tag{5.10}$$

A fourth density is for the signal response time conditional on both no observable event τ sec prior to the signal and no additional signal between the given one and the response. This is, in essence, the one calculated by Egan et al. (1961) except, of course, their presentation schedule was not Poisson. This density, for $t > \tau$, is given by

$$f_4(t) = (1-q)(\nu+\lambda)e^{-(\nu+\lambda)t}/[1+(\lambda q/\nu)(R_{-\lambda}/R_\nu)]. \tag{5.11}$$

The corresponding probability is

$$1-(1-q)e^{-(\nu+\lambda)\tau}/[1+(\lambda q/\nu)(R_{-\lambda}/R_\nu)]. \tag{5.12}$$

A special case of this model is the lock-out one, which is the queuing model with $\rho = 0$. In this model signals that arrive during the processing of other signals are simply lost because there is no queue for them to enter. This was the model tested by Green and Luce (1967) and in an improved replication by Luce and Green (1970). We ran studies with brief, difficult-to-detect pure tones in a noise background. Using $\tau = 2$ sec, which seems quite conservative, we estimated η from the tails of densities 1 and 3 (Eqs. 5.3 and 5.9) and $\nu + \lambda$ from densities 2 and 4 (Eqs. 5.7 and 5.11). Since λ is known—it is selected by the experimenter—q and ν may be calculated. The probability expression for density 2, Eq. 5.8, was then fit to the data for that case in order to estimate $R_\nu/R_{-\lambda}$. Thus, all of the parameters entering into the probability expression for density 4, Eq. 5.12, are known, and so it can be predicted. This is shown in Figure 5.2; it is abundantly clear that the lock-out model is not satisfactory.

The question remains whether the queuing model is more adequate. A direct test was not carried out and the data are no longer available, so we will have to follow the indirect argument of Luce and Green. According to Eq. 5.8, assuming the lock-out model instead of the queuing one causes a misestimate of $R_{-\lambda}/R_\nu$ by a factor of

$$B = \rho(\nu+\rho\lambda)/(1-\rho)\nu.$$

Note that $B-1 = \rho(\nu+\lambda)/(1-\rho) > 0$ and so $B > 1$. If we let

$$A = (\lambda q/\nu)R_{-\lambda}/R_\nu,$$

then the error in estimating the probability in Figure 5.2 is, according to Eq. 5.12,

$$(1-q)e^{-(\nu+\lambda)\tau}[1/(1+A)-1/(1+AB)]$$
$$= (1-q)e^{-(\nu+\lambda)\tau}A(B-1)/(1+A)(1+AB)$$
$$< (1-q)e^{-(\nu+\lambda)\tau}A(B-1)$$
$$< (1-q)qe^{-(\nu+2\lambda)\tau}(\lambda/\nu)[(\nu+\lambda)/\nu][\rho/(1-\rho)],$$

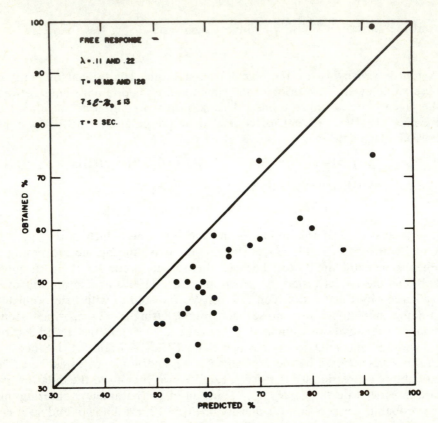

FIG. 5.2 Observed proportion of a signal-response interval that is not preceded within 2 sec by a signal or a response and during which no second signal occurs versus the predicted value for that probability in the lock-out model. The model and method for estimating the parameters is described in the text. There are between 100 and 400 observations per data point. [Figure 3 of Luce and Green (1970); copyright 1970; reprinted by permission.]

where we have used the fact that $R_{-\lambda}/R_\nu < e^{-\lambda\tau}$. In the data, $\lambda \leq \nu$, of course $(1-q)q \leq \frac{1}{4}$, and $\rho = \eta E(\mathbf{R}) < \frac{1}{2}$, so the error is less than $e^{-3\lambda\tau}E(\mathbf{R})$. Since λ and τ are experimentally controlled ($\lambda \geq .11 \sec^{-1}$ and $\nu = 2 \sec$), it suffices to bound η and $E(\mathbf{R})$. According to Green and Luce (1967, Figures 4 and 5), for λ in the same range, $\eta < .5 \sec^{-1}$. In Figures 8 and 9 of the same paper they showed interresponse times that must arise from signals in the queue, and they appear to be much like simple RTs. Thus, it is probably safe to assume $E(\mathbf{R}) < .2$ sec. In which case, the error in estimating $\int_0^\tau f_4(x)\,dx$ does not exceed .06. Actually, the error is probably a good deal less since our bounds have been generous. In any event, we see from Figure 5.2 that shifting the points up by .06 is not adequate to make the model fit.

Observe that the analysis does not really provide any insight into what about the model is wrong, but studies discussed below indicate that something more than simple queuing is involved.

As none of these models resolved the difficulties of signals close together in the Green and Luce data, we had two options. One, which we took, was to try to eliminate the source of the problem by changing the experimental design. We were led away from vigilance experiments as such and turned to simple reaction time designs in which the foreperiod was exponential (this has been discussed in Sections 2.4.3 and 4.1.3). The other strategy, which was underway much earlier in Great Britain and Australia in connection with tracking and skilled motor skills, was to make a direct frontal attack on the question of what subjects do when two signals occur close together. I turn to this next.

5.4 INTERACTION OF TWO SIGNALS IN CLOSE SUCCESSION

5.4.1 *The Major Phenomenon: Psychological Refractoriness*

Telford (1931) was one of the first to report an interaction in the response times to two signals that are presented in rapid succession, and he spoke of a "refractory phase" following the occurrence of each signal. This term was invoked because he thought the phenomenon to be one of recovery, somewhat analogous to the refractoriness of nerves; however, careful work in the 1950s made clear that this is really a very poor analogy. Among other things, neural refractoriness is measured in msec whereas behavioral interference lasts as long as a few hundred msec. As a result, the phenomenon is no longer called that but rather the "psychological refractory period," still a potentially misleading term.

Several surveys have been published on this topic, among them Bertelson (1966), Herman and Kantowitz (1973), Kahneman (1973), Kantowitz (1974), Smith (1967c), and Welford (1980c). Much of the work goes considerably beyond issues of detection, ranging into rather more complex cognitive tasks. For example, Posner (1978) has extensively used a probe technique in which a stimulus is presented and some more-or-less difficult cognitive task is begun. But on some trials after the main task is underway a probe stimulus is presented, and the subject is to respond to the probe as rapidly as possible. This procedure is obviously related to the topic of the chapter. To encompass this more general class of experiments, Kantowitz uses the term "double stimulation." In contrast, in this chapter I shall take a relatively narrow view of the matter and concentrate on simple detection and the simplest of identification designs.

Since the empirical literature has been covered quite thoroughly in these reviews, I shall not attempt to deal with all of its nuances here. The situation in this literature, and we shall see much the same thing again in Section 6.5 when we examine sequential effects in the choice reaction-time context, is agreement about the major outlines of the phenomenon but with considerable disagreement about some of the fine details. A good deal of the motivation for the work was not simple reaction times as such or even choice ones, but rather more complex tasks involving more-or-less skilled motor activities. The work began with an inquiry into the nature of continuous tracking, such as arises in the control of various vehicles, and more recently has focused on extremely rapid discrete activities such as typing or piano playing. I shall focus my attention entirely on the interaction that is relevant to reaction times and avoid the temptation to enter into a discussion of the literature on skilled motor activity. The interested reader should examine the following references and those listed there: Cooper (1983), Stelmach (1978), and Stelmach and Requin (1980).

Let us turn now to psychological refractoriness itself. An early study, following on the pioneering work of Craik (1947, 1948), is that of Vince (1948) in which the subject viewed a rotating drum through a narrow slit whose width corresponded to about 50 msec. On the drum was a line that mostly was constant, but every now and then changed, either up or down, by 2.5 cm. These changes were described as occurring at random, although I doubt if they were programmed as a Poisson process; rather, it appears that a limited set of ISI intervals was chosen and these were equally likely to be selected. The subject controlled a lever that was to be moved as rapidly as possible in the direction of the change. The data of interest were comparisons of reaction times to successive changes in opposite directions as a function of the time between them, the ISI. She found that for an interval of 50 msec the MRT to the first change was 290 msec (to an accuracy of 10 msec), whereas that to the second was 510 msec, some 220 msec more. As the ISI was increased the magnitude of the effect decreased until at 500 msec there was no noticeable difference.

A number of questions can be raised about the source of the slowing. For one, the subject had to reverse very rapidly the movement of the hand, and so the effect could simply have been a motor limitation. Also, it is certainly conceivable that there is some sort of peripheral sensory interaction, something of the sort suggested by Telford. Davis (1956, 1957, 1959), Fraisse (1957), and Welford (1952, 1959) ruled out these possibilities and made clear that the phenomenon is probably central in origin. For example, Davis (1959) ran four conditions involving a visual stimulus first and either a visual or an auditory one second. The first visual stimulus was a 40-msec flash of a neon bulb just left of center and at the end of a 3-ft tube. The second visual one was a similar light just right of center at the end of the same tube, and the auditory one was a highly audible click. If a response was required to the first stimulus, it was made by pressing a key with a finger of the left hand, and the response to the second signal was always with a right finger. Four conditions were run: either a visual or an auditory second signal and either a response to each signal or just to the second one. The two visual conditions were interleaved as were the two auditory ones. The data are shown in Figure 5.3.

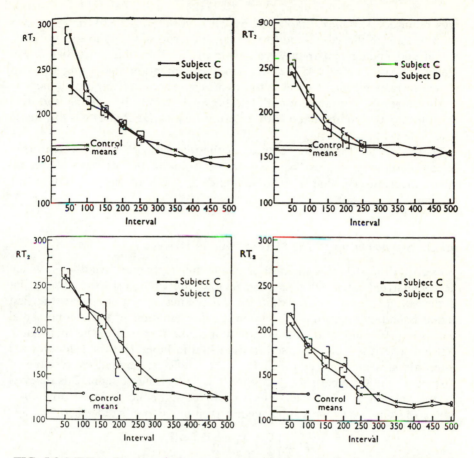

FIG. 5.3 MRT to the second of two signals versus interstimulus interval (ISI) for the Davis (1959) experiment described in the text. The first signal was visual. The data in the first row are for a visual second signal and in the second row for an auditory one; the data in the left panels arose when the subject responded to both signals and in the right, when the subject responded only to the second one. There were 40 observations per data point. [Figures 1 and 2 of Davis (1959); copyright 1959; reprinted by permission.]

Four aspects of these data are striking: The psychological refractory period was complete by 250 msec, which seems to be the pattern of most of the later studies; its existence did not depend upon the two stimuli being in the same modality; it did not arise through some conflict of the response mechanisms since they were carried out by different hands [this was also ruled out by Welford (1959) using a similar response procedure]; and it depended very little upon any response being carried out to the first stimulus [which was also shown by Fraisse (1957) and Smith (1967b)]. The impact of the first signal on the response to the second depended to some degree upon the repeated alternation of conditions in which response to the first signal was required. This was established by running the same subjects some two months later in the visual-auditory case with responses only to the auditory signal and finding that they were substantially faster than they had been. Earlier, Davis (1956, 1957) addressed the contention that using the two hands to respond might involve the two hemispheres of the brain, thereby introducing a communication delay between them, by having the two responses occur on one hand with different fingers. He found that this made little difference.

These then are the major features of the phenomenon about which there is considerable consensus. We turn now to some of the attempts to understand theoretically what is involved and to some of the less consistent findings.

5.4.2   Signal Queuing: The Single-Channel Hypothesis

Welford (1952, 1959) is the author of the single-channel hypothesis, which he summarized carefully in his 1980 review. In its simplest form, it says that if the second signal arrives while the processing or responding to the first signal is underway, then some buffered representation of the second signal enters a queue and awaits the completion of the response to the first signal. At that time it is then processed in the usual fashion. Thus, if I denotes the inter-stimulus interval (ISI) and $\mathbf{T}_i$ is the undisturbed random variable of response time to signal i, $i = 1, 2$, then the processing of signal 2 is delayed by the amount $\mathbf{T}_1 - I$, if that time is positive, and is not delayed otherwise. Thus, the observed time to the second stimulus is predicted to be

$$\mathbf{T}_2' = \begin{cases} \mathbf{T}_2 + \mathbf{T}_1 - I, \text{ if } I \leq \mathbf{T}_1, \\ \mathbf{T}_2, \text{ if } I > \mathbf{T}_1, \end{cases}$$
$$= \mathbf{T}_2 + \max(\mathbf{T}_1, I) - I. \tag{5.13}$$

On a priori grounds, the model has at least two defects. First, if we think of simple reaction times as composed of three additive components—the conduction time $\mathbf{C}$, decision time $\mathbf{D}$, and response activation time $\mathbf{R}$—then queuing should only arise if the decision time for $\mathbf{T}_1$, $\mathbf{D}_1$, overlaps that for $\mathbf{T}_2$. If we assume $\mathbf{C}_1$ and $\mathbf{C}_2$ are identically distributed, which is plausible if both signals are in the same modality and of the comparable magnitude, then the model really should read

$$\mathbf{T}_2' = \mathbf{T}_2 + \max(\mathbf{D}_1, I) - I.$$

Since $\mathbf{D}_1 < \mathbf{T}_1$, the observed $\mathbf{T}_2'$ is thus predicted to reach its asymptotic value well before I exceeds $\mathbf{T}_1$. As we shall see, this result does not happen, suggesting that the a priori model is defective. Welford (1959) formulated a variant in which a signal that arrives during $\mathbf{D}_1$ is stored until that process is completed, whereas a signal that arrives during $\mathbf{R}_1$ is stored until the response process is completed. Second, it is assumed that the act of storing the signal in the queue has no effect on the subsequent reaction time or on the quality of performance. This is tantamount to assuming no degradation of the representation as a result of its being stored and that it takes no time to retrieve the representation from the queue.

Ignoring these criticisms, we work with Eq. 5.13. Welford typically has substituted $E(\mathbf{T})s$ for the $\mathbf{T}s$ in Eq. 5.13, but that is incorrect and potentially misleading. Following Ollman (1968), who was more general in that he treated I as an independent random variable, we compute $E(\mathbf{T})$ exactly. In doing so, we do not need to assume that $\mathbf{T}_1$ and $\mathbf{T}_2$ are independent. Let $\mathbf{Y} = \max(\mathbf{T}_1, \mathbf{I})$, F the distribution function of $\mathbf{Y}$, F_1 that of $\mathbf{T}_1$, and G that of $\mathbf{I}$, which when $\mathbf{I}$ is constant is simply

$$G(x) = \begin{cases} 0, & \text{if } x < I, \\ 1, & \text{if } x \geq I. \end{cases}$$

Since $\mathbf{T}_1$ and $\mathbf{I}$ are independent, we see $F(x) = F_1(x)G(x)$. Using this relationship, assuming that density functions exist, and carrying out an integration by parts,

$$E(\mathbf{Y}^n) = \int_0^\infty x^n f(x)\, dx$$

$$= n \int_0^\infty x^{n-1}[1 - F(x)]\, dx$$

$$= n \int_0^\infty x^{n-1}[1 - F_1(x)G(x)]\, dx$$

$$= n \int_0^I x^{n-1}\, dx + n \int_I^\infty x^{n-1}[1 - F_1(x)]\, dx$$

$$= I^n + n \int_I^\infty x^{n-1}[1 - F_1(x)]\, dx. \tag{5.14}$$

Thus, setting $n = 1$

$$E(\mathbf{T}_2') = E(\mathbf{T}_2) + E(\mathbf{Y}) - I$$

$$= E(\mathbf{T}_2) + \int_I^\infty [1 - F_1(x)]\, dx. \tag{5.15}$$

Observe,

$$\lim_{I \to 0} E(\mathbf{T}_2') = E(\mathbf{T}_1) + E(\mathbf{T}_2), \tag{5.16}$$

$$\lim_{I \to \infty} E(\mathbf{T}_2') = E(\mathbf{T}_2). \tag{5.17}$$

As an example of how Eq. 5.14 behaves, suppose $f_1 = f_2$ is a displaced exponential

$$f(t) = \begin{cases} \mu e^{-\mu(t - t_0)}, & \text{if } t \geq t_0, \\ 0, & \text{if } t > t_0. \end{cases}$$

Then it is easy to calculate the integral in Eq. 5.15, yielding

$$E(\mathbf{T}_2') = m + t_0 + \begin{cases} m + t_0 - I, \text{ if } I \le t_0, \\ me^{-(I-t_0)/m}, \text{ if } I > t_0, \end{cases}$$

where $m = 1/\mu$.

Observe that by differentiating Eq. 5.14 with respect to I,

$$dE(\mathbf{T}_2')/dI = -[1 - F_1(I)] \ge -1. \tag{5.18}$$

It is entirely possible for the minimum slope to be achieved as follows. Suppose that the density of $\mathbf{T}_1$ lies entirely between two bounds, say, a and b—that is,

$$f_1(x) = 0 \text{ if } x < a \text{ or } x > b,$$

then from Eq. 5.14 we see that

$$E(\mathbf{T}_2') = E(\mathbf{T}_2) + \begin{cases} E(\mathbf{T}_1) - I, \text{ if } I < a, \\ 0, \text{ if } I > b. \end{cases}$$

So, the model predicts that $E(\mathbf{T}_2')$ will initially decrease with slope -1, provided $I < a$, and the slope will gradually increase until $E(\mathbf{T}_2')$ asymptotes at $E(\mathbf{T}_2)$. Moreover, since $E(\mathbf{T}_2')$ is decreasing, Eq. 5.16 implies

$$E(\mathbf{T}_2') \le E(\mathbf{T}_1) + E(\mathbf{T}_2). \tag{5.19}$$

Before looking into this empirically, we deduce two other properties of the model.

In the following calculations for the variance of $\mathbf{T}_2'$ and for its correlation with $\mathbf{T}_1$, we assume that $\mathbf{T}_1$ and $\mathbf{T}_2$ are independent random variables. Then, using Eq. 5.14,

$$V(\mathbf{Y}) = E(\mathbf{Y}^2) - E(\mathbf{Y})^2$$

$$= I^2 + 2 \int_I^\infty x[1 - F_1(x)]\, dx - I^2 - 2I \int_I^\infty [1 - F_1(x)]\, dx$$

$$- \left[\int_I^\infty [1 - f_1(x)]\, dx \right]^2. \tag{5.20}$$

Taking the derivative with respect to I,

$$dV(\mathbf{Y})/dI = -2I[1 - F_1(I)] - 2 \int_I^\infty [1 - F_1(x)]\, dx + 2I[1 - F_1(I)]$$

$$+ 2[1 - F_1(I)] \int_I^\infty [1 - F_1(x)]\, dx$$

$$= -2F_1(I) \int_I^\infty [1 - F_1(x)]\, dx$$

$$< 0.$$

Thus, $V(\mathbf{Y})$ is decreasing, so the maximum occurs for $I = 0$, whence by Eqs.

5.14 and 5.20,

$$V(\mathbf{T}_2') \leq V(\mathbf{T}_1) + V(\mathbf{T}_2). \tag{5.21}$$

Next we turn to the correlation of $\mathbf{T}_2'$ with $\mathbf{T}_1$:

$$
\begin{aligned}
\mathrm{COV}(\mathbf{T}_2', \mathbf{T}_1) &= E\{[\mathbf{T}_2 + \mathbf{Y} - I - E(\mathbf{T}_2) - E(\mathbf{Y})][\mathbf{T}_1 - E(\mathbf{T}_1)]\} \\
&= E\{[\mathbf{T}_2 - E(\mathbf{T}_2)][\mathbf{T}_1 - E(\mathbf{T}_1)]\} + E\{\mathbf{Y}[\mathbf{T}_1 - E(\mathbf{T}_1)]\} \\
&\quad + E\{[E(\mathbf{Y}) - I][\mathbf{T}_1 - E(\mathbf{T}_1)]\} \\
&= 0 + I \int_0^I [x - E(\mathbf{T}_1)]f_1(x)\, dx + \int_I^\infty x[x - E(\mathbf{T}_1)]f_1(x)\, dx + 0 \\
&= V_1(I) + [E(\mathbf{T}_1) - I]E_1(I),
\end{aligned}
$$

where

$$E_1(I) = \int_I^\infty [x - E(\mathbf{T}_1)]f_1(x)\, dx,$$

$$V_1(I) = \int_I^\infty [x - E(\mathbf{T}_1)]^2 f_1(x)\, dx.$$

So the correlation is given by

$$\rho = \frac{V_1(I) + [E(\mathbf{T}_1) - I]E_1(I)}{V(\mathbf{T}_2')^{1/2} V_1^{1/2}}. \tag{5.22}$$

Again the limiting cases are interesting. Note that for $I < a$, $V_1(I) = V_1$ and $E_1(I) = 0$, and for $I > b$ both quantities are 0, so

$$\rho = \begin{cases} V_1^{1/2}/[V_1 + V_2]^{1/2}, & \text{if } I < a, \\ 0, & \text{if } I > b. \end{cases} \tag{5.23}$$

Observe that if $V(\mathbf{T}_1) = V(\mathbf{T}_2)$, which is certainly plausible when the two signals are identical, then for $I < a$, $\rho = 1/\sqrt{2} = 0.707$.

The idea of studying how various experimental manipulations, such as the ISI, introduce delays in processing times as a means to infer something of the mental processing network—in this case, to conclude that it exhibits a serial aspect—is much generalized in Sections 12.4.6 to 12.4.8. There it is shown how more elaborate manipulations can be used to infer the entire network of processing stages—provided there are such distinct stages.

5.4.3 Data Relevant to the Single-Channel Model

The model yields at least six major predictions.

1. For sufficiently short ISI, the slope of $E(\mathbf{T}_2')$ versus ISI is -1 (Eq. 5.18).
2. For sufficiently long ISI, $E(\mathbf{T}_2')$ approaches $E(\mathbf{T}_2)$, the simple reaction time to signal s_2 (Eq. 5.17).

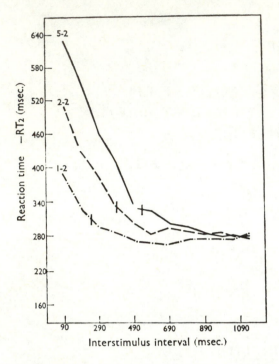

FIG. 5.4 MRT to the second of two signals versus ISI when the first signal was selected at random from among 1, 2, or 5 digits and the subject was to identify the digit presented and the second signal was one of two tones that was also to be identified. See the text for discussion. Each data point is based on 360 observations—90 each from four subjects. [Figure 1 of Karlin and Kestenbaum (1968); copyright 1968; reprinted by permission.]

3. For $I < \mathbf{T}_1$, a change in $\mathbf{T}_1$, however effected, will be reflected as a comparable change in $\mathbf{T}_2'$ (Eq. 5.13).
4. Assuming that $\mathbf{T}_1$ and $\mathbf{T}_2$ are of comparable size, as is the case when the two signals are the same, then $E(\mathbf{T}_2') \leq 2E(\mathbf{T}_2)$ (Eq. 5.19), and also assuming their independence, then $V(\mathbf{T}_2') \leq 2V(\mathbf{T}_2)$ (Eq. 5.21).
5. $\mathbf{T}_1$ is affected neither by ISI nor by s_2 (Eq. 5.13).
6. The correlation between $\mathbf{T}_1$ and $\mathbf{T}_2'$ is 0.707 when ISI = 0 and $\mathbf{T}_1$ and $\mathbf{T}_2$ are independent random variables with equal variances; but when the ISI is sufficiently large, the correlation drops to 0 (Eq. 5.23). I do not know if the correlation is at its maximum when ISI = 0.

In evaluating these predictions, as well as some other theoretical ideas, an experiment of Karlin and Kestenbaum (1968) is crucial. A similar experiment with similar results is reported by Smith (1969). They used either 1, 2, or 5 alternatives for s_1, which was the 35-msec flash of a digit responded to by different fingers of the left hand. Signal s_2 was either a 600-Hz or a 3000-Hz tone of 35-msec duration, and was responded to by either one or two fingers of the right hand. The conditions were intermixed, but the four paid subjects knew which condition was in force at the start of each trial. The impact of ISI on MRT_2, the empirical estimate of $E(\mathbf{T}_2)$, is shown in Figures 5.4 and 5.5.

1. The prediction of an initial slope of -1 or greater seems, by and large,

well sustained in the data. For example, in all of the curves shown in Figures 5.3 to 5.5, there is only one minor discrepancy: subject D in upper left of Figure 5.3 has a slope slightly less than -1. All of the others are either approximately -1 or larger. It is not surprising that the slopes are larger than -1 since all ISIs are well above 0. Other data not shown here are also consistent with this prediction (Welford, 1980c).

2. Figures 5.3 to 5.5 suggest that for larger ISIs T_2' may approach simple reactions times since the values achieved are in the typical range. However, there has been no direct verification of that fact. If we were to discover an effect of s_1 on T_2 for such long ISIs, it would have consequences for running simple reaction-time experiments in order to avoid unwanted sequential effects. In Figure 5.6, the asymptote is about 84 msec slower when s_2 involves a choice than when it does not; as we shall see in Section 6.1, this is typical of choice data. What is quite surprising, however, is the fact that this difference disappears as the ISI becomes shorter. This is clearly inconsistent with Eq. 5.13, and it suggests that something else is involved for short ISIs.

3. Smith (1967a) manipulated T_1 by varying the intensity of s_1, which was a light flash, and she found a systematic change in MRT_2' as a function of ISI except, possibly, for the shortest value of ISI, 60 msec. So, except for the shortest ISI, the data are consistent with the model.

4. Ollman (1968) reanalyzed the data of Davis (1959) and found that while the means satisfy the predicted inequality, the variances definitely do

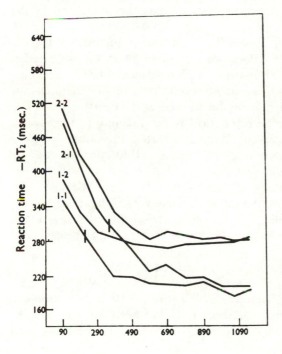

FIG. 5.5 This figure is the same as Figure 5.4 except that the numbers of alternatives are 1 and 2, in all four pairings with first and second signal position. See the text for discussion. [Figure 3 of Karlin and Kestenbaum (1968); copyright 1968; reprinted by permission.]

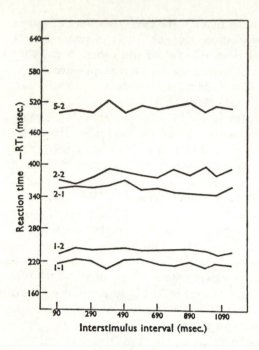

FIG. 5.6 MRT to the first signal in the experiment of Figures 5.4 and 5.5. [Figure 4 of Karlin and Kestenbaum (1968); copyright 1968; reprinted by permission.]

not. In all four cases, the estimate of $V(\mathbf{T}'_2)$ was at least four times as large as that of $V(\mathbf{T}_2)$, and in one of them it was larger by a factor of 20. This clear violation of the model seems largely to have been ignored in the secondary sources.

5. The effect of ISI and s_2 on MRT_1 is shown in Figure 5.6 for the Karlin and Kestenbaum data. ISI does not appear to affect $\mathbf{T}_1$, but whether s_2 entails a choice or not definitely matters. This result is not predicted by the single channel model. Ollman (1968) pointed out that a simple reaction-time experiment with a warning signal can be viewed as a special case of this two-signal paradigm in which the foreperiod is the ISI and no response is made to the first signal. Nickerson (1965b) reported such data in which MRT was examined as a function of the family of foreperiods used in different conditions. The model says that $\mathbf{T}'_2$ should depend only on the actual foreperiod, not the family. This was not the case. Although this finding appears inconsistent with the model, it may very well not be terribly telling if the subject is controlling a response criterion that is changed with foreperiod family in order to keep the level of anticipations below some small proportion.

6. For an ISI of 50 msec, Davis (1959) reported an estimate of $\rho = 0.77$. Welford (1967, p. 20) reported a correlation of 0.473 for all cases of his 1959 data for which $\mathrm{ISI} < \mathrm{MRT}_1$; however, Welford (1959, p. 205) seems to say that the correlation was zero for short ISIs, but he is not very specific about it. Karlin and Kestenbaum (1968) report correlations for each of their

four subjects in three experimental conditions for the following ISIs: $90 +n100$ msec ($n = 0, \ldots, 9$), 1050, and 1150 msec. Although the individual correlations seem somewhat variable, they decrease approximately linearly from a mean of 0.69 at 90 msec to less than 0.10 for all ISIs beyond 590 msec except 790, which is 0.14. This finding appears to be consistent with Eqs. 5.22 and 5.23 but it does not inform us about what happens at very short ISIs.

In sum, this simple queuing model accounts for some of the major features of the data, but it fails on some points. Thus, almost certainly, the model does not describe all that is involved in the interaction of two nearby signals. As we shall see, a more detailed examination of the data suggests additional complications, and we know from Section 5.3.2 that the queuing model did not fit the weak signal data of Green and Luce. Both in his 1959 paper and in the 1980 survey, Welford gave consideration to two refinements of the theory that are designed to handle some discrepancies between the model and the data. The one, which I shall not go into in detail, entails distinguishing between the effects that arise when signal 2 arrives during the perceptual processing of signal 1 and those that arise when it arrives after that has been completed and the response selection process is underway. He assumed that in the former case the processing of s_2 is initiated when the perceptual processing of s_1 is completed, but that in the latter case processing of s_2 is not started until the response to s_1 is made and there is feedback to the CNS that the response is complete. Salthouse (1982) reported an empirical study whose findings he interpreted in terms of two mechanisms: one complete at about 100 msec, which he suggested may be masking of the first signal by the second, and the other lasting to about 200 msec, which he interpreted as the second signal interrupting the central processing of the first one. The argument for two mechanisms is the following. Signal 2 was either the same or different from signal 1. When the signals are the same, the probability of a correct judgment was independent of ISI, but when they were different it was at chance for an ISI of 20 msec rising to that of the other case by about 100 msec. Equally well, the duration of the same case was constant and that of the different one was some 100 msec slower at an ISI of 20 msec, it fell with increasing ISI, but did not reach the other value until an ISI of about 200 msec. The case for two mechanisms is not compelling, however, for as we shall see in Section 8.4.2 sometimes a single mechanism can account for two quite different time courses. The other phenomenon is discussed in Section 5.4.4.

5.4.4 Signal Grouping

Studies have shown repeatedly that when the ISI is quite brief, say less than 100 msec, Welford's model breaks down, and it appears as if the two signals are sometimes treated as a single entity. If this is true and if the grouped and ungrouped cases are not separated in the data analysis, then on average $\mathbf{T}_2'$

responses will be somewhat briefer than would be expected by the model, and this has been found (Elithorn & Lawrence, 1955; Koster & Bekker, 1967; Marill, 1957). Welford (1980c) pointed out that such grouping of nearby signals really comes as no surprise since it appears to be an essential feature of all fast, highly skilled activities such as typing or playing an instrument.

Karlin and Kestenbaum questioned whether the signals can be viewed as grouped at all. They observed that if any grouping of the two signals occurs, then both response times should exhibit a comparable delay due to ISI, but their plots of MRT_1 against ISI are quite constant (Figure 5.7). However, this fact does not seem relevant since their shortest ISI was 90 msec, which is at the very top of the range within which grouping is thought to occur. The most notable effect in this analysis was the fact that MRT_1 depended upon the number of alternatives for s_2 as well as the number for s_1: when s_2 has two possibilities rather than one, then MRT_1 is some 30 msec slower. This result is not predicted by the single channel model.

5.4.5 Quantized Perception

One theoretical idea that leads naturally to some sort of signal grouping was pointed out by Broadbent (1958), who raised the possibility that visual perception (it is extremely doubtful if anything comparable is true in audition) is partitioned into discrete temporal "snapshots" of the environment. Such discreteness of sensory intake over time appears to have been first proposed by Stroud (1956). These perceptual quanta, as they are called, are thought to be of the order of 100 to 300 msec in duration—they would have to be near the latter value to account for the present data. According to this view, unless ISI is quite small, in which case s_1 and s_2 are dealt with as a single signal, signal s_1 captures the time quantum in which it occurs. Should s_2 be presented during the same quantum, it must be held in a buffer until that quantum ends and a new one begins. To be quite explicit about what is assumed, suppose the quanta are of duration Q time units, that relative to the onset of a quantum, s_1 is presented at a random time $\mathbf{X}$ that is uniformly distributed over the interval 0 to Q, and the time between s_1 and s_2 is I. For simplicity, assume that the processing times to the two signals are independent and identically distributed, say $\mathbf{Y}_1$ and $\mathbf{Y}_2$. Then we obtain as the model for the case where the signals are not grouped:

$$\mathbf{T}_1 = \mathbf{Y}_1,$$

$$\mathbf{T}_2' = \begin{cases} \mathbf{Y}_2, & \text{if } I > Q - \mathbf{X}, \\ \mathbf{Y}_2 + Q - \mathbf{X} - I, & \text{if } I < Q - \mathbf{X}. \end{cases}$$

At least two empirical observations cast considerable doubt on this model. Observe that since $\mathbf{Y}_1$ is independent of both $\mathbf{Y}_2$ and $\mathbf{X}$, it implies that $\mathbf{T}_1$ and $\mathbf{T}_2'$ are independent, which as we have seen above is far from the case.

The second argument is based on the data of Karlin and Kestenbaum (1968), which show that the more alternatives there are for s_1, the larger must be the value of the ISI before $T_2' = T_2$ (see Figures 5.5 and 5.6). One striking empirical fact is that the effect of the ISI on MRT_2 changes with the number of alternatives, and there is nothing in the quantal theory to account for that, whereas it is exactly what one expects if the single channel hypothesis holds and if, as is generally true (Section 6.1 and Chapter 10), MRT_1 increases with the number of stimulus alternatives.

5.4.6 *Perceptual and/or Response Preparation*

A still different and important approach to understanding these phenomena, as well as some we consider in Section 6.5, is to suppose that subjects vary in their state of readiness to receive, process, and respond to signals. Summaries of this point of view—which is largely conceptual and has not been stated as a detailed model comparable to the single-channel hypothesis—can be found in Bertelson (1966), Smith (1967c), and Welford (1980c). The idea of preparation can be partitioned into two distinct ideas: preparation to receive the signal, which is referred to as an *expectancy theory*, and preparation to make the response, which is referred to as a *readiness theory*.

In an expectancy theory, the ISI serves as a foreperiod for the presentation of s_2, and experience with the ISIs used should serve to develop an expectancy for some waits and not others. The obvious test of this concept is a design in which ISI is constant either in blocks over trials in a within-subjects design (Borger, 1963) or over subjects in a between-subjects design (Creamer, 1963). In neither case was the effect of ISI eliminated. Smith (1967c) discussed several other relevant studies.

A readiness theory also likens the ISI to a foreperiod during which the subject is developing a readiness to make the required response. As was mentioned above, Nickerson (1965b) demonstrated a significant effect of foreperiod duration on simple RT to visual signals. Perhaps the most directly relevant study is Kay and Weiss (1961) in which they formed many of the possible combinations of constant or variable foreperiod to s_1, constant or variable ISI, and responses to both signals or only to s_2. They found that MRT_2' was longer when a response was required to s_1 than when it was not, and it was longer when the foreperiod to s_1 was variable than when it was constant. Indeed, when the foreperiod is variable and the ISI is constant, MRT_2' is longer than when the foreperiod is constant and the ISI is variable, which is rather different from what one expects from a readiness theory. The conclusion is that the delay is due largely to the processing of the first signal and not upon the nature of the ISI per se.

Welford (1980c, p. 206) remarked that the substantial correlations between T_1 and T_2 are not explicable on the basis of changes in uncertainty about the onset of s_2. It appears to me that this claim may be incorrect. If the level of readiness is both variable and relatively slow to change, then it should be at approximately the same level for both s_1 and s_2 when the ISI is sufficiently small, in which case the two response times should be correlated. The consequence of signal uncertainty would be to alter the distribution of levels, which would change but not necessarily eliminate the correlation. My argument is not valid if, however, the presentation of s_1 rapidly decreases the level of readiness so that it is at a very low level when s_2 arrives, and so the response time to it is slow. Of course, intuitively, one might have suspected that s_1 would serve as a signal to raise, not lower, the level of readiness.

The data shown in Figure 5.5 also seem to cast considerable doubt upon the readiness hypothesis because the pattern of effects due to ISI was identical in all conditions, and yet there was considerable additional impact of uncertainty about s_1 on MRT_2.

5.4.7 Capacity Sharing

One of the most elusive, yet plausible, ideas to arise in accounts of response times is the "mental" capacity needed to carry out a task, and the assumption that the total amount of relevant capacity is distinctly limited. Two things make the concept particularly slippery. First, the nature of capacity is rarely specified in much detail. In a few models it is identified with some parameter of the model. For example, in the model of Section 11.3.4 capacity will be the decay parameter of an exponential process, and in another model it has been identified with the sample size of the information on which a decision is based. But for the most part, it is a verbal concept whose use is little constrained by agreed-upon properties. Second, if the network of processing stages is also treated as something unspecified, to be ascertained from the data, and if capacity can be shifted more-or-less freely from one task to another, then making decisive inferences about either the network or the capacity is really very difficult. For example, a serial system such as is suggested by the single-channel hypothesis can be mimicked easily by a parallel system with capacity sharing. These issues are developed in some detail in Sections 11.3.3, 11.3.4, and 12.2. Here I will merely report one set of data in which the single-channel hypothesis is placed into doubt, at least for tasks in two different modalities, and in which capacity considerations provide a plausible, but partial, account of what is going on.

Greenwald (1970, 1972) pointed out that some stimulus-response pairs are so overlearned and/or "natural" that they draw on far less capacity than do other pairs, even ones we may feel are quite compatible. One example involves the presentation of a spoken *A* or *B*. A compatible, but not overlearned, response is for the subject to say "one" to *A* and "two" to *B*. An overlearned response is to say "*A*" to *A* and "*B*" to *B*. The former are called SR pairs and the latter IM pairs, where IM stands for his term "ideomotor," which seems to be little specified beyond meaning overlearned and natural. In this example, the stimulus is the same in both cases, but the response differs. In the next example, which is visual, the response is the same, moving a key to either the left or the right, but the stimulus differs. In the SR case the stimulus is either a light flash to the left or right of a midpoint, and in the IM case the light flash is, in fact, an arrow pointing either left or right, in accord with the response desired.

Greenwald assumed that the capacity used in simple IM tasks is sufficiently small so that two such tasks can be carried out simultaneously with no loss in performance, whereas that is not true for SR tasks. This assumption was confirmed in the 1972 paper. Greenwald and Shulman (1973) extended this idea to the study of the psychological refractory period. They used the visual stimulus mentioned above for s_1 and the auditory one for s_2, and then ran all four combinations of SR and IM with six ISIs ranging from 0 to 1000 msec. The 0 case was the same as that studied in the 1972 paper. To their initial chagrin, the usual psychological refractory decay in MRT_2' was found in all four cases, with the curves essentially the same except for overall vertical shifts, the IM-IM case being the fastest and SR–SR the slowest. Not only did the psychological refractory period remain, but they failed to replicate the 1972 result. In addition, they noted the surprising fact that MRT_1 actually increased with ISI, and that the average of the two times is constant for the IM-IM condition and not for the others. These results suggested to them that, for some reason, capacity had in fact been shifting between the two tasks in the IM-IM case, contrary to what they had anticipated. They argued that perhaps this was because the instructions had not made clear that the ISI could, in fact, be 0. So the experiment was rerun with two changes. The instructions made clear that the ISI could be 0, and two of the intermediate ISIs were dropped and a control, denoted C, of just s_1 and just s_2 was added. The data are shown in Figure 5.7, where we see that MRT_2' is independent of ISI and the duration of the ISI effect is much attenuated (to less than 100 msec) in the IM-SR case as compared with its full-blown development in both cases where the first task was SR. In addition, there continues to be a pronounced effect of ISI on MRT_1, with significant slowing during the first 200 msec. This they attribute to capacity shifts as ISI changes.

The natural way to test capacity shift arguments is to observe the correlation between the two responses. If there is such a shift and if there is any degree of trial-by-trial variation in the amount, then it should be reflected as a negative correlation between the two response times. When no shifting is required, then a zero correlation should occur. Unfortunately, these correlations were not provided. It is unclear to me how capacity arguments are to be adapted to account for the positive correlations that others have reported, at least when both tasks are substantially the same.

In Section 12.4.2, on applications of the method of additive factors, a study by Pashler (1984) is described in which it is concluded that capacity sharing is not the major source of the psychological refractory period.

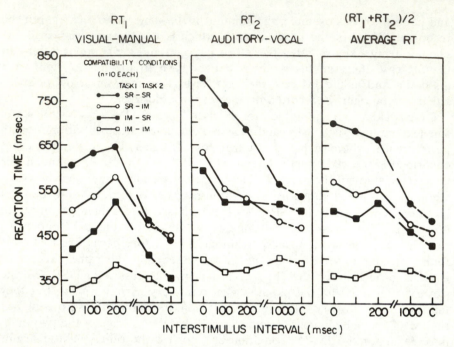

FIG. 5.7 MRT to the first and second of two signals versus ISI for four conditions of stimulus-response compatibility described in the text. Each data point is based on 300 observations, 30 from each of 10 subjects. [Figure 3 of Greenwald and Schulman (1973); copyright 1973; reprinted by permission.]

Moreover, by selective manipulations of the several stages of processing thought to exist, the locus of the single channel bottleneck is argued to exist at the decision stage, not the perceptual or response initiation stages.

5.5   CONCLUSIONS

There is not a great deal to say in conclusion. Although Poisson or other irregular temporal presentations seem far more natural than do trial designs, the problems of analysis are considerable. Either we use a Poisson schedule—which aids considerably in carrying out mathematical analyses of the resulting process but inevitably leads to the presentation of pairs of signals in close succession—or we use a modified schedule that eliminates such pairs, in which case detailed analyses appear to be quite difficult. Empirically, there is no doubt whatsoever that when two signals are close together, the response time to the second one is slowed considerably. To some extent, this appears to be a delay of the sort expected if there is a single channel and the processing of the second signal must await the completion of the processing of the first one—a queue. But the phenomenon is more complex than that as is evidenced by various deviations from that model, including the possible grouping of the two signals when they are sufficiently close, and the possibility of shifting capacity. Unfortunately, these additional complexities are not yet understood in sufficient detail to define a proper model. For the rest of the book we deal with both experiments and models for trial designs that largely, although not altogether, bypass the possible interaction of successive signals.

II
IDENTIFICATION PARADIGMS

6

Two-Choice Reaction Times:
Basic Ideas and Data

6.1 GENERAL CONSIDERATIONS

6.1.1 Experimental Design

The simplest choice-reaction time experiment has much in common with the simple-reaction time design. The major difference is that on each trial one of several signals is presented that the subject attempts to identify as rapidly as is consistent with some level of accuracy. This attempted identification is indicated by making one of several responses that correspond systematically to the stimuli. In terms of the driving example, not only must dangerous obstacles be detected, but they must be identified and appropriate responses—braking, swerving, or accelerating—be made, which one depending upon the exact identity, location, and movement of the obstacle.

Formally, we shall suppose that the signal is one of a fixed set of possible signals, $s_1, \ldots, s_k$, and the corresponding responses are $r_1, \ldots, r_k$, so that the subject responds r_i if he or she believes s_i to have been presented. One may view the selection of a signal by the experimenter as a random variable, which we denote as $\mathbf{s}_n$ on trial n, and the response is another random variable $\mathbf{r}_n$. When there are only two signals and two responses, as will be true throughout this and the following three chapters, I shall avoid the subscripts and, depending upon the context, use either of two notations. In most two-choice situations, I use $\{a, b\}$ and $\{A, B\}$ for the names of the stimuli and corresponding responses; the generic symbols are s and r, $s = a$ or b, $r = A$ or B. Occasionally when the experiment was clearly a Yes-No detection one in which the subject responded Yes if a signal was detected and No otherwise, I will denote the presentation set by $\{s, n\}$, where n stands for no signal or noise alone, and the response set by $\{Y, N\}$.

Many aspects of the design do not differ from the simple case. There is always a foreperiod—either the time from the preceding response, in which case it is called the response—stimulus interval, RSI, or from a warning signal—and it may be variable or constant. Catch trials can be used (e.g., Alegria, 1978, and Ollman, 1970), although it is not common to do so. Payoffs may be based upon response time as well as on its accuracy. But more interesting are the new possibilities that arise from the increased complexity of the design. I list five:

1. Because a discriminative response is being made, it is more plausible to

use a fixed foreperiod design than in the simple reaction case; indeed, it is entirely possible to have a well-marked time interval during which the signal is presented (this is often used in Yes-No and forced-choice designs). Basically, the argument is that if a discriminative response is made, the subject must wait for the signal to occur and so there is no need to worry about anticipations. This argument is compelling so long as the signals are perfectly discriminable and no response errors occur; but the minute some inaccuracy in the performance is present, then the claim becomes suspect. For a discussion of this and the effective use of random foreperiod in a choice experiment to suppress anticipatory responses, see Green, Smith, and von Gierke (1983). And as we shall see in Section 6.6.5, considerable evidence exists that anticipations may be a problem in many choice-reaction time experiments.

2. Since the experimenter has total control over the sequence of signals presented, it is possible to use that schedule in an attempt to elicit information about what the subject is doing. The most commonly used schedule is a purely random one, but in some studies the stimuli are not presented equally often and in a few sequential dependencies are built into the schedule in order to affect locally the decision strategies employed by the subjects.

3. In addition to payoffs based upon the observed reaction times, there is clearly the possibility of introducing information feedback and payoffs based upon the accuracy of the responses. By varying the values of the payoffs for both response time and accuracy, the experimenter sets up different monetary conflicts between accuracy and speed. If people are able to alter their strategies to take advantage of this tradeoff—and they are—then we may exploit this technique to gain some information about what those strategies are.

4. The relation between the signals can be manipulated over experimental runs in order to study how that variable affects behavior. For example, one can use two pure tones of frequencies f and $f + \Delta f$, where the separation Δf is manipulated. Clearly, the dependence of reaction-time performance may very well vary with the value of f used and almost surely will depend upon the intensity of the two tones, which can vary from threshold to very loud.

5. As was true for simple reactions, there are many options for the signals—indeed, there are all the possible differences signals may exhibit beyond simple presence and absence. And there are many options for the response, although the most common continues to be finger presses of highly sensitive keys. For an empirical study of the use of different fingers and hands, see Heuer (1981a, b). What is new, and complicating, is the multiple ways in which the possible responses can be related to the possible signals. In most studies, aside from those that undertake to study the impact of different mappings between responses and signals, experimenters attempt to select a mapping that on intuitive grounds is as natural, compatible, and symmetric as possible. Of course, one can study directly the impact of stimulus-response compatibility on response time, and we will do so in

Section 10.2.3. In the two-choice situation, three closely related designs are the most common. In each there are two highly sensitive keys, and either the two forefingers are used, each being held over a key, or the subject's preferred forefinger rests on a well-defined spot between the two keys and is moved to the appropriate key, or the forefinger and middle finger of the preferred hand are placed over the two keys.

6.1.2   Response Measures

In any choice experiment there are at least two dependent measures—namely, the choices made and the times they take. One may, in addition, ask of the subject other things such as the confidence felt about the judgment. I shall focus primarily on the first two measures—to my mind the most natural ones. It will prove convenient to partition the story into a number of subpieces. In Sections 6.2 and 6.4 I discuss matters that do not entail much, if any, interaction between the two measures or between the measures on successive trials. In Section 6.5 the focus turns to the interaction between response times and errors—the so-called speed-accuracy tradeoff—that arises when the times are manipulated. Section 6.6 examines interactions of responses and their associated times with the events on preceding trials—sequential effects in the data. The following three chapters discuss a number of models that have been proposed to account for some of these as well as other phenomena. After that, in Chapter 10, attention turns to response times when more than two signals are to be identified.

There is, of course, some option in the exact measures of accuracy and time to be collected and reported. For the choices there is little debate (perhaps there should be) about what data to collect: one postulates the existence of a conditional probability, $P(r \mid s)$, of response r being made when signal s is presented. Of course, we must be sensitive to what aside from the current signal may affect this probability. For example, it may well depend upon some previous signals and responses. Much of the literature tacitly assumes otherwise and, ignoring any dependencies that may exist, relative frequencies of responding are used to estimate these simple conditional probabilities. Some of the data in Section 6.6 should lead to some concern about this practice.

Suppose the signals a, b and the responses A, B are in natural $1:1$ correspondence; then there are just two independent conditional probabilities since

$$P(A \mid a) + P(B \mid a) = 1 \quad \text{and} \quad P(A \mid b) + P(B \mid b) = 1.$$

We usually elect to use $P(A \mid a)$ and $P(A \mid b)$. The study of the behavior of these probabilities is the province of much of traditional psychophysics, a topic that is alive and well today in part because of the theory of signal detectability. This literature offers several possible summary measures of performance accuracy, the most famous of which is d'. We will go into this question more thoroughly in Sections 6.4 and 6.5.3.

For reaction times, a distribution of times can be developed for each of the four signal-response pairs and, unlike the choice probabilities, these are not logically constrained to be related in any particular way. Of course, these distributions may also depend upon something else, such as preceding signals and responses. Again, much of the literature implicitly assumes no such dependence; but as we shall see in Section 6.6, that assumption is highly optimistic. As with simple reaction times, the distributions can be presented in a variety of ways, but in practice little has been published about actual distributions or their hazard functions. For the most part, only mean reaction times have been reported, although in a few recent studies some other statistics, usually the variance, skew, and kurtosis (see Sections 1.3.4 and 1.4.5), have also been provided.

6.2 RELATIONS TO SIMPLE REACTION TIMES

6.2.1 *Means and Standard Deviations*

Perhaps the best established fact about choice reaction times is that, with everything else as similar as possible, these times are slower than the comparable simple ones by 100 to 150 msec, and they are usually, but not always, somewhat more variable. This has been known for a very long time and has been repeatedly demonstrated; I shall cite just two studies in which the relationship has been explored with some care. The first does not involve any feedback-payoff manipulation; the second does.

In his Experiment 4, Laming (1968) ran 20 subjects for 120 trials in each of five conditions that were organized in a Latin square design. The signals, white bars of width 0.50 in. and height 2.83 in. and 4.00 in., were presented singly in a tachistoscope and the subject had to identify each presentation as being either the longer or shorter stimulus. Signals were presented according to an equally likely random schedule. There were three general types of conditions. In the simple-reaction time design subjects were to respond as rapidly as possible to both signals. In one variant they used only their right forefinger and in a second only their left forefinger. In the choice design, they used the right forefinger response for one signal and the left for the other. And in the recognition design, the situation was as in the choice one except that one of the two responses was withheld. That is, they had to identify the signals and respond to just one of them. In a certain sense, the recognition design resembles a choice one in which withholding a response is itself a response. Table 6.1 presents the median reaction times and the median over subjects of the standard deviation of reaction times. The pattern of medians is typical: the simple reaction times of about 220 msec are normal for visual stimuli; the choice values are about 200 msec slower; and the recognition times are some 35 msec faster than the choice ones. The

TABLE 6.1. Response time data from Experiment 4 of Laming (1968)

Condition	Response time in msec	
	Median	Median standard deviation
Simple		
Right forefinger	228	87
Left forefinger	220	88
Choice	419	88
Recognition		
4 in.	384	81
2.83 in.	385	85

variability, which appears to be the same in all conditions, is not so typical. I will say more about it below.

Snodgrass, Luce, and Galanter (1967) ran three subjects in four conditions, including the three run by Laming plus a simple design in which just one of the signals was presented. The two simple cases are identified as simple-1 and simple-2, depending on the number of signals used. The warning and reaction signals were pure tones of 143 msec duration; the foreperiod was 2 sec. The warning signal was a 1100-Hz tone and the two reaction signals were 1000- and 1200-Hz tones, both of which were quite audible. Payoffs were used. They were defined relative to one of two time bands: the fast band ran from 100 to 200 msec following signal onset, and the slow one, from 200 to 300 msec. Responses prior to the band in force were fined 5¢, and those within each successive third of the band received rewards of 3¢, 2¢, and 1¢, respectively. In the choice and recognition designs, correct responses each received 1¢ and incorrect ones lost 5¢ each. At the completion of a trial, the subject was provided information feedback about the amounts won or lost. A total of from 210 to 240 observations were obtained in each combination of band and condition that was run (several possible combinations were omitted). The resulting data are shown in Figure 6.1. The pattern closely resembles that of the Laming experiment. Mean times to both simple conditions fall within the appropriate band and are virtually identical, whereas both the recognition and choice mean times either lie in the slow band or exceed 300 msec independent of which payoff band is used. Apparently, it was impossible for these subjects to identify the signals in less than 200 msec, and the payoff structure was such that to abandon accuracy completely would have been costly. The mean recognition data are from 75 to 100 msec slower and the choice ones are from 100 to 150 msec slower than simple reaction times.

The plot of standard deviations, shown in Figure 6.2, exhibits a similar pattern. These data differ appreciably from Laming's, which showed the same variability in all conditions. It is, perhaps, worth noting that his

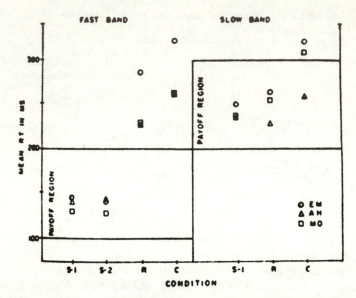

FIG. 6.1 MRT to pure tones of 1000 and 1200 Hz under four conditions: simple reactions to a single signal; simple reactions to either signal; recognition of and response to just one of the two signals; and choice reactions where the signal presented is to be identified. Two reinforcement bands, 100–200 msec and 200–300 msec, were used. Each data point is based on a sample of 240 reactions. [Figure 2 of Snodgrass et al. (1976); copyright 1967; reprinted by permission.]

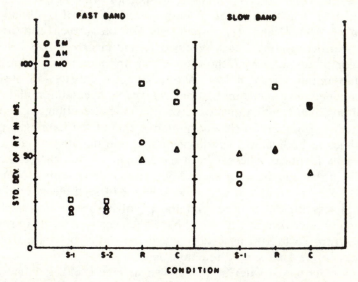

FIG. 6.2 Estimated standard deviations for the experiment discussed in Figure 6.1. [Figure 3 of Snodgrass et al. (1967); copyright 1967; reprinted by permission.]

variability for simple reaction times is rather large—the coefficient of variation (σ/μ) being about .40 as compared with about .17 in the Snodgrass et al. data—whereas the variability for the choice conditions is similar in the two experiments. There are a number of differences that might underlie this difference in results. The two most notable are the modality, auditory versus visual, and the use of feedback and payoffs in the one and not the other.

Although recognition data typically are somewhat faster than comparable choice reactions, this is not always true. For example, Smith (1978) (as reported in Smith, 1980) found the recognition times (248 msec) to be slower than the choice ones (217 and 220) in a study of vibrotactile stimuli to the index fingers with keypress responses by the stimulated fingers. This reversal of choice and recognition times will reappear as an issue in Section 6.2.2.

Turning to another phenomenon, we know (Section 2.4.1) that simple MRTs become slower as the proportion of catch trials is increased. Alegria (1978) examined their impact in a choice situation where, of course, we must ask both how the error rate and the MRT is affected. A fixed foreperiod of 700 msec was defined by a spot of light moving from left to right, and the signal interval began when it passed a vertical line. The signals were tones of 900 and 2650 Hz, and responses were key presses of the right index and middle fingers. The three conditions of catch trial frequency were 0%, 20%, and 77%. As can be seen in Table 6.2, the error rate was little affected by the proportion of catch trials or by whether the trial previous to the one being examined was a catch or a signal trial. Figure 6.3 shows that MRT is greatly affected by the nature of the preceding trial, and the effect cumulates over trials, but MRT seems little affected by the actual proportion of catch trials. These data are not consistent with the idea that subjects speed up by relaxing their criterion for what constitutes a signal and thereby increase the number of anticipatory responses. The reason for this conclusion is the fact that the error rate is, if anything, smaller following a signal trial than it is following a catch trial.

Section 2.4.3, on the impact of exponential foreperiods in simple reaction time, reported that MRT increases gradually with the actual foreperiod wait,

TABLE 6.2. Percent error as a function of type of preceding trial and proportion of catch trials (Alegria, 1978)

Proportion of catch trials	Preceding trial	
	Catch	Signal
.77	11.1	7.6
.20	9.5	5.2
0	—	7.7

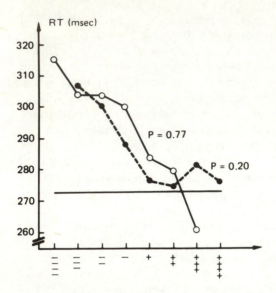

FIG. 6.3 MRT for choice reactions to two tone frequencies with ether 20% or 77% catch trials versus the length of the preceding run of catch trials (−) or of signal trials (+). The solid line, which is ordinary simple reactions, involved 44,800 observations per subject; the 20% condition involved 164,000 observations per subject; and the 77%, 234,000. There were six subjects. Depending upon the number n of conditioning events, these sample sizes are reduced by a factor of $1/2^n$. [Figure 1 of Alegria (1978); copyright 1978; reprinted by permission.]

an increase of from 50 to 100 msec over a range from half a second to 30 sec. For choice reaction times, Green, Smith, and von Gierke (1983) ran a closely comparable auditory experiment in which the signals differed in frequency. They found substantially the same pattern—a rise of about 30 msec in the range from 200 msec to 6 sec. Error responses are slightly faster than correct ones making the same response (see Section 6.4.3), but the curves exhibit basically the same shape. For waits less than 200 msec, the reaction time increases rather sharply as the wait decreases, rising some 20 msec over that interval. The impact of an exponentially distributed foreperiod, therefore, appears to be substantially the same in the choice and simple-reaction time paradigms.

6.2.2   *Donders' Subtraction Idea*

Donders (1868), in a highly seminal paper, proposed that the time to carry out a specific mental subprocess can be inferred by running pairs of experiments that are identical in all respects save that in the one the subject must use the particular process whereas in the other it is not used. He put the idea this way (Koster's 1969 translation):

> The idea occurred to me to interpose into the process of the physiological time some new components of mental action. If I investigated how much this would lengthen the physiological time, this would, I judged, reveal the time required for the interposed term. (Donders, 1969, p. 418)

He proceeded then to report data for several different classes of stimuli for both simple- and choice-reaction times (some for two-stimulus designs and much for a five-stimulus one), which he spoke of as, respectively, the *a*-and *b*-procedures. The difference between the two times he attributed to the difference in what is required—namely, both the identification of the signal presented and the selection of the correct response to make.

He next suggested that the times of the two subprocesses could be estimated separately by collecting times in the recognition or, as he called it, the *c*-procedure. As we have seen above, this entails a schedule of presentations like that used in the choice design, but instead of there being as many responses as there are stimuli, there is just one. It is made whenever one of the signals is presented and is withheld whenever the other(s) occur. Using vowels as stimuli and himself as subject, he reported the difference in times between the *c*- and *a*-procedures was 36 msec, which he took to be an estimate of the recognition time, and the $b-c$ difference was 47 msec, an estimate of the time to effect the choice between responses. The comparable numbers for the Laming data are 161 and 34 msec and for the Snodgrass et al. data they are 110 and 40 msec.

Data in which choices are faster than recognitions, such as Smith (1978), should be impossible in Donders' framework. They may result from subjects using different criteria for responding in the two procedures.

Indeed, Donders expressed one concern over the *c*-procedure:

> [Other people] give the response when they ought to have remained silent. And if this happens only once, the whole series must be rejected: for, how can we be certain that when they had to make the response and did make it, they had properly waited until they were sure to have discriminated? . . . For that reason I attach much value to the result of the three series mentioned above and obtained for myself as a subject, utilizing the three methods described for each series, in which the experiments turned out to be faultless. (Donders, 1969, p. 242)

Although the subtraction method was very actively pursued during the last quarter of the 19th century and today is often used with relatively little attention given to its theoretical basis (e.g., Posner, 1978), it has not found favor in this century among those who study response times as a speciality. The criticisms have been of four types:

First is the one mentioned by Donders himself—namely, that the recognition method may not, in fact, induce the subjects always to wait until the signal actually has been identified. (This may be a difficulty for the other two methods, as well.) His proposed method of eliminating those runs in which errors occur is not fully satisfactory because, as we noted in Sections 2.2.5 and 2.2.6, it is highly subject to the vagaries of small sample statistics. As we shall see below in Section 6.6.5, there is evidence from choice designs that anticipations also occur when the time pressure is sufficiently great. This problem can probably be greatly reduced by using a random (exponential) foreperiod, as in the simple-reaction-time design (see Green et al., 1983). The reason that this should work better than catch trials is the greater opportunity it provides the lax criterion to evidence itself since each trial affords an opportunity to anticipate. Working against it is the fact that many foreperiods are relatively brief.

The second concern, which was more in evidence in the 1970s than earlier, centers on the assumption of a purely serial process in which all of the times of the separate stages simply add. As we know from Chapter 3, this assumption has not been clearly established for the decision latency and the residue. Sternberg (1969a, b), in his classic study on the method of additive factors, suggested a method for approaching the questions of whether the times associated with the several stages are additive, provided that one has empirical procedures for affecting the stages individually. A special case of the method was discussed in Section 3.3.4, and it will be discussed more fully in Section 12.4. This means that we have methods, perhaps not yet as perfected as we would like, to investigate empirically the truth of this criticism.

The third criticism, which is the least easy to deal with, was the one that turned the tide against the method at the turn of the century. It calls into question the assumption of "pure insertion"—namely, that it is possible to add a stage of mental processing without in any way affecting the remaining stages. Sternberg (1969b, p. 422) describes the attack in this way.

> [I]ntrospective reports put into question the assumption of pure insertion, by suggesting that when the task was changed to insert a stage, other stages might also be altered. (For example, it was felt that changes in stimulus-processing requirements might also alter a response-organization stage.) If so, the difference between RTs could not be identified as the duration of the inserted stage. Because of these difficulties, Külpe, among others, urged caution in the interpretation of results from the subtraction method (1895, Secs. 69, 70). But it appears that no tests other than introspection were proposed for distinguishing valid from invalid applications of the method.
>
> A stronger stand was taken in later secondary sources. For example, in a section on the "discarding of the subtraction method" in his *Experimental Psychology* (1938, p. 309), R. S. Woodworth queried "[Since] we cannot break up the reaction into successive acts and obtain the time of each act, of what use is the reaction-time?" And, more recently, D. M. Johnson said in his *Psychology of Thought and Judgment* (1955, p. 5), "The reaction-time experiment suggests a method for the analysis of mental processes which turned out to be unworkable."

As Donders seemed unaware of the problem and as introspection is not a wholly convincing argument, an example of the difficulty is in order. Suppose that the decision latencies of simple reaction times are as was described in Section 4.4—namely, a race between change and level detectors, where a level detector is nothing more than the recognition process being put to another use. If in a recognition or choice situation the identification mechanism is no longer available to serve as a level detector because it is being used to identify which signal has been presented, then the insertion of the identification task necessarily alters the detection mechanism, changing it from a race to the use of just the change detector. This being so means that the detection of signal onset, particularly of a weak signal, is somewhat slower and more variable than it would have been if the same mechanisms for detection were used as in simple reaction time, and so the recognition times will be somewhat overestimated.

The idea of stages of processing is very much alive today, as we shall see in Part III, but very few are willing to bank on the idea of pure insertion. It is not to be ruled out a priori, but anyone proposing it is under considerable obligation to explain why the other stages will be unaffected by the insertion.

The fourth criticism, first pointed out by Cattell (1886b), is that the c-reaction involves more than pure identification since the subject must also decide either to respond or to withhold the response, which in a sense is just as much of a choice as selecting one of two positive responses. Wundt suggested a d-procedure in which the subject withholds the response until the signal is identified, but in fact makes the same response to every signal. This procedure caused difficulty for most subjects and has rarely been used. It is possible, although not necessary, to interpret Smith's slow c-reactions as direct evidence favoring Cattell's view.

For additional discussion of these matters see Welford (1980b), who summarized the matter as follows (p. 107):

> The evidence suggests that Donders' approach was correct in that, except under very highly compatible or familiar conditions, the c-reaction involves less choice of response than the b-reactions, but was wrong in assuming that all choice of response was eliminated. The difference between b- and c-reactions will therefore underestimate the time taken by choice, and the difference between c- and a-reactions will overestimate the time taken to identify signals.

6.2.3 Subtraction with Independence

An obvious assumption to add to Donders' additivity and pure insertion is statistical independence of the times for the several stages. This, it will be recalled, was the basic assumption of Chapter 3. The main consequence of adding this is the prediction that not only will the mean times add, but so will all of the cumulants (Section 1.4.5).

Taylor (1966) applied these ideas to the following design. Donders conditions b and c were coupled with two modified conditions. Using the same stimulus presentation schedule as in b and c, condition b' involves substituting for one of the signals ordinary catch trials, and the subject is required to make the discriminative response. In condition c', the presentation is as in b', but only a single response is required on signal trials. The model assumes a total of four stages: signal detection, signal identification, response selection, and response execution. The first and last are common to

TABLE 6.3. Presence of stages in Taylor (1966) design (see text for description of conditions)

	Stage	
Condition	Signal identification	Response selection
b	Yes	Yes
c	Yes	No
b'	No	Yes
c'	No	No

all four conditions, and so they can be ignored. The second and third are assumed to be invoked as they are needed, and the pattern assumed is shown in Table 6.3. Assuming that this is correct, then we see that the difference between *b* and *c'* is both stages, that between *c* and *c'* is just the signal identification stage, and that between *b'* and *c'* is just the response selection stage. So if we let $\mathbf{T}(i)$ denote the response time observed in condition *i*, the following equation embodies the additivity and pure insertion assumptions

$$\mathbf{T}(b) - \mathbf{T}(c') = \mathbf{T}(c) - \mathbf{T}(c') + \mathbf{T}(b') - \mathbf{T}(c'),$$

which is equivalent to

$$\mathbf{T}(b) - \mathbf{T}(c) - \mathbf{T}(b') + \mathbf{T}(c') = 0.$$

Taylor tested this null hypothesis in an experiment in which the stimuli were red and green disks, the warning signal was a 500-Hz tone, and foreperiods of 800, 1000, 1300, and 1500 msec were equally likely. The sample size in each condition was the 32 responses of the preferred hand of each of eight subjects, for a total of 256 per condition. He tested the additivity prediction for the mean, variance, and third cumulant, and none rejected the null hypothesis.

Were this to be repeated today, one would probably use the Fast Fourier Transform to verify the additivity of the entire cumulative generating function; however, I am not sure what statistical test one should employ in that case.

As was pointed out in Section 3.2.3, if the component inserted is exponential with time constant λ and the density is *f* with it in and *g* without it, then

$$\lambda = g(t)/[G(t) - F(t)].$$

So an easy test of the joint hypothesis of pure insertion, independence, and the insertion of an exponential stage is that the right side of the above expression be independent of *t*. Ashby and Townsend (1980) examined this for data reported by Townsend and Roos (1973) on a memory search procedure of the type discussed in Section 11.1, and to a surprising degree constancy was found. Thus, while there are ample a priori reasons to doubt all three assumptions, an unlikely consequence of them was sustained in one data set. This suggests that additional, more detailed work should be carried out on Donders' model.

6.2.4 Varying Signal Intensity

The effect of intensity on simple reaction times is simple: both MRT and VRT decrease systematically as signal intensity is increased (Sections 2.3.1 and 2.3.2), and for audition but not vision an interaction exists between signal intensity and response criterion (Section 2.5.2). Neither of these statements appears to be true for choice reaction times, as was made evident by Nissen (1977) in a careful summary of the results to that point. The independence for visual stimuli was found. For example, Pachella and Fisher (1969) varied the intensity and linear spacing of 10 lights and imposed a deadline to control response criterion, and did not find evidence for an interaction of intensity with the deadline, although there was one between intensity and spacing. Posner (1978) varied the intensity of visual signals, and using conditions of mixed and blocked intensities he found no interaction. However, since no interaction was found in simple reactions for visual stimuli, the question of what would happen with auditory signals was not obvious. In 1977 the evidence was skimpy.

This question was taken up by van der Molen, Keuss, and Orlebeke in a series of papers. In 1979 van der Molen and Keuss published a study in which the stimuli were 250 msec tones of 1000 Hz and 3000 Hz with intensities ranging from 70 to 105 dB. There were several foreperiod conditions, which I will not go into except to note that the foreperiods were of the order of a few seconds. Both simple and choice reactions were obtained. The major finding, which earlier had been suggested in the data of Keuss (1972) and Keuss and Orlebeke (1977), was that for the choice condition the MRT is a U-shaped function of intensity. The simple reactions were decreasing, as is usual. This result makes clear that the impact of intensity in the choice context is by no means as simple as it is for simple reactions, where it can be interpreted as simply affecting the rate at which information about the signal accumulates. They raised the possibility that a primary effect of intensity is in the response selection stage of the process rather than just in the accumulation process. That was not a certain conclusion because the error rate had not remained constant as intensity was altered. Additional U-shaped data were exhibited by van der Molen and Orlebeke (1980).

To demonstrate more clearly the role of response selection, van der Molen and Keuss (1981) adapted a procedure introduced by J. R. Simon (1969; Simon, Acosta, & Mewaldt, 1975; Simon, Acosta, Mewaldt, &

Speidel, 1976). The signals were as before with a range of 50 to 110 dB. They were presented monaurally through ear phones, and responses were key presses with the two hands corresponding to signal frequency. Lights and digits presented just before the beginning of the foreperiod provided additional information about what was to be presented. The digit code was the following: 000 indicated to the subject that the signal was equally likely to be presented to either ear, 001 that it would go to the right ear, and 100 that it would go to the left ear. One colored light indicated that the ear receiving the signal and its frequency would be perfectly correlated, whereas the other color indicated no correlation of location and frequency. Note that the correct response could be either ipsilateral or contralateral to the ear to which the signal was presented. The data showed that responding was fast and a monotonic decreasing function of intensity when the correlated presentation was used and the response was ipsilateral. In any contralateral or uncorrelated ipsilateral condition, MRT was slower and U-shaped. They concluded that these results support the hypothesis that a major impact of intensity in choice reactions is on the response selection stage.

In still another study, Keuss and van der Molen (1982) varied the foreperiod—either a fixed one of 2 sec or a variable one of 20, 25, 30, 35, or 40 sec—and whether the subject had preknowledge of the intensity of the presentation. The effect of preknowledge was to reduce MRT by about 10 msec. More startling was the fact that both simple and choice MRTs decreased with intensity except for the briefer 2-sec foreperiod, where again it was found to be U-shaped. Moreover, the error rate was far larger in this case than in the others. They seemed to conclude that the foreperiod duration was the important factor, although it was completely confounded with constant versus variable foreperiod. Assuming that it is the duration, they claimed this to be consistent with the idea of intensity affecting the response selection process. I do not find it as compelling as the earlier studies.

6.3   A CONCEPTUAL SCHEME FOR TRADEOFFS

6.3.1   Types of Parameters

A major theoretical feature of cognitive psychology is its attempt to distinguish both theoretically and experimentally between two classes of variables and mechanisms that underlie behavior. The one class consists of those experimental manipulations that directly affect behavior through mechanisms that are independent of the subjects' motivations. For example, most psychologists and physiologists believe that the neural pulse patterns that arise in the peripheral nervous system, immediately after the sensory transducer converts the physical stimuli into these patterns, are quite independent of what the subject will ultimately do with that information. This means that these representations of the signal are independent of the type of experiment—reaction time, magnitude estimation, discrimination—, of the questions we pose to the subject, and of the information feedback and payoffs we provide. Such mechanisms are often called *sensory* or *perceptual* ones, and the free parameters that arise in models of the mechanism are called *sensory parameters*. The experimental variables that activate such mechanisms have no agreed upon name. In one unpublished manuscript, Ollman (1975) referred to them as "display variables," but in a later paper (1977) he changed it to "task variables." I shall use a more explicit version of his first term, *sensory display variables*.

The other type of mechanism is the decision process that, in the light of the experimental task posed, the subject brings to bear on the sensory information. These are mechanisms that have variously been called control, decision, motivation, or strategy mechanisms. Ollman refers in both papers to the experimental variables that are thought to affect these mechanisms directly as strategy variables. I shall follow the terminology of *decision mechanism*, *decision parameters*, and *decision strategy variables*. The latter include a whole range of things having to do with experimental procedure: the task—whether it is detection, absolute identification, item recognition, and so on—the details of the presentation schedule of the signals, the payoffs that are used to affect both the tradeoff of errors and to manipulate response times, and various instructions aimed at affecting the tradeoffs established among various aspects of the situation.

It should be realized that there is a class of motivational variables, of which attention is a prime example, that I shall not attempt to deal with in a systematic fashion. Often, attentional issues lie not far from the surface in our attempts to understand many experiments, and they certainly relate to the capacity considerations of Chapters 11 and 12. Moreover, they are a major concern of many psychologists (Kahneman, 1973). Some believe that such variables affect the sensory mechanism, which if true only complicates the story to be outlined.

To the degree that we are accurate in classifying sensory display and decision strategy variables, the former affect the sensory parameters and the latter the decision parameters. But a major asymmetry is thought to exist. Because the decision parameters are under the subject's control, they *may* be affected by sensory display variables as well as by decision strategy ones; whereas, it is assumed that the sensory parameters are not affected by the decision strategy variables. What makes the study of even the simplest sensory or perceptual processes tricky, and so interesting, is the fact that we can never see the impact of the sensory display variables on the sensory mechanism free from their impact on the decision parameters. Even if we hold constant all of the decision strategy variables that are known to affect the decision mechanism, but not the sensory ones, we cannot be sure that the decision parameters are constant. The subject may make changes in these parameters as a joint function of the sensory display and decision strategy variables.

One major issue of the field centers on how to decide whether a particular experimental design has been successful in controlling the decision parameters as intended. This is a very subtle matter, one that entails a careful interplay of theoretical ideas and experimental variations. During the late 1960s and throughout the 1970s this issue was confronted explicitly as it had never been before, and out of this developed considerable sensitivity to the so-called speed-accuracy tradeoff.

In Section 6.3.2 I shall try to formulate this general conceptual framework as clearly as I know how, and various special cases of it will arise in the particular models examined in Chapters 7–10.

6.3.2   Formal Statement

Assuming the distinction just made between sensory and decision mechanisms is real, we may formulate the general situation in quite general mathematical terms. Each experimental trial can be thought of as confronting the subject with a particular environment. This consists not only of the experimentally manipulated stimulus presented on that trial, but the surrounding context, the task confronting the subject, the reward structure of the situation, and the previous history of stimuli and responses. We can think of this environment as described by a vector of variables denoted by $\vec{E}$. We may partition this into a subvector $\vec{S}$ of sensory display variables and a subvector $\vec{D}$ of decision strategy variables: $\vec{E} = (\vec{S}, \vec{D})$. The observable information obtained from the trial are two random variables, the response $\mathbf{r}$ and some measure $\mathbf{T}$ of time of occurrence. We assume that $(\mathbf{r}, \mathbf{T})$ is governed by a joint probability density function that is conditioned by the environmental vector, and it is denoted

$$f(r, t \mid \vec{E}) = \Pr(\mathbf{r} = r \text{ and } \mathbf{T} = t \mid \vec{E}). \tag{6.1}$$

In order to estimate f from data, it is essential that we be able to repeat the environment on a number of trials, and so be able to use the empirical histograms as a way to estimate f. Obviously, this is not possible if $\vec{E}$ really includes all past stimuli and responses, and so in practice we truncate the amount of the past included in our definition of $\vec{E}$. For more on that, see Section 6.6.

The theoretical structure postulates the existence of a sensory mechanism with a vector $\vec{\sigma} = (\sigma_1, \ldots, \sigma_l)$ of sensory parameters and a decision mechanism with a vector $\vec{\delta} = (\delta_1, \ldots, \delta_m)$ of decision parameters. In general, $\vec{\sigma}$ and $\vec{\delta}$ should be thought of as random vectors; that is, their components are random variables and they have a joint distribution that is conditional on $\vec{E}$. If $\vec{\sigma}$ and $\vec{\delta}$ are numerical l- and m-tuples, respectively, we denote the joint density function of $\vec{\sigma}$ and $\vec{\delta}$ by

$$\Phi(\sigma, \delta \mid \vec{E}) = \Pr(\vec{\sigma} = \vec{\sigma} \ \& \ \vec{\delta} = \vec{\delta} \mid \vec{E}). \tag{6.2}$$

When we have no reason to distinguish between the two types of parameters, we simply write $\vec{\epsilon} = (\vec{\sigma}, \vec{\delta})$. For each set of parameter values, it is assumed that the sensory and decision processes relate the $(\mathbf{r}, \mathbf{T})$ pair probabilistically to the parameters and to them alone. In particular, it is assumed that $(\mathbf{r}, \mathbf{T})$ has no direct connection to $\vec{E}$ except as it is mediated through the parameters. We denote the joint density function of $(\mathbf{r}, \mathbf{T})$ conditional on $\vec{\epsilon}$ by

$$\Psi(r, t \mid \vec{\epsilon}) = \Pr(\mathbf{r} = r \ \& \ \mathbf{T} = t \mid \vec{\epsilon}). \tag{6.3}$$

So Ψ is the theory of how the sensory and decision processes jointly convert a particular set of parameter values into the $(\mathbf{r}, \mathbf{T})$ pair. By the law of total probability applied to the conditional probabilities of Eqs. 6.2 and 6.3, we obtain from Eq. 6.1

$$f(r, t \mid \vec{E}) = \int \Psi(r, t \mid \vec{\epsilon}) \Phi(\vec{\epsilon} \mid \vec{E}) \, d\vec{\epsilon}, \tag{6.4}$$

where the integral is to be interpreted as just that in the case of continuous parameters and as a sum in the case of discrete ones. We will always assume that the densities are of such a character that the integral exists in some usual sense (Riemann or Lebesgue).

A special case of considerable interest is where $\mathbf{r}$ and $\mathbf{T}$ are independent random variables for each set of parameters; that is, if $P(r \mid \vec{\epsilon})$ and $f(t \mid \vec{\epsilon})$ denote the marginal distributions of Ψ,

$$\Psi(r, t \mid \vec{\epsilon}) = P(r \mid \vec{\epsilon}) f(t \mid \vec{\epsilon}). \tag{6.5}$$

We speak of this as *local* (or conditional) *independence*. Observe that it does *not* in general entail that $f(r, t \mid \vec{E})$ also be expressed as the product of its marginals. [It is perhaps worth noting that conditional independence is the keystone of the method of latent structure analysis sometimes used in sociology (Lazarsfeld, 1954)]. Among the models we shall discuss in Chapters 7 to 9, local independence holds for the fast guess and counting models, but not for the random walk or timing models. One happy feature of local independence is the ease with which the marginal distributions are calculated.

Theorem 6.1. *If Eqs. 6.4 and 6.5 hold, then*

$$P(r \mid \vec{E}) = _{\text{DEF}} \int f(r, t \mid \vec{E}) \, dt = \int P(r \mid \vec{\epsilon}) \Phi(\vec{\epsilon} \mid \vec{E}) \, d\vec{\epsilon}, \tag{6.6}$$

$$f(t \mid \vec{E}) = _{\text{DEF}} \sum_r f(r, t \mid \vec{E}) = \int f(t \mid \vec{\epsilon}) \Phi(\vec{\epsilon} \mid \vec{E}) \, d\vec{\epsilon}. \tag{6.7}$$

The easy proof is left to the reader.

6.3.3 An Example: The Fast-Guess Model

A specific, simple example should help fix these ideas and those to follow (especially Section 6.5). I shall use a version of the fast-guess model of Ollman (1966) and Yellott (1967, 1971), which will be studied more fully in

Section 7.4. Suppose that prior to the presentation of the signal the subject opts to behave in one of two quite distinct ways. One is to make a simple reaction to signal onset without waiting long enough to gain any idea as to which signal was presented. We assume that the simple-reaction-time density to both signals is $g_0(t)$ and, quite independent of that, response r is selected with probability β_r, $r = A, B$, where $\beta_A + \beta_B = 1$. The other option is to wait until the information is extracted from the signal and to respond according to that evidence. This time is assumed to have density $g_1(t)$ for both signals and that, independent of the time taken, the conditional probability of response r to signal s is P_{sr}, where $s = a, b$, $r = A, B$, $P_{sA} + P_{sB} = 1$. Note that we have built in local independence of $\mathbf{r}$ and $\mathbf{T}$ for each of the two states, 0 representing fast guesses (simple reactions) and 1 the informed responses. Denote by ρ the probability that the subject opts for the informed state. In arriving at the general form for $f(r, t \mid \vec{E})$, let us suppress all notation for $\vec{E}$ save for the signal presented, s. From Eqs. 6.4 and 6.5 we obtain

$$f(r, t \mid s) = \rho g_1(t) P_{sr} + (1-\rho) g_0(t) \beta_r. \tag{6.8}$$

Observe that this model has two decision parameters—namely, ρ and β_A (recall, $\beta_B = 1 - \beta_A$)—, two sensory functions—g_0 and g_1—, and two discrimination (sensory) parameters—P_{sA}, $s = a, b$ (recall, $P_{sB} = 1 - P_{sA}$). For some purposes we can reduce the functions to their means, ν_0 and ν_1. Implicitly, I assume $\nu_0 < \nu_1$ (see Section 6.2.1).

Either by direct computation from Eq. 6.8 or by using Eqs. 6.6 and 6.7, we obtain for the marginals

$$f(t \mid s) = \rho g_1(t) + (1-\rho) g_0(t), \tag{6.9}$$

$$P(r \mid s) = \rho P_{sr} + (1-\rho) \beta_r. \tag{6.10}$$

Note that $f(t \mid s)$ is actually independent of s. From Eq. 6.9 we can compute the overall expected reaction time to the presentation of a particular signal s:

$$E(\mathbf{T} \mid s) = \int t f(t \mid s) \, dt = \rho \nu_1 + (1-\rho) \nu_0. \tag{6.11}$$

For some purposes it is useful to compute $E(\mathbf{T})$ for each (s, r) pair separately—that is, the mean of $f(t \mid r, s) = f(t, r \mid s) / P(r)$, which from Eq. 6.8 we see is

$$E(\mathbf{T} \mid s, r) = [\rho \nu_1 P_{sr} + (1-\rho) \nu_0 \beta_r] / P(r \mid s), \tag{6.12}$$

where $P(r \mid s)$ is given by Eq. 6.10.

A few words may be appropriate at this point about how one attempts to confront such a model with data. One immediately obvious problem is that the data provide us with estimates of $f(r, t \mid \vec{E})$ whereas the theory as stated in Eq. 6.8 has a number of parameters that are not explicit functions of $\vec{E}$.

Of course, from the interpretation of the model the parameters ρ and β_r belong to the decision process and the others belong to the sensory process. Thus, we do not anticipate any dependence of the latter parameters on manipulations of the decision strategy, but the former may depend upon any aspect of $\vec{E}$. It is quite typical of models throughout psychology—not just those for response times—that no explicit account is offered for the dependence of the parameters on environments. This is a fact and limitation, not a virtue, of our theorizing.

Because we cannot compute the parameters from knowing $\vec{E}$, in practice we estimate them in some fashion from the data and then attempt to evaluate how well the model accounts for those data. For example, this will be done for the fast guess model in Section 7.4. If the fit is reasonably satisfactory and if enough data have been collected, which often is not the case, we can then study empirically how the parameters vary with the different experimental manipulations. Sometimes quite regular relations arise that can be approximated by some mathematical functions and that are then used in later applications of the model to data.

6.3.4 Discrimination of Color by Pigeons

In some data, however, it is reasonably clear without any parameter estimation that something like fast guesses are involved because the two distributions g_0 and g_1 are unimodal and are so separated that the overall response-time distribution is bimodal. The clearest example of this that I know is not with human data, but with pigeons. During the training phase, Blough (1978) reinforced the birds for responding to the onset of a 582-nm light (S^+) and the onset of the signal was delayed a random amount whenever a response (peck) was made at a time when the light was not on. This is a discrimination, not a choice design. In the test phase, all lights from 575- to 589-nm in 1-nm steps were presented equally often except for 582 nm, which was three times more frequent than the others and was reinforced on one third of its occurrences. Response probability was a decreasing function of the deviation from 582 and it was approximately the same decay on both sides. To keep the figure from being too complex, only the data for the smaller wave lengths are shown. The pattern of response times, shown for one bird in Figure 6.4 is strikingly bimodal. The earlier mode, the unshaded region of these distributions, clearly does not differ from signal to signal in frequency of occurrence, location in time, or general shape. Since that mode had a central tendency of about 170 msec, I suspect they were simple reaction times to signal onset—that is, fast guesses. However, I am not aware of any simple reaction time data for pigeons with which to compare that number. The second mode, the shaded region, is clearly signal dependent in that the number of responses of this type decreases as the signal deviates from the reinforced S^+ (582 nm); however, its location did not seem to change and its central tendency was about 350 msec. These data,

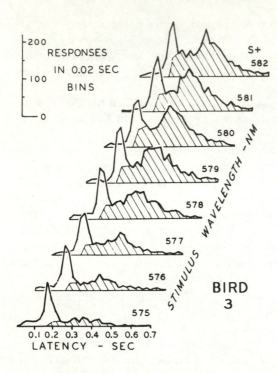

FIG. 6.4 Histograms of response times of a pigeon to signal lights of several frequencies, of which the one marked S^+ was reinforced during training and partially reinforced during testing. The sample size for each distribution was 1760. Note the striking bimodality of the histograms and the relative independence of the first mode as the wavelength of the light varies. [Figure 4 of Blough (1978); copyright 1978; reprinted by permission.]

which are completely consistent with the fast-guess model, suggest that pigeons's reactions to visual signals are similar to those of people; the mean of 170 msec for simple reactions may be a trifle faster, but the additional delay of about 180 msec for accurate responding is, as we saw in Section 6.2.1, very similar to people.

6.4 DISCRIMINABILITY AND ACCURACY

6.4.1 *Varying the Response Criterion: Various ROC Curves*

By now it is a commonplace that either by varying the relative frequency of *a* to *b*, or by differential payoffs for the four possible signal-response pairs, or just by instructing the subject to favor *A* or *B*, one can cause $P(A \mid a)$ and $P(A \mid b)$ to vary all the way from both conditional probabilities being 0 to both being 1—that is, from no *A* responses at all to all *A* responses. Note that nothing about the stimulating conditions, and so presumably nothing about the sensory mechanism, is altered. Just the presentation probability or the payoffs or the instructions are varied. Moreover, the locus of these pairs of points is highly regular, appearing to form a convex function when $P(A \mid a)$ is plotted against $P(A \mid b)$—that is, an increasing function with a decreasing slope. Typical data are shown in Figure 6.5. Such functions are called *ROC curves*, the term stemming from the engineering phrase "receiver operating characteristic." Detailed discussions of these curves, of data, and of mathematical models to account for them can be found in Green and Swets (1966, 1974) and Egan (1975). In the case of Yes-No detection in which $A = Y$, $B = N$, $a = s =$ signal, and $b = n =$ noise, we speak of $P(A \mid s)$ as a "hit," $P(N \mid s)$ as a "miss," $P(Y \mid n)$ as a "false alarm," and $P(N \mid n)$ as a "correct rejection."

Let us work out the ROC for the fast-guess model, which we do by eliminating β_A from Eq. 6.10, where $s = a, b$, $r = A$:

$$P(A \mid a) = P(A \mid b) + \rho(P_{aA} - P_{bA}),$$

which is simply a straight line with slope 1. Other models yield different, usually curved, ROCs. For example, the standard model of the theory of signal detectability assumes that each stimulus is internally represented as a Gaussian random variable and the continuum of possible values is partitioned by a cut—called the response criterion—and the subject responds according to whether the observation is larger or smaller than the criterion. This model is sketched in Figure 6.5.

For some time it had been noted that as the criterion was varied, subjects exhibited a tendency to respond faster when the internal representation of the signal was far from the criterion, as judged by confidence ratings, and slower when it was close to the criterion (Emmerich, Gray, Watson, & Tanis, 1972; Fernberger, Glass, Hoffman, & Willig, 1934; Festinger, 1943a, b; Gescheider, Wright, Weber, Kirchner, & Milligan, 1969; Koppell, 1976; Pike, 1973; and Pike & Ryder, 1973). Pike and Ryder (1973) refer to the assumption that $E(T) = f(|x - c|)$, where c is the criterion, as the *latency function hypothesis*. Festinger (1943a, b), Garrett (1922), and Johnson (1939) all reported no evidence that the relation between confidence and reaction time is affected by instructions emphasizing either speed or accu-

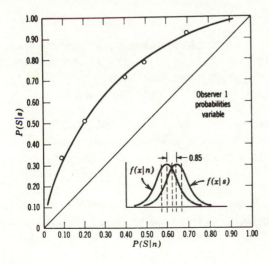

FIG. 6.5 Example of auditory ROC data obtained under fixed signal conditions with varied payoffs. The theoretical curve arises from Gaussian decision variables postulated in the theory of signal detectability. The inset indicates how the ROC is generated by varying the response criterion. [Figure 4.1 of Green and Swets (1966); copyright 1966; reprinted by permission.]

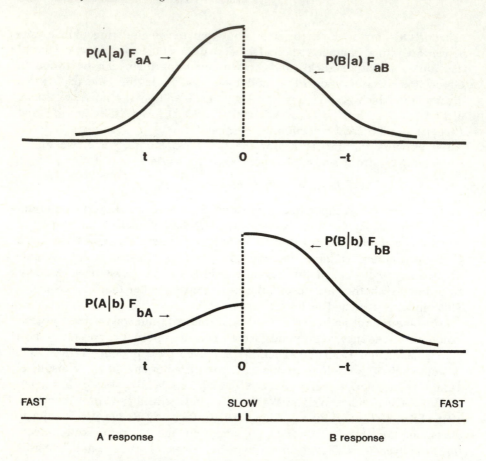

FIG. 6.6 Schematic of how latency ROC curves are constructed; see text for explanation.

racy of responding (Section 6.5). As a result confidence and reaction time were assumed to be very closely related. Recently, however, Vickers and Packer (1981) carried out a careful study using line length discriminations and found a decided difference as a function of instruction. The reason for this difference in results is uncertain.

The earlier apparent relation between confidence and reaction time together with the fact that ROC curves can be quite accurately inferred from confidence judgments led to the idea of trying to infer the ROC curve from response-time data. One method was proposed by Carterette, Friedman, and Cosmides (1965) and another, closely related, one by Norman and Wickelgren (1969), which is illustrated in Figure 6.6. The idea is this: For each signal, place the two subdistributions, weighted by their probabilities of occurring, back to back, with the A response on the left. From these artificial densities we generate the ROC as follows: Align them at the point of transition from A responses to B responses and vary the criterion. To be more explicit, the locus of points (x, y) is generated as follows. For $x \leq P(A \mid a)$, let t be such that

$$F(t \mid a, A)P(A \mid a) = x$$

and set

$$y = F(t \mid b, A)P(A \mid b).$$

For $x > P(A \mid a)$, let t be such that

$$[1 - F(t \mid a, B)]P(B \mid a) = x - P(A \mid a)$$

and set

$$y = [1 - F(t \mid b, B)]P(B \mid b) + P(A \mid b).$$

This locus of points has been called both the *latency operating characteristic*, abbreviated LOC, and the RT-ROC. It is important to note that Lappin and Disch (1972a, b and 1973) used the term LOC for a speed-accuracy measure that others call the conditional accuracy function (see Section 6.5.4).

The construction we have just outlined is really quite arbitrary; it does not stem from any particular theoretical view about what the subject is doing. The major motive for computing it is the intuition that reaction time serves as a proxy for the subject's confidence in the response made. According to Gescheider et al. (1969) in a model with a response criterion, such as that of the theory of signal detectability, this function has to do with how far the evidence about the stimulus is from the response criterion.

The only serious theoretical study of the relation between the ROC and RT-ROC is Thomas and Myers (1972). The results, which are rather complicated and will not be reported very fully here, were developed for both discrete and continuous signal detection models; that is, there is an internally observed random variable $\mathbf{X}_s$ for signal s, which is either discrete or continuous and has density function $f(x \mid s)$, and there is a response criterion β such that the response is A when $\mathbf{X}_s > \beta$ and B when $\mathbf{X}_s < \beta$. They assumed that the latency is a decreasing function of $|\mathbf{X}_s - \beta|$. They considered the somewhat special case where the distributions are simply a shift family; that is, there is a constant k_{ab} such that for all x, $f(t \mid a) = f(t - k_{ab} \mid b)$, and that the slope of the ROC curve is decreasing (which they showed is equivalent to $-d^2 \log f(x \mid s)/dx^2 \geq 0$). Under these assumptions, they proved that the RT-ROC lies below the ROC except, of course, at the point $(P(A \mid a), P(A \mid b))$, which, by construction, they have in common.

Emmerich et al. (1972) reported a detection study of a 400-Hz tone in noise in which detection responses and confidence judgments were made; in addition, without the subjects being aware of it, response times were recorded. The confidence and RT-ROCs are shown in Figure 6.7. Note that these are not plots of $P(A \mid a)$ versus $P(A \mid b)$, but of the corresponding Gaussian z-scores {i.e., $z(r \mid s)$ is defined by $P(r \mid s) = \Phi[z(r \mid s)]$, where Φ is the unit Gaussian distribution}, which results in straightline ROCs if the

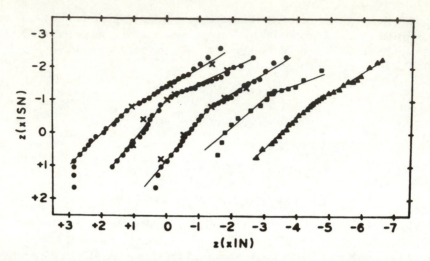

FIG. 6.7 ROC data of several types presented in z-score coordinates (displaced along the abscissa for clarity), in which case the Gaussian ROCs are straight lines. The three curves on the left are latency ROCs, and the two on the right are conventional ones obtained from choice probabilities, with the squares data from Emmerich (1968) and the triangles from Watson et al. (1964). [Figure 4 of Emmerich et al. (1972); copyright 1972; reprinted by permission.]

underlying distributions are Gaussian. Ordinary Yes-No and confidence ROCs are usually rather closely fit by straight lines in z-score coordinates, but as can be seen the RT-ROCs exhibit a rather distinct elbow. This result is typical of all that have been reported: Moss, Meyers, and Filmore (1970) on same-difference judgments of two tones; Norman and Wickelgren (1969) using the first of memorized digit pairs as the stimuli; and Yager and Duncan (1971) using a generalization task with gold fish. The conclusion drawn by Emmerich et al. (1972, p. 72) was:

> Thus latency-based ROCs should probably not be viewed as a prime source of information about sensory processing alone. Response latencies are known to be influenced by many factors, and this is undoubtedly also the case for latency-based ROCs. Yager and Duncan (1971) reach a similar conclusion . . . .

Additional cause for skepticism is provided by Blough's (1978) study of wavelength discrimination by pigeons, which was discussed previously in Section 6.3.4. Using the response-time distributions, RT-ROC curves were developed with the result in Figure 6.8. These do not look much like the typical ROC curves. For example, from other pigeon data in which rate of responding was observed, one gets the more typical data shown in Figure 6.9. The reason for the linear relations seen in Figure 6.8 is the bimodal character of the response-time distributions seen in Figure 6.4 (Section 6.3.4).

6.4.2 Varying the Discriminability of the Signals

The most obvious effect of altering the separation between two signals that differ on just one dimension—for example, intensity of lights—is to alter the probability of correctly identifying them. This information was traditionally presented in the form of the *psychometric function*: holding signal *b* fixed and varying *a*, it is the plot of $P(A \mid a)$ as a function of the signal separation,

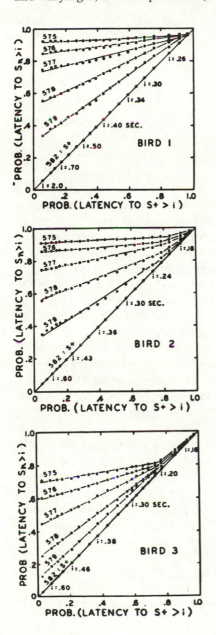

FIG. 6.8 Latency ROCs for pigeons; an example of the distributions from which these were constructed was shown in Figure 6.4. [Figure 2 of Blough (1978); copyright 1978; reprinted by permission.]

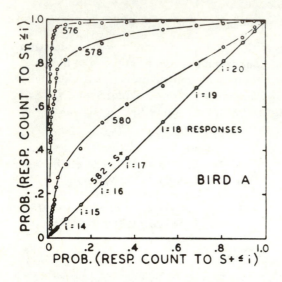

FIG. 6.9 Conventional choice probability ROCs for pigeons responding to light stimuli. [Figure 3 of Blough (1978); copyright 1978; reprinted by permission.]

usually either the difference, the ratio, or log ratio of the relevant physical measures. This function begins at about $\frac{1}{2}$ for two identical signals and grows to 1 when they are sufficiently widely separated—approximately a factor of 4 in intensity. However, given the impact of response criterion just discussed, it is clear that there is no unique psychometric function but rather a family of them. For example, in the fast-guess model (Section 6.3.3) with the interpretation given the parameters above, the impact of signal difference will be on P_{sr} and not directly on ρ or β_A, which are thus parameters of the family of psychometric functions for this model (Eq. 6.10).

For very careful and insightful empirical and theoretical analysis of psychometric functions, see Laming (1985). He makes very clear the importance of plotting these functions in terms of different physical measures depending on the exact nature of the task. He also provides a most interesting theoretical analysis concerning the information subjects are using in the basic psychophysical experiments.

In order to get a unique measure it is necessary to use something that captures the entire ROC curve. The most standard measure is called d', and its calculation is well known (see Green and Swets, 1966, 1974, or Egan, 1975, or any other book on signal detection theory); it is the mean separation of the underlying distributions of internal representations normalized by some average of their standard deviations.

Navon (1975) showed under the same assumptions made by Thomas and Meyers (1972) that if the false-alarm rate is held constant as stimulus discriminability is varied, then $E(\mathbf{T} \mid a, A) - E(\mathbf{T} \mid b, A)$ is a monotonic function of d'_{ab}.

The second, and almost equally obvious, effect is that subjects are slower when the signals are close and faster when they are farther apart. Moreover, this phenomenon occurs whether the conditions of signal separation are run blocked or randomized. Among the relevant references are Birren and Botwinick (1955), Botwinick, Brinley, and Robbin (1958), Crossman (1955), Henmon (1906), Festinger (1943a, b), Johnson (1939), Kellogg (1931), Lemmon (1927), Link and Tindall (1971), Morgan and Alluisi (1967), Pickett (1964, 1967, 1968), Pike (1968), Vickers (1970), Vickers, Caudrey, and Willson (1971), Vickers and Packer (1981), and Wilding (1974). The fact that it appears using randomized separations means that the phenomenon is very much stimulus controlled since the subject cannot know in advance whether the next discrimination will be easy or difficult.

As Johnson (1939) made clear and as has been replicated many times since, the stimulus range over which these two measures—accuracy and time—vary appears to be rather different. At the point the response probability appears to reach its ceiling of 1, response times continue to get briefer with increasing signal separation. Moreover, the same is true for the subject's reports of confidence in the response, which is one reason that reaction time is often thought to reflect confidence in a judgment (or vice versa, since it is not apparent on what the confidence judgments are based). It is unclear the degree to which this is a real difference or a case of probabilities being very close to 1 and estimated to be 1 from a finite sample. In the latter case, it may be the ranges corresponding to changes in d' and $E(\mathbf{T})$ may actually be comparable.

Some debate has occurred over what aspect of the stimulus separation is controlling, differences or ratios or something else. Furthermore, there is no very good agreement as to the exact nature of the functions involved (see Vickers, 1980, pp. 36–38). If accuracy increases and time decreases with signal separation, then they must covary and one can be plotted as a function of the other. This plot, however, is not what is meant when one speaks of a speed-accuracy tradeoff, which is discussed in Section 6.5.

The only study of the dependence of response time on signal separation I shall present here in any detail is Wilding (1974), because he gives more information about the reaction-time distributions than do the others. The task for each of his seven subjects was to decide on each trial if a 300-msec spot of light of moderate brightness was to the right or left of the (unmarked) center of the visual field. There were four possible locations on each side forming a horizontal line, numbered from 1 on the left to 8 on the right, spanning a visual angle of about 0.4°. So 1 and 8 were the most discriminable stimuli and 4 and 5, the least. The data were collected in runs of 110 trials, the first 10 of which were discarded. There were four runs in each of two sessions which differed according to instructions, the one emphasizing accuracy and the other speed.

In analyzing the data for certain things, such as the fastest or the slowest response, one must be cautious about sample sizes. For signals 1 and 8 the probability of being correct was virtually 1, whereas it was very much less

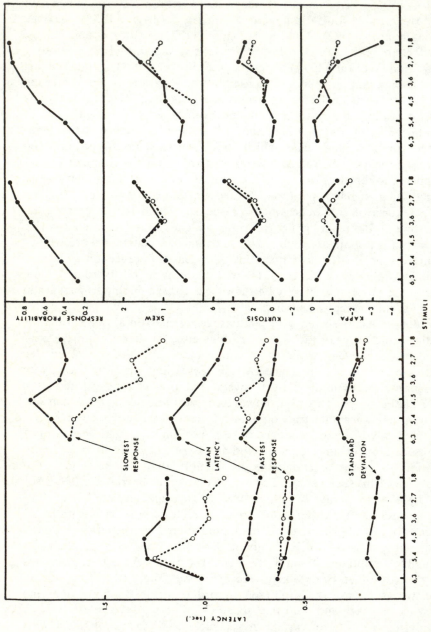

FIG. 6.10 For signal positions to be discriminated as being to the right or left of an unmarked point, various summary statistics about the response times as a function of signal location and whether the response was correct or in error. (1, 8), (2, 7), (3, 6), (4, 5) are all correct responses from the most distant to the least, and (5, 4) and (6, 3) are incorrect ones for the least distant and the next position. The data on the left of each subpanel were obtained with the subjects instructed to be fast, and on the right, to be accurate. Each subject participated in 400 trials; there were seven subjects. [Figure 1 of Wilding (1974); copyright 1974; reprinted by permission.]

than that for 4 and 5, and so the sample sizes of, say, correct responses were not the same. Wilding, therefore, forced comparability by choosing randomly from the larger sets samples of the same size as smaller ones, and he reported the results both for the original and the truncated samples. Figure 6.10 shows a number of statistics. The measures all come in pairs, with the left one arising from the speed instructions and the right one from the accuracy instructions. We see a number of things. First, all of the times are very slow, indeed, much slower than the choice data discussed in Section 6.2.1. I do not understand why this was so. One possibility is that the stimuli were actually weak, but I cannot be certain from the paper. Second, the effect of the instructions is to produce a mean difference of nearly 500 msec. Third, the times that arise from errors, the pairs denoted (6, 3) and (5, 4), are slower than the times from the corresponding correct responses, (3, 6) and (4, 5). Fourth, easy discriminations are, of course, both faster and less prone to error than are difficult ones. Fifth, the pattern of the standard deviations mimics rather closely that of the means. And sixth, the skewness and kurtosis are both positive and increasing with ease of discrimination. This is in agreement with data of Vickers, Caudrey, and Willson (1971) discussed in Section 8.5.1.

Figure 6.11 shows the latency frequency histograms for each subject for the accuracy condition; the columns correspond to (1, 8), (2, 7), ..., (6.3), as in Figure 6.9. There are not enough data here to tell much about the mathematical form involved except that both the mean and variance increase as stimulus discriminability decreases.

6.4.3   Are Errors Faster, the Same as, or Slower than the Corresponding Correct Responses?

This question has loomed important because a number of the models to be discussed in Chapters 7 to 9 make strong (and often nonobvious) predictions about the relation. I know of three appraisals of the situation—Swensson (1972a), Vickers (1980), and Wilding (1971a)—and they are inconsistent. The earlier ones, which Vickers seems to have ignored, are the more accurate.

It is actually clear from the data already presented that there is no simple answer to the question. For the pigeons attempting to make a difficult discrimination, but doing it quite rapidly, the data in Figure 6.7 make clear that errors are faster than correct responses; in fact, the larger the error the faster it is. But for people also engaged in a visual discrimination, we see in Figure 6.10 that errors are slower than the corresponding correct response. The source of the difference probably is not the species of the subject, although no directly comparable data exist.

According to Swensson the important difference, at least for human beings, can be described as follows. Errors are faster than correct responses when two conditions are met: the discrimination is easy and the pressure to

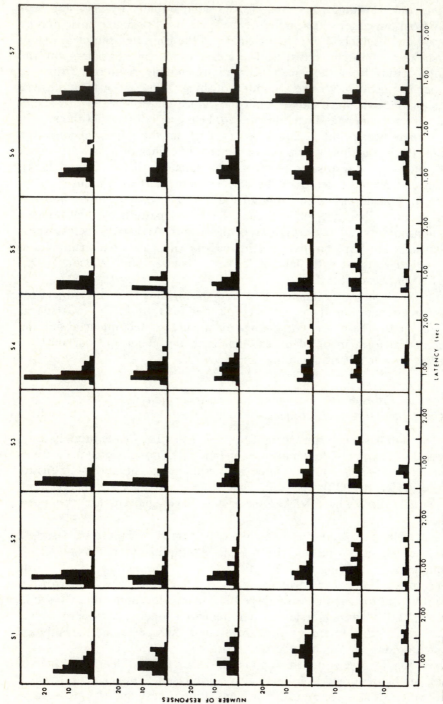

FIG. 6.11 For the experiment of Figure 6.10, histograms for response times in the accuracy condition. The rows correspond, from top to bottom, to the abscissa code of Figure 6.10 with (1, 8) at the top; the columns are different subjects. [Figure 2 of Wilding (1974); copyright 1974; reprinted by permission.]

234

be fast is substantial. This is true of the data of Egeth and Smith (1967), Hale (1969a), Laming (1968), Lemmon (1927), Ollman (1966), Rabbitt (1966), Schouten and Bekker (1967), Swensson (1972a), Swensson and Edwards (1971), Weaver (1942), and Yellot (1967). A near exception to this rule are the results of Green et al. (1983). In this study well-practiced observers each making over 20,000 frequency identifications exhibited virtually the same mean times for errors and correct responses. A careful analysis of the distributions, however, did show a difference in the direction of faster errors. I will go into this experiment in detail in Section 8.5. Continuing with Swensson's rule, errors are slower than correct responses when two conditions are met: the discrimination is difficult and the pressure to be accurate is substantial. This is true of Audley and Mercer (1968), Emmerich et al. (1972), Hecker, Stevens, and Williams (1966), Henmon (1911), Kellogg (1931), Pickett (1967), Pierrel and Murray (1963), Pike (1968), Swensson (1972a), Vickers (1970), and Wilding (1971a, 1974).

There are fewer studies in which the discrimination is difficult and the pressure to be fast is great. Henmon (1911) showed that under such conditions the fastest and slowest response times involved higher proportions of errors than did the intermediate times, suggesting that the subjects may have oscillated between two modes of behavior. Rabbitt and Vyas (1970) suggested that errors can arise from a failure of either what they call perceptual analysis or response selection. They state (apparently their belief) that when the failure is in response selection, errors are unusually fast; but when it is in perceptual analysis, error and correct RT distributions are the same. Apparently, perceptual analysis corresponds to what I call the decision process and is the topic of most modeling. In Blough's experiment, the pigeons exhibited fast errors, and judging by the times involved the pigeons were acting as if they were under time pressure. Of course, Wilding found errors to be slower than correct responses under both his speed and accuracy instructions, but one cannot but question the effectiveness of his speed instructions when the fastest times exceeded 450 msec. Link and Tindall (1971) combined four levels of discriminability with three time deadlines—260 msec, 460 msec, and ∞ msec—in a study of same-different discrimination of pairs of line lengths successively presented, separated by 200 msec. Their results are shown in Figure 6.12. Note that under the accuracy condition and for the most difficult discriminations, errors are slower than correct responses; whereas at the 460-msec deadline the pattern is that errors are faster than correct responses and the magnitude of the effect increases with increased discriminability; and at 260 msec, which is only slightly more than simple reaction times, the mean times are constant, a little less than 200 msec, independent of the level of discriminability and of whether the response is correct or in error. The latter appear to be dominated by fast guesses—that is, simple reactions—but they cannot be entirely that since accuracy is somewhat above chance. A careful analysis of these data will be presented in Section 7.6.2. Thomas (1973) reported a

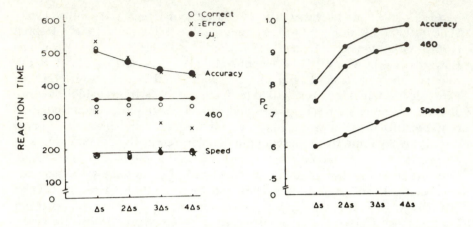

FIG. 6.12 For same-different judgments of pairs of lines, MRT and proportion of correct judgments as a function of signal discriminability (abscissa) under three deadline conditions. In the MRT plot, the solid circles are obtained by using the fast-guess model's correction for guessing. [Figure 1 of Link and Tindall (1971); copyright 1971; reprinted by permission.]

study in which errors were fast for one foreperiod distribution and one group of subjects and slow for another distribution and group of subjects; I cannot tell from the experimental description if the signals were easy or difficult to discriminate. Heath (1980) ran a study on the discrimination of the order of onset of two lights, where the time between onset varied, and he imposed response deadlines. Unfortunately, the data do not seem to be in a form suited to answering the question of this section.

6.5   SPEED-ACCURACY TRADEOFF

6.5.1   General Concept of a Speed-Accuracy Tradeoff Function (SATF)

Within any response-time model of the type formulated in Section 6.3.3, as the decision parameters are varied, changes occur in $\Psi(r, t \mid \vec{\sigma}, \vec{\delta})$, which in turn are reflected in $f(r, t \mid \vec{E})$. The general intuition is that these changes are such that the marginal measures of probability of choice, $P(r \mid \vec{E})$, and of response time, $f(t \mid \vec{E})$, covary. The more time taken up in arriving at a decision, the more information available, and so the better its quality. This statement is, perhaps, overly simple since if a great deal of time is allowed to pass between the completion of the signal presentation and the execution of the response, then the accuracy of responding may deteriorate because of some form of memory decay. But for a reasonable range of times the statement appears to be correct. What is probably most relevant is the portion of the stimulus presentation that can be processed before an order to respond is issued. Usually we attempt to control that time indirectly through time deadlines on the response time.

As usual, the theory involves a covariation due to changes in parameters, and the data a covariation due to changes induced in $\vec{E}$. For example, suppose the experimenter imposes a time deadline on the subject such that any response occurring after signal onset but before the deadline is rewarded for accuracy, but those that are slower than the deadline are fined independent of their accuracy. The effect of changes in the deadline is to vary both the accuracy and the mean response time. Suppose that we suppress all of the notation for $\vec{E}$ except for the two things that vary from trial to trial—namely, the signal presented, s, and the deadline, δ, imposed. The averaged data then consist of four pairs of numbers:

$$\langle P(r \mid s, \delta), \mathrm{MRT}(s, r, \delta)\rangle, \; s = a, b, r = A, B,$$

for each value of δ. If we think of these as functions of δ, then we may solve for the one in terms of the other, eliminating δ, yielding four empirical functions of the form

$$P(r \mid s) = G_{rs}[\mathrm{MRT}(s, r)], \; s = a, b, r = A, B.$$

These are called empirical *speed-accuracy tradeoff functions* (SATF) or latency-probability functions (LPF). I use the former term and abbreviation. As four separate functions are a bother, especially since they probably contain much the same information, in practice some simplification is made. Usually a single measure of accuracy—four different ones will be mentioned below—is plotted against the overall MRT, and that is referred to as *the* SATF. Other terms are found in the literature such as the speed-accuracy operating characteristic or S-A OC (Pew, 1969) and the macro tradeoff (Thomas, 1974). The rationale for the latter term will become apparent later. One must be ever sensitive to the fact that such a collapse of information may discard something of importance.

Observe that if we vary something in the environment, different from the deadline, that affects both speed and accuracy, we may or may not get the same SATF. As an example of a different procedure, Reed (1973) signaled the subjects when to respond, and he varied the time during the presentation of the reaction signal when the response was to be initiated. Theoretically, what SATF we get depends upon which decision parameters are affected by the experimental manipulation. Since we do not usually have a very firm connection between $\vec{E}$ and $\vec{\delta}$, there can be disagreement about which theoretical tradeoff goes with which empirical one. For the fast guess model this is not really an issue, since the only decision parameter affecting $E(T \mid s)$ (Eq. 6.11) is ρ. So if we eliminate it between Eqs. 6.10 and 6.11 we obtain the unique theoretical SATF,

$$P(r \mid s) = E(\mathbf{T} \mid s) \frac{P_{sr} - \beta_r}{\nu_1 - \nu_0} + \beta_r - \frac{\nu_0}{\nu_1 - \nu_0} (P_{sr} - \beta_r), \tag{6.13}$$

which is the simplest possible relation, a linear one.

Swensson and Thomas (1974) described a broad class of models, called fixed-stopping ones, that yields a relation that has played a role in empirical investigations. Suppose that there is a series of n distinct observations $\mathbf{X}_i$ each taking time $\mathbf{T}_i$, $i = 1, \ldots, n$, where all of the random variables are independent, the $\mathbf{X}_i$ are identically distributed, and the $\mathbf{T}_i$ are also identically distributed. The density of $\mathbf{X}_i$, $f(x \mid s)$, depends on the signal presented whereas that of $\mathbf{T}_i$ does not. If $\mathbf{R}$ is the residual time, then the response time is

$$\mathbf{T} = \sum \mathbf{T}_i + \mathbf{R}.$$

So

$$E(\mathbf{T}) = nE(\mathbf{T}_i) + r_0.$$

Assume the decision variable to be the logarithm of the likelihood of the observations; that is,

$$\mathbf{Y}_n = (1/n) \sum \ln[f(\mathbf{X}_i \mid a)/f(\mathbf{X}_i \mid b)].$$

For n reasonably large, the Central Limit Theorem (Appendix A.1.1) implies that $\mathbf{Y}_n$ is distributed approximately as a Gaussian with mean $E(\mathbf{Y}_n \mid s) = \mu_s$ and variance $V(\mathbf{Y}_n \mid s) = \sigma_s^2/n$, $s = a, b$. If a response criterion c is selected for responding A when $\mathbf{Y}_n > c$, then we see that

$$P(A \mid s) = \Pr(\mathbf{Y}_n > c) = \int_{-\infty}^{c} \Phi(\mu_s, \sigma_s^2/n) = \int_{-\infty}^{(c-\mu_s)\sqrt{n}/\sigma_s} \Phi(0, 1).$$

Denoting the z-score of $P(A \mid s)$—that is, the upper limit on the unit normal that yields this probability, by $z(s)$—then eliminating c between $z(a)$ and $z(b)$ yields the linear ROC curve

$$z(a) = (\sigma_b/\sigma_a)z(b) + \sqrt{n}(\mu_b - \mu_a)/\sigma_a.$$

There are several ways to define a so-called d' measure of the accuracy of performance described by the ROC curve; perhaps the simplest is that value of $z(a)$ corresponding to $z(b) = 0$; that is,

$$d' = \sqrt{n}(\mu_b - \mu_a)/\sigma_a.$$

Now, if the speed-accuracy tradeoff is achieved by varying n, we see that it is given by

$$(d')^2 = K[E(\mathbf{T}) - r_0]. \tag{6.14}$$

They also describe another class of models with an optional stopping rule, in which the value of n depends upon the observations actually made; it is more complex and versions of it are described in detail in Sections 8.2 and 8.3.

With more complicated models in which $E(\mathbf{T}|s)$ and/or $P(r|s)$ depend upon two or more decision parameters, then there can be a great deal of uncertainty as to what theoretical relation to compare with what data. Weatherburn (1978) pointed this out as a serious issue for a number of the models we shall discuss in Chapter 8. Pike and Dalgleish (1982) attempted to counter his admittedly correct observations by showing that for some of the models the locus of possible pairs of speed and accuracy values is sufficiently constrained under all possible (or plausible) values of the parameters that the model can, in principle, be rejected. Weatherburn and Grayson (1982) replied, reemphasizing that the rejoinder rested on interpretations of model parameters, which may not be correct. The fact is that the models they were discussing indeed do have a wide range of possible speed-accuracy pairs consistent with them, not a simple function. Great caution must be exercised when a model has more than one decision parameter that affects both speed and accuracy. This point, which I believe to be of considerable importance, has not been as widely recognized as it should be by those who advocate the use of SATFs. In a sense, whether a tradeoff plot is useful depends, in part, on the complexity of the model one assumes to underlie the behavior. However, ignoring the tradeoff or assuming that certain parameters can be held constant by empirically trying to achieve constancy of accuracy or of time is subject to exactly the same difficulties.

A substantive realization of these observations can be found in Santee and Egeth (1982), in which they argue that in some cognitive tasks—they use letter recognition—experimental procedures that permit the use of accuracy measures draw upon a different aspect of the cognitive processing than do procedures that use response-time measures. In their study they manipulated exposure duration. They argued that for brief exposures the accuracy is affected by limitations on data processing by the subject, whereas with long exposures, which is typical of cognitive experiments, the behavior studied has to do with response limitations. For example, in their Experiment 1, there were two letters on either side of a fixation point, and an arrow under one indicated that the subject was to respond whether that letter was an *A* or an *E*. There were three conditions involving the other letter: it could be the same as the indicated one, or the other target letter, or an irrelevant letter (*K* and *L* were used). I refer to these as same, different, and irrelevant, respectively. With the tachistoscope timed to produce about 75% overall accuracy in each subject (8 to 20 msec exposure durations), it was found that subjects were most accurate in the different condition and least accurate in the same one. With an exposure of 100 msec and instructions to respond as rapidly as possible while maintaining a high degree of accuracy, they were fastest for same and slowest for different. They believe these findings to be inconsistent, and so conclude that different aspects of the process are being tapped.

6.5.2   Use of the SATF

Consider assessing the impact of some variable, say the amount of alcohol ingested, upon performance. If as the dosage level is increased both accuracy and MRT change in the same direction, then it can be quite unclear whether there has been a change in the quality of performance or merely a change in the speed-accuracy tradeoff. In particular, it may be quite misleading to plot just one of the two measures against dosage level. For a summary of references in which ambiguous results about alcohol have been presented, see Jennings, Wood, and Lawrence (1976).

Some experimenters have attempted to overcome this problem by experimentally controlling one of the two variables. For example, one can use some sort of time payoff scheme, such as band payoffs or a deadline, to maintain MRT within a narrow range as the independent variable—in this case, amount of alcohol ingested—is manipulated, and to evaluate the performance in terms of accuracy. Alternatively, one can attempt to control accuracy. This approach is widely used in the study of short term memory, as we shall see in Chapter 11. Often an attempt is made to keep the error rate low, in the neighborhood of 2% to 5%. Not only is it difficult to estimate such a rate with any degree of accuracy, but if the SATF is changing rapidly in the region of small errors—which as we shall see it often appears to be—then this is a region in which very large time changes can correspond to very small changes in the error rate, making it very unlikely that the intended control is effective. Furthermore, one can easily envisage a model having more than one sensory state, one of which exhibits changes only in accuracy and another of which involves a speed-accuracy tradeoff. If experimentally we control accuracy through the first stage, then we will have done nothing whatsoever to control the SATF, which is under the jurisdiction of the second stage.

Because of these difficulties in keeping control of one of the variables, some authors (most notably Wickelgren and those associated with him, but also Ollman, Swensson, and Thomas) have taken the position that the only sensible thing to do is to estimate the entire SATF and to report how it as a whole varies with the experimental manipulation. This attitude parallels

TABLE 6.4. Mean slopes and intercepts of the best-fitting linear regression for each alcohol condition (Jennings et al., 1976)

	Dose (mg/kg)				
	0	.33	.66	1.00	1.33
Slope (bits/sec)	6.45	5.71	4.92	4.90	3.38
Intercept (msec)	168	162	161	173	150

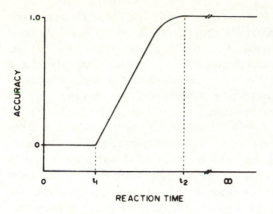

FIG. 6.13 Schematic of the general tradeoff relation (SATF) believed to hold between some measure of accuracy and response time. For any time below t_1 accuracy is nil; for times above t_2 accuracy does not change; and in between it is monotonic increasing. [Figure 1 of Wood and Jennings (1976); copyright 1976; reprinted by permission of the publisher.]

closely that expressed by those who say discrimination can only be studied via the ROC curve, and any measure of discriminability should relate to that curve.

As an example, Jennings et al. (1976) studied the SATF for choice reactions involving the identification of 1000 Hg and 1100 Hg tones. To manipulate the tradeoff they used a variety of deadlines, and subjects were paid for accuracy when responses were faster than the deadline and were fined for the slower responses. Measuring accuracy in terms of information transmitted (see Section 6.5.3 for a general discussion of accuracy measures), they fit linear functions to the curves and Table 6.4 shows how the intercept and slope varied with alcohol dose level. The slope is affected systematically, and the intercept somewhat irregularly.

6.5.3   Empirical Representations of SATFs

A certain amount of discussion has been devoted to the best way to present the empirical SATF. The initial studies* (Fitts, 1966; Pachella & Pew, 1968) separately plotted percent correct and MRT as functions of the decision strategy variable manipulated by the experimenter. Schouten and Bekker (1967), using a somewhat different measure of performance, which will be discussed in detail in Section 6.5.4, plotted their measure of accuracy against MRT. They, and others, who have plotted a probability measure of accuracy against MRT, have found the general pattern shown in Figure 6.13, which is composed of three separate pieces that can, to a rough first approximation, be thought of as linear pieces. Up to a certain time, the accuracy level remains at chance, after which it grows linearly until it reaches its ceiling of

---

* Perhaps the earliest relevant study is Garrett (1922) in which he said (p. 6), "Everyday knowledge seems to indicate that, in general, accuracy diminishes as speed increases, but there is little detailed information beyond the bare statement." He then went on to study how accuracy is affected by stimulus exposure time, but he did not directly manipulate the overall response time, as such, and so it was not really an example of a SATF.

1, after which it stays at perfect accuracy with increases in time. The important facts are that for sufficiently short times, accuracy is nil; beyond another time, changes in MRT, which do occur, do not seem to affect the accuracy, which is virtually perfect; and between the two times there is a monotonic increase in accuracy. As was noted earlier, it is unclear whether accuracy really does become perfect or whether we are dealing with an asymptotic phenomenon. The models usually imply the latter.

Taylor, Lindsay, and Forbes (1967) replotted the Schouten and Bekker data, replacing the probability measure of accuracy by the d' measure of signal detectability theory, and they showed that $(d')^2$ was approximately linear with MRT. Pew (1969), noting that log odds $= \log P_c/(1 - P_c)$, where P_c is the probability of being correct, is approximately linear with $(d')^2$ in the 2-alternative case, replotted the data existing at the time in log odds, which is shown in Figure 6.14. Another set of data, plotted in the same way, will be presented in Figure 9.6 (Section 9.3.4) when we discuss the timing and counting models. Lappin and Disch (1972a) raised the question as to which of several measures of accuracy gave the most linear plot against MRT. They compared d'; $(d')^2$ (see Eq. 614); information transmitted, that is,

$$-\sum_r P(r) \log_2 P(r) + \sum_{s,r} P(r, s) \log_2 P(r \mid s)$$

(see Section 10.2 for a rationale); and

$$-\ln \eta = -\tfrac{1}{2} \ln \frac{P(B \mid a)P(A \mid b)}{P(A \mid a)P(B \mid b)},$$

which becomes log odds in a symmetric situation and was suggested by Luce (1963). For each they established the best linear regression and evaluated the fit by the percent of variance accounted for; it had the small range of .86 to .91 with d' having a very slight edge over the others. Swensson (1972a) made a similar comparison with similar results. Salthouse (1981) reported for each of four subjects the correlations of MRT with P_c, d', $(d')^2$, log odds, and information transmitted. Again, the range of values was not large—.706 to .924. Ranking the five measures for each subject and adding the ranks show information transmitted to be best, $(d')^2$ the worst, and the other three about midway with little difference among them. So among these measures of accuracy none provides a clearly better correlation with MRT, and as we shall see, different theories suggest different choices.

Why do we concern ourselves with the question of which accuracy measures lead to linear SATFs? One reason is ease of comparison, but that is hardly overriding since as we shall see shortly in certain memory studies comparisons are readily made among exponential fits. A more significant reason is formulated as follows by Thomas (1974, p. 449): "*Capacity* [of an information processing system] is usually defined as the maximum *rate* at which *information* is processed, and it is measured by finding that monotonic

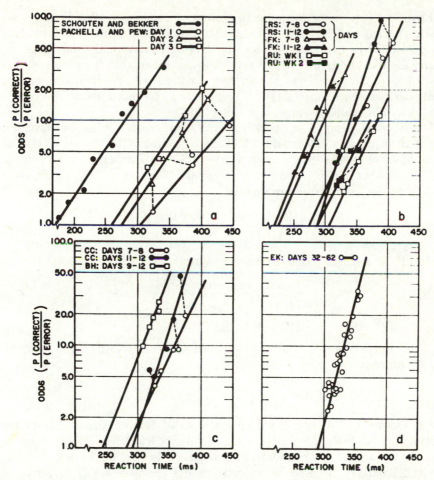

FIG. 6.14 SATF, with accuracy measured as log odds, from four studies: *a* is Schouten and Bekker (1967) and Pachella and Pew (1968), *b* and *c* are data from P. Fitts, and *d* is data from R. Swensson. [Figure 1 of Pew (1969); copyright 1969; reprinted by permission.]

function of accuracy which is linear with reaction time. The slope of this line is taken to be the measure of capacity . . . ." To a considerable degree, this appears to be definitional rather than descriptive. It is, however, disconcerting that the linear function usually does not pass through the origin. For further discussion of the concept and modeling of capacity, see Townsend and Ashby (1978, 1984).

Kantowitz (1978), in response to a general survey of SATFs and their role in cognitive research by Wickelgren (1977), was highly critical of our current uncertainty about which accuracy measure to use. He cited Townsend and

Ashby (1978, p. 122) as suggesting some reasons why the Lappin and Disch (1972a) and Swensson (1972a) studies were inconclusive, including the possibility of too variable data, the fact that some of the measures are nearly identical (although not d' and its square), and that the range of RTs from 100 to 300 msec was simply too small to see much in the way of nonlinearities. Wickelgren's (1978) response, while sharp about other matters, does not really disagree with this point.

Those working on memory rather than sensory discrimination have not found d' to be very linear with MRT, as a summary by Dosher (1979) of some of these studies makes clear. Corbett (1977), Corbett and Wickelgren (1978), Dosher (1976), and Wickelgren and Corbett (1977) all fit their SATFs by the cumulative exponential

$$d'(t) = \begin{cases} \lambda\{1 - \exp[-\beta(t-\delta)]\}, & t > \delta, \\ 0, & t \le \delta. \end{cases}$$

Reed (1973) used the somewhat more complex

$$d'(t) = \begin{cases} \dfrac{\lambda\{1 - \exp[-\beta(t-\delta)]\}}{\beta(t-\delta)[\sigma^2 + (t-\delta)^{-1}]^{1/2}} & t > \delta, \\ 0, & t \le \delta \end{cases}$$

in order to account for a drop in d' with sufficiently large times. Ratcliff (1978) proposed

$$d'(t) = \begin{cases} \lambda/[1 + \nu^2/(t-\delta)]^{1/2}, & t > \delta, \\ 0, & t \le \delta, \end{cases}$$

which Dosher (1979) noted is a special case of Reed's formula. Both the exponential and Reed's formula are ad hoc; Ratcliff's follows from a continuous random walk model to be discussed in Section 11.4.4.

McClelland (1979) used his cascade model (Section 4.3.2) to arrive at another possible formula for the SATF. He assumed that for each s, r pair the level of activation is the deterministic one embodied in Eq. 4.12 perturbed by two sources of noise. One of these is purely additive and he attributed it to noise associated with activation of the response units. He took it to be Gaussian with mean 0 and variance 1, thereby establishing a unit of measurement. Let it be denoted $\mathbf{X}$. The other source is assumed to be additive on the scale factor A_s that multiplies the generalized gamma $\Gamma_n(t)$. This random variable $\mathbf{Y}$ is also assumed to be Gaussian with mean 0 and variance σ_s^2. Moreover, the residual time is $\mathbf{R}$. Putting this together, the decision variable is

$$\mathbf{X} + (A_s + \mathbf{Y})\Gamma_n[t - E(\mathbf{R})], \quad t > E(\mathbf{R}).$$

Assuming the random variables are independent, then its expected value and variance are

$$a_s\Gamma_n[t - E(\mathbf{R})] \qquad \text{and} \qquad 1 + \sigma_s^2\Gamma_n[t - E(\mathbf{R})]^2.$$

Using the usual signal detection approach to this Gaussian decision variable, d' between signals a and b is easily seen to be

$$d'_{ab} = \frac{(A_a - A_b)\Gamma_n[t - E(\mathbf{R})]}{\{1 + \sigma^2\Gamma_n[t - E(\mathbf{R})]^2\}^{1/2}},$$

where $\sigma^2 = \frac{1}{2}(\sigma_a^2 + \sigma_b^2)^{1/2}$. He showed numerically that for appropriate choices of the parameters, this equation is virtually indistinguishable from Wickelgren's cumulative exponential.

6.5.4 *Conditional Accuracy Function* (CAF)

For the joint density $f(r, t \mid \vec{E})$, the plot of

$$P(r \mid t, \vec{E}) = f(r, t \mid \vec{E})/f(t \mid \vec{E}) \qquad (6.15)$$

versus t is a tradeoff function of some interest. Thomas (1974) called it the micro tradeoff in contrast to the macro tradeoff of the SATF; Lappin and Disch (1972a, b) used the term *latency operating characteristic* (which of course has also been suggested for other things); Rabbitt and Vyas (1970), the T-function; and Ollman (1977) the *conditional accuracy function*, (CAF), which Lappin (1978) has adopted as better than LOC. And as I think CAF is the most descriptive, I too shall use it.

A major difference between the CAF and SAFT is that the former can be computed in any experimental condition for which sufficient data are collected to estimate the density functions, whereas the latter is developed only by varying the experimental conditions. For example, by using several response time deadlines one can generate the SATF, and one can compute a CAF for each deadline separately.

To get some idea of just how distinct the CAF is from the SATF, we compute it for the fast guess model. By Eqs. 6.8 and 6.9.

$$P(r \mid t, s) = [\rho g_1(t)P_{sr} + (1 - \rho)g_0(t)\beta_r]/[\rho g_1(t) + (1 - \rho)g_0(t)].$$

Obviously, the form of $P(r \mid t, s)$ as a function of t depends entirely upon the forms of g_0 and g_1, whereas the SATF of Eq. 14 is linear in MRT independent of their forms.

Actually, we can establish the general relationship between the CAF and SATF as follows (Thomas, 1974). Let r' denote the response other than r, then by Bayes' theorem (Section 1.3.2),

$$P(r \mid t, s) = \frac{P(r \mid s)f(t \mid s, r)}{f(t \mid s)}$$

$$= \frac{P(r \mid s)f(t \mid s, r)}{P(r \mid s)f(t \mid s, r) + [1 - P(r \mid s)]f(t \mid s, r')}. \qquad (6.16)$$

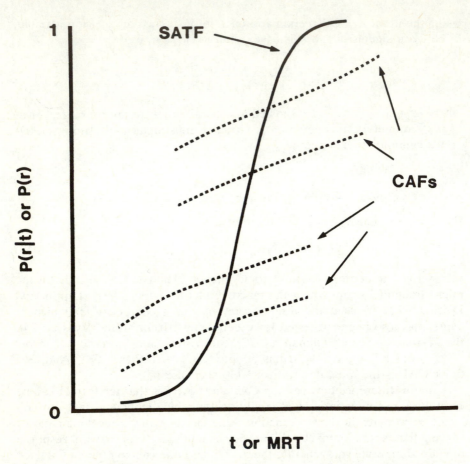

FIG. 6.15 A possible relation between SATF and conditional accuracy function (CAF).

Substituting the SATF for $P(r \mid s)$ establishes the general connection between them. Observe that,

$$E[P(r \mid \mathbf{T}, s)] = \int \frac{f(r, t \mid s)}{f(t \mid s)} f(t \mid s) \, dt$$

$$= \int f(r, t \mid s) \, dt$$

$$= P(r \mid s). \tag{6.17}$$

Thus, the general character of the pattern relating the CAF and SATF as one varies MRT must be something of the sort shown in Figure 6.15.

One nice result involving the CAF has been established by Ollman (unpublished, 1974).

Theorem 6.2. *Suppose in a two-choice situation, r' denotes the other response from r. Let $\mathbf{T}$ denote the response time random variable and suppress the notation for the environment except for the signal presented. If $P(r \mid s) > 0$ and $P(r' \mid s) > 0$, then*

$$E(\mathbf{T} \mid s, r) - E(\mathbf{T} \mid s, r') = \mathrm{COV}[P(r \mid \mathbf{T}, s), \mathbf{T}]/P(r \mid s)P(r' \mid s). \quad (6.18)$$

Proof. We use

$$f(t \mid s, r) = f(r, t \mid s)/P(r \mid s) = f(r \mid t, s)f(t \mid s)/P(r \mid s)$$

and Eq. 6.17 in the following calculation:

$$E(\mathbf{T} \mid s, r) - E(\mathbf{T} \mid s, r')$$

$$= \int tf(t \mid s, r)\, dt - \int tf(t, s, r')\, dt$$

$$= \int t\frac{P(r \mid t, s)f(t \mid s)}{P(r \mid s)}\, dt - \int t\frac{P(r' \mid t, s)f(t \mid s)}{P(r' \mid s)}\, dt$$

$$= \frac{P(r' \mid s)\int tP(r \mid t, s)f(t \mid s)\, dt - P(r \mid s)\int t[1 - P(r \mid t, s)]f(t \mid s)\, dt}{P(r \mid s)P(r' \mid s)}$$

$$= \left[\int tP(r \mid t, s)f(t \mid s)\, dt - P(r \mid s)\int tf(t \mid s)\, dt\right]\Big/ P(r \mid s)P(r' \mid s)$$

$$= \{E[P(r \mid \mathbf{T}, s)\mathbf{T}] - E[P(r \mid \mathbf{T}, s)]E(\mathbf{T} \mid s)\}/P(r \mid s)P(r' \mid s)$$

$$= \mathrm{COV}[P(r \mid \mathbf{T}, s)\mathbf{T}]/P(r \mid s)P(r' \mid s). \qquad \blacksquare$$

So, whether errors to a given signal are faster or slower than the corresponding correct responses depends on whether the correlation embodied in the CAF is positive or negative. Note, this is not the correct versus error comparison made in Section 6.3.3 since there it was the response, not the stimulus, that was constant in the comparison.

For the fast-guess model,

$$\mathrm{COV}[P(r \mid \mathbf{T}, s)\mathbf{T}] = E[P(r \mid \mathbf{T}, s)\mathbf{T}] - E[P(r \mid \mathbf{T}, s)]E(\mathbf{T} \mid s)$$

$$= \rho\nu_1 P_{sr} + (1 - \rho)\nu_0\beta_r$$

$$\quad - [\rho P_{sr} + (1 - \rho)\beta_r][\rho\nu_1 + (1 - \rho)\nu_0]$$

$$= \rho(1 - \rho)(\nu_1 - \nu_0)(P_{sr} - \beta_r). \qquad (6.19)$$

Since $\rho(1 - \rho) > 0$ and $\nu_1 > \nu_0$, the covariance is positive or negative as $P_{sr} - \beta_r$ is positive or negative.

6.5.5   Use of the CAF

Lappin and Disch (1972a) and Harm and Lappin (1973) explored the question: does a subject's knowledge of the presentation probability affect

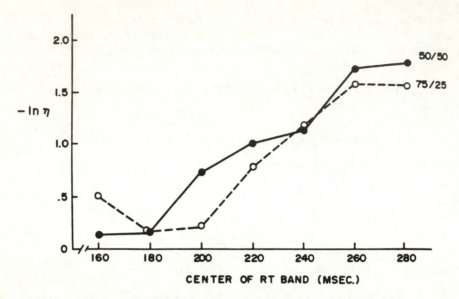

FIG. 6.16 CAF for subjects identifying random dot patterns with two different presentation schedules, where response time is manipulated by 20-msec reward bands. The accuracy measure is $\frac{1}{2}\ln P(B \mid a)P(A \mid b)/P(A \mid a)P(B \mid b)$. [Figure 1 of Lappin (1978); copyright 1978; reprinted by permission.]

the subject's ability to discriminate signals? Using the CAF, with accuracy measured by

$$-\ln \eta = -\tfrac{1}{2}\ln[P(B \mid a)P(A \mid b)/P(A \mid a)P(B \mid b)],$$

they found the CAF to be essentially unaffected. This was done with perfectly discriminable signals, so Lappin (1978) repeated the study using difficult-to-discriminate signals—namely, pairs of random patterns of eight dots located in an invisible 8×8 matrix. Subjects were required to confine their responses to a 100-msec wide band that was located so as to get about 75% correct responses. There were two conditions: 50:50 and 75:25 presentations schedules. The resulting CAF is shown in Figure 6.16, and we see that the CAF has a slight tendency to be flatter in the biased condition, but without additional data it is probably unwise to assume any real effect. By contrast, the bias measure of choice theory,

$$\ln \beta = \tfrac{1}{2}\ln[P(A \mid a)P(A \mid b)/P(B \mid a)P(B \mid b)],$$

is much affected, as seen in Figure 6.17.

6.5.6 Can CAFs be Pieced Together to get the SATF?

Apparently the first appearance of CAFs in the reaction-time literature was in the Schouten and Bekker (1967) study in which they manipulated reaction time rather directly. The reaction signals were lights, one above the other, which the subject identified by key presses. In addition, three 20-msec acoustic "pips" spaced at 75 msec were presented, and subjects were instructed to respond in coincidence with the third pip. The time between that pip and the signal onset was manipulated experimentally. The data were reported in terms of CAFs, although that term was not used. In principle, a CAF can be estimated in its entirety for each speed manipulation, but because of the fall off of the RT density on either side of the mean the sample sizes become quite small for times more than a standard deviation away from the mean. For this reason, it is tempting to try to piece them together to get one overall function. Schouten and Bekker's data, the means of which were replotted by Pew in Figure 6.14, are shown in Figure 6.18. Their conclusion was that these CAF lie on top of one another and so, judging by Figure 6.15, they may actually reconstruct the SATF.

Wood and Jennings (1976) discussed whether it is reasonable to expect this piecing together to work—of course, we already know from the example of fast-guess model that it cannot always work. They presented data from the end of the training period of their alcohol study. The CAFs calculated for each deadline are shown in Figure 6.19 and as is reasonably apparent—they confirmed it by a non-parametric analysis of variance—these estimated CAFs are not samples from a single function.

At a theoretical level Ollman (1977) raised the question under what conditions would the CAF and SATF coincide. He found a set of sufficient conditions that he dubbed the Adjustable Timing Model (ATM). Because the framework given in Eq. 6.4 is somewhat more general than that postulated by Ollman, we must add a condition not mentioned explicitly in his ATM. This is the postulate that the sensory parameters are fixed, not random variables, which we denote $\vec{\sigma} = \vec{\sigma}(\vec{E})$. Thus, $\Phi(\vec{\epsilon} \mid \vec{E}) = \Phi(\vec{\delta} \mid \vec{E})$, where $\vec{\delta}$ is the decision parameter vector. Introducing this assumption into

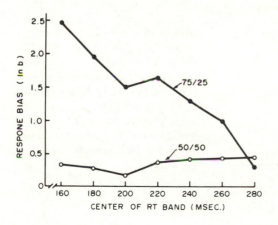

FIG. 6.17 For the experiment of Figure 6.16, response bias as measured by $\frac{1}{2} \ln P(A \mid a) \times P(A \mid b)/P(B \mid a)P(B \mid b)$ versus band location. Note the substantial shifts due to changes in presentation probability. [Figure 2 of Lappin (1978; copyright 1978; reprinted by permission.]

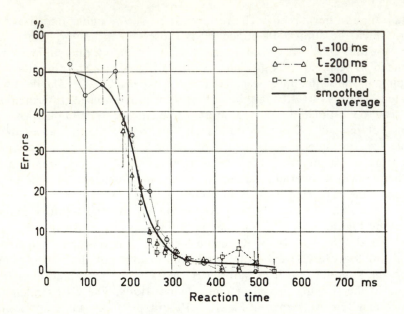

FIG. 6.18 SATF pieced together from a number of CAFs, where the stimuli were lights and the subjects were induced to use different response times by a series of three auditory pips (duration 20 msec each, separated by 75 msec) and the reaction to the signal light was to coincide with the third pip. These were set at the values $\tau = 100, 200, 300, 400, 600,$ and 800 msec. The data are averaged over 20 subjects and have 4000 responses per CAF. [Figure 4 of Schouten and Bekker (1967); copyright 1967; reprinted by permission.]

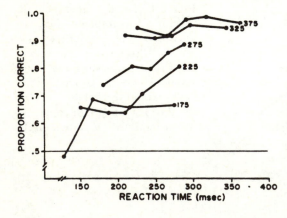

FIG. 6.19 CAFs for the identification of 1000- and 1100-Hz tones with response deadlines and payoffs for responses within the deadline. They do not appear to be samples from a single function. [Figure 2 of Wood and Jennings (1976); copyright 1976; reprinted by permission of the publisher.]

250

Eqs. 6.4 and 6.15,

$$P(r \mid t, \vec{E}) = \frac{\displaystyle \int \Psi(r, t \mid \vec{\sigma}, \vec{\delta}) \Phi(\vec{\delta} \mid \vec{E}) \, d\vec{\delta}}{\displaystyle \sum_r \int \Psi(r, t \mid \vec{\sigma}, \vec{\delta}) \Phi(\vec{\delta} \mid \vec{E}) \, d\vec{\delta}}$$

$$= \frac{\displaystyle \int P(r \mid t, \vec{\sigma}, \vec{\delta}) f(t \mid \vec{\sigma}, \vec{\delta}) \Phi(\vec{\delta} \mid \vec{E}) \, d\vec{\delta}}{\displaystyle \int f(t \mid \vec{\sigma}, \vec{\delta}) \Phi(\vec{\delta} \mid \vec{E}) \, d\vec{\delta}}, \tag{6.20}$$

where we have used the fact $\sum_r P(r \mid t, \vec{\sigma}, \vec{\delta}) = 1$. Ollman's major assumption is that the impact of the decision parameter vector $\vec{\delta}$ on r is completely indirect, via its impact on t; that is,

$$P(r \mid t, \vec{\sigma}, \vec{\delta}) = P(r \mid t, \vec{\sigma}). \tag{6.21}$$

From Eqs. 6.20 and 6.21, which embody the assumptions of the ATM, it is easy to see that

$$P(r \mid T, \vec{E}) = P(r \mid T, \vec{\sigma}). \tag{6.22}$$

The significance of this is that any manipulation of $\vec{E}$ that affects $\vec{\delta}$, and so t, but not $\vec{\sigma}$, will generate the same CAF, namely, $P(r \mid t, \vec{\sigma})$.

It does not follow that this function is the same as the SATF; in general, they will differ. However, as Ollman has pointed out, if the ATM holds and if the CAF is linear—that is,

$$P(r \mid t, \vec{\sigma}) = kt + c,$$

where k and c are independent of t but may very well depend on r and on σ—then the SATF is

$$P(r \mid \vec{E}) = kE(\mathbf{T} \mid \vec{E}) + c.$$

To show this, consider

$$P(r \mid \vec{E}) = \int P(r \mid t, \vec{E}) f(t \mid \vec{E}) \, dt$$

$$= \int P(r \mid t, \sigma) f(t \mid \vec{E}) \, dt$$

$$= \int (kt + c) f(t \mid \vec{E}) \, dt$$

$$= kE(\mathbf{T} \mid \vec{E}) + c.$$

To my knowledge, no good a priori reasons exist to expect ATM to hold. Indeed, the whole philosophy of the theory of signal detectability is exactly the opposite—namely, that decision parameters do in fact directly affect the

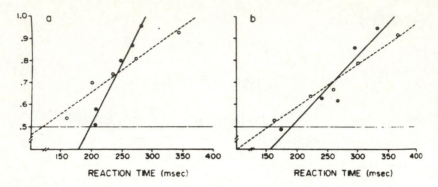

FIG. 6.20 SATF (solid circles) and CAF (open circles) calculated from the same set of data for two subjects. Note that both are approximately linear, but they are distinct functions. [Figure 3 of Wood and Jennings (1976); copyright 1976; reprinted by permission of the publisher.]

choice probabilities and most of the models we shall examine in the next two chapters fail to meet the conditions of ATM. Moreover, Wood and Jennings (1976) have presented data where both the CAF and SATF appear to be linear, but quite different, as can be seen in Figure 6.20.

6.5.7   Conclusions about SATFs

I believe the SATF may prove to be of comparable importance to the ROC curves of error tradeoffs in giving us a way to describe the compromises subjects make between accuracy and time demands. In general, enough data should be obtained in order that some summary of the SATF can be reported. As yet, there is no consensus about the best way to summarize the SATF. Presumably, as we better understand the empirical SATFs, we will arrive at a simple measure to summarize them, something comparable to d' for ROC curves. Some authors have attempted to find an accuracy measure that leads to a linear relation, in which case two parameters summarize it. However, apparent linearity seems to be relatively insensitive to what appear, on other grounds, to be appreciable nonlinear changes in the accuracy measures. Other authors, working with search paradigms (see Chapter 11) have attempted to fit the resulting function of d' versus MRT by one or another of several families of curves, and they then study how the several parameters of the fitted family vary with experimental manipulations; however, there are no compelling theoretical reasons underlying the choice of some of these families and no real consensus exists as to which is best to use.

Wickelgren (1977) has presented a very spirited argument for preferring SATF analysis to either pure reaction time or pure error analysis. As was noted, Kantowitz (1978) took exception on, among other grounds, that we do not really know which accuracy measure to use. Weatherburn (1978) observed that if two or more parameters are involved, then the SATF is simply not a well-defined function, but rather a region of possible speed-accuracy pairs that can sometimes be thought of as a family of functions. Schmitt and Scheiver (1977) took exception to the attempts to use SATFs on the grounds that one does not know which family of functions to use, and they claimed that the analysis of data had, in several cases, been incomplete in terms of the family chosen. Dosher (1979), one of those attacked, provided a vigorous defense, pointing out gross errors in the critique, and giving a careful appraisal of the situation.

Without denying our uncertainty about how to summarize the data and the real possibility that because of multiple parameters there may be no single function relating speed and accuracy, there can be little doubt that presenting SATFs in some form is more informative than data reported just in terms of MRTs with error rates either listed, usually in an effort to persuade the reader that they have not varied appreciably, or merely described as less than some small amount. As was mentioned previously the problem is that in many of the plots such as the exponential relation between d' and MRT, small changes in the accuracy measure can translate into far larger changes in the MRT when the error rate is small than when it is large. This parallels closely the problem of ill-defined psychometric functions arising because at small values of $P(A \mid b)$ a change of one percentage point corresponds to a very large change in $P(A \mid a)$; that is, the ROC is steep for small $P(A \mid b)$.

The CAF, which has been invoked by some as almost interchangeable with the SATF, is in fact completely distinct from the SATF, and there really is no justifiable reason to treat them as the same. Despite the fact that the CAF is defined for each experimental condition, on the whole I think it is the less useful of the two measures. The CAF does not clearly address the tradeoff of interest, it is certainly far more difficult to pin down empirically over a wide range of times, and in most theoretical models it is analytically less tractable than the SATF.

6.6   SEQUENTIAL EFFECTS*

Up to now I have treated the data as if successive trials are independent. On that assumption, it is reasonable to suppose that $f(r, t \mid \vec{E})$ on a trial depends

---

* I am particularly indebted to D. R. J. Laming for severe, and accurate, criticism of an earlier version of this section. I suspect that he will view my changes as inadequate, especially since his primary recommendation was that I drop the section entirely, in part at least, on the grounds that too little consensus exists about the empirical facts for the material to be of any real use to model builders. My judgment is that, in spite of its complexity and inconsistencies, this literature is simply too important to ignore.

on the signal presented on that trial and upon the entire experimental context, but not on the preceding history of stimuli and responses. If that were so, then this density function could be estimated by collecting together all trials on which a particular stimulus was presented and forming the $(\mathbf{r}, \mathbf{T})$ histogram. But if the trials are not independent, we are in some danger when we make such an estimate. At the very least, the usual binomial computation for evaluating the magnitude of the variance of an estimate based upon a known sample size is surely incorrect (Norman, 1971). Depending upon the signs of the correlations, the dependence can either make the estimate too large or too small. Beyond that, if the trials are not independent, then we face the major theoretical problem of trying to account systematically for the dependencies.

The evidence for the existence of such dependencies or sequential effects is very simple: we determine whether the estimate of some statistic, usually either the response probabilities $P(r \mid s)$ or the corresponding expected reaction time $E(\mathbf{T} \mid s, r)$, differs appreciably depending upon how much of the history is taken into account. As stated by Kornblum (1973b, p. 260), "The term *sequential effect* may be defined as follows: If a subset of trials can be selected from a series of consecutive trials on the basis of a particular relationship that each of these selected trials bear to their predecessor(s) in the series, and the data for that subset differs significantly from the rest of the trials, then the data may be said to exhibit sequential effects." Let it be very clear that the principle of selection depends on events prior to the trial in question and does not in any way depend upon the data from that trial.

6.6.1   Stimulus Controlled Effects on the Mean

The most thoroughly studied sequential effects are those arising when the signal on the current trial is the same as or different from that on the preceding trial. These trials are referred to, respectively, as *repetitions* and *alternations* (in the case of two stimuli) or as *non-repetitions* (in the case of more than two stimuli).

The discussion of sequential effects begins here for the two-stimulus, two-response situation, and I draw heavily upon the survey articles of Kirby (1980) and Kornblum (1973b). One notable omission from the Kirby review is the extensive set of experiments and their detailed analysis in Laming (1968); among other things, his sample sizes (averaged over the subjects) are appreciably larger than any of the other studies except Green et al. (1983), who report very large samples on a few subjects. Although we can clearly demonstrate the existence of such effects in the two-choice experiment and discover a number of their properties, many of the hypotheses that arise can only be tested in k-choice designs with $k > 3$. So our discussion of sequential effects will resume in Section 10.3 when we turn to these more complex reaction-time experiments.

An illustration of the limitations of the $k = 2$ case may be useful. Suppose we have reason to believe that the magnitude of the sequential effects depends both upon the relative frequency with which the signals are presented, $\Pr(\mathbf{s}_n = a) = p$, where $\mathbf{s}_n$ is the signal presented on trial n, and upon the tendency for the signals to be repeated in the presentation schedule (which is sequential structure imposed by the experimenter), which we make independent of the particular signal—that is, $P(\mathbf{s}_n = a \mid \mathbf{s}_{n-1} = a) = P(\mathbf{s}_n = b \mid \mathbf{s}_{n-1} = b) = P$. Since $P(\mathbf{s}_n = a)$ is independent of n, it must satisfy the constraint

$$p = P(\mathbf{s}_n = a)$$
$$= P(\mathbf{s}_n = a \mid \mathbf{s}_{n-1} = a)P(\mathbf{s}_{n-1} = a) + P(\mathbf{s}_n = a \mid \mathbf{s}_{n-1} = b)P(\mathbf{s}_n = b)$$
$$= Pp + (1 - P)(1 - p),$$

and solving, either $P = 1$ or $p = \frac{1}{2}$. Thus, if we wish to vary p and P independently, we must either use more than two signals or abandon the condition that the probability of repetition is the same for both signals.

Another problem in studying sequential effects is reduced sample sizes. Suppose we consider the purely random schedule, and we wish to partition the history of stimulus presentations back m trials. If the overall sample is of size N, then each history has an expected sample size of $N/2^m$ and so the standard error of the resulting mean estimate is $2^{1/2m}\sigma/N^{1/2}$. So, for example, if the true MRT is 400 msec with a standard deviation of 75 msec and the basic sample N is 2000, the standard error of the overall MRT for one signal is 2.37 msec, that of a two step history is 3.35 and that of a four step one is 6.71 msec. Many of the differences in the data are under 10 msec, and so they must be viewed with some skepticism.

The first two studies in which the data were partitioned according to their history of stimuli were Laming (1968, Ch. 8) and Remington (1969). The latter experiment involved five subjects who responded by key presses to one of two lights. A warning light and a 1-sec foreperiod was used prior to the signal presentation. Subjects were asked to respond as rapidly as possible, consistent with an error rate of less than 5%. The actual overall level was about 1%. The average interstimulus interval was about 4 secs. (I begin to report this time because, as will soon be evident, it is an important independent variable for sequential effects.) There were two experimental conditions: one with equally likely presentations (50:50) and the other with a ratio of 70:30. Some data were rejected as not having achieved stability. What remained were 800 observations per subject in the 50:50 condition and 1000 in the 70:30. These were partitioned into histories up to five trials back, and they are shown in Figures 6.21 and 6.22. Observe in Figure 6.21 the pronounced repetition effect. Note that in this figure the symbol A denotes the stimulus on the trial under consideration and B the other stimulus, and the past history is read from the current trial on the right and back to the left. Thus, a string of the other stimulus B before and the current A presentation makes for a slow response, the time increasing as the

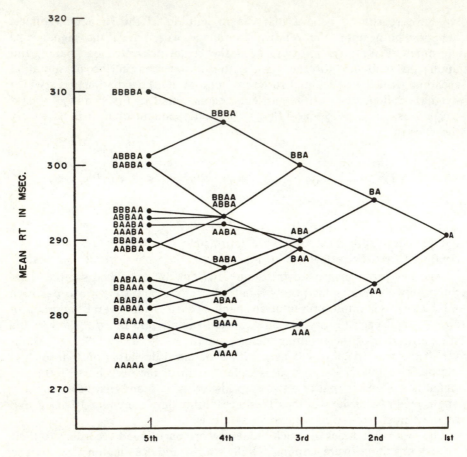

FIG. 6.21 MRT versus previous stimulus history for two equally likely lights. The sample size was 800 for the signal not partitioned into any previous history and it decreases to $800/2^n$ for a history of length n. The symbol A designates the signal being responded to and B the other signal. The stimulus history is read from right to left. [Figure 2 of Remington (1969); copyright 1969; reprinted by permission.]

number of Bs increases; a string of As before an A makes for a rapid response. The pattern for the 70:30 data is similar with, of course the less frequent signal distinctly slower than the more frequent one.

An experiment by Falmagne, Cohen, and Dwivedi (1975) in essence replicated these results of Remington, but in some ways is more striking. The span of times from the slowest to the fastest as a function of presentation pattern is some two to five times as large as in Remington's data. This may be because a fairly brief response-stimulus interval (200 msec) was used by Falmagne et al. as compared with Remington's average of four seconds. Since the data are not qualitatively different and they will be described in some detail relative to a sequential model (Section 7.6.4), I do not present them here.

As was mentioned earlier, Laming's experiments involved the identification of two white bars on a black background presented tachistocopically. His Experiment 3, which was run without automation, had a 2500-msec RSI interval. Twenty-four subjects participated in five series of 200 trials

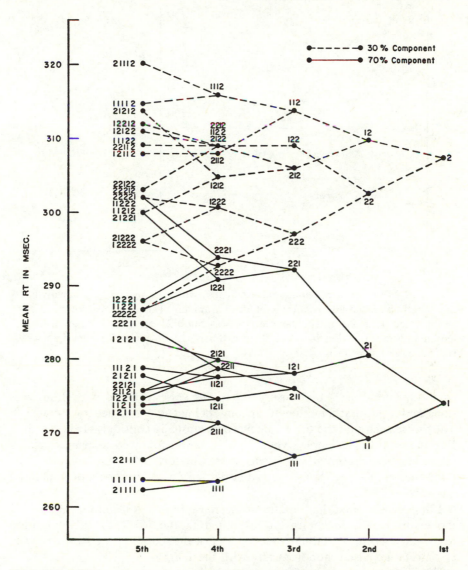

FIG. 6.22 MRT versus previous stimulus history with 70:30 presentation probability. Here 1 denotes the more probable signal and 2 the less probable one. [Figure 3 of Remington (1969); copyright 1969; reproduced by permission of the publisher.]

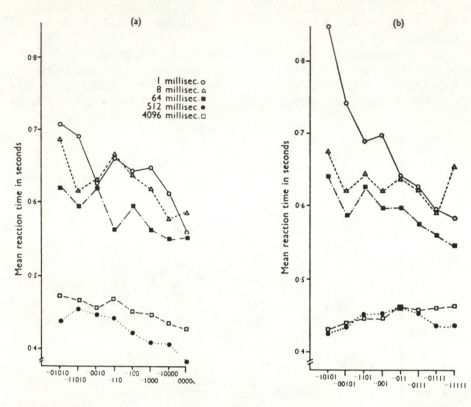

FIG. 6.23 MRT versus previous stimulus history when the signals were equally likely line lengths with the intertrial interval as a parameter. The code used for the history is explained in the text. The sample size was $5000/2^n$ per stimulus per history of length n (see discussion in text). [Figure 8.5 of Laming (1968); copyright 1968; reproduced by permission.]

each, for a total of 24,000 observations. The series differed in both instructions and a point scheme aimed at influencing the speed-accuracy tradeoff. They were such that the error rate was intentionally considerably larger than Remington's. For example, when an alternation followed a string of six or seven identical presentations, it was approximately 20%. As there was little difference among the series, they were pooled for the purposes of sequential analyses.

Laming also found that repetitions decreased the MRT and they decreased the errors made. In contrast to Remington, the MRT to an alternation following a string was largely independent of the length of the string, but the error rate increased monotonically with the length.

His Experiment 5 was automated, which permitted use of the intertrial interval as an experimental variable. The same general experiment was run with intertrial intervals of 1, 8, 64, 512, and 4096 msec, arranged in a Latin square design. Each of 25 subjects was run for 100 trials at each ITI, yielding 12,500 observations. The MRT data for selected histories are shown in Figure 6.23 and the corresponding error data in Figure 6.24. The code is read from left to right in time up to the trial before the signal in question. A 0 means that the signal in that position (trial) was the same as the one for which the data are being plotted, and a 1 means that it was the other signal. Thus, for example, 0100 arises either from the sequences on trials $n-4$, $n-3$, $n-2$, $n-1$, and n of either *abaaa* or *babbb*. It is quite clear that the shorter the ITI, the slower the response and the more likely an error, especially after particular histories. Laming (1968, p. 109) summarized the results as follows:

> The sequential analyses of Experiments 1, 2, and 3 suggested that if the subject experiences a run of one signal or an alternating sequence, he expects those patterns to continue. On this basis the subjective expectation of ... the signal actually presented ... increases from left to right [in the left panels of Figures 6.23 and 6.24] and from right to left [in the right panels]. When the intertrial interval is long the mean reaction times and proportions of errors behave as one would expect; they both decrease as the subjective expectation of [the signal] increases. But when the intertrial interval is short they behave differently: after a run of either kind of signal the mean reaction times and proportion of errors all decrease, while after an alternating sequence they increase greatly, irrespective of which signal might have been most expected.

Later Kirby (1976b), apparently unaware of Laming's work, ran a study in which he manipulated the interval between a response and the next presentation, the RSI. His data presentation was the same as Remington's except that he separated it into first and second halves. These are shown in Figure

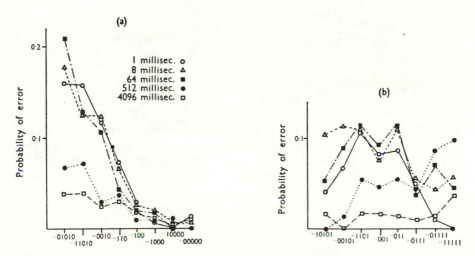

FIG. 6.24 The response proportions corresponding to Figure 6.23. [Figure 8.6 of Laming (1968); copyright 1968; reprinted by permission.]

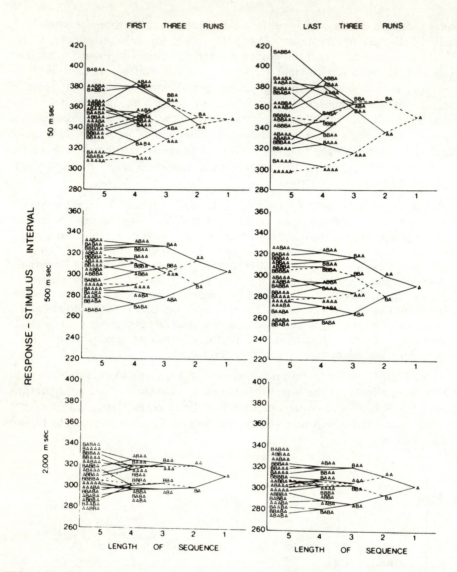

FIG. 6.25 Effect of response-stimulus interval (RSI) and experience on MRT versus previous stimulus history. The stimulus history code is as in Figures 6.21 and 22. The sample is 100 trials per run and three runs per panel. [Figure 4.1 of Kirby (1980); copyright 1980; reprinted by permission.]

6.25. The most striking fact can be seen in the first-order sequential effects—namely, that a repetition of a signal, AA in his notation, speeds up the MRT for the 50-msec RSI, but slows it down for the 500- and 2000-msec RSIs. It should be noted, however, that at all RSIs the effect of additional repetitions is to speed the MRT slightly from the one step repetition; however, for any length of history at the two longer RSIs, the fastest time arises with pure alternation.

Certain inconsistencies exist between Laming and Kirby's data, and one wonders what might account for them. Two notable differences in the studies are the sample sizes (12,500 versus 3,600) and the fact that Laming included all responses whereas Kirby discarded error responses (less than 4.5%). The first means that for the smaller sample size, it is entirely possible that more of the orderings are inverted due to sampling variability, and so not all differences can be assumed to be real. The second raises the possibility that the experiments were run at different speed-accuracy tradeoffs and that this affects the sequential pattern in some way. Another fact, much emphasized by Green et al. (1983) as probably contributing to instability in all of these experiments, is the use of many, relatively inexperienced subjects for relatively few trials each. In their work, which I discuss more fully in Section 8.4, only three subjects were used, but each was practiced for at least 3500 trials and was run for 21,600 trials. There was evidence of changes in MRT during at least the first 7200 trials of the experiment. Another factor they emphasize is their use of random (exponential) foreperiods, in contrast to most other studies that use constant foreperiods (i.e., RSI). No matter which, if any or all, of these factors are relevant to the different results, the fact is that considerable uncertainty obtains about the basic facts.

That the RSI affects in some manner the significance of alternations and repetitions had been noted earlier.

> The point at which this change from a repetition to an alternation effect takes place appears to be approximately half a second. Thus, repetition effects have been found for RSIs of less than approximately half a second by Bertelson (1961, 1963), Bertelson and Renkin (1966), Hale (1967), Kornblum (1967), Hale (1969a), Eichelman (1970), Kirby (1976b) and alternation effects with intervals greater than half a second by Williams (1966), Hale (1967), Moss, Engel, and Faberman (1967), Kirby (1972, 1976b). At intervals of, or close to, half a second, repetition, alternation, and nonsignificant sequential effects have been reported (e.g., Bertelson, 1961; Hale, 1967; Schvaneveldt and Chase, 1969; Eichelman, 1970; Kirby, 1976b). (Kirby, 1980, p. 132)

And, of course, we know from Section 5.4 that a significant interaction exists even in simple reaction times when two signals are separated by less than 300 msec. So far as I know, no attempt has been made to use those ideas in the study of sequential effects in choice paradigms or to place both sets of phenomena in a common framework.

Kirby went on to point out that there are at least four anomolous studies in which a repetition effect was in evidence at long RSI: Bertelson and Renkin (1966), Entus and Bindra (1970), Remington (1969), and Hannes (1968). To this list, we must add Laming's (1968) data. As I just remarked, we do not know the source of these differences, but it is interesting that in a second experiment Kirby (1976) was able to produce either repetition or alternation effects at long RSI by instructing the subjects to attend to repetitions or alternations; whereas, at short RSI the instructions had little effect, with a repetition effect occurring under both instructions.

6.6.2   *Facilitation and Expectancy*

The data make clear that at least the previous signal and probably a considerable string of previous signals affect the MRT. Moreover, the nature of that effect differs depending upon the speed with which new stimuli occur. It seems likely, therefore, that two mechanisms are operative: one having a brief temporal span and the other a much longer one. In terms of the types of mechanisms we have talked about, I suspect the brief one is part of the sensory mechanism and the longer lasting one involves memory phenomena that last some seconds and are a part of the decision process. In this literature, the relevant sensory mechanism is spoken of as "automatic facilitation" (Kirby, 1976; also "intertrial phenomenon" by Bertelson, 1961, 1963, and "automatic after effect" by Vervaeck and Boer, 1980) and the decision one as a "strategy" (or "subjective expectancy" or "anticipation"). And, as we shall see below, there is reason to suspect that there may be at least two distinct strategy mechanisms involved.

The facilitation mechanism is thought to be of one of two types. The first is that the signal leaves some sort of sensory trace that decays to a negligible level in about 750 msec. Sperling (1960) used masking techniques to provide evidence for such a trace. When a second signal occurs in less time than that, the traces are "superimposed." If the two signals differ, there is little gain and perhaps some interference in the superimposed representation. If they are the same, however, the residual trace somehow facilitates the next presentation of the signal. This could involve either some sort of direct addition of the old to the new representation, making it stronger than it would otherwise be and, thereby, allows the identification to proceed more rapidly than usual, or it could entail some sort of priming of a signal coding mechanism, for example, by influencing the order in which certain features are examined. In either event, a repetition effect results. The facts that MRTs in a choice situation run from 300 to 400 msec with signals of 100-msec duration and that the repetition effect gives way to an alternation one at about an RSI of 500 msec suggest that the trace has largely disappeared after 700 to 800 msec.

The other facilitation mechanism is somewhat less clearly formulated. It supposes that the effect of a repeated signal is to bypass some of the signal processing that is normally involved. Since exactly what is bypassed is unclear, it is not evident how to distinguish facilitation from trace strengthening.

If a sensory-perceptual facilitation mechanism were the whole story, then since it is entirely driven by the stimulus schedule we should not see any impact of previous experience or instructions on it. Kirby (1976) tested this idea in his third experiment, again using lights as signals. There were six conditions, half of which were at an RSI of 1 msec and the others at 2000 msec. Within each condition, the last third of the trials were run at a 50:50 ratio of repetitions and alternations. The first two-thirds were run at three ratios: 70:30, 50:50, and 30:70. He found that for the longer RSI, a repetition effect in the 70:30 condition and an alternation effect in the 30:70 condition persisted into the last third of the data. For the short RSI, the effects did not persist. These data are consistent with the idea that for short RSIs the sequential effects are stimulus determined, but for the long ones something other than the stimulus pattern affects the behavior.

So one considers possible decision strategies. The fact that faster responses occur with alternations suggests that the subjects in some sense anticipate the occurrence of alternations. This is reminiscent of the famed negative recency effect uncovered in probability learning experiments (Jarvik, 1951). It appears that many people have a powerful tendency to act as if a local law of averages exists—that is, as if there were a force altering conditional probabilities in a random sequence—so as to keep the local proportions very close to 50:50. Such a rule or belief would lead to an exaggerated expectation for alternations.

This idea that the subject is predicting, albeit incorrectly, which signal will be presented has led to a series of attempts to have the subject make the predictions overt and to see how MRT depends on the prediction. The major idea is that if we single out successive pairs of correct predictions, then the sequential effects on those trials should vanish. This literature was discussed in detail by Kirby (1980, pp. 143–144), who concluded that there is just too much evidence that the act of predicting directly affects the response times, and so overt prediction fails to be a useful experimental strategy. The relevant papers are DeKlerk and Eerland (1973), Geller (1975), Geller and Pitz (1970), Geller, Whitman, Wrenn, and Shipley (1971), Hacker and Hinrichs (1974), Hale (1967), Hinrichs and Craft (1971a), Schvaneveldt and Chase (1969), Whitman and Geller (1971a, b; 1972), and Williams (1966).

Kirby (1980, pp. 145–148) examined the evidence as to whether the strategy effect is, as he appears to believe, one of preparation and/or expectancy or whether the strategy develops after the signal is presented. Although the argument is protracted, it appears to me that its main thread goes as follows. If the strategy comes into play after signal onset, then shortening the RSI should only accentuate it since it reduces the time for memory to decay. Any effect to the contrary must be due to sensory facilitation, which as we have seen comes into play with RSIs under half a second. On the other hand, if the strategy is set prior to signal presentation, the shorter the RSI the less time it has to be developed, and so at the shortest times its effect should be negligible. And Kirby contends that the data are more consistent with the latter view. For example, the fact that some well-practiced subjects develop the ability to produce alternation or repetition effects at will, even at short RSIs, he interprets as their becoming more efficient at preparing their strategies. However, these data could just as well be interpreted in terms of a shift from a preparation strategy, which at short RSI does not have time to be effective, to a reactive one that is established after the signal onset. I find the arguments unpersuasive, and I believe that the basic nature of these strategy effects is still an open question. I shall, nonetheless, explore some rather detailed, specific suggestions about them in Section 6.6.5.

Vervaeck and Boer (1980) made some important observations in this connection. First, they noted that an expectancy hypothesis predicts not only that the expected signal will be responded to faster than when no expectancy is involved, but that the unexpected one will be responded to more slowly. In contrast, a general facilitation mechanism of any sort predicts that an increase of the facilitation factor leads to faster responses and a decrease to slower responses independent of which signal is presented. At short RSI, Kirby (1976) reported sequential effects that differed according to whether the signal was a repetition or an alternation, whereas Laming (1968, Experiment 5) obtained facilitation that did not depend upon the signal. Vervaeck and Boer pointed out a significant procedural difference: Laming measured his RSI from the onset of the response key, and Kirby measured it from the offset. They judged from other data that the typical duration of a key press was from 100 to 200 msec. They repeated both experiments under the same conditions, found a difference of 106 msec between the two observed RSIs, and replicated both Laming's and Kirby's results.

6.6.3　Stimulus-Response Controlled Sequential Effects

Our discussion of sequential effects to this point should seem a bit odd since nothing has been said about the responses except that their MRT is used as the dependent variable. What about previous responses as a source of sequential effects? To my knowledge, this has never been examined with anything like the care that has gone into stimulus effects. In particular, I do not know of any two-choice studies, analogous to those reported in Figures 6.20–6.24, that partition the data according to the past history of responses or, better, the joint past history of signals and responses. Laming (1968, Section 8.4) reports some linear regression results, but no very clear pattern is evident. There are, however, several studies in which the joint past history for one trial back is examined, and I discuss them here. Concerning the sequential effects exhibited jointly by response probability and time, there is but one study, which is reported in the next section. Within the general psychophysical literature there is a fair amount of data about sequential effects in absolute identification and magnitude estimation, but with many more than two signals. The only data for two-stimulus designs of which I am aware are concerned primarily with the impact of an error on the next trial. Some of these data, particularly those in Rabbitt (1966), are based upon more than two signals, but they are too relevant to postpone until Chapter 10.

In his studies, Rabbitt has used a short RSI, often 20 msec and never more than 220 msec. The task was the identification of one of several lights appearing in different positions. His data showed: that errors are faster than correct responses (Section 6.4.3), that the MRT on the trial preceding an error did not differ significantly from the overall MRT, and that the MRT following an error is slower than the overall MRT. The fact that the MRT before an error is not unusually fast suggests that the fastness of the error trials is not part of some overall waxing and waning of the reaction time. Rabbitt and Rogers (1977) and Rabbitt (1969), using Arabic numerals as signals and key presses as responses, showed that the delay following an error was considerably greater when the alternative signal was used (and so to be correct in the two choice situation the response was a repetition of the previously erroneous one) than when the signal was repeated.

Laming (1979b), in discussing Rabbitt's work, cited the data from Experiment 5 of Laming (1968) (described earlier) in which he varied the RSI and found appreciable changes in performance. Recall, at long RSI the probability of an error following an error is sharply reduced below the average error rate independent of whether the signal was repeated or alternated; whereas, at short RSI the error probability is reduced for a repeated signal and greatly increased when the signal is alternated. For Experiments 1, 2, and 3—where the first two were slight variants in which the presentation probability was varied and in 3 the error rate was varied by instructions— the RSI was long: 2500 msec, 1500 msec, and 2500 msec. Because of the pronounced effects that the previous stimulus history is known to have (Section 6.6.1), Laming corrected for it both in his error probabilities and MRTs using a multiple regression analysis described in Appendix C of Laming (1968). The data are broken up according to whether the error stimulus is repeated or alternated, and so the erroneous response is either alternated or repeated in order to be correct. The data are shown in Figure 6.26 as a function of the number of trials since the preceding error. Error probabilities are presented directly whereas times are presented in terms of deviations from the overall MRT for that stimulus history. We see, first, that error trials are faster by about 50 msec than the overall mean times. Second, immediately following an error the time is slower than average, which is true whether the stimulus is repeated or alternated. The effect is somewhat larger for alternations than repetitions. Third, following an error, the error rate for both types of trials is reduced below average (except for the alternative

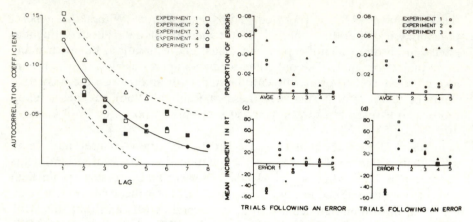

FIG. 6.26 For three experiments in which the subject is attempting to identify length, the probability of an error and the deviation of MRT from the overall mean versus the number of trials since an error. The data on the left are when the stimulus in question is the same as the one for which an error was made, and on the right, when they differ. The sample sizes were as follows:

Exp	No. of Conditions	Ss/Cond	Obs/S
1	4	6	1000
2	4	6	1000
3	8	3	1000
4	10	2	800
5	5	5	1000

[Figure 1 of Laming (1979b); copyright 1979; reprinted by permission.]

signal of Experiment 3). Fourth, the recovery of MRT to its normal value is comparatively rapid; in the case of repeated signals it is complete in one trial. Fifth, the recovery of error probability to its normal level is, except for Experiment 3, not achieved even after five trials. The fact that the recovery patterns for MRT and error probability are quite different suggests two distinct mechanisms, but this is not a necessary conclusion. For example, Laming has shown how a single mechanism can suffice (Section 6.6.5). First, however, it is desirable to examine the sequential problem empirically from the point of view of the SATF.

6.6.4   *Are the Sequential Effects a Speed-Accuracy Tradeoff?*

The answer to the question of the title is not obvious from what has been presented. It could be Yes, but equally well it could be No in that the SATF itself is changed as a result of the previous history. Obviously, the answer to the question may very well depend upon the RSI.

Swensson (1972b) performed the following relevant experiment. There were five distinct but unmarked horizontal locations on a cathode ray tube, and a square with one of the two diagonals was shown successively in these locations from left to right, with the choice of the diagonal made at random for each location. The subjects responded by key presses to identify the direction of the diagonal at each presentation. At the end of each sequence of five stimuli, information was fed back on the number of correct responses and the sum of the five response times. Two subjects were run. One major manipulation was the time between each response and the presentation of the next signal in the sequence, the RSI. One at 0 msec was called the immediate serial task (IS) and the other at 1000 msec was called delayed serial (DS). Another manipulation was to shift the emphasis between speed and accuracy between blocks of 50 or 100 trials. In addition, for subject RG an explicit monetary payoff was used to effect the speed-accuracy tradeoff. The total number of trials (each a sequence of five stimuli) run in each condition for each subject varied from 1500 to 3000. The data were pooled over blocks of trials having comparable error rates into four groups. The SATF presented is log odds versus MRT.

Because of the design into five presentations per trial, the first question to be raised is whether serial position effects are in evidence. Figure 6.27 shows that a considerable serial position effect exists for the IS condition and is very slight for the DS condition. This is not surprising if memory traces dominate studies with brief RSIs.

To study the sequential effects, the data from positions 2 through 5 were combined and then partitioned into four categories according to whether the response (not the signal) in question is a repetition or alternation (coded in

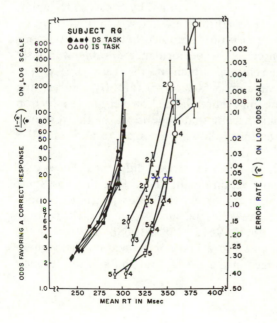

FIG. 6.27 SATF for one of two subjects for each serial position of a sequence of five presentations on each of which the subject was to identify orientation of a line. The IS condition is with zero RSI and DS with a 1000-msec RSI. Sample sizes varied from 1500 to 3500 per condition. The bars show ±1 standard deviation. [Figure 3 of Swensson (1972b); copyright 1972; reprinted by permission.]

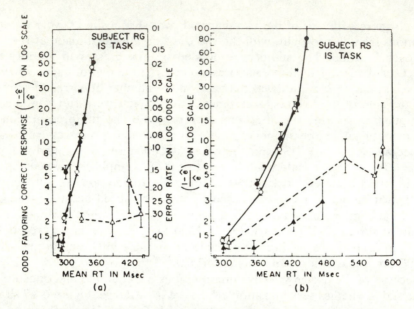

FIG. 6.28 SATF sequential effects for two subjects in the zero RSI condition of Figure 6.27. Open symbols are repeated responses and solid ones are alternated ones; circles mean the previous response was correct and triangles means it was in error. [Figure 5 of Swensson (1972b); copyright 1972; reprinted by permission.]

the figures as open and closed symbols, respectively) and whether the response follows an error or a correct response (coded by circles or triangles, respectively). The data for the IS condition are shown in Figure 6.28. Following a correct response there is little difference between alternations and repetitions, but following an error the performance is rather seriously degraded, the more so for alternations which in the case of RG are exceedingly fast and have approximately a 50% error rate. By contrast, the data from the DS condition, shown in Figure 6.29, show very little effect on the SATF of these categorizations except that repetitions of the response may be slightly poorer than alternations following a correct response for RG and following an error for RS.

Once again it is clear that RSI makes an important difference. These data seem to accord with earlier evidence that with short RSI there is some tendency for the subject to attempt to correct the error just made, which leads to an unusually fast and, relative to the next signal, largely random response (Burns, 1971; Rabbitt, 1966, 1967, 1968a, 1968b, 1969). For the long RSI this tendency disappears and to a first approximation the sequential effects appear to be not changes in the SATF, but shifts in the tradeoff on that function.

6.6.5   Two Types of Decision Strategy

Judging by Swensson's data, the most obvious idea to account for the impact of an error with a long RSI is as some sort of adjustment on the SATF, the subject becoming more conservative and so more accurate at the expense of being slower. The difficulty with this view is that it predicts that changes in MRT and error probability should covary, even though we know from Figure 6.26 that during the recovery phase following an error they do not.

Laming (1968, pp. 80–82) suggested another possibility. This arose in his discussion of the important classical random walk model (Sections 8.2, 8.3.1, and 8.4.2) which model has as one of its predictions that the distributions of error and of correct responses (same response, different signals) should be identical. As this is contrary to the data, Laming asked if some plausible mechanism would account for the fact that errors are usually faster than correct responses. He suggested that when the subject is under time pressure he or she may err as to the actual onset of the signal. Laming described this tendency as arising from time estimation, but it is just as plausible that the subject adjusts the detection criterion to the point where on a significant

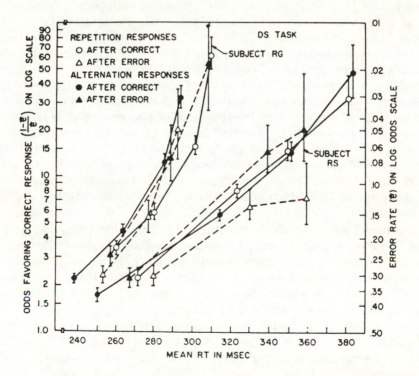

FIG. 6.29   Same plot as Figure 6.28 for the 1000-msec RSI. [Figure 6 of Swensson (1972b); copyright 1972; reprinted by permission.]

fraction of the trials the pre-stimulus background "noise" triggers a detection response in the system. Either way, if a premature cue serves to begin the information accumulation on which a decision is to be based, then the response is both more likely to be in error and to be somewhat faster than it would otherwise be. According to this view, then, there are two criteria at the subjects' disposal. The one has to do with the point at which information for the decision begins to be accumulated—either the criterion for detection or the setting of the parameters of the time estimation process. The other is the criterion for making a response once information begins to be collected.

Laming made the interesting observation that the differential recovery of MRT and error probability following an error can, in fact, be accounted for by just the anticipation mechanism grafted onto a standard decision model (the SPRT model of Section 8.3.1). He showed that if the subject starts to accumulate information well in advance of signal presentation, the error rate is substantially increased from what it would have been had accumulation begun exactly at signal presentation. That result is not surprising, but what is surprising is the fact that $E(\mathbf{T})$ is reduced by only a few milliseconds. This arises because the information accumulated prior to the signal does not itself tend to lead to a decision, but rather introduces variability in the starting point of information accumulation at signal onset. He assumed that following an error, the subject becomes really very conservative and begins accumulating information well after signal onset. This tendency both greatly reduces the error probability (on the assumption that signal information is continuing to be available) and delays $E(\mathbf{T})$ by the amount of the delay after signal onset plus the amount of anticipation that was in effect at the time of the error. If on the next trial the time at which accumulation is initiated is moved forward, then $E(\mathbf{T})$ is moved forward by the same amount, but the error probability does not change. In fact, the initiation time can shorten until it coincides with signal onset before the error probability begins to rise to its original value. Clearly, this single mechanism is sufficient qualitatively to account for the apparently separate recovery of MRT and error probability.

This model illustrates nicely Weatherburn's point that there may well be more than one source of tradeoff between speed and accuracy. The time to begin accumulating information establishes one tradeoff, and the criterion for responding on the basis of the information accumulated establishes a second one. At the present time, we do not know of any reliable way experimentally to evoke just one of them.

Some authors in discussing the sequential data have spoken of selective preparation for one response rather than the other (Bertelson, 1961; Falmagne, 1965), and others of nonselective preparation (Alegria, 1975; Bertelson, 1967; Granjon & Reynard, 1977). It is difficult to know for sure what is meant by these concepts, but one possibility is the two sorts of mechanisms just discussed, with the criterion for signal detection being non-selective.

One final point. Laming (1969b) developed an argument, based on his 1968 data, that the same theoretical ideas that account for the sequential patterns may also underlie the so-called signal-probability effect. This effect is the fact that the more probable signal is responded to more rapidly and more accurately than the less probable one. It is clear that the more probable signal will, in general, be preceded by a longer run of repetitions than the less probable one. Thus to the extent that repetitions lead to both speed and accuracy, the effect follows. He worked out this idea in some detail for the SPRT model. We will return to the relation between sequential effects and presentation probability in Section 10.3.1.

6.7   CONCLUSIONS

Comparing choice-reaction times with simple-reaction times leaves little doubt that somewhat more is going on. It usually takes 100 msec and sometimes more to respond to the identity of a signal than to its presence. Many believe that most of the additional time has to do with the processing of information required to distinguish among the possible signals. Others believe that some and perhaps much of the time is required to select among the possible responses. This point of view is argued by Sternberg (1969a). To some degree, this distinction can be examined by uncorrelating the number of responses from the number of signals; some of those studies are taken up in Chapters 11 and 12.

It is also clear from data that subjects effect important compromises or tradeoffs. Perhaps the best known of these is between the two types of error, which is represented by the ROC curves and has become a standard feature not only of modern psychophysics but of much of cognitive psychology. Some models assume that the mind is able to partition the internal evidence about stimuli into categories corresponding to the responses. Once the experimenter records response times as well as choices, a number of questions arise about how the response times relate to the responses made. One controversial question has been how the time depends upon whether the response is correct or in error. The result tends to be this: for highly discriminable signals responded to under considerable time pressure, errors are faster than the corresponding correct responses, but for signals that are difficult to discriminate and with pressure for accurate responding, the opposite is the case. A few studies fail to conform to this pattern, and there is little work on time pressure coupled with difficult-to-discriminate signals.

Another major tradeoff is between speed and accuracy, which is thought to arise when the subject varies the amount of information to be accumulated and processed prior to a response. There is at least the possibility that this tradeoff is a strategy distinct from another tradeoff—namely, the selection of a criterion to determine the actual response to be made once the information is in hand. In the fast-guess and fixed stopping-rule models they were distinct; in some of the other models studied in later chapters they are not.

The last body of data examined in the chapter concerned sequential effects. Here we were led to believe that there may be at least three distinct mechanisms at work, the last of which is probably a manifestation of the speed-accuracy tradeoff just discussed. The first is the possibility of direct sensory interaction between successive signal presentations, which some authors have suggested arises from the superposition of sensory traces when a signal is repeated sufficiently rapidly. The evidence for this came from the different effects that occur as the time from a response to the next signal presentation is varied. But even after eliminating this sensory effect by using long SRIs, there is still a rather complex pattern of sequential effects following an error. After an error both the MRT slows and accuracy increases, but on subsequent trials the former returns rapidly—in some cases in one trial—to its overall mean value whereas the error rate increases only slowly over a number of trials. Some have interpreted this as evidence for both a type of non-selective preparation that is not long sustained and a selective one that is. Within the information accrual framework, Laming has suggested that the non-selective one is some mechanism—perhaps time estimation, perhaps a signal detector that is causing anticipations—that often initiates the accrual process prior to the actual signal onset. The other mechanism appears to be some sort of speed-accuracy tradeoff for which there are a number of models (Chapters 7 to 10).

Most theories attempt to provide accounts of the ROC and SATF. Relatively little has been done to account in detail for the sequential effects, in part because it leads to messy mathematics and in part because the phenomena to be explained remain somewhat uncertain. There are a few attempts to wed stochastic learning processes to otherwise static models. Laming has coupled a time estimation model with the random walk one, which was originally designed only to provide an account of the ROC and SATF. I am not aware of any models for the sensory effect found with brief RSIs.

I have elected to partition this theoretical work into three broad classes. In Chapter 7 the models assume that the subject can opt, as in the fast-guess model, to be in one of several states, each of which has its characteristic time and error pattern. Chapters 8 and 9 explore information accrual models for two-signal experiments. They differ only in whether we assume that time is quantized independently of the information accrual process or by that process itself. And Chapter 10 deals with identification data and models when there are more than two signals, a topic far less fully developed than the two-signal case.

7

Mixture Models

Beginning with this chapter, we examine a series of models that attempt to formulate what information the mind has about the signals presented and how it makes decisions about what and when to respond. In some earlier chapters, especially Chapter 4, we have already encountered mathematical processes that unfold in time, but we did not explore them in much depth. To study such processes in the detail required to compare them with data, it becomes necessary to be explicit about the mathematical formulations, which technically are stochastic processes. In this chapter, only Markov chains will play a role. In Chapter 8, the major focus is on discrete-time random walks. Chapter 9 rests mainly on diffusion and renewal counting processes in continuous time.

To the extent that I can, I will keep the presentation self-contained. As an aid to those having limited familiarity with the fundamental concepts of stochastic processes, some of the basic definitions were listed in Section 1.5. And, of course, there are a number of well-known introductions to stochastic processes; among my standbys are Karlin and Taylor (1975) and Parzen (1962). An advanced treatment is Gihman and Skorohod (1974).

The topic of this chapter is the fast-guess model, which we have already explored briefly (Section 6.3.3), and various generalizations of it. First, I take up the general concept of a mixture of distributions and work out some of their general properties. Second, the possibility is explored of formulating sequential effects within the mixture framework. Third, the more specific fast-guess model is examined in some depth and several important predictions are derived from it. Fourth, a blend of fast guesses and a simple model of memory scanning that involves two response states is shown to exhibit something close to the correct sequential effects in both times and errors. And finally quite a number of experiments that have been run are used to evaluate the models. The conclusion I shall draw from this is double pronged: two-state models are too simple to account for all aspects of the data, but the idea that subjects may revert to fast guesses when under sufficient time pressure seems well sustained. In fitting any other model to a body of data, it is wise first to check whether the data are contaminated by fast guesses and either to remove those responses before carrying out further analyses or model them as in the promising three-state memory model.

7.1   TWO-STATE MIXTURES

Psychologists as well as those not formally trained in the area generally believe that performance is greatly influenced by the degree to which one is prepared to perform. This preparedness is thought to consist of three distinct aspects: overall attention to the task at hand, focusing upon one or a very few of the possible stimuli, and preparation to carry out particular responses. These factors are easily illustrated in the example of driving under adverse conditions. The very fact that the conditions are adverse—say mist and fog—is usually enough, in the absence of alcohol, to bring attention fully to the task of driving so that one is unlikely to converse or to recall what was said or played on the radio. Further, one is likely to be particularly focused upon certain possible stimuli—namely, those signaling the greatest danger such as colliding with another vehicle or striking a pedestrian. Stimuli such as road signs are likely to require more response time than normal and certainly more than is required for something that is interpreted as a car or a person. And finally, one is highly prepared to make the braking response rather than something else (e.g., accelerating and passing).

One of the early explicit models for choice reaction time attempted to capture at least part of this idea. It, and most other models, take for granted the overall attention to the task at hand, and they attempt to model the focus-preparation aspect. In fact, the framework of the initial model is sufficiently general that it is unclear which of the three aspects—overall attention, focus, or preparation—is actually involved. Falmagne (1965) suggested that for the choice reaction time situation the observer is in one of two states where responses are slower in one than in the other. Various interpretations are possible for the states, but level of motivation to respond rapidly is the most obvious. The variable to be manipulated experimentally is the probability of being in each state. Let us denote by $\rho(\vec{E})$ the probability of being in the slow state when experimental state $\vec{E}$ is used. The experimental condition is part of the environment which, except for the conditions being manipulated including the stimulus presented, is presumed to be invariant over trials. Thus, in addition to the stimulus presented, $\vec{E}$ can refer to the instructions, the probability distribution of presentations, and/or the payoffs, and so on. Denote by $G_1(t)$ the distribution function of response times when in the slow state and by $G_0(t)$ the distribution when in the fast state. On these assumptions, the distribution of observed response times is

$$F(t \mid \vec{E}) = \rho(\vec{E})G_1(t) + [1 - \rho(\vec{E})]G_0. \qquad (7.1)$$

This is a *two-state mixture model*, an example of which is the fast-guess model.

The generalization of the two-state model to multistate mixtures is obvious, but only one, a three-state model, has been developed in detail (Section 7.5). The conclusion will be that at a minimum three states are needed in general. For a more general discussion of mixture models and their associated statistical theory, see Everitt and Hand (1981).

One drawback of the model formulated by Eq. 7.1 is that it fails to say anything at all about the relation between stimuli and responses. The simplest assumption, the one made by Falmagne, is that the stimuli are perfectly discriminable and no errors are made in either the fast or slow states. This assumption is unlikely if one thinks of the two states as different levels of attention, but quite acceptable if they are thought of as levels of response preparation. Under that assumption, Eq. 7.1 may apply to the identification of any finite number of stimuli. The generalization to imperfect performance when there are just two stimuli and two responses is embodied in the fast-guess model of Ollman (1966, 1970) and Yellott (1967, 1971), who assumed that no stimulus discrimination is made in the fast state, whereas some, albeit not necessarily perfect, discrimination is made in the slow state. As was noted earlier, this could arise if the fast responses are based merely on the detection of a signal, whereas the slower ones involve identification as well. This model is discussed in Section 7.4 and is compared with data in Sections 7.6 and 7.7.

7.1.1 Linear Functions

The mixture model of Eq. 7.1 is, for many purposes, usefully re-expressed as

$$F(t \mid \vec{E}) = \rho(\vec{E})[G_1(t) - G_0(t)] + G_0(t). \tag{7.2}$$

Observe that by differentiating one finds the same mixture property for densities

$$f(t \mid \vec{E}) = \rho(\vec{E})[g_1(t) - g_0(t)] + g_0(t). \tag{7.3}$$

The density exhibits one of the most characteristic features of mixtures—namely, that if g_0 and g_1 are unimodal and the modes are well separated, then f is bimodal. Recall, we saw evidence of this in the pigeon discrimination data of Figure 6.4 (Section 6.3.4).

Because the expectation operator is linear, a mixture relation holds for the moment generating function (mgf),

$$\mathcal{M}(s \mid \vec{E}) = E(e^{s\mathbf{T}} \mid \vec{E})$$
$$= \rho(\vec{E})[E(e^{s\mathbf{T}_1} \mid \vec{E}) - E(e^{s\mathbf{T}_0} \mid \vec{E})] + E(e^{s\mathbf{T}_0} \mid \vec{E})$$
$$= \rho(E)[\mathcal{M}_1(s \mid \vec{E}) - \mathcal{M}_0(s \mid \vec{E})] + \mathcal{M}_0(s \mid \vec{E}), \tag{7.4}$$

where, of course, $\mathcal{M}_i$ is the mgf of G_i. From this follows immediately that all of the raw moments are mixtures of the corresponding component raw moments:

$$\mu(\vec{E})^{(r)} = \rho(\vec{E})[\nu_1(r) - \nu_0(r)] + \nu_0(r), \tag{7.5}$$

where $\nu_i(r)$ is the rth raw moment of G_i and $\mu(\vec{E})^{(r)}$ is that of $F(. \mid \vec{E})$.

We see that there is an endless list of linear relations that arise by eliminating $\rho(\vec{E})$ between any two mixture equations. One example is the linear relation between the first and second raw moments—namely,

$$\mu(\vec{E})^{(2)} = \alpha\mu(\vec{E})^{(1)} + \beta, \tag{7.6}$$

where

$$\alpha = [\nu_1(2) - \nu_0(2)]/[\nu_1(1) - \nu_0(1)],$$

$$\beta = \nu_0(2) - \alpha\nu_0(1).$$

Another, slightly less obvious one, is that between the distribution function itself and the mean—namely,

$$F(t \mid \vec{E}) = \alpha(t)\mu(\vec{E})^{(1)} + \beta(t), \tag{7.7}$$

where

$$\alpha(t) = [G_1(t) - G_0(t)]/[\nu_1(1) - \nu_0(1)],$$

$$\beta(t) = G_0(t) - \alpha(t)\nu_0(1).$$

This can be plotted for any value of t by manipulating the experimental state represented by $\vec{E}$. Examples will be provided in Section 7.3.1.

Another family of relations arise by taking the difference of any equation for two values of $\vec{E}$, call them $\vec{E}$ and $\vec{E}'$. For example, from Eq. 7.2 we see that

$$F(t \mid \vec{E}) - F(t \mid \vec{E}') = [\rho(\vec{E}) - \rho(\vec{E}')][G_1(t) - G_0(t)]. \tag{7.8}$$

And if we run a third distinct condition, $\vec{E}''$, it follows by division that

$$\frac{F(t \mid \vec{E}) - F(t \mid \vec{E}')}{F(t \mid \vec{E}) - F(t \mid \vec{E}'')} = \frac{\rho(\vec{E}) - \rho(\vec{E}')}{\rho(\vec{E}) - \rho(\vec{E}'')}, \tag{7.9}$$

which predicts an invariance in the data—namely, that the left side is independent of t.

Thomas (1969) noted that one can always express $F(t \mid \vec{E})$ as a linear mixture of the two most extreme observable distributions. To show this, suppose $\rho(\vec{m}) < \rho(\vec{E}) < \rho(\vec{M})$. Then from Eq. 7.1 with $\vec{E} = \vec{m}$ and $\vec{E} = \vec{M}$, we solve explicitly for $G_0(t)$ and $G_1(t)$ as functions of $F(t \mid \vec{m})$, $F(t \mid \vec{M})$, $\rho(\vec{m})$, and $\rho(\vec{M})$. Substitute into Eq. 7.1 with general $\vec{E}$ to obtain

$$F(t \mid \vec{E}) = \eta(\vec{E})F(t \mid \vec{M}) + [1 - \eta(\vec{E})]F(t \mid \vec{m}), \tag{7.10}$$

where

$$\eta(\vec{E}) = [\rho(\vec{E}) - \rho(\vec{m})]/[\rho(\vec{M}) - \rho(\vec{m})].$$

All of these relations provide partial ways of testing the model and of estimating parameters.

7.1.2 Fixed Points

In any of the linear expressions involving functions—for example, Eqs. 7.2, 7.3, and 7.4—the following fixed-point property holds (Falmagne, 1968), which I will illustrate for Eq. 7.3. Suppose that for some t^*, $g_0(t^*) = g_1(t^*)$, which for densities is surely plausible if they overlap at all. Then for all $\vec{E}$,

$$f(t^* \mid \vec{E}) = g_0(t^*), \tag{7.11}$$

that is, all of the densities pass through the same fixed point. Observe that the condition $g_0(t^*) = g_1(t^*)$ fails to hold only when g_0 and g_1 do not overlap, in which case $f(t \mid \vec{E})$ must be a perfectly bimodal density function, a property easily checked in the data. The only difficulty in checking Eq. 7.11 is that one is forced to work with histograms, not density functions, and there will be some uncertainty as to whether the fixed-point property holds.

The comparable fixed-point property of the distribution function is rather less revealing because there is no compelling reason to suppose G_0 and G_1 intersect at any value intermediate between 0 and 1. For example, if they are Gaussian with equal variances, then there will be no intermediate fixed point. The same is true for the mgf in the Gaussian case.

*7.1.3 Statistical Test

Thomas (1969) has provided a statistical test of the hypothesis Eq. 7.10 that derives from the general mixture hypothesis. To my knowledge it has not been systematically applied. The assumed data are samples of observations from each of three distributions, $(t_{\bar{h}1}, t_{\bar{h}2}, \ldots, t_{\bar{h}n(\bar{h})})$, $\bar{h} = \vec{E}$, $\bar{m}$, $\vec{M}$. Now select triples consisting of an observation from each set, say $(t_{\vec{E}i}, t_{\bar{m}j}, t_{\vec{M}k})$, and rank order them. The ranking is a permutation of $(1, 2, 3)$. Assign to the triple the number 0 if the permutation is effected by an even number of interchanges of adjacent numbers and 1 if the number is odd. Let $\mathbf{Z}$ denote that assignment, and let $\mathbf{Z}_n^*$, where $n = \min[n(\vec{E}), n(\bar{m}), n(\bar{m})]$, denote the average of this statistic over all possible distinct triples:

$$\mathbf{Z}_n^* = \frac{1}{n(\vec{E})n(\bar{m})n(\vec{M})} \sum_{i=1}^{n(\vec{E})} \sum_{j=1}^{n(\bar{m})} \sum_{k=1}^{n(\vec{M})} \mathbf{Z}[(t_{\vec{E}i}, t_{\bar{m}j}, t_{\vec{M}k})].$$

Thomas established the following facts about $\mathbf{Z}_n^*$, which I do not prove here. First, as $n \to \infty$, $(\mathbf{Z}_n^* - \frac{1}{2})/\sqrt{n}$ approaches the Gaussian distribution with zero mean and unit variance. Second, the variance of $\mathbf{Z}_n^*$ is given by

$$V(\mathbf{Z}_n^*) = \left[\frac{28}{n} + \frac{1-8\theta}{n}\right][1 - \varphi(1-\varphi)],$$

where

$$\theta = 2[\tfrac{2}{3} - \beta_{\bar{m}} - \beta_{\vec{M}}] - (\alpha - \tfrac{1}{2})^2,$$

$$\phi = \int_{-\infty}^{\infty} F_{\bar{m}}(t)\, dF_{\vec{M}}(t),$$

$$\beta_{\bar{h}} = \int_{-\infty}^{\infty} F_{\bar{m}}(t) F_{\vec{M}}(t)\, dF_{\bar{h}}(t), \quad h = \bar{m}, \vec{M}.$$

Thomas developed a method to estimate θ and φ, and so a test of the hypothesis is easily made. It is important to realize that the test statistic may have a mean of $\frac{1}{2}$ for relations other than mixtures, so the null hypothesis must be accepted with caution.

7.2 A LINEAR OPERATOR MODEL FOR SEQUENTIAL EFFECTS

7.2.1 The Model

Falmagne (1965) suggested a simple learning mechanism to describe the way the mixture parameter $\rho(\vec{E})$ might be selected. It is of such a character as to provide a possible account of the sequential effects seen in much reaction-time data. Later, Falmagne, Cohen, and Dwivedi (1975) formulated a somewhat different Markov chain model within the conceptual framework of memory search, and they compared it in great detail and with considerable success for one subject to sequential data of the type discussed in Section 6.5.1. Although that work belongs conceptually with the memory search ideas of Chapter 11, I elect to discuss it now (Section 7.5) because the ideas are easy to state. It is an important example of a mixture model.

Turning to the linear operator approach, suppose there are k stimuli, one of which is presented on each trial, and suppose further that the probability of being in state 1 rather than state 0 depends upon which stimulus is presented. Note that this is a rather surprising assumption. The more obvious one would be that G_0 and G_1 are affected by the stimulus. Pursuing Falmagne's assumption, denote by $\rho_n(s)$ the probability that state 1 arises on trial n if stimulus s is presented. The basic mechanism postulated for passing from $\rho_n(s)$ to $\rho_{n+1}(s)$ is this. If some stimulus other than s, say s^*, is presented on trial n, then with some fixed probability α^* the system moves into state 0, and with probability $1-\alpha^*$ it remains in state 1. And if s is presented, there is a fixed probability α that the system moves into state 1, and with probability $1-\alpha$ no change is made. So, letting s^* denote any stimulus different from s,

$$\rho_{n+1}(s) = \begin{cases} (1-\alpha)\rho_n(s)+\alpha, & \text{if } s \text{ occurs on trial } n, \\ (1-\alpha^*)\rho_n(s), & \text{if } s^* \text{ occurs on trial } n. \end{cases} \quad (7.12)$$

The mixture distribution on trial $n+1$ when s is presented is obviously

$$F_{n+1}(t \mid s) = \rho_{n+1}(s)G_1(t)+[1-\rho_{n+1}(s)]G_0(t). \quad (7.13)$$

Substituting Eq. 7.12 into Eq. 7.13 yields

$$F_{n+1}(t \mid s) = \begin{cases} (1-\alpha)F_n(t \mid s)+\alpha G_1(t), & \text{if } s \text{ on trial } n. \\ (1-\alpha^*)F_n(t \mid s)+\alpha^* G_0(t), & \text{if } s^* \text{ on trial } n. \end{cases} \quad (7.14)$$

Consider, now, a situation where beginning with trial n and running through trial $n + k - 1$, a sequence of k repetitions of stimulus s occurs, then by a very simple induction we obtain

$$F_{n+k}(t \mid s) = (1-\alpha)^k [F_n(t \mid s) - G_1(t)] + G_1(t). \tag{7.15}$$

In like manner, a sequence of k stimuli different from s yields

$$F_{n+k}(t \mid s) = (1-\alpha^*)^k [F_n(t \mid s) - G_0(t)] + G_0(t). \tag{7.16}$$

From these equations, very simple expressions for the moments of the reaction times arise; for example, the means are

$$E(\mathbf{T}_{n+k} \mid s) = \begin{cases} (1-\alpha)^k [E(\mathbf{T}_n \mid s) - \nu_1] + \nu_1, & \text{if a run of } k \text{ } s\text{'s,} \\ (1-\alpha^*)^k [E(\mathbf{T}_n \mid s) - \nu_0] + \nu_0, & \text{if no } s \text{ from } n \text{ to } n+k-1. \end{cases}$$

$$\tag{7.17}$$

Clearly, a strong sequential structure is imposed on the mean reaction-time data, which can be predicted once the parameters ν_0, ν_1, α, and α^* are estimated.

It is evident that from Eqs. 7.12 and 7.13 an explicit equation for $E(T_{n+k} \mid s)$ can be calculated for any particular sequence of stimuli beginning with trial n; I will not, however, write these down.

7.2.2 Parameter Estimation

Observe from Eq. 7.17 that the one-step transitions of mean reaction times are given by

$$E(\mathbf{T}_{n+1} \mid s) = \begin{cases} (1-\alpha)E(\mathbf{T}_n \mid s) + \alpha\nu_1, & \text{if } s \text{ on trial } n, \\ (1-\alpha^*)E(\mathbf{T}_n \mid s) + \alpha^*\nu_0, & \text{if } s^* \text{ on trial } n. \end{cases} \tag{7.18}$$

In principle, then, if we have estimates of the mean times on successive trials, then the plot of one against the other should be linear. Thus $1 - \alpha$ and $1 - \alpha^*$ could be estimated as the slopes and $\alpha\nu_1$ and $\alpha^*\nu_0$ as the intercepts. The problem in carrying this out is that $E(\mathbf{T}_n \mid s)$ is not an observable. So the task is to try to transform this scheme into one that does involve observables.

The major idea for doing so rests on the process settling down to a stationary stochastic process after a sufficiently long time, in which case the transitions becomes independent of n. And if that is so, then one can (with care) average over trials and thereby estimate mean reaction times. There are two problems to consider: when is the process asymptotically stationary and what averaging should be done?

For the first, it is enough to give a sufficient condition. Consider the class of experiments in which the probability of presenting signal s is a constant, $\pi(s)$, that is independent of the trial, where $\sum_s \pi(s) = 1$. Consider the state transitions for signal s. Suppose that on trial n the system is in state 1, so

$\rho_n(s) = 1$, then using Eq. 7.12 we see that

$$\rho_{n+1}(s) = (1 - \alpha + \alpha)\pi(s) + (1 - \alpha^*)[1 - \pi(s)]$$
$$= 1 - [1 - \pi(s)]\alpha^*. \tag{7.19}$$

And if the system is in state 0, so $\rho_n(s) = 0$, then

$$\rho_{n+1}(s) = \alpha\pi(s). \tag{7.20}$$

So the transition matrix among the states is trial independent, and that process forms a Markov chain (Section 1.5.2). It is a well-known property of Markov chains that there is an asymptotic distribution of states that is easily determined from Eqs. 7.19 and 7.20. Let $\rho(s)$ be the asymptotic probability of state 1 for signal s, then

$$\rho(s) = \{1 - [1 - \pi(s)]\alpha^*\}\rho(s) + \alpha\pi(s)[1 - \rho(s)].$$

Collecting terms and solving,

$$\rho(s) = \pi(s)\alpha/\{\pi(s)\alpha + [1 - \pi(s)]\alpha^*\}. \tag{7.21}$$

So the condition that the stimulus presentation schedule is random, independent of trial number, is sufficient to lead to an asymptotically stationary process.

Let us turn, therefore, to the issue of averaging in order to use Eq. 7.18. The key problem is that while the process is overall stationary, there are all sorts of local run properties that must be taken into account. So we estimate a number of different $E(\mathbf{T}_n \mid s)$ terms depending upon the length of the run leading up to the presentation of s on trial n: s^*s, s^*ss, s^*sss, s^*ssss, and so on, where s^* denotes any stimulus different from s. These means are all kept distinct. Now, what do we use to estimate $E(\mathbf{T}_{n+1} \mid s)$? If we are in the situation where stimulus s was presented on trial n, then the answer is simple: to the mean time estimated from a run of k s's, associate the mean estimated from a run of $k + 1$ s's. The problem is trickier when we deal with the second half of Eq. 7.18 in which the condition is that stimulus s was not presented on trial n. Then the relevant past history is of the form $s^*\overbrace{s \cdots s}^{k}s^*$, and so $E(\mathbf{T}_{n+1} \mid s)$ is estimated over all histories of this type, which were called "intervals" by Falmagne, and it is compared with the $E(\mathbf{T}_n \mid s)$ estimated from $s^*\overbrace{s \cdots s}^{k}ss$, which history was called a "repetition."

Each stimulus and each value of k yields a pair of mean times for each half of Eq. 7.18, and if they exhibit sufficient range, then a way to estimate the parameters is provided. Obviously when $\pi(s)$ is small, runs rapidly become very scarce with increasing k.

A second method for estimating the parameters arises from the expression for the asymptotic probabilities, Eq. 7.21. From Eq. 7.14,

$$E(\mathbf{T}_n \mid s) = \rho_n(s)\nu_1 + [1 - \rho_n(s)]\nu_0.$$

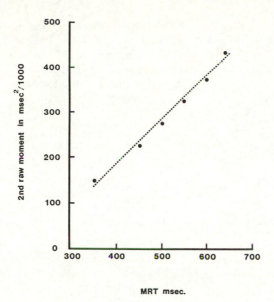

FIG. 7.1 Second raw moment versus MRT from a six-choice digit experiment with non-uniform presentation probabilities (Falmagne, 1965). There were 1400 trials per subject and seven subjects. According to two-state mixture model, this should be linear (Eq. 7.6).

Let $n \to \infty$ and substitute from Eq. 7.21,

$$E(\mathbf{T}_\infty \mid s) = \frac{\pi(s)\alpha\nu_1 + [1 - \pi(s)]\alpha^*\nu_0}{\pi(s)\alpha + [1 - \pi(s)]\alpha^*}. \tag{7.22}$$

Observe that only α/α^* is identifiable, not α and α^* separately. The parameter estimates can be chosen so as to minimize the mean square error for the times over the stimuli.

7.3 DATA WITH FEW RESPONSE ERRORS

7.3.1 Linear Functions

Falmagne (1965) reported a study in which each of seven subjects responded as rapidly as possible, subject to maintaining near error-free performance, as to which of six digits appeared on a display. The instructions were successful in holding down the error rate to about 3%. In the data analysis, all error trials were discarded. Responses were carried out by three fingers of each hand. Considerable care was taken to counterbalance the design, and the data were averaged over subjects, digits, and fingers. The major manipulation was the likelihood of the digits, which appeared with probabilities 0.01, 0.03, 0.06, 0.10, 0.24, and 0.56. The data were analyzed from three points of view: linear functions (in this subsection), fixed points in the density of reaction times (Section 7.3.2), and sequential effects (Section 7.3.3).

Figure 7.1 shows the relation between the first two raw moments, Eq. 7.6;

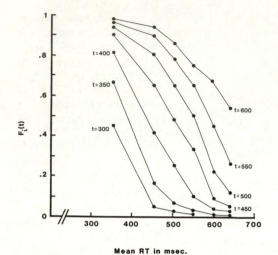

Mean RT in msec.

FIG. 7.2 For the same experiment as Figure 7.1, estimated $F(t)$ as a function of MRT, with t a parameter. By Eq. 7.7 this should be linear in the two-state mixture model.

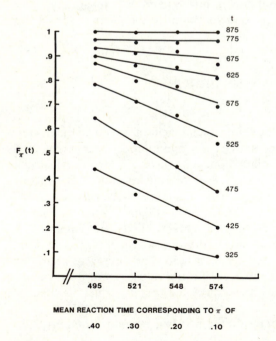

MEAN REACTION TIME CORRESPONDING TO π OF

.40   .30   .20   .10

FIG. 7.3 This is the same plot as Figure 7.2 for data of Lupker and Theios (1977), which I adapted from an unpublished manuscript of D. Noreen.

there appears to be a very slight departure from linearity. Figure 7.2 shows the distribution function $F(t \mid s)$ for several values of s against the mean reaction time (Eq. 7.7). Quite obviously these curves are not linear, and so the model surely does not fit these data terribly well, although as we shall see in Section 7.3.3 it gives a partial account of the sequential effects.

Lupker and Theois (1977) conducted a similar experiment using four digits and presentation probabilities of 0.10, 0.20, 0.30, and 0.40 with the results shown in Figure 7.3. Superficially, these data appear rather more linear, but in relation to the Falmagne data they correspond only to the 100-msec range from 400 to 500 msec, where his data are also fairly linear.

7.3.2   Fixed Points

Falmagne (1968) first pointed out to psychologists the striking fixed-point property of the mixture model, Eq. 7.11, and he plotted the distributions for his 1965 experiment. These are shown in Figure 7.4, and quite obviously they do not exhibit the fixed-point property since the top two histograms intersect at the dotted line and that line does not go through the point of intersection of the top histogram with any of the others.

Lupker and Theios (1975) ran both a four- and six-digit version of the experiment with unequal presentation probabilities. The design differed, however, in having a key stimulus that was selected to be presented with probability π, and the remaining digits were equally likely with a total probability of $1 - \pi$. The values of π used were 0.10, 0.25, 0.40, 0.55, and 0.70. The key stimulus for each subject was the same throughout the conditions, but differed among subjects. In the four-digit experiment there

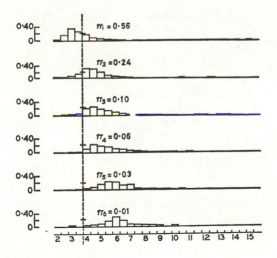

FIG. 7.4 Response-time histograms from the digit study of Falmage (1965) in which the total sample size is 9800. In the two-state mixture model, the densities underlying these histograms should have a fixed point. [Figure 1 of Falmagne (1968); copyright 1968; reprinted by permission.]

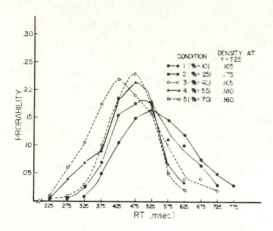

FIG. 7.5 For a four-digit experiment similar to that of Figure 7.4, the response-time histograms for several probability distributions. The distributions are based on 608, 1620, 2632, 3644, and 4856 observations with increasing π. [Figure 1 of Lupker and Theios (1975); copyright 1975; reprinted by permission.]

were a total of 20 subjects, five per key digit. In the six-digit case, the same pattern was used, leading to 30 subjects. Figures 7.5 and 7.6 show the estimated density functions for the four- and six-digit experiments, respectively. The fixed-point property that all histograms should meet at a common point is well sustained in the four-digit case, and less well so in the six-digit case, although it does not fail nearly so badly as in the Falmagne data. Lupker and Theois suggested that the extremely small presentation probabilities used by Falmagne were the source of the problem because, they

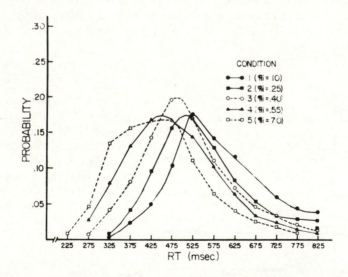

FIG. 7.6 The same as Figure 7.5 for a six-digit experiment. The sample sizes, with increasing π, were 912, 2280, 3648, 5016, and 6484. [Figure 2 of Lupker and Theios (1975); copyright 1975; reprinted by permission.]

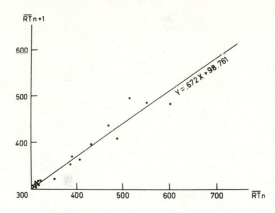

FIG. 7.7 For Falmagne's (1956) digit experiment, MRT for repetition sequences of length $n+1$ versus MRT for repetition sequences of length n, where a repetition sequence is defined in the text (Section 7.2.2). [Figure 3 of Falmagne (1965); copyright 1965, reprinted by permission.]

conjectured, the subjects treated the three least probable stimuli in a way quite different from the others. In any event, it seems clear that the two-state mixture model is not sufficiently general to account for even these simple experiments; nonetheless, in some cases the data do in fact exhibit the fixed-point property.

7.3.3 Estimation of Parameters and Fitting Sequential Data

There are two major ways to estimate the parameters. One is to use the asymptotic mixing probability given by Eq. 7.21 in the expression for the mean reaction time, Eq. 7.5. This yields estimates of ν_0, ν_1, and α/α^*. The other is to examine the one-step sequential effects on the reaction times, as was outlined at the end of Section 7.2.2. Figures 7.7 and 7.8 show the repetition and interval scatter diagrams for Falmagne's (1965) data, the former yielding α and ν_0, the latter α^* and ν_1. The results of these estimation schemes are shown in Table 7.1. The correspondence is good.

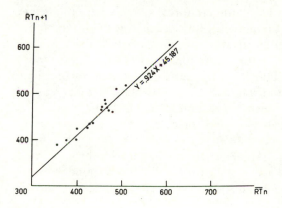

FIG. 7.8 Same as Figure 7.7 but for interval sequences (see Section 7.2.2). [Figure 4 of Falmagne (1965); copyright 1965; reprinted by permission.]

TABLE 7.1. Parameters estimated by Falmagne (1965)

Source	α	α^*	α^*/α	ν_0	ν_1
MRT			.210	295	611
Sequential MRT	.328	.076	.232	300	593

Using those estimated from the one-step sequential data, predictions can be made for repetitions and intervals of various lengths, and these are shown in Table 7.2. There are, as one might expect by now, substantial discrepancies for the low probability presentations where, for example, the total sample of presentations at the 0.01 probability over the seven subjects was only 378. Splitting this up into sequences is bound to produce highly unstable estimates.

Remington (1969), whose experiment and data were presented in Section 6.5.1, interpreted his results as inconsistent with a two-state mixture model. Theois and Smith (1972) pointed out that this is incorrect. They fit the model to the data in two ways under the restriction that $\alpha = \alpha^*$. Either the value of α can be assumed independent of the experimental manipulation of presentation probability or to depend on it. Under the former assumption, the fit to all of the sequential MRTs had an average absolute error of 8.6 msec, and under the latter assumption the error was reduced to 2.8 msec. The numbers resulting from the latter assumption, shown in Table 7.3, is impressive.

7.4   THE FAST-GUESS ACCOUNT OF ERRORS

7.4.1   The Simple Fast-Guess Model

Ollman (1966) proposed a generalization of Falmagne's mixture model that allows for errors in responses. He stated it only for means, and Yellott (1967, 1971) generalized it to distributional form and pointed out some problems with Ollman's test of the model. More detailed tests of the model are included in Ollman's (1970) dissertation and in Yellott (1971).

As we recall from Section 6.3.3, the basic idea is that in the fast mode, which has response-time distribution G_0, the subject is unable to discriminate at all between the signals and responds simply by guessing; whereas, in the slower identification mode, which has response-time distribution G_1, the subject is able to discriminate between the signals, although not necessarily perfectly. Ollman (1966) assumed that in advance of the trial the subject decides either just to detect the signal onset and make a preprogrammed response or to wait until the signal is identified and then respond. So, G_0 should be the simple-reaction-time distribution. Yellott (1967) suggested

TABLE 7.2. Observed and theoretical MRT for the various repetition and interval histories (parameter values: $v_1 = 611$, $v_0 = 300$, $\alpha^*/\alpha = 0.232$)

Probability		Interval								Repetition										
		1	2	3	4	5	6	7	8	0	1	2	3	4	5	6	7	8	9	10
0.56	Pre.	358	376	392	407	421	434	446		373	352	335	324	316	311	307	305	303	302	301
	Obs.	376	399	400	422	427	434	434		389	352	320	316	309	314	314	308	310	302	305
0.24	Pre.	423	436	448	459	470	480	498	506	465	416	381	357							
	Obs.	455	464	470	463	479	461	487	512	471	434	391	367							
0.10	Pre.									511	448	404	373							
	Obs.									419	491	406	362							
0.06	Pre.									555	478									
	Obs.									557	482									
0.03	Pre.									604	513									
	Obs.									607	479									

Note: Pre. = predicted; Obs. = observed.

TABLE 7.3. Mean reaction time (in milliseconds) on trial n given preceding stimulus sequence

| | | | | | | Stimulus presentation probability | | | | | |
| | | | | | | .3 | | .7 | | .5 | |
Order	S_n	S_{n-1}	S_{n-2}	S_{n-3}	S_{n-4}	Obs.	Pre.	Obs.	Pre.	Obs.	Pre.
First	1					307	308	274	273	290	290
Second	1	1				302	300	269	269	284	284
	1	2				310	311	280	281	295	296
Third	1	1	1			297	293	267	267	278	280
	1	1	2			309	304	276	274	288	289
	1	2	1			306	306	278	278	290	292
	1	2	2			314	314	292	288	300	301
Fourth	1	1	1	1		292	288	263	266	276	276
	1	1	1	2		301	295	271	270	280	284
	1	1	2	1		309	298	275	272	283	286
	1	1	2	2		309	304	279	278	293	293
	1	2	1	1		309	302	278	276	292	288
	1	2	1	2		305	308	280	282	286	295
	1	2	2	1		308	309	291	285	293	296
	1	2	2	2		316	315	294	293	305	304
Fifth	1	1	1	1	1	287	283	264	265	273	274
	1	1	1	1	2	296	290	262	268	279	279
	1	1	1	2	1	296	292	273	269	277	281
	1	1	1	2	2	302	297	266	273	283	286
	1	1	2	1	1	303	295	273	271	285	283
	1	1	2	1	2	311	300	278	275	281	288
	1	1	2	2	1	309	302	275	277	293	290
	1	1	2	2	2	309	305	285	282	294	295
	1	2	1	1	1	303	300	279	275	292	285
	1	2	1	1	2	312	304	276	279	292	291
	1	2	1	2	1	314	306	283	281	282	292
	1	2	1	2	2	300	309	276	286	290	298
	1	2	2	1	1	308	308	287	284	288	294
	1	2	2	1	2	308	312	300	289	300	300
	1	2	2	2	1	320	313	288	291	301	301
	1	2	2	2	2	315	316	302	297	310	307

Note: Obs. = observed; Pre. = predicted.

that the mechanism might actually be one of time estimates from the warning signal. I will discuss the evidence on that point in Section 7.5.3.

The source of tradeoff between speed and accuracy in this, the simplest, version of fast guessing is attending or not to the identity of the stimulus. If one does attend, then there is assumed to be a fixed distribution of response times and a fixed error rate. One of the major empirical tasks is to decide, given that the subject attends to the stimulus, whether or not there is a further speed-accuracy tradeoff beyond that of attention. If there is, as appears to be the case, then it too must be modeled, which is the topic of Chapters 8 and 9.

Recall that $\rho = \rho(\vec{E})$ is the probability of being in state 1 (i.e., wait to identify the signal), β_A and β_B are the two guessing probabilities, where $\beta_A + \beta_B = 1$, and P_{sr} is the probability of making response r to stimulus s when in state 1, where $P_{sA} + P_{sB} = 1$. Then the response probabilities are (Eq. 6.10)

$$P(r \mid s) = \rho P_{sr} + (1 - \rho)\beta_r, \qquad s = a, b, \quad r = A, B. \tag{7.23}$$

Although in his work Falmagne assumed that ρ is not only a function of the past history of the experiment, but also of the signal on the current trial, given the interpretation of the fast-guess model, dependence on the signal presented is implausible. Moreover, the analyses suggested by Ollman and Yellott do not go through if that is the case. So we explicitly assume that ρ is independent of the signal presented although it still depends upon other aspects of the environment.

It is easy to see that the response-time densities are given by

$$f(t \mid r, s) = [\rho g_1(t)P_{sr} + (1 - \rho)g_0(t)\beta_r]/P(r \mid s)$$
$$= \eta_{sr}g_1(t) + (1 - \eta_{sr})g_0(t), \tag{7.24a}$$

where

$$\eta_{sr} = P_{sr}/P(r \mid s), \tag{7.24b}$$

and $P(r \mid s)$ is given in Eq. 7.23. This form is exactly the same as Eq. 7.1 except that the mixture parameter η_{sr} is a function of both s and r as well as the condition.

7.4.2 Two Predictions

In addition to the fixed-point property, which holds since Eq. 7.24a is a special case of Eq. 7.3, the model embodied in Eqs. 7.23 and 7.24 makes two major predictions about the data. The first seems not to have been noted in the literature, even though it provides a very stringent and useful test of the simple fast-guess model. Keeping in mind that the denominator of Eq. 7.24b is $P(r \mid s)$ and using the local independence of the model,

$$f(t \mid s) = f(t \mid s, A)P(A \mid s) + f(t \mid s, B)P(B \mid s)$$
$$= \rho g_1(t)P_{sA} + (1 - \rho)g_0(t)\beta_A$$
$$\quad + \rho g_1(t)P_{sB} + (1 - \rho)g_0\beta_B$$
$$= \rho g_1(t) + (1 - \rho)g_0(t), \tag{7.25}$$

which is completely independent of the signal s; that is, for all t,

$$f(t \mid a) = f(t \mid b), \tag{7.26a}$$

and in particular

$$E(\mathbf{T} \mid a) = E(\mathbf{T} \mid b). \tag{7.26b}$$

This will be checked below in several bodies of data, but we already know that it is at considerable variance with some of the data reported in Section 6.5. (For example, with unequal presentation probabilities, the more probable signal is responded to more rapidly than is the less probable one.)

The second prediction follows a similar line of argument, originally stated by Ollman (1966) for means. Following Yellott (1971) and using the subscript notation c and e on P and f for "correct" and "error" responses, we first define

$$P_c = \tfrac{1}{2}[P(A \mid a) + P(B \mid b)], \qquad (7.27a)$$

$$P_e = \tfrac{1}{2}[P(B \mid a) + P(A \mid b)]. \qquad (7.27b)$$

Then we establish that

$$2f_c(t) = f(t \mid a, A)P(A \mid a) + f(t \mid b, B)P(B \mid b)$$

$$= \frac{[P_{aA} + P_{bB}]g_1(t) - g_0(t)}{P_{aA} + P_{bB} - 1}(P_c - P_e) + g_0(t) \qquad (7.28a)$$

and

$$2f_e(t) = f(t \mid a, b)P(B \mid a) + f(t \mid b, A)P(A \mid b)$$

$$= \frac{[2 - P_{aA} - P_{bB}]g_1(t) - g_0(t)}{P_{aA} + P_{bB} - 1}(P_c - P_e) + g_0(t). \qquad (7.28b)$$

These are proved as follows. First, observe that by definition of P_c and P_e and Eq. 7.23,

$$P_c - P_e = P(A \mid a) + P(B \mid b) - 1$$

$$= \rho P_{aA} + (1 - \rho)\beta_A + \rho P_{bB} + (1 - \rho)\beta_B - 1$$

$$= \rho(P_{aA} + P_{bB} - 1). \qquad (7.29)$$

Next, substitute Eq. 7.24a into the definitions of f_c and f_e, and then use Eq. 7.29 to eliminate ρ and get Eq. 7.28.

If we define

$$M_c = (1/P_c)\int tf_c(t)\, dt, \qquad (7.30a)$$

$$M_e = (1/P_e)\int tf_e(t)\, dt, \qquad (7.30b)$$

then from Eqs. 7.28 and 7.29, we obtain the important relations

$$2P_c M_c = \frac{(P_{aA} + P_{bB})\nu_1 - \nu_0}{P_{aA} + P_{bB} - 1}(P_c - P_e) + \nu_0, \qquad (7.31a)$$

$$2P_e M_e = \frac{(2 - P_{aA} - P_{bB})\nu_1 - \nu_0}{P_{aA} + P_{bB} - 1}(P_c - P_e) + \nu_0. \qquad (7.31b)$$

By Eq. 7.27, $P_c + P_e = 1$, and so adding Eqs. 7.31a and 7.31b, we see

$$E(\mathbf{T}) = P_c M_c + P_e M_e$$

$$= (\nu_1 - \nu_0) \frac{2P_c - 1}{P_{aA} + P_{bB} - 1} + \nu_0. \qquad (7.31c)$$

Equation 7.31c follows immediately from Eqs. 6.13 and 7.26b. The first two of this trio of equations say that when ρ is varied by some experimental manipulation, the data should exhibit linear relations between estimates of $2P_c M_c$ and $2P_e M_e$ and estimates of $P_c - P_e$. Moreover, they have a common intercept at the mean guessing time ν_0. These are two speed-accuracy tradeoffs in terms of the observables. The third combines these two more detailed results into a single linear SATF between $E(\mathbf{T})$ and P_c (see, also, Eq. 6.13). As was noted earlier, these tradeoffs arise in the data without our having to postulate any direct tradeoff between speed and accuracy in the underlying mechanism.

Another important property of the model arises by subtracting Eq. 7.28b from Eq. 7.28a, yielding

$$g_1(t) = [f_c(t) - f_e(t)]/(P_c - P_e). \qquad (7.32)$$

For $P_c - P_e$ not too near 0, this provides us with a means of testing the hypothesis that g_1 is invariant under changes of conditions in the experiment. If it is, one can use Eq. 7.32 to estimate g_1 from the data. Such a formula is known as a "correction for guessing." The general question about techniques for correcting various response measures for the effect of guessing was explored by Link (1982).

It follows immediately from Eq. 7.32 that the means satisfy the linear relation

$$P_c M_c - P_e M_e = \nu_1(P_c - P_e), \qquad (7.33)$$

in which the slope is the mean identification time.

7.4.3 *Estimation of the Mean Identification Time*

The obvious way to estimate the mean identification time is to estimate P_c, P_e, M_c, and M_e from the data in the usual way and then compute an estimate of ν_1 from Eq. 7.33. Is this a satisfactory estimate? Since we have made no assumptions about the distributions G_0 and G_1, we do not know the sampling distribution of ν_1 unless we can in some manner invoke the central limit theorem (Appendix A). Basically, we would like to know the conditions under which the estimate from Eq. 7.33 converges in probability to ν_1 as the sample size goes to ∞. Yellott (1971) presented the following sufficient conditions: (1) G_0 and G_1 have finite mean and variances, (2) $\lim E[P(A \mid a) + P(B \mid b) - 1] > 0$, and (3) the convergence of $E(\boldsymbol{\rho}_m \mid \mathbf{s}_n, \mathbf{r}_n, \mathbf{T}_n)$ to $E(\boldsymbol{\rho}_m)$ is not too slow—geometric or better will do—where $\mathbf{s}_n$, $\mathbf{r}_n$, and

$\mathbf{T}_n$ denote, respectively, the stimulus, response, and latency on trial n and $\boldsymbol{\rho}_m$ is the probability of attending to a signal on trial m. Since these conditions seem plausible, it is reasonable to use Eq. 7.33 to estimate ν_1. The proof may be found on pp. 168–169 of Yellott (1971).

The intercept of Eq. 7.31c yields an estimate of ν_0, and with both of those means known, then the slope provides an estimate of $P_{aA} + P_{bB}$.

7.4.4   Generalized Fast-Guess Model

Ollman, in his original presentation, stated a somewhat more general model than the simple fast-guess one. This generalized model supposes that G_1 depends both on the signal presented and the response made, and so is replaced by $G_{1,sr}$ and that G_0 depends on the response, and so is replaced by $G_{0,r}$. The question, then, is the extent to which the two predictions of Section 7.4.2 are changed.

First, nothing as simple as Eq. 7.26—that $f(t \mid s)$ is independent of the signal presented—obtains. Second, the linear relation given in Eq. 7.33 still obtains with ν_1 replaced by

$$\frac{\nu_{1,aA} + \nu_{1,bB}}{2} - \frac{P_{bA}(\nu_{1,aA} - \nu_{1,bA}) + P_{aB}(\nu_{1,bB} - \nu_{1,aB})}{2(P_{aA} + P_{bB} - 1)}. \qquad (7.34)$$

This result is verified in exactly the same way that Eq. 7.33 was. Thus, if we find Eq. 7.26 rejected but Eq. 7.33 sustained in data, we know that the simple fast-guess model is wrong but the generalized one might be correct.

7.4.5   Sequential Effects

Since we know there are sequential effects in the data (Section 6.5), it is reasonably important to see if there is reason to expect them to affect the predictions of the fast-guess model. Basically, one wants to graft Falmagne's linear operator model onto the fast-guess structure. The most obvious way of doing so—namely, to suppose ρ is trial- and stimulus-dependent and changes according to Eq. 7.12—will not do, the reason being that if the subject knows which signal was presented then the fast mode would not also be a guessing mode. Rather, Yellott (1971, p. 194) suggested that the impact is on the guessing strategy as follows. On trial n there is a probability φ_n that the subject is "set for" or "prepared for" stimulus a and $1 - \varphi_n$ for stimulus b. Set affects the process in two ways. If the subject elects to guess, which is done with probability $1 - \rho$, then the response is A when the set is for a and B when it is for b. If, however, the subject elects to attend to the stimulus, the response times and probabilities differ depending upon whether or not the signal is the one for which the subject is set. We use unprimed and primed symbols to indicate whether or not the signal is the one for which the subject is set. The generalized fast-guess model is restricted to the extent that no distinction is made as to the type of correct and error response; that is,

$$P_c = P_{aA} = P_{bB},$$

$$P_{c'} = P_{a'A} = P_{b'B},$$

$$\nu_{1,c} = \nu_{1,aA} = \nu_{1,bB},$$

$$\nu_{1,e} = \nu_{1,aB} = \nu_{1,bA},$$

$$\nu_{1,c'} = \nu_{1,a'A} = \nu_{1,b'B},$$

$$\nu_{1,e'} = \nu_{1,a'B} = \nu_{1,b',A}.$$

The sequential process is to change φ_n according to Eq. 7.12 (with $\varphi_n = \varphi_{a,n}$). As was remarked in arriving at Eq. 7.21, because the transitions between the two states of "set" form a Markov chain, the probability φ_n of being set for stimulus a has an asymptotic value. Using that and following the argument that led to Eq. 7.33 again yields a linear relation between $P_c M_c - P_e M_e$ and $P_c - P_e$ with ν_1 replaced by an expression similar to Eq. 7.34 and with aA replaced by c', bB by c, aB by e', and bA by e. Thus, the linear prediction of Eq. 7.33 is unaffected by the existence of sequential effects described by this type of Markov chain.

A more interesting attempt to deal with sequential effects in the context of fast guesses is taken up in Section 7.5.

7.4.6 A Donderian Assumption

Consider the following further specification of the simple fast-guess model. First, suppose, as Ollman suggested, that the difference between the two states 0 and 1 is that only detection occurs (say, by means of a change detector) in the former, whereas in the latter it is followed by an independent stage of identification. This is a typical Donderian assumption of the type discussed in Section 6.2.2. Second, let us explicitly suppose that the time for identification is independent of the time for detection. If so, then g_1 is the convolution of g_0 with the identification distribution, call it g_I. Putting this together with Eq. 7.24 and calculating the mgf yields

$$\mathcal{M}(x \mid r, s) = \mathcal{M}_0(x)[\eta_{sr} \mathcal{M}_I(x) + 1 - \eta_{sr}], \tag{7.35}$$

where η_{sr} is given by Eq. 7.24b.

In principle, this can be used as follows, although it has yet to be applied to data. By experimental manipulation, run the experiment for two values of ρ: $\rho(1)$ and $\rho(2)$. Let $\eta_{sr}(i)$, $i = 1, 2$, be the corresponding values of Eq. 7.24b, then it follows immediately that

$$\left[\frac{\mathcal{M}(x \mid s, r)}{\mathcal{M}_0(x)} \right]_1 = \frac{\eta_{sr}(1)}{\eta_{sr}(2)} \left[\frac{\mathcal{M}(x \mid s, r)}{\mathcal{M}_0(x)} \right]_2 + 1 - \frac{\eta_{sr}(1)}{\eta_{sr}(2)}. \tag{7.36}$$

This linear relation can be tested by obtaining $\mathcal{M}(x \mid s, r)$ from the choice situation for two experimental manipulations run on the same subject under the same conditions. If three levels of ρ are run, then Eq. 7.23 yields six probabilities and the six parameters: p_{aA}, P_{bB}, β_A, $\rho(1)$, $\rho(2)$, and $\rho(3)$. This permits us to compute $\eta_{sr}(i)$ from Eq. 7.24b and to insert these values in Eq. 7.35, so the predicted relation is parameter free. And, of course, we can compute $\mathcal{M}_I(x)$ from Eq. 7.35. It would be of interest to do this in a situation where the general fast-guess model appears to hold.

7.5   A THREE-STATE, FAST-GUESS, MEMORY MODEL

Falmagne, Cohen, and Dwivedi (1975) suggested combining two sets of ideas—fast guessing and memory scanning—as a way to account for the sequential effects found in two-choice reaction times. Unlike Falmagne's 1965 model, this one is sufficiently general to account for the sequential effects in error data as well as time data. Although the general issues of memory scanning are not dealt with until Chapter 11, the ideas used in this model are sufficiently self-contained and simple that introducing them now does not present any real difficulty. It should be recognized, however, that the assumptions of serial and self-terminated scanning are controversial.

Without a doubt, the subject has some sort of stored representation of each of the two signals, a or b. Suppose on each trial, the subject elects either to base the decision on a comparison of the information arising from the signal with the representation held in memory or to make a fast guess. In the former case suppose memory is organized so that a comparison is first made with one of the representations and then, sometimes, with the other— that is, either in the order (a, b) or (b, a). This is the serial aspect of memory. If this is true, then the organization of the memory can serve to reflect the subject's expectancy about which signal is more likely or more important.

The model has two distinct components: how the responses are affected by both the signal presented and the state of the subject's memory, and how the state of memory is altered. The response part is taken up in Section 7.5.2. Basically three things are involved: under what conditions does the memory search terminate after comparing the information from the signal and the first item in memory; what response is made in each case; and how long does each response take? The temporal structure of this response system is a three-state mixture in which fast guesses have one distribution, single scans have another, slower one, and double scans a still slower one. In addition, these distributions are assumed to differ depending upon which response is made; this is necessary if, for example, the subject's response times for the two hands differ.

The other component of the model, which is developed in detail in Section 7.5.1, is a description of the possible states of memory and a model for how these change. This leads to a Markov chain representation of memory states in which the experience on a trial has some tendency to alter the state of memory. We will be interested only in these dynamics after steady state has been reached, in which case they are the source of sequential effects in this model.

7.5.1 Memory Transitions

In describing this model, I find it convenient to continue using a notation similar to that used so far; it differs somewhat from that of Falmagne et al. I use a and b to refer, in context, to the particular stimuli, the particular responses used to identify them, and the corresponding representations in memory. Context will make quite clear which of the three levels is involved. Generic stimuli and responses are denoted s and r, respectively. The stimulus other than s is denoted s^*, so if $s = a$, then $s^* = b$. The same convention is followed for responses. For trial n, the stimulus presented, the response made, and the response time are all observable realizations of random variables, denoted as usual, s_n, r_n, and T_n. In addition, there is assumed to be an unobserved random variable, M_n, describing the state of the subject's memory. This variable is discussed next.

There are four possible states of memory which will be denoted a_F, b_F, a, and b. The first two are the fast-guess states, with the former biased toward a and the latter, b_F, toward b. The other two states determine the order of scanning: a indicating that the representation of a is scanned first and b second, and b indicating the opposite order.

The intuitive idea about how memory changes is that if the signal presented agrees with the bias in memory, then that bias remains or becomes more severe, where s_F is a more severe bias than is s, $s = a$ or b. If, however, the signal presented does not agree with the bias, then memory ends up at one or the other of the less biased states, the probability of each depending upon where it was. The following matrix of transition probabilities from the states on trial n to trial $n + 1$ captures these ideas explicitly: if signal s is presented, then the transitions among memory states are:

$$
\text{Trial } n \quad
\begin{array}{c}
 \\ s_F \\ s \\ s^* \\ s_F^*
\end{array}
\overset{\displaystyle \text{Trial } n+1}{
\begin{array}{c}
s_F \quad\; s \quad\;\; s^* \quad\;\; s_F^* \\
\left[
\begin{array}{cccc}
1 & 0 & 0 & 0 \\
\beta_s & 1-\beta_s & 0 & 0 \\
0 & \alpha_s & 1-\alpha_s & 0 \\
0 & \delta_s & 1-\delta_s & 0
\end{array}
\right].
\end{array}}
\tag{7.37}
$$

Note, there are two distinct matrices depending on whether $s = a$ or b, and that they introduce a total of six parameters.

So far as I can tell, the assumptions embodied in Eq. 7.37 have no basis in any observations aside from the data they help explain. They seem plausible, and certainly memory for simple signals might work this way. But it is not difficult to think of other quite plausible ways it might work, and so their real test comes later, in accounting for sequential data.

Before turning to the response model, it is useful to introduce an assumption about the experiment to which the model will be applied— namely, that the probability of presenting a signal depends upon nothing but the signal. Formally, if we let $\mathbf{W}_n$ be the entire history of random variables up to and including trial n—that is, $\mathbf{s}_i$, $\mathbf{r}_i$, $\mathbf{T}_i$, $\mathbf{M}_i$, $i = 1, 2, \ldots, n$, then the postulate is

$$\Pr(\mathbf{s}_n = s \mid \mathbf{M}_n, \mathbf{W}_{n-1}) = \pi_s, \tag{7.38}$$

where $\sum_s \pi_s = 1$. On that assumption, one can calculate the transitions among the memory states. For example, consider,

$$\Pr(\mathbf{M}_{n+1} = a \mid \mathbf{M}_n = b, \mathbf{s}_n, \mathbf{W}_{n-1})$$
$$= \Pr(\mathbf{M}_{n+1} = a \mid \mathbf{M}_n = b, \mathbf{s}_n = a, \mathbf{W}_{n-1}) \Pr(\mathbf{s}_n = a \mid \mathbf{M}_n = b, \mathbf{W}_{n-1})$$
$$+ \Pr(\mathbf{M}_{n+1} = a \mid \mathbf{M}_n = b, \mathbf{s}_n = b, \mathbf{W}_{n-1}) \Pr(\mathbf{s}_n = b \mid \mathbf{M}_n = b, \mathbf{W}_{n-1})$$
$$= \alpha_a \pi_a + 0.$$

The first term arises from Eq. 7.37 by noting that with $s = a$, the memory states are $\mathbf{M}_n = s^*$ and $\mathbf{M}_{n+1} = s$, and so the transition probability is α_a. With $s = b$, the memory states are s and s^*, which has a transition probability of 0. Thus, we derive that this transition probability is a constant, independent of n and of $\mathbf{W}_{n-1}$, $\mathbf{r}_n$, and $\mathbf{T}_n$. As this is true of all other pairs of states, the memory transitions form a Markov chain with the following transition matrix:*

Trial $n+1$

	a_F	a	b	b_F
a_F	π_a	$\pi_b(1-\delta_b)$	$\pi_b\delta_b$	0
a	$\pi_a\beta_a$	$\pi_a(1-\beta_a)$ $+\pi_b(1-\alpha_b)$	$\pi_b\alpha_b$	0
b	0	$\pi_a\alpha_a$	$\pi_a(1-\alpha_a)$ $+\pi_b(1-\beta_b)$	$\pi_b\beta_b$
b_F	0	$\pi_a\delta_a$	$\pi_a(1-\delta_a)$	π_b

The fact that memory transitions form a Markov chain very much simplifies the calculations involved (see Section 7.5.3).

---

* The matrix in Falmagne et al. (Table 6, p. 329) appears to be in error, in that it has a pair of parameters in addition to the four pairs postulated. These appear to arise from having the last row of Eq. 7.37 written as $(\gamma_s, \delta_s, 1-\gamma_s-\delta_s, 0)$, thereby allowing a direct transition from one guessing state to the other. In fitting the model to data, they clearly assumed $\gamma_s = 0$.

7.5.2   *Responses and Response Times*

The postulated response rule is simple. When the memory is in one of the fast-guess states, the response is that of the state. So assume memory is in one of a or b. The assumption is that if the signal agrees with the memory state—that is, there is a match between the signal and the first memory scan—then that response is made and it is error free. If, however, a mismatch exists, then either of two things can happen. The mismatch may be perceived as a match, in which case the response is that of the memory, and it is an error. Such a misperception is presumed to occur with some probability η_{s^*s} when s is presented and, as before, s^* denotes the opposite symbol. If, however, the mismatch is correctly perceived, then the second memory is scanned, a match is found, and the correct response is made. It is easiest to summarize this in terms of the conditional error probabilities:

$$\Pr(\mathbf{r}_n = s^* \mid \mathbf{s}_n = s, \mathbf{M}_n, \mathbf{W}_{n-1}) = \begin{cases} 1, & \text{if} \quad \mathbf{M}_n = s_F^*, \\ \eta_{s^*s}, & \text{if} \quad \mathbf{M}_n = s^*, \\ 0, & \text{if} \quad \mathbf{M}_n = s \text{ or } s_F, \end{cases} \tag{7.39}$$

This rule introduces two new parameters, η_{ab} and η_{ba}.

For the response times, six different distributions are introduced. For fast guesses, they are $G_{r,F}$, where $r = a, b$. For a single scan of the memory, they are $G_{r,1}$, where $r = a, b$. Recall, this occurs whenever the response matches the memory, either because the signal matches the memory or because it does not and an erroneous response is made. For two scans of the memory, they are $G_{r,2}$, and this occurs when the response and memory do not agree. Presumably, for each r, the means are ordered $\nu_{r,F} < \nu_{r,1} < \nu_{r,2}$. Formalizing this assumption:

$$\Pr(\mathbf{T}_n \leq t \mid \mathbf{s}_n, \mathbf{t}_n, \mathbf{r}_n = r, \mathbf{M}_n, \mathbf{W}_{n-1}) = \begin{cases} G_{r,F}(t), & \text{if} \quad \mathbf{M}_n = r_F, \\ G_{r,1}(t), & \text{if} \quad \mathbf{M}_n = r, \\ G_{r,2}(t), & \text{if} \quad \mathbf{M}_n = r^*. \end{cases} \tag{7.40}$$

This completes the formal statement of the assumptions of the model. There are a lot of parameters: six mean times, two η_{s^*s}, and six transition probabilities. However, considering the variety of probabilities and mean times that can be generated by partitioning the data by its history, the model can certainly be tested. We turn next to how this is done.

7.5.3   *A Strategy for Data Analysis*

Unlike the fast-guess model or even the more general two-state models, few simple properties of this model have been found that can be used to evaluate it. The main test is to estimate all of the parameters and see how well the model reproduces the sequential data. I outline that procedure in this subsection, but first I derive the only known testable property, which also serves to simplify slightly the estimation problem. Consider the class of histories: $(\mathbf{r}_{n+1} = s^*, \mathbf{s}_{n+1} = s, \mathbf{T}_n, \mathbf{r}_n, \mathbf{s}_n = s, \mathbf{W}_{n-1})$. Observe that the memory state on trial $n + 1$ must be s^*. The reasoning is as follows. Since $\mathbf{s}_n = s$, we know that $\mathbf{M}_{n+1}$ cannot be s_F^* because the final column of the memory matrix, Eq. 7.37, is all 0's. And since $\mathbf{r}_{n+1}$ is an error, we know by Eq. 7.39 this is possible only if $\mathbf{M}_{n+1}$ is either s^* or s_F^*. As the latter is impossible, the former must hold. Knowing that, consider $\mathbf{T}_{n+1}$. Since $\mathbf{M}_{n+1} = s^* = \mathbf{r}_{n+1}$, we see by Eq. 7.40 that the distribution $G_{s^*,1}$ must be used, so

$$E(\mathbf{T}_{n+1} \mid \mathbf{r}_{n+1} = s^*, \mathbf{s}_{n+1} = s, \mathbf{T}_n, \mathbf{r}_n, \mathbf{s}_n = s, \mathbf{W}_{n-1}) = \nu_{s^*,1}. \qquad (7.41)$$

This affords both a test of the model since, for example, one can partition the data on $\mathbf{r}_n$ and, of course, $\mathbf{W}_{n-1}$, and see if the estimated values are the same or not. Assuming they are, it affords an estimate of these parameters.

Beyond that, it is necessary to deduce explicit expressions for the various conditional probabilities. These deductions are straightforward, once one gets the knack of it, but they never cease being tedious. To illustrate in a simple case the type of calculation involved, consider the special case of no guessing states—that is, $\beta_s = 0$ (this is called model I in Falmagne et al.). Using first the law of total probability, next Eq. 7.39, and then Bayes' rule, we can develop an explicit expression for the error probabilities (in which I suppress the notation for much of the past history):

$$\begin{aligned}
\Pr(\mathbf{r}_n = s^* \mid \mathbf{s}_n = s) &= \Pr(\mathbf{r}_n = s^* \mid \mathbf{s}_n = s, \mathbf{M}_n = s)P(\mathbf{M}_n = s \mid \mathbf{s}_n = s) \\
&\quad + \Pr(\mathbf{r}_n = s^* \mid \mathbf{s}_n = s, \mathbf{M}_n = s^*)P(\mathbf{M}_n = s^* \mid \mathbf{s}_n = s) \\
&= 0 + \eta_{s^*s}\Pr(\mathbf{M}_n = s^* \mid \mathbf{s}_n = s) \\
&= \eta_{s^*s}\Pr(\mathbf{s}_n = s \mid \mathbf{M}_n = s^*)\Pr(\mathbf{M}_n = s^*)/\Pr(\mathbf{s}_n = s) \\
&= \eta_{s^*s}\Pr(\mathbf{M}_n = s^*),
\end{aligned}$$

where we have cancelled the two presentation terms that, despite different conditioning, are by assumption (Eq. 7.38) just the probability π_s. This result becomes useful when we let $n \to \infty$ and note that, because the memory transitions form a Markov chain and so have an asymptotic distribution, $\lim_{n \to \infty} \Pr(\mathbf{M}_n = m) = p(m)$. The asymptotic distribution can be calculated explicitly in terms of the parameters of the transition matrix, but there is no need to do so here.

This illustrates the general strategy. Since the equations are algebraically complex, Falmagne et al. programmed a computer to do the work for them. They then did a numerical exploration of the 12-dimensional parameter space, finding a numerical minimum for χ^2. The experiment to which this was applied and the results are described in Section 7.6.4.

7.6 DATA WITH RESPONSE ERRORS: HIGHLY DISCRIMINABLE STIMULI

7.6.1 *Identification of Color, Auditory Frequency, and Auditory Intensity*

Yellott (1967, 1971) ran a series of studies modeled on a design first introduced by Ollman (1966), except that Yellott's stimuli were far more discriminable than were Ollman's. The design involved manipulating a deadline, such that responses after the deadline were fined and those before it were paid off for accuracy. The deadlines used by Yellott were 150, 200, 250, 300, 350, 400, 500, and 800 msec. Following each trial, information feedback was provided. The stimuli to be identified were all highly discriminable. In Experiment 1, which was partially analyzed in his 1967 paper, the stimuli were red and green lights on a display screen. The signals were equally likely to appear, and the symmetric payoffs were not varied. In addition to the eight deadline conditions, there were two other conditions: "speed" in which subjects were pressed for speed and asked to ignore accuracy, and "accuracy" in which there was no deadline and they were urged to be as accurate as possible. There were 960 trials per condition and three subjects. Experiment 2 was similar to 1 except that the payoffs were varied in order to alter the accuracy of performance over a wider range. There were 500 trials per condition and four subjects. Experiment 3 changed the stimuli to 1000- and 1500-Hz, 70-dB SPL tones, reduced the deadlines to three (250, 300, 400 msec), and varied the presentation probabilities (.1, .3, .5, and .7). Of the possible deadline-probability pairs, nine were run. There were 500 trials per condition and four subjects.

Only for Experiment 3 were the data reported in sufficient detail (see Appendix C.1) to compute MRT(a) and MRT(b) and so to check their equality (Eq. 7.26b). With mean reaction times in range from 200 to 300 msec, the mean differences of the estimated means and standard deviations of those differences were: 1.84 ± 18.64, 3.77 ± 12.88, and -8.83 ± 12.81 msec. This does not reject the null hypothesis of Eq. 7.26b.

The plot of $P_c M_c - P_e M_e$ versus $P_c - P_e$ for the first experiment is shown in Figure 7.9. The linearity of these functions seems very satisfactory, supporting one of the main predictions of any of the fast-guess models. The data from the second and third experiments were comparable. The major deviations from linearity were the accuracy condition in Experiment 1 and, perhaps, the 800-msec deadline in Experiment 2 (condition 9). As Yellott pointed out, in the accuracy condition the subject has no motive to respond as rapidly as is consistent with perfect accuracy, and so this failure probably should not be taken very seriously.

The major evidence in these data that there may be some difficulty with the model is the fact that when the estimate of ν_1 is correlated with

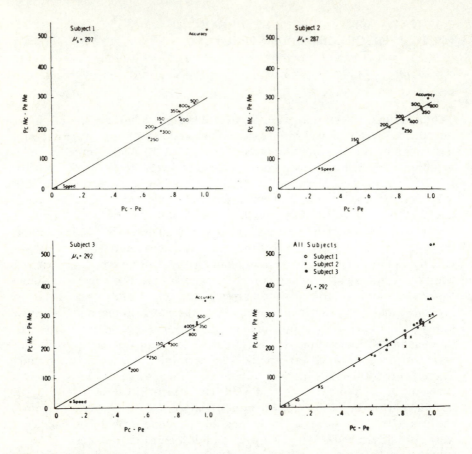

FIG. 7.9 $P_cM_c - P_eM_e$ versus $P_c - P_e$ for the identification of highly discriminable red and green lights collected under various response deadlines. There are 960 observations per condition. The linear function is predicted by the fast-guess model (Eq. 7.33) and the value μ_s—in my notation, ν_1—is the slope of the line. [Figure 2 of Yellott (1971); copyright 1971; reprinted by permission.]

accuracy, P_c, the correlation is significantly different from 0 for the four subjects of Experiment 2.

Recall that for the simple fast-guess model, there are in addition to the linear prediction of Eq. 7.33 the two separate linear predictions of $2P_cM_c$ and $2P_eM_e$ versus $P_c - P_e$, for which ν_0 is the common intercept (Eqs. 7.31a, b). With ν_1 known, one can use one slope—Yellott used the error one—to estimate $P_{aA} + P_{bB}$ and so predict the slope of the other. The estimates and predictions for the deadline conditions of Experiment 1 are shown in Figure 7.10. The model seems in close accord with the data, as it does for the other two experiments except for one deadline in Experiment 2.

In his unpublished dissertation Ollman (1970) reran his earlier 1966 study (see Section 7.7.1 below), but with several changes in design and one of analysis. He introduced catch trials and variable foreperiods in order either to induce the subjects not to time-estimate from the warning signal or to detect it if they did; the evidence was that they were not estimating time. And he used asymmetric distributions of the stimuli—20% catch trials, 50% signal *a*, and 30% signal *b*—in order to avoid symmetric guessing probabilities (i.e., $\beta_A = \beta_B = \frac{1}{2}$), which in certain cases cause estimation problems. The signals were 900-Hz tones of 100-msec duration that differed by 19 dB. The conditions differed according to the instructions, which attempted to vary the speed-accuracy tradeoff. Appendix C.2 presents the data.

Letting *a* denote the more probable signal, then the mean value of

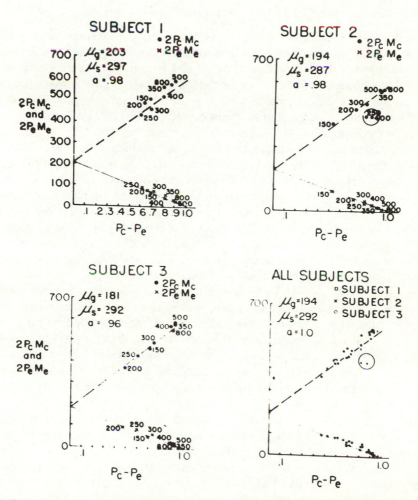

FIG. 7.10 Estimates and predictions from the fast-guess model of $2P_cM_c$ and $2P_eM_e$ versus P_c-P_e for the experiment of Figure 7.9. [Figure 3 of Yellott (1971); copyright 1971; reprinted by permission.]

$\mathrm{MRT}(a) - \mathrm{MRT}(b)$ over conditions is 30.1 msec with standard deviations of 22.3, 23.6, and 14.1 msec for the three subjects. The difference is negative only once in 17 cases for the first subject and only once in 13 cases for the second. Thus, the simple fast-guess model surely is not correct.

To test the more general model, Ollman estimated ν_0 and ν_1 for each condition and plotted them against $P(A \mid a) + P(B \mid b) - 1 = P_c - P_e$. In 9 out of 10 cases when $P(A \mid a) + P(B \mid b) - 1 > 0.8$, the estimates of ν_0 were actually negative. It is clear that these data are not consistent with any of the fast-guess models. Within the fast-guess framework, one is forced to conclude there is some covariation of P_{aA} and P_{bB} with ν_1.

7.6.2   *Identification of Length, Orientation, and Digits*

Laming (1968) performed a number of experiments to test the version of the random walk model known as the sequential probability ratio test (SPRT) model, which will be described in detail in Chapter 8. Of these experiments, only Experiments 1 and 2 are reported in sufficient detail for our purposes here, and since 2 is a refinement of 1, I report only those data. The task, it will be recalled, was to identify which of two vertical white stripes on a black background had been presented in a tachistoscope. The main experimental manipulation was the presentation probability, which varied over blocks of trials. The order of presentation of these conditions was varied among four groups of six observers each. The instructions were to respond rapidly "without worrying too much about accuracy." No information feedback was provided. There were 200 trials per condition, for a total of 4800 observations over the 24 observers. The mean data over observers are summarized in Appendix C.3.

In general, I believe it unwise to try to test models using data averaged over groups of subjects because there may be individual differences of, at least, parameter values. Two exceptions to that rule are when only ordinal comparisons are involved or when, as in this case, the relations being studied are all linear. The latter follows from the fact that any probability mixture of linear functions is itself linear. So the objection to group data is less salient here, but it will be for some of the models tested in Chapter 8. Figure 7.11 presents the plot of $\mathrm{MRT}(b)$ versus $\mathrm{MRT}(a)$, and there is little doubt that they are not equal—indeed, the correlation is nearer to -1 than it is to $+1$.

Link (1975) ran a similar study in which the two stimuli were outlines of squares each with just one of the two possible diagonals. Presentation of one or the other followed a 1000-msec foreperiod, and the signal was response terminated. The major experimental manipulation was the presentation probabilities that, unlike Laming's experiment, were interleaved at random, and the observer was told prior to each presentation which probability was in use. Information feedback about performance was not used. Seven hundred observations were collected from each observer in each condition.

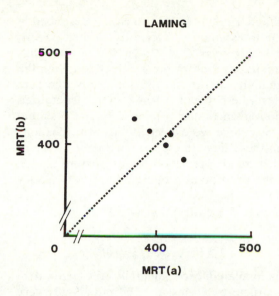

FIG. 7.11 MRT of stimulus *a* versus MRT of *b* in an experiment on the identification of length for which presentation probability was varied (Laming, 1968) (Appendix C.3). There are 4800 observations per point. The line is the prediction of the fast guess-model.

The mean data for the four observers are provided in Appendix C.4. The plot MRT(*b*) versus MRT(*a*) is shown in Figure 7.12, and again the prediction of Eq. 7.26b is violated about as badly as is possible.

For these two data sets, the simple fast-guess model is clearly wrong. And because these data exhibit very little variation in $P_c - P_e$, it is impossible to study the linearity of $P_c M_c$ and $P_e M_e$ with $P_c - P_e$, and so we have no test of the general model.

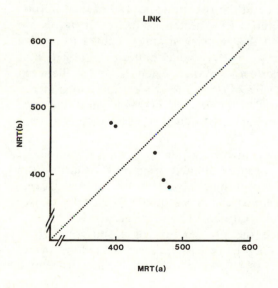

FIG. 7.12 The same as Figure 7.11 for identification of orientation (Link, 1975) (Appendix C.4). There are 2800 observations per condition.

Another relevant study is Link and Tindall (1971), which was described in Section 6.3.3. They used Eq. 7.33 to estimate v_1 (called μ_D in their paper), and these estimates were shown in Figure 6.12 (p. 236). Not only are they not constant between deadline conditions, but for the accuracy condition the estimates vary with the discriminability of the signals. So, clearly, the data are inconsistent with the simple fast-guess model. Turning to the generalized model, we see from the discussion given that the slope of Eq. 7.33 should depend on P_{aA} and P_{bB}, which of course we expect to vary with deadline conditions. So there is nothing in these facts to cause rejection of the more general model. However, the other major prediction of any mixture model, including the fast-guess ones, is the fixed point property, and it was grossly violated in their data.

Falmagne (1972) pointed out that if identification is perfect in state 1, then Eq. 7.23 yields

$$P(B \mid a) = (1-\rho)\beta_B \quad \text{and} \quad P(A \mid b) = (1-\rho)\beta_A.$$

Thus, if both ρ and β_A are manipulated experimentally, the error data should exhibit a simple product structure. To test this, he ran a study very similar to his 1965 one and checked this hypothesis; it was rejected, casting doubt on the fast-guess model. He did not report the time data in his paper.

7.6.3   Persistent Strategies in the Location of a Light

Perhaps the most conclusive study favoring the idea of two distinct strategies as in the fast-guess model, although not some other features of that model, is that of Swensson and Edwards (1971). They noticed in their data something that had been neither assumed nor predicted theoretically, but which makes studying the processes far more direct and convincing. Their subjects tended to persist using one of the two strategies rather than shifting frequently between them. Sometimes one strategy appeared to be in use throughout an entire session, and the guessing strategy seemed to involve not random guessing but rather a highly regular pattern. Although it is impossible to estimate with perfect accuracy when a switch between strategies occurred, the fact that runs of one strategy were quite long means that slight errors in estimating the boundaries between runs does not introduce gross errors into the estimates of either accuracy or mean times associated with a strategy.

For their first experiment, they arrived at the following definition of guessing or what they called "preprogrammed responses." Such a run consisted of any maximal sequence of successive responses using just one key and involving at least three error trials. Any sequence lying between two such preprogrammed runs was defined to be a run of the accuracy strategy.

The experiment itself involved the presentation of a small square of bright, easily detectable light in one of two easily discriminable locations to the left or right of a fixation point. The foreperiod was uniformly distributed

TABLE 7.4. Accurate and preprogrammed-response (PPR) performance for each subject in Experiment 1 of Swensson and Edwards (1971) during homogeneous and mixed sessions with equiprobable stimuli

| | Type of session | | | | | |
| | Homogeneous | | | Mixed | | |
Strategy	JD	TW	JM	JD	TW	JM
Accurate						
(No. response)	(1350)	(2611)	(899)	(1084)	(513)	(758)
Mean block length[a]	—	—	—	64	259	253
Error rate	.0052	.0356	.0222	.0266	.0409	.0435
MRT (msec)	228.3	200.1	210.8	223.3	198.8	201.0
PPR						
(No. response)	—	(448)	(1797)	(1124)	(343)	(592)
Mean block length[a]	—	—	—	70	58	59
Error rate	—	.493	.506	.487	.492	.503
MRT (msec)	—	185.8	189.0	203.4	187.2	182.9
MRT difference	—	14.3	21.8	19.9	11.6	18.1

[a] Mean number of consecutive trials before S switched to the other strategy during mixed-strategy sessions.

in the sense that it lay in the interval from 1 to 3 sec with each individual millisecond in that interval being equally likely. Subjects were severely fined for anticipations, they were rewarded for time inversely to the response time measured from signal onset, and they were paid off for accuracy of responding. The sums of money involved were sufficiently large that wins and losses of as much as $50 occurred in a session. Feedback was provided on a trial-by-trial basis. The experimental manipulations were three levels of presentation probability, 0.5, 0.7, and 0.9, and three payoff matrices, including a symmetric one and two asymmetric ones. This resulted in 18 conditions, to which were added the two extremes of 0 and 1 presentation probabilities, in which case no discrimination was required.

For some conditions, the evidence suggested that a single, simple strategy was in force throughout the condition. For others, a mix of the two strategies seemed to be used. The data were segregated accordingly. As can be seen in Table 7.4, the three subjects are quite similar. First, for both of the estimates of accuracy and mean time, the values are substantially the same whether a run came from an entire session (called homogeneous) or from a mixed session. Second, under the accuracy strategy, the error rate was less than 5%, whereas for the preprogrammed (guessing) strategy it was close to 50%. And third, mean reaction times for the "accurate" responses were some 12 to 22 msec slower than the preprogrammed ones. The times for the preprogrammed responses are about those found in most visual, simple-reaction time studies, but those for the accurate responses seem remarkably fast as compared with other estimates of the time required for accurate identifications.

The major effect of the experimental conditions—payoffs and presentation probabilities—was to determine the proportion of time a strategy was used. In particular, the payoffs had no significant effect on the error rate in the accuracy condition. This fact is inconsistent with all of the models to be discussed in Chapters 8 and 9. Moreover, mean reaction time increased with decreasing signal probability when the subject was operating under the accuracy strategy and it also decreased for the incorrect responses under the preprogrammed strategy. These effects are not consistent with the fast-guess model.

Experiments 2 and 3 undertook a more careful study of the speed-accuracy trade off, in particular, to see if it is possible to induce some form of intermediate responding of the type described in the next two chapters. The results, except perhaps for one subject, strongly confirmed the existence of just two types of strategy, although they found it necessary to admit into the definition of preprogrammed patterns two additional ones besides simple repetition of one response—namely, strict alternation and always giving the response that was appropriate to the preceding signal.

Aside from Swensson (1972a)—which experiment I take up in Section 7.7.3—the only other person I am aware of analyzing their data in this fashion is Wilding (1974). However, because his subjects were so slow, it made no difference. I believe that such an analysis should be used routinely since it provides simple definitions of guessing strategies, thereby permitting one not only to check if there was guessing in experiments where one hopes no guessing was involved, but to identify the runs of guesses and remove them for separate analysis.

7.6.4 Sequential Effects in the Identification of Orientation

In a study mentioned earlier (Section 6.5.1), Falmagne et al. (1975) ran three subjects in the identification of two isosceles triangles presented on a CRT. The bases were vertical and the apex faced either right or left, to which right and left keys corresponded. The vertical and horizontal visual angles were about 2.4° and 1.2°. The presentation probabilities were 0.65 and 0.35, which on half the sessions were assigned to right and left, respectively, and on the other half to left and right. The stimuli were response terminated, and the response-stimulus interval was 200 msec. Each session consisted of 100 practice trials followed by three blocks of 300 trials each. Following each block, subjects were informed of error rates and were urged to speed up when it was less than 0.10 and to be more careful when it was greater than 0.12. A total of 20,000 trials were run, of which 2600 were practice and were not included in the analyses. As the two hands made a difference, the data were partitioned accordingly.

As was noted in Section 7.5.3, the model was fit to the data by means of a

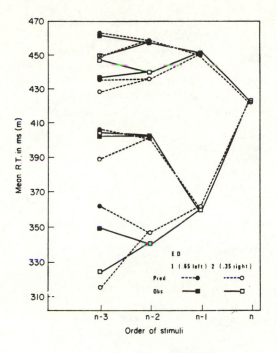

FIG. 7.13 MRT versus stimulus history, similar to Figures 6.21 and 22 for Remington (1969), for an unequal presentation probability experiment of Falmagne et al. (1975). The sample size for the pair of rightmost points is 8700 and is reduced to 1087 for any corresponding pair of leftmost points. The theoretical predictions are for the three-state model described in the text. [Figure 13 of Falmagne et al. (1975); copyright 1975; reprinted by permission.]

numerical search. For one subject, two states of memory (no fast guesses) sufficed, but for the other two fast-guessing states had to be included. Only one data set was fully analyzed because of the expense of the parameter search. To gain some idea of how the model fits some of these data, Figures 7.13 and 7.14 show the time and error sequential data for the 0.35 probability signal. The code is this: squares are data points and circles are predictions from the model. Filled symbols are signals that are the same as the one on trial n, whereas unfilled symbols are the opposite signal. Thus, if $s_n = a$, $s_{n-1} = a$, and $s_{n-2} = b$, then the symbol over n is filled, that over $n-1$ is also filled, but that over $n-2$ is unfilled since b differs from a. The ability of the model to mimic the data is striking.

The estimated mean latencies (in msec) for the several scanning conditions are

$$v_{a,F} = 123, \quad v_{a,1} = 305, \quad v_{a,2} = 439,$$
$$v_{b,F} = 23,^* \quad v_{b,1} = 373, \quad v_{b,2} = 469.$$

In this case, b corresponded to the less preferred hand, and we see that for the identification responses it is slower.

The value of χ^2 for these data was 104 with 34 degrees of freedom (46 nodes less 12 estimated parameters, ignoring the two times that were estimated separately). This is, of course, highly significant. Nevertheless, the model is mimicking the pattern of the data exceedingly well. The authors

---

* I have verified with Falmagne that this is not a typesetting error.

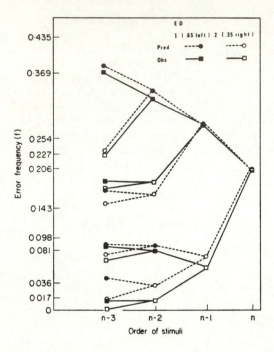

FIG. 7.14 Error probability versus stimulus history for the same experiment as in Figure 7.13. [Figure 15 of Falmagne et al. (1975); copyright 1975; reprinted by permission.]

were unable to find any systematic pattern to the erroneous predictions, which was not the case when they attempted to fit the simpler model to the same data. Clearly, the model is not quite correct, but nevertheless it does an impressive job in reproducing a highly complex set of results. As they note, no doubt with a bit of tinkering the fit could be improved.

The greatest difficulty in this approach is how to generalize it. This has been the dilemma of much model building in psychology, and has proved especially acute with Markov chain models. As one goes to more signals, the number of parameters proliferates rapidly. This would not be too bad if they could be partitioned into subgroups that could be estimated from simpler experiments, but so far that goal has not been achieved. Part of the difficulty is in understanding how the parameters relate to the subject and to the stimuli being used. To what extent can we assume the memory parameters are a fixed property of the subject, and to what extent are they experiment dependent? All too often, they seem to depend on both.

7.7 DATA WITH RESPONSE ERRORS: CONFUSABLE SIGNALS

7.7.1 *Identification of Auditory Frequency*

Ollman (1966) reported a study using three subjects and a monaural presentation of 100 msec pure tones. One pair of stimuli were 900 and

907 Hz of the same intensity, the other 900 and 920 Hz. The payoff involved a deadline such that responses occurring after the deadline lost one point and those before it were paid off according to a symmetric matrix of payoffs; the points were converted to money. The deadlines used were 300, 400, and 500 msec. One subject was insensitive to the deadline. For the other two, $P_c M_c$ and $P_e M_e$ were plotted against $P_c - P_e$, as shown in Figure 7.15. The lines fitted to the data are those of Eq. 7.31a, b (with the notation $a = \frac{1}{2}[P_{aA} + P_{bB}]$, $K = \nu_0$, and $H = \nu_1$). These data seem supportive of the fast-guess model.

7.7.2   Detection of Auditory Intensity

In this section I report some additional data sets which were run for quite different reasons (taken up in Chapters 8 and 9). Carterette, Friedman, and Cosmides (1965) reported a Yes-No experiment involving the detection of a relatively weak 1000-Hz tone in noise. At the end of a 750-msec warning light, a 100-msec listening interval began that might or might not contain the tone. The observers, who were already extensively experienced in detection, were practiced for two weeks in the task. They thought it just a detection task and were unaware that their response times were being recorded and were, in fact, the primary focus of the study. (This is a good example of where I am reluctant to speak of reaction times.) Each experimental condition involved one of two intensities called high and low, although both were quite near threshold, and one of three presentation

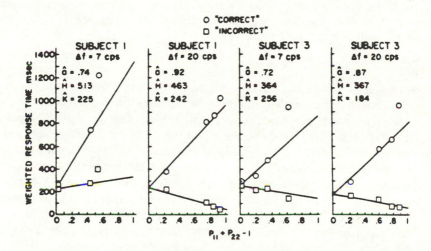

FIG. 7.15 Fit of Eq. 7.31 of the fast-guess model to data from the identification of auditory frequency in which errors cannot be avoided. I have not been able to ascertain the sample size. [Figure 1 of Ollman (1966); copyright 1966; reprinted by permission.]

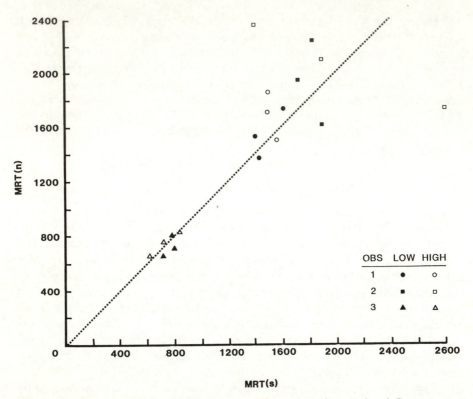

FIG. 7.16 MRT(s) versus MRT(n) for an auditory detection study of Carterette et al. (1965). There were two intensity levels and three presentation probabilities (see Appendix C.5). For each observer, there are 1800 observations per condition. The line is the prediction of the fast-guess model.

probabilities—0.2, 0.5, and 0.8. A total of 1800 observations were obtained in each condition from each observer. The response probabilities and mean response times are provided in Appendix C.5. Figure 7.16 compares MRT(s) with MRT(n). They may be equal for observer 3 but certainly not the other two. Estimates of ν_1 obtained from Eq. 7.33 are shown in Table 7.5. As they are quite variable it seems doubtful if the generalized fast-guess model holds for these subjects. The exceedingly erratic values for Observer 3 arise primarily from the fact that $P_c - P_e$ was very small for all conditions.

Green and Luce (1973) reported a detection study whose basic data have not been published in full (Link, 1978, published the averages over the three observers from one part of the study); they are given in Appendix C.6. The signals were near-threshold, 1000-Hz tones in noise that were response terminated. Each condition involved a deadline and the following payoff structure: Anticipations were each fined 25 points, responses later than the deadline were fined 4 points, and responses within the deadline were paid

TABLE 7.5. Estimate of ν_1 (msec) from the equation $(P_cM_c - P_eM_e)/(P_c - P_e)$ for data from Carterette et al. (1965), Appendix C.5

	Experimental conditions					
	Low intensity			High intensity		
Observer	.2	.5	.8	.2	.5	.8
1	1413	1630	499	1660	898	1269
2	2626	1660	1138	3088	2076	2766
3	1167	678	42610	−434	826	−32

off according to a matrix of the following character:

	Responses	
Stimuli	Yes	No
s	x	−10
n	−10	y

The points were converted to money at the end of the experiment. In one manipulation, $x = y = 10$, and the deadline was varied. In another manipulation, the deadline was fixed at 600 msec and the following (x, y) pairs were used: (20, 1), (15, 5), (10, 10), (5, 15), and (1, 20). Two types of deadline were run. In the s-deadline condition, the deadline applied only on those trials when a signal was presented, in which case there was no fine for slow responses on non-signal trials; in the sn-deadline condition, the deadline applied to all types of trials. (The motivation for this design will become apparent in Section 9.3.) Information feedback followed each response. Each condition had approximately 1500 trials for each observer.

Figure 7.17 plots MRT(n) versus MRT(s) for this experiment. It is clear that the simple fast-guess model fails for the s-deadline procedure. Figure 7.18 shows $P_cM_c - P_eM_e$ versus $P_c - P_e$ for the sn-deadline data; those for the s-deadline are similar. Obviously, for the weak signal case the relation is not linear, and so none of the fast-guess models describe these data.

7.7.3 *Persistent Strategies in the Identification of Orientation*

In a study closely resembling Swensson and Edwards (1971) (Section 7.6.3), Swensson (1972a) used stimuli that were somewhat confusable. They were rectangles in one of two 45° orientations with the ratio of the sides sufficiently near to 1 that each subject had an error rate of 1% to 2% when

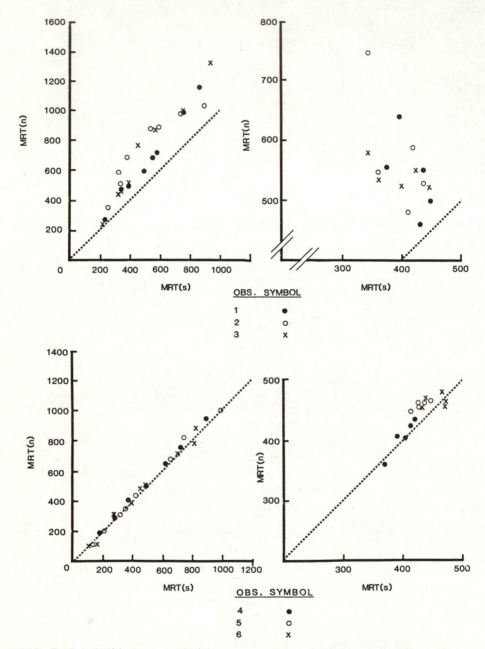

FIG. 7.17 MRT(s) versus MRT(n) for an auditory detection study with response deadlines of Green and Luce (1973) (see Appendix C.6). The upper row is for the condition in which the deadline applied only to signal trials, and the bottom for the deadline on all trials. The left column is the data generated with a fixed payoff matrix and varied deadline. The right column is the data with a fixed deadline and varied payoffs. For each observer there are 1100 observations per condition.

time was not a factor. As before, anticipatory responses were severely fined, accuracy was rewarded, and time was charged according to a proportional cost function. Other aspects of the design were essentially as before.

Preprogrammed guesses were identified in two ways. The first was the definition used in the earlier study—namely, any unbroken sequence of responses that included at least three errors or any pattern of strict alternation or any pattern of making the response that would have been appropriate to the preceding signal. The second criterion was based on the observation that the response-time distributions were, in fact, bimodal with very few times falling in the interval from 240 to 280 msec. So, any response that had not been classed as preprogrammed under the first definition was so classed if it was faster than 250 msec. As can be seen in Figure 7.19, the error rate of the preprogrammed responses was very close to 50%, whereas, the other, more accurate ones have an error rate of 10% or a bit less. The times for the accurate responses—those greater than 250 msec—are about 200 msec slower than the preprogrammed ones, which at about 200 msec is typical of simple reaction times to intense visual signals. Note the enormous difference in the time estimated for accurate responding in this experiment and in Swensson and Edwards (1971). I do not understand what accounts for the difference.

Because the error rates found among the accurate responses exceeded the 1% or 2% the subjects were capable of in an ordinary discrimination experiment, and because there was no evidence for a speed-accuracy tradeoff to account for it, two additional experiments were conducted. In both an attempt was made to vary the monetary tradeoff between speed and accuracy over a wider range, thereby encouraging a speed-accuracy tradeoff.

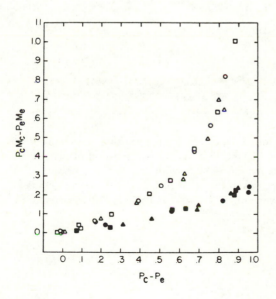

FIG. 7.18 $P_cM_c-P_eM_e$ versus P_c-P_e for the sn-deadline condition of the experiment of Figure 7.17. The open symbols are for the weak signals and the closed ones are for intense signals. [Figure 2 of Green and Luce (1973); copyright 1973; reprinted by permission.]

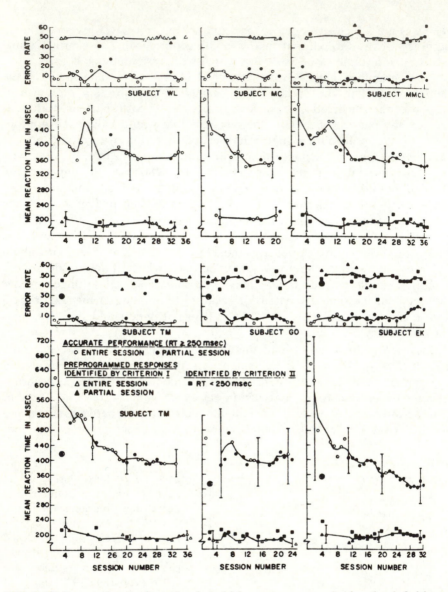

FIG. 7.19 In a study of orientation for which errors occur and using the definition of guessing and accurate trials described in the text, plots of proportion of errors and MRT versus sessions. There are data for six subjects, with 350 trials per session. The guessing trials appear as the upper curves in the error panels and the lower curves in the MRT panels. [Figure 2 of Swensson (1972a); copyright 1972; reprinted by permission.]

314

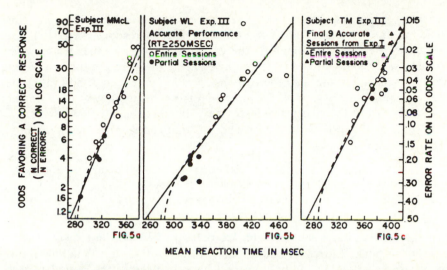

FIG. 7.20 SATFs for three subjects of the study cited in Figure 7.19. The open circles are data from accurate trials and the closed ones are from guessing trials. [Figure 5 of Swensson (1972a); copyright 1972; reprinted by permission.]

The second of these additional experiments had the added feature of taking into account a finding of the first—namely, that following a detection there is a substantial time before any accurate identification is possible. This time appears to the subject as a fixed cost in electing to be accurate rather than fast. So the payoff structure was revamped to take this into account. For two of the subjects the costless delay was set at 250 msec and for a third at 300 msec. The resulting pattern of tradeoff for responses greater than 250 msec is shown in Figure 7.20. The measure of accuracy used is log odds—that is, $\log(P_c/P_e)$. It seems clear that there is a substantial speed-accuracy tradeoff of a type different from that envisaged in the fast-guess model. Also, it should be noted in Experiment 2 that some subjects exhibited a clear ceiling effect in the sense that additional time devoted to the task did not have any effect on accuracy.

Swensson discussed at some length the possibility of accounting for this tradeoff by combining the fast-guess model with one or another of the models to be discussed in Chapter 8. At that time, no one allowed for error responses to be faster than correct ones, as is needed for the responses classed as accurate.* This is now possible within the original random walk framework using either Laming's modification or the version developed by Link and Heath (Section 8.3.3). Because nothing seemed available, Swensson urged the simpler deadline model of Nickerson (1969) in which the

---

* Apparently Swensson, like many others at the time, was not yet aware of Laming's (1968) idea of sampling prior to the signal onset in the SPRT random walk model in order to account for this fact.

accurate responses result from a race between a subject-imposed time deadline and an accrual process with some sort of response criterion. The responses that are determined by the deadline, necessarily the slowest ones, are also more likely to be errors simply because the criterion for responding was not satisfied at the time the response was in fact effected. So that model has the qualitatively correct features of errors being slower than correct responses, given that the fast guesses have been excluded.

Wilding (1974) pointed out a number of predictions of the model, among them these three (p. 484):

(1) A subsidiary peak in the latency distribution should occur at the longest latency obtained, due to the deadline responses.
(2) This peak will be relatively larger for errors.
(3) The peak will be greater when the deadline comes earlier.

His distribution data, shown in Figure 6.10 (p. 234), do not reveal such a secondary peak. Moreover, additional predictions of the deadline model were also rejected. The only concern I have is whether the verbal instructions that Wilding used were adequately effective in establishing a deadline at all. Recall that Swensson's data had a mean response time for fast guesses of about 200 msec and a mean time for accurate responses of about 400 msec, whereas Wilding's data (which involved the identification of the location of an 800 msec flash to the right or left of a fixation point) had no responses faster than 450 msec. I suspect that subjects were exhibiting quite different styles of behavior in the two experiments, at least to the extent that Wilding's subjects did not seem to produce any fast guesses.

7.8 CONCLUSIONS

Although it is rare to find an empirical study for which simple two-state mixture models, such as the fast-guess one, actually fit the data accurately, in a number of cases it appears as if something like fast guesses occur. Perhaps the most vivid demonstrations of this are Blough's pigeon data (Figure 6.4, p. 224) and the human studies by Swensson and by Swensson and Edwards in which subjects sustained for prolonged periods either of two quite different patterns of responding. When subjects are put under severe time pressure it is probably advisable for experimenters to examine their data for fast guesses, possibly using Swensson's (1972a) criteria and, if they are interested in testing other models, eliminating those responses from the data analyzed. The fast guesses appear to be just what had been postulated—simple reactions to signal onset that exhibit virtually no accuracy at all. It is less clear what happens when subjects are not guessing.

It seems to me that if one attempts to encompass all of the data presented in this chapter within a framework of mixtures of finitely many states of attention, then there can be no less than three states, including one of pure guessing (and quite possibly there are more than three).

The argument is as follows. The fact that perfectly identifiable stimuli can, under sufficient time pressure, be incorrectly identified (Yellott, 1971) forces one to at least two states, one of which is a guessing state. Although Yellott's data appeared consistent with the simple fast-guess model, those of Laming (1968), Link (1975), Link and Tindall (1971), and Ollman (1970), all of which also involved easily identified stimuli, made clear that the simple fast-guess model is not sufficient, and certainly one possibility is at least two states of more-or-less accurate responding. Such a model was realized in the striking work of Falmagne et al. (1975) on sequential effects, which suggests that four states of memory leading to mixtures of three different latency distributions (complicated by a response effect, which doubles the number of distributions) are very nearly sufficient to account fully for the data. Such a conclusion is, however, tentative since the model has only been studied intensively for one subject.

Next consider the data obtained from perfectly identifiable stimuli and for which few response errors occurred. The lack of error rules out the guessing state playing any role, and the data are not easily understood in terms of a single state. For example, two states seem needed to encompass sequential effects. So, at least two states in addition to the guessing one are needed. If there were just two, then the data histograms should exhibit the fixed-point property. Those of Lupker and Theois (1975) seemed to, but those of Falmagne (1965, 1968) and of Link and Tindall (1971) grossly violated it. If we hold to the simple assumption that each state has a single response-time distribution, then we are forced to conclude that there must be more than two states of perfect discrimination. The alternative—an example of which was developed in Section 7.5—is that there are different distributions for the two responses in each state. Then, in the case of two states, the fixed-point property would not follow for the overall reaction times but only when they are partitioned according to responses. I am unaware of such plots in the literature.

Data arising from confusable stimuli (Carterette et al., 1965; Green and Luce, 1973; Ollman, 1970; Swensson, 1972a) uniformly reject all versions of the two-state, fast-guess models, and so within the finite-state framework require a minimum of two states of stimulus identification. So far as I can tell, these data do not clearly implicate a third non-guessing state, although the results of Swensson (1972a) and Swensson and Edwards (1971), with their vastly different mean times for accurate responses and with the speed-accuracy tradeoff of the former paper appearing to lie outside the fast-guess model, are easier to understand with more than two non-guessing states.

Thus, to encompass all of the data in a unified framework, we appear to need at least three states, $0, 1, 2, \ldots$, with reaction time distributions G_i having means ν_i with the property that $\nu_i < \nu_{i+1}$ and state identification probabilities $P_{sr}(i)$ with the following plausible properties:

$$P_{ar}(0) = P_{br}(0) = \beta_r,$$
$$P_{aA}(i) \leq P_{aA}(i+1), \quad i > 0,$$
$$P_{bB}(i) \leq P_{bB}(i+1), \quad i > 0,$$

where state 0 is a guessing state and the slower a state the more accurate the identification. This model, although quite plausible given the data, has not been much pursued (except of course in the various special two- and three-state subcases discussed above) because it has so many parameters— $\rho(0), \ \rho(1), \ldots, \rho(i), \ \nu_0, \nu_1, \ldots, \beta_A, \ P_{aA}(1), P_{bB}(1), \ldots,$ where $\sum_i \rho(i) = 1$.

Thus, with three states there are 10 and with four states 14 parameters (some subject to inequalities) to account for just six pieces of independent data per experimental condition. Even assuming that some parameters are invariant under experimental manipulations, the problems of estimation and finding adequate ways to test the model are formidable, as we saw in the work of Falmagne et al. (1975). It appears clear that only by insisting such models account for sequential effects do we have any hope of evaluating them.

The primary alternative that has been pursued is to suppose that in addition to a special guessing state, a continuum of accuracy states exist, establishing a continuous tradeoff between speed and accuracy, and that any experimental condition elicits just one of these states. Under that assumption, the observed speed-accuracy tradeoff provides indirect evidence about the underlying tradeoff. For this approach to be successful, considerable care must be taken once again not to become overwhelmed with free parameters. Attempts along these lines are the topics of the next two chapters.

8

Stochastic Accumulation
of Information in Discrete Time

This chapter and the next one examine several closely related models for possible processes underlying choice reaction time. Except for Section 8.4.2, it is implicitly assumed in all of the models that the subject knows when to begin accumulating information, the only uncertainty being the signal presented, which is to be identified rapidly and accurately. In practice, signal onset is known either because there is an intense signal in another modality that identifies the onset time, or because the signals themselves are sufficiently intense that they alert the subject (perhaps via a change detector) to their presence. However it is done, we usually attempt to insure that we do not have to contend with the complication of information accumulation during periods when the signal is not present—which raises questions about how to deal with signal termination. One possibility is to avoid the problem experimentally by using response-terminated signals; that technique has been used only rarely. Another possibility is simply to assume that information is collected only during the duration of the signal. For the most part, the problem has simply been ignored by model builders. It conceivably can be treated by using time-dependent parameters; however, we are forever in danger of being overwhelmed with free parameters.

The major ideas for these accrual processes were presented in Section 4.2.1, and the reader is urged to reread that material because what was said there will be taken for granted here. In this chapter I assume that information about the signal accrues at discrete, brief times as samples of it are "observed" in the nervous system. These internal observations are assumed to arise from a process that is unitary in the sense that it is not possible experimentally to manipulate one observation independently of the others. This assumption is the reason that the models of this chapter (and the next) are treated as having just a single stage rather than many. Further, most of these models are classed as optional stopping in the sense that the decision to respond rests upon the observations that have been obtained (Swensson and Thomas, 1974).

As in the preceding chapter, we concentrate on a two-choice reaction-time experiment in which just one of two signals, a or b, is presented on each trial. The subject is to try to identify the signal presented rapidly and accurately, attempting to respond A to a and B to b.

8.1 ACCUMULATOR MODELS

In the first two subsections of the chapter (in contrast to the others), information is assumed to be binary. At each instant, the information registers a single count in favor of one of the two responses, A or B. LaBerge (1962), who also admitted the possibility of the information not favoring either response, cast this in terms of sampling stimulus elements in the sense of Estes (1950). Audley (1960) referred to these observations as implicit responses. If signal s is presented, we assume that the probability of a count in favor of A is p_s and in favor of B is $q_s = 1 - p_s$, $s = a$ or b. Obviously, we anticipate that $p_a > p_b$. There are two distinct response rules in the literature, which we now explore.

8.1.1 The Simple Accumulator

LaBerge (1962), who worked out this model, called it recruitment theory; later Audley and Pike (1965) called it a simple accumulator, which strikes me as more graphic. There are two constants k_A and k_B and the decision rule is that the system responds whenever either the count favoring A reaches k_A or the count favoring B reaches k_B, and the response is A in the former case and B in the latter. What we need to compute is the probability that a particular response, say A, occurs after a fixed number of observations. Since it takes k_A observations in favor of A, the least number that can occur is k_A. And the most is $k_A + k_B - 1$, since if k_B occurs favoring B, then that response would be made. So we need to consider $k_A + j$ observations where $0 \le j \le k_B - 1$. Clearly, the last observation must favor A, and so the j observations favoring B must be distributed in $k_A - 1$ locations, and it is well known that there are

$$\binom{k_A + j - 1}{j}$$

ways for that to happen. So the probability distribution is

Pr(response A at step $k_A + j$ | given signal s)

$$= \binom{k_A + j - 1}{j} p_s^{k_A} q_s^i. \tag{8.1}$$

In order to calculate the moments of this distribution, it is very convenient to put the distribution in the form of a generating function (see Section 1.4.6),

$$\mathcal{G}_{sA}(z) = p_s^{k_A} z^{k_A} \sum_{j=0}^{k_B - 1} \binom{k_A + j - 1}{j} q_s^i z^i. \tag{8.2}$$

For some purposes it is convenient to reexpress this in terms of the incomplete beta function:

$$I_x(m, n) = \frac{(m+n-1)!}{(m-1)!(n-1)!} \int_0^x t^{m-1}(1-t)^{n-1} \, dt, \tag{8.3}$$

To do so we use the following known relations among the cumulative negative binomial distribution, the binomial one, and the incomplete beta function (Eq. 8.3) (see, e.g., Beyer, 1966, p. 202–203):

$$\sum_{i=0}^{n} \binom{m+i-1}{i} p^m q^i = \sum_{j=m}^{m+n} \binom{m+n}{j} p^j q^{m+n-j}$$

$$= I_p(m, n+1).$$

Keeping in mind that $p_s z$ is not $1 - q_s z$ and substituting this expression for I into the right side of Eq. 8.4a immediately yields the right side of Eq. 8.2, so

$$\mathcal{G}_{sA}(z) = \left(\frac{p_s z}{1 - q_s z}\right)^{k_A} I_{1-q_s z}(k_A, k_B). \tag{8.4a}$$

By interchanging A and B and p_s and q_s,

$$\mathcal{G}_{sB}(z) = \left(\frac{q_s z}{1 - p_s z}\right)^{k_B} I_{1-p_s z}(k_B, k_A). \tag{8.4b}$$

From these equations it is easy to derive explicit expressions for the response probabilities and the mean number of steps to a response. In carrying out the latter, one uses the following known identity:

$$I_p(m, n) - I_p(m+1, n) = \frac{(m+n-1)!}{m!(n-1)!} p^m q^n.$$

We obtain

$$P(A \mid s) = \lim_{z \to 1} \mathcal{G}_{sA}(z) = I_{p_s}(k_A, k_B), \tag{8.5}$$

$$E(\mathbf{J} \mid s, A) = \lim_{z \to 1} \frac{d}{dz} \mathcal{G}_{sA}(z) = \frac{k_A}{p_s} \frac{I_{p_s}(k_A + 1, k_B)}{P_{As}}, \tag{8.6a}$$

$$E(\mathbf{J} \mid s, B) = \lim_{z \to 1} \frac{d}{dz} \mathcal{G}_{sB}(z) = \frac{k_B}{q_s} \frac{I_{q_s}(k_B + 1, k_A)}{P_{Bs}}, \tag{8.6b}$$

where $\mathbf{J}$ is the random variable representing the number of steps to a decision. Assuming that there is a constant conversion factor Δ from discrete time to physical time and an additive mean residual time r_0, the expression for expected response time is

$$E(\mathbf{T} \mid s, r) = \Delta E(\mathbf{J} \mid s, r) + r_0. \tag{8.7}$$

Weatherburn (1978) has expressed some doubt about the assumption of a constant conversion factor, but there is little to do with the model if one does not assume it.

Since there are six independent equations and a total of six parameters—p_a, p_b, k_A, k_B, Δ, and r_0—it is clear that, except for possible degeneracies, the model can always fit the data from one experimental condition. The only effective test, therefore, is to manipulate some experimental variable and observe how the estimated parameters vary with the manipulation. For example, in Section 8.5 we will examine data from four experiments in each of which at least the presentation probability or the payoff matrix was manipulated. Given the apparent meanings of the parameters, we would expect p_a, p_b, Δ, and r_0 to be invariant and for k_A and k_B to vary.

8.1.2   The Runs Model

Audley (1960), in a continuous time context, and later Audley and Pike (1965), introduced a variant on the accumulator idea. They postulated that the relevant accumulation toward an alternative is the total number of counts in favor of it following the most recent count favoring the other alternative. That is to say, response A occurs at the end of the first run of k_A implicit observations favoring A that is not preceded by a run of k_B observations favoring B. This makes distant past history irrelevant to the current decision.

To calculate the generating function, we may argue as follows. The overall process is a convolution of alternating runs with the following properties. The last run is a sequence of k_A favoring A. Those runs preceding it must not exceed $k_A - 1$ favoring A and $k_B - 1$ favoring B. We will make use of the fact that the generating function of a convolution is the product of the generating functions of the component distributions of the convolution.

Letting p_s be the probability of an implicit response favoring a given stimulus s, then

$$\alpha_s(z) = p_s z + (p_s z)^2 + \cdots + (p_s z)^{k_A - 1}$$
$$= \frac{1 - (p_s z)^{k_A}}{1 - p_s z} - 1$$

characterizes the generating function of all possible lengths of a single run favoring A that does not lead to a response. Similarly,

$$\beta_s(z) = \frac{1 - (q_s z)^{k_B}}{1 - q_s z} - 1$$

does the same thing for a run favoring B. Now, prior to the last run favoring A, either there is no run, which has a generating function of 1, or a run favoring B, represented by $\beta_s(z)$, or one of that type preceded by one favoring A, represented by $\alpha_s(z)\beta_s(z)$, and so on. Thus, the overall generating function is

$$\mathcal{G}_{sA}(z) = (p_sz)^{k_A}[1 + \beta_s(z) + \alpha_s(z)\beta_s(z) + \alpha_s(z)\beta_s(z)^2$$
$$+ \alpha_s(z)^2\beta_s(z)^2 + \alpha_s(z)^2\beta_s(z)^3 + \cdots]$$
$$= (p_sz)^{k_A}[1 + \beta_s(z)] \sum_{i=1}^{\infty} [\alpha_s(z)\beta_s(z)]^i$$
$$= \frac{(p_sz)^{k_A}[1 + \beta_s(z)]}{1 - \alpha_s(z)\beta_s(z)}$$
$$= \frac{(p_sz)^{k_A}/[1 + \alpha_s(z)]}{\dfrac{1}{1 + \alpha_s(z)} + \dfrac{1}{1 + \beta_s(z)} - 1}$$
$$= \frac{P_s(z)}{S_s(z)},$$

where

$$P_s(z) = (p_sz)^{k_A}(1 - p_sz)/[1 - (p_sz)^{k_A}]$$

and

$$S_s(z) = \frac{1}{1 + \alpha_s(z)} + \frac{1}{1 + \beta_s(z)} - 1.$$

If we let

$$Q_s(z) = (q_sz)^{k_B}(1 - q_sz)/[1 - (q_sz)^{k_B}],$$

then

$$S_s(z) = P_s(z) + 1 - p_sz + Q_s(z) + 1 - q_sz - 1$$
$$= P_s(z) + Q_s(z) + 1 - z.$$

So,

$$\mathcal{G}_{sA}(z) = \frac{P_s(z)}{P_s(z) + Q_s(z) + 1 - z}. \tag{8.8a}$$

Similarly,

$$\mathcal{G}_{sB}(z) = \frac{Q_s(z)}{P_s(z) + Q_s(z) + 1 - z}. \tag{8.8b}$$

We now derive the equations for the response probabilities and mean response times:

$$P(A \mid s) = \lim_{z \to 1} \mathcal{G}_{sA}(z) = \frac{P_s(1)}{P_s(1) + Q_s(1)}$$

$$= \frac{1}{1 + \left(\dfrac{q_s^{k_B - 1}}{p_s^{k_A - 1}}\right)\left(\dfrac{1 - p_s^{k_A}}{1 - q_s^{k_A}}\right)} \tag{8.9}$$

$$E(\mathbf{J} \mid s, A) = \lim_{z \to 1} \frac{\mathcal{G}'_{sA}(z)}{P(A \mid s)}$$

$$= \lim_{z \to 1} \frac{d}{dz} \ln \mathcal{G}_{sA}(z)$$

$$= \lim_{z \to 1} \frac{P'_s(z)}{P_s(z)} - \lim_{z \to 1} \frac{S'_s(z)}{S_s(z)}.$$

Taking the derivative of $\ln P_s(z)$ yields

$$\frac{P'_s(z)}{P_s(z)} = \frac{k_A}{z} - \frac{p_s}{1 - p_s z} + \frac{k_A (p_s z)^{k_A - 1} p_s}{1 - (p_s z)^{k_A}}$$

and so

$$\lim_{z \to 1} \frac{P'_s(z)}{P_s(z)} = k_A - \frac{p_s}{q_s} + \frac{k_A p_s^{k_A}}{1 - p_s^{k_A}}.$$

Turning to S'_s/S_s,

$$\lim_{z \to 1} \frac{S'_s(z)}{S_s(z)} = \lim_{z \to 1} \frac{P'_s(x) + Q'_s(x) - 1}{S_s(z)}$$

$$= \lim_{z \to 1} \left[\frac{P_s(z)}{S_s(z)} \frac{P'_s(z)}{P_s(z)} + \frac{Q_s(z)}{S_s(z)} \frac{Q'_s(z)}{Q_s(z)} - \frac{1}{S_s(z)} \right]$$

$$= P(A \mid s)\left[k_A - \frac{p_s}{q_s} + \frac{k_A p_s^{k_A}}{1 - p_s^{k_A}} \right]$$

$$+ P(B \mid s)\left[k_B - \frac{q_s}{p_s} + \frac{k_B q_s^{k_B}}{1 - q_s^{k_B}} \right] - \frac{1}{S_s(1)}.$$

Substituting

$$E(\mathbf{J} \mid s, A) = P(B \mid s)\left[k_A - k_B + \frac{1}{p_s} - \frac{1}{q_s} + \frac{k_A p_s^{k_A}}{1 - p_s^{k_A}} - \frac{k_B q_s^{k_B}}{1 - q_s^{k_B}} \right]$$

$$+ \frac{1}{\dfrac{q_s}{1 - p_s^{k_A}} + \dfrac{p_s}{1 - q_s^{k_B}} - 1}. \tag{8.10}$$

A similar expression follows for $E(\mathbf{J} \mid s, B)$ with A and B interchanged and p and q interchanged. As before, Eq. 8.7 relates $E(\mathbf{T} \mid s, r)$ to $E(\mathbf{J} \mid s, r)$, and there are six parameters and six equations.

Audley and Pike (1965) generalized the model to m alternatives.

8.1.3 The Strength Accumulator

Vickers (1970) proposed a variant on LaBerge's simple accumulator in which magnitudes favoring the two alternatives are accumulated as follows. Suppose that at each instance of time i during which the signal s is present a Gaussian random variable $\mathbf{X}_i(s)$ with mean μ_s and variance σ_s^2 is observed. We anticipate $\mu_a > 0$ and $\mu_b < 0$. Suppose further that the $\mathbf{X}_i(s)$ are independent random variables.

If $\mathbf{X}_i(s) > 0$, this is interpreted as evidence favoring the presence of a, and that has the probability $P_s = \int_0^\infty \Phi(\mu_s, \sigma_s)$. Similarly, $\mathbf{X}_i < 0$ is evidence favoring b. However, unlike LaBerge's model, which registered a count one way or the other, Vickers suggested that the evidence is the more persuasive the further it is from 0, and so the total amount of evidence is tallied for each alternative:

$$\mathbf{T}_A(s) = \sum_{i \in \mathcal{A}} \mathbf{X}_i(s) \qquad \text{and} \qquad \mathbf{T}_B(s) = \sum_{i \in \mathcal{B}} \mathbf{X}_i(s),$$

where $\mathcal{A} = \{i \mid \mathbf{X}_i(s) > 0\}$ and $\mathcal{B} = \{i \mid \mathbf{X}_i(s) < 0\}$. Let

$$m_{sA} = E(\mathbf{X}_i(s) \mid \mathbf{X}_i(s) > 0) \qquad \text{and} \qquad m_{sB} = E(\mathbf{X}_i(s) \mid \mathbf{X}_i(s) < 0),$$

which are, of course, completely determined by μ_s and σ_s. The response criteria are assumed to be of the form

$$K_A = c\sigma_a, \qquad K_B = c\sigma_b,$$

and the response rule is to keep a running tally of $K_A - \mathbf{T}_A$ and $K_B + \mathbf{T}_B$ and respond according to whichever first becomes negative. McCarthy (1947) is quoted as showing that the expected total number of instances prior to a response is

$$\frac{K_{sA}}{p_s} I_{p_s}(K_{sA} + 1, K_{sB}) + \frac{K_{sB}}{q_s} I_{q_s}(K_{sB} + 1, K_{sA}), \qquad (8.11)$$

where $K_{sr} = K_r/m_{sr}$ and I_p is the incomplete beta function.

No other analytic results seem to be known; in particular, it has not been possible to derive the four mean times separately.* Assuming a symmetric case, $\sigma = \sigma_a = \sigma_b$ and $\mu = \mu_a = -\mu_b$, Vickers simulated the process for a range of values of σ/μ and c, and plotted the mean time versus the response probability. These are shown in Figure 8.1. In Section 8.5.1 we compare this model with some data; however, the comparisons are still rather incomplete.

---

* Note added in proof: Vickers (personal communication) has informed me that P. L. Smith and he have recently arrived at quite detailed analytic results.

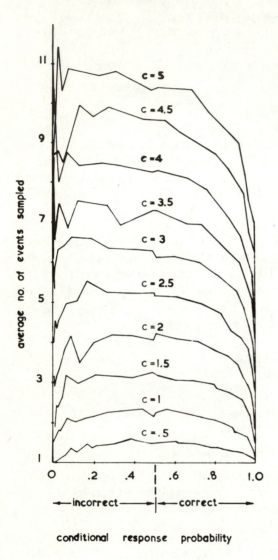

FIG. 8.1 For the accumulator model, the relation between MRT and response probability computed from simulations of 500 runs for each condition (10 values of the criterion C and 20 values of σ/μ. [Figure 3 of Vickers (1970); copyright 1970; reprinted by permission.]

8.2 RANDOM WALKS WITH BOUNDARIES

Assuming discrete counts favoring either A or B, another natural model to consider is one in which decisions are based upon the difference in counts favoring A and favoring B. If we denote that difference on the ith observation by $\mathbf{N}_i$, the natural decision rule is to respond A if $\mathbf{N}_i > k_A$ occurs before $\mathbf{N}_i < -k_B$ and to respond B the other way round. This process is the simplest example of a random walk, and its analysis will be subsumed under a rather more general model I now describe.

8.2.1 The Model

Assume that at each discrete time i a new piece of information, $\mathbf{Y}_i$, accrues; moreover, assume that these random variables are independent and identically distributed. Let their common density be denoted f_a when signal a is presented, f_b when b is presented. Suppose further that there is a monotonic transformation h that takes $\mathbf{Y}_i$ into $\mathbf{X}_i = h(\mathbf{Y}_i)$ and that decisions are based upon the partial sums

$$\mathbf{S}_n = \sum_{i=1}^{n} \mathbf{X}_i. \tag{8.12}$$

The stochastic process $\{\mathbf{S}_n\}$ is called a random walk on the line (see Section 1.5.2).

Assume that the random variables $\mathbf{X}_i$ are such that the walk tends in one direction, say to the right, when a is presented and in the opposite direction when b is presented. Introducing a symbol for the mean of $\mathbf{X}_i$, the assumption is

$$\mu_a = E(\mathbf{X}_i \mid a) > 0,$$
$$\mu_b = E(\mathbf{X}_i \mid b) < 0.$$

The decision rule for the process is as follows. Place the origin of the line at the initial point of the process. The process is assumed to terminate when enough evidence has accumulated to provide good reason to believe it is tending in one direction or the other. Obviously, the direction is ambiguous only when $\mathbf{X}_i$ can take on both positive and negative values. The simplest way to decide about the tendency is to establish criteria both to the right and left of 0 such that when $\mathbf{S}_n$ crosses a criterion, a response is made—namely, A when the right one is crossed and B when the left one is. There will be no confusion in letting A and B have double meanings, both as the name of a response and as the absolute numerical value of the corresponding criterion. So the decision rule at the nth observation is:

If $-B < \mathbf{S}_n < A$, proceed to observe $\mathbf{X}_{n+1}$,

If $\mathbf{S}_n \geq A$, respond A, $\qquad\qquad$ (8.13)

If $\mathbf{S}_n \leq -B$, respond B.

The theoretical problem is to understand the distribution of times at which a response occurs and the probability of that happening. Observe that by moving a boundary toward 0, the corresponding responses will tend to speed up and become more error prone.

Obviously, the problem just formulated is very general and of much broader interest than just choice reaction time. The literature on the subject began with Wald's (1947) original and seminal book, *Sequential Analysis*, which was motivated largely by the problem of reducing sample sizes when it is very expensive to collect data. Although there is considerable statistical literature on the subject, a tiny fraction of which I shall reference (for a reasonably recent treatment, see Wetherill, 1975), most of the reaction-time work is focused on two restrictive assumptions about the distribution of $\mathbf{X}_i$. The reason is that it appears to be very difficult to get usable results except under these assumptions. And even then, the attack on the problem requires some indirection.

8.2.2   *The Assumption of Small Steps and Wald's Identity*

It is not immediately obvious whether or not the process just defined always ends in a response; it is conceivable that there is a positive probability that for all integers n the condition $-B < \mathbf{S}_n < A$ will hold, in which case no response would be made. Were that to happen, we would need to take it into account. As a matter of fact, it cannot, as is proved in Theorem 8.1 (see Section 8.2.6).

We turn now to the major device used to analyze such processes. I do not know how to motivate the approach intuitively; suffice to say that it works. Let the mgf of $\mathbf{X}$ given signal s be denoted

$$\mathcal{M}_s(\theta) = E(e^{\theta \mathbf{X}} \mid s), \text{ where } s = a, b.$$

Observe that for a fixed integer n, Eq. 1.44 together with the independence of the $\mathbf{X}_i$ leads to

$$\mathcal{M}_s(\theta)^n = E(e^{\theta \mathbf{S}_n} \mid s),$$

which can be rewritten as

$$E[e^{\theta \mathbf{S}_n}/\mathcal{M}_s(\theta)^n \mid s] = 1.$$

It does not follow from this observation that the same equality holds generally when n is replaced by an integer-valued random variable. (The reason is that with infinite sums and integrals, an argument is needed to justify interchanging them.) However, what Wald's identity asserts is that it does in fact hold for a broad class of distributions for $\mathbf{X}$ when n is replaced by the trial number at which criterion is crossed. This fact is stated as a formal theorem, which is proved in Section 8.2.6.

Theorem 8.2 (Wald, 1947, p. 159).   *In a random walk on the line of the type described above, let* $\mathbf{N}$ *denote the least integer such that either* $\mathbf{S}_N < -B$ *or* $\mathbf{S}_N > A$. *Then for all* θ *for which* $|M_s(\theta)| \geq 1$,

$$E[e^{\theta \mathbf{S}_N}/\mathcal{M}_s(\theta)^{\mathbf{N}} \mid s] = 1, \qquad s = a, b, \qquad (8.14)$$

where the expectation is the joint one over the $\mathbf{X}_i$ *and* $\mathbf{N}$.

Equation 8.14 is Wald's identity. It becomes of value only if we are willing to assume that the mean and standard deviation of $\mathbf{X}_i$ are very small relative to A and to B, in which case the value of $\mathbf{S}_N$ is approximately either

$-B$ or A at the time the criterion is satisfied. We state this formally:

The Assumption of Small Steps: *The value of $\mathbf{S_N}$ is either $-B$ or A.*

In the context of sequential sampling, where the error probabilities are usually set at 0.05 or 0.01 or even smaller, this assumption is not unreasonable. But those importing the random walk model to the study of reaction times seem to have been unaware that the circumstances under which the assumption holds and at the same time leads to typical error rates—say in the range 0.1 to 0.3—are somewhat unusual. For the Gaussian case, this is explored more fully in Section 8.2.4.

If one thinks of the size of the steps as becoming vanishingly small and the number of them infinitely large, the discrete case passes into a continuous one. We deal with that in the next chapter.

Under the assumption of small steps, we may immediately rewrite Eq. 8.14 as: for $s = a, b$,

$$1 = P(A \mid s)e^{\theta A}E[\mathcal{M}_s(\theta)^{-N} \mid s, A] + P(B \mid s)e^{-\theta B}E[\mathcal{M}_s(\theta)^{-N} \mid s, B], \quad (8.15)$$

where $P(A \mid s)$ and $P(B \mid s)$ are, respectively, the probabilities of an A and B response occurring (i.e., the probability the corresponding criterion being crossed) when signal s is presented.

We make use of Eq. 8.15 in two ways. First, we search for those values of θ for which $\mathcal{M}_s(\theta) = 1$, in which case both expectations become 1 and we thus obtain an equation involving only $P(A \mid s)$, $P(B \mid s)$, A, and B. Obviously, $\theta = 0$ leads to $\mathcal{M}_s(0) = 1$, but that only results in the triviality (given Theorem 8.1) that $P(A \mid s) + P(B \mid s) = 1$. The important question is values of $\theta \neq 0$ for which $\mathcal{M}_s(\theta) = 1$. Once those are found, then $P(A \mid s)$ is determined explicitly as a function of the parameters of the model. Second, we can then substitute those values for $P(A \mid s)$ in Eq. 8.15 in order to study $E[\mathcal{M}_s(\theta)^{-N} \mid s, r]$, $s = a, b$, $r = A, B$. If we think of $1/\mathcal{M}_s(\theta) = z$ as a variable, then we are studying $E[z^N \mid s, r]$, which is the generating function of the random variable $\mathbf{N}$. In principle it tells us the distribution of $\mathbf{N}$ and, in practice, it permits us to compute the mean and variance of $\mathbf{N}$ fairly easily.

8.2.3 *Response Probabilities and Mean Decision Latencies*

If we assume that the distribution of $\mathbf{X}_i$ is so restricted that the mgf satisfies

1. $\lim_{\theta \to \pm\infty} \mathcal{M}_s(\theta) > 1$, and
2. $\mathcal{M}'_s(0) \neq 0$,

then it can be shown (Section 8.2.6) that there is a unique value of θ distinct from 0, call it θ_{1s}, such that $\mathcal{M}_s(\theta_{1s}) = 1$. These assumptions must be verified each time we make a specific choice for the distribution of $\mathbf{X}_i$ or the existence of θ_{1s} must be shown directly, which is often easy to do. Assumption 1 holds if the random variable $\mathbf{X}_i$ straddles the origin and $\mathcal{M}_s(\theta)$ exists for all θ. Thus, any entirely positive or entirely negative random variable necessarily violates the first condition. For the special case that the transformation h is the log of the probability ratio (see Section 8.3.1), the second condition is equivalent to the distributions corresponding to the two signals not being identical.

Inserting θ_{1s} into Eq. 8.15 and taking into account that $P(A \mid s) + P(B \mid s) = 1$ yields

$$1 = P(A \mid s)e^{\theta_{1s}A} + [1 - P(A \mid s)]e^{-\theta_{1s}B}.$$

Setting

$$\alpha_s = -\theta_{1s}A, \tag{8.16a}$$

$$\beta_s = -\theta_{1s}B, \tag{8.16b}$$

we obtain for the two response probabilities

$$P(A \mid s) = \frac{e^{\beta_s} - 1}{e^{\beta_s} - e^{-\alpha_s}}. \tag{8.17a}$$

$$P(B \mid s) = \frac{1 - e^{-\alpha_s}}{e^{\beta_s} - e^{-\alpha_s}}. \tag{8.17b}$$

The computation of the mean decision latency is based upon the following property of generating functions

$$L_{sA} = E(\mathbf{N} \mid s, A) = \frac{d}{dz} E(z^{\mathbf{N}} \mid s, A)|_{z=1}.$$

From this we show in Section 8.2.6 that

$$L_{sA} = \frac{1}{\mu_s} [AP(A \mid a) - BP(B \mid s)] \frac{e^{\beta_s}}{e^{\beta_s} - 1}$$

$$+ \frac{1}{\gamma_s \mu_s} [AP(A \mid s) - BP(B \mid s)e^{\alpha_s + \beta_s}] \frac{e^{-\alpha_s}}{e^{\beta_s} - 1}, \tag{8.18a}$$

$$L_{sB} = -\frac{1}{\mu_s} [AP(A \mid s) - BP(B \mid s)] \frac{e^{-\alpha_s}}{1 - e^{-\alpha_s}}$$

$$- \frac{1}{\gamma_s \mu_s} [AP(A \mid s)e^{-(\alpha_s + \beta_s)} - BP(B \mid s)] \frac{e^{\beta_s}}{1 - e^{-\alpha_s}}, \tag{8.18b}$$

where γ_s is a parameter of the distribution of $\mathbf{X}$ defined by

$$\gamma_s = -\frac{1}{\mu_s} \mathcal{M}'_s(\theta)|_{\theta = \theta_{1s}}. \tag{8.19}$$

At this point we have a total of six equations—one each for $P(A \mid a)$, $P(A \mid b)$, L_{aA}, L_{bA}, L_{aB}, and L_{bB}—and eight parameters—A, B, θ_{1a}, θ_{1b}, μ_a, μ_b, γ_a, and γ_b. Despite the fact that the unit of the underlying scale of the process is arbitrary, we cannot reduce the number of parameters because the relation between physical time and distance in the random walk is unspecified. As that leaves us with two more parameters than equations, it is tempting to derive more equations from the moment generating function. For example, we can calculate four more equations for the variance of the response times. Unfortunately, that adds four more parameters—the variances of $\mathbf{X}_i$ for a and b and two values analogous to γ_s.

Even though the model is not completely determined, there are nevertheless constraints imposed by it and, in principle, these can be tested. Unfortunately, none of any use have been derived. An example of the difficulty may be instructive. From Eq. 8.15 it can be shown that the overall mean decision latency time and the response probabilities satisfy

$$L_s = L_{sA}P(A \mid s) + L_{sB}P(B \mid s)$$

$$= \frac{1}{\mu_s}[AP(A \mid s) - BP(B \mid s)]. \tag{8.20}$$

Link (1978, Eq. 5) derived this relation for the special case of symmetric stimulus representation (8.3.3), but it holds generally (see Section 8.2.6, Eq. 8.25a).

Equation 8.20 would be of use if we could perform an experiment in which L_s and $P(A \mid s)$ are manipulated while holding A/μ_s and $B/_{\mu s}$ fixed, in which case we could test for a linear relation between them. Observe that from Eqs. 8.17 and 8.18 that this is possible only if θ_{1s} is varied while holding everything else fixed. For all practical purposes, this entails finding a manipulation that affects the variance of $\mathbf{X}_i$ without affecting either its mean or the boundaries A and B. No one has had an idea about how to do that. So our only recourse is to restrict the model further, which means the imposition of some assumptions on the distribution of $\mathbf{X}_i$. One possibility is to limit attention to a specific parametric family of distributions, which is done in Section 8.2.4. Another, more useful, approach is to limit attention to broad classes of distributions that lead to tractable results. In Section 8.3.1 we study the case where the two moment generating functions are translations of one another (Theorem 8.3) and in Section 8.3.3 where they are reflections of each other (Theorem 8.5).

8.2.4 Gaussian Steps

The most obvious tack, although probably not the best, is to limit one's self to very specific, well-known families of distributions. For example, if we assume that $\mathbf{X}_i$ has a Gaussian distribution with mean μ_s and variance σ_s^2, then since (Eq. 1.50)

$$\mathcal{M}_s(\theta) = \exp[\mu_s\theta + \tfrac{1}{2}\sigma_s^2\theta^2],$$

it follows that

$$\theta_{1s} = -2\mu_s/\sigma_s^2 \qquad \text{and} \qquad \gamma_s = 1.$$

The model now has five free parameters, and so in principle can be tested. No attempt to do so exists in the literature, probably, in part, because two other classes of models have attracted a good deal of attention and, in part, because one would have to explore a five-dimensional parameter space by Monte Carlo methods, which used to be expensive and difficult—although that is rapidly becoming a non-issue. We study the other two classes of models in Section 8.3.

Heath (1981) noted the following non-parametric test of the Gaussian model. From Eqs. 8.18a and b, we see

$$L_{sA} - L_{sB} = \frac{1}{\mu_s}\left(1 + \frac{1}{\gamma_s}\right)\left[\frac{A}{1 - e^{-\alpha_s}} - \frac{B}{e^{\beta_s - 1}}\right] + \frac{1}{\mu_s}\left(\frac{A}{1 - e^{-\alpha}}\right)(e^{\beta_s} + e^{-\alpha_s}).$$

And from Eqs. 8.17a and b,

$$e^{\beta_s} + e^{-\alpha_s} = 2 + (e^{\beta_s} - e^{-\alpha_s})[2P(A \mid s) - 1].$$

Assuming that $\theta_{1s} = -2\mu_s/\sigma_s^2$ is small, and so

$$e^{\beta_s} - 1 \cong -(2\mu_s/\sigma_s^2)B \qquad \text{and} \qquad 1 - e^{-\alpha_s} \cong -(2\mu_s/\sigma_s^2)A,$$

yields

$$L_{sA} - L_{sB} \cong 2\{(1/\mu_s) - (\sigma_s/\mu_s)^2(A + B)[2P(A \mid s) - 1]\}.$$

This says that in the Gaussian model with σ_s substantially larger than μ_s, then the slope of $L_{sA} - L_{sB}$ versus $2P(A \mid s) - 1$ must be negative since $(\sigma_s/\mu_s)^2(A + B)$ necessarily is positive. We return to this prediction in Section 8.5.6.

The context of the Gaussian model is a good place to examine the magnitude of the error that has been introduced by the assumption of small steps. In the Gaussian case

$$\alpha_s = 2\mu_s A/\sigma_s^2, \qquad \beta_s = 2\mu_s B/\sigma_s^2.$$

To simplify, suppose $A = B$, then $\alpha_s = \beta_s$ and so by Eq. 8.17a,

$$P(A \mid s) = \frac{e^{\alpha_s} - 1}{e^{\alpha_s} - e^{-\alpha_s}}.$$

For $\alpha_s = 1$, $P(A \mid s) = .731$; for $\alpha_s = 2$, $P(A \mid s) = .881$. This is the normal range of probabilities, but in the latter case it means that $A = \sigma_s^2/\mu_s$. If we let $k = \sigma_s/\mu_s$, then $A = k\sigma_s$. Thus, in order for the small step assumption to be satisfied, it is necessary that the mean be small compared to the variance and the boundary large compared with the variance. The most natural way for the former condition to arise is for **X** to be the difference of two random variables with nearly the same mean.

In Section 8.2.5 I examine some simulations to see how accurate the equations are.

8.2.5 *Distributions of Decision Latencies*

At a theoretical level, the title of this subsection is misleading because explicit expressions for the distributions are not arrived at; rather, I derive their characteristic functions. In the process use is made of the Wald identity which, as an examination of the proof in Section 8.2.6 shows, holds for characteristic as well as moment generating functions. Recall that the characteristic function of **N** is

$$E(e^{i\omega \mathbf{N}}), \quad \text{where} \quad i = (-1)^{1/2} \quad \text{and} \quad \omega \text{ is real.}$$

To do this, Wald proceeded as follows. Search for those values of θ such that

$$e^{i\omega} = 1/\mathcal{M}_s(\theta), \tag{8.21}$$

which causes Eq. 8.15 to become an identity in conditional characteristic functions. Assuming $\mathcal{M}'_s(\theta) \neq 0$ for $\theta = 0$ and θ_{1s}, then we know that for sufficiently small $|\theta|$, there are just two roots $\theta_{0s}(\omega)$ and $\theta_{1s}(\omega)$ to Eq. 8.21 such that

$$\lim_{\theta \to 0} \theta_{0s}(\omega) = 0 \quad \text{and} \quad \lim_{\theta \to 0} \theta_{1s}(\omega) = \theta_{1s}.$$

Substituting these into Eq. 8.15 and, for simplicity, dropping the conditioning on s throughout,

$$1 = P(A)e^{\theta_0(\omega)A}E[e^{i\omega \mathbf{N}} | A] + P(B)e^{-\theta_0(\omega)B}E[e^{i\omega \mathbf{N}} | B],$$
$$1 = P(A)e^{\theta_1(\omega)A}E[e^{i\omega \mathbf{N}} | A] + P(B)e^{-\theta_1(\omega)B}E[e^{i\omega \mathbf{N}} | B].$$

Solving,

$$E[e^{i\omega \mathbf{N}} | A] = \frac{1}{P(A)} \left[\frac{e^{-\theta_1(\omega)B} - e^{-\theta_0(\omega)B}}{e^{-\theta_1(\omega)B + \theta_0(\omega)A} - e^{-\theta_0(\omega)B + \theta_1(\omega)A}} \right], \tag{8.22a}$$

$$E[e^{i\omega \mathbf{N}} | B] = \frac{1}{P(B)} \left[\frac{e^{-\theta_0(\omega)A} - e^{-\theta_1(\omega)A}}{e^{-\theta_1(\omega)B + \theta_0(\omega)A} - e^{-\theta_0(\omega)B + \theta_1(\omega)A}} \right]. \tag{8.22b}$$

Suppose that **X** is Gaussian distributed, then Eq. 8.21 becomes

$$\mu\theta + \tfrac{1}{2}\sigma^2\theta^2 = -i\omega,$$

and the two solutions are easily seen to be

$$\theta_0(\omega) = -\frac{\mu}{\sigma^2}[1 - (1 - 2i\omega\sigma^2/\mu^2)^{1/2}],$$

$$\theta_1(\omega) = -\frac{\mu}{\sigma^2}[1 + (1 - 2i\omega\sigma^2/\mu^2)^{1/2}].$$

On substitution into Eqs. 8.22a and 8.22b we have the characteristic functions for the reaction times. To my knowledge, these have not been inverted in general.

For the special case where B approaches ∞—simple reaction times—observe that since

$$\lim_{\omega \to 0} \theta_1(\omega) = \theta_1 < 0 = \lim_{\omega \to 0} \theta_0(\omega),$$

we know that for small $|\theta|$, the real part of $\theta_1(\omega) <$ real part of $\theta_0(\omega)$, thus

$$\lim_{B \to \infty} e^{[\theta_1(\omega) - \theta_0(\omega)]B} = \lim_{B \to \infty} e^{\theta_1(\omega)B} = 0.$$

So

$$\begin{aligned}
E(e^{i\omega \mathbf{N}} \mid A) &= \lim_{B \to \infty} \frac{1}{P(A)} \left[\frac{1 - e^{[\theta_1(\omega) - \theta_0(\omega)]B}}{e^{\theta_0(\omega)A} - e^{[\theta_1(\omega) - \theta_0(\omega)]B} e^{\theta_1(\omega)A}} \right] \\
&= e^{-\theta_0(\omega)A} \\
&= \exp\left\{ \frac{\mu}{\sigma^2} \left[1 - \left(1 - \frac{2i\omega\sigma^2}{\mu^2} \right)^{1/2} \right] \right\}.
\end{aligned}$$

This can be shown (Wald, 1947, p. 193, or Johnson and Kotz, 1970, Vol. 1, p. 139) to be the characteristic function of the Wald distribution:

$$\frac{A}{\sigma(2\pi)^{1/2} n^{3/2}} \exp\left[-\frac{(A - \mu n)^2}{2\sigma^2 n} \right].$$

The reaction-time distribution is rather more sensitive to the exact form of the distribution of $\mathbf{X}$ than one might have anticipated. For example, suppose the distribution of $\mathbf{X}$ is the gamma $\lambda^m x^{m-1} e^{-\lambda x}/(m-1)!$. This arises when $\mathbf{X}$ is the sum of m-independent, identical exponential random variables, which it is if $\mathbf{X}$ is the sum of n interarrival times of a Poisson process. This fact suggests that for large m, the reaction-time distribution should be much like the Wald since by the central limit theorem the gamma approaches the Gaussian. We show that this conjecture is not so. The distribution of crossing times and distances are the concatenation of m gamma distributions with shape parameter m and, therefore, are gamma distributed with shape parameter nm when $\mathbf{N} = n$. As is well known, to achieve a fixed distance, A in the case $B = \infty$, the distribution of the number of steps, $\mathbf{N}m$, is necessarily Poisson. Going to a continuous generalization,

$$f(t) = \Pr(\mathbf{T} = t) = g(A\lambda)(A\lambda)^{mt} e^{-A\lambda}/\Gamma(mt + 1),$$

where $g(A\lambda)$ is simply a normalizing factor and Γ is the gamma function, we see

$$-\frac{d}{dt} \ln f(t) = -mA + -m\psi(mt + 1),$$

where ψ is the diagamma function, and it is known to be increasing. Thus, by Theorem 1.1, the hazard function of $\mathbf{T}$ is increasing, which of course is not true of the Wald distribution.

TABLE 8.1. Comparison of theoretical and simulated (50,000 trials) observables in the Gaussian random walk model

Parameter values		$P(A/a)$	$P(B/b)$	MRT			
				aA	*bA*	*aB*	*bB*
$A = B = 500$	Theory	.83	.83	332	332	332	332
$\sigma = 25, \mu = 1$	Simulated	.84	.84	340	340	334	345
$A = B = 35,$	Theory	.75	.75	17.4	17.4	17.4	17.4
$\sigma = 8, \mu = 1$	Simulated	.77	.77	22.1	21.7	22.1	21.8
$A = 50, B = 25$	Theory	.80	.87	23.7	14.4	23.7	14.4
$\sigma = 8, \mu = 1$	Simulated	.65	.88	28.9	18.4	28.6	18.3

Apparently, therefore, the observed reaction-time distribution is quite sensitive to the exact nature of the decay in the tail of the distribution of **X**. The faster decay of $\exp(-x^2)$ as compared with $\exp(-x)$ is reflected in a peaked as compared with an increasing hazard function for the reaction-time distribution.

Since, to my knowledge, the form of the reaction-time distribution is not known in the choice case for any particular assumption about the distribution of **X**, I had the Gaussian process simulated.* Figure 8.2 gives some examples of the simulated density and hazard functions, based upon samples of 50,000 trials. The main thing to observe is that qualitatively they are of the same general shape as the Wald distribution with hazard functions that asymptote to a constant and that may or may not have a peak. Perhaps more important is the observation that for these simulations, and many others we have done, the estimated mean reaction times are substantially larger than the theoretical ones. Table 8.1 gives some examples. Presumably this is due to a failure of the small step assumption. This fact raises serious questions about attempts to fit random walk models to data (see Section 8.5).

*8.2.6 Proofs

Theorem 8.1 (Wald, 1974, p. 157).   *With probability 1, for some n,* $\mathbf{S}_n \geq A$ *or* $\mathbf{S}_n \leq -B$.

Proof.   Let $\mathbf{X}_1, \mathbf{X}_2, \ldots, \mathbf{X}_n, \ldots$ be the sequence of independent, identical random variables. Let k be an integer, and partition the sequence into successive subsequences of length k. Let $\mathbf{S}_j^{(k)}$ be the sum of the jth such subsequence. If the process does not terminate in a boundary crossing, then for every j, $|\mathbf{S}_j^{(k)}| < A + B$. Let P_j be the probability that $|\mathbf{S}_j^{(k)}| < A + B$. Since the $\mathbf{X}_n$ are independent and identically distributed, $P_j = P$ independent of j. Thus, the probability of all inequalities holding is $\lim_{j \to \infty} P^j = 0$, provided $P < 1$.

---

* This calculation was carried out by R. M. Nosofsky.

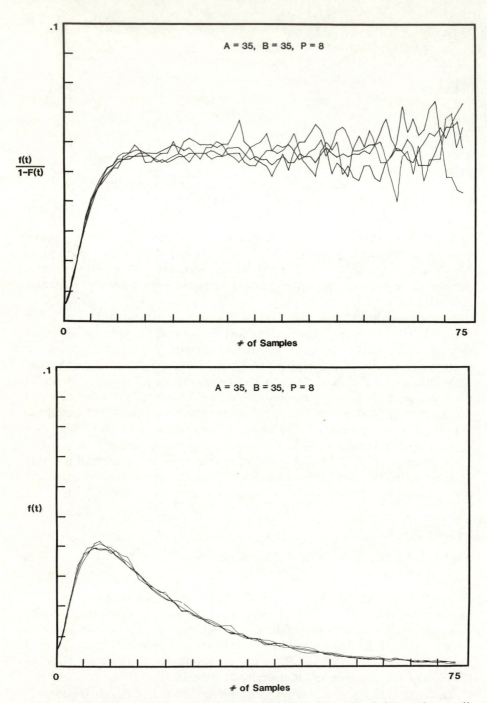

FIG. 8.2 Density and hazard functions for the Gaussian case of the random walk computed from simulations of 50,000 runs with $\mu = 1$ and $\sigma = 8$. Parts a and b are, respectively, the density and hazard functions for the symmetric case $A = B = 35$; c and d are $A = 50$, $B = 25$.

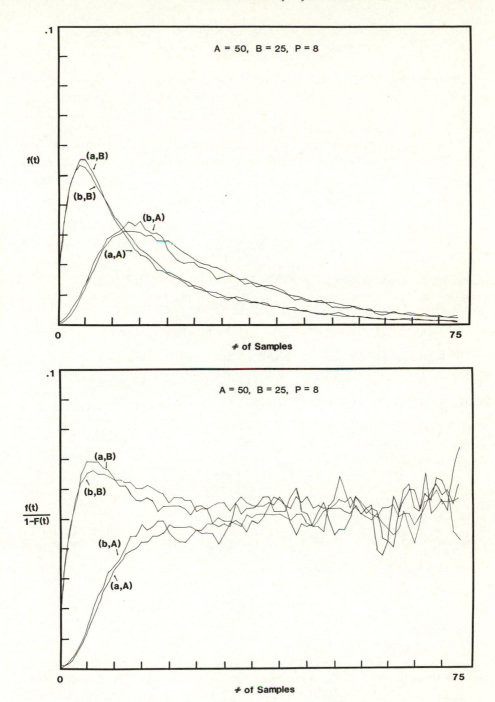

But we may select k sufficiently large to insure $P < 1$ because $E(\mathbf{X}_n) \neq 0$ and so $|E[\mathbf{S}_j^{(k)}]|$ can be made arbitrarily large. ∎

Theorem 8.2 (Wald, 1947, p. 159). *Let $\mathbf{N}$ be the least integer such that either $\mathbf{S_N} \leq -B$ or $\geq A$. Then for all θ for which $|M_s(\theta)| > 1$,*

$$E[e^{\theta \mathbf{S_N}} / M_s(\theta)^{\mathbf{N}} \mid s] = 1, \qquad s = a, b.$$

Proof. Let n be any integer and let P_n denote the probability that a barrier is crossed on or before n. Since $\mathbf{S}_n$ is the sum of identical and independent random variables,

$$E[e^{\mathbf{S_N}\theta + (\mathbf{S}_n - \mathbf{S_N})\theta} \mid s] = E(e^{\mathbf{S}_n\theta} \mid s) = M_s(\theta)^n.$$

Let E_n denote the expectation operator conditional on the crossing occurring on or before n and E_n^* the operator conditional on the crossing after n. Then,

$$M_s(\theta)^n = P_n E_n[e^{\mathbf{S_N}\theta + (\mathbf{S}_n - \mathbf{S_N})\theta} \mid s] + (1 - P_n)E_n^*(e^{\mathbf{S}_n\theta} \mid s).$$

Since for each value of $\mathbf{N}$, $\mathbf{S}_n - \mathbf{S_N}$ is independent of $\mathbf{S_N}$,

$$E_n[e^{\mathbf{S_N}\theta + (\mathbf{S}_n - \mathbf{S_N})\theta} \mid s] = E_n[e^{\mathbf{S_N}\theta} M_s(\theta)^{-\mathbf{N}} \mid s] M_s(\theta)^n.$$

Substituting and dividing by $M_s(\theta)^n$,

$$1 = P_n E_n[e^{\mathbf{S_N}\theta} M_s(\theta)^{-\mathbf{N}} \mid s] + (1 - P_n)E_n^*[e^{\mathbf{S}_n\theta} \mid s] / M_s(\theta)^n.$$

By Theorem 8.1, $\lim_{n \to \infty} P_n = 1$. Because E^* is conditional on crossing after n, $|E_n^*[e^{\mathbf{S}_n\theta} \mid s]|$ is bounded by $e^{A\theta} + e^{-B\theta}$. And by hypothesis, $|M_s(\theta)| > 1$. Thus,

$$1 = \lim_{n \to \infty} P_n E_n[e^{\mathbf{S_N}\theta} M_s(\theta)^{-\mathbf{N}} \mid s] + \lim_{n \to \infty} (1 - P_n)E_n^*[e^{\mathbf{S}_n\theta} \mid s] / M_s(\theta)n$$

$$= E[e^{\mathbf{S_N}\theta} M_s(\theta)^{-\mathbf{N}} \mid s]. \qquad ∎$$

Lemma 8.1. *If (1) $\lim_{\theta \to \pm\infty} M_s(\theta) > 1$ and (2) $M_s'(0) \neq 0$, then there exists a unique $\theta_{1s} \neq 0$ such that $M_s(\theta_{1s}) = 1$.*

Proof. Observe that

$$M_s'(\theta) = E(\mathbf{X}e^{\theta\mathbf{X}} \mid s),$$
$$M_s''(\theta) = E(\mathbf{X}^2 e^{\theta\mathbf{X}} \mid s) > 0,$$

hence there is only one value of θ, say θ_{0s}, such that $M_s'(\theta_{0s}) = 0$. By hypotheses 1 and 2, θ_{0s} must be a minimum of $M_s(\theta)$. By hypothesis 2, $\theta_{0s} \neq 0$, so $M_s(\theta_{0s}) < M_s(0) = 1$. Thus, there exists a unique $\theta_{1s} \neq 0$ with $M_s(\theta_{1s}) = 1$. ∎

Proof of Eqs. 8.18a and 8.18b. Take the derivative of Eq. 8.15 with respect to $z = \mathcal{M}_s(\theta)^{-1}$:

$$0 = P(A \mid s)e^{\theta A}\frac{dE(z^{\mathbf{N}} \mid s, A)}{dz} + P(A \mid s)e^{\theta A}A\frac{d\theta}{dz}E(z^{\mathbf{N}} \mid s, A)$$

$$+ P(B \mid s)e^{-\theta B}\frac{dE(z^{\mathbf{N}} \mid s, B)}{dz} + P(B \mid s)e^{-\theta B}B\left[-\frac{d\theta}{dz}\right]E(z^{\mathbf{N}} \mid s, B). \quad (8.23)$$

To evaluate $d\theta/dz$, observe

$$1 = \frac{dz}{dz} = -\frac{\mathcal{M}_s'(\theta)}{\mathcal{M}_s(\theta)^2}\frac{d\theta}{dz},$$

whence

$$\frac{d\theta}{dz} = -\frac{\mathcal{M}_s(\theta)^2}{\mathcal{M}_s'(\theta)}.$$

Since

$$\mu_s = E(X \mid s) = \mathcal{M}_s'(0),$$
$$\mathcal{M}_s(0) = 1,$$

we see

$$\left.\frac{d\theta}{dz}\right|_{\theta=0} = -\frac{1}{\mu_s}. \quad (8.24)$$

Define γ_s by

$$\left.\frac{d\theta}{dz}\right|_{\theta=\theta_{1s}} = -\frac{\mathcal{M}_s(\theta_{1s})^2}{\mathcal{M}_s'(\theta_{1s})}$$

$$= -\frac{1}{\mathcal{M}_s'(\theta_{1s})}$$

$$= \frac{1}{\gamma_s\mu_s}. \quad (8.19)$$

Using Eqs. 8.24 and 8.19 and setting $\theta = 0$, then $\theta = \theta_{1s}$ in Eq. 8.23 yields

$$0 = P(A \mid s)[L_{sA} - A/\mu_s] + P(B \mid s)[L_{sB} + B/\mu_s] \quad (8.25a)$$

$$0 = P(A \mid s)e^{-\alpha_s}[L_{sA} + A/\gamma_s\mu_s] + P(B \mid s)e^{\beta_s}[L_{sB} - B/\gamma_s\mu_s], \quad (8.25b)$$

where

$$L_{sR} = E(\mathbf{N} \mid s, R).$$

Solving for L_{sA} and L_{sB} yields Eqs. 8.18a and 8.18b. ∎

Note that Eq. 8.25a is the same as Eq. 8.20.

8.3   RESTRICTIONS ON THE RANDOM WALK MODEL

8.3.1   *The Classical Optimum Model:*
Sequential Probability Ratio Test (SPRT)

If the observed random variables underlying the decision process—call them $\mathbf{Y}_i$, $i = 1, 2, \ldots$—have the common distributions g_a and g_b, depending on which signal is presented, then by definition the likelihood ratio that a rather than b was presented, given that Y was observed, is $g_a(Y)/g_b(Y)$. Under repeated, independent observations, the overall likelihood ratio is the random variable

$$\prod_{i=1}^{n} \frac{g_a(\mathbf{Y}_i)}{g_b(\mathbf{Y}_i)}.$$

Taking the logarithm leads to a sum of independent and identically distributed random variables, and that suggests we define

$$\mathbf{X}_i = \ln g_a(\mathbf{Y}_i)/g_b(\mathbf{Y}_i) = h(\mathbf{Y}_i), \tag{8.26}$$

where $h = \ln(g_a/g_b)$. This is the model Wald (1947) developed and that Stone (1960) suggested as a choice reaction-time model.

Of course, $\mathbf{X}_i$ has one distribution, f_a, when a is presented and another, f_b, when b is presented. The relation between these two distributions is indirectly, but adequately, captured in the next result, which is Swensson and Green's (1977) adaptation of a result in Thomas (1975).

Theorem 8.3.   *Equation 8.26 holds if and only if* $\mathcal{M}_b(\theta) = \mathcal{M}_a(\theta - 1)$.

We use this result shortly to see how the general random walk model is constrained by the assumption that decisions are based upon likelihood ratios.

As one can see, using products of likelihood ratios to generate a decision is exactly the same method of updating as in Bayes' Theorem (Section 1.3.2). Moreover, it generalizes the normative theory of signal detectability (Green & Swets, 1966, 1974); in that theory there is just one observation and a single criterion with no region of indeterminancy. Wald and Wolfowitz (1948) showed that this sampling procedure is optimal in the following sense: if the error probabilities are fixed, then the number of observations before a decision is reached is, on average, no greater than it would be for any other decision rule. Of course, there is no assurance whatsoever that the brain is optimal in this sense, and as we shall see there is ample reason to believe it is not.

Theorem 8.4.   *Under the conditions of Theorem 8.3,*

$$\theta_{1a} = -\theta_{1b} = -1, \tag{8.27}$$

$$A = \alpha_a = -\alpha_b = \ln \frac{P(A \mid a)}{P(A \mid b)}, \tag{8.28}$$

$$B = \beta_a = -\beta_b = \ln \frac{P(B \mid b)}{P(B \mid a)}, \tag{8.29}$$

$$L_s = \frac{1}{\mu_s} \left[P(A \mid s) \ln \frac{P(A \mid a)}{P(A \mid b)} - P(B \mid s) \ln \frac{P(B \mid b)}{P(B \mid a)} \right], \tag{8.30}$$

$$\gamma_a = 1/\gamma_b = -\mu_b/\mu_a, \tag{8.31}$$

$$E(z^{\mathbf{N}} \mid a, r) = E(z^{\mathbf{N}} \mid b, r), \qquad r = A, B. \tag{8.32}$$

Of these properties, the most striking is the last. It says that the distribution of response times depends on the response made, but, surprisingly, it is quite independent of the signal presented. Assuming the model to be correct, the testable prediction that response times are independent of the signal presented follows only if the distribution of residual times also does not depend upon the signal.

The next most striking fact, embodied in Eqs. 8.28 and 8.29, is that the boundaries A and B are determined entirely by the response probabilities, independent of the response times. This simplifies appreciably the estimation problem, which we discuss in Section 8.3.2.

This last fact, together with Eq. 8.20, yields the relation embodied in Eq. 8.30. If one assumes there is an experimental manipulation that does not affect μ_s, but does vary the response times and probabilities, then Eq. 8.30 formulates a speed-accuracy tradeoff function for the model.

For some purposes, it may be useful to know more about the response-time distribution than the mean. For the SPRT model, Ghosh (1969) has developed approximate expressions for the first four moments; I do not reproduce them here as they are quite lengthy.

8.3.2 On Testing SPRT

Let us begin by considering the parameters to be estimated. In SPRT the unit of the underlying decision axis has already been selected; it is determined by Eq. 8.26. If one wishes to change the unit—to assign to the likelihood ratio of 1 a value different from 1—it is necessary to multiply Eq. 8.26 by a constant k, which in turn will appear in Theorem 8.3 as $\mathcal{M}_b(\theta) = \mathcal{M}_a(\theta - k)$ and will also appear in some of the expressions of Theorem 8.4. So that degree of freedom is lost. That leaves us with four model parameters: A, B, μ_a, μ_b. As we noted, A and B are determined uniquely by, and uniquely determine, the response probabilities.

So we turn to the latency equations. There are two complications. First, the model describes the mean number of discrete steps prior to a decision, and that must be converted into real time. Normally, one assumes there is a constant factor, Δ, that converts steps into time, but as Weatherburn (1978) has pointed out, the constancy of the conversion is not necessarily correct. Because no one really knows what to do in the more general case, I shall assume that the conversion is independent of the number of steps. As a result, the equations for the mean reaction times will have the factor Δ/μ_s to be estimated, and we will be unable to identify Δ and μ_s separately. The second complication is the existence of residual times for which we have no theory. If we assume them to be the same, independent of signal and response, then we obtain from Eqs. 8.18a and 8.18b the following two equations in the three parameters Δ/μ_a, Δ/μ_b, and r_0:

$$E(\mathbf{T} \mid a, A) = E(\mathbf{T} \mid b, A) = r_0 + \frac{\Delta}{\mu_a} \eta_{aA} + \frac{\Delta}{\mu_b} \eta_{bA}, \tag{8.33a}$$

$$E(\mathbf{T} \mid a, B) = E(\mathbf{T} \mid b, B) = r_0 + \frac{\Delta}{\mu_a} \eta_{aB} + \frac{\Delta}{\mu_b} \eta_{bB}, \tag{8.33b}$$

where

$$
\begin{aligned}
\eta_{aA} &= \left[A - B \frac{P(B \mid a)}{P(A \mid a)} \right] \frac{e^B}{e^B - e^{-A}}, \\[2mm]
\eta_{bA} &= \left[A - B \frac{P(B \mid b)}{P(A \mid a)} \right] \frac{e^{-B}}{e^{-B} - e^A}, \\[2mm]
\eta_{aB} &= \left[B - A \frac{P(A \mid a)}{P(B \mid a)} \right] \frac{e^{-A}}{e^B - e^{-A}}, \\[2mm]
\eta_{bB} &= \left[B - A \frac{P(A \mid b)}{P(B \mid b)} \right] \frac{e^A}{e^{-B} - e^A}.
\end{aligned}
\tag{8.34}
$$

In practice few attempts have been made to estimate these parameters because most data grossly violate the condition that

$$E(\mathbf{T} \mid a, r) = E(\mathbf{T} \mid b, r), \qquad r = A, B,$$

as we have seen in Section 6.3.3. This means that this model, including the assumption that the subject starts processing information at signal onset (Section 8.4.2), can be saved only by making the residual a function of either the signal or the response or both. Once that is done, the model is indeterminate unless one varies conditions and assumes that some of the parameters are invariant under those changes. For example, suppose that the presentation probabilities are varied and it is assumed that this affects A and B, but not the two stimulus parameters μ_s. If, in addition, one were to assume the residuals depend on either the signal or the response but not both, then if there are m different conditions of presentation probabilities, there are a total of four parameters to estimate from $2m$ equations. Note, however, that this strategy will not succeed if the residuals are also assumed to depend upon the presentation probabilities.

8.3.3 Symmetric Stimulus Representation (SSR)

Because the data clearly reject SPRT with constant residuals, other specializations of the general random walk model are clearly of interest. Link

(1975) and Link and Heath (1975) have made the only other suggestion, which Laming (1979c, p. 433) has concluded may well be the only other tractable alternative. The suggestion, once again, is that the two densities of X are very closely related. In SSR it is assumed that the tendency to go in the A direction when a is presented is exactly the same as the tendency to go in the B direction when b is presented.* Stated formally, for all real x,

$$f_a(x) = f_b(-x). \tag{8.35}$$

It is trivial to see that:

Theorem 8.5. *Equation 8.35 holds if and only if $\mathcal{M}_a(\theta) = \mathcal{M}_b(-\theta)$.*

Theorem 8.6. *Under the conditions of Theorem 8.5,*

$$\theta_{1a} = -\theta_{1b}, \tag{8.36}$$

$$\alpha_a = -\alpha_b = \ln \frac{P(A \mid a)}{P(A \mid b)}, \tag{8.37}$$

$$\beta_a = -\beta_b = \ln \frac{P(B \mid b)}{P(B \mid a)}, \tag{8.38}$$

$$\mu_a = -\mu_b, \tag{8.39}$$

$$\gamma_a = \gamma_b, \tag{8.40}$$

If we set $\theta_{1a} = -1$, which determines the unit of the decision axis, then Eqs. 8.37 and 8.38 become Eqs. 8.28 and 8.29 of SPRT, and A and B are determined by the response probabilities. Moreover, the speed-accuracy Eq. 8.20 then becomes exactly that of SPRT, Eq. 8.30. The major difference in the relations among the parameters is that there is but one mean, $\mu = \mu_a = -\mu_b$, and $\gamma = \gamma_a = \gamma_b$, rather than $\gamma_a = 1/\gamma_b$. The most important consequence of this is that the mean times for the same response need not be the same. We can see that by using the properties of Eqs. 8.37–8.40 in Eq. 8.18, we obtain

$$L_{Aa} - L_{Ab} = \frac{A}{\mu} \left[\frac{\gamma - 1}{\gamma} \right],$$

$$L_{Bb} - L_{Ba} = \frac{B}{\mu} \left[\frac{\gamma - 1}{\gamma} \right].$$

The equality of SPRT holds if and only if $\gamma = 1$, which in fact is a special case of SPRT. Recall that $\gamma = 1$ is a property of the Gaussian model.

Observe that the relations between the response probabilities and A and

---

* It is easy to become confused about terminology. Link (1975, 1978) speaks of "relative judgment theory" (RJT), by which he means that the observations X_i arise by comparing an internal observation relative to a standard; however, in these papers he imposed Eq. 8.35, which he did not name and which need not arise from relative judgments, and some have come, incorrectly in my view, to refer to that assumption as RJT.

B are exactly the same in both models. Furthermore, so long as A and B are otherwise unconstrained, absolutely any pair of response probabilities $P(A \mid a)$ and $P(A \mid b)$ can occur. Thus, neither SPRT nor SSR imposes any constraints whatsoever on the ROC curve—the relation between $P(A \mid a)$ and $P(A \mid b)$ that arises when the signal is held fixed and the error tradeoff is manipulated, usually by varying the presentation probabilities, the payoff matrix for accuracy, or the instructions. This observation is not inconsistent with Link and Heath's (1975) emphasis on the fact that SSR encompasses the ROC curves of many well-known psychophysical theories, such as low thresholds and the theory of signal detectability; however, the significance of the fact is much undercut when it is realized that SSR and SPRT both encompass every conceivable ROC curve!

Noreen (1976) was perhaps the first to note and certainly the first to exploit the fact that Eqs. 8.18a and 8.18b become the following linear system in $1/\mu$ and $1/\gamma\mu$:

$$L_{aA} = \frac{1}{\mu}\,\eta_A + \frac{1}{\gamma\mu}\,(\eta_A - A),$$

$$L_{bA} = \frac{1}{\mu}\,(\eta_A - A) + \frac{1}{\gamma\mu}\,\eta_A,$$

$$L_{aB} = \frac{1}{\mu}\,(\eta_B - B) + \frac{1}{\gamma\mu}\,\eta_B,$$

$$L_{bB} = \frac{1}{\mu}\,\eta_B + \frac{1}{\gamma\mu}\,(\eta_B - B),$$

(8.41)

where the η's arise from Eq. 8.18 and simplify to

$$\eta_A = \frac{P(B \mid b)}{P(A \mid a) + P(B \mid b) - 1}\{AP(A \mid a) - B[1 - P(A \mid a)]\},$$

$$\eta_B = \frac{P(A \mid a)}{P(A \mid a) + P(B \mid b) - 1}\{BP(B \mid b) - A[1 - P(B \mid b)]\}.$$

(8.42)

8.3.4 On Testing SSR

The situation is similar to that of SPRT, but simpler. For A and B, the models are the same. For the mean response times, there are four equations and two parameters, Δ/μ and $\Delta/\gamma\mu$, associated with the steps of the random walk. Of course, nothing can be done if we assume the residuals are affected by both the signals and the responses. So, I consider two special cases. The first is that the residuals are a function only of the signal. Then

$$E(\mathbf{T} \mid a, r) = r_s + \Delta L_{sr}, \qquad s = a, b, \qquad r = A, B, \qquad (8.43)$$

where L_{sr} is given by Eq. 8.41, is a system of four equations linear in the

TABLE 8.2. Mean and standard deviations of the parameter estimates of the perturbed MRTs using $A = 5$, $B = 2$, $\mu = 10$, $\gamma = 2$, $r_a = .100$, and $r_b = .125$

Size of perturbation		$\hat{\mu}/\Delta$	$\hat{\gamma}$	$\hat{r}_a$	$\hat{r}_b$
.05	Mean	10.05	2.02	.100	.125
	standard deviation	0.72	0.16	.016	.021
.10	Mean	10.21	2.08	.100	.125
	standard deviation	1.51	0.38	.031	.043

four unknowns Δ/μ, $\Delta/\gamma\mu$, r_a, and r_b, and it can be solved explicitly for any set of data.

There is some question about the sensitivity of the estimation given that there is error in the time estimates. To get some idea how bad the estimations might be I had the following calculations carried out.* For the parameter values

$$A = 5, \quad B = 2, \quad \frac{\mu}{\Delta} = 10, \quad \gamma = 2, \quad r_a = .100, \quad \text{and} \quad r_b = .125,$$

the four values of $E(\mathbf{T} \mid s, r)$ were computed. Then they were systematically perturbed by the factors $(1 + \epsilon)$, 1, and $(1 - \epsilon)$, which results in 81 quadruples of mean reaction times. The estimated parameters were obtained for each. As a crude measure of failure of the model to fit the data, I used any of the following as a definition of failure:

$$\frac{\hat{\mu}}{\Delta} < 0, \quad \hat{\gamma} < 0, \quad \hat{r}_s < 50 \text{ msec}, \quad \hat{r}_s > \text{MRT}_{sr} \quad (s = a, b, \quad r = A, B).$$

Using $\epsilon = .05$, there were no failures of this sort; using $\epsilon = .10$, there were five failures, all of them cases where $\hat{r}_s < 50$ msec. (This will be important later in evaluating fits of the model to data.) To get some idea of the deviation of the estimates from the "true" values of the parameters, the means and standard deviations, over the 81 cases, are given in Table 8.2.

The obvious alternative model is to suppose that the residuals depend upon the responses, not on the signals. Unfortunately, the resulting linear system

$$E(\mathbf{T} \mid s, r) = r_r + \Delta L_{sr}, \quad r = A, B, \quad s = A, B,$$

is singular since

$$E(\mathbf{T} \mid a, r) - E(\mathbf{T} \mid b, r) = (L_{ar} - L_{br}) = \frac{\Delta}{\mu\gamma}(\gamma - 1)r, \tag{8.44}$$

* A. F. Smith carried out these calculations.

and so eliminating $\Delta(\gamma - 1)/\mu\gamma$,

$$E(\mathbf{T} \mid a, A) = E(\mathbf{T} \mid b, A) + \frac{A}{B}[E(\mathbf{T} \mid b, B) - E(\mathbf{T} \mid a, B)].$$

It follows that we cannot estimate all of the parameters, but as a check on the model we do have two independent estimates of $\Delta(\gamma - 1)/\mu\gamma$.

Except for Laming (1979c), the published attempts to test SSR (Link, 1975, 1978, and Link and Heath, 1975) have not involved estimation of the parameters μ/Δ and γ and an evaluation of their plausibility or how they vary over experimental conditions. Rather, the emphasis has been on linear relations, such as the speed-accuracy tradeoff of Eq. 8.30, that follows from parts of the linear system. As we shall see, this can be grossly misleading.

8.3.5   Restrictions on the Boundaries

One way to reduce the number of parameters in SPRT and SSR is to entertain hypotheses about how the boundaries are selected. I give three examples.

First, let us suppose that response symmetry, $A = B$, is imposed. Then from Eq. 8.20 we see that the speed accuracy tradeoff becomes

$$L_s = \frac{A}{\mu_s}[2P(A \mid s) - 1].$$

And from Eqs. 8.16a and 8.16b we see $\alpha_s = \beta_s$ and so by Eqs. 8.28 and 8.29 of SPRT and the corresponding Eqs. 8.37 and 8.38 of SSR, either $P(A \mid a) = P(A \mid b)$ or $P(A \mid a) = P(B \mid b)$. As the former represents no stimulus discrimination, so then the latter—that is, response symmetry— must obtain.

Second, let us suppose that the separation between the boundaries is held constant—that is, for some K, $A + B = K$. As we shall see in Figures 8.9 to 8.11, this appears to be approximately correct for at least two experiments. For either SPRT or SSR, using Eq. 8.36 and substituting into Eqs. 8.37 and 8.38 and eliminating A, we obtain as the ROC curve

$$P(A \mid a) = \frac{CP(A \mid b)}{1 + (C - 1)P(A \mid b)}, \qquad C = \exp(-\theta_{1a}K).$$

The area under this curve is

$$\frac{C}{(C - 1)^2}(C - 1 - \ln C).$$

The third approach, due to Edwards (1965), assumes that there are payoffs for the four signal-response pairs and a cost that is proportional to the decision latency. Let the payoffs be V_{sr} and the cost per unit time be $-U$, where $U > 0$. If π denotes the probability of presenting a, then the expected value on each trial in SPRT and SSR is easily seen to be

$$
\begin{aligned}
EV = {} & P(A \mid a)\pi(V_{aA} - V_{bB}) + P(B \mid b)(1-\pi)(V_{bB} - V_{bA}) \\
& + \pi V_{aB} + (1-\pi)V_{bA} \\
& - U\frac{\pi}{\mu_a}\left[P(A \mid a)\ln\frac{P(A \mid a)}{1 - P(B \mid b)} - [1 - P(A \mid a)]\ln\frac{P(B \mid b)}{1 - P(A \mid a)}\right] \\
& - U\frac{(1-\pi)}{\mu_b}\left[[1 - P(B \mid b)]\ln\frac{P(A \mid a)}{1 - P(B \mid b)} - P(B \mid b)\ln\frac{P(B \mid b)}{1 - P(A \mid a)}\right].
\end{aligned}
$$

Let us suppose that A and B are chosen so as to maximize expected value. Since selecting A and B is equivalent (in these two models) to selecting $P(A \mid a)$ and $P(B \mid b)$, it suffices to solve the two equations

$$
\frac{\partial EV}{\partial P(A \mid a)} = 0, \qquad \frac{\partial EV}{\partial P(B \mid b)} = 0.
$$

This leads to the pair of equations

$$
0 = \varphi_a - \ln\frac{\Omega_A}{\Omega_B} - \rho\left[\frac{1}{\Omega_A} - \frac{1}{\Omega_B}\right],
$$

$$
0 = \varphi_b + \ln\frac{\Omega_A}{\Omega_B} - \frac{1}{\rho}[\Omega_A - \Omega_B],
$$

where

$$
\varphi_a = (V_{aA} - V_{aB})\frac{\mu_a}{U},
$$

$$
\varphi_b = (V_{aB} - V_{bA})\frac{\mu_b}{U},
$$

$$
\rho = \left[\frac{1 - \pi}{\pi}\right]\frac{\mu_a}{\mu_b},
$$

$$
\Omega_A = \frac{P(A \mid a)}{1 - P(B \mid b)},
$$

$$
\Omega_B = \frac{1 - P(A \mid a)}{P(B \mid b)}.
$$

These can be solved numerically for Ω_A and Ω_B, and so for A and B. To my knowledge, this has not been done.

8.3.6 Proofs

Theorem 8.3. $\mathbf{X} = \ln g_a(\mathbf{Y})/g_b(\mathbf{Y})$ iff $\mathcal{M}_b(\theta) = \mathcal{M}_a(\theta - 1)$.

Proof. Denoting $\mathbf{X} = h(\mathbf{Y})$, then

$$
\mathcal{M}_a(\theta - 1) = \int_{-\infty}^{\infty} e^{(\theta-1)h(y)} g_a(y)\, dy
$$

$$
= \int_{-\infty}^{\infty} [g_a(y)/g_b(y)]^{\theta-1} g_a(y)\, dy
$$

$$
= \int_{-\infty}^{\infty} [g_a(y)/g_b(y)]^{\theta} g_b(h)\, dy
$$

$$
= \int_{-\infty}^{\infty} e^{\theta h(y)} g_b(y)\, dy
$$

$$
= \mathcal{M}_b(\theta).
$$

Conversely,

$$
\int_{-\infty}^{\infty} e^{\theta h(y)} g_b(y)\, dy = \mathcal{M}_b(\theta)
$$

$$
= \mathcal{M}_a(\theta - 1)
$$

$$
= \int_{-\infty}^{\infty} e^{(\theta-1)h(y)} g_a(y)\, dy
$$

$$
= \int_{-\infty}^{\infty} e^{\theta h(y)} e^{-h(y)} g_a(y)\, dy.
$$

By the uniqueness theorem for moment generating functions,

$$
g_b(y) = e^{-h(y)} g_a(y),
$$

and so

$$
h(y) = \ln g_a(y)/g_b(y). \qquad \blacksquare
$$

Theorem 8.4. *Under the conditions of Theorem 8.3,*

$$
\theta_{1a} = -\theta_{1b} - 1, \tag{8.27}
$$

$$
A = \alpha_a = -\alpha_b = \ln \frac{P(A \mid a)}{P(A \mid b)}, \tag{8.28}
$$

$$
B = \beta_a = -\beta_b = \ln \frac{P(B \mid b)}{P(A \mid a)}, \tag{8.29}
$$

$$
L_s = \frac{1}{\mu_s} \left[P(A \mid s) \ln \frac{P(A \mid a)}{P(A \mid b)} - P(B \mid s) \ln \frac{P(B \mid b)}{P(B \mid a)} \right], \tag{8.30}
$$

$$
\gamma_a = 1/\gamma_b = \mu_a/\mu_b, \tag{8.31}
$$

$$
E(z^{\mathbf{N}} \mid a, r) = E(z^{\mathbf{N}} \mid b, r), \qquad r = A, B. \tag{8.32}
$$

Proof. Since $\mathcal{M}_a(0) = 1 = \mathcal{M}_b(0)$, then $\mathcal{M}_b(\theta) = \mathcal{M}_a(\theta - 1)$ yields $\mathcal{M}_b(1) = \mathcal{M}_a(1 - 1) = 1$ and $\mathcal{M}_a(-1) = \mathcal{M}_b(0) = 1$, and so $\theta_{1a} = -1 = -\theta_{1b}$. Substituting into Eqs. 8.16 and 8.17 yields Eqs. 8.28 and 8.29. Substituting these into Eq. 8.20 yields Eq. 8.30.

Observe that $\mathcal{M}_b'(\theta) = \mathcal{M}_a'(\theta - 1)$, so

$$\mu_b = \mathcal{M}_b'(\theta)\,|_{\theta=0} = \mathcal{M}_a'(-1) = \mathcal{M}_a'(\theta)\,|_{\theta=\theta_{1a}} = -\gamma_a\mu_a,$$

$$\mu_a = \mathcal{M}_a'(\theta)\,|_{\theta=0} = \mathcal{M}_b'(1) = \mathcal{M}_b'(\theta)\,|_{\theta=\theta_{1b}} = -\gamma_b\mu_b,$$

from which it follows that $\gamma_a = 1/\gamma_b$.

To show Eq. 8.32, substitute $e^A = P(A \mid a)/P(A \mid b)$ and $e^{-B} = P(B \mid a)/P(B \mid b)$ into Eq. 8.15 with $s = b$:

$$1 = P(A \mid b)[P(A \mid a)/P(A \mid b)]^{\theta}E[\mathcal{M}_b(\theta)^{-N} \mid b, A]$$
$$+ P(B \mid b)[P(B \mid a)/P(B \mid b)]^{\theta}E[\mathcal{M}_b(\theta)^{-N} \mid b, B].$$

Now replace θ by $\theta + 1$ and, by Theorem 8.3, substitute $\mathcal{M}_a(\theta) = \mathcal{M}_b(\theta + 1)$,

$$1 = P(A \mid b)[P(A \mid a)/P(A \mid b)]^{\theta+1}E[\mathcal{M}_a(\theta)^{-N} \mid b, A]$$
$$+ P(B \mid b)[P(B \mid a)/P(B \mid b)]^{\theta+1}E[\mathcal{M}_a(\theta)^{-N} \mid b, B]$$
$$= P(A \mid a)[P(A \mid a)/P(A \mid b)]^{\theta}E(\mathcal{M}_a(\theta)^{-N} \mid b, A]$$
$$+ P(B \mid a)[P(B \mid a)/P(B \mid b)]^{\theta}E[\mathcal{M}_a(\theta)^{-N} \mid a, B].$$

But setting $s = a$ in Eq. 8.15,

$$1 = P(A \mid a)[P(A \mid a)/P(A \mid b)]^{\theta}E[\mathcal{M}_a(\theta)^{-N} \mid a, A]$$
$$+ P(B \mid a)[P(B \mid a)/P(B \mid b)]^{\theta}E[\mathcal{M}_a(\theta)^{-N} \mid b, B].$$

Since these equations must hold for all θ,

$$E[\mathcal{M}_a(\theta)^{-N} \mid b, A] = E[\mathcal{M}_a(\theta)^{-N} \mid a, A]$$

and

$$E[\mathcal{M}_a(\theta)^{-N} \mid b, B] = E[\mathcal{M}_a(\theta)^{-N} \mid a, B]. \qquad \blacksquare$$

The proof of Theorem 8.6 is very similar to that just given and is left as an exercise.

8.4 MODIFICATIONS OF THE RANDOM WALK

The literature includes several attempts to preserve the main features of the two major, tractable random walk models while making them more consistent with the data, especially the lack of equality of error and correct responses. Two of these modifications I treat here and the others fit more naturally into Chapter 9. The basic ideas involved are the following: to assume systematic changes in the boundaries as a function of time, to assume variability in the location of the boundaries, and to assume variability in the time at which the subject begins processing information aimed at making a response. The first and third are taken up here—in that order which does not correspond to chronological order—and the second is dealt with in Chapter 9.

8.4.1   Linear Boundary Changes: Biased SPRT Model

In the presentation of SPRT in Section 8.3.1, we suggested that the decision variable at each step is the log-likelihood ratio. As Laming (1968) was clearly aware and as Ashby (1983) reiterated, this seems unduly restrictive in the light of modern psychophysics because the evidence favors the idea of bias being introduced into likelihood ratio.

Laming (1968) suggested the Bayesian formulation

$$\sum_i \mathbf{X}_i = \ln k + \ln \prod_i g_a(\mathbf{Y}_i)/g_b(\mathbf{Y}_i),$$

where $k = \Pr(s = a)/\Pr(s = b)$. This does not alter the theory in any serious way except to replace the boundary A by $A - \ln k$ and B by $B + \ln k$; that is, it shifts the starting point by $\ln k$.

Ashby (1983) suggested a more pervasive bias, one that affects each observation, not the entire set. So he assumed

$$\mathbf{X}_i = \ln[k g_a(\mathbf{Y}_i)/g_b(\mathbf{Y}_i)], \quad k > 0. \tag{8.45}$$

Thus,

$$\sum_i \mathbf{X}_i = n \ln k + \ln\left[\prod_i g_a(\mathbf{Y}_i)/g_b(\mathbf{Y}_i)\right].$$

Observe that

$$-B \le \sum_i \mathbf{X}_i \le A$$

is equivalent to

$$-B - n \ln k \le \ln \prod_i g_a(\mathbf{Y}_i)/g_b(\mathbf{Y}_i) \le A - n \ln k,$$

which is the standard random walk model with boundaries that begin at A and $-B$ and change linearly with n with slope $-\ln k$.

On this assumption, the proof of Theorem 8.3 is readily modified to show:

Theorem 8.7.   *Equation 8.45 holds if and only if $\mathcal{M}_b(\theta) = k\mathcal{M}_a(\theta - 1)$.*

The line of argument used to prove Theorem 8.4 does not go through for this generalized model. In lieu of this, Ashby developed the special case in which $\mathbf{Y}_i$ is Gaussian distributed with mean μ_s when signal s is presented and variance σ^2, independent of s. In that case,

$$\mathbf{X}_i = \ln k + [(\mathbf{Y}_i - \mu_a)^2 - (\mathbf{Y}_i - \mu_b)^2]/2\sigma^2$$
$$= \ln k - [\mu_b^2 - \mu_a^2 + 2\mathbf{Y}_i(\mu_a - \mu_b)]/2\sigma^2.$$

Thus $\mathbf{X}_i$ is linear with $\mathbf{Y}_i$ and so it, too, is Gaussian, and as is easily verified,

$$E(\mathbf{X}_i \mid a) = \ln k + d,$$
$$E(\mathbf{X}_i \mid b) = \ln k - d,$$
$$V(\mathbf{X}_i \mid s) = 2d,$$

where

$$d = (\mu_a - \mu_b)^2/2\sigma^2.$$

If these are entered into the general Wald model, a system of equations, similar to those previously derived (Section 8.3.2) can be developed (see Ashby, 1983, p. 288). The model was fitted to the *sn*-deadline data of Green and Luce (Appendix C.6). Although it fits slightly better than SPRT and SSR, the estimates of k were 1.00 to two decimal places, suggesting no real difference from the standard Gaussian model.

8.4.2 Premature Sampling

As I noted in Section 6.6.5, Laming (1968) made the important observation that all of the random walk models, and in particular SPRT, presuppose that signal onset is so accurately detected that the subject knows exactly when to begin accumulating discriminative information. As is known from simple reaction-time data (Section 2.4 and Chapter 4), anticipations are common when the time pressure is considerable, and so they may also occur in the choice situation although they are much less noticeable because the response does not usually occur until discriminative information has accumulated. If this happens, then the noise that is being processed tends not to affect the discrimination, but it does introduce variability in the position of the random walk when useful information begins to accumulate. In essence, then, the starting point is a random variable, which means that it is almost always closer to one of the boundaries than it would be if sampling were to begin at signal onset. The major consequence of this is that error times are in fact faster than correct ones.

In particular, suppose that for the N_0 steps prior to signal onset the subject is sampling noise information, which is assumed to be a random variable $\mathbf{Z}$ with the following properties: $\mathbf{Z}$ is independent of the signal to be presented, $E(\mathbf{Z}) = 0$, and $\mathbf{Z}$ has the moment generating function $\mathcal{M}_0(\theta)$. Let $\mathbf{S}_0$ denote the sum of these N_0 observations. Then Wald's identity is easily seen to be modified from Eq. 8.14 to

$$1 = E\{\exp[\theta(\mathbf{S_N} + \mathbf{S}_0)]/\mathcal{M}_s(\theta)^N \mathcal{M}_0(\theta)^{N_0}\}. \tag{8.46}$$

Making the assumption of small steps, Eq. 8.15 is replaced by

$$1 = P(A \mid s)[e^{\theta A}/\mathcal{M}_0(\theta)^{N_0}]E[e^{\theta \mathbf{S}_0}/\mathcal{M}_s(\theta)^N \mid s, A]$$
$$+ P(B \mid s)[e^{-\theta B}/\mathcal{M}_0(\theta)^{N_0}]E[e^{\theta \mathbf{S}_0}/\mathcal{M}_s(\theta)^N \mid s, B]. \tag{8.47}$$

If we now assume that S_0 is independent of N—it is far from clear that this assumption is valid although it may be if, as Laming assumes, the distribution of Z, and so S_0, is symmetric—then Eq. 8.47 can be rewritten as

$$\mathcal{M}_0(\theta)^{N_0}/E[e^{\theta S_0}] = P(A \mid s)e^{\theta A}E[\mathcal{M}_s(\theta)^{-N} \mid s, A]$$
$$+ P(B \mid s)e^{-\theta B}E[\mathcal{M}_s(\theta)^{-N} \mid s, B]. \qquad (8.48)$$

The right side is as before (Eq. 8.15), but the left side depends on θ. If one now proceeds as in Section 8.2.6 by taking the derivative of Eq. 8.48 with respect to $z = \mathcal{M}_s(\theta)^{-1}$ and sets $\theta = 0$ and θ_{1s} (Section 8.2.3), the right side develops as before but the left side, instead of going to 0, involves the parameters N_0, $\mathcal{M}_0(\theta_{1s})$, $E[\exp(\theta_{1s}S_0)]$, and $E[S_0\exp(\theta_{1s}S_0)]$. Clearly, one can solve, as before, for the latencies, but four parameters have been added.

Laming (1968) reduced them to two by assuming that θ_{1s} is sufficiently small so that only the first-order terms need be retained in the last two constants, reducing them to 1 and a negligible term. Since in SPRT $\theta_{1s} = -1$, the assumption that higher-order terms of the exponential can be neglected seems implausible. Accepting that approximation, the second constant can then be incorporated into the definitions of α_s and β_s (Eq. 8.16), which then leaves only N_0 to affect the latencies. This leads to a difference of $2N_0$ in the correct and error latencies, which at the expense of an additional parameter brings SPRT back into the running. Aside from Laming, little attention has been paid to this modification of the model, and in my opinion more work developing it is warranted.

As was described in Section 6.5.3, Laming (1979b, c) has used this idea with systematic changes in N_0 as a possible way to account for sequential effects. No really detailed analysis of specific data has been presented for this model.

8.5   DATA

The models of this chapter all include two distinct types of parameters. One describes the nature of the information accrual process, including always some measure of the rate of accrual and, in some models, the variability of that process. The other describes the conditions under which responses are made. Although there is nothing in the structure of the models to force any particular identification of model parameters with experimental manipulations, there is in fact fairly wide consensus that certain pairings make intuitive sense. The information accrual process is assumed to be affected both by properties of the stimuli, such as their discriminability, and by properties of the observer that are not under voluntary, trial-by-trial or condition-by-condition control. The conditions for making a response are also affected by the stimuli, but, in addition, with the stimuli fixed, they can be significantly altered by variables that affect an observer's motivation.

Among these manipulations are the probability of presenting a signal, the instructions used, and the payoffs both for accuracy of performance and for the time to respond.

These beliefs about the models lead to two strategies of experimental testing. The one attempts to manipulate the accrual process while holding constant the response conditions, and the other attempts to hold constant the accrual process while manipulating the response conditions. I say "attempts" advisedly because I fear we do not always succeed in these manipulations. The ones that are most suspect, in my opinion, are some attempts to manipulate the accrual process. A problem arises when the stimulus manipulation is such that it may also result in systematic changes in the response process. This means that if the trials are run in blocks—which has almost always been the case—we have no reason whatsoever to believe that the response parameters are the same from block to block. Only by randomizing the stimulus manipulation on a trial-by-trial basis can we hope that the response parameters may be the same from trial to trial. This possibility casts doubt upon at least the first study discussed in Section 8.5.1.

8.5.1 Attempts to Vary Accumulation of Information

Pickett (1967) used matrices of dot patterns for stimuli, where the dots were selected according to two-state Markov chains in which the average density of dots was constant but the transition probabilities varied. Subjectively, the stimuli varied from appearing clustered to quite evenly distributed. The observers were required to classify them as such and their times and accuracy were recorded. Error feedback was provided. The primary result was that the distribution of incorrect times was uniformly slower than that of correct ones—the two distributions did not overlap at all. The major conclusion was the SPRT does not fit these data. However, Pickett did argue that these data might be consistent with a random walk model in which the boundaries approach each other with time.

Sanders and Ter Linden (1967) undertook to design stimuli so as to manipulate the accrual process locally without altering the overall character of the stimuli per se. This design appears to avoid the problem of affecting the response parameters as well as the accrual ones. There were two colored lights, and a stimulus was a sequence of flashes fluctuating between the two lights. For one class of stimuli the lights appeared in the proportion 60:40; for the other in the proportion 40:60. The observers were to identify on each trial which proportion was being used. A payoff scheme was employed in which each error of identification was fined 100 points and each observation of a flash cost one point. The prior probability of each stimulus was $\frac{1}{2}$. With that prior, the Bayesian strategy to minimize the expected loss of points is to respond whenever the difference is four in the total number of flashed by each source. The basic experimental manipulation was to control the position in a sequence when the evidence became decisive. For example, in their first experiment there were two classes of sequences: class I in which the difference remained small during the first part of the sequence and became large in the second part, and class II in which the difference became large early in the sequence. They found that observers responded on average when the difference reached 5.3 for class I and 7.0 for class II. Experiment 2 altered the rate at which the flashes occurred, and Experiment 3 caused a difference of 5 to occur at various places in the sequence. The results were as in Experiment 1: the later the response, the smaller the difference.

If one assumes that a binary random walk is involved, these data force the conclusion that the boundaries diminish with time. However, as Vickers, Caudrey, and Willson (1971) pointed out, the observed pattern is exactly what one expects from LaBerge's simple accumulator. Consider, for example, the following two sequences of length 26 and a ratio of 62:38. The one is obtained from the other by interchanging the first and second halves:

```
1 1 0 1 0 1 1 1 1 1 0 0 1 0 1 1 0 0 1 0 1 0 1 1 0 1
0 1 1 0 0 1 0 1 0 1 1 0 1 1 1 0 1 0 1 1 1 1 1 0 0 1
```

If $k = 8$, then the response occurs at the 10th observation with a difference of 6 for the first sequence and at the 14th observation with a difference of 2 for the second sequence.

The fourth experiment investigated the impact of runs by presenting sequence of the following character, where the runs of 1's are indicated by parentheses:

```
(1 1) 0 (1 1) 0 (1 1) 0 1 0 (1 1) 0 1 0 1 0 1 0 0 (1 1 1 1 1 1) 0 0 0 1
1 0 1 0 (1 1 1) 0 1 0 (1 1 1) 0 1 0 1 0 1 0 0 (1 1 1 1 1 1) 0 0 0 1
1 0 1 0 1 0 1 0 (1 1 1 1 1) 0 1 0 1 0 1 0 0 (1 1 1 1 1 1) 0 0 0 1
```

A difference of 5 is achieved at the end of the initial string of 13, after which the sequences are the same. Each initial sequence differs in its run pattern. The data did not provide any evidence that these patterns mattered, and they concluded that the runs model is not correct.

Vickers et al. (1971) employed stimuli of the same type, using the proportions 68:32, 64:36, 60:40, 56:44, and 52:48. No error feedback was provided. They controlled for possible practice effects by means of a latin-square design. Their basic data summary consisted of plots of the following statistics versus the experimental proportion: probability of responding A together with the mean, standard deviation, skew and kurtosis of the response-time distribution. These were compared with the predictions of four, somewhat specialized, models: the simple accumulator (recruitment model) with $k_A = k_B = k$ (Section 8.1.1); the runs model with $k_A = k_B = k$ (Section 8.1.2); the binary random walk (in which a unit step is taken toward the appropriate boundary with probability p and a unit step away from it with probability $1 - p$) with equal boundaries, $A = B = k$ (Section 8.2.1); a

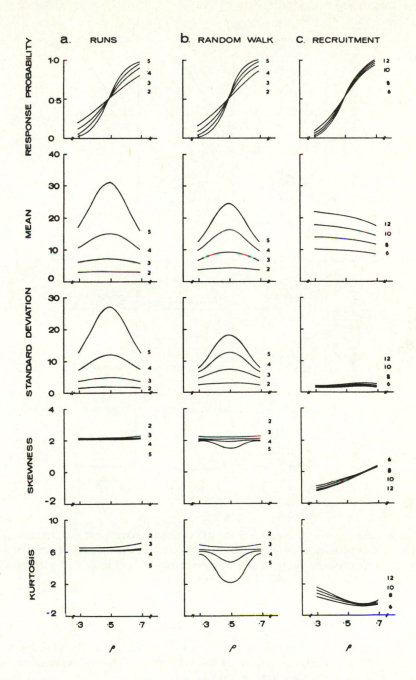

FIG. 8.3 Plots of various statistics as a function of the parameters p (shown as ρ in the plot) and k (listed as a column of numbers in each panel) for the runs, random walk, and recruitment models. See text for a discussion of the meaning of the parameters for each model. [Figure 1 of Vickers et al. (1971); copyright 1971; reprinted by permission.]

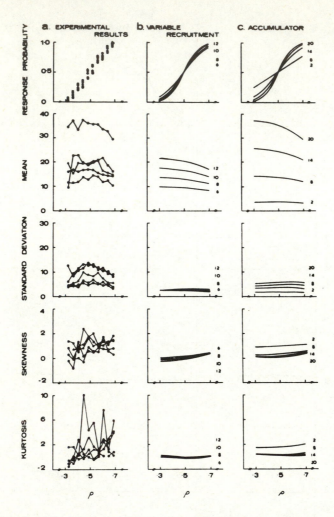

FIG. 8.4 Continuation of Figure 8.3 for the variable recruitment and accumulation models and experimental data of Vickers et al. (1971) on stimulus sequences with different proportions of the two types of signals (see text). [Figure 2 of Vickers et al. (1971); copyright 1971; reprinted by permission.]

variable recruitment model in which *k* is a Gaussian random variable with mean *k* and standard deviation $\sigma (= 0.5$ in plot). The relevant plots are shown in Figures 8.3 and 8.4.

On the assumption that the *p* of each model is the same as the probability of the experimental manipulation—not a necessary assumption—the conclusion has to be that no single model is fully satisfactory. The slower subjects exhibit an asymmetry of the mean and to a lesser degree of the skewness and kurtosis that is similar to the recruitment model and unlike the symmetry of the runs and random walk models. The faster subjects, however, seem far more symmetric. Pike (1968) noted this same pattern in other bodies of data, including his own. There are two other facts, however, that argue against both of the recruitment models—namely, that the standard deviation is symmetric and more widely spread out than can be accounted for by these models, and the skewness data are mostly positive for the data whereas they are mostly negative for the models in the range of probabilities used. Although it is not perfect, the most promising model for these data is Vickers' strength accumulator model. Qualitatively it seems to have most of the correct features. In summarizing this study, Vickers et al. (1971, p. 169) say: "It would be premature, however, to offer any firm verdict on the adequacy of the [strength] accumulator model in this context, while there remains no obvious rationale for assigning a value to σ, upon which the whole pattern of predictions depend."

8.5.2   Accumulator Model Analyses of Attempts to Manipulate the Response Parameters

Attempts were made to fit the data of Section 7.7.2 (Appendix C.5 and C.6) by the accumulator model using computer search techniques,* but we were unsuccessful in finding an adequate fit—the estimated parameters always drifted off to extreme values. The conclusion we came to was that the model was radically inappropriate for these data.

8.5.3   SPRT Analysis of Attempts to Manipulate the Response Parameters

The empirical literature on attempts to manipulate the response parameters, mostly by varying the presentation probabilities, is sufficiently extensive and the raw data are available (see Appendix C) that we report the several analyses in separate sections.

   Of the several bodies of data given in Appendix C, it is evident that with the possible exception of the Green and Luce data for the *sn*-deadline condition (C.6) and those of Green, Smith, and von Gierke (1983) (C.7), the mean time for a particular response depends upon which signal was presented. Recall that their equality is a prediction of SPRT. Figure 8.5, based on the Laming data, makes clear the systematic nature of the failure. The *aA* curve appears to be the *bA* curve increased by a positive constant, whereas the *aB* curve appears to be the *bB* curve reduced by a constant. It is therefore not possible to account for these data by choices of the mean residual time r_a and r_b. Laming (1968, 1979c) discussed with great care the inability of SPRT to account for these and a number of other sets of data,

---

* R. M. Nosofsky did the computer programming.

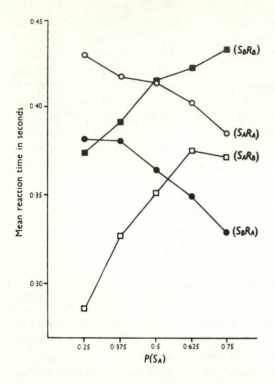

FIG. 8.5 MRT versus presentation probability for experiment 2 of Laming (1968) (see Appendix C.3). The sample size is 4800 observations per condition. According to SPRT each pair of curves with symbols of the same shape should be the same. [Figure 5.2 of Laming (1968); copyright 1968; reprinted by permission.]

and by now there is general concensus that SPRT in its original form is completely inadequate as a general model for choice reaction times.

There are, however, two exceptional studies in which the appropriate invariance was found. In the first, Kornbrot (1977), the stimuli were eight classes of random dot patterns, with the same number of dots in each pattern of a class. Each of the four subjects made absolute identifications. There were five experimental conditions in which different patterns of payoffs were used. A χ^2 test on the reaction-time distributions led her to accept the null hypothesis of no difference as a function of the signal presented for a fixed response. She mentions that in two-choice pilot data, this property was rejected.

In the other study by Green et al. (1983), whose data are summarized in Appendix C.7, the experiment was designed to overcome some of the potential sources of discrepancy. In particular, highly practiced subjects were run for many trials, the warning and response signals were in different modalities—a visual countdown and a 70-dB response signal of either 1000 or 1700 Hz—and a random (exponential) foreperiod with a mean wait of 1 sec. Payoffs were employed that aimed at fast and correct responding, but severely punished anticipations. Presentation probabilities of .25, .50, and .75 were used. The main reason for all of these features was to attempt to reduce the tendency for subjects to begin the accumulation of information that will lead to a decision prior to signal onset, which as Laming (1968, 1979a) had argued was possibly happening (Sections 6.6.5 and 8.4.2). As can be seen from Appendix C.7, the mean times nearly conform to the prediction, and indeed the fit of the SPRT model (with *A* and *B* varying with presentation probability and with the sensory parameters fixed) is satisfactory. However, a detailed comparison of the response distributions, using the Kolmorgorov-Smirnov maximum deviation test, showed that in 14 out of 18 comparisons the distributions differed at the 1% level. Autocorrelations of the responses showed a much attenuated pattern as compared with Laming's (1979b) data, and for one subject there was no correlation at all. Another happy feature of these data is the fact that when the presentation probabilities were changed to 0 and 1—simple reaction times—the values obtained were very close to the estimated values of the residuals. This has not been true by some 50 to 100 msec in some other experiments (Laming, 1979c, Swensson, 1972).

8.5.4   SSR Analysis With Signal-Dependent Residuals

Link (1975, 1978) examined the data of Appendix C.1–C.4 and C.6 from the point of view of SSR. As Laming (1979) pointed out, Link's strategy has been one of giving partial analyses of the data, centering primarily on some of the linear relations predicted by SSR or, in the case of a favorite plot, Eq. 8.30, by both SSR and SPRT. Laming criticized this strategy and he concluded from other analyses that SSR is also inadequate to account for any of these bodies of data. I shall draw the same conclusion, although my approach, which was outlined above, is somewhat different from Laming's.

Assuming the residuals are affected only by the signal, the linear system Eq. 8.43 has been solved* for all of the conditions of all the experiments. As a first pass at the data, let us class the model as a failure if any of the estimates exhibit any of the inequalities in Section 8.3.4—namely,

$$\frac{\hat{\mu}}{\Delta} < 0, \quad \hat{\gamma} < 0, \quad \hat{r}_s < 50 \text{ msec}, \quad \text{or} \quad \hat{r}_s > \text{MRT}_{sr}.$$

The reasoning is as follows. If $\hat{\mu}/\Delta < 0$, then $\hat{\mu} < 0$ and the random walk is actually in the opposite direction to the responses. The assumptions made imply $\gamma > 0$. If $\hat{r}_s < 50$ msec, then one has an estimate of the residual far less than anyone believes possible. If $\hat{r}_s > \text{MRT}_{sr}$, then at least one of the decision latencies is forced to be negative, which is clearly untenable. Using these criteria for failure, we find the pattern in Table 8.3.

Consider first the Green and Luce data, which on the face of it are grossly inconsistent with the SSR model. Several observations should be made. First, judging by the sensitivity analysis provided in Section 8.3.4, it is doubtful if experimental error is sufficient to account for this number of

---

* A. F. Smith carried out this computation.

TABLE 8.3. Number of failures of SSR/Number of Conditions, where a failure is defined by any parameter estimate meeting the conditions $\hat{\mu}/\Delta < 0$, $\hat{\gamma} < 0$, $MRT_{R_s} < \hat{r}_s$ or $\hat{r}_s < 50$ msec

Carterette et al. (1965)		Obs. 1,	0/6		
		Obs. 2,	0/6		
		Obs. 3,	3/6		

| Laming (1968) | 0/5 | | | | |
| Link (1975) | 1/6 | | | | |

Green and Luce (1974)		*s*-deadline	*s*-ROC	*sn*-deadline	*sn*-ROC
	Obs. 1	6/8	3/5	3/9	0/5
	Obs. 2	3/8	3/5	6/9	2/5
	Obs. 3	6/8	4/5	4/9	2/5

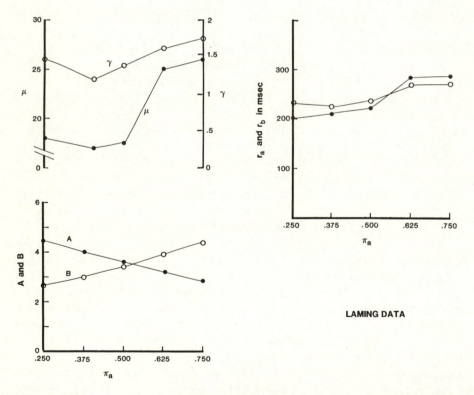

FIG. 8.6 Estimated parameters obtained by fitting the system of equations given in Eq. 8.43 for the SSR model with signal dependent residual times to the data of Laming (1968, Experiment 2) (Appendix C.3).

failures. Second, the 42 failures in these 90 conditions break down as follows: two were singular matrices, 22 were either $\hat{\mu}/\Delta < 0$ (and these were mostly accompanied by some $\hat{r}_s > \text{MRT}_{sr}$) or $\hat{\gamma} < 0$, and 16 were $\hat{r}_s < 50$ msec, and of these 14 were actually $\hat{r}_s < 0$. This is compared with the five failures in the 81 conditions of 10% perturbations of the data, all of which were $\hat{r}_s < 50$ msec and none of which involved $\hat{r}_s < 0$. Third, on the basis primarily of the speed–accuracy tradeoff, Link (1978) concluded these data tended to support SSR, which in my opinion is an erroneous conclusion.

Given the asymmetry that usually appears in Yes-No psychophysical detection experiments, it is not terribly surprising that a model that assumes a highly symmetric stimulus representation fails to account for the data.

Turning to the other sets of data, except for observer 3 of Carterette et al. and one condition of the Link data, one can plot the several estimated parameters as a function of the experimental manipulation. These are shown in Figures 8.6 through 8.9. First, the pattern of A and B is very much as one would expect if manipulating the presentation probability had had the intended effect. Moreover, the hypothesis that $A + B$ is a constant seems moderately consistent with these data, which is plausible for fixed signals. Second, there is sufficiently little difference between the estimates of r_a and

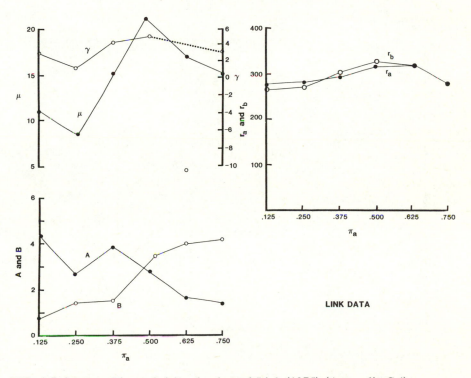

FIG. 8.7 Same as Figure 8.6 for the data of Link (1975) (Appendix C.4).

Carterette et al Obs 1

○────────○ LOW INTENSITY

□·········□· HIGH INTENSITY

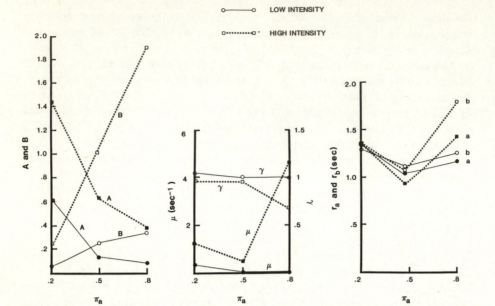

FIG. 8.8 Same as Figure 8.6 for observer 1 of Carterette et al. (1965) (Appendix C.5).

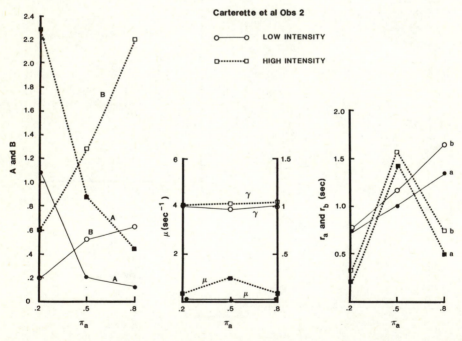

FIG. 8.9 Same as Figure 8.6 for observer 2 of Carterette et al. (1965) (Appendix C.5).

r_b to lead one to believe that they are probably equal. Third, while there is some trend in the values of γ, the hypothesis that it is a constant independent of the presentation probability is not untenable. Fourth, except for observer 2 of Carterette et al., the estimate of μ/Δ is consistently and appreciably larger for high presentation probabilities than for smaller ones. Fifth, the pattern in the change of r_a and r_b closely parallels that of μ/Δ, which suggests that the one change is compensating the other one. This could arise if there were systematic misestimates of the A and B parameters and therefore in the coefficients of the linear equations.

Because of this last observation, I have computed* those values of μ/Δ, γ, r_a, and r_b that minimize the quantity

$$\sum_s \sum_{\pi_s} \sum_r [\text{MRT}_{sr}(\pi_s) - r_s - L_{sr}]^2 P(r \mid s)\pi_s.$$

For the Laming and Link data this leads to

	μ/Δ	γ	r_a	r_b
Laming	30.2	1.96	297	293
Link	16.5	10.87	311	306

The scatter diagram of the MRTs is shown in Figure 8.10, and there does not appear to be any systematic pattern to the plots, especially when one recalls that there is probably a substantial error in the equations for the mean reaction times (recall Table 8.1).

Heath (1981) pointed out that there are signs of trouble in the parametric analyses as evidenced by the non-constancy of the estimated parameter μ/Δ, shown in Figures 8.6 through 8.9. He demonstrated it in a slightly different fashion. Equation 8.20 can be written

$$L_s = (1/\gamma\mu)z_s,$$

where

$$z_s = \gamma[AP(A \mid s) - BP(B \mid s)].$$

The scatter plot of L_s versus z_s should be constant if $\gamma\mu$ is constant. For the Green and Luce *sn*-data, this was not the case.

8.5.5 SSR Analysis With Response-Dependent Residuals

Turning to the other model in which the residuals depend upon A and B and not on a and b, we can do little more than estimate $\dfrac{\Delta}{\mu}\left(\dfrac{\gamma-1}{\gamma}\right)$ from Eq.

---

* Carried out by A. F. Smith.

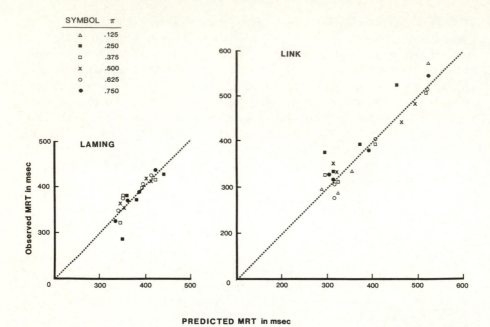

FIG. 8.10 Observed versus predicted MRT for data of Link (1965) and Laming (1968), where the prediction is from the SSR model with the parameter values reported in Figures 8.6 and 8.7.

8.44. There are two estimates—one from the A equations and another from the B equations. On the average, half of the A ones should be larger than the B ones, and half smaller. Table 8.4 shows that this prediction seems not to be true in the Carterette et al. data ($p < .01$ by the sign test) and surely not true in the Green and Luce data ($p < .001$ by the sign test). Moreover,

TABLE 8.4. The number of cases where the estimate of $\dfrac{\Delta}{\mu}\left(\dfrac{\gamma-1}{\gamma}\right)$ from the A equations exceeds that from the B equations

Carterette et al. (1965)		Obs. 1	1/6		
		Obs. 2	0/6		
		Obs. 3	2/6		
Laming (1968)	2/5				
Link (1975)	3/6				
Green and Luce (1974)			s-deadline	s-ROC	sn-deadline	sn-ROC
		Obs. 1	1/8	0/5	3/9	2/5
		Obs. 2	0/8	0/5	0/9	0/5
		Obs. 3	3/8	2/5	2/9	1/5

in the Carterette et al. data, both positive and negative estimates arise. For the Laming and Link data, where there is no evidence of a problem, the scatter plot is shown as Figure 8.11. It is not as tight as one might wish. Green et al. (1983) carried out this analysis on their data, and the fit was slightly, but not significantly, better than that of the SPRT model. For all subjects, the estimate of γ (Eq. 8.40) was approximately 1.2, which predicts a latency difference for the same response to different signals of $.167r\Delta/\mu$, were $r = A, B$, which for these data corresponds to a difference of from 3 to 15 msec.

8.5.6   A Gaussian Analysis

As was noted in Section 8.2.4, for the Gaussian model with small θ_{1s} it follows that the slope of $L_{sA} - L_{sB}$ versus $2P(A \mid s) - 1$ must be negative. To test this, Heath (1981) carried out a study in which subjects were to identify which of two lights came on first. He varied the interstimulus interval (5, 10, 20, and 40 msec), imposed deadlines (250, 400, and 900 msec), and also ran an accuracy condition with no deadline. The mean times of the four deadline conditions were 231, 319, 460, and 712 msec. The slope of $L_{sA} - L_{sB}$ versus $2P(A \mid s) - 1$ was decidedly positive for the three deadline conditions and decidedly negative for the accuracy one. This is strong evidence against the Gaussian model. Since comparable predictions do not exist for the more general models, we can reach no new conclusions about them.

Heath outlined a model—called the tandem random walk model—to account for such data; however, as it is not worked out in sufficient detail to test it, I do not present it.

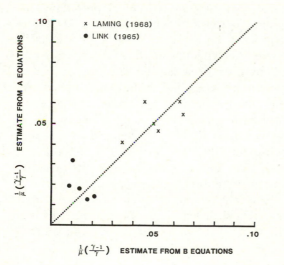

FIG. 8.11 Estimates of $(\gamma - 1)/\mu\gamma$ from independent parts of the Link (1965) and Laming (1968) data.

8.6   CONCLUSIONS

It is clear that the major idea underlying all of the models of this chapter—namely, differential accumulation of information with different signals and a decision rule based on that accumulation—results in models that exhibit some of the gross features of much data. The problems arise as one attempts to examine matters in closer detail. Although, in principle, the models characterize the four response-time distributions, in practice relatively little is known about these distributions beyond their means, and most of the data analysis has been in terms of mean latencies. Because there tend to be as many or more parameters than the six independent pieces of data—the two conditional response probabilities and the four mean times—one is forced into one of three possible strategies. (1) Additional assumptions—such as symmetry in the information representation or residual times that do not depend on the stimulus presented—can be invoked in order to reduce the numbers of parameters. (2) Vary some experimental condition and in the light of the intended meaning of the parameters assume that some are invariant under the changes in conditions. Or (3) seek out properties of the model that are free, or relatively free, of parameter estimates.

In the attempts to fit the SPRT and SSR random walk models to the several bodies of data in Appendix C, a mixture of strategies 1 and 2 has been used with, in my opinion, only partial success. In general, parameters that we believe should not be affected by manipulations were less constant than one would have wished. The cleanest results involved the use of strategy 3 in the SPRT model; most of the data do not support the prediction that for a given response, error and correct distributions are identical. As the experiments are usually run, that prediction is clearly false. Laming (1968) argued that this is likely due to premature sampling of the sensory information flow, and he suggested how to modify SPRT—indeed, the general random walk model—to take this into account. Approximations are required in order to avoid adding four new parameters, and the resulting equations have not been fitted to data in the same detail as SPRT itself. Rather than modify the model, with its attendent complications, Green et al. (1983) suggested that the tack should be to revise the experiment so that subjects no longer engage in premature sampling. Although a statistically significant difference between the two distributions still remained, most of the discrepancy had in fact vanished by introducing three changes: highly practiced subjects, warning and reaction signals in different modalities, and random foreperiods. This suggests that SPRT (or SSR with $\gamma = 1$) may be more accurate than had been thought for a while and Laming may be correct in attributing the failures to premature sampling. Further work on the premature sampling model seems in order. It is especially important that some attempt be made to couple it with a learning process, much as was done in Chapter 7, in an attempt to see if the sequential effects can actually be reproduced.

9

Stochastic Accumulation
of Information in Continuous Time

9.1 INTRODUCTION

The models of this chapter are similar in spirit to those we have just discussed. The major difference is that the accumulation of information is assumed to occur not at discrete times, but in some sense at continuous times. This does not mean that the accumulation is necessarily continuous in time, although it may be, but rather that it does not occur at periodic intervals. Perhaps the best known example of such a process with a continuous-time parameter is the Poisson process in which discrete events occur in such a fashion that the interevent times are independently, identically, and exponentially distributed. This is an example of a counting process, so called because one can simply count the number of events that have occurred prior to each instant in time.

Each of the models to be discussed can be thought of as a continuous generalization of the discrete case in which the time between observations is made arbitrarily small. If so, the question arises: what is the point—why not work with the discrete approximation, especially since it will almost surely be used in carrying out numerical solutions? The reasons are several. First, in some cases the limiting process is rather delicate to carry out, and errors easily result. Nevertheless, as we shall see in Section 9.2.2, careful use of limiting processes can be most helpful in getting detailed results. Second, analytically, the relation between a continuous process and the continuous asymptotic results often seems more natural, and many questions that are complex combinatorially in the discrete case are easily understood as differential equations. Third, at least one class of processes—the continuous random walks—are more readily generalized to non-constant boundaries and non-constant rates of accumulation than are their discrete analogues. Fourth, renewal processes, which arise as a natural generalization of the Poisson, are not nearly so natural as generalizations of the geometric process, which is the discrete analogue of the Poisson. Last, and perhaps most compelling, is the lack of any substantial evidence for synchronization in the nervous system comparable to that found in a digital computer. A discrete stochastic process, of course, involves temporal regularity, which usually is the first step toward synchronization.

Since the mathematics of continuous processes can become quite formidable as the models are made increasingly complex and, presumably, more realistic, I shall limit attention only to the simplest cases. And of those, I shall discuss only the few for which substantial attempts have been made to apply them to response-time data. References will be given to some of the more complex variants not outlined in detail.

Two main types of models are described. First I take up continuous analogues of the random walk models of the last chapter. That is followed by models based on the idea that information accumulates in a punctate manner according to a renewal counting process, which leads to models that differ somewhat from those of the preceding chapter.

9.2   ADDITIVE PROCESSES

Let $\{\mathbf{X}(t)\}$ be the stochastic process that represents the information available to the subject at time t, where, of course, it will be necessary later to subscript $\mathbf{X}$ according to the conditions obtaining on a particular trial of the experiment. We shall say that the process is *additive* if and only if the difference random variables $\mathbf{X}(t+s) - \mathbf{X}(t)$ over the intervals $(t, t+s)$ are independent for non-overlapping intervals, and they have the additive property

$$\mathbf{X}(t+s) = \mathbf{X}(t) + \mathbf{X}(s) - \mathbf{X}(0). \tag{9.1}$$

Note that by defining $\mathbf{Y}(t) = \mathbf{X}(t) - \mathbf{X}(0)$, this equation can be simplified to

$$\mathbf{Y}(t+s) = \mathbf{Y}(t) + \mathbf{Y}(s). \tag{9.2}$$

Obviously such a process is stationary (see Section 1.5). A random walk on the line is a simple discrete example of such an additive process.

Following Bartlett (1962) consider the cumulant generating function

$$K(\omega, t) = \ln E[e^{i\omega \mathbf{Y}(t)}],$$

which by Eq. 9.2 and the independence of the intervals yields the following functional equation:

$$\begin{aligned}
K(\omega, t+s) &= \ln E[e^{i\omega \mathbf{Y}(t+s)}] \\
&= \ln E[e^{i\omega[\mathbf{Y}(t+s) - \mathbf{Y}(s) + \mathbf{Y}(s)]}] \\
&= \ln\{E[e^{i\omega[\mathbf{Y}(t+s) - \mathbf{Y}(s)]}]E[e^{i\omega \mathbf{Y}(s)}]\} \\
&= \ln\{E[e^{i\omega \mathbf{Y}(t)}]E[e^{i\omega \mathbf{Y}(s)}]\} \\
&= K(\omega, t) + K(\omega, s). \tag{9.3}
\end{aligned}$$

Since K is continuous, being the logarithm of an integral, this functional equation is known to have a unique solution of the form (Aczél, 1966, p. 34)

$$K(\omega, t) = tK(\omega). \tag{9.4}$$

So the general problem of continuous additive processes is equivalent to finding all processes that satisfy Eq. 9.4.

A result that is beyond the scope of this book (see Cramér, 1937) is that the most general solution is composed of weighted sums of two processes characterized by

$$K(\omega) = mi\omega - \sigma^2\omega^2/2 \tag{9.5}$$

and

$$K(\omega) = m(e^{i\omega} - 1). \tag{9.6}$$

We examine Eq. 9.5 in Sections 9.2.1 and 9.2.2, generalizations of it in Section 9.2.3, Eq. 9.6 in Section 9.2.4, and a blend of the two in Section 9.2.5.

9.2.1 Diffusion Processes

A process satisfying Eq. 9.5 goes under two main names—diffusion process and Wiener process—named after the mathematician Norbert Wiener who studied them as a model for Brownian motion. We see from the definition of K in terms of the characteristic function $\mathscr{C}$—namely,

$$K(\omega, t) = \ln \mathscr{C}(\omega, t),$$

and Eqs. 9.4 and 9.5,

$$\frac{\partial \mathscr{C}(\omega, t)/\partial t}{\mathscr{C}(\omega, t)} = \frac{\partial K(\omega, t)}{\partial t} = K(\omega) = mi\omega - \frac{\sigma^2\omega^2}{2}. \tag{9.7}$$

Recall (see Section 1.4.4) that if $\mathscr{C}_n$ denotes the characteristic function of the nth partial derivative with respect to x of the density function $f(t, x)$ of the random variable in question, then

$$(-i\omega)^n \mathscr{C}(\omega, t) = \mathscr{C}_n(\omega, t).$$

Thus, by multiplying Eq. 9.7 by $\mathscr{C}(\omega, t)$ and integrating,

$$\int e^{i\omega x} \frac{\partial f(t, x)}{\partial t} dx = -m \int e^{i\omega x} \frac{\partial f(t, x)}{\partial x} dx + \frac{1}{2}\sigma^2 \int e^{i\omega x} \frac{\partial^2 f(t, x)}{\partial x^2} dx.$$

Since this must hold for all ω for which the integrals are defined, it follows that f satisfies the partial differential equation:

$$\frac{\partial f}{\partial t} + m \frac{\partial f}{\partial x} = \frac{\sigma^2}{2} \frac{\partial^2 f}{\partial x^2}. \tag{9.8}$$

This is often called the *diffusion equation with drift*. When the *drift parameter* $m = 0$, it is referred to as the *diffusion equation* or, in the physical literature, as the Fokker-Planck equation. In probability theory it also goes under the name of the *backward equation*, which is a general type of equation used in studying Markov processes. The parameter $\sigma^2/2$ is called the *diffusion coefficient*.

It is not difficult to show that an unrestricted solution to Eq. 9.8 under the assumption that the process begins at 0 at time 0 is

$$f(t, x) = \frac{1}{(2\pi\sigma^2 t)^{1/2}} \exp\left[-\frac{(x - mt)^2}{2\sigma^2 t}\right]. \tag{9.9}$$

Ratcliff (1978) employed Eq. 9.9 to arrive at a SATF as follows. He assumed the parameter m actually to be a random variable with mean μ_s depending upon the signal s presented and a variance η^2, which is independent of the signal. Calculating

$$\int f(t, x)\Phi(\mu, \eta^2)\, dm$$

yields an equation just like 9.9 but with m replaced by μ_s and the variance term $\sigma^2 t$ replaced by $t(\eta^2 t + \sigma^2)$. This, then, is the effective variance to use in a d' calculation (i.e., difference in the mean normalized by a standard deviation). The result is

$$d' = \frac{(\mu_a - \mu_b)}{\eta(1 + \sigma^2/\eta^2 t)^{1/2}}$$

This equation was listed in Section 6.4.3 [with $\lambda = (\mu_a - \mu_b)/\eta$ and $\nu = \sigma/\eta$] as one of several proposed SATFs.

In the study of reaction-time distributions, Eq. 9.9 itself is of little direct interest, since one is concerned with first passage times—that is, times when the process first crosses one of the boundaries and so initiates a response. So the key question is the distribution of first passage times. It turns out that the easiest way to get at that is via a discrete-time approximation to the process.

9.2.2　An Alternative Derivation

The absolutely simplest—and classical—random walk is the one in which the process makes unit jumps, one unit up with probability p and one unit down with probability $q = 1 - p$. It is assumed that the process begins at Z and that there are boundaries at A and 0. This is a special case of the random walk model of Chapter 8, one having two virtues: its properties are very well understood and, under an appropriate limiting procedure, it approaches the above diffusion process. This discrete process goes under the name *gamblers ruin* because of its interpretation in terms of two gamblers, having amounts of money Z and $A - Z$ to begin with, and who gamble for one unit at a time until one or the other possesses all of the money.

Let $P(Z)$ denote the probability that the process is ultimately absorbed at 0. Observe that if $0 < Z < A$, then after the first step the process is either at $Z + 1$ with probability p or at $Z - 1$ with probability q, so $P(Z)$ must satisfy the recursive equation

$$P(Z) = pP(Z + 1) + qP(Z - 1), \qquad 0 < Z < A, \tag{9.10}$$

and the boundary conditions

$$P(0) = 1 \qquad \text{and} \qquad P(A) = 0.$$

Following Feller (1957, p. 314), when $p \neq q$, it is easy to verify that

$$P(Z) = 1 \qquad \text{and} \qquad P(Z) = (q/p)^Z$$

are particular solutions to Eq. 9.10. The general solution is well known to be a linear combination of the two particular ones, which when we take into account the boundary conditions yields the unique solution

$$P(Z) = \frac{(q/p)^A - (q/p)^Z}{(q/p)^A - 1}, \qquad q \neq p \tag{9.11}$$

For $p = q = \frac{1}{2}$, the two particular solutions just used are not distinct; however, in this case it is easy to verify that $P(Z) = 1$ and $P(Z) = Z$ are distinct solutions, and so

$$P(Z) = 1 - Z/A, \qquad p = q = \tfrac{1}{2} \tag{9.12}$$

is the general solution meeting the boundary conditions.

More generally, one would like to consider the probability that the process beginning at Z first gets absorbed at 0 on trial n; denote this $P(Z, n)$. As above, we see that it satisfies the recursion

$$P(Z, n+1) = pP(Z+1, n) + qP(Z-1, n), \qquad 1 < Z < A, \tag{9.13}$$

along with the boundary conditions

$$P(0, n) = P(A, n) = 0 \text{ for } n > 0,$$

$$P(0, 0) = 1 \qquad \text{and} \qquad P(Z, 0) = 0 \text{ if } Z > 0.$$

Next we want to show that by taking appropriate limits, this process evolves into the diffusion one. We want to shift both our unit of time and of distance from 1 to small quantities we call Δ and δ. In particular, if t and z are fixed quantities, we let n and Z go to ∞ and Δ and δ to 0 in such a way that $n\Delta = t$ and $Z\delta = z$. Moreover, we let Δ and δ go to zero in such a way that δ^2/Δ is constant, and $p - q = 2p - 1$ approaches 0 in such a way that $(p - q)\delta/\Delta$ is constant. In fact, select the constants to be

$$(p - q)\delta/\Delta = -m \qquad \text{and} \qquad 4pq\delta^2/\Delta = \sigma^2.$$

Then, formally, Eq. 9.13 in the units Δ and δ becomes

$$P[Z\delta, (n+1)\Delta] = pP[(Z+1)\delta, n\Delta] + qP[(Z-1)\delta, n\Delta],$$

that is,

$$P(z, t+\Delta) = pP(z+\delta, t) + qP(z-\delta, t).$$

Doing a certain amount of elementary algebra,

$$
\begin{aligned}
P(z, t+\Delta) - P(z, t) &= pP(z+\delta, t) + qP(z-\delta, t) - P(z, t) \\
&= p[P(z+\delta, t) + P(z-\delta, t) - 2P(z, t)] \\
&\quad + (p-q)[P(z, t) - P(z-\delta, t)] \\
&= \sigma^2[P(z+\delta, t) - P(z-\delta, t) - 2P(z, t)]\Delta/4q\delta^2 \\
&\quad - m[P(z, t) - P(z-\delta, t)]\Delta/\delta.
\end{aligned}
$$

Dividing by Δ and taking the limits as Δ and δ approach 0, we see that the diffusion equation 9.8 follows.

We may also carry out the limiting process on Eq. 9.11 for the probability of absorption, as follows. Observe from the definition of m,

$$
p/q = 1 - m\Delta/\delta q,
$$

and so under the above limiting process

$$
\begin{aligned}
\lim (p/q)^Z &= \lim_{\Delta\delta \to 0} (1 - m\Delta/\delta q)^Z \\
&= \lim_{\Delta\delta \to 0} (1 - 4m\Delta\delta Xp/4pq\delta^2 Z)^Z \\
&= \lim_{x \to \infty} (1 - 4pmx/\sigma^2 Z)^Z \\
&= \exp(-2mx/\sigma^2).
\end{aligned}
$$

Letting $a = \delta A$, we see that Eq. 9.11 becomes

$$
P(z) = \frac{\exp(-2ma/\sigma^2) - \exp(-2mz/\sigma^2)}{\exp(-2ma/\sigma^2) - 1}. \tag{9.14}
$$

Considering the difficulty experienced in developing explicit expressions for the distribution of first passage times in the general random walk model of Chapter 8, it is rather remarkable that one can in fact do so for the general diffusion problem. One way to do it is to develop explicit expressions for the distribution of the trial of the gambler's ruin, and then take limits to derive expressions for the distribution of first passage times in the general diffusion problem with barriers. The detailed development is given in a number of sources including Feller (1957), Karlin and Taylor (1975), Ratcliff (1978, Appendix), and Sampath and Srinivasan (1977). The result is that the density of first passage times at the 0 boundary is simply a weighted sum of exponentials (recall that this was also the conclusion of the cascade model, Section 4.3.2):

$$
f(t) = A \sum_{k=1}^{\infty} B(k) \exp[-C(k)t],
$$

where

$$A = (\pi\sigma^2/a^2) \exp(zm/\sigma^2) > 0,$$
$$B(k) = k \sin(\pi zk/a),$$
$$C(k) = \tfrac{1}{2}[(m/\sigma)^2 + (\pi k\sigma/a)^2] > 0.$$

The expression for a crossing of the other boundary is obtained by replacing z by $a - z$ and m by $-m$. The hazard function corresponding to this density is

$$\lambda(t) = \frac{B(1) + \sum\limits_{k=2}^{\infty} B(k) \exp\{-[C(k)-C(1)]t\}}{[B(1)/C(1)] + \sum\limits_{k=2}^{\infty} [B(k)/C(k)] \exp\{-[C(k)-C(1)]\}}.$$

Since $C(k) > C(1)$, the limit as $t \to \infty$ is $C(1)$. I do not know the shape of this hazard function.

We return to Ratcliff's successful application of this model to memory data in Section 11.3.6.

9.2.3   Generalizations

Several generalizations of the standard diffusion process are worth referencing. The first of these investigated time-dependent absorbing boundaries. Anderson (1960) examined the case of a linear time change. Later Kryukov (1976) assembled together and generalized a number of results in the literature in which the boundaries are of the form

$$st^{1/2} + ut^\beta + d \qquad \text{and} \qquad r_\infty + (r_0 - r_\infty)e^{-\alpha t}.$$

He also studied decaying jump-like processes, somewhat analogous to those of Section 4.3.2. These generalizations have been motivated primarily by data on neural spike trains, and they have not been applied to reaction-time models. A detailed survey of the neural models is provided by Sampath and Srinivasan (1977).

The other major generalization, due to R. Ratcliff, assumes that the drift parameter is itself a random variable, Gaussian distributed with mean and variance as parameters of the model. This generalization is relatively easy to analyze primarily because the diffusion equation is linear with constant coefficients. And it is, to my knowledge, the only version of the diffusion model that has been applied to reaction-time data, specifically to matching experiments in which two strings of symbols are presented successively and the subject is required to say whether they are the same or different. As this experiment and the models for it comes more naturally in Chapter 11, I postpone discussion until then (Sections 11.3.6 and 11.4.4).

9.2.4 Poisson Processes

As was mentioned at the beginning of Section 9.2, the second basic additive (Eq. 9.4) continuous-time stochastic process is the one with the cumulant generating function (Eq. 9.6)

$$K(\omega, t) = mt(e^{i\omega} - 1).$$

Recall that for a Poisson process with parameter m the distribution of counts during duration t is the Poisson distribution with parameter mt:

$$\Pr[\mathbf{X}(t) = n] = (mt)^n e^{-mt}/n!, \qquad n = 0, 1, 2, \ldots,$$

and so

$$
\begin{aligned}
K_{\mathbf{X}}(\omega, t) &= \ln E[e^{i\omega \mathbf{X}(t)}] \\
&= \ln \sum e^{i\omega n}(mt)^n e^{-mt}/n! \\
&= \ln e^{-mt} \sum (mte^{i\omega})^n/n! \\
&= \ln e^{-mt} \exp(mte^{i\omega}) \\
&= mt(e^{i\omega} - 1).
\end{aligned}
$$

Thus, we see that the second solution to the additive property is the Poisson process—that is, a counting process in which the times between counts are independently, identically, and exponentially distributed. Put another way, it is a process with a constant hazard function. As was noted earlier, such processes are very basic.

Judging by data on the electrical activity of single peripheral neurons, Poisson processes can serve as first approximations to the spike trains generated in the peripheral nervous system when a constant signal is imposed. But in detail, such a model is incorrect on at least two counts. First, when a signal comes on, the hazard function of the neural spike train usually exhibits a significant overshoot and then drops back to a constant level as long as the signal remains present. (This is not unlike the hazard functions discussed in Chapter 4.) Second, after each spike occurs, the neuron is refractory for something on the order of half a millisecond, after which it rapidly recovers to its normal level. In terms of the hazard function, it drops to zero immediately after a firing, and at about $\frac{1}{2}$ msec it rises to its constant level until the next firing. So, it is really necessary to modify the model somewhat, which means we can no longer assume a purely additive process.

The literature includes a number of modifications, each of which has virtues and faults. Many of them are summarized in Sampath and Srinivasan (1977). Here I mention three—two of which are described more fully in the next sections. The first postulates a generalized Poisson process in which spiking is governed by a hazard function that is locked to the signal and is distinctly not constant. Some such process is strongly implicated by data on the patterning of interspike distributions that, in the auditory system at least, are multimodal and phase locked to the frequency of a pure tone signal.

This can be modeled readily by having the hazard function vary with the signal. Such models fail in one major respect—namely, they do not deal with the refractoriness of the neuron. Models of this type with applications to detection can be found in Siebert (1968, 1970) and are summarized briefly by Green and Luce (1974). So far as I know, they have not played a direct role in reaction-time analyses.

A second generalization, which I discuss in Section 9.2.5, entails a curious blending of the Poisson and diffusion processes. The former is used to model the accumulation of sensory information, much in the spirit of the Grice and McClelland models (Sections 4.3.1–2), and the diffusion process with drift is used to model a variable response threshold.

A third approach is to generalize the Poisson process to a general renewal counting process in which the times between successive spikes are independent, identically distributed random variables—but not exponential. It is obviously easy in this model to encompass refractoriness simply by setting the density equal to zero for the first $\frac{1}{2}$ msec. It is equally obvious that the model fails to capture the phase-locked character of the data since, by assumption, the successive intervals are independent, which is just what they cannot be in a phase-locked system. Despite the latter weakness, these models have been developed in some detail and provide interesting accounts of some data. They are developed in Section 9.3.

9.2.5 Diffusion Boundaries and Poisson Accumulation

Viviani (1979a, b; Viviani & Terzuolo, 1972) has presented a model that incorporates both of the additive processes—diffusion and Poisson—into a generalization of the strength or information accumulation models we have examined earlier (see Sections 4.3.2 and 4.3.3). As in all such models, information about the stimulus accumulates gradually, and when it crosses a boundary criterion a response is initiated. In Viviani's model, the boundary is assumed to be a diffusion process with drift. In a two-stimulus discrimination study, this introduces a total of four parameters: the two initial values of the boundaries, a drift parameter (it being assumed that both boundaries drift at the same rate), and a diffusion coefficient (also assumed to be identical for both boundaries, and called by Viviani "the spectral density of the threshold noise").

The assumption that the boundaries drift towards each other with time is motivated by the data described below. The Gaussian variability of the boundary is as in Grice's model, but its increasing magnitude with time is different and is motivated by two considerations, one empirical and the other a feature of Viviani's accumulator model. His data, like most, indicate that the variability of response times grows with their mean, but his model for accumulation exhibits reduced variability with increasing information. So, if the accumulator model is accepted, there is little option but to assign increasing variability to the boundary.

The accumulator model is unusual in two respects. First, the stimulus postulated is not a simple signal of the type usually employed in choice reaction times, but rather a string of brief pulses of two types—red and green in his experiment—that are randomly interleaved in different proportions. Stimuli of a similar type were encountered earlier in Section 8.5.1 where I summarized work of Sanders and Ter Linden (1967) and Vickers et al. (1971). In fact, Viviani assumed that the stimuli can be treated as the sum of two Poisson processes, one for each color. Of course, the parameters of the two processes can be manipulated by the experimenter.

Each process is assumed to set up a strength or information variable in the following manner. Let $\mathbf{X}(t)$ denote one of the Poisson processes and let $\mathbf{Y}(t)$ be a strength variable associated with that process. Assume that $\mathbf{Y}$ is governed by the following stochastic differential equation:

$$d\mathbf{Y}(t)/dt = \mathbf{X}(t)e^{-\psi\mathbf{Y}(t)} - \varphi, \qquad (9.15)$$

where φ is called the decay constant and ψ the increment saturation constant. Recall that in previous models of this general character, the dependence was of the general form $d\mathbf{Y}/dt = -\psi\mathbf{Y} - \varphi$, which is sometimes referred to as a leaky integrator. Thus, one can think of the present model as a leaky, nonlinear, cascade integrator. Viviani assumed that the decision variable is the difference in the strengths associated to the two Poisson processes:

$$\mathbf{Y}_D(t) = \mathbf{Y}_G(t) - \mathbf{Y}_R(t). \qquad (9.16)$$

The formal solution to Eqs. 9.15 and 9.16 is easily seen to be

$$\mathbf{Y}(t) = \frac{1}{\psi} \log\left[e^{\psi(y_0 - \varphi t)} + \psi \int_0^t \mathbf{X}(t)e^{-\varphi\psi(t-x)} \, dx \right], \qquad (9.17)$$

where $y_0 = \mathbf{Y}(0)$. In the appendix to Viviani (1979b), this solution was recast in another form, and by using cumulant and Taylor-series arguments he developed approximate expressions for the mean and variance of $\mathbf{Y}$. He verified the adequacy of his approximations by simulating the process. There is no need to reproduce those formulas here.

9.2.6 A Flash-Rate Experiment

The above model was then applied with considerable success to the data reported in Viviani (1979a). That experiment had three parameters: d the duration of time during which the two Poisson processes controlling the stimuli were identical and so, on average, the same number of red and green flashes occurred; and the two Poisson parameters ν_R and ν_G, which characterize the imbalance introduced after duration d. The Poisson parameters may be reported in terms of their sum $\nu = \nu_R + \nu_G$ and their ratio $r = \nu_R/\nu_G$. In the latter notation, the values used were 3 and 5 pulses per second (pps) for ν and $\frac{1}{2}, \frac{2}{3}, 1, \frac{3}{2}$, and 2 for r. (In some of the data plots, the $\frac{1}{2}$ and 2 and the

$\frac{2}{3}$ and $\frac{3}{2}$ data are collapsed in the obvious way.) The values selected for d were 8, 10, 12, 14, and 16 sec. Thus, there were $2 \times 5 \times 5$ experimental conditions, and each was run 20 times for a total of 1000 sequences per subject. This was carried out by randomizing them over 10 sessions. Ten subjects were run; however, three failed to complete the 5 pps rate. Judgments occurring during the d-interval, which were few, were eliminated from the analysis.

A hierarchical clustering analysis revealed four patterns of behavior. One subject was little affected by either r or d; three were mainly affected by d and not by r; three were affected about equally by both d and r; and three were intermediate between the last two cases. Ignoring the isolated subject, each of the other three groups were pooled and analyzed separately.

The data to which the model was fitted were the mean response times and the two independent response probabilities. For the latencies and one of the response probabilities, the pooling resulted in 5×3 rather than 5×5 data points and the other response probability contributed 5×5, for a total of 55 points. The number of parameters estimated from the data are fewer than might first be anticipated. The choice of ψ is an arbitrary scaling of $\mathbf{Y}$ and so was set at 1, and the value of $\varphi\psi$ was set at .0361 on the basis of the data from Viviani and Terzuolo (1972). It was assumed there were no color biases in the sense that the initial boundary values were taken to be equal with their common value called T_0. The other two parameters were the drift and diffusion constants. So there were three or four parameters depending upon how one views the choice of $\varphi\psi$. The data and model fit shown in Figure 9.1 are for the three subjects who were affected equally by d and r. Although no statistical analysis of the adequacy of the fit was provided, it is obvious that this three- (perhaps four-) parameter model is doing quite well in accounting for the data.

The nature of the tradeoff existing between the model for the accumulation process and that for the boundary is quite unclear. For example, why was Eq. 9.15 chosen to govern the accumulation process rather than a linear leaky integrator? Obviously, that would have entailed a different boundary model, but there is nothing especially compelling about the boundaries evolving as a drifting diffusion process.

It should be noted that the evidence for a drift in the boundary is the fact that the response performance becomes faster as the value of d is increased—this despite the fact that no useful information accumulates during the initial interval.

As we recall from Chapters 6 and 8, the pattern of times for error and correct responses is often a problem to model. Viviani's data are much like those obtained in ordinary choice reaction time when the signals are easy to discriminate and there is substantial pressure to respond quickly—namely, errors are faster than the corresponding correct response (see Section 6.3.3). For these data, the error times as a function of r and the predictions of the model are shown in Figure 9.2. Again, the fit of the model is impressive, and

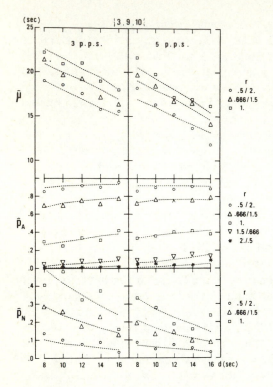

FIG. 9.1 From an experiment of Viviani (1979a), which is described in the text, involving random mixed sequences of red and green flashes, plots of MRT, probability of responding, and probability of no response as a function of the "foreperiod" parameter *d* for one subgroup of similar subjects. The parameter *r* is the ratio of Poisson parameters governing the two light sequences; the left panels have an overall Poisson rate of 3 pps and the right ones, 5 pps. The data represent averaged results of three subjects, with a total of 300 observations per point. The dotted lines show the theoretical values predicted by the model described in the text [Figure 2 of Viviani (1979b); copyright 1979; reprinted by permission of the publisher.]

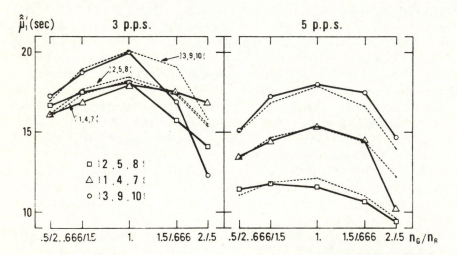

FIG. 9.2 MRT to errors as a function of the Poisson ratio ν_R/ν_G (denoted n_R/n_G on plot) for the experiment of Figure 9.1. The legend shows the code for each of the groups of similar subjects, whose data are plotted separately. The dotted lines are predictions from the theory. [Figure 6 of Viviani (1979b); copyright 1979; reprinted by permission of the publisher.]

it is clear that the worse the error (largest and smallest values of *r*) the faster the response.

Viviani discussed briefly the possibility of other models accounting for his data. For example, he argued—correctly I believe—that the accumulation models of Section 8.1 will not do since if certain particular sequences were sufficient to trigger a response, then all subjects should be sensitive to changes in *r*, but some are not. The SPRT model is, of course, rejected because observed mean time to respond depends on whether a response is correct or an error. The SSR model was not disposed of by a qualitative argument nor was any attempt made to fit it to his data. Two other models will be considered shortly.

9.3   RENEWAL PROCESSES

As I pointed out earlier, if information accumulation forms a counting process, there are two quite distinct types of decision rule. One is familiar: an information boundary is established and its crossing initiates a decision. This determines the response time. But there is a major difference from earlier models because in a counting process, the count can never decrease. The difference between two signals is found not in the barrier crossed, but the rate at which the count tends to increase. The value of the number of counts that have occurred—which is equivalent to the location of the boundary—divided by the time to reach the boundary is an estimator of the rate of accumulation of information. If the signals differ in their rates, as is the case for intensity discrimination, then the estimated rate can serve as a decision variable, as in the theory of signal detectability. Note that in this model all decisions are based upon the same sample size, which is uniquely specified by the boundary.

Because the random variable observed is the time to achieve a fixed count, these are called *timing* models. The specific model worked out below is somewhat more complex than this because the information is accumulated in parallel as well as in series.

The other decision procedure is to fix a time boundary on the accumulation—that is, a fixed observation time. This time, which may be a random variable, determines the response time. Again the decision is based on an estimate of the rate, this time estimated by the ratio of the observed count to the fixed observation time.

Because the observed random variable is a count, these are called *counting* models.

In each type of model it is plausible to suppose that the total sample of information is obtained by making observations on all of the neural fibers activated by the signal. Although it is surely somewhat of an oversimplification, let us suppose that all of the active fibers are statistically identical, and so each carries the same amount of information about the signal. [Wandell

(1977) has shown that this is not a serious restriction in, at least, the Poisson case.] Aside from the fact that physiological observation indicates massive parallelism in peripheral sensory systems, it is moderately clear from what we know that something of this sort must be the case. Decisions are reached in a matter of a few hundreds of milliseconds, and neural firing rates are of the order of a hundred spikes per second. Thus, a single channel provides only tens of spikes in the time available, and such small samples simply are not sufficient to permit the accuracy of discrimination that is observed. Thus, the central nervous system must have available more information than is carried by a single fiber.

Before turning to the specific models, several a priori observations are in order. First, each type of model requires some form of timer and some form of counter. Hypothetical neural networks can be devised to count and to time. In a counting model the timer is used to determine the observation interval (i.e., the time boundary) and the counter to count the spikes that occur. In a timing model the counter is used to determine the sample size (i.e., the count boundary) and the timer to time how long it takes to achieve the count. Thus, if the relevant sensory nervous system is capable of being reprogrammed, we should anticipate finding evidence for neither model or evidence for both.

Second, in experiments with signals of fixed, brief duration—as is typical of most psychophysics—the counting model seems more appropriate because, by setting the observation window to correspond to signal duration, the exactly relevant information can be collected and processed by the nervous system. Were the subject to use the timing procedure, the fixed sample size would have to compromise between the different values that would be appropriate for the weaker and stronger signals, and a compromise choice must fail to use all of the available information when the strong signal is presented and to include irrelevant information (outside the signal interval) when the weak signal is presented.

Third, if the organism is faced with signals of irregular durations and intensities, then the counting procedure may well be inferior to the timing one. The counting procedure guarantees a fixed response time independent of the signal presented, but the quality of discrimination must vary greatly, being exceedingly poor for weak signals and very good for intense ones. The timing procedure maintains equal quality of discrimination, but it does so at the expense of being slower to weak signals than to strong ones.

Since the ordinary world is surely populated with signals of irregular durations and intensities, and the laboratory tends to use fixed durations, we cannot ignore the possibility that our training procedures serve, in part at least, to reprogram subjects from timing to counting modes of behavior. If so, our data may systematically misinform us about most ordinary human processing of discriminative stimuli. In any event, it seems clear that if we wish to study the availability of these two strategies, it will be necessary to design experiments aimed at eliciting both strategies and to some extent, therefore, they will have to differ from the standard mold.

9.3.1 A Counting Model

The psychological literature on counting models is modest, but growing. Much of it focuses on discrimination, and somewhat less on the speed-accuracy tradeoff. Some of the relevant discrimination papers are: Lachs & Teich (1981), Luce & Green (1972, 1974), McGill (1960, 1967), McGill & Goldberg (1968), Prucnal & Teich (1983), Teich & Cantor (1978), Teich & Lachs (1979), Teich & McGill (1976), and Vannucci & Teich (1978). The major references to speed-accuracy tradeoffs are fewer still: Green & Luce (1973, 1974), Luce & Green (1972), Wandell (1977), and Wandell & Luce (1978).

Since in a discrimination paradigm the signals are really quite similar, it is not unreasonable to suppose that both activate the same number, J, of channels. Undoubtedly the observation time really is a random variable, but we shall treat it as a constant, δ, and assume all of the observed variability in the response times is due to other times such as the residual time and computation time. As an approximation, assume that the data collected from each of the J channels over the observation interval δ is the same as if the data had been collected from a single channel for a total time of $J\delta$. Further, assume that the renewal process generating the spike train has interspike random variables with finite mean μ and variance σ^2 and that the firing rate, $1/\mu$, is sufficiently large so that the number of counts observed in time $J\delta$, $\mathbf{N} = \mathbf{N}(J\delta)$, can be considered to have a distribution close to the asymptotic distribution. Then, according to Theorem A.3, the distribution of $\mathbf{N}$ is approximately Gaussian with mean $J\delta/\mu$ and variance $J\delta\sigma^2/\mu^3$. (As I noted after that theorem, the variance expression is not particularly intuitive.)

Consider two signals s_i, $i = 1, 2$, whose stochastic representations are renewal processes with means μ_i and variances σ_i^2. Suppose $\mu_1 > \mu_2$, which means that s_2 is the more intense signal. The z-scores corresponding to the response probabilities

$$P(Y \mid s_i) = \int_{-\infty}^{z_i} \Phi(0, 1)$$

obtained by using a response criterion N_0 are (following a development parallel to that of Section 6.4.3 for the fixed-stopping rule model)

$$z_i = z(Y, s_i) = \frac{N_0 + J\delta/\mu_i}{(J\delta\sigma_i^2/\mu_i^3)^{1/2}}.$$

Eliminating N_0 from the two equations and solving for z_2, we obtain the following equation for the ROC curve:

$$z_2 = \frac{\sigma_1}{\sigma_2}\left[\frac{\mu_2}{\mu_1}\right]^{3/2} z_1 + (J\delta)^{1/2}\left[1 - \frac{\mu_2}{\mu_1}\right]\left[\frac{\mu_2}{\sigma_2^2}\right]^{1/2}. \tag{9.18}$$

Suppose μ^3/σ^2 is an increasing function of μ—which it is in the Poisson case since $\mu^3/\sigma^2 = \mu$ and will most likely be for any reasonable process—then since $\mu_1 > \mu_2$, we see that the ROC curve is a straight line in z-score coordinates with a slope less than 1. Furthermore, if we treat the right term of Eq. 9.18—which is the value of z_2 corresponding to $z_1 = 0$—as a measure of discriminability, called d', and if we eliminate δ between the expressions for d' and $E(\mathbf{T}) = r_0 + \delta$, we obtain as the speed-accuracy tradeoff

$$d' = \begin{cases} A[E(\mathbf{T}) - r_0]^{1/2}, & \text{for } E(\mathbf{T}) > r, \\ 0, & \text{for } E(\mathbf{T}) \leq r. \end{cases} \qquad (9.19)$$

Recall from Section 6.4.3 that such a square-root relation has been arrived at from other models as well as having been proposed as an empirical approximation to the speed-accuracy tradeoff function.

It should be recognized that in this model the reaction-time distribution is a function neither of the response made nor of the signal presented. That is not typical of most of the data we have previously encountered—for example, Viviani's above—which therefore cannot possibly be fitted by a counting model. However, as was noted above, the counting model may entail reprogramming of the subject that will occur only in experiments with fixed duration signals and for which a great deal of data is collected from each subject. Viviani's experiment did not satisfy the first condition, and many "cognitive" experiments do not meet the second one.

We turn next to a model that is better suited to signals of indefinite duration.

9.3.2   A Timing Model

Assume exactly the same set up as for the counting model, except that instead of a fixed observation time there is a fixed count, κ, on each channel. We again assume that the total sample, now $J\kappa$, is sufficiently large so that the decision variable can be assumed to be approximately distributed according to the central limit theorem. Thus, the total time to observe this many counts is distributed approximately as a Gaussian with a mean of $J\kappa\mu$ and a variance of $J\kappa\sigma^2$. If the response is determined by a temporal response criterion, T_0, then the two z-scores are given by

$$z_i = \frac{T_0 - J\kappa\mu_i}{(J\kappa\sigma_i^2)^{1/2}},$$

and so eliminating T_0 we find for the ROC curve

$$z_2 = \frac{\sigma_1}{\sigma_2} z_1 + (J\kappa)^{1/2} \frac{\mu_1 - \mu_2}{\sigma_2^{1/2}}. \qquad (9.20)$$

Observe that if σ is an increasing function of μ, which is generally the case, then since $\mu_1 > \mu_2$, the slope of this ROC is larger than 1—quite different from that predicted by the counting model. In the Poisson case, the two slopes are $(\mu_2/\mu_1)^{1/2}$ and μ_1/μ_2, respectively. Assuming that the two rates μ_1

and μ_2 are not too similar, this provides a striking criterion for deciding which model is better suited to a body of data.

As in the counting model, a measure of similarity is the d' value given by the right term of Eq. 9.20. However, working out the speed-accuracy tradeoff equation is more complex because the observations times are not fixed—indeed, they are intimately involved with what happens in the discrimination. No one has yet worked out useable expressions for the $E(\mathbf{T})$ as a function of both the signal and response to it. Formally, the problem to be solved is this: let $\mathbf{T}_i$, $i = 1, 2, \ldots, J$, be independent and identically distributed random variables (i.e., the times observed on the separate channels, to find the distribution of $\max(\mathbf{T}_i)$ subject to the condition that $\sum \mathbf{T}_i < T_0$).

All that has been successfully computed is the mean reaction time for each signal not partitioned according to the response. To do this, we note (dropping the signal subscript) that the total time to respond is the sum of two times, the residual plus the maximum time over the channels to achieve a sample of κ in each. So far as I know, there is no exact solution to finding the maximum time over the several channels, even in the simplest Poisson case. So we proceed approximately, making the none-too-good assumption that κ is sufficiently large that the distribution of times for each channel is approximately Gaussian. To achieve κ intervals, we need $\kappa + 1$ counts, and so we are dealing with a Gaussian having mean $\mu(\kappa + 1)$ and variance $\sigma^2(\kappa + 1)$. If we denote the Gaussian with mean μ and variance σ^2 by $\Phi(t, \mu, \sigma)$, then the mean of the maximum over J channels is simply

$$J \int_0^\infty t\Phi[t, (\kappa+1)\mu, (\kappa+1)^{1/2}\sigma] \left[\int_0^t \Phi[x, (\kappa+1)\mu, (\kappa+1)^{1/2}\sigma]\, dx \right]^{J-1} dt.$$

Changing variables to $y = [t - (\kappa+1)\mu]/(\kappa+1)^{1/2}\sigma$ and letting $H(J)$ denote the mean of the maximum of J Gaussian random variables with mean 0 and variance 1, we see that the mean reaction time to the signal is

$$E(T \mid s_i) = r_0 + (\kappa+1)\mu_i + (\kappa+1)^{1/2}\sigma_i H(J)$$
$$= r_0 + \mu_i + \sigma_i H(J)$$
$$+ \mu_i\{\kappa + [(\kappa+1)^{1/2} - 1](\sigma_i/\mu_i)H(J)\}, \qquad (9.21)$$

where I have written this so that the first three terms form the irreducible minimum time when $\kappa = 0$ and so $d' = 0$. Observe that this minimum time is somewhat larger than it is in the counting model, and unlike that model the mean times differ for the two signals. If we introduce the variable

$$M_i = E(\mathbf{T} \mid s_i) - r_0 - \mu_i - \sigma_i H(J),$$

and then eliminate κ between the d' and $E(\mathbf{T} \mid s_i)$ expressions, we get a formula for the speed-accuracy tradeoff. The equation can be found in Green and Luce (1974, p. 390). Suffice it to say that the initial rise of the function $(d')^2$ versus M_i at $M_i = 0$ exceeds the initial rise of comparable expression in the counting model by a factor of μ_1/μ_2 when signal 1 is presented and by the square of that when signal 2 is presented. So the tradeoff is predicted to start later and to be appreciably steeper in the timing model than in the counting model.

Equation 9.21 affords another prediction when $\sigma_i = \mu_i$, which holds in the Poisson case—namely, that

$$E(\mathbf{T} \mid s_2) = (\mu_2/\mu_1)E(\mathbf{T} \mid s_1) + r_0(1 - \mu_2/\mu_1). \qquad (9.22)$$

So, to the extent that the assumption holds, the slope of this curve should be exactly that of the ROC curve, Eq. 9.20.

9.3.3 Flash-Rate Data

Viviani's (1979b) experiment seems to invite timing behavior: the stimuli are themselves counting processes of the sort envisaged in the model and they continue until the subject makes a response. He did not attempt to fit the model to the data because of the following argument. If a fixed sample size is used, then the ratio of times to achieve that sample in the conditions with rates of 3 and 5 presentations per second should stand in the ratio $\frac{5}{3} = 1.67$. The empirically observed ratio of response times was about 1.5, from which he concluded the timing model is incorrect for these data. The argument is unconvincing to me on two counts. First, it is not clear why one should assume that subjects will necessarily maintain the same sample size for the two rates; it is plausible that they might use a smaller one for the slower rate in order to accelerate the pace of the experiment, which was very slow. Second, the argument makes the implicit assumption that the difference between information accumulation time and response time is negligible. Given that the response times were 10 to 15 sec, the usual estimated residual time of 100 msec is surely negligible, but that may not be a very good estimate for the following reason. After the information has been accumulated, a certain amount of data processing is necessary, and it is not difficult to envisage such, possibly cognitive, processing taking a matter of seconds. For example, suppose the response times to the slow and fast rates are 15 sec and 10 sec, giving the observed ratio of 1.5, and that the "residual" time is 2.5 sec, then the accumulation ratio is $(15 - 2.5)/(10 - 2.5) = 1.67$, as it should be on the assumption of constant sample size. It appears to me that a more serious attempt to fit the timing model is needed before it can be rejected as wrong for these data.

9.3.4 Deadline Data

To test these models, Green and Luce (1973) ran a simple Yes-No detection experiment for auditory signals in noise (Appendix C.6 and Section 7.7.2). Recall that from the point of view of psychophysics the experiment was unusual in two respects: the signals were response terminated and response deadlines were imposed. In one condition, the deadline was applied on all trials, in which case the counting strategy, if available, is appreciably more

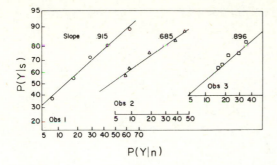

FIG. 9.3 ROC data from Green and Luce's (1973) auditory detection study with response deadline on all trials (Appendix C.6). For each observer, there are 1500 observations per condition. [Figure 4 of Green and Luce (1973); copyright 1973; reprinted by permission.]

efficient than the timing strategy in making use of the information generated by the stimulus on each trial. In another condition, the deadline was applied only on signal trials, in which case the timing strategy, if available, with the count chosen to complete the signal trials just under the deadline, is the more efficient strategy. The reason is that on noise trials the rate is slower, and so the count will often exceed the deadline for signal trials, but that does not matter since it is not applied on noise trials. For quality of decision, however, it is better to have a larger than a smaller sample size. The speed-accuracy curves were developed by varying the deadline from 300 msec to 2000 msec, and the ROC curves were developed by varying the payoffs at the 600-msec deadline.

Except for the longest deadlines, the MRT data for the sn-deadline condition seem relatively independent of the signal and the response, as must be the case for the counting model. The times in the s-deadline data are clearly longer for noise trials than for signal ones. As I noted above, exact predictions do not exist for the mean time partitioned by responses, $E(\mathbf{T} \mid s, r)$, but some qualitative deductions seem plausible. An error response occurs when the total time observed was on the wrong side of the criterion, which suggests that in the case of signal trials the mean response time for errors should be unusually slow—that is, $E(\mathbf{T} \mid s, N) > E(\mathbf{T} \mid s, Y)$—whereas for noise trials the errors should be unusually fast—that is, $E(\mathbf{T} \mid n, N) > E(\mathbf{T} \mid n, Y)$. Of the 78 comparisons, eight (or 10%) violate these inequalities. Of the eight, several differences are so small that they probably can be attributed to chance, and five arise either at the longest or the shortest times, both of which may be somewhat peculiar. The short ones may well be contaminated by fast guesses and the longer ones, by a shifting criterion.

The most striking confirmations of the theory are found in the plots of the ROC curves, of MRT(n) versus MRT(s), and the speed-accuracy tradeoffs. The sn-deadline ROC data shown in Figure 9.3 all exhibit slopes less than 1, which is usual in psychophysical data, and the s-deadline ROC data shown in Figure 9.4 all have slopes greater than 1, as predicted by the timing model. The MRT plots for the s-deadline experiment, Figure 9.5, have slopes virtually identical to those for the ROC curve, also as predicted.

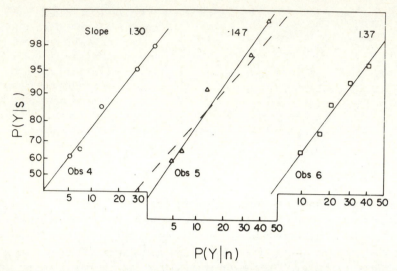

FIG. 9.4 For the same study as Figure 9.3, the ROC data when the response deadline is imposed only on signal trials. Again, there are 1500 observations per condition for each observer. [Figure 9 of Green and Luce (1973); copyright 1973; reprinted by permission.]

Finally, the speed-accuracy tradeoff shown in Figure 9.6 exhibits just the predicted features of the two models: the functions d' versus MRT for the s-deadline data rise from 0 both somewhat later and much more rapidly than for the sn-deadline data, as should be the case if the former is governed by the timing model and the latter by counting.

Wandell (1977) replicated and extended this experiment using visual rather than auditory stimuli. He added the condition of a deadline only on

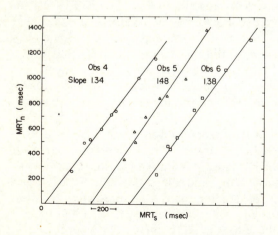

FIG. 9.5 For the same study as Figure 9.3, MRT(n) versus MRT(s) for the s-deadline procedure. Note the similarity of these slopes with those of Figure 9.4. [Figure 7 of Green and Luce (1973); copyright 1973; reprinted by permission.]

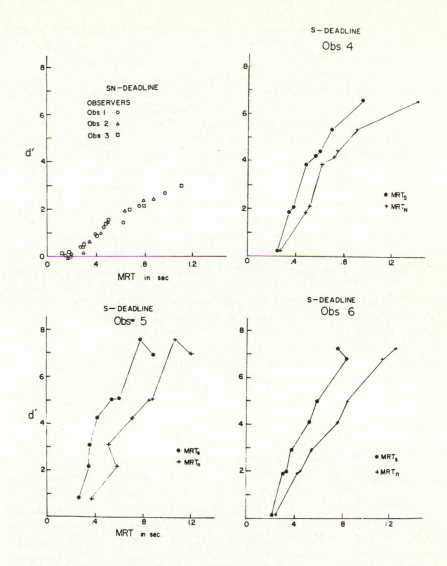

FIG. 9.6 For the same study as Figure 9.3, SATF with accuracy measured by d'. The upper left panel is for the condition where the deadline applies to all trials, and it combines the data for all three observers. The other three panels show the data for each observer separately for the condition where the deadline applied only on signal trials. [Figure 11 of Green and Luce (1973); copyright 1973; reprinted by permission.]

noise trials because, as he observed, the s-deadline and n-deadline predictions differ. As we have argued, the s-deadline invites timing behavior. But the n-deadline does not since if the sample size is selected to get the response in by the deadline on noise trials, then on signal trials the sample will be achieved appreciably before the deadline. This means that timing behavior entails less complete use of the available information about the signal presented as compared with counting, and that is inefficient. His data were as predicted: the ROC slopes were >1 for the s-deadline condition and <1 for both the sn- and n-deadline conditions.

Wandell and Luce (1978) raised the following question. So far we have assumed without discussion that the information gathered on the several channels is summed in order to arrive at a decision variable. There are other ways a discriminative decision can be reached, the simplest probably being to use the slowest observation over the channels. From Theorems A.5 and A.6 we know that for the types of interspike time distributions we are assuming, the asymptotic distribution should then be the double exponential, not the Gaussian. The whole theory can be reworked on that assumption, transforming the probabilities according to that distribution to get their analogue of the z-scores and then to construct their ROC curves. To our surprise, the data were as linear in these coordinates as in the Gaussian ones, but the slopes were much more extreme. This fact was sufficient to reject the model since slopes of the timing ROC curve and MRT curve were again predicted to be equal, which they were not.

9.4 CONCLUSIONS

One is left feeling considerable lack of closure. In this and the preceding two chapters we have examined a number of stochastic models, each attempting to account in detail for the interplay of errors and response times in two-alternative designs. And a variety of experiments have been conducted in relatively isolated attempts to check the adequacy of, usually, particular models, and each can be said to have found some support in data and most have also been shown to fail for some data. There have not been, however, any truly comprehensive attempts to fit all models to one body of data, and we do not really have any taxonomy of experiments that would permit us to say, for broad categories of designs, which models appear to be adequate. One can well believe that it matters whether signal duration is fixed or response terminated, whether deadlines are used or not, and whether the signal is a single flash of light at threshold or a mixed sequence of moderately bright light flashes of different colors in a fixed ratio or one of two letters of the alphabet. But no one can say today with any confidence which, if any, of these models is appropriate to each design, although some models are definitely known to fail in certain designs. This is not a satisfactory state of affairs.

10

Absolute Identification
of More Than Two Signals

10.1 TYPES OF DESIGNS WITH MORE THAN TWO SIGNALS

Once we admit more than two signals, quite a variety of experimental designs become possible. Some special ones, designed to investigate specific issues, crop up every now and then, but most of the literature is dominated by two designs. The earlier, and perhaps the most natural extension of the two-signal, two-response design of Chapter 6, involves N signals and N responses that are in one-to-one correspondence, so each response uniquely identifies a signal. One signal is presented on each trial, usually but not always selected according to a random schedule, and the subject attempts to identify it absolutely by responding with the "correct" response. Some major reaction-time results for this design are presented in this chapter.

Much of the experimental literature involves easily discriminated signals and nearly error-free responding. The impact of number of signals is treated in Section 10.2 and sequential effects in Section 10.3. What there is involving errors and speed-accuracy tradeoffs, and the corresponding theories, is dealt with in Section 10.4. In addition, of course, the psychophysical literature includes quite a number of papers involving uni-dimensional signals varying along one physical dimension, such as tones varying in intensity, for which the error rate is quite high; however, for the most part, reaction times have not been reported for these studies and so they are not treated here. Since there are pronounced sequential effects in the reaction times for the error-free case and in the probabilities of errors in the error-prone case, it is evident that not only should speed-accuracy be studied more fully, but so should its sequential structure. This is a major lacuna.

The other major design—one version of which is called memory scanning and another is called visual search—is a slightly more complex task with a simpler response. Prior to each trial, or sometimes prior to a run of trials, the subject in a memory scanning experiment is presented with a set of stimuli called the memory set, which is to be commited to (possibly short-term) memory. An experimental trial involves the presentation of a single signal that is either from the memory set or from another distractor set. The subject is to report, as rapidly as is consistent with highly accurate perfor-mance, whether or not it was a member of the memory set. The dependent variable—the time to respond—presumably reflects something of the search process of short-term memory. Visual search designs differ from memory scanning ones by inverting the order of the single signal and the set of signals to which it is matched; the single signal comes first and it is followed by the sequential presentation of possible matches. Again, the response set remains at two, independent of the size of the set of stimulus alternatives. Some of these experiments and proposed interpretations are initially treated in Chapter 11. As the theoretical issues that have grown up around them are rich and somewhat complex, they are treated separately in Chapter 12.

10.2   EXPERIMENTS WITH FEW ERRORS: MEAN TIMES

Once we go beyond two signals, a number of variables can be manipulated—although doing so without confounding them is virtually impossible, as we shall see. We focus initially on three of them: the number of signals, the probability that a particular signal is presented, and the conditional probability of one signal following another.

The following qualitative facts are well established. First, assuming the signals are equiprobable, MRT increases or, under certain circumstances (see Section 10.2.3), is constant as the number of alternatives increase (Hick, 1952; Merkel, 1885). This is simply a generalization of the fact that the $N = 2$ times are slower than the $N = 1$ (simple) ones. Second, MRT decreases with increasing probability of a signal (Falmagne, 1965; Krinchik, 1969; Leonard, Newman, & Carpenter, 1966). Since as N increases the probability of each signal, $1/N$, decreases, the first result is conceivably just a consequence of the second; but, as we shall see, matters are not so simple. Third, MRT to a repeated signal is faster than to a non-repeated one (Kornblum, 1967).

The major question facing a theorist is to try to specify more precisely these regularities and to understand how they relate to one another, with an eye to spelling out the underlying mechanisms.

10.2.1   *The Stimulus Information Hypothesis*

An initial bold theoretical attempt of the 1950s, much influenced by the then new and very fashionable theory of information of Shannon (1948), was the hypothesis that MRT is simply a function of—indeed, is linear with—the information transmitted (in a technical sense to be specified) by the signal presentations. The idea was first formulated by Hick (1952) for the N equally likely alternative case. Following the major constructive device of information theory, he argued that the decision to make a response involves repeated partitions of the signal set into equally likely subsets, and he assumed that, independent of the size of the subset, the same time was needed to decide which subset included the signal presented. The latter, apparently unlikely, assumption is discussed more fully below. At least for N of the form 2^n these assumptions imply that the response time should be proportional to $\log_2 N$. Obviously, this cannot be correct since for $N = 1 = 2^0$, it implies zero reaction time. To deal with this, Hick compared

$$E(\mathbf{T}) = a \log_2 N + r_0 \tag{10.1}$$

and

$$E(\mathbf{T}) = a \log_2(N + 1) \tag{10.2}$$

with his and Merkel's data and concluded that Eq. 10.2 fitted somewhat better. He then argued that this equation is plausible because, in reality, there are $N + 1$ choices to be made when we take into account that a discrimination between something and nothing is involved. Of course, Eq. 10.1 simply incorporates the familiar idea of a residual response time.

Hick pointed out that his selection model, as stated, should lead to individual reaction times that are integral multiples of the simple reaction time. It comes as no surprise that he did not find such periodicities in the data. This fact does not seem particularly telling since, to be rid of the periodicities, one need only replace the assumption of a constant inspection time with a random variable.

From one perspective, a major assumption of the Hick model seems almost to contradict the data it is intended to explain. On the one hand, the data say that the larger the set of possible signals, the longer it takes to isolate one of them and to respond. On the other hand, the model says that successive decisions about which half of the remaining possible response alternatives includes the signal take equally long, no matter how many alternatives remain. One way to interpret Hick's assumption, the way he suggested, is to suppose that each signal is a bundle of (unspecified) features or attributes, and a signal is identified by sequentially ascertaining whether or not it has one feature and then another, until it becomes clear which of a limited class of signals it is. If the signal presented exhibits a particular feature, the response set is thereby reduced to just those alternatives having that feature; if it does not have the feature, then the response set is limited to the complementary set of alternatives—that is, to those not having the feature. Assuming that each feature is exhibited by half the possible signals and that the several relevant features are uncorrelated over the set of possible signals (neither of which is easy to guarantee when the features are not explicitly known to the experimenter), then the number of features that must be examined on average in order to isolate the signal is the number of halvings required—that is, $\log_2 N$.

In contrast to such feature isolation, there are two other types of theories in which the signal is treated wholistically. One of these, the more prevalent, is called "template matching," although to me that term conjures up more about the matching of silhouettes than is intended. If comparisons of the encoded test signal are carried out sequentially among the encoded representations (or memories) of the possible signals, then the number of comparisons taken to achieve a match should, on average, be proportional to the number of signals. While this prediction does not accord with data from the absolute identification design, it does with those from memory scanning designs (see Section 11.1.2). A careful comparison of the template matching and feature extraction points of view was provided by Smith (1968).

Another wholistic point of view, taken up in Section 10.4.2, supposes the process to consist of a sequence of successive discards of possible responses. At each stage of the process, the discard takes some time, but it reduces the choice set by one, at which point the process is assumed to begin anew as if the reduced set were the possible choice set. In this model, unlike Hick's, the times are increasingly faster as each discard occurs, but under certain circumstances this leads to predictions not unlike the data. No interpretation is given to the mechanism that leads to discarding alternatives.

Since Hick's argument was essentially identical to the partitioning used in the theory of information, Crossman (1953) and Hyman (1953) independently generalized the hypothesis to a linear relation between MRT and stimulus information, where the latter is defined as follows. Suppose the stimuli are selected on each trial according to independent random variables with the distribution $P(s)$, $s = 1, 2, \ldots, N$, then by definition the information in the selection is

$$H = - \sum_{s=1}^{N} P(s) \log_2 P(s). \tag{10.3}$$

If there are one-step sequential dependencies $P(s \mid s')$ and the asymptotic distribution of choices is $P(s)$, then the information measure is altered to

$$H = - \sum_{s'=1}^{N} P(s') \sum_{s=1}^{N} P(s \mid s') \log_2 P(s \mid s'). \tag{10.4}$$

Hyman systematically varied the number of equally likely alternatives, the probability distribution, and the one-step sequential dependencies. His correlations between MRT and stimulus information for these three manipulations were .983, .975, and .938.

Although his data were generally supportive of the hypothesis, detailed aspects cast the model into doubt. First, the response time to a particular signal with probability p of occurring does not depend upon p alone, but is also affected by the distribution of probabilities over the other signals. Second, in the sequential design there were cases where if a signal had just occurred it could not possibly occur on the next trial. Rather than speeding up the response on the next trial (because the effective N was reduced by 1), it was slowed. Third, as Laming (1968, p. 89) has demonstrated, the overall MRT versus H function is very different from that obtained when the data are partitioned according to the response made, which in these error-free data is tantamount to the stimulus presented, and plotted against the corresponding information value. It thus appears that the stimulus information model does not really provide an accurate summary. As we shall see in the Section 10.3.1, the hypothesis is quite incomplete.

Laming (1968) devoted the first chapter of his monograph on choice reaction times to a detailed and useful critique of the approach to reaction time based on information theory—which he calls communication theory because he uses the word information in a different way. Among other things, he pointed out that the basic conceptual framework of information theory entails the use of asymptotic theorems. For example, the information measure given in Eq. 10.4 for sequential dependencies states how many binary choices are required on average by a maximally efficient coding scheme working on an indefinitely long sequence of signals. Since the subject must respond trial-by-trial and cannot wait to take advantage of the sequential dependencies, at best Eq. 10.4 sets a lower bound on the number of covert partitionings required, and one really should not expect MRT to be linear with H.

10.2.2   Alternative Accounts of Hick's Logarithmic Relation

There are a number of conceptually distinct ways that the logarithm, or something close to it, can arise. The one most fully studied is called a parallel, exhaustive search. It assumes that each possible stimulus is being held in memory and that on presentation of a signal a comparison is made simultaneously with each of the stored representations. The response occurs following the completion of all the comparisons. If we assume that the comparisons are independent and each is distributed according to the same exponential random variable, then we are in the case of the parallel model dealt with in Appendix A.2, and so, adding a residual time, it is easy to see that the mean time is

$$E(\mathbf{T}) = r_0 + \frac{1}{\lambda} \sum_{j=1}^{N} \frac{1}{j}. \tag{10.5}$$

Independently, Laming (1966) and Rapoport (1959) noted that for large N

$$\sum_{j=1}^{N} \frac{1}{j} \cong A \log_2 N + C, \tag{10.6}$$

where $A = \ln 2$ and C is Euler's constant. Rapoport reported an elaborate experiment in an attempt to evaluate the model, but as I do not find it especially illuminating, I do not report it.

Laming observed that Hick's "law" can be rewritten using

$$E(\mathbf{T}) = a \log(N+1) + r_0$$

$$= a \sum_{j=1}^{N+1} \frac{1}{j} + C + r_0$$

$$= a \left[1 + \sum_{j=1}^{N} \frac{1}{j+1} \right] + C + r_0, \tag{10.7}$$

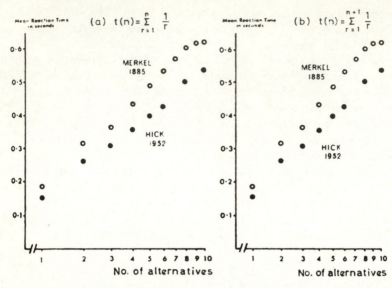

FIG. 10.1 For identification experiments with various numbers of stimuli (Merkel, 1885; Hick, 1952), the fit of Eq. 10.8a with $k = 0$ on the left and $k = 1$ on the right. [Figure 1 of Laming (1966); copyright 1966; reprinted by permission.]

and he noted that a function that encompasses both this and Eq. 10.5 is

$$E(\mathbf{T}) = r_0 + a \sum_{j=1}^{N} \frac{1}{j+k}, \qquad (10.8a)$$

where $k = 0$ corresponds to Eq. 10.5 and $k = 1$ to Eq. 10.7. The fit of these two extreme functions to Merkel's and Hick's data are shown in Figure 10.1.

Laming then raised the question of whether there is some distribution F with the following property: the mean of the maximum of N independent random variables distributed according to F is given by Eq. 10.8a. He showed that such a function exists, that it is unique, and that it can be characterized indirectly. Moreover, he derived an expression for the variance

$$\sigma^2(k, N) = 2 \sum_{i=1}^{N} \sum_{j=1}^{N} \frac{1}{(i+k)(j+k)} - \sum_{j=1}^{N} \frac{1}{(j+k)^2}, \qquad (10.8b)$$

which for $k = 0$ and $k = 1$ is compared with the data in Figure 10.2.

The main point of this example is to illustrate, early on, that data fit by a serial model, Hick's, often can be fit equally by a parallel one. This will be explored thoroughly in Section 12.2. And there are other models that are conceptually distinct that also lead to an approximately linear relation between stimulus information and MRT. I do not delve into them in detail here because they all face a very serious problem—namely, that they require

MRT to grow with *N*, whereas as we see in Section 10.2.3, that does not necessarily happen empirically.

10.2.3 Practice and Stimulus-Response Compatibility

Since the early 1950s a number of papers on absolute identification have explored two major classes of variables. One class is the amount of practice the subject has had either through previous experience or in the experimental procedure—the latter has varied from a few tens of trials to tens of thousands. The other class of variables has been termed the compatibility between the responses and the signals. Actually two quite different things are meant by the term "compatibility." The more special meaning has to do with whether the one-to-one relation between signals and responses is "natural." For example, suppose signals are the illumination of one of a semicircle of small light bulbs before each of which is a response key, then the "natural" relation is to respond using the key nearest the lighted bulb; but many unnatural ones are also possible. One is to place the fingers of the two hands on the keys and to respond with the corresponding key of the hand opposite to the "natural" response. For the present, I do not mean this type of compatibility. Rather, there is thought to be some sort of mental compatibility between the modality of the signal and the nature of the response. For example, responding vocally to the visual or auditory presentation of digits is thought to be more compatible than responding by a key press, no matter how compatible in the first sense the ordering of the keys is.

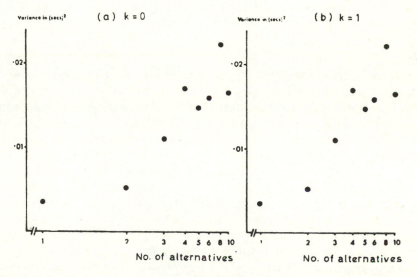

FIG. 10.2 Predictions based on Eq. 10.8b for the variance for the data discussed in Figure 10.1. [Figure 2 of Laming (1966); copyright 1966; reprinted by permission.]

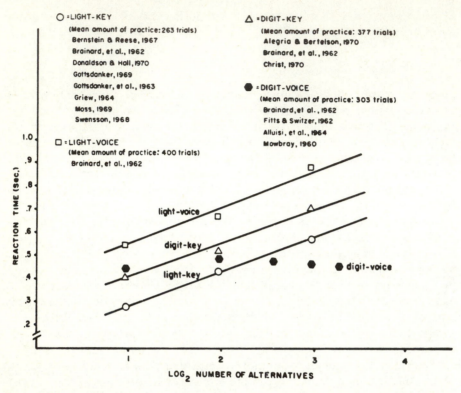

FIG. 10.3 MRT versus log N (N = number of alternatives) for the various stimulus-response pairings shown in legend. (Not all sources listed in the legend are included in the present bibliography.) Note the flatness for the digit-voice case. [Figure 1 of Teichner and Krebs (1974); copyright 1974; reprinted by permission.]

Over the years a good deal has been published on these two topics and fortunately Teichner and Krebs (1974) performed an heroic survey of that part of the literature—which is most of it—having to do with visual signals. There appear to be some reasonably simple patterns to this mass of data. The reader is urged to consult their paper, for I shall summarize only part of it. Theios (1975) reviewed some of the same material.

Consider, first, minimally practiced subjects, and let us compare their performance with different pairings of stimulus and response modalities. The stimuli are either the presentation of one of N lights or the visual presentation of one of N digits. The responses are either key presses, arranged in a "natural" fashion, or voice response. The data are summarized in Figure 10.3. Three aspects are noteworthy: the linear growth with log N, the degree of parallelism of three of the four pairings, and the fact that the digit-voice curve is constant, independent of N.

The key question is what to make of the constancy of the digit-voice data.

If it says what it seems to say, all of the models we have discussed are clearly wrong. Laming (1968), however, suggested that it does not really mean what it seems to. He noted that the times involved, about 450 msec, are really quite slow for two-choice visual reaction times, which are usually about 300 to 350 msec. He suggested the reason for this is that digits are so over-learned that, despite subjects being told that only two are being used in a particular run, they continued to behave as if there were ten. If that is so, then the growth of the digit-key curve with *N* must be due to response aspects, not decision ones. Evidence that this is true, provided by Theios (1973), is shown in Figure 10.4. Here the stimuli are digits and the response is either to name them or to identify them by pushing a button. The difference is striking. This immediately raises the question of the effect of practice on such performance.

Another, widely quoted study, in which MRT did not change with the number of stimuli, is Leonard (1959). The stimuli were vibrations of the fingers and the response on each trial was movement of the finger stimulated, an exceedingly compatible response. For values of *N* = 2, 4, and 8, the mean time for the right forefinger to react was independent of *N*. Recently Ten Hoopen, Akerboom, and Raaymakers (1982) repeated the study, varying both the frequency (40 Hz and 150 Hz) and intensity (difference of 9.5 dB) of the stimuli as well as the RSI. They reported data for all fingers. They found no interaction of RSI with the number of choices, comparatively little difference among the fingers, and the plot of MRT was fairly flat (but with a significantly non-zero slope) for the 150-Hz, more intense signals and quite steep for the 40-Hz less intense signals. Leonard's stimuli were comparable to the former. The authors demonstrated that the effects over stimulus type are not attributable to a speed-accuracy tradeoff.

Practice data for the digit-key task are shown in Figure 10.5 and for the light-key task in Figure 10.6, with the number of alternatives as a parameter of the plot. From the linear functions fit in Figure 10.5, one can infer how

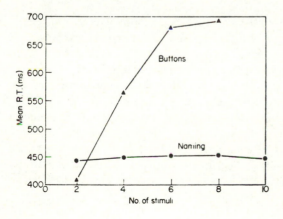

FIG. 10.4 MRT versus number of digits, *N*, in two conditions: when the response was to name the digit presented and when it was to push a button in a compatible arrangement. The data are averaged over 12 subjects, with each contributing 296 observations per point [Figure 5 of Theios (1975); copyright 1975; reprinted by permission.]

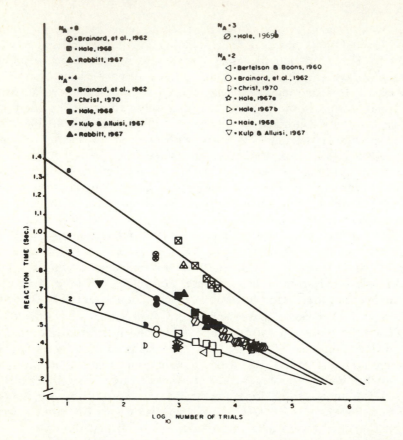

FIG. 10.5 MRT versus log of the number of trials of experience in the identification of a digit by a key response with the number of alternative as a parameter. The legend identifies the sources of the data, not all of which are included the present bibliography. [Figure 2 of Teichner and Krebs (1974); copyright 1974; reprinted by permission.]

MRT grows with number of alternatives, with practice shown as the parameter of the plot. This is shown in Figure 10.7. We see that they extrapolate the data to a constant function at something less than 250 msec with over a million practice trials. This suggests that Laming may well have been correct that the digit-voice case is flat because the subjects, who are not practiced in the experiment, are treating all runs as a choice out of 10. It also suggests—but no more than that since the million practice trials have not been run—that with practice the effect of number of alternatives disappears.

Some of Hick's data—those involving about 8000 trials of practice—were not used in developing Figure 10.5. Using the 8000 trial curve estimated from Figure 10.6, Teichner and Krebs made the parameter-free fit to Hick's data shown in Figure 10.8. It is strikingly good.

The model builder is posed with a dilemma. The data suggest, but by no means yet prove, that with adequate practice the times get shorter and become independent of *N*. If true, the models should exhibit this property, which means a different class of models from those we have been considering. But we do not know for sure that the data say this because they have never been collected; we are working with extrapolations, at best a risky business.

10.3   EXPERIMENTS WITH FEW ERRORS: SEQUENTIAL EFFECTS

10.3.1   *First-Order Stimulus Effects*

The most systematic attack on the stimulus information hypothesis of Hick is that of Kornblum (1967, 1968, 1969, 1973b, 1975), with the 1969 and

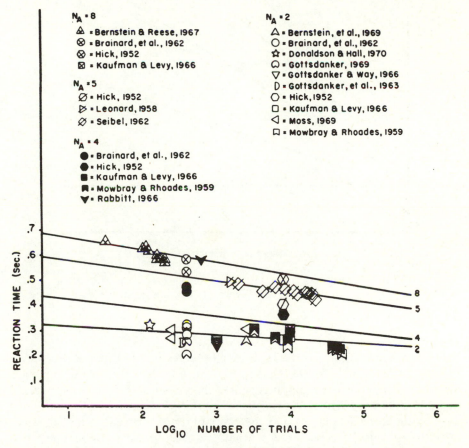

FIG. 10.6 Data similar to Figure 10.5 for pairings of lights with key presses. [Figure 5 of Teichner and Krebs (1974); copyright 1974; reprinted by permission.]

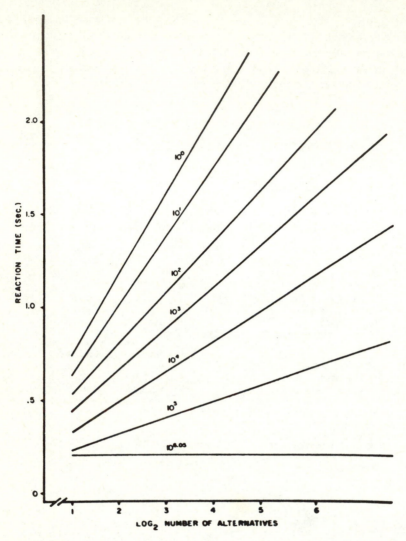

FIG. 10.7 MRT versus $\log_2 N$ as inferred from Figure 10.5 with practice as a parameter. [Figure 8 of Teichner and Krebs (1974); copyright 1974; reprinted by permission.]

1973 papers providing overviews. Basically he pointed out that earlier work, mostly in the two-signal setting (see Section 6.6), had shown that reaction times are faster when a signal is repeated than when it is not, and in most of the $N > 2$ studies performed prior to his work there was a serious confounding of stimulus information and the probability of a signal being repeated. The question to be considered is what are the relative roles of these two variables as well as set size itself.

It is useful to examine closely the nature of the confounding. Suppose signal presentations are governed by a Markov chain with asymptotic distribution $P(s)$ and with transition probabilities for successive trials of $P(s \mid s')$. Then the probability of a non-repetition, P_{NR}, is given by

$$P_{NR} = \sum_{s'} P(s') \sum_{s \neq s'} P(s \mid s'), \qquad (10.9a)$$

and so that of a repetition, P_R, is

$$P_R = 1 - P_{NR}. \qquad (10.9b)$$

Consider the three ways Hyman varied stimulus information H.

1. N equiprobable alternatives. In this case

$$P(s \mid s') = 1/N \qquad \text{and} \qquad P(s) = 1/N$$

and so

$$P_{NR} = \sum_{s'} \frac{1}{N} \sum_{s \neq s'} \frac{1}{N} = \frac{N-1}{N}$$

and of course

$$H = \log_2 N.$$

It is thus obvious that P_{NR} and H are monotonically related.

2. N fixed, no sequential dependencies, and variable distribution of presentations. Although explicit formulas are of little help in the case, note that H and P_{NR} each achieve their maximum value when the distribution is uniform. They covary, but not in a simple way.

3. N fixed, uniform distribution, and Markov sequential dependencies. Consider the case where there is a difference between the probability of repetitions and non-repetitions, and all of the latter probabilities are the

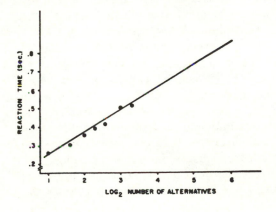

FIG. 10.8 MRT versus $\log_2 N$ as inferred for 8000 trials of experience from Figure 10.6 and the data of Hick (1952), which was not used in constructing Figure 10.6. [Figure 9 of Teichner and Krebs (1974); copyright 1974; reprinted by permission.]

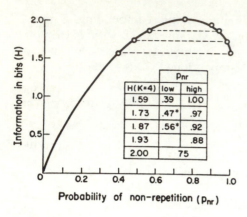

FIG. 10.9 Pairs of sequential probabilities of repetitions that were chosen for experimental study because each pair yields the same value of the measure of information transmitted. [Figure 1 of Kornblum (1969); copyright 1969; reprinted by permission.]

The figure's y-axis reads "Information in bits (H)" and the x-axis reads "Probability of non-repetition (P_{nr})". The embedded table:

H(K=4)	P_{nr} low	high
1.59	.39	1.00
1.73	.47*	.97
1.87	.56*	.92
1.93		.88
2.00	75	

same—that is,

$$P(s \mid s') = \begin{cases} 1-p & \text{when } s = s', \\ p/(N-1) & \text{when } s \neq s'. \end{cases}$$

Then

$$P_{NR} = \sum_{s'} \frac{1}{N} \sum_{s \neq s'} \frac{p}{N-1} = p$$

and

$$H = -\sum_{s'} \frac{1}{N} \left[\sum_{s \neq s'} \frac{p}{N-1} \log_2 \frac{p}{N-1} + (1-p) \log_2(1-p) \right]$$

$$= -p \log\left(\frac{p}{N-1}\right) - (1-p) \log_2(1-p).$$

Observe that H is an increasing function of p for $0 \leq p \leq (N-1)/N$ and decreasing for $(N-1)/N \leq p \leq 1$. Thus, P_{NR} and H are functionally related, but non-monotonically.

The last calculation suggests the key idea for an experiment run by Kornblum—namely, that pairs of values of p exist for which H is identical and P_{NR} is not. Those pairs that Kornblum (1969) studied for $N = 4$ are shown in Figure 10.9. Two sets of stimuli were used. One was an array of lights, which he called the "serial" design. The other was the appearance of one of the first four digits on a CRT, which he called the "discrete" experiment. The responses were key presses. The MRT and error data are shown in Figure 10.10, and they make very clear that both variables, P_{NR} and H, have an impact on response time and that there probably is an interaction between them. The conclusion is that the pure information hypothesis generalization of Hick's logarithmic relation is not correct.

To see in better detail the role of repetitions versus non-repetitions, the data are partitioned accordingly in Figure 10.11. To a good approximation,

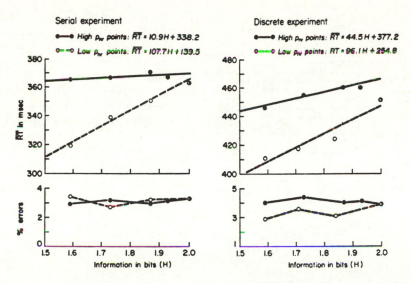

FIG. 10.10 MRT and proportion of error versus stimulus information when both values of P_{NR} yield the same value for information transmitted. The serial experiment involved one light from an array being presented and then responded to by a key in natural correspondence. The discrete experiment was the presentation on a video screen of one of the first four digits, and responses were again key presses. Each observer yielded 300 observations in the serial case and 150 in the discrete case per point. The number of observers was not stated. [Figure 2 of Kornblum (1969); copyright 1969; reprinted by permission.]

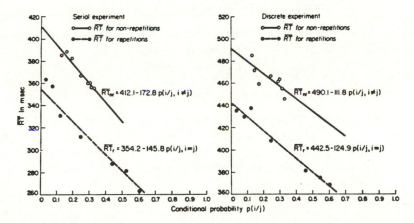

FIG. 10.11 For the experiment of Figure 10.10, MRT versus the actual value of P_{NR} used partitioned according to whether or not the stimulus presented was in fact a repetition. [Figure 3 of Kornblum (1969); copyright 1969; reprinted by permission.]

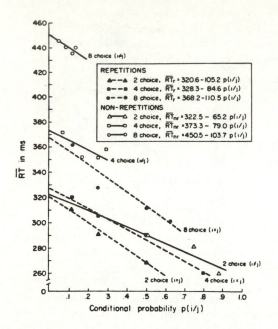

FIG. 10.12 For the experiment of Figure 10.10, MRT versus P_{NR} partitioned according to the number of alternatives and whether or not the stimulus was a repetition. [Figure 5 of Kornblum (1969); copyright 1969; reprinted by permission.]

MRT is a linear decreasing function of the probability of the type of event in question and that, for each level of probability, repetitions are approximately 50 msec faster than non-repetitions. If one assumes that the slopes are identical, which oversimplifies the data a bit, then we can approximate the data by

$$MRT_R = -mP(s \mid s) + b_R,$$
$$MRT_{NR} = -mP(s \mid s', s' \neq s) + b_{NR}.$$

(10.10)

And if we assume that no other effects than these are relevant, which is doubtful (see Kornblum, 1967), then by definition

$$MRT = P_R MRT_R + P_{NR} MRT_{NR}$$
$$= -p^2 N(N-1)m + p(N-1)(b_{NR} - b_R + 2m) - m + b_R,$$

which is quadratic in p. [Kornblum expressed the same result in terms of the variable $p' = p/(N-1)$, which is the probability of a non-repetition.] As he pointed out, for the relatively narrow ranges of H involved in studies with fixed N, it is not easy to distinguish between a linear dependence on H and a quadratic one on p.

He also examined the impact of N on MRT using the data of the 1967 paper. The relevant plot is shown in Figure 10.12, where we see that the major impact of N on the linear relations between MRT and $P(s \mid s)$ or $P(s \mid s')$, Eq. 10.10, is to affect b_R and b_{NR}, the intercepts, with by far the greater impact on b_{NR}. He used this fact to account for what appears to be a change in slope of MRT versus H when the data are segregated according to the number of signals employed. This, in turn, may explain why Hick's law fails to account for the MRTs of single signals as a function of $-\log P(s)$ in Hyman's data. The reason is that the low probability events arise from data with larger numbers of alternatives and the high probability events arise from those with smaller numbers of alternatives, and so have quite different temporal structures.

Kornblum (1975) reported data that suggest the impact of the size of the stimulus set is primarily on the non-repetitions rather than the repetitions. This agrees with earlier studies of Hale (1969b) and Remington (1969, 1971), but Schvaneveldt and Chase (1969) found the effect to be about the same for repetitions and non-repetitions. In Kornblum's experiment one signal, called the critical one, had a probability of $\frac{1}{2}$ of occurring independent of the total of number of signals employed. In what was called the experimental condition, the critical signal was responded to by the forefinger of one hand whereas all other signals were responded to by the other hand. In the control condition, all signals were responded to using the same hand. Not using thumbs, N could be varied from 2 to 5 in the experimental condition and from 2 to 4 in the control. We see in Figure 10.13 that with sufficient experience (five days of running versus three), the MRT to the critical signal is largely independent of the number of alternatives, which is not true of the other signals (see also Section 10.2.3).

The upshot of all this work is a very firm conviction that sequential effects in the signal presentations have a major impact on the response times, and that any model or experiment that ignores this or fails to predict it surely is incomplete and likely is wrong, as well. Often attempts to manipulate something about the signal presentations result in an unintended confounding with sequential effects which is not taken into account. For example, this appears to be an issue in some of Hinrichs' work (Hinrichs, 1970; Hinrichs & Craft, 1971a, b; Hinrichs & Krainz, 1970). As a case in point, in Hinrichs and Craft (1971b) the stimuli are one of three digits on a visual display with one response associated with s_1 and the other with both s_2 and s_3. The experimental manipulation was the relative frequencies of the signals: $2:1:1$, $1:1:1$, $1:1:2$, and $1:1:4$. The subjects were required to predict which signal would be presented and then to react with the appropriate response when it appeared. The MRTs exhibited two main features. Times to correct predictions were faster than to incorrect ones. And in the $1:1:4$ case, the time to predict s_3 correctly was significantly faster than the times to the other two correct predictions. No analyses of sequential effects were presented, but since the probability of repetitions of s_3 is rather high in the $1:1:4$ condition, such effects may very well underlie the apparent effect of signal frequency.

At the present time, there are no sequential models for $N > 2$. Should a model builder attempt to attack the problem, it would be wise also to take into account some of the recent psychophysical studies of sequential matters

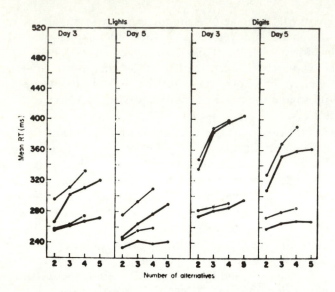

FIG. 10.13 MRT for a signal that, independent of *N*, had a probability of $\frac{1}{2}$ (and all others were equally likely) versus *N*. In one condition, the special signal was responded to with the other hand (heavier lines with a value for *N* = 5); in another condition the same hand was used for all responses (lighter lines with no values for *N* = 5, since the thumb was not used). The data are partitioned both as to the type of stimulus and the amount of experience the subject had had in the task. There were 12 observers, each of whom contributed 216 observations per point. [Figure 3 of Kornblum (1975); copyright 1975; reprinted by permission.]

in absolute identification, among them Purks, Callahan, Braida, and Durlach (1980); Luce, Nosofsky, Green, and Smith (1982); Nosofsky (1983); Treisman (1984); and Ward and Lockhead (1970). In some of these papers the data are analyzed in terms of a Thurstonian model in which sensitivity is measured by *d'* and response bias by the location of category boundaries. The evidence suggests that there are sequential effects both on the value of *d'* and on the category boundaries. The *d'* effects tend to be small or non-existent unless the signals on several successive trials are close together on the continuum on which they vary, in which case the changes in *d'* can be quite sizable. In the random presentation design, the boundaries around the signal just presented appear to separate, making it more likely that a repeated signal will be correctly identified. Presumably the reaction-time effects are related to the changes in category boundaries, although this statement has not been established empirically. Kirby (1975), in discussing data described below in Section 10.3.3, proposed a theoretical scheme not unlike the anchoring ideas that have arisen in the work of Braida, Durlach, and their colleagues (Berliner and Durlach, 1973).

10.3.2 Higher-Order Stimulus Effects

Recall that for the two-choice situation, the impact of signal repetitions did not end after just one trial (Section 6.6.1). It seems plausible that the same should be true of data involving more signals, which Kornblum (1973b) has shown for his 1969 data. Figure 10.14 presents MRTs as a function of the number of intervening items between repetitions and, separately, as a function of the number of repetitions. In each case, the absolute probability of the signal presentation is a parameter of the plot. It is clear that repetitions speeded the process and non-repetitions slowed it down.

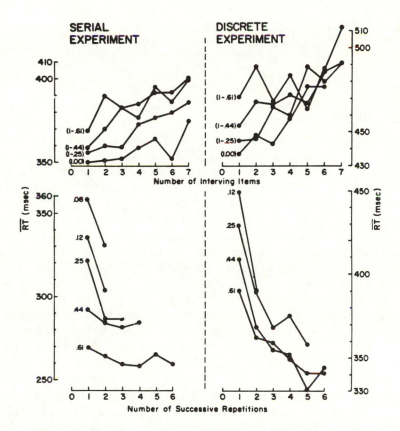

FIG. 10.14 MRT versus the number of successive repetitions for the experiment of Kornblum (1969), Figure 10.9. The upper panel is for the number of repetitions just prior to a non-repetition, and the lower panel is for the number of repetitions since the last non-repetition. The parameters of the curves are the probabilities of a repetition. For sample size, see Figure 10.10. [Figure 2 of Kornblum (1973b); copyright 1973; reprinted by permission.]

TABLE 10.1. Mean reaction times (msec) for different classes of transitions between signals and responses (Rabbitt, 1968, table II adapted)

(R, S) Group	Nature of signal	Nature or response	Trials 301–600	Trials 1201–1500
2, 4	New	New	584	424
	Equivalent	Same	567	394
	Identical	Same	491	383
2, 8	New	New	608	484
	Equivalent	Same	580	416
	Identical	Same	510	377
4, 8	New	New	725	592
	Equivalent	Same	720	532
	Identical	Same	652	416
8, 8	New	New	970	770
	Identical	Same	693	461

10.3.3   First-Order Response Effects

Confounded with the stimulus effects just discussed may very well be response ones. For example, Rabbitt (1965) ran an $N = 10$ design in which all eight fingers and two thumbs were used to make responses. The signal presentations were random except that no signal repetitions were permitted, which was intended to eliminate the major effect of signal repetitions on MRT. This, of course, also means that with accurate responding there were no exact response repetitions; however, there were repetitions involving the same hand, which can be compared with hand alternations. He reported MRTs of 534 msec and 581 msec for hand repetitions and alternations, respectively.

Bertelson (1965) used an $N = 4$ design in which pairs of signals received the same response. He distinguished repetitions of identical signals, of equivalent ones for which the response was repeated, and new ones for which the response was different. The times for identical and equivalent signals were both considerably faster than for new ones, with the identical ones being slightly faster than the equivalent ones. Rabbitt (1968b) elaborated this idea in order to distinguish between stimulus and response effects and to study the impact of practice. He used digits on a CRT as stimuli and key responses with up to eight fingers. The stimuli were partitioned in a natural way into equal-sized equivalence classes, forming the conditions $2R/8S$, $4R/8S$, $8R/8S$, and $2R/4S$, where the latter replicates Bertelson's experiment. The error pattern was similar across conditions and was about 7.8% for trials 301–600 and 4.4% for trials 1201–1500. Table 10.1 shows

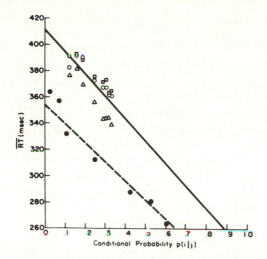

FIG. 10.15 MRT versus P_{NR} from Kornblum's (1969) four-choice, serial experiment. The solid circles are repetitions (*HF*) and the open symbols are for non-repetitions of various sorts. The triangles are $H\bar{F}$, the squares $\bar{H}F$, and the circles $\bar{H}\bar{F}$. For sample size, see Figure 10.10. [Figure 3 of Kornblum (1973b); copyright 1973; reprinted by permission.]

the data from these two runs. With sufficient practice, Bertelson's finding is reproduced; but with little practice equivalent signals are closer to new ones than to identical ones. Perhaps the most notable feature of these data is the fact that following practice neither the stimulus entropy (compare $2R/4S$ and $2R/8S$) nor the response entropy (compare $2R/8S$, $4R/8S$, and $8R/8S$) has much effect on the identical responses (he provided the necessary statistical tests). Similarly, equivalent responses are not much affected by stimulus entropy, but in contrast they are affected by response entropy.

Kornblum (1973b) analyzed his 1969 data in a fashion similar to that of Rabbitt (1965): hand repetitions, H, or not, $\bar{H}$, and finger repetitions, F, or not, $\bar{F}$. Thus, *HF* means an exact repetition of the same finger of the same hand. By $\bar{H}F$ is meant the use of the same finger of the opposite hand. We see in Figure 10.15 that pure repetitions, *HF*, are much the fastest, $H\bar{F}$ next, and the other two are indistinguishable.

In a review of sequential effects, Kirby (1980) pondered both these and the $N = 2$ data and attempted to tease out whatever qualitative conclusions that he could. He argued that we are dealing with a preparatory or facilitatory effect and that "... the only firm conclusion that the evidence reviewed allows is that repetition effects are predominantly caused by central processes involved in the choice rather than peripheral stimulus identification and response execution processes." (p. 164) At present the model builder is faced with a bewildering array of data that leaves little doubt that sequential effects, both in reaction times and in accuracy of performance, are pervasive and must be an integral part of any accurate model of the process. So far we do not have any such models aside from those of Sections 7.2 and 7.5.

10.4 EXPERIMENTS WITH ERRORS

10.4.1 *Empirical Speed-Accuracy Tradeoff Functions*

Exactly the same concerns as those expressed in Chapter 6 about errors for the two-signal case apply here. It is very difficult both to control the error level with sufficient precision and to measure it with sufficient accuracy to be confident that measured reaction times are uncontaminated by inadvertent speed-accuracy tradeoffs. The advice, once again, is: do not ignore the tradeoff, study it.

Hick (1952) was the first to do so. By instructions to speed up, he caused himself and another subject to increase appreciably the error rate. He first calculated the information transmitted from the signal to the response, which is Eq. 10.3 evaluated for the *response* probabilities less Eq. 10.4, where $p(s' \mid s)$ is replaced by the conditional probability of response r given the presentation of signal s, $p(r \mid s)$—that is,

$$T = H(r) - H(r \mid s). \tag{10.11}$$

He next converted that result to the equivalent number of error-free responses, N_e, and then showed that the MRT followed the same law, proportional to $\log(N_e + 1)$, as the (relatively) error-free data.

Somewhat later this tradeoff was studied more fully in a series of papers (Hale, 1969b; Pachella, Fisher, & Karsh, 1968; Pachella & Fisher, 1969, 1972; Stanovich, Pachella, & Smith, 1977). Hale used the digits 1, 2, and 3 with key presses as the responses, and Pachella and Fisher used a visual marker in one of N unmarked locations and corresponding response keys, where N was 2, 4, and 8 in one study and 10 in the others. Hale manipulated the tradeoff by instruction. Pachella and Fisher used four response deadlines—none, 1000 msec, 700 msec, and 400 msec. The accuracy measure in all studies was again the amount of information transmitted, Eq. 10.11. The major finding, which is completely consistent with Hick's observations, is a linear tradeoff between information transmitted and MRT. This is shown in Figures 10.16 and 10.17. Note that for the location of a position, the tradeoff is approximately 3.5 bits per sec, independent of the number of response alternatives; whereas, for the digits it is approximately 14 bits per sec, larger than that for location by a factor of 4.

According to Swensson's rule of thumb stated in Section 6.4.3, since the digits in the Hale study were easy to discriminate and the data were collected under time pressure, we anticipate that errors will be faster than the corresponding correct responses. The data are shown in Figure 10.18, with time plotted as a function of the error probability. The decline with probability is extremely systematic.

Judging by Figure 10.18, even with unlimited time in the Pachella and Fisher experiments, errors are being made and therefore the signals must be difficult to discriminate. So, according to Swenson's rule of thumb, a response in error should be slower than the same response when correct, but

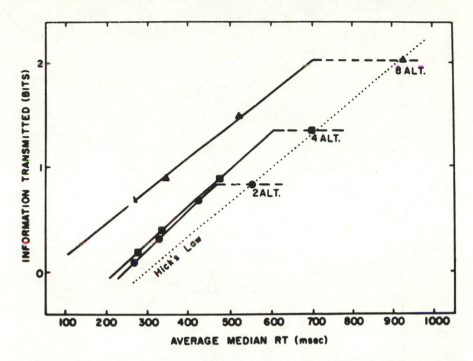

FIG. 10.16 SATF in the form of information transmitted (Eq. 10.11) versus MRT with number of alternatives as a parameter. The SATF was achieved by means of response deadlines. There were 12 observers each of whom contributed 192 observations per point [Figure 2 of Pachella and Fisher (1972); copyright 1972; reprinted by permission.]

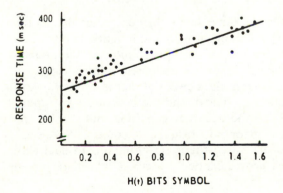

FIG. 10.17 SATF in the form of MRT versus information transmitted with $N = 3$ and the tradeoff effected by instructions. Each data point is based on 184 observations; there are data from three subjects on the graph. [Figure 6 of Hale (1969b); copyright 1969; reprinted by permission.]

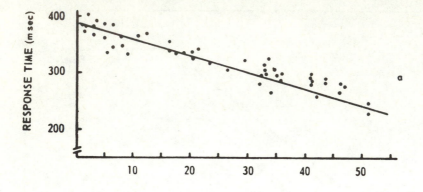

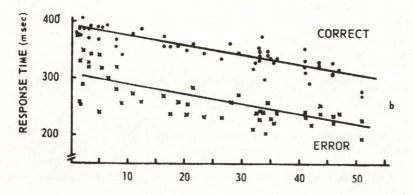

FIG. 10.18 For the experiment of Figure 10.17, MRT as a function of the proportion of errors. The top panel is overall MRT whereas the bottom panel has the MRT partitioned by whether the response was correct or in error. [Figure 5a,b of Hale (1969b); copyright 1969; reprinted by permission.]

these data were not reported. On the other hand, they do report that as the subjects are pressed for speed the fraction of response repetitions increases. For example, with eight signals, the proportion of repetitions in the presentation was reported to be .05 (which is low as compared with a theoretical .125, and which apparently results from the constraint that in every block of 64 trials each stimulus appeared eight times), and the proportion of repetitions in the responses was .08 for the accuracy condition and .15 for the 300 msec one. Presumably, these errors are faster than correct responses.

To my knowledge, there are only three theoretical attempts to deal with the *N*-alternative case in which errors explicitly occur. I take them up in chronological order.

10.4.2 A Response Discard Model

Luce (1960) suggested* a process for reducing a choice from N alternatives to a single one; it is in spirit somewhat different from Hicks model. Denote by R the set of response alternatives which are $1:1$ correspondence with the set S of signals. Denote by $P(r, t \mid s, R)$ the joint probability density that response r is made at time t given that stimulus s was presented and that R is the response set. [In my 1960 presentation I was not explicit about the conditioning on the signal presented. Indeed, the way the paper was written suggests that I had in mind overall response probabilities $P(r) = \sum_s P(r \mid s)P(s)$. I cannot recall exactly what I intended, but in any event I now believe that it should have been stated in terms of $P(r \mid s)$, and that is how I will formulate it here.] The assumed mechanism for responding is that the subject discards, one-by-one, possible responses until only one alternative remains, which is then the response made. Denote by $Q(k, \tau \mid s, R)$ the probability of discarding response k at time τ given response set R and signal s. The following convolution describes the process if we assume that the subsequent choice probability following a discard is an event independent of the discard:

$$P(r, t \mid s, R) = \sum_{r' \in R - \{r\}} \int_0^t Q(r', \tau \mid s, R)P(r, t - \tau \mid s, R - \{r'\}) \, dt. \quad (10.12)$$

This is the first major postulate of the theory. If the discard and choice probabilities are families of gamma distributed random variables, the parameters can be selected so Eq. 10.12 holds (Luce, 1960, Theorem 5).

By definition, the choice probabilities are the marginals obtained by integrating out the time, and as a technical postulate it is assumed that they can be obtained from their moment generating functions by taking limits:

$$P(r \mid s, R) = \int_0^\infty P(r, t \mid s, R) \, dt.$$

$$= \lim_{\theta \to 0} \int_0^\infty e^{-\theta t} P(r, t \mid s, R) \, dt, \quad (10.13)$$

$$Q(r \mid s, R) = \int_0^\infty Q(r, \tau \mid s, R) \, d\tau.$$

$$= \lim_{\theta \to 0} \int_0^\infty e^{-\theta \tau} Q(r, \tau \mid s, R) \, d\tau. \quad (10.14)$$

---

* Laming (1977a) pointed out that I had made an error in the proof and by a counter example showed that the theorem, as asserted, is false. He stated a modified result, but that proof makes use of an assumption that was not explicitly stated. In correspondence, he has convinced me that it is a plausible assumption, and so I will state the corrected version of Laming's theorem. I will make clear which assumption is implicit in his paper, to which the reader is referred for a proof of the result.

The second major postulate of the theory is that the choice axiom (Luce, 1959) holds among these probabilities; namely, if they differ from 0 and 1, then for $r \in A \subseteq R$,

$$P(r \mid s, A) = \frac{P(r \mid s, R)}{\sum\limits_{r' \in A} P(r' \mid s, R)}. \tag{10.15}$$

This simply says that the response probabilities of a subset of alternatives can be obtained from those of a superset by normalizing them over all alternatives in the subset.

The mean reaction time of response r to signal s when the response alternative set is r is obtained by computing it from $P(r, t \mid s, R)$, and we again assume as a somewhat technical postulate that it can be obtained in the usual limiting fashion from the moment generating function:

$$\begin{aligned} E(\mathbf{T} \mid s, t, R) &= \int_0^\infty t \frac{P(r, t \mid s, R)}{P(r \mid s, R)} \, dt \\ &= \lim_{\theta \to 0} \frac{\partial}{\partial \theta} \int_0^\infty e^{-\theta t} \frac{P(r, t \mid s, R)}{P(r \mid s, R)} \, dt, \end{aligned} \tag{10.16}$$

and the mean discard latency is

$$\begin{aligned} \mu(s, r, R) &= \int_0^\infty \tau \frac{Q(r, \tau \mid s, R)}{Q(r \mid s, R)} \, d\tau \\ &= \lim_{\theta \to 0} \frac{\partial}{\partial \theta} \int_0^\infty e^{-\theta \tau} \frac{Q(r, \tau \mid s, R)}{Q(r \mid s, R)} \, d\tau. \end{aligned} \tag{10.17}$$

The next major assumption of the theory is that for each stimulus s, a continuous function f_s exists such that

$$E(T \mid s, r, R) = f_s[P(r \mid s, R)]. \tag{10.18}$$

This postulates a somewhat strong form of a SATF (Section 6.5.1) not unlike those found in some, but not all, models for two-stimulus experiments.*

Finally, the implicit assumption in Laming's proof is that if r is in R and if we consider a series of process P_i satisfying the other assumptions and such that

$$\lim_{i \to \infty} P_i(s, r, R) = 0,$$

then for $r' \neq r$,

$$\lim_{i \to \infty} \mu_i(s, r', R) = \mu_i(s, r', R - \{r\}). \tag{10.19}$$

---

* In my 1960 paper I assumed a weaker form of this—namely, that f depended on both s and R, and this was shown by Laming (1977a) not to be sufficient to get the result. I have subsequently shown that a variant of my original assumption will do, but the proof has not been published.

In words, if a response has no chance of being selected, then in terms of the mean discard latency it does not matter whether that response is in the choice set or not.

Theorem 10.1.   *If the assumptions embodied in Eqs.* 10.12 *through* 10.19 *are satisfied, then for each stimulus s there exist constants* $A(s)$ *and* $B(s) > 0$ *such that*

$$E(\mathbf{T} \mid s, r, R) = A(s) - B(s) \ln P(r \mid s, R). \qquad (10.20)$$

The proof can be found in Laming (1977a).

Two immediate consequences of Eq. 10.19 are worthy of note. First, if we denote the N signals by $s_1, s_2, \ldots, s_N$ and the corresponding responses by $r_1, r_2, \ldots, r_N$, then for each i,

$$
\begin{aligned}
E(\mathbf{T} \mid s_i, r_j, R) &- E(\mathbf{T} \mid s_i, r_i, R) \\
&= B(s) \ln[P(r_i \mid s_i, R)/P(r_j \mid s_i, R)]. \qquad (10.21)
\end{aligned}
$$

So, on the assumption (which seems always to be satisfied) that any error probability is smaller than the correct response probability to the same stimulus, then the corresponding mean error latency is longer than the corresponding correct one. Note that this does not have anything to do with the generalizations made in Section 6.4.3 about correct and error latencies for the same response, not signal. Here we are talking about rows of the stimulus-response matrices, and there we were talking about columns of the same matrix.

In fact, to the extent that the stimuli admit error-free performance, so $P(r_j \mid s_i)$, $i \neq j$, approaches 0, the mean time approaches infinity. Laming (personal communication) feels that this is an absolutely fatal flaw of the model—so bad, in fact, that he feels the model should be forgotten. His argument is that when stimuli are perfectly identifiable, errors tend to be very fast, not very slow. The question to my mind is whether those fast errors can reasonably be considered a part of the same mechanism. As we have seen, there is substantial reason to suppose that they may be fast guesses or some other type of anticipatory response that is not really a part of what is being modeled here. Moreover, when the signals are actually confused to a substantial degree, as in Laming's own data (see Appendix C.8), the error responses to a signal are slower than the correct ones to it.

The second consequence of Eq. 10.20 is this

$$
\begin{aligned}
E(\mathbf{T} \mid s, R) &= \sum_r E(\mathbf{T} \mid s, r, R) P(r \mid s, R) \\
&= A(s) - B(s) \sum_r P(r \mid s, R) \ln P(r \mid s, R). \qquad (10.22)
\end{aligned}
$$

On the surface this resembles somewhat the empirical hypothesis that mean reaction time is linear with transmitted information. So we should look into the relation—or, as will become apparent, the lack of clear relation—between the present model and that hypothesis. Consider, first, the error-free case in which $P(r_i \mid s_i, R) = 1$ and so $\sum_r P(r \mid s, R) \log P(r \mid s, R) = 0$. So $E(\mathbf{T} \mid s, R) = A(s)$. We are not really sure what function A is of s, but if the information theory hypothesis were correct, then

$$A(s) = a - b \log P(s).$$

Of course, we know from Hyman's work, this is not really accurate. Nonetheless, proceeding as if it were true, then from Eq. 10.21,

$$E(\mathbf{T} \mid R) = \sum_s E(\mathbf{T} \mid s, R)P(s)$$

$$= a - b \sum_s P(s) \ln P(s) - \sum_s B(s) P(s) \sum_r P(r \mid s, R) \ln P(r \mid s, R). \quad (10.23)$$

This has some resemblance to the generalized information theory hypothesis that

$$\mathrm{MRT}(R) = a' + b'[H(r) - H(r \mid s)]$$

$$= a - b' \sum_r P(r) \ln P(r) + b' \sum_s P(s) \sum_r P(r \mid s, R) \ln P(r \mid s, R), \quad (10.24)$$

but a careful examination reveals major differences. The $\sum p \ln p$ term on the left of Eq. 10.23 differs from that on the left of Eq. 10.24 in that the former is totally about stimulus probabilities and the latter about response probabilities. However, to the extent that response probabilities match response ones, which is quite common in data, they are the same. The double sum terms on the right are the same except for the factor $B(s)$ under the s-summation in Eq. 10.23. To the extent $B(s)$ is constant, these terms are the same. So while there is no formal identity between Eqs. 10.23 and 10.24, there may be a practical one.

Let us turn to data. Luce (1960) compared some data of Kellogg (1931), even though they were really not appropriate, to Eq. 10.20, and the fit was poor. Laming (1968) reported appropriate data in his Experiment 6, which was an $N = 5$ absolute identification of lengths in which the signal probabilities were varied from $\frac{1}{15}$ to $\frac{5}{15}$. Two groups of 12 subjects were run, the one with probabilities increasing from the thumb to the little finger and the other with the pattern reversed. These data, which Dr. Laming has kindly provided me, are presented in Appendix C.8 with the two groups of subjects combined so that signals of the same prior probability, regardless of which finger was used, are averaged. Laming (1968, Fig. 7.3) plotted

$$E(\mathbf{T} \mid r) = \left[\sum_s E(\mathbf{T} \mid s, r, R)P(s)P(r \mid s, R) \right] \Big/ P(r \mid R), \quad (10.25)$$

where

$$P(r \mid R) = \sum_s P(r \mid s, R)P(s),$$

versus $-\log P(r \mid R)$. Because he believed the theory to predict a linear

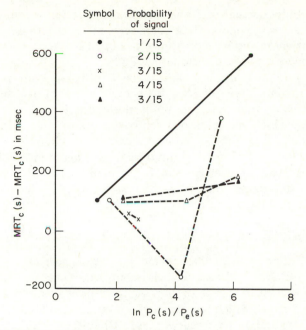

FIG. 10.19 $\mathrm{MRT}_{ij}-\mathrm{MRT}_{ii}$ versus $\ln P(r_i \mid s_i)/P(r_j \mid s_i)$, which should be linear with slope a function of s_i if Eq. 10.21 is true, for Laming data of Appendix C.8.

relation between these variables and the plot was non-monotonic, he concluded the model to be in error. [Laming's discussions in 1968 and, especially, in 1977b make clear that he was perplexed by my failure to make explicit reference to a stimulus in my 1960 paper. My presentation and attempt to use Kellogg's data reasonably lead one to conclude that I was talking about marginal response times and probabilities rather than conditional ones.]

If, as I now believe is a reasonable interpretation of the assumptions, the model holds for probabilities conditioned on the stimulus, then substituting Eq. 10.20 into Eq. 10.25 yields

$$E(\mathbf{T} \mid r) = \left[\sum_s A(s)P(s)P(r \mid s, R) \right.$$

$$\left. - \sum_s B(s)P(s)P(r \mid s, R) \ln P(r \mid s, R) \right] \Big/ P(r \mid R),$$

which predicts nothing unless A and B are known functions of s.

Probably the best test is to plot Eq. 10.21 because one of the two unknown functions drops out. This is shown for Laming's data in Figure 10.19. Aside from the apparently anomalous point at -165 msec and having a response probability of 0.013, these data are not inconsistent with the hypothesis of a linear fan through the origin, but with a slope that decreases as signal probability decreases. To be sure, this is not a stringent test of the model, but I do not believe these data are adequate to reject it. An experiment with more stimuli more densely packed so as to guarantee more confusions is needed to tax the model adequately.

The theory—although not necessarily the conclusion embodied in Eq. 10.20—can, of course, be rejected by showing any of its three major assumptions to be wrong. At this point there are considerable data to suggest that the choice axiom is not valid when the set of alternatives is highly structured (Luce, 1977), which is the case when they are one-dimensional. Laming (1968) studied this directly and again in 1977b when he published a corrected and somewhat more detailed analysis. His conclusion, which accords with other studies, is that the choice axiom is incorrect in this situation.

10.4.3   *A Generalization of SPRT*

Laming (1968) appears to have been the first to suggest a version of the random walk for $N > 2$ alternatives. Basically, the idea is that at each instant t there is associated with each possible response r an "information" random variable $I(r, t)$, which represents the accumulated evidence favoring response r. As in the two-alternative case (Chapter 8), different models result depending upon how $I(r, t)$ is assumed to develop in time. For example, in Section 8.3 we explored two distinct models, and another arose in Section 9.2.1. The one proposed by Laming in Section 3.3 of his monograph and worked out in detail in his Appendix B is a continuous generalization of the SPRT two-choice model (Section 8.3.1). It can be stated as follows.

At time t there is a probability $\pi(r, t)$ that r is a correct response, where $\sum_r \pi(r, t) = 1$. This is assumed to be related to the information favoring r by a log odds expression:

$$I(r, t) = \ln \frac{\pi(r, t)}{1 - \pi(r, t)}.$$

The response rule is as follows: associated with each possible response is an error criterion λ_r, with $0 < \lambda_r < 1$ and $\lambda_r + \lambda_{r'} < 1$, such that response r is made at time t if and only if, for all r' and all $\tau < t$, $\pi(r', \tau) < 1 - \lambda_{r'}$, and $\pi(r, t) \geq 1 - \lambda_r$. The major assumptions of the theory are equivalent (by Laming's Theorem 3.1) to the following assertion: For each $\delta t > 0$, there exists a series of independent random variables $\mathbf{X}_{s,i}$, $s = 1, \ldots, N$, and $i = 1, 2, \ldots$, with distribution functions $F_i(x \mid s)$, such that the products $\prod_{i=1}^{k} F_i(x_i \mid s)$ are all distinct for sufficiently large k and for some $x_i, \ldots, x_k$,

$$I(s, k\delta t) = \ln \frac{P(s) \prod_{i=1}^{k} dF_i(x_i \mid s)}{\sum_{u=1}^{N} \prod_{i=1}^{k} dF_i(x_i \mid u)},$$

where $P(s)$ is the presentation probability of signal s. This is, in essence, a Bayesian information accumulation assumption.

Laming proved a number of technical results about the process he postulated as well as the following important substantive prediction (Theorem 3.6): The response distribution is independent of whether the response is correct or incorrect. Recall that this was a major property of the SPRT model, and that it was seriously violated by most of the two-choice data. It is also incorrect for Laming's (1968) five-choice data (Appendix C.8) as we summarize:

	Response alternative corresponding to signal with probability				
	$\frac{1}{15}$	$\frac{2}{15}$	$\frac{3}{15}$	$\frac{4}{15}$	$\frac{5}{15}$
MRT (correct) − MRT (error)	70	6	−100	−100	−191

We see that there is a strong interaction with the probability of the signal, with errors being fast for the low probability signal and slow for the three highest probability signals. The data clearly do not agree with the SPRT model.

Little additional work seems to have been done with this model, so I do not pursue it further here.

10.4.4 Accelerating Cycle Model

G. A. Smith (1977, 1980) described a sequential model I find difficult to formulate to my satisfaction. Part of my discomfort is that several of the assumptions seem entirely ad hoc, explicitly chosen to yield just the right properties. To the degree that this is true, the model lacks both elegance and depth. Another part of my discomfort is that the stochastic process involved is not made explicit, and the equations derived for the deterministic case do not provide much insight into the general case.

Suppose that initially each possible signal s has associated with it an amount of excitation $e(s)$, where this variable is normalized so that $\sum_s e(s) = 1$. Suppose that when s_0 is presented,

$$e(s_0) > e(s) \text{ for all } s \neq s_0$$

and

$$e(s) = e(s') \text{ for all } s, s' \neq s_0.$$

The excitement associated with non-presented signals is considered the noise level of the system.

Next, a sensory processor is assumed to cycle over all the potential signal alternatives, on each cycle extracting information that is ultimately going to determine the response. For a specified signal-response mapping, $r = \theta(s)$, there is assumed to be some associated time $\alpha(s)$, the time devoted to processing signal s is $\alpha(s)e(s)$, for a total cycle time of $\sum \alpha(s)e(s)$. However, and this seems most ad hoc, it is assumed that each cycle gets faster in proportion to its cycle number. In particular, on the mth cycle, the cycle time is assumed to be $\sum \alpha(s)e(s)/m$. I can see no very principled reason for assuming this, although the motive for doing so is that it produces a logarithm. In particular, suppose that the cycling process terminates after k cycles, then the total mean time is

$$E(\mathbf{T}) = r_0 + \sum_{m=1}^{k} \frac{1}{m} \sum_{s} \alpha(s)e(s),$$

and replacing the first sum by an integral one obtains the approximation

$$E(\mathbf{T}) = r_0 + (\ln k) \sum_{s} \alpha(s)e(s). \tag{10.26}$$

The next question is how to determine k. Smith observed that if $E(\mathbf{T})$ is to be linear with $\ln N$, then it is necessary that k be proportional to N. One way this might come about is to assign each response the prior probability $1/N$, which is then modified on each cycle by the excitement accorded the signal that corresponds under the mapping θ to response r; that is, after $k - 1$ cycles we have

$$\sum_{i=1}^{k-1} \frac{e[\theta^{-1}(r)]}{N} = \frac{e(\theta^{-1}(r))}{N}(k-1).$$

If we suppose there is a response criterion $\lambda(r)$ for each response, then for the response r to occur at cycle k requires

$$\lambda(r) = \frac{e[\theta^{-1}(r)]}{N}(k-1).$$

Solving for k and substituting into Eq. 10.26 yields

$$E(\mathbf{T} \mid r) = A + B \ln\left[N + \frac{e[\theta^{-1}(r)]}{\lambda(r)} \right],$$

where

$$A = r_0 + \sum_{s} \alpha(s)e(s) \ln \frac{\lambda(r)}{e[\theta^{-1}(r)]},$$

$$B = \sum_{s} \alpha(s)e(s).$$

Fundamentally, very little has been shown at the expense of two highly arbitrary assumptions. Moreover, the model does not make clear—as was done for the Wald model in Chapter 8 and for both of the two preceding models—how the response probabilities and response times covary. One reason is that, as stated, it is deterministic; presumably it could be made stochastic by making $e(s)$ a random variable. It also lacks freedom to handle unequal presentation probabilities. By playing on the enormous freedom existing in the three unspecified functions—$e(s)$, $\alpha(s)$, and $\lambda(r)$—Smith attempted to give an account of various phenomena in the literature (see pp. 201–210 of Smith, 1980), but it is far from compelling.

10.5 CONCLUSIONS

The chapter has been relatively brief and so will be my conclusions. It is evident that we don't have as much solid empirical information about the absolute identification of more than two signals as we do for two, and the development of theoretical ideas about them is also not as rich. This is by no means unique to response times. In psychophysics, generally, detection and discrimination experiments and theory are far more extensively developed for two signals than for more than two signals. Part of the reason is the difficulty in getting adequate sample sizes in a reasonable length of time and part is the difficulty of avoiding an exponential explosion of free parameters in the models.

The major empirical findings are that MRT grows approximately linearly with information transmitted, although in detail this statement is surely incorrect. No detailed generalization seems to exist, especially when one attempts to take into account the very pervasive sequential effects. They are complex and ill understood. There are also substantial practice effects, and with some overlearned stimuli the MRT appears to be virtually independent of the size of the stimulus set, although that may result from an inability to confine attention to subsets of the overlearned set. Models that attempt any sort of detailed analysis are very few and at present lack any substantial empirical support. All in all, the situation is very unsatisfactory.

III
MATCHING PARADIGMS

11

Memory Scanning, Visual Search, and Same-Different Designs

11.1 MEMORY SCANNING AND VISUAL SEARCH

11.1.1 The Experimental Designs

In the memory scan or the item recognition task, as Sternberg (1966, 1967a, b, 1969a, b, 1975), who made it popular, called it, the set of N stimuli are partitioned into two parts. The one, composed of M items, is presented to the subject and is called either the memory or positive set. The other, consisting of $D = N - M$ items, is the distractor or negative set. On each trial an item is presented and the subject is simply to recognize whether or not it is from the memory set. So, independent of N and M, there are always two possible responses. Items and responses are called positive and negative according to which set they are drawn from or associated to. The scheme is shown in Figure 11.1.

The basic data are response accuracy and response time. Typically, the instructions are ambiguous as to the speed-accuracy tradeoff, emphasizing both responding as rapidly as possible consistent with highly accurate performance, which can be nearly perfect since the items are not ambiguous. Error rates of less than 2% to 5% are usually obtained and are considered acceptable. So for most of the studies (but see Sections 11.3.6 and 11.3.7) the analysis is entirely in terms of response times, often just the MRT but more recently in terms of other aspects of the response-time distribution. Of course, it is important to examine the times separately for positive and negative items. It may also be important to consider sequential effects, but they have not been much attended to in this literature.

The experimenter has a number of choices to make. Usually M and N are parameters to be manipulated. The class of items must be selected. Often letters or digits are used, but other more-or-less homogeneous classes have been employed. The positive set and/or the negative set can be fixed throughout a long run of trials or they can be varied from trial to trial. Usually the union of the positive and negative sets is constant throughout the experiment. When the positive set is held fixed, the procedure is called fixed- or consistent-set; when it is varied on each trial, varied-set. Since the stimuli are usually highly recognizable and the error rates are low, there is little reason to provide trial-by-trial feedback about accuracy. Often after a block of trials feedback is provided and payoffs are used in an attempt to hold the error rates to a low level. There is, of course, the possibility of

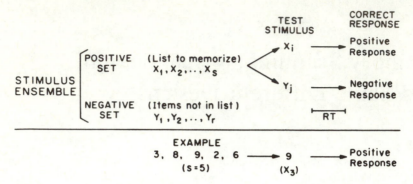

FIG. 11.1 Scheme for the memory scan experiment [Figure 2 of Sternberg (1969b); copyright 1969; reprinted by permission.]

some sort of feedback about the response times. For example, one can attempt to manipulate the speed-accuracy tradeoff by means of time-based or deadline payoffs, although little research of that sort has been done. Another choice is how to present the positive set—either sequentially or simultaneous. Sternberg used a sequential presentation, presumably to insure the same exposure to each item, which cannot be controlled if all items are present at once.

The visual search task differs from memory scanning in two major ways. First, the order of presentation of the test item and memory set are reversed, in which case these names are inappropriate. They are called the target and the search list. Second, since our interest is in how long the subject takes to process the items in the search list, it cannot be presented one item at a time. And when presented simultaneously, there are questions of how best to display the items. For example, if they form a linear array, then reading habits as well as changes in visual angle with number of items become issues.

11.1.2 *Typical Memory Scanning Data*

In Sternberg (1969b) we find a varied-set procedure involving the ten digits: $0, 1, \ldots, 9$. On each trial a positive set of from one to six digits was presented visually and sequentially at a rate of 1.2 sec/digit. Two seconds after the last positive item was completed, a warning signal occurred and it was followed by a test item. The response was to pull one of two levers corresponding to the test item being positive or negative. Average data for eight subjects are shown in Figure 11.2. These data are noteworthy in two ways. First, in sharp contrast to those from absolute identification (Section 10.2.1), MRT increases linearly with M, not with $\log M$. Second, the search time per item is the same for positive and negative items. The experiment, using both fixed- and varied-set presentation and using visual search as well as memory scanning designs, has been repeated by many researchers, all finding basically the same result: linear growth with the same rate, about 40 msec per item, independent of whether the item is positive or negative. These are robust results. A review of the earlier studies can be found in Nickerson (1972).

A recent study by Hockley (1984) compared memory and visual search tasks in the following way. He fitted the distributional data by the ex-Gaussian distribution (Section 3.2.1 and Appendix B.2), and then plotted the three parameters, μ and σ of the Gaussian and λ of the exponential, as a function of set size, separating positive and negative cases. In the visual search, the slope of μ with number of items was about 70 msec/item for positive ones and 90 for negative ones, whereas σ and λ had much smaller slopes, under 30 msec/item. By contrast, in memory search μ and σ showed little change, less than 12 msec/item, and λ was greater than 30 msec/item. It is unclear exactly what interpretation to give to these result since the ex-Gaussian distribution is ad hoc, with no theoretical basis. There is an additional empirical concern, as S. Sternberg (personal communication) has noted: these data are unusually variable, with a standard deviation $2\frac{1}{2}$ times greater than Sternberg found in comparable data.

11.2 THE SERIAL, EXHAUSTIVE SEARCH MODEL

11.2.1 The Model

Sternberg (1966) proposed the following, now classical, account of these data. Suppose the items in memory are coded serially. The items are drawn

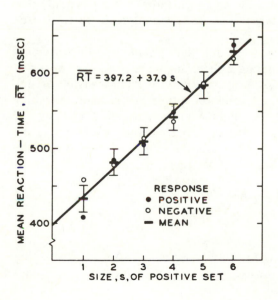

FIG. 11.2 MRT versus the size of the memory (or positive) set in a memory search design described in text. The data are averaged over eight subjects, for a total of about 95 observations per point. Standard errors of the means are shown by vertical bars. [Figure 1 of Sternberg (1966); copyright 1966; reprinted by permission.]

singly from memory, compared with the code of the test item, and so on until the memory is exhausted. Each comparison either achieves an acceptable match or not. After exhausting the memory, the positive response is initiated if a match has occurred; otherwise, the negative response is initiated. The search is assumed to be serial in the sense that items are drawn from memory, compared, and a match is achieved or not prior to the next comparison. The search is exhaustive in the sense that the entire memory is exhausted before initiating a response. If the mean time per comparison is k, the mean residual time is r_0, and there are M items in memory, then

$$E(\mathbf{T}) = kM + r_0, \tag{11.1}$$

independent of the test item. As we noted, for these experiments k is in the neighborhood of 40 msec.

The assumption of a serial search of memory did not, at first, attract nearly as much attention as the assumption that the search is exhaustive. On the face of it, exhaustive search seems less efficient than a self-terminating one. For if it were self-terminating and assuming no correlation between the signal presented and the order in which memories are extracted, then when the test item is positive it will require on average $M/2$ comparisons to achieve a match. Thus, the prediction is that Eq. 11.1 will continue to hold for negative test items and

$$E(\mathbf{T}) = \tfrac{1}{2}kM + r_0 \tag{11.2}$$

would hold for positive ones. Note that the slope is half of that in Eq. 11.1. Accepting the serial assumption, the data seem to leave no choice—the search appears to be exhaustive rather than self-terminating. Certainly that is consistent with these data, but it is not, in fact, forced by them (see Section 11.3.1).

Sternberg (1969b, p. 444) suggested that the optimality argument could be made to favor exhaustive scanning if the scanning process were very fast compared to a process that yields an output exactly when a match occurs. This could happen, for example, if considerable time is consumed in passing from the scanning process to examining the counter that registers whether or not a match has occurred. If the switching time plus that of examining the counter is, on average, h, then instead of Eqs. 11.1 and 11.2 we have for the exhaustive search

$$E(\mathbf{T}_E) = kM + h + r_0,$$

and for the self-terminating search

$$E(\mathbf{T}_{ST}) = \begin{cases} (k+h)M + r_0, \text{ for a negative test item,} \\ \tfrac{1}{2}(k+h)M + r_0, \text{ for a positive test item.} \end{cases}$$

Thus, on a positive item, if $k \ll h$,

$$E(\mathbf{T}_{ST}) - E(\mathbf{T}_E) \cong h(\tfrac{1}{2}M - 1),$$

which is positive for $M > 2$.

To demonstrate that this may really be the case, Sternberg ran a study just like the memory scanning one except that the subject was to report which item in memory was the immediate successor to the item that matched the test stimulus. The evidence supports a self-terminating search, but with a much slowed scanning rate of 124 msec per item, which means an actual rate of 248 msec per item, some six times slower than simple scanning.

11.2.2 Reactions to the SES Model

The attack on Sternberg's interpretation of his data has been intensive and sustained. It can be partitioned into three major phases that overlap in time. The first to appear consisted of experiments and data analyses intended to show that the SES model fails to give a satisfactory account of aspects of the data other than the simple means. This is taken up in Section 11.2.3. Second alternative models were proposed that are either not serial, or not exhaustive, or neither serial nor exhaustive but that give at least as satisfactory an account of the data. The role of these models has been to make clear that the serial, exhaustive search model is by no means uniquely forced by the original data. One of the principal features of some of these models has been to add another conceptual element to the modeling—the idea of limited capacity to carry out comparison processes. Some of these alternative models are discussed in Section 11.3. The third phase has been to study, as generally as possible, consequences of each of the three major conceptual building blocks of these mental models of memory. The first is the structure of the search process with the two most extreme cases being serial and parallel systems. The second is the nature of the termination of the search with the two simplest cases being exhaustive and self-terminating search. The third is the availability of resources (sometimes called capacity, other times attention) to each of the several comparisons that are being carried out. These distinctions are initially sharp but they become blurred in various ways. Nonetheless, the goal is, so far as possible, to see if we can devise differential predictions and appropriate experiments that allow us to make decisions about each aspect, more-or-less independently of the others. The most general results to date, which are taken up in Chapter 12, concern the structure of the search process.

11.2.3 Failures of Prediction

According to Townsend and Ashby (1983), four aspects of the data are inconsistent with the SES model. The first two arise simply as a result of additional analyses. The other two entail some, but not very major, changes in the experimental design.

The first is what happens to the variances. According to the serial exhaustive model and assuming that comparisons are independent of each other and of the residual processes, then for each test item whether in the memory set or not,

$$V(\mathbf{T}) = \sigma_C^2 M + \sigma_R^2,$$

where σ_C^2 is the variance attributable to a comparison and σ_R^2 is that of the residual process. (Even if there were correlations, the variance should not differ between positive and negative test items, unless the occurrence of a match were to alter the correlation.) The data are otherwise: the variance of the positive items grows more rapidly with M than does that of the negative items. For example, Schneider and Shiffrin (1977), using memory set sizes of 1, 2, and 4 symbols and independent of that choice a test display of 1, 2, or 4 symbols, showed a differential growth of variance occurs with the varied mapping procedure but not with the consistent one. Note that such a differential growth in variance is to be expected in a self-terminating model since for the positive items the number of comparisons, $\mathbf{K}$, required for termination is a random variable that adds to the total variance as

$$\sigma_C^2 E(\mathbf{K}) + k V(\mathbf{K}),$$

where k is the mean comparison time. Of course, these data do not imply self-terminating search; they merely cast doubt on the serial, exhaustive search model.

A second aspect of the data are the serial position curves; these are a further partition of the data by the location of the test item in the sequential presentation of the memory set. So for each memory size, there is a curve of MRT as a function of the serial position of the test item. According to the serial-exhaustive model, these curves should be flat, with the larger memory sets being slower than the smaller ones. The same prediction is true of the serial, self-terminating model if the memory is accessed randomly, but not if it is retrieved according to the order of presentation. Sternberg reported flat curves, but a number of other authors have found recency effects (Atkinson, Holmgren, & Juola, 1969; Clifton & Birenbaum, 1970; Corballis, 1967; Morin, De Rosa, & Stultz, 1967; Morin, De Rosa, & Ulm, 1967; Townsend & Roos, 1973). Sternberg (1969b) suggested that it may be due to highly rapid presentations of both the items in the memory set and the test item. Nonetheless, there surely are circumstances when the serial-exhaustive model breaks down.

A slight modification of the visual search design is to include more than one copy of the target item in the search list. The finding is that MRT decreases with increased numbers of replicas of the target items (Bjork & Estes, 1971; Baddeley & Ecob, 1973; Van der Heijden & Menckenberg, 1974). No such effect is predicted by the original serial-exhausitive model.

By itself, this effect can be incorporated into the model simply by supposing target items are processed more rapidly than nontarget items, which could occur if features are compared and a sufficient number of feature matches leads to a match (see Section 11.4.2). For if k_T is the mean target time, k ($>k_T$) is the mean nontarget time, and τ the number of targets, we see

$$E(\mathbf{T}) = k_T\tau + k(M - \tau) + r_0$$
$$= kM + (k_T - k)\tau + r_0.$$

The effect is to alter the intercept, but it does not alter the common value of the slope for target and nontarget items.

Townsend and Ashby (1983, Chapter 7) suggested that a way around these problems is to use designs with τ targets and M items in memory and to vary (τ, M) so that the mean number of items searched to the first target—namely, $(M + 1)/(\tau + 1)$—is a constant. So, for example, $(1, 3)$, $(2, 5)$, and $(3, 7)$ all have a mean of 2. Under self-termination the mean time to respond on target trials is

$$\left[\frac{M + 1}{\tau + 1} - 1\right]k + k_T = \left[\frac{M - \tau}{\tau + 1}\right]k + k_T,$$

which is constant. By contrast, under serial exhaustive search the times are

$$(M - \tau)k + \tau k_T.$$

If $(M + 1)/(\tau + 1) = C$, then $M - \tau = (C - 1)(\tau + 1)$, and so the serial exhaustive search time can be rewritten as

$$\tau[k_T + (C - 1)k] + (C + 1)k,$$

which is not constant. To my knowledge, this experiment has not yet been performed.

The first modification that raises problems about the serial aspect of the model is to present the search set of a visual search experiment in a circular rather than a linear array (Egeth, Jonides, & Wall, 1972; Gardner, 1973; Van der Heijden & Menckenberg, 1974). This design change greatly reduces the slope of the MRT versus M curve, even being flat in some cases. This means either that the model is wrong or that, under these display conditions, the scanning rate is incredibly fast.

11.3 ALTERNATIVE MODELS

This section is devoted to specific models intended to account for at least as much of the data as the serial, exhaustive search model. In addition to the serial or parallel, self-terminating or exhaustive, and various capacity models we discussed below, several others of a similar nature have appeared in the literature. Many of these are due to Townsend with various collaborators, and they are summarized in Chapters 6 and 7 of Townsend and Ashby (1983). Included are a self-terminating model in which the scanning rate is not constant, an exhaustive model in which the scanning rate differs for positive and negative items, a broad class of serial self-terminating models that is rejected by the data (Townsend and Roos, 1973), and an experimental design intended to force self-terminating behavior and so to permit a choice between serial and parallel models (Taylor, Townsend, and Sudevan, 1978).

11.3.1 A Serial, Self-Terminating Search Model: Push-Down Stack

The first, and perhaps best known, of these alternative models is a serial self-terminating search model developed by Falmagne and Theios (1969), Theios and Smith (1972), Theios, Smith, Haviland, Traupman, and Moy (1973), and Theios (1973). It is called a push-down stack model and it demonstrates that exhaustive search is not a necessary consequence of the data even if the search is assumed to be serial. Memory search is assumed to be ordered from top to bottom, it is serial, and it is self-terminating. Memory acquisition is push down in character, with two major exceptions. First, if an item is presented that is already in memory, say at location i, then instead of there being two representations of it, one at $i+1$ and the new one at 1, there is a single representation at j, where $1 \leq j \leq i$. The items previously at $j, j+1, \ldots, i-1$ each move down one level: $j+k$ to $j+k+1$. Second, the lowest level of memory is identified with long-term memory. Unlike the other levels, which can hold only a single item, long-term memory holds many. It is searched only after the other levels have been searched. A major difference from the Sternberg model is the assumption that all items presented enter the memory stack, so it includes both positive and negative items, labeled accordingly.

Since the model is serial and self-terminating, it predicts the same linear relation for both positive and negative items provided they are presented with the same probability. Moreover, because of its built-in assumption about the effect of repetitions and the push-down character, it admits sequential effects.

11.3.2 Comparison of Serial-Exhaustive and Self-Terminating Models

One notable difference between the two models, as stated, is that the push-down model is greatly influenced by the probability of a stimulus being presented. Theios et al. (1973) investigated this in an experiment designed to unconfound presentation probability and set size. In their design the positive and negative sets, consisting of digits, were of the same size and varied from one to five. Except for the case of one item, presentation probabilities were varied according to the same pattern in both sets. At each set size, presentation probability had comparable effects for both positive and negative items. For example, in going from 30% to 5% in set size 3, the MRT increased about 80 msec. Using an analysis of variance, the effects were significant. In addition, at each probability level there was an effect of set size. Various versions of the push-down stack model were simulated and fit to the data quite successfully. However, the exhaustive model is also able to account for them, with more parameters, by assuming that the encoding process depends upon the presentation probability.

In this study no significant interaction between presentation probability and set size was found. None is predicted by the exhaustive model and although a correlation is predicted by the self-terminating model, it was too small to be seen. Theios and Walter (1974) repeated Sternberg (1967b), and they did find a significant interaction. Snodgrass (1972) also presented data favoring self-terminating over exhaustive search (see Section 12.3.4).

In a still unpublished paper, however, Sternberg (1973) raised distributional arguments against the self-terminating serial models. Assume that N stimuli, presented equally often, are in the buffer. Let $F_i(t)$ be the probability distribution that it takes time t to search for and respond to an item when it is in memory location i—this is assumed to depend on the location, but not on the particular item in store. The main assumption made about these distributions is that they are ordered by their location, later ones taking longer than earlier ones: for all $t > 0$ and all $j < k$,

$$F_j(t) \geq F_k(t). \tag{11.3}$$

Next, let α_{ij} be the probability of item i being located at memory site j. Since every item is somewhere and every location is filled,

$$\sum_{i=1}^{N} \alpha_{ij} = \sum_{j=1}^{N} \alpha_{ij} = 1. \tag{11.4}$$

Now let $G_{i,N}(t)$ denote the probability distribution of a response to item i when N states are involved, and let G_N denote the average distribution. Then,

$$G_{i,N}(t) = \sum_{j=1}^{N} \alpha_{ij} F_j(t)$$

and

$$G_N(t) = \frac{1}{N} \sum_{i=1}^{N} \alpha_{ij} F_i(t)$$

$$= \frac{1}{N} \sum_{i=1}^{N} \sum_{j=1}^{N} \alpha_{ij} F_j(t)$$

$$= \frac{1}{N} \sum_{j=1}^{N} \left(\sum_{i=1}^{N} \alpha_{ij} \right) F_j(t)$$

$$= \frac{1}{N} \sum_{i=1}^{N} F_i(t). \tag{11.5}$$

It is interesting that G_N does not depend upon the α_{ij}.

Now, suppose $M < N$, then by Eq. 11.5,

$$MG_M(t) = \sum_{j=1}^{M} F_j(t)$$

$$\leq \sum_{j=1}^{N} F_j(t)$$

$$= NG_N. \tag{11.6}$$

Sternberg called this the short-RT property. Note that its derivation does not depend upon Eq. 11.3, but merely on Eq. 11.5 and $F_j(t) \geq 0$.

To derive the long-RT property, suppose $0 < M < N$. From Eq. 11.3, we know that for $j \leq M$, $F_j \geq F_{M+1}$, so

$$G_M = \frac{1}{M} \sum_{j=1}^{M} F_j$$

$$\geq \frac{1}{M} \sum_{j=1}^{M} F_{M+1}$$

$$= F_{M+1}.$$

And for $M+1 \leq j$,

$$G_M \geq F_{M+1} \geq F_j.$$

Using these two inequalities, we see that

$$G_N = \frac{1}{N} \sum_{j=1}^{N} F_j$$

$$= \frac{1}{N} \left(\sum_{j=1}^{M} F_j + \sum_{j=M+1}^{N} F_j \right)$$

$$\leq \frac{M}{N} F_{M+1} + \frac{N-M}{N} F_{M+1}$$

$$\leq G_M. \tag{11.7}$$

Combining Eqs. 11.6 and 11.7,

$$\frac{N}{M} G_N(t) \geq G_M \geq G_N.$$

Sternberg tested this prediction using $N = 4$, $M = 2$, and $N = 8$, $M = 2$, so

$$2G_4 \geq G_2 \geq G_4 \quad \text{and} \quad 4G_8 \geq G_2 \geq G_8,$$

in a study of the absolute identification of digits. As we would anticipate, MRT was linear with $\log N$. The long-RT property was satisfied, but the short-RT property was grossly violated. He also applied the method to memory scanning data, and again rejected the serial, self-termination hypothesis.

11.3.3 A Parallel, Exhaustive Search, Capacity Reallocation Model

Atkinson, Holmgren, and Juola (1969) and, independently, Townsend (1969, 1974) proposed the following parallel, exhaustive search model to account for Sternberg's data. Suppose the test item is simultaneously compared with the M items stored in memory. The assumption is that the hazard function $h_i(t)$ of the ith comparison represents the part of some finite total capacity that is devoted to that activity. Let v denote the total, then the assumption is that

$$\sum_i h_i(t) = v. \qquad (11.8)$$

As we know (Theorem 2.3), in a race among independent processes the hazard function to the first completion is the sum of the individual hazard functions, and so is v. When that first completion occurs, it is assumed that the capacity is then redistributed among the remaining $M-1$ alternatives, at which point the process continues as a race between $M-1$ independent process with overall hazard function v. This repeats until all M comparisons have been completed. Thus, the overall time to complete the memory search, which since it is exhaustive is independent of whether the test item is positive or negative, is gamma distributed with parameters M and v. The mean is, of course, M/v.

Note that because of the reallocation, the random variables describing the overall times for each comparison are not independent. Sternberg (1966) showed that no independent, parallel model with fixed distributions for the processes can yield a time proportional to M. If, however, the distributions are allowed to depend upon M, then, as Townsend (1974) has shown by example, it is possible to get the desired prediction.

These models share the weakness of the serial, exhaustive search model in being unable to account for serial position effects and incorrectly predicting the variances to grow linearly with M.

11.3.4 An Optimal, Capacity-Reallocation Model

During World War II a theory of optimal search (for submarines) was developed (Koopman, 1956a, b, 1957; see Stone, 1975, for a more recent review). Shaw and Shaw (1977) and Shaw (1978) proposed to adopt it as a psychological theory. Basically, the model assumes that attention is allocated over time to several possible locations as in Eq. 11.8. If the target is in location i, it is assumed that the probability of a response—namely, spotting the target—by time t, has the distribution corresponding to the hazard function $h_i(t)$; that is, by Eq. 1.8,

$$F_i(t) = 1 - \exp\left[-\int_0^t h_i(x)\,dx\right]$$

$$= 1 - \exp[-H_i(t)], \qquad (11.9)$$

where

$$H_i(t) = \int_0^t h_i(x)\, dx.$$

Stone (1975, Theorem 2.25) showed the following. Suppose the cost of the search is proportional to the effort expanded, that is, to total capacity

$$H(t) = \sum_{i=1}^N H_i(t);$$

and, for each i, the detection function $f_i(t)$ is what he calls regular—namely, it is 0 if $H_i(t) = 0$ and $F_i'(t) = h_i(t) \exp[-H_i(t)]$ is continuous, positive, and strictly decreasing. Then there is an allocation function $\vec{h}^*(t) = [h_1^*(t), h_2^*(t), \ldots, h_N^*(t)]$ of capacity that is uniformly optimal in the sense that for any other allocation function $\vec{h}(t)$ meeting the cost requirement, the probabilities of detection satisfy

$$F_i(t, \vec{h}^*) \geq F_i(t, \vec{h}). \tag{11.10}$$

Since, by Feller (1966, p. 148), for any random variable $\mathbf{T}_i$ with distribution F_i,

$$E[\mathbf{T}_i(\vec{h})] = \int_0^\infty [1 - F_i(t, \vec{h})]\, dt,$$

it follows immediately from Eq. 11.10 that

$$E[\mathbf{T}_i(\vec{h}^*)] \leq E[\mathbf{T}_i(\vec{h})],$$

that is, the uniformly optimal search also minimizes expected search time. This simultaneous optimization of two variables, which we do not normally expect, arises in this case because cost is proportional to h_i, which is functionally related to response time.

Shaw erred in thinking that Eq. 11.9 insured that F_i would be concave down, as is needed for Stone's theorem to apply. It has to be an added assumption.

Assume that detection is exponential—that is, for some t_0,

$$H_i(t) = v_i t, \qquad t \geq t_0, \tag{11.11}$$

where v_i is the capacity allocated to the search in location i, and assume that total capacity is constant,

$$\sum_{i=1}^N v_i = v. \tag{11.12}$$

Suppose the alternatives have been numbered so that the prior probabilities of target location are $P_1 \geq P_2 \geq \cdots \geq P_N$, and let t_i be the first time that the prior probability equals the posterior probability of the region i being searched (i.e., a region i is searched at time t if $h_i(t) > 0$). Then it can be shown (Stone, 1975, p. 55) that $t_1 \leq t_2 \leq \cdots \leq t_N$ and that the optimal allocation function satisfies for $i \leq j$ and $t > t_j$

$$P_j e^{-H_j(t)} = P_i e^{-H_i(t)}. \tag{11.13}$$

From this it follows (Shaw, 1978, Appendix B; see Section 11.3.5) that the expected time to discovery of a target at location j is given by

$$E(\mathbf{T}_j) = \frac{1}{v} \left[\sum_{i=1}^{j} \frac{P_i}{P_j} + \sum_{i=j+1}^{N} \left(1 - \ln \frac{P_j}{P_i} \right) \right]. \tag{11.14}$$

For the experiment to which she applied the model, there were two levels of prior probability, P_a and P_b, $P_a \geq P_b$, with n_a locations having probability P_a and n_b with probability P_b. In that case, it follows from Eq. 11.14 that

$$\frac{1}{v} = [E(\mathbf{T}_a) - E(\mathbf{T}_b)] / [n_a(1 - P_a/P_b) + n_b \ln P_b/P_a], \tag{11.15}$$

and so one test of the model is to estimate $1/v$ from different choices of P_a and P_b. In such an experiment Shaw (1978) found satisfactory agreement for 10 of 14 subjects.

In terms of the memory search experiment we see that the model is self-terminating, but it is neither serial nor parallel, but rather hierarchal. It predicts a linear growth with the number of items because when the target locations are equally likely—that is, $P_i = 1/N$, the term $\ln P_j/P_i$ of Eq. 11.14 drops out and so $E(T_j) = N/v$. Adding a residual time yields the linear relation. Note that no serial position effect is predicted. As it stands, the model does not deal with the absence of a target.

*11.3.5   Proof of Eq. 11.14

The following proof is taken from Appendix B of Shaw (1978):

$$E(\mathbf{T}_j) = \int_0^\infty t F_j'(t) \, dt$$

$$= \int_0^\infty t h_j(t) \exp[-H_j(t)] \, dt \qquad \text{(Eq. 11.9)}$$

$$= \frac{1}{v} \int_0^\infty \sum_{i=1}^{N} H_i(t) h_j(t) \exp[-H_j(t)] \, dt \qquad \text{(Eqs. 11.11, 11.12)}$$

$$= \frac{1}{v} \sum_{i=1}^{N} G_{ij},$$

where

$$G_{ij} = \int_0^\infty H_i(t) h_j(t) \exp[-H_j(t)] \, dt.$$

We evaluate G_{ij}. First, suppose $i \leq j$, then for $t \leq t_j$ we know by definition of

t_j that $h_j(t) = 0$ and for $t > t_j$ by Eq. 11.13 that

$$\exp[-H_j(t)] = (P_i/P_j) \exp[-H_i(t)].$$

Differentiating and substituting,

$$G_{ij} = \frac{P_i}{P_j} \int_{t_j}^{\infty} H_i(t) h_i(t) \exp[-H_i(t)] \, dt$$

$$= \frac{P_i}{P_j} \int_{u(t_j)}^{u(\infty)} \ln u \, du, \qquad \text{where } u = \exp[-H_i(t)]$$

$$= \frac{P_i}{P_j} [u \ln u - u]_{u(t_j)}^{u(\infty)}.$$

Observe that for $t > t_N$, $H_i(t) = vt/N$, so $u(\infty) = 0$ and

$$u(t_j) = \exp[-H_i(t_j)] = (P_j/P_i) \exp[-H_j(t_j)] = P_j/P_i.$$

Substituting,

$$G_{ij} = 1 - \ln(P_j/P_i).$$

Next, suppose $i > j$; then for $t < t_i$, $h_i(t) = 0$ and so

$$G_{ij} = \int_{t_i}^{\infty} H_i(t) h_j(t) \exp[-H_j(t)] \, dt$$

$$= \frac{P_i}{P_j} [u \ln u - u]_{u(t_i)}^{u(\infty)}.$$

As before, $u(\infty) = 0$ and $u(t_i) = \exp[-H_i(t_i)] = \exp(-0) = 1$, so

$$G_{ij} = P_i/P_j.$$

Putting these two terms together yields Eq. 11.14.

11.3.6   A Parallel, Self-Terminating Search Based on a Continuous Random Walk

Perhaps the most sweeping theoretical model in this general area is the memory retrieval model of Ratcliff (1978). It assumes that whenever a person must compare a signal presented with items stored in memory, it is done by carrying out in parallel and independently as many searches as are needed. If a match is found in any of the searches, then all processing ceases and a match response is made. Assuming that, the only question is how an individual match is carried out.

Ratcliff assumed that it can be described as a continuous random walk of the type discussed in some detail in Section 9.2.1. Recall, there are four parameters: a diffusion rate m and variance σ^2, boundaries at 0 and a, and the starting point z. As was noted then, the analytic development of this model is surprisingly complete. Of course, when there are two classes of stimuli, those in the memory set and those not, we anticipate two diffusion rates—one positive and one negative—which Ratcliff denoted u and v, respectively. He assumed that σ^2 (which he symbolized by s^2) is the same for both. The original wrinkle introduced at this point, one that has given this model a great deal of flexibility, is that the rates are in fact random variables over otherwise identical trials. He initially assumed them to be Gaussian with means u and v and variance η^2. This added freedom is adequate to permit the model to mimic a great deal of somewhat surprising data. In his 1978 paper, he examined five sets of data, some old and some new, and was able to use the same values for the two variances for all of the experiments (of which I shall only mention one here and another in Section 11.4.4). Thus, in any particular experiment he had the four parameters u, v, z, and a, to which he added a mean residual time r_0 (he called it T_{er}).

As an aside, let me mention his somewhat unusual way of fitting the model to data. As we know, this is a delicate matter when we study response distributions. For example, fitting the moments of, say, the response-time distribution, to the empirical moments is not usually a very good idea if more than the first two moments are involved. The reason is that increasingly they become dominated by a very few observations in the tails because their values are being raised to powers ≥ 3, and so these estimates simply are not very stable quantities. The major alternative is to attempt some sort of smoothing of the expirical histogram, and then fit the theory to the smoothed data. The two most common ways of doing that are to run the histogram through some sort of weighted averaging or to approximate it by a spline (see Section 3.2.5). Rather than that, Ratcliff took seriously the fact that, for reasons unknown, the ex-Gaussian—the convolution of an exponential with a Gaussian—fits response-time distributions well. This was demonstrated in Section 3.2.1, although it is equally clear that for weak signals it is a poor approximation since its hazard function is increasing whereas the data indicate that it must be increasing and then decreasing to a constant (Sections 4.1 and 4.4). In any event, he did optimal fits of this three-parameter family to the data, and then he fitted the random walk model to that approximation. The danger in this approach is having data not well fitted by the Ex-Gaussian; the fit must be verified each time the technique is used.

It is not intuitively obvious that this model can reproduce the Sternberg results for mean times. To check that, Ratcliff (1978) ran a memory set-size experiment resulting in typical data shown in Figure 11.3. Of course, in fitting his model many more parameters are involved than the two needed for an SES model. But it is equally true that with these parameters one accounts for far, far more data than just the means. For example, the predicted values for the response-time distributions to correct responses are shown in Figure 11.4. The fit is clearly very satisfactory. The same cannot be said for the error distributions, since the model predicts far more long times than are observed. Whether this is a serious criticism of the model is not

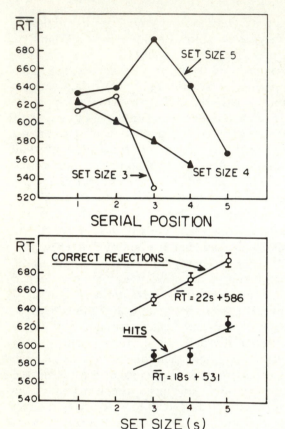

FIG. 11.3 MRT versus serial position and set size for Ratcliff's memory set-size experiment. Each of two observers contributed 1280 observations per set size. One standard deviation error bars are shown. [Figure 13 of Ratcliff (1978); copyright 1978; reprinted by permission.]

clear. Ratcliff claimed not, arguing that the prediction rests largely on the form of the tails of the Gaussian governing the rate of information accumulation. By simulating the process, he showed that a somewhat truncated Gaussian, in which the tail probability is spread about as a uniform distribution over the center of the empirical distribution, had the appropriate properties.

11.3.7 *Distributive Memory Model*

Anderson (1973) pointed out that the estimated memory-search rate of 30–40 msec per item arising from the serial search models is simply too fast, given what is known about neural switching times, to make plausible the existence of a detailed item-by-item comparison. He suggested instead a quite different type of model for the memory involved, one derived from his earlier discussions of the nature of long-term memory (Anderson, 1970,

1972). For more recent developments, see Anderson, Silverstein, Ritz, and Jones (1977), Hinton and Anderson (1982), Kohonen (1977), and Levy, Anderson, and Lehmkuhle (1984).

Memory is assumed to draw upon some large number K of individual neural systems in the following fashion. Each signal s_i results in a characteristic pattern of activity over these systems. If we assume the level (this

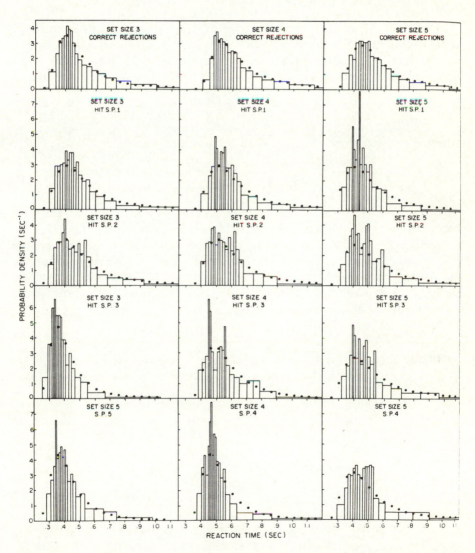

FIG. 11.4 Response-time distributions fit by the memory retrieval model for the data of Figure 11.3. [Figure 15 of Ratcliff (1978); copyright 1978; reprinted by permission.]

could be a voltage or a firing rate) of activity on subsystem k is f_{ik}, then the signal is represented by the vector

$$\vec{f}_i = (f_{i1}, f_{i2}, \ldots, f_{iK}).$$

The memory of a series of presentations $s_1, s_2, \ldots, s_M$ is simply a weighted sum of these vectors

$$\vec{M} = \sum_{i=1}^{M} C_i \vec{f}_i = \left(\sum_{i=1}^{M} C_i f_{ij}, \ldots, \sum_{i=1}^{M} C_i f_{iK} \right). \qquad (11.16)$$

At first glance, it appears that all the information about an individual signal is lost by summing over all of them. This, however, is not as severe as it seems. To take an extreme case, suppose all signals, both in the memory set and in the distractor set, have orthogonal representations in the sense that

$$\vec{f}_i \cdot \vec{f}_j = \sum_k f_{ik} f_{jk} = \begin{cases} P, & \text{if } i = j, \\ 0, & \text{if } i \neq j, \end{cases} \qquad (11.17)$$

where $\cdot$ denotes inner product. Then we see that

$$\vec{f}_j \cdot \vec{M} = \sum_i C_i f_j \cdot f_i = \begin{cases} C_j P, & \text{if } s_j \text{ is in the memory set,} \\ 0, & \text{if } s_j \text{ is not in memory set.} \end{cases} \qquad (11.18)$$

This model implies that a correct recognition, although not an absolute identification, can be based upon the calculation of the scalar $\vec{f}_j \cdot \vec{M}$.

Anderson generalized this property by supposing that the stimuli actually form a random sample from a population of stimuli whose representations are generated by independent selections from K independent random variables $\mathbf{f}_k$. In addition to the independence assumptions, several somewhat inessential ones are made:

$$E(\mathbf{f}_k) = 0 \qquad \text{and} \qquad V(\mathbf{f}_k) = \sigma^2. \qquad (11.19)$$

It follows that if $\vec{\mathbf{f}}_i$ and $\vec{\mathbf{f}}_j$ are independent selections so that $\mathbf{f}_{ik}$ and $\mathbf{f}_{jk}$, $k = 1, \ldots, K$, are mutually independent random variables, then using Eq. 11.19.

$$E(\vec{\mathbf{f}}_i \cdot \vec{\mathbf{f}}_j) = \sum_{k=1}^{K} E(\mathbf{f}_{ik} \mathbf{f}_{jk}) = \sum_{k=1}^{K} E(\mathbf{f}_{ik}) E(\mathbf{f}_{jk}) = 0,$$

$$E(\vec{\mathbf{f}}_i \cdot \vec{\mathbf{f}}_i) = \sum_{k=1}^{K} E(\mathbf{f}_{ik}^2) = \sum_{k=1}^{K} V(\mathbf{f}_{ik}) = K\sigma^2.$$

Thus,

$$E(\vec{\mathbf{f}}_j \cdot \vec{\mathbf{M}}) = \sum_i C_i E(\mathbf{f}_j \cdot \mathbf{f}_i) = \begin{cases} C_j K\sigma^2 & \text{if } s_j \text{ is in memory set,} \\ 0 & \text{otherwise.} \end{cases} \qquad (11.20)$$

Anderson estimated a signal-to-noise ratio for this process, but following my previous practice I shall compute d'. We need to know the variance of the criterion variable when a random signal not in the memory set is presented. Suppose its representation is $\vec{\tilde{g}}$. Then using independence freely,

$$E(\vec{\tilde{g}} \cdot \vec{M}) = \sum_{i=1}^{M} C_i E(\vec{\tilde{g}} \cdot \vec{f}_i) = 0 \qquad \text{(using Eq. 11.19)}$$

$$V(\vec{\tilde{g}} \cdot \vec{M}) = \sum_{i=1}^{M} C_i^2 V(\vec{\tilde{g}} \cdot \vec{f}_i). \tag{11.21}$$

Observe,

$$V(\vec{\tilde{g}} \cdot \vec{f}_i) = \sum_{k=1}^{K} V(\mathbf{g}_k \mathbf{f}_{ik})$$

$$= \sum_{k=1}^{K} [E(\mathbf{g}_k^2 \mathbf{f}_{ik}^2) - E(\mathbf{g}_k \mathbf{f}_{ik})^2]$$

$$= \sum_{k=1}^{K} [E(\mathbf{g}_k^2) E(\mathbf{f}_{ik}^2) - E(\mathbf{g}_k)^2 E(\mathbf{f}_{ik})^2] \qquad \text{(Theorem 1.2)}$$

$$= \sum_{k=1}^{K} \sigma^4 \qquad \text{(using Eq. 11.19)}$$

$$= K\sigma^4.$$

So

$$V(\vec{\tilde{g}} \cdot \vec{M}) = K\sigma^4 \sum_{i=1}^{M} C_i^2. \tag{11.22}$$

For simplicity, assume $C_i = C$, then

$$V(\vec{\tilde{g}} \cdot \vec{M}) = K\sigma^4 M C^2. \tag{11.23}$$

On this assumption, we may calculate d' from Eqs. 11.19, 11.21, and 11.23,

$$d' = \frac{CK\sigma^2 - 0}{K^{1/2}\sigma^2 M^{1/2} C} = \left(\frac{K}{M}\right)^{1/2}. \tag{11.24}$$

Thus performance grows as the square root of the number of neuronal systems dedicated to memory and inversely as the square root of the number of items in the memory.

To get a reaction-time prediction, Anderson simply postulated that $E(\mathbf{T})$ is linear with the number of items in memory, the rationale apparently having to do with the summing operations to form M. To my mind, this does not seem at all sensible. After all, the memory is formed prior—in some experiments a long time prior—to the presentation of the test item, whereas response time is measured from that point. According to the model, the subject calculates $\vec{\tilde{g}} \cdot \vec{M}$ and that calculation clearly depends upon K but not obviously on M. There is a way out; however, it is quite ad hoc. If we are dealing with short-term memory, perhaps the subject is able, up to a point, to dedicate increasing numbers of neuronal systems to the task as the memory load is increased. In particular, if it is done so that the error rate is

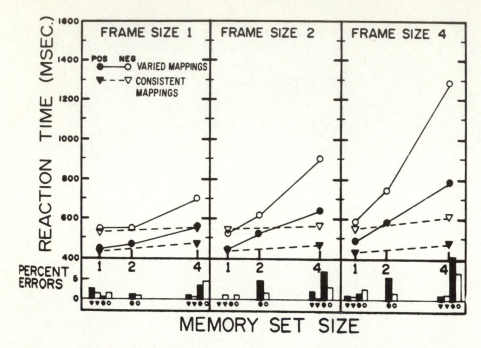

FIG. 11.5 MRT versus memory set size for varied and consistent mappings. Each data point is based on a sample size of 60 from each of two subjects. Note that the consistent mapping leads to the faster search (smaller slope). [Figure 5 of Schneider and Shiffrin (1977); copyright 1977; reprinted by permission.]

fixed—that is, d' is constant—then by Eq. 11.24, $K = (d')^2 M$, whence

$$E(\mathbf{T}) = aK + r_0$$
$$= a(d')^2 M + r_0,$$

which produces the Sternberg result.

Observe that this model automatically exhibits no impact of memory set size on $E(\mathbf{T})$ once K reaches its maximum value, which presumably is not large for short-term memory and is large but possibly not flexible for long-term memory. Figure 11.5 shows data of Schneider and Shiffrin (1977) in which MRT is examined for both varied- and consistent-set procedures. MRT changes very little for the consistent procedure, as would be expected if the memory set is in long-term store, and increases appreciably for the varied-set procedure.

These ideas are very attractive for recognition, but they do not automatically generalize to absolute identification so far as I can see.

11.4 SAME-DIFFERENT EXPERIMENTS

Perhaps the simplest version of the memory search task is one in which the memory set includes just one stimulus (which may, in fact, consist of a string of items such as letters), and the task is to decide whether the test stimulus is the same as or different from the memorized stimulus. Since this is a two-stimulus, two-response design, it logically belongs in Chapter 6. However, the fact that in general the stimuli consist of L distinct items such as letters or digits and that some sort of search is assumed to be carried out over these items make it more appropriate to treat these experiments here. Because L, the length of the stimulus string, is often varied, some concern must be given to whether the stimuli are apprehended in a single fixation or not; presumably what goes on within a glance differs from what happens in shifting from one portion of the stimulus to another (Krueger, 1978).

11.4.1 The Basic Data

The experiment has been run in many variants and discussed by many people. The major references are: Bamber (1969a, b, 1972), Beller (1970), Burrows (1972), Egeth (1966), Eichelman (1970), Grill (1971), Krueger (1973, 1978), Krueger and Shapiro (1980, 1981), Nickerson (1965a, 1969, 1971, 1972), Posner and Mitchell (1967), Ratcliff and Hacker (1981), Silverman (1973), Silverman and Goldberg (1975), Taylor (1976a, b), and Tversky (1969). The four most conspicuous features of these data are:

1. On trials when the stimuli do not match and with L fixed, the MRT decreases with the number D of individual elements that differ. For example, if the memory stimulus is XBMF, then on average the response of "different" is faster to XPME than it is to XPMF.
2. On non-match trials, longer strings are slower than shorter ones. These two facts are illustrated in Figure 11.6.
3. The MRT when the "same" response is made is faster on average than when the "difference" response is made; indeed, in Bamber's data the former time is approximately the same as the fastest difference case—that is, when $D = L$. This can be seen by comparing Figure 11.6 with Figure 11.7. Krueger (1978, p. 290) reported that in the 57 experiments he found involving stimuli with just one element and for which times were reported, 35 exhibited faster "same" responses than "different" ones. However, at least one later study (Ratcliff & Hacker, 1981) demonstrated that this relation is affected by instructions and so, presumably, is under subject control.
4. The pattern of errors is also systematically related to the experimental parameters. In particular,

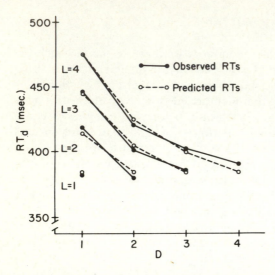

FIG. 11.6 MRT versus the number, *D*, of elements that differ in strings of length *L* in a same-different experiment. There were four subjects, each of whom contributed from 120 to 240 observations per point. The predicted values are from the serial, self-terminating model. [Figure 1 of Bamber (1969a); copyright 1969; reprinted by permission.]

(a) The probability of an error is larger when the response is "same" than when it is "different." Krueger (1978, p. 290) stated this was true in 42 of 65 single-element experiments that he examined.

(b) The probability of an error when the response is "different" increases with *L* and decreases with *D*. This is evident in Figure 11.8.

Two things are noteworthy. First, the rapidity of the "same" responses relative to the "different" ones is somewhat surprising since, after all, only one difference need be noted to warrant a "different" response whereas all elements must be identical to warrant a "same" response. Second, the facts

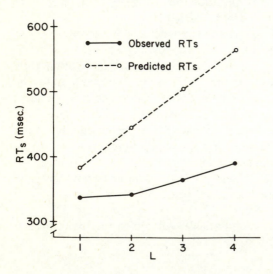

FIG. 11.7 MRT versus list length *L* for "same" responses of the experiment reported in Figure 11.6. Again there were four subjects, each of whom contributed from 240 to 540 observations per point. The predicted values are from the serial, self-terminating model. [Figure 2 of Bamber (1969a); copyright 1969; reprinted by permission.]

that both times and errors vary systematically with the nature of the stimulus—same or different—and with the experimental parameters L and D strongly suggest that a speed-accuracy tradeoff should flow naturally from any plausible model of the process.

11.4.2 Modified Error-Free Stage Models

The fact that for strings of fixed length L, MRT decreases with increasing numbers of different elements D suggests (but by no means proves) a self-terminating search process. Bamber (1969a) fit the serial self-terminating model to the different responses, with the satisfactory results we have already seen in Figure 11.6. Only two parameters are involved—a residual time of 384 msec, which seems a bit long, and a scan rate of 60 msec per item, which is 50% slower than that estimated by Sternberg. But the real problem is not these estimates but the fact that for each length L the model predicts the slowest search should be to stimulus pairs that match; that prediction is often grossly wrong (see Figure 11.7). In addition, the estimated scan rate has speeded up to 25 msec per item—more than twice as fast as the other estimate—which is an unhappy lack of invariance. And, of course, as is generally true of stage models, there is no place for errors. This model will not do.

Bamber suggested a two-process model in which, in addition to a relatively slow serial scan, there is a more rapid "identity" reporter. This will explain the data since it was designed to do so, but it is neither particularly plausible nor has it been shown to be a useful device for explaining other data. As Taylor (1976b) has noted, a device that can rapidly spot a match can presumably also rapidly spot a mismatch; it seems odd not to invoke it

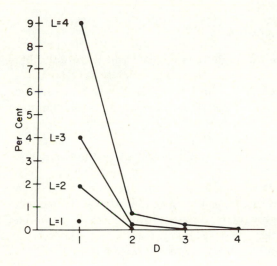

FIG. 11.8 Percentage of same responses to the non-matching stimuli versus the number D of mismatches and list length L for the experiment of Figure 11.6. The sample sizes are as in Figure 11.7 [Figure 4 of Bamber (1969a); copyright 1969; reprinted by permission.]

on all trials. Moreover, as Bamber (1972) showed, the results do not change if the match is conceptual (*A* and *a*) instead of identical (either *A* and *A* or *a* and *a*), which belies any sort of direct template comparisons.

Taylor (1976a) undertook a comprehensive survey of a variety of stage models that had arisen to that point. He (1976b) systematically attempted to fit each of these models to the data in Bamber's study as well as his replication of it and a variant in which the subject was to report either "all different" or "some different." Without going into the details of how he went about it, he found that a number of the models were suitable provided they were somehow modified to generate fast "same" responses. In particular, all acceptable models were self-terminating, and there was some evidence favoring parallel over serial models. Moreover, those favored exhibited limited capacity, one consequence of which is that the performance on one item is affected by what has happened on other items. But no model in its simple form gave a satisfactory account of the "same" data. To handle that, Taylor explored three modifications, two of which yielded identical predictions for the mean times. One was Bamber's fast identity reporter. Indistinguishable from it as far as MRTs are concerned is a decision bias that increases, by a constant factor, the decision times to items that differ. The third is a guessing model having the following features. After any identical item is compared and no mismatch has been found up to that point, there is a fixed probability that the entire process, whether serial or parallel, is terminated and the response "same" is emitted. (In the variant mentioned above, this guessing rule was applied to non-identical items but the guessed response is that all comparisons are different.) All three modifications were adequate to bring all of the partially acceptable models into approximate accord with the data. Again, as in Bamber's identity model, the add-on seems ad hoc and to be acceptable it must be useful in understanding a great deal of other data. So far, that has not been demonstrated.

11.4.3   *Serial, Exhaustive, Imperfect Search*

Krueger (1978) suggested a somewhat different approach to these data that blends the simple search ideas with some stochastic models developed for two-choice response times (Sections 8.2 and 8.3). His general qualitative assumptions are three. First, the process of comparing pairs of stimulus features is less than perfect, which places the decision system in a situation of selecting a response on the basis of a random variable—namely, the count of the number of mismatches of individual features (possibly stimulus items, but not necessarily). Second, the imperfection is asymmetric in the sense that the effect of "noise" is far more likely to change a match into a mismatch than vice-versa. This seems plausible since almost any change will corrupt a match whereas only highly selected ones convert a mismatch into a match. Third, because mismatches arise so easily from noise, the system must be designed to be conservative about reporting mismatches and so is likely to recheck the stimuli whenever a non-zero mismatch count occurs in an attempt to develop more certain evidence of an actual mismatch. In a sense, then, he assumed a random walk model on the number of mismatches.

Qualitatively, the model has the correct properties. It is slower on average when there is an actual mismatch because that condition generally leads to an observed mismatch and unless it is extreme, it is likely to be rechecked. In contrast, on those trials where the stimuli match and no observed mismatches occur, there will be no rechecking and so a certain fraction of the same responses are faster than most of the difference responses. It is built into the second assumption that there must be more errors when the pair is a match than when it is a mismatch. And with the number of items held fixed, the proportion of errors decreases with the number of mismatched items, D, because the conversion of an actual mismatch into a perceived match is more probable when the number of mismatches is smaller than when it is larger.

Let us make the model more specific. Let n denote the number of distinct features defining the stimulus for the subject. This is almost certainly not the number of letters in a stimulus—for example, Krueger assumed $n = 100$ when $L = 1$. Let d be the number of mismatched features among these n, so on trials when the pair is a match, $d = 0$. Assume that feature comparisons are statistically identical and independent, and let p denote the probability that a feature pair is incorrectly perceived—that is, either a match being a mismatch or the other way around. Symmetry is assumed here, but leads to overall asymmetry because $p \neq 1 - p$. Let $\mathbf{M}$ be the random variable that gives the total count of perceived mismatches. On these assumptions, for the match trials, the distribution of M is obviously the binomial

$$P(\mathbf{M} = m) = \binom{n}{m} p^m (1 - p)^{n-m}.$$

For trials with d actual mismatches, $\mathbf{M}$ can be thought of as the sum of the observed mismatches, $\mathbf{M}_d$, arising from the d mismatches and the observed mismatches, $\mathbf{M}_{n-d}$, arising from the $n - d$ matches. Each is again binomial:

$$P(\mathbf{M}_d = m) = \binom{d}{m}(1 - p)^m p^{d-m}$$

$$P(\mathbf{M}_{m-d} = m) = \binom{n-d}{m} p^m (1 - p)^{n-d-m}.$$

So the distribution of $\mathbf{M}$ is the convolution of these two distributions, which we do not need to write out explicitly.

For stimuli composed of a single letter, Krueger assumed $n = 100$ and he treated d and p as free parameters to be estimated from the data. For the random walk, he established barriers at values of $\mathbf{M}$ corresponding to likelihood ratios of 1 to 25 and 25 to 1. Whenever a rechecking occurred,

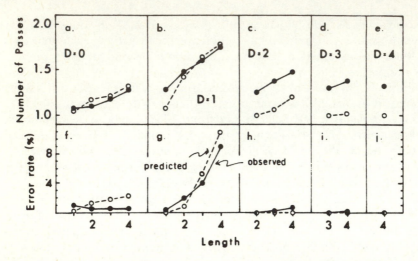

FIG. 11.9 Data and predictions for a replication of Bambers (1969a) experiment. The predicted values arise from a model in which mismatches tend to be rechecked (see text). I could not infer the sample sizes. [Figure 6 of Krueger (1978); copyright 1978; reprinted by permission.]

the several random variables were added and the boundaries were recomputed so as to maintain the same likelihood ratios. The parameter space was searched numerically. To compare the model with the response-time data, it is necessary to add another parameter, namely, the time equivalent for each cycle of comparisons of the several features. The choice varied from case to case, but in the one shown here it was chosen to be 125 msec per cycle. That choice was not part of the numerical parameter search. For stimuli with strings of L (≤ 4) letters, it was assumed that the entire stimulus consisted of $nL = 100L$ features. Letting D denote the number of letter mismatches, it was found that the value of p must vary considerably with D. Rather than estimate the number of feature mismatches and p separately for each D, he assumed that the former to be given by dD, where d is the value for a single mismatched letter, and that the latter, p, arises from a rather ad hoc formula I will not spell out.

Six distinct experiments, three involving $L = 1$ and the other three having values from $L = 1$ to 4, were reported. I present the data for just case 4, which replicates Bamber (1969). The fit of the model to both MRT and error data is shown in Figure 11.9. The major failing of the model is the underestimation of the response time for $D \geq 2$. Presumably this could have been greatly improved by making separate estimates of p, which reflects a change in the subject's criterion for what constitutes a match of a feature pair. The fit of the other data are comparable, and they certainly encourage further work on the model.

One prediction of the model, which is not made by either Bamber's or the several examined by Taylor but is widely true of the data, is that erroneous (i.e., same) responses to non-matched stimuli are actually slower than the correct responses. This presumably arises in the model because the count has hovered longer in the region of indeterminancy before the erroneous response is finally made, which can happen because of the asymmetry of distributions of steps in the random walk.

A variant on the Krueger model was proposed by Miller and Bauer (1981). The basic difference is that rechecking occurs not because found differences are suspected to be unreal, but because they may simply be irrelevant to the discrimination being made.

11.4.4   A Continuous Random Walk Model

Probably the most successful model to have been proposed so far is the parallel, self-terminating, continuous random walk model of Ratcliff (1978). It is similar in some ways to Krueger's model, but does not invoke a rechecking mechanism. The general model was described in Section 11.3.6 in connection with the memory scanning experiment. Its main features, it will be recalled, are that the memory is searched by independent, parallel processes; a response is initiated as soon as a match is established or, barring that, when all processes have been completed without finding a match; the individual processes are modeled by a continuous random walk in which the rate parameter is a random variable over trials, its mean value being larger the more similar two stimuli are; and the boundaries of the random walk are parameters adjusted by the subject to effect a speed-accuracy tradeoff.

In that first paper he fitted the model to several studies, including one from Ratcliff and Murdock (1976) in which subjects saw, and attempted to remember, 16 words and were tested with 32 words of which 16 were the memory set. The task for the subject was to identify which of the 32 words were "old" words from the memory set. A quite decent fit was provided by the model, as can be seen in Figures 11.10 and 11.11. (The plots of μ and τ in Figure 11.10 are the mean and time constant of the Gaussian and exponential whose convolution was fitted to the data.) He also accounted for the response-time distributions, which no other theory attempts to do, with the excellent results shown in Figure 11.12.

In subsequent papers he has repeatedly shown the flexibility of his model to account for data. For example, in 1981 he observed that of the major contenders neither Bamber nor Taylor could produce a SATF since in both models the mechanism for error is independent of that for time. Although Krueger's model could do so, as I mentioned earlier, it entailed the curious change in one of the parameters. And in Ratcliff (1981) he took up in detail some of the properties exhibited by order of presentation—which had been reported and modeled by Lee and Estes (1977, 1981)—and he was able to provide an account of them in terms of his random walk model.

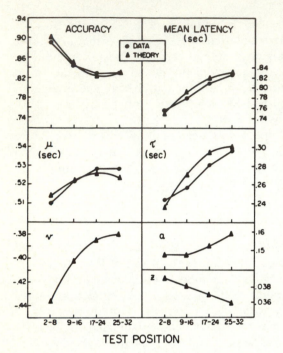

FIG. 11.10 Comparison of data from a memory search experiment of Ratcliff and Murdock (1976) in which 16 of 32 words were in the memory set with predictions from Ratcliff's memory retrieval model. In addition to accuracy and MRT versus serial position, the parameters μ and τ are the means of the Gaussian and exponential of the ex-Gaussian fit to the data, and v, a, and z are parameters of the diffusion model. Each of four subjects contributed 192 positive and 192 negative observations. [Figure 9 of Ratcliff (1978); copyright 1978; reprinted by permission.]

One of the more striking successes of the model was to account for the data from Ratcliff and Hacker (1981), who not only showed empirically that they could shift, by instructions, the temporal relation between "same" and "different" responses, but that there are some odd speed-accuracy effects. The study involved memory sets of four letters selected at random and without replacement from a set of 10 consonants. The test stimulus was also a set of four letters that involved replacing either 0, 1, 2, 3, or 4 of the letters of the memory set by other consonants from the 10. The two experimental conditions were: say "same" only when absolutely sure of a match, and say "different" only when absolutely sure of a non-match. With a sample size of about 575 per condition, the results were as shown in Table 11.1. I find two features of these data noteworthy. First, in the condition where the subject is instructed to be sure of the "same" response, the MRT on matching trials is slower than that for three of the four non-match conditions. And second, accuracy on matching trials was *poorer* when the subject was attempting to be sure—and presumably that means more accurate—in making a "same" response than when attempting to be sure in making a "different" response. The parallel result is true on non-match trials when the instructions are to be sure of the different response—times are longer and accuracy is reduced. This fact, which apparently is not contested, is not accounted for in any of the other models, including a verbally formulated one of Proctor (1981) and a modification of it by

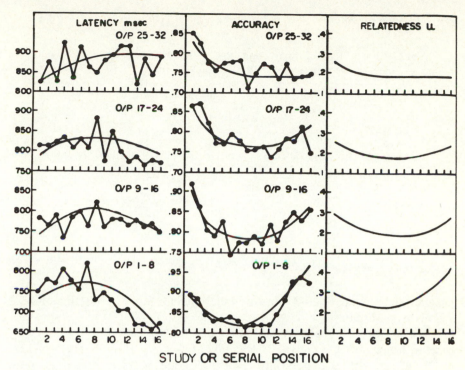

FIG. 11.11 Plots of MRT, accuracy, and a parameter of the model versus study position and partitioned according to the output position (O/P) for same experiment as Figure 11.10. [Figure 10 of Ratcliff (1978); copyright 1978; reprinted by permission.]

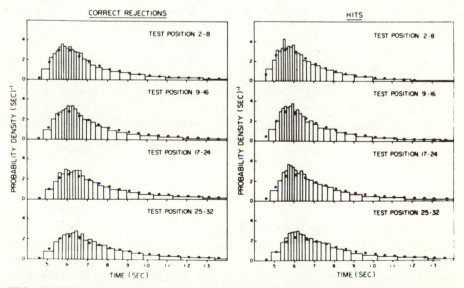

FIG. 11.12 For the same experiment as Figure 11.10, comparison of distributions and predictions of the memory retrieval model. [Figure 11 of Ratcliff (1978); copyright 1978; reprinted by permission.]

TABLE 11.1. Effect of instructions on MRT and percent correct in a Same-Different experiment (Ratcliff and Hacker, 1981)

Number of letters switched	Instruction			
	Sure of "same"		Sure of "different"	
	MRT (msec)	Percent correct	MRT (msec)	Percent correct
Match 0	573	.89	472	.97
1	605	.80	695	.65
2	517	.96	484	.89
3	480	.98	531	.94
4	461	.97	518	.97

Krueger and Shapiro (1981), but when the data are fitted by Ratcliff's model this arises naturally.

There has ensued a considerable debate (Proctor and Rao, 1982, 1983; Proctor, Rao, and Hurst, 1983; Ratcliff, 1984; and Ratcliff and Hacker, 1982), which, although not fully resolved, seems to have ended up with acceptance of the flexibility of Ratcliff's model to handle the data and acknowledgement of the difficulty that other models have with it. I believe that one reason it has taken so long to accept Ratcliff's model is the fact that it is not as well understood analytically as one would like. For example, we do not understand the hazard function of the first passage time, and it is difficult to get clear-cut predictions that one can seek to see in the data. Rather, this is a case where the only option seems to be to search the parameter space numerically for a best fit, and then the quality of the fit is demonstrated pictorially as we have seen above in Figures 11.10–11.12. I find it difficult to sense intuitively what properties the model will and will not exhibit. Perhaps additional theoretical work will illuminate it more completely, although since it is a classical, well-studied stochastic process it is hard to be optimistic about finding simple results.

11.5   CONCLUSIONS

The evidence is that the basic MRT data from all three types of matching experiments should be approached with considerable theoretical caution. The most obvious interpretation is surely not the only one and may very well be wrong. A complex tradeoff exists among at least three major ways in which the mind might be organized: (i) the pattern of memory search—serial and parallel being the two simplest cases—which conceivably may differ for overlearned versus just-learned stimuli; (ii) the nature of the stopping rule—

self-terminating and exhaustive being the simplest but others exist, such as Krueger's repeated checking of a mismatch; and (iii) the possibility, which is especially important in parallel systems, of shifting "mental resources" or capacity, as it is called, from a completed process to those not yet completed.

It should be clear at this point that MRT data from a single paradigm cannot lead to a clearcut decision among these possibilities. More of the response-time distributions than the mean should be explained by a model, SATFs should be studied explicitly, and tightly interlocked designs in which the same processes are used in different ways should be jointly explained by a theory. And, although there is little precedent for it in this literature, I suspect that sequential effects should be examined and accounted for. The next, and last, chapter examines some of the research that has resulted from attempts to understand how to make inferences about these three basic aspects of mental organization. It is quite astonishingly difficult to answer what seem to be the simplest and most basic questions about mental organization: Do we search memory serially or in parallel? When does a search stop? To what extent are mental resources shared and reallocated as they are no longer needed? These are the questions, and although we will understand better how to get at the first two, we are very far from having evolved ways to resolve them conclusively.

12

Processing Stages and Strategies

12.1 INTRODUCTION

Previously, especially in the preceding chapter, three general questions have arisen about models of mental processing. One is: may we think of the process as partitioned into distinct, autonomous stages of activity and, if so, what is the network that establishes the temporal relations among the stages? The second is: what strategy is followed in deciding when to respond, with the two extremes being exhaustive and self-terminating searches? And the third is: can processing capacity be reallocated when one stage is completed and others are still being processed? These interrelated questions have previously arisen in a variety of specific models. In addition, they have led to some quite general considerations about the equivalence of models and about experimental strategies to attempt to reach decisions about them. These more general considerations are our present topic.

In Section 12.2, I focus on the ability of serial and parallel models to mimic either an arbitrary response-time distribution or just one another. The results vary both in what is assumed to be observable and what is assumed about the process: for example, self-terminating or exhaustive, and the nature of the independence among stages. The upshot of that work is simple. It is virtually impossible to identify the network being used from just data on the distributions of response times in a single experiment; however, with data on intermediate completion times and on the order of completion of stages, neither of which is usually available, it is possible to reject some models. This failure has led to two distinct experimental strategies, which are outlined in Sections 12.3 and 12.4. The first of these involves running a series of closely related experiments based on a limited set of stimuli, and to demand that they be accounted for in a consistent way using the same set of underlying parameters (usually, mean latencies). The second is to confine attention to a single paradigm, but to introduce experimental manipulations designed to affect the stages differentially. The pattern of overall times as a function of the manipulations allows some inferences about the nature of the network involved.

A substantial fraction of the work covered in Sections 12.2 and 12.3 is due to J. T. Townsend together with students and collaborators. Anyone interested in these and related topics in greater detail than I shall treat them should consult the book by Townsend and Ashby (1983) and/or the original papers cited below.

12.2 SERIAL-PARALLEL EQUIVALENCES

12.2.1 General Nomenclature

If we are willing to suppose that information processing is carried out by distinct mechanisms that, under certain input conditions, do just one thing and then yield an output, we may schematically think of them as forming the nodes of a flow diagram in which the arrows represent precedence relations. The activity represented by a node is begun when and only when all of the nodes that feed into it have completed their tasks. This is the so-called "stage" conception of information processing. It is vaguely plausible if one thinks of the brain as highly compartmentalized, but many doubt if it is a good general model of processing. At a minimum, they argue, there may be substantial temporal overlap of function, with one stage beginning to operate on a partial output of another stage that has not fully completed its activities. One such theory, called cascade theory, was discussed in Section 4.3.2. We also note that the stage conception is not really consistent with most of the models that have been proposed for two-choice situations, in particular the various forms of information accumulation in Chapters 4, 8, and 9. Nonetheless, the stage conception has received the attention of many cognitive psychologists throughout the 1970s, and I shall report some of their results.

If the network of a process is a simple chain in which each node, except for the initial one, follows just one other, then the system is said to be *serial*. If the network is a fan of arrows from one node to all but one of the others and a reverse fan from these to the remaining one, it is called a *parallel* system. Suppose that the nodes are numbered $1, 2, \ldots, n$ and that the time from initiation to completion of the processing stage i is a random variable $\mathbf{T}_i$. A realization of $\mathbf{T}_i$ is referred to as the *actual processing time* of the stage. The distribution of $\mathbf{T}_i$ may depend upon aspects of the system other than the stage itself. In a serial system the time at which the ith stage is completed, assuming the nodes are numbered as they occur, is $\sum_{j=1}^{i} \mathbf{T}_i$. In a parallel system matters are far more complex since the order of completion of stages is not fixed in advance; it depends upon the actual realizations of the n random variables $\mathbf{T}_i$. In general, any order of completion can arise. Such an order is a permutation ρ of the set $\{1, 2, \ldots, n\}$ of indices for the stages. Let the associated completion times be denoted $\tau_1 \leq \tau_2 \leq \cdots < \tau_k < \cdots \tau_n$, where $\tau_k = \mathbf{T}_{\rho^{-1}(k)}$. We speak of

$$t_1 = \tau_1, \; t_2 = \tau_2 - \tau_1, \ldots, t_k = \tau_k - \tau_{k-1}, \ldots, t_n = \tau_n - \tau_{n-1}$$

as the *intercompletion times* of the parallel process. Obviously, one set of intercompletion times looks exactly like a realization of a serial process with nodes in the same order as the times. But the intercompletion times, except for the first one, are not the actual processing times of the nodes of the parallel system. Rather,

$$\tau_1 = t_1, \ \tau_2 = t_1 + t_2, \ldots, \tau_n = \sum_{j=1}^{n} t_j$$

are the actual processing times. In a serial system, the intercompletion times are identical to the actual processing times.

The reader should be alerted to a potential terminological confusion. I use the word "stage" to refer to a unitary processing activity occurring in an underlying network of nodes. My usage is consistent with that of Sternberg and his followers. In contrast, Townsend and his followers speak of such an activity as a "subsystem" or "subprocess," which is only a problem because they use the word "stage" to refer to something else—namely, the number identifying an intercompletion time. It thus refers not to any locus in the system, but to a defined random variable.

It is obvious, without any further analysis, that rigid serial and parallel systems cannot mimic each other at this level of detail. The reason is that the order of the one is invariant and that of the other depends upon the exact realizations of the random variables. But this is probably not a particularly relevant observation for two reasons. First, in many situations we simply do not have observational access to the order of completion and usually not to the intercompletion times themselves, but only to the overall time. This is certainly typical of most response-time studies treated in this book. Second, in many processing models we do not assume that the order of events in the serial system is rigidly determined to be the same trial after trial, in which case it is far less clear that the two processes are so distinct.

12.2.2 Mimicking Overall Decision Times

Consider any system where overall response time $\mathbf{T}$ has some distribution F. Can it be mimicked by either a serial or parallel system of n stages with exhaustive search? The answer is that it is trivial to do so using a serial system having perfectly correlated and identically distributed stages or with a parallel system having independent and identically distributed stages. There are infinitely many other ways of partitioning such a distribution into n stages. For the serial system, let the random variable of each of the n stages be $\mathbf{T}_i = \mathbf{T}/n$, in which case they are perfectly correlated and their distribution functions are

$$F_i(t) = \Pr(\mathbf{T}_i \leq t) = \Pr(\mathbf{T}/n \leq t) = \Pr(\mathbf{T} \leq nt) = F(nt).$$

Observe that

$$\sum_{i=1}^{n} \mathbf{T}_i = n(\mathbf{T}/n) = \mathbf{T},$$

and so the process is mimicked.

Next consider a parallel system with n independent stages having actual completion times $\mathbf{T}_i$ with distribution functions $F_i(t) = F(t)^{1/n}$. Since the search is exhaustive, the observed time is $\max(\mathbf{T}_i)$, which we know (Appendix A, Eq. A.7) has the distribution function

$$\prod_{i=1}^{n} F_i(t) = \prod_{i=1}^{n} F(t)^{1/n} = F(t).$$

Consider next processes that are self-terminating. For the serial case, place the terminating stage in the first position and let $F_1 = F$. For the parallel process, let all of the independent stages have the same distribution $G_i = F$, then independent of what happens on the other stages, the process is determined just by the terminating stage and so has distribution F.

Summarizing,

Theorem 12.1. *For any distribution of overall response time and any integer n, there exist both serial and parallel and both exhaustive and self-terminating search processes of n stages that have the given distribution; in the parallel case, the stages may be selected to be independent.*

12.2.3 Mimicking Intercompletion Times by Serial and Parallel Exhaustive Searches

To make the mimicking tasks more difficult, let us suppose next that all of the intercompletion times are known, although the order of the stages to which they are attached is not specified. Numbering the intercompletion times by their order of occurrence, suppose that they have the joint distribution $F(t_1, t_2, \ldots, t_n)$. Mimicking this by the serial exhaustive search is trivial: simply identify the stages with the intercompletion times. For the parallel exhaustive search simply let the actual processing times be

$$t_1, t_1 + t_2, \ldots, \sum_{i=1}^{n} t_i,$$

with their joint distribution induced by F. Summarizing,

Theorem 12.2. *For any joint distribution of n intercompletion times, there exist serial and parallel, exhaustive search processes of n stages whose intercompletion times have the given distribution.*

12.2.4 Mimicking Intercompletion Times and Order by Serial and Parallel Exhaustive Searches

As we noted at the end of Section 12.1, it is impossible for a rigid serial search to mimic both the times and orders of a parallel search. To be able to do this one must drop the fixed order of processing. It suffices to suppose that the order, a permutation ρ of $\{1, 2, \ldots, n\}$, is selected at random with some probability $P(\rho)$. We refer to this as a variable order serial system.

Theorem 12.3 (Vorberg, 1977). *For any joint distribution of n intercomple-tion times and order of stages, there exist variable-order serial and parallel, exhaustive search processes whose intercompletion times and order of stages have the given distribution.*

Proof. Let $H(t_1, t_2, \ldots, t_n, \rho)$ be the distribution of the given process. To mimic it by a variable-order, serial process, let

$$P(\rho) = H(\infty, \infty, \ldots, \infty, \rho)$$

and

$$F(t_1, t_2, \ldots, t_n \mid \rho) = H(t_1, t_2, \ldots, t_n, \rho)/P(\rho).$$

This yields the given process since $H = FP$.

   To mimic it by a parallel process, let $\tau_1 \leq \tau_2 \leq \cdots \leq \tau_n$, and define the joint distribution for the parallel process with the temporal order described by ρ as follows:

$$G(\tau_{\rho(1)}, \tau_{\rho(2)}, \ldots, \tau_{\rho(n)}) = H(\tau_1, \tau_2 - \tau_1, \ldots, \tau_n - \tau_{n-1}, \rho)$$

This obviously yields the desired mimicking. ∎

12.2.5 Mimicking Intercompletion Times and Order by Physically Realizable Searches

Vorberg's Theorem 12.3 is simply too flexible to be of interest. It does not attempt to distinguish systems that can be realized by physical processes from those in which the temporal dependencies are not physically possible because an event is modified by something yet to happen. Consider, for example, serial systems of three stages. The distribution of times in the first stage to occur can depend upon the fact that it is first and on the order in which the other two will occur, which is assumed known in advance, but it must not depend upon the actual (inter)completion times t_2 and t_3. Similarly, the distribution of $\mathbf{T}_2$ cannot depend upon the value assumed by $\mathbf{T}_3$, but it can depend upon the value of $\mathbf{T}_1$, which has already been selected and so can be known. When we turn to parallel systems, the problem of dependen-cies is a great deal more difficult to formulate. At the onset, there really cannot be any conditioning, since everything is in the future, but during the course of information processing in the several stages it is entirely possible for interactions to develop. For example, the completion of the processing within any one stage can alter the hazard functions for the other stages, thereby introducing a dependence among the processes. This is exactly what was postulated in the capacity allocation models of Sections 11.3.3 and 11.3.4. Far and away the easiest assumption to make about parallel proces-ses is that between successive completions, the stages are independent stochastic processes. Such processess can be called *locally stage independent*. Townsend, who used the term "stage" to refer to intercompletion times, called this "within-stage independence."

For initial simplicity, let us begin by formulating the two-stage processes, after which we generalize this to n stages. A variable order, two-stage serial process is said to be *realizable* if there are unconditional density functions f_{ij}, where i denotes the stage and j the position in the temporal ordering, and a probability P such that the distribution of ordered pair of intercompletion times (t_1, t_2) is given by

$$Pf_{11}(t_1)f_{22}(t_2 \mid \mathbf{T}_1 = t_1) \tag{12.1}$$

when stage 1 precedes stage 2 and by

$$(1 - P)f_{21}(t_1)f_{12}(t_2 \mid \mathbf{T}_2 = t_1) \tag{12.2}$$

when stage 2 precedes stage 1.

For a local stage-independent parallel system, which is of course realizable, there are four density functions g_{ij}, where again i denotes the stage and j the position in the temporal ordering. The distribution of the ordered pair of intercompletion times (t_1, t_2) is given by

$$g_{11}(t_1)[1 - G_{21}(t_1)]g_{22}(t_2 \mid t_1), \tag{12.3}$$

when stage 1 is completed before stage 2 and by

$$g_{21}(t_1)[1 - G_{11}(t_1)]g_{12}(t_2 \mid t_1), \tag{12.4}$$

when stage 2 is completed before stage 1. We may think of the two intercompletion times as being generated separately. The first is described by the term $g_{i1}(t_1)[1 - G_{\bar{i}1}(t_1)]$, which is the density that stage i is completed at time t_i and the complementary stage $\bar{i}$ fails to be completed in that time. This is on the assumption that both processes unfold independently. Once stage i is completed, however, the stage $\bar{i}$ process comes to be governed by a new conditional density function namely, $g_{i2}(t_2 \mid t_1)$.

To generalize these processes to n stages, proceed as follows. In the serial case, the stages are dealt with in some order that can be thought of as a permutation ρ of $\{1, 2, \ldots, n\}$. The process terminates either when all n stages are completed, which is exhaustive search, or when a critical item is reached in some stage k, which is self-terminating search. For present purposes, it is quite immaterial which search procedure is used. Let $P(\rho)$ be the probability that order ρ is used. We suppose that the processing of a particular stage depends upon three things: the stage itself, the order in which it is done, and the preceding intercompletion times. We could also assume that it depends upon the order of processing yet to come, but for simplicity I do not. So the relevant densities are of the form $f_{ij}(t \mid .)$ where i is the stage being processed, j the rank order, and the conditioning is on preceding intercompletion times. In that case, the joint distribution of the first k intercompletion times $t_1, t_2, \ldots, t_k$ and order is given by

$$P(\rho)f_{\rho^{-1}(1),1}(t_1)f_{\rho^{-1}(2),2}(t_2 \mid t_1) \cdots f_{\rho^{-1}(k),k}(t_k \mid t_1, t_2, \ldots, t_{k-1}). \tag{12.5}$$

For the locally stage-independent parallel process, assume that as each stage is completed new hazard functions are established on each of the remaining stages and the processes are carried out independently until the next completion, at which point new hazard functions govern the remaining stages, and so on. So, once again, we assume that the density function of a stage depends upon that stage, the number but not identity of the stages already completed, and the actual intercompletion times. Suppose ρ is a permutation of $\{1, 2, \ldots, n\}$, then let

$$A_j(\rho) = \{1, 2, \ldots, n\} - \{\rho^{-1}(1), \ldots, \rho^{-1}(j)\}.$$

Now suppose we are in the situation where $j-1$ stages have been completed and the intercompletion times were $t_1, t_2, \ldots, t_{j-1}$. Then each of the remaining stages enters a race to be the jth completion. We suppose that each process is now governed by a conditional density function $g_{ij}(t_j \mid t_1, t_2, \ldots, t_{j-1})$, where i denotes the stage and j the order of the intercompletion time under consideration. So, if the jth intercompletion time is t_j and the order of intercompletion times being considered is ρ, then the conditional density function is

$$g_{\rho^{-1}(j),j}(t_j \mid t_1, t_2, \ldots, t_{j-1})$$
$$\times \prod_{r \in A_j(\rho)} [1 - G_{r,j}(t_j \mid t_1, t_2, \ldots, t_{j-1})] \qquad (12.6)$$

Theorem 12.4 (Townsend, 1976a). *Any locally stage-independent, parallel process described by Eq. 12.6 can be mimicked by a realizable serial one described by Eq. 12.5. The converse is true only under special conditions.*

Proof. Let the parallel process be given. For any ρ, let $P(\rho)$ be the probability obtained by integrating the factors given by Eq. 12.6 from 0 to ∞ and then forming the product over j. Let $f_{\rho^{-1}(j),j}(t_j \mid t_1, t_2, \ldots, t_{j-1})$ be defined to be Eq. 12.6 normalized by its integral. This serial process clearly mimics the parallel one.

To mimic a serial process that terminates in k steps by a parallel one, it is necessary and sufficient that the intercompletion time distributions agree for each order ρ. Thus, by Eqs. 12.5 and 12.6,

$$P(\rho)^{1/k} f_{\rho^{-1}(j),j}(t_j \mid t_1, t_2, \ldots, t_n)$$
$$= g_{\rho^{-1}(j),j}(t_j \mid t_1, t_2, \ldots, t_{j-1})$$
$$\times \prod_{r \in A_j(\rho)} [1 - G_{r,j}(t_j \mid t_1, t_2, \ldots, t_{j-1})] \qquad (12.7)$$

Let A be a fixed subset of $n-j+i$ elements of $\{1, 2, \ldots, n\}$. For each i in A, define the subset of permutations

$$R_i = \{\rho \mid \rho(j) = i \text{ and } A_j(\rho) = A - \{i\}\}.$$

Note that the number of elements in R_i is independent of i; denote it by K. Define $P(R_i) = \sum_{\rho \in R_i} P(\rho)^{1/k}$. From Eq. 12.7 (but suppressing the notation for

$t_1, t_2, \ldots, t_{j-1}$ and writing $t_j = t$),

$$P(R_i)f_{ij}(t\,|\,.) = \sum_{\rho \in R_i} P(\rho)^{1/k} f_{\rho^{-1}(j),j}(t\,|\,.)$$

$$= \sum_{\rho \in R_i} g_{\rho^{-1}(j),j}(t\,|\,.) \prod_{r \in A_j(\rho)} [1 - G_{r,j}(t\,|\,.)]$$

$$= \sum_{\rho \in R_i} g_{i,\,j}(t\,|\,.) \prod_{r \in A - \{i\}} [1 - G_{r,j}(t\,|\,.)]$$

$$= K g_{i,j}(t\,|\,.) \prod_{r \in A - \{i\}} [1 - G_{r,j}(t\,|\,.)]. \tag{12.8}$$

Summing over A,

$$\sum_{i \in A} P(R_i)f_{i,j}(t\,|\,.) = K \sum_{i \in A} g_{i,j}(t\,|\,.) \prod_{r \in A - \{i\}} [1 - G_{r,j}(t\,|\,.)]$$

$$= K \frac{d}{dt} \prod_{r \in A} [1 - G_{r,j}(t\,|\,.)].$$

Integrating and taking into account the boundary condition $F_{i,j}(\infty\,|\,.) = G_{i,j}(\infty\,|\,.) = 1$,

$$\sum_{i \in A} P(R_i)[1 - F_{i,j}(t\,|\,.)] = K \prod_{r \in A} [1 - G_{r,j}(t\,|\,.)]. \tag{12.9}$$

Dividing Eq. 12.8 by Eq. 12.9,

$$\frac{P(R_i)f_{i,j}(t\,|\,.)}{\sum P(R_i)[1 - F_{i,j}(t\,|\,.)]} = \frac{g_{i,j}(t\,|\,.)}{1 - G_{i,j}(t\,|\,.)} = h_{i,j}(t\,|\,.). \tag{12.10}$$

Thus, given k, $P(\rho)$, and the $f_{i,j}$, Eq. 12.10 determines the hazard function of the $g_{i,j}$ that mimics it. This is a hazard function of a probability density function if and only if both $h_{i,j} \geq 0$ and

$$\int_0^\infty h_{i,j}(t\,|\,.)\,dt = \infty. \qquad \blacksquare$$

There is absolutely no assurance that the second of these two conditions is satisfied. For example, if the $f_{i,j}$ are assumed to be exponential, then the condition can be shown to hold if and only if the intensity parameters of the several exponentials are identical, in which case the $h_{i,j}$ are constant, corresponding to exponential $g_{i,j}$. Townsend (1976b) gave two sufficient conditions, neither implying the other, for this condition on the hazard function to be met. One is

$$\lim_{t \to \infty} \frac{f_{i,j}(t\,|\,.)}{f_{k,j}(t\,|\,.)} = c, \quad 0 < c < \infty. \tag{12.11}$$

The other is, for some constants a, b, and c,

$$\lim_{t \to \infty} f_{i,j}(t\,|\,.)/(a + bt) = c. \tag{12.12}$$

Ross and Anderson carried out a memory retrieval study, which was motivated by the assumption in Anderson's (1976) ACT theory of parallel retrieval processing, to see if it was possible for such a parallel structure to mimic a serial one. The test was of Eq. 12.11, and it was judged to be sustained in these data.

12.2.6   Subconclusion

The upshot of these exercises is very simple. As long as the behavior of the stages is unspecified, it is quite impossible to use the observed reaction-time distributions to decide whether we are dealing with serial or parallel (or other) systems. This is true not only when the overall response-time distribution is given (Theorem 12.1), but even when it is also assumed that the intercompletion times are known (Theorem 12.2). Adding finally the information of the precise order in which the stages are completed fails to narrow things down if we ignore the question of physical realizability (Theorem 12.3); however, adding physical realizability does mean there are serial systems that cannot be mimicked by parallel ones, although the other mimicking is always possible.

Since we do not usually have either order or intercompletion time information, the message is clear: the decision about the structure of the mental network will have to be reached using information that is richer than can be obtained from a single response-time experiment. We describe in Sections 12.3 and 12.4 two ideas about how to gain and use additional information for this purpose.

12.3   SIMULTANEOUS ACCOUNTS OF SEVERAL EXPERIMENTS

To overcome our inability to infer the order of processing from the data of a single experiment, two major ideas have been pursued. The one—the topic of the present section—is to run several different designs using the same stimuli and subjects and to assume that the same processing stages, network, and optimal search strategy underlie the observed behavior. It is then possible to show that certain non-equivalences hold among models and so, in principle, it is possible to select among them. The other idea—the topic of Section 12.4—is to remain within a single design, but to introduce manipulations of the stimuli and/or the procedure that affect some but not all of the durations of processing stages. The pattern of observed effects on response times sometimes sheds light upon the processing network and/or search strategy.

12.3.1   A Serial or Parallel, Exhaustive or Self-Terminating Testing Paradigm

The ideas discussed in this subsection are found in Snodgrass and Townsend (1980), Townsend (1976b), Townsend and Ashby (1983), and Townsend and Snodgrass (1974); they simplify an earlier proposal of the same general type first described by Snodgrass (1972). The basic paradigm is to have a target, A, followed by the presentation of two alternatives, one of which may be the target and the other, of similar type, we may call B. In procedure I, either AB or BA is presented and the subject is to report whether the target is on the right or the left. In procedures II and III, there are four different presentations, each equally likely: AA, AB, BA, and BB. In II the subject is to distinguish AA from the other three presentations; that is, one response is made if no B is present and the other if at least one B is present. In III, the distinction is between BB and the rest—that is, one response if no A is present and the other if at least one A is present. The goal of the design is to force distinctions between serial versus parallel and between self-terminating versus exhaustive search procedures based upon the assumption that any $A - A$ comparison and any $A - B$ comparison is like any other of the same type carried out in the same temporal order and in the same physical location.

For initial simplicity, let us suppose that neither the order nor the location matter—the only relevant factor being whether the comparison is the same or different. Let $\mathbf{X}_S$ and $\mathbf{X}_D$ denote the decision latencies (random variables) for same and different decisions, respectively. We may then write out the total decision time for each case, which is assumed to differ from the observed reaction time only by a residual time independent of the decision. This analysis is shown in Table 12.1, where in the serial self-terminating column the parameter p denotes the probability that the search is carried out from left to right.

Let us examine several cases so it becomes clear how the table is constructed. For exhaustive searches, the random variable $\mathbf{X}_S$ arises when an A appears and $\mathbf{X}_D$ when a B appears. In the serial case, they are added; in the parallel case, the slower one determines the overall time, and so the maximum of the two is calculated. Nothing is assumed about independence at this point; later we will assume the parallel processes to be locally stage independent.

TABLE 12.1. Type of search (see text for explanation)

Experimental	Exhaustive		Self-terminating	
Condition	Serial	Parallel	Serial	Parallel
I AB	$\mathbf{X}_S + \mathbf{X}_D$	$\max(\mathbf{X}_S, \mathbf{X}_D)$	$p\mathbf{X}_S + (1-p)\mathbf{X}_D$	$\min(\mathbf{X}_S, \mathbf{X}_D)$
BA	$\mathbf{X}_D + \mathbf{X}_S$	$\max(\mathbf{X}_D, \mathbf{X}_S)$	$p\mathbf{X}_D + (1-p)\mathbf{X}_S$	$\min(\mathbf{X}_S, \mathbf{X}_D)$
II AA	$\mathbf{X}_S + \mathbf{X}_S$	$\max(\mathbf{X}_S, \mathbf{X}_S)$	$\mathbf{X}_S + \mathbf{X}_S$	$\max(\mathbf{X}_S, \mathbf{X}_S)$
AB	$\mathbf{X}_S + \mathbf{X}_D$	$\max(\mathbf{X}_S, \mathbf{X}_D)$	$p\mathbf{X}_S + \mathbf{X}_D$	$\mathbf{X}_D$
BA	$\mathbf{X}_D + \mathbf{X}_S$	$\max(\mathbf{X}_D, \mathbf{X}_S)$	$(1-p)\mathbf{X}_S + \mathbf{X}_D$	$\mathbf{X}_D$
BB	$\mathbf{X}_D + \mathbf{X}_D$	$\max(\mathbf{X}_D, \mathbf{X}_D)$	$\mathbf{X}_D$	$\min(\mathbf{X}_D, \mathbf{X}_D)$
III AA	$\mathbf{X}_S + \mathbf{X}_S$	$\max(\mathbf{X}_S, \mathbf{X}_S)$	$\mathbf{X}_S$	$\min(\mathbf{X}_S, \mathbf{X}_S)$
AB	$\mathbf{X}_S + \mathbf{X}_D$	$\max(\mathbf{X}_S, \mathbf{X}_D)$	$(1-p)\mathbf{X}_D + \mathbf{X}_S$	$\mathbf{X}_S$
BA	$\mathbf{X}_D + \mathbf{X}_S$	$\max(\mathbf{X}_D, \mathbf{X}_S)$	$p\mathbf{X}_D + \mathbf{X}_S$	$\mathbf{X}_S$
BB	$\mathbf{X}_D + \mathbf{X}_D$	$\max(\mathbf{X}_D, \mathbf{X}_D)$	$\mathbf{X}_D$	$\max(\mathbf{X}_D, \mathbf{X}_D)$

The self-terminating search is more complex. For the serial structure, it is necessary to consider the order in which comparisons are made. For procedure *I*, only one observation need be made because the other must be the other stimulus. So, for the presentation *AB*, with probability p the *A* is examined and takes time $\mathbf{X}_S$ and with probability $1-p$ the *B* is examined and takes time $\mathbf{X}_D$, and the response is determined. The overall random variable is thus $p\mathbf{X}_S+(1-p)\mathbf{X}_D$. In the parallel case, the process terminating first determines the response, and so the minimum of the two times is the relevant time variable. For procedure II, where the subject is attempting to decide if a *B* is present, the *AA* presentation must be examined exhaustively, and the others need not be. For example, consider *AB*. In the serial analysis, either *A* is examined first, with probability p, and then *B* for a total time of $\mathbf{X}_S+\mathbf{X}_D$, or *B* is examined first, with probability $1-p$, and the response is determined with time $\mathbf{X}_D$. So the overall random variable is $p(\mathbf{X}_S+\mathbf{X}_D)+(1-p)\mathbf{X}_D = p\mathbf{X}_S+\mathbf{X}_D$. The parallel analysis is simpler; the subject must wait until the *B* process is completed, which takes time $\mathbf{X}_D$; however, keep in mind that this examination is carried out while *A* is being examined, and so the distribution of $\mathbf{X}_D$ may be altered when *A* is completed. The other analyses are similar.

12.3.2   How Distinct are the Predictions?

The perfect parallelism of the serial and parallel columns of the exhaustive search make clear that these two cannot be discriminated by this paradigm. We now establish that the other pairs can be distinguished at the level of mean response times.

A major distinction between exhaustive and self-terminating models lies in comparing IIAA with IIIAA. In both of the exhaustive models these times are identical and in both of the self-terminating models IIAA is slower than IIIAA. The remaining question concerns the serial-parallel distinction within the self-terminating class.

Theorem 12.5 (Townsend, 1976c; Townsend & Ashby, 1983). *Assuming that $\mathbf{X}_S$ and $\mathbf{X}_D$ have distinct continuous distribution functions, it is impossible for serial and locally stage-independent parallel models to mimic each other at the level of mean times simultaneously for procedures* I, II, *and* III.

Proof.   Observe that for the serial case, the mean time for IAB added to the mean time for IBA is

$$pE(\mathbf{X}_S)+(1-p)E(\mathbf{X}_D)+pE(\mathbf{X}_D)+(1-p)E(\mathbf{X}_S)= E(\mathbf{X}_S)+E(\mathbf{X}_D).$$

Similarly, adding IIBB to IIIAA also yields $E(\mathbf{X}_S)+E(\mathbf{X}_D)$. For the parallel model, the two sums are, respectively,

$$E[\min(\mathbf{X}_S, \mathbf{X}_D)]+E[\min(\mathbf{X}_S, \mathbf{X}_D)] \qquad (12.13)$$

and

$$E[\min(\mathbf{X}_S, \mathbf{X}_s)] + E[\min(\mathbf{X}_D, \mathbf{X}_D)]. \qquad (12.14)$$

It is, thus, sufficient to show that the latter two times are not equal when we assume independent realizations of the random variables within the different comparisons. Recall that when $\mathbf{X}$ and $\mathbf{Y}$ are locally independent random variables,

$$E[\min(\mathbf{X}, \mathbf{Y})] = \int_0^\infty \bar{F}_\mathbf{X}(t)\bar{F}_\mathbf{Y}(t)\, dt,$$

where $\bar{F} = 1 - F$ and F is a distribution function. So for Eq. 12.13 to equal Eq. 12.14, we must have

$$2\int_0^\infty \bar{F}_S(t)\bar{F}_D(t)\, dt = \int_0^\infty \bar{F}_S(t)^2\, dt + \int_0^\infty \bar{F}_D(t)^2\, dt.$$

Rewriting,

$$\int_0^\infty [\bar{F}_S(t) - \bar{F}_D(t)]^2\, dt = 0.$$

But this is impossible because $[\bar{F}_S(t) - \bar{F}_D(t)]^2 \geq 0$, $F_S \neq F_D$, and the distribution functions are continuous. So the two equations must not be equal. ∎

This suggests that, in principle, data can be used to choose among models.

12.3.3 An Experiment

Following a technique first used by Snodgrass (1972), which will be discussed in Section 12.3.4, Townsend and Snodgrass (1976) used stimuli that can be thought of as arising from 2×2 matrices of the letters Q, R, T, and Z. The subjects were to focus only on the columns. A column is a target, or type A, item if both entries are the same and a non-target, or type B, item if the two entries differ. So, for example, $\begin{bmatrix} QT \\ QT \end{bmatrix}$ is one version of an AA presentation whereas $\begin{bmatrix} QT \\ ZT \end{bmatrix}$ is one version of a BA presentation. The procedure involved the visual presentation of the top row for 300 msec, followed by a 400-msec blank, and then the bottom row for 300 msec. Response time was measured from the onset of the bottom row. Thus, the task was to compare the second presentation, column by column, with the memory of the first presentation. Depending upon the condition, the response is affected by the location and existence or not of a match. Data were collected from four subjects, and their mean times (and the sample sizes underlying them) are shown in Table 12.2.

The most obvious fact about these data is that the mean times for IIAA and IIIAA, 347 and 352 msec, are virtually identical, which is consistent

TABLE 12.2. Mean data, averaged over four subjects, from Townsend and Snodgrass (1974)

Condition	No. of trials	MRT in msec
I *AB*	720	381
BA	720	352
II *AA*	2160	347
AB	720	400
BA	770	394
BB	720	367
III *AA*	720	352
AB	770	437
BA	720	440
BB	2160	464

with an exhaustive model but not with a self-terminating one. However, that is about all that is consistent with the exhaustive model. For example, the model says that the *AB* and *BA* presentations should all take the same time, but the values of 381, 356, 400, 394, 437, and 440 are far too variable to be explained by sampling variability. If the population standard deviation is 30% of the mean, then with a sample size of 720 the sampling standard deviation is only 4.5 msec.

One possible difficulty is the assumption that only a single random variable is associated with each type of stimulus. Perhaps their location, right or left, and/or the order in which the processing occurs makes a difference. Of course, admitting this possibility increases the number of mean latencies from two to eight, which together with the order of search probability p means nine parameters to account for ten pieces of data. Even so, the model is still not satisfactory since it still requires that the four times of procedure II should equal the corresponding ones of procedure III, and 367 and 464 cannot possibly arise from the same distribution based on samples of 720 and 2160, respectively.

Townsend and Ashby (1983, Chapter 13) proceeded as follows. To get around the fact that IIAA and IIIAA are nearly identical, which is quite inconsistent with the self-terminating model, they suggested that matches in both columns are dealt with differently from the other cases. They phrased it that such stimuli are treated as a gestalt. To my taste this is unacceptably ad hoc, although it certainly has precedent in the literature (Section 11.4). It adds one more parameter, which leaves no degrees of freedom for the serial case and just one for the parallel one. They worked out the equations for the means on the assumption of exponential random variables and fitted the parallel, self-terminating model to the data and found that it cannot be rejected by a χ^2 test. I do not find it a very convincing test of the models. The most reasonable conclusion for this one set of data is that none of the four models really accounts for what is going on.

TABLE 12.3. Snodgrass (1972) experimental conditions[a]

A	B	C	D
$\begin{bmatrix} 1 \\ 1 \end{bmatrix} \to$ Same	$\begin{bmatrix} & 1 \\ 2 & 1 \end{bmatrix} \to$ Right	$\begin{bmatrix} 2 & 1 \\ & 1 \end{bmatrix} \to$ Right	$\begin{bmatrix} 2 & 1 \\ 3 & 1 \end{bmatrix} \to$ Right
$\begin{bmatrix} 1 \\ 2 \end{bmatrix} \to$ Diff	$\begin{bmatrix} & 1 \\ 1 & 2 \end{bmatrix} \to$ Left	$\begin{bmatrix} 1 & 2 \\ & 1 \end{bmatrix} \to$ Left	$\begin{bmatrix} 2 & 1 \\ 2 & 3 \end{bmatrix} \to$ Left

E	F	G	H
$\begin{bmatrix} & 1 \\ 1 & 2 \end{bmatrix} \to$ Same	$\begin{bmatrix} 1 & 2 \\ & 1 \end{bmatrix} \to$ Same	$\begin{bmatrix} 1 & 2 \\ 1 & 2 \end{bmatrix} \to$ Same	$\begin{bmatrix} 1 & 2 \\ 1 & 3 \end{bmatrix} \to$ Same
$\begin{bmatrix} & 1 \\ 2 & 1 \end{bmatrix} \to$ Same	$\begin{bmatrix} 2 & 1 \\ & 1 \end{bmatrix} \to$ Same	$\begin{bmatrix} 1 & 2 \\ 2 & 1 \end{bmatrix} \to$ Same	$\begin{bmatrix} 1 & 2 \\ 2 & 3 \end{bmatrix} \to$ Same
$\begin{bmatrix} & 1 \\ 2 & 3 \end{bmatrix} \to$ Diff.	$\begin{bmatrix} 2 & 3 \\ & 1 \end{bmatrix} \to$ Diff.	$\begin{bmatrix} 1 & 2 \\ 1 & 3 \end{bmatrix} \to$ Diff.	$\begin{bmatrix} 2 & 1 \\ 3 & 1 \end{bmatrix} \to$ Same
		$\begin{bmatrix} 1 & 2 \\ 2 & 3 \end{bmatrix} \to$ Diff.	$\begin{bmatrix} 2 & 1 \\ 3 & 2 \end{bmatrix} \to$ Same
		$\begin{bmatrix} 1 & 2 \\ 3 & 1 \end{bmatrix} \to$ Diff.	$\begin{bmatrix} 1 & 2 \\ 3 & 4 \end{bmatrix} \to$ Diff.
		$\begin{bmatrix} 1 & 2 \\ 3 & 2 \end{bmatrix} \to$ Diff.	

[a] Table 1 of Snodgrass (1972) is misleading in that the last two Differences of *G* and the last two Same Cases of *H* are omitted, although they enter into the calculations to follow.

12.3.4 A Variant on the Paradigm*

Prior to the developments just outlined, Snodgrass (1972) proposed essentially the same idea but in a somewhat more complex procedure. She used 2×2 matrices and subsets of them as stimuli with the top row presented for 2.5 sec, a 2.5 sec wait, and then the bottom row. Subjects had to consider all possible comparisons between items in the top row and the bottom row, not just the column pairs. So in the full 2×2 case, there were four comparisons. The stimuli and responses are shown in Table 12.3.

The increased complexity of the comparisons forces some increase in the complexity of analysis and requires added assumptions. Snodgrass assumed the following rule of search. The subject randomly chooses one of the presented elements from the bottom row. Memory is then searched for either the only element in it (Cases *A*, *B*, and *E*) or in the general case a column is examined at random. If the pair exhibits a match, delete that pair. Depending upon the condition and the model, that either determines the

---

* Dr. Snodgrass was helpful in making clear to me exactly what assumptions she used to arrive at the predictions discussed in this section.

response or a comparison is made of what remains. If, however, the first pair is not a match, then the subject examines what remains with priority being given to the diagonal, if it exists, involving the same lower element and the other upper one. Following this, if necessary, the other diagonal is examined. It should be noted that this is but one of many possible search strategies, and it is unclear why it is to be preferred.

Let us work out a few cases of serial self-terminating search in order to see how the rule is applied. Let $\mathbf{X}_S$ denote the time required for a match and $\mathbf{X}_D$ that for a non-matching pair. For condition A, the presentation $\begin{bmatrix} 1 \\ 1 \end{bmatrix}$ takes $\mathbf{X}_S$ whereas $\begin{bmatrix} 1 \\ 2 \end{bmatrix}$ takes $\mathbf{X}_D$. For condition B, either presentation takes $\mathbf{X}_S$ or $\mathbf{X}_D$ according to the order of the search, and so on average it is $(\mathbf{X}_S + \mathbf{X}_D)/2$, assuming equally likely presentations. Conditions C, D, E, and F are all treated similarly. For condition G, same response, if $\begin{bmatrix} 1 & 2 \\ 1 & 2 \end{bmatrix}$ is presented, either $\begin{bmatrix} 1 \\ 1 \end{bmatrix}$ or $\begin{bmatrix} 2 \\ 2 \end{bmatrix}$ is first checked and eliminated. The remaining comparison determines the response, and so takes $\mathbf{X}_S + \mathbf{X}_S = 2\mathbf{X}_S$. If $\begin{bmatrix} 1 & 2 \\ 2 & 1 \end{bmatrix}$ is presented, then either vertical comparison takes $\mathbf{X}_D$, which then is followed by both diagonal comparisons for a total of $\mathbf{X}_D + 2\mathbf{X}_S$. Averaging $2\mathbf{X}_S$ and $\mathbf{X}_D + 2\mathbf{X}_S$ yields $(4\mathbf{X}_S + \mathbf{X}_D)/2$. For the four different responses we have the display shown in Table 12.4. Averaging yields $(2\mathbf{X}_S + 7\mathbf{X}_D)/4$. The analysis of the parallel models is nearly the same, except instead of adding one either takes the maximum of the random variables when all must be completed or the minimum when the first to be completed yields the response. All of this is summarized in Table 12.4.

From the table one can deduce quite a number of inequalities among the means on the assumption the $E(\mathbf{X}_S) < E(\mathbf{X}_D)$. For example, in the serial self-terminating case,

$$E(\mathbf{T}_A) = [E(\mathbf{X}_S) + E(\mathbf{X}_D)]/2 = E(\mathbf{T}_B) = E(\mathbf{T}_C) = E(\mathbf{T}_D)$$
$$< [2E(\mathbf{X}_S) + 5E(\mathbf{X}_D)]/4 = E(\mathbf{T}_E) = E(\mathbf{T}_F)$$
$$< [10E(\mathbf{X}_S) + 9E(\mathbf{X}_D)]/8 = E(\mathbf{T}_G) \quad \text{if } 6E(\mathbf{X}_S) > E(\mathbf{X}_D)$$
$$< [4E(\mathbf{X}_S) + 22E(\mathbf{X}_D)]/8 = E(\mathbf{T}_H) \quad \text{if } 2E(\mathbf{X}_D) > E(\mathbf{X}_S).$$

Without the additional assumptions, it is impossible to conclude how $E(\mathbf{T}_E)$ relates to $E(\mathbf{T}_G)$ and it to $E(\mathbf{T}_H)$. The inequalities for the two exhaustive searches are easy to derive. These results together with Snodgrass' data are shown in Figure 12.1. There is a slight reason to favor the serial self-terminating model, but note that this conclusion rests entirely on the comparison of $E(\mathbf{T}_A)$ and $E(\mathbf{T}_B)$. Indeed, if we average the data for B, C, and D, it is slightly less than that of A, giving a slight edge for the parallel self-terminating model. Significance tests are needed to tell if there is really an empirical difference.

TABLE 12.4. Random variables arising in the different conditions and for each of the models on the assumption that a same comparison is governed by $\mathbf{X}_S$ and a difference by $\mathbf{X}_D$

Condition	Response	Serial exhaustive	Serial self-terminating	Parallel exhaustive	Parallel self-terminating
B, C, D	Same	$\mathbf{X}_S$	$\mathbf{X}_S$	$\mathbf{X}_S$	$\mathbf{X}_S$
	Diff.	$\mathbf{X}_D$	$\mathbf{X}_D$	$\mathbf{X}_D$	$\mathbf{X}_D$
E, F	Same	$\mathbf{X}_S + \mathbf{X}_D$	$(\mathbf{X}_S + \mathbf{X}_D)/2$	$\max(\mathbf{X}_S, \mathbf{X}_D)$	$\min(\mathbf{X}_S, \mathbf{X}_D)$
	Diff.	$\mathbf{X}_S + \mathbf{X}_D$	$\mathbf{X}_S + \mathbf{X}_D/2$	$\max(\mathbf{X}_S, \mathbf{X}_D)$	$\mathbf{X}_S$
	Diff.	$2\mathbf{X}_D$	$2\mathbf{X}_D$	$\max(\mathbf{X}_D, \mathbf{X}_D)$	$\max(\mathbf{X}_D, \mathbf{X}_D)$
G	Same	$2\mathbf{X}_S + 2\mathbf{X}_D$	$(4\mathbf{X}_S + \mathbf{X}_D)/2$	$\max(\mathbf{X}_S, \mathbf{X}_S, \mathbf{X}_D, \mathbf{X}_D)$	$\max(\mathbf{X}_S, \mathbf{X}_S)$
	Diff.	$\mathbf{X}_S + 3\mathbf{X}_D$	$(2\mathbf{X}_S + 7\mathbf{X}_D)/4$	$\max(\mathbf{X}_S, \mathbf{X}_D, \mathbf{X}_D, \mathbf{X}_D)$	$\max(\mathbf{X}_S, \mathbf{X}_D)$
H	Same	$\mathbf{X}_S + 3\mathbf{X}_D$	$(2\mathbf{X}_S + 3\mathbf{X}_D)/2$	$\max(\mathbf{X}_S, \mathbf{X}_D, \mathbf{X}_D, \mathbf{X}_D)$	S
	Diff.	$4\mathbf{X}_D$	$4\mathbf{X}_D$	$\max(\mathbf{X}_D, \mathbf{X}_D, \mathbf{X}_D, \mathbf{X}_D)$	$\max(\mathbf{X}_D, \mathbf{X}_D, \mathbf{X}_D, \mathbf{X}_D)$

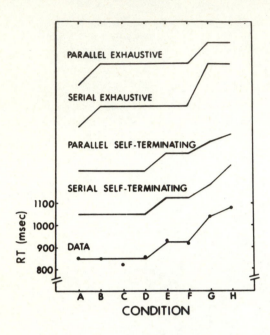

FIG. 12.1 Comparison of the several models described in the text with the data of Snodgrass (1972). Each of five subjects contributed 720 observations for each of conditions *A, B, C, E, F,* and *G,* and 1080 for conditions *D* and *H.* [Figure 6 of Snodgrass (1972); copyright 1972; reprinted by permission.]

Additional data of the same type are reported by Snodgrass and Townsend (1980), and they continue to favor serial self-termination.

12.4   SELECTIVE MANIPULATION OF STAGES

If the processing is in fact carried out in distinct stages, another way to try to infer the temporal network among the stages is to affect differentially the latencies of the stages. There are at least four different attempts to make use of this general idea. The oldest is Donders' method of subtraction or, as Sternberg (1969b) called it, pure insertion (see Section 6.2.2). The goal is to find manipulations that bypass or eliminate one or more of the stages without affecting the remaining ones. Assuming a serial process, as Donders did, then the distribution of times associated with the subtracted stage is simply the deconvolution of the distributions with it in and with it out. I discussed some of the drawbacks of this idea in Section 6.2.2. The next oldest method, which in fact is quite recent, was first proposed to find if there is some serial link in the network. This is the single-channel hypothesis discussed in Section 5.4, and its study is based upon observing how the response to the second of two signals presented in rapid succession is affected by the time interval between them. Next came a modification of Donders in which one does not try to bypass a stage but rather tries to affect it selectively and alter its latency. The first discussion of this idea, known as additive factors methodology and due to S. Sternberg, was limited to serial systems, as was Donders' work. We encountered it in Section 3.3.4, and it is described in some detail in Section 12.4.1; an illustrative application is given in Section 12.4.2. Next in Section 12.4.3 the question is considered of when the means of an additive search can be mimicked by the means of a parallel, independent one. Criticisms of the method of additive factors are taken up in Section 12.4.4. Very recently a scheme has been proposed that largely subsumes the earlier ones and is able to uncover the nature of the network of stages. Its major limitation at present is that it is entirely deterministic, and it has not yet been worked out for latencies that are random variables. It is described in the final three subsections.

12.4.1   *The Additive Factors Method*

Sternberg (1966, 1969a, b) revived and revised Donders' discredited, although still widely used, method of subtraction (Section 6.2.2). Recall that Donders assumed both a strictly serial system and the existence of procedures, such as comparing simple and choice response times, that he believed resulted in the use—or insertion—of an additional stage of mental processing while leaving the other stages unchanged. Sternberg pointed out that a much weaker hypothesis was often equally useful, namely, that certain experimental manipulations may affect—not eliminate—some stages but not others, and these effects will show up as revealing patterns in the overall response times. For example, suppose in the standard memory search design the test stimulus is purposely degraded in quality, then the perceptual processing that transforms the stimulus into a form that can be compared with the items in memory should be slowed down. As this processing is thought to be a single stage of processing that presumably is prior to any memory search, we should find the entire plot of time to respond versus number of memory items displaced upward, but the slope (search time) should not be affected. Such data are shown in Figure 12.2.

Note that if the experimental manipulation were to affect each stage of the comparison process, then we would expect a systematic change in the slope. For example, that should happen in a procedure that makes it impossible for the subject to hold the memorized list in active, short-term memory. To effect that, Sternberg had subjects memorize a list of digits, for some subjects a list of 1, others of 3, and still others 5 items. On each trial a new list of 7 letters was presented. On a random third of the trials subjects were required to recall the list of letters—a manipulation that was designed to keep short-term memory fully active by rehearsing the letters. On the remaining trials, a test digit was presented and the subject was required to decide whether it was in the memorized list of digits. Presumably these memorized digits had to be withdrawn from long-term memory and placed into active memory, which should be slower for each item than just searching short-term memory. The results are shown in Figure 12.3, and we see that both the slope and the intercept were affected.

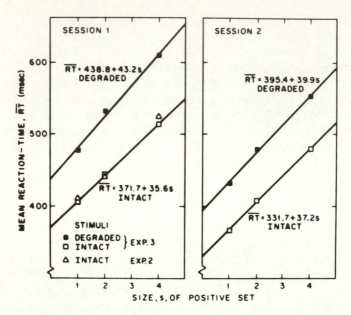

FIG. 12.2 Effect of degrading stimulus quality in a standard memory search design. The data are based on averages from 12 subjects. [Figure 4 of Sternberg (1967b); copyright 1967; reprinted by permission.]

The basic mathematical idea underlying what we have just illustrated is this. Suppose there are n serial stages of search and m other serial stages whose latencies are, respectively, $\mathbf{T}_1, \mathbf{T}_2, \ldots, \mathbf{T}_n, \mathbf{S}_1, \mathbf{S}_2, \ldots, \mathbf{S}_m$, and so the overall response time is

$$\mathbf{T} = \sum_{i=1}^{m} \mathbf{S}_i + \sum_{j=1}^{n} \mathbf{T}_j.$$

Now, if we assume that these latencies are independent random variables, so each rth-order cumulant (Section 1.4.5) is the sum of the component rth-order cumulants, we will be led to simple results. For example, working just with the means (in which case we need not assume independence) and assuming that a manipulation affects a single stage—for example, changing $\mathbf{S}_1$ into $\mathbf{S}_1'$, we see the following change in mean times:

$$\Delta T = E(\mathbf{T}') - E(\mathbf{T}) = E(\mathbf{S}_1') - E(\mathbf{S}_1).$$

In contrast, a manipulation that affects all of the times of a group, say $\mathbf{T}_1, \ldots, \mathbf{T}_n$, then yields

$$\Delta T = \sum_{j=1}^{n} [E(\mathbf{T}_j') - E(\mathbf{T}_j)]$$

$$= n\delta \quad \text{if } E(\mathbf{T}_j') - E(\mathbf{T}_j) = \delta \text{ independent of } j.$$

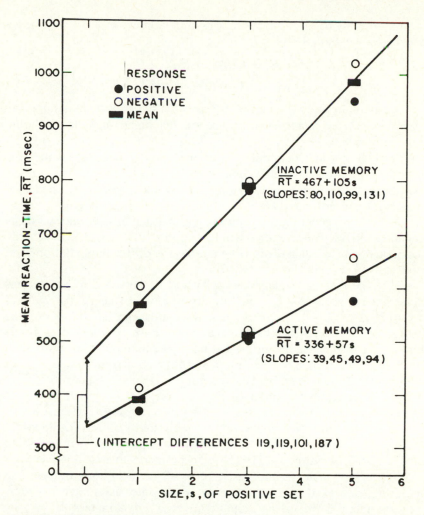

FIG. 12.3 Effect of keeping short-term memory occupied with another activity in a standard memory search design. The data were averaged over 12 subjects, but the number of observations per subject was not stated. [Figure 16 of Sternberg (1969b); copyright 1969; reprinted by permission.]

Now we may formulate the major idea of the method of additive factors. Suppose we have two independent experimental manipulations. If the first affects only stage 1, changing its latency from S_1 to S_1', and the second one affects only stage 2, changing its latency from S_2 to S_2', then the two changes can be described by

$$\Delta T_1 = E(S_1') - E(S_1)$$
$$\Delta T_2 = E(S_2') - E(S_2).$$

Now consider applying both manipulations simultaneously. Since they affect distinct stages, we should find

$$\Delta T_{12} = E(\mathbf{S}_1') + E(\mathbf{S}_2') - E(\mathbf{S}_1) - E(\mathbf{S}_2)$$
$$= \Delta T_1 + \Delta T_2.$$

So the incremental effects should be additive. On the additional assumption of independence, the incremental effects on the higher cumulants should also be additive.

In contrast, if the first manipulation affects stage 1 but the second one affects both stages 1 and 2, then we may very well not obtain additive effects because the simultaneous application of the two manipulations need not, and in general will not, have additive effects on the stage they both affect, stage 1. Indeed, the general philosophy of the method is such that were the manipulations to be additive one would suppose that stage 1 is actually composed of two serial stages, one affected by one of the manipulations and the other by the second one.

If, in fact, the system of stages is serial and if there are manipulations available that affect each stage individually, then in principle the method permits us to establish the number of stages, although it tells us nothing about their order of occurrence. That can sometimes be guessed by interpreting the role of the stage from the nature of the manipulations that affect it (see Section 12.4.2), but such interpretations are somewhat risky. A modified method (see Section 12.4.7) goes further and permits us, in principle, to infer either the order or its converse.

Although Sternberg proposed his method as a substitute for Donders' pure insertion, the latter continues to be widely used, often with apparent success (e.g., see Section 6.2.3). The possibility of using both in the same design was raised by Salthouse (1981), who pointed out that this increases one's ability to make clear which treatments affect the inserted stage. For example, suppose task II involves inserting a stage into task I, and that some pair of experimental treatments exhibit an interaction in task II but are additive in task I, then the conclusion suggested is that the treatments affect separate stages of task I and both affect the inserted stage of task II. He carried out a study illustrating the methods.

12.4.2   Illustrative Applications of the Model

Sternberg (1971) reported a number of applications of the additive-factors method, and subsequently it has often been used by others—although not always well. I merely illustrate it by summarizing one of Sternberg's experiments. The stimuli were numerals the subject was to identify. Three ways of slowing the response were effected by the manipulations: degrading the quality of the visual presentation; increasing the number of possible stimuli from two to eight; and requiring the subject to respond to the digit n with

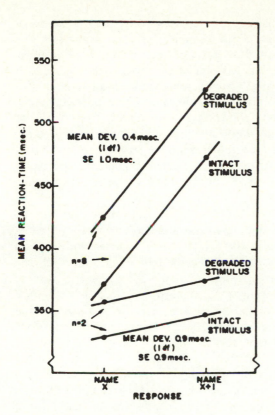

FIG. 12.4 A memory search experiment with three manipulations designed to effect response delays: degrading the stimulus quality; two or eight stimuli; respond with the digit presented or its successor. Additive stages should not produce interactions. [Figure 8 of Sternberg (1969a); copyright 1969; reprinted by permission.]

$n + 1$ rather than n. Intuitively, it seems clear that degrading the stimulus should affect the time to encode it. Varying the number of possible responses and the compatibility of the responses should not affect the encoding, but they should affect respectively the search and response processes. One might anticipate the three effects to be additive. The mean data are shown in Figure 12.4, and there is a surprise. A sizable interaction exists between the manipulation of the number of stimuli and response compatibility, whereas stimulus quality is additive with each. The tentative conclusion to be drawn is that the data are compatible with a two-stage, serial model. However, in Section 12.4.6, we shall see that an additional analysis of the data actually suggests the three-stage, serial model may indeed be correct.

To illustrate further some of the current uses of the method, I cite three papers. Sanders and Andriessen (1978) used four vowels as signals. The manipulations were: intensity—45 dBA or 85 dBA; foreperiod duration—1 sec and 10 sec; and stimulus-response compatibility—respond by indicating the vowel presented or the one after it in the alphabet. At high intensity, but not at low, they found evidence of interaction between compatibility and foreperiod duration. Sanders, Wijnen, and van Arkel (1982) varied sleep

loss, signal degradation, stimulus-response compatibility, and signal modality. They found only one interaction—namely, between sleep loss and
degradation—which they interpreted in terms of several theories of arousal
and motivation. Simon (1982) presented one of two visual stimuli, an X or
an O, and a tone to either ear. The visual signals were either degraded or
not. With exactly the same visual display, subjects either responded by key
presses to just the visual display (single task) or to both the visual and
auditory (dual task). The experimenters interpreted the pattern of interactions as evidence of parallel initial stages—not too surprising—followed by a
common stage—also not too surprising since the same hand was involved.
Nonetheless, it is interesting that the method could tease this out from the
response times.

Another use of the additive-factors methodology is Pashler (1984), who
attempted to infer which processing stages are affected in the overlapping,
dual task that leads to the so-called psychological refractory period (Section
5.4). He assumed that the second task can be thought of as composed of a
minimum of three main stages—a perceptual one, followed by a stage of
decision making and response selection, in turn followed by response
initiation and execution. The delay in response time to the second task due
to there being another, immediately prior task, has in one paper or another
been attributed to postponement of each of these three stages while the
preceding stage is taken up with the first task. The general magnitude of the
effect makes reasonably clear that not all of it can possibly be due just to
delays in the perceptual stage, and some authors—for example, Duncan
(1980)—hold that such activity goes on automatically and in parallel and
definitely is not a source of delay. Welford (1980c) and his colleagues have
suggested that the bottleneck lies in the use of a single, central processor
during the decision stage. And Keele (1973) and Keele and Neill (1978)
have argued for the delay lying in the response execution stage.

In an attempt to get evidence on these alternatives, Pashler (1984)
reasoned as follows. If the delay in the second task is due to a particular
stage being taken up with task-one activities, then experimental manipulations that affect that stage directly should manifest themselves as additive
effects in the response time to the second task. If, however, the delay is due
to a later stage, then manipulations affecting the earlier one should exhibit
no effect (at least until these delays are sufficiently long so that they further
delay the start of the later stage), and so empirically it should appear as
underadditivity. Thus, carrying out separate manipulations that are believed
to affect the perceptual and decision stages should result in patterns of
response delays that permit the localization of the bottleneck, if one exists.

When there was a first task (on half of the trial blocks), it was to identify
which of two horizontal bars, one above and one below a fixation point,
had been presented. The response was before the second task. The second,
experimental task, involved search for a target letter in a display of M ($= 2$,
4, or 6) letters. Some of the manipulations carried out on the second task

were signal contrast (aimed at affecting the perceptual stage), presence or absence of the target letter and display size (both aimed at affecting the decision stage), and length of the SOA (time between signal onsets in tasks 1 and 2). Experiment 1 involved a fixed SOA of 100 msec and a fixed set size (4), and it varied both target present or absent and signal contrast. A substantial underadditivity was found for signal contrast, whereas target absent or present had an additive effect. Experiment 2, again at an SOA of 100 msec, involved target absent or present and varied set size. Again, target absent or present exhibited additivity, but set size was underadditive. At an SOA of 300 msec (Experiment 3), both variables were additive. The conclusion is that the delay is not in the response execution stage and that the decision stage is divided into two substages, with the first substage affected by set size and the second affected by target presence or absence. Additional experiments were performed aimed at deciding between the bottleneck and capacity sharing accounts of the delays. As the arguments involved are less convincing to me, I do not go into them here.

After this book was in production, I became aware, via Mudd (1983), of the research program of George E. Briggs in the late 1960s and during the first half of the 1970s in which he systematically applied Sternberg's method, information theory ideas, and Bayesian calculations to data from a series of experiments. This led him to a surprisingly detailed model of the several stages involved. I do not attempt to insert a description of this work, but those interested in generalizations of Sternberg's approach will find that Mudd (1983) has provided a comprehensive summary. In addition, the following original references are of interest: Briggs (1972, 1974); Briggs and Blaha (1969); Briggs and Johnsen (1973); Briggs, Johnsen, and Shinar (1974); Briggs, Peters, and Fisher (1972); Briggs and Shinar (1972); Briggs and Swanson (1969, 1970); Briggs, Thomason, and Hagman (1978); Johnsen and Briggs (1973); Swanson and Briggs (1969); and Swanson, Johnsen, and Briggs (1972).

12.4.3 Can a Parallel System Mimic the Means of a Serial System?

Although Theorem 12.4 and its proof provides general conditions under which a realizable serial process can be mimicked by a locally stage-independent parallel process, within the framework of additive factors we should consider the conditions under which an observed additivity of factors precludes the possibility of a parallel interpretation. This is, after all, a less stringent demand. Townsend and Ashby (1983, pp. 372–375) have dealt with this question.

Suppose i and j are manipulations and we have

$$E(\mathbf{T}_{ij}) = E(\mathbf{X}_i) + E(\mathbf{X}_j).$$

(12.15)

It is obvious that if l and k are also manipulations, then

$$E(\mathbf{T}_{ij}) - E(\mathbf{T}_{ik}) = E(\mathbf{T}_{ij}) - E(\mathbf{T}_{lk}).$$ (12.16)

Further, it is not difficult to show that Eq. 12.16 is equivalent to the manipulations satisfying what is known in the measurement literature as the Thomson condition (Krantz, Luce, Suppes, and Tversky, 1971):

If $E(\mathbf{T}_{ij}) = E(\mathbf{T}_{lk})$ and $E(\mathbf{T}_{lm}) = E(\mathbf{T}_{nj})$,

then $E(\mathbf{T}_{im}) = E(\mathbf{T}_{nk})$.   (12.17)

Furthermore, Eq. 12.15 implies the following condition that is known as monotonicity or independence:

$$E(\mathbf{T}_{ij}) \geq E(\mathbf{T}_{ik})   \text{iff}   E(\mathbf{T}_{lj}) \geq E(\mathbf{T}_{lk})$$ (12.18a)

and

$$E(\mathbf{T}_{ij}) \geq E(\mathbf{T}_{lj})   \text{iff}   E(\mathbf{T}_{ik}) \geq E(\mathbf{T}_{lk}).$$ (12.18b)

It is also known that under somewhat restrictive additional conditions on the manipulations (restricted solvability and Archimidean) Eqs. 12.17 and 12.18 imply Eq. 12.15 (Krantz, et al, 1971, Ch. 6). So we will work with its consequence, Eq. 12.16.

Now, suppose the underlying mechanism is not serial stages, but rather parallel ones with times $\mathbf{T}_a$ and $\mathbf{T}_b$, where the one class of manipulations affects process a and the other affects b. Let

$$G_{ab,ij}(t) = \Pr[\max(\mathbf{T}_{a,i}, \mathbf{T}_{b,j}) \leq t],$$

then as we have seen before we may write

$$\mu_{ij} = E[\max(\mathbf{T}_{a,i}, \mathbf{T}_{b,j})] = \int_0^\infty [1 - G_{ab,ij}(t)] \, dt.$$ (12.19)

Our question is when is it impossible for Eq. 12.19 to satisfy Eq. 12.16. Observe that

$$\mu_{ij} - \mu_{ik} = \int_0^\infty [G_{ab,ik}(t) - G_{ab,ij}(t)] \, dt,$$

and so a sufficient condition for Eq. 12.16 to fail in the parallel model is that for all $t > 0$,

$$G_{ab,ik}(t) - G_{ab,ij}(t) > G_{ab,lk}(t) - G_{ab,lj}(t).$$ (12.20)

Another sufficient condition is to replace $>$ by $<$ in Eq. 12.20.

Consider the special case when the parallel process are independent, then there are distributions of the component processes, $G_{a,i}$ and $G_{b,j}$, such that

$$G_{ab,ik}(t) = G_{a,i}(t) G_{b,i}(t),$$ (12.21)

in which case Eq. 12.20 is equivalent to

$$[G_{a,i}(t) - G_{a,l}(t)][G_{b,k}(t) - G_{b,j}(t)] > 0 \qquad (12.22)$$

or equally well <0 for all t. Equation 12.22 amounts to saying that the effect of a change in treatment is to alter the distribution function so that the two do not have a common point. An example is a shift family where for some constant α_{ij}

$$G_{a,i}(t) = G_{a,i}(t - \alpha_{ij}).$$

Thus, to the degree Eq. 12.22 is plausible, which it seems to be, it is impossible for independent parallel processes to mimic a finding of additive means using the additive-factors method.

12.4.4 Cautions and Concerns

In presenting the additive-factors method, Sternberg was very cautious in discussing its use. He made the following points.

1. The analysis of variance model is exactly appropriate for additive, independent stages; however, the usual tests of significance are not very appropriate and if used incautiously will lead too easily into accepting the additive independence of response times as a function of the manipulations. As there is no fully satisfactory statistical procedure to decide this, one must be conservative and attempt to run a sufficiently precise experiment so that additivity can be rejected when it is false.

2. The method can isolate serial processing stages, if they exist, but it in no way isolates processes. It is a considerable theoretical leap to decide exactly which processes have been affected and to infer their order of occurrence.

3. If the temporal network is not in fact serial, the inferences can be totally misleading. In particular, under some circumstances, independent parallel processes can be interpreted as interactive serial ones. The circumstances appear likely to hold (Section 12.4.3). Moreover, as McClelland (1979) first established and Ashby (1982b) confirmed, the cascade model, which is a serial, but overlapping, strength model, produces approximate additivity of means when the component processes are manipulated. This result is numerical in character and its analytic basis is not understood. Both authors give rules-of-thumb indicating when they believe additivity will appear in the cascade model.

4. Unlike Donders' scheme, this method provides no information whatsoever about the latencies associated with individual stages.

Others have raised different issues. I shall cite five that strike me as the most pervasive.

First, the method does not confront speed-accuracy tradeoff concerns.

Sternberg assumed that subjects could and would perform as rapidly as is consistent with perfect performance. In practice, however, error rates up to 5% are usually considered acceptable. Others have argued that this is inadequate and one must analyze explicitly the class of speed-accuracy tradeoff models that are consistent with the additive-factors methodology. To some extent, I have already examined these issues in Section 6.4, and I go into it further in Section 12.4.5.

Second, even if one accepts the idea of stages that are temporally quite distinct, surely it is possible that they are not organized serially. One can imagine a stage with several inputs that does not begin processing until all of the inputs to it are completed, or equally one can imagine a stage that begins processing as soon as any input occurs but does not output anything until the processing of the previous stage is completed. Nevertheless, one may be able to infer the network involved by using methods that affect the stages differentially. This I take up in Section 12.4.6.

Third, many of those who have commented on the matter very strongly question the existence of stages at all, at least as conceived by Sternberg. A number of the more popular two-stimulus, response-time models, such as most of those in Chapters 8 and 9, do not postulate anything resembling stages except for the distinction between decision and residual processes. Others who accept the idea of separate processing mechanisms question whether the sharp temporal order postulated by Sternberg is plausible. The cascade model of Section 4.3.2 is an example of one involving temporally overlapping stages. Perhaps the most systematic attack against the stage idea is that found in Taylor (1976a). Other relevant references are Blackman (1975), Pachella (1974), Smith (1980), and Stanovich and Pachella (1977).

Fourth, a variety of what may be lumped together as statistical issues have been raised. Perhaps the most sweeping attack of this sort was by Pieters (1983). I shall mention three major points from this paper. (i) The use of ANOVA was questioned on two counts: the power of the test, about which Sternberg had early cautioned, and the assumption that the variance is independent of the mean. As we know from many sources of data, the latter is almost always false in response-time data—the mean and variance covary in a highly regular fashion. This seems a highly telling argument against using ANOVA in this context. (ii) The data analyzed are usually group data, whereas the idea of stages is clearly about the operation of individual minds. Sufficient conditions are known (Thomas and Ross, 1980) for when a family of individual distributions lead to group data that can be modeled in the same family of distributions. Such conditions are not so easily satisfied that the issue can afford to be ignored; it usually is, however. (iii) Assuming independent stages and studying the additivity of cumulants may well lead to the introduction of artificial stages. Consider for example a stage having a Gaussian distribution with mean μ and variance σ^2, where μ is substantially larger than σ (so the Gaussian approximation does not lead to much trouble with negative times). We know (Eq. 1.56) that the first two cumulants are μ

and σ^2. Now if we have experimental procedures that affect these two parameters of the Gaussian independently, then we will be led to believe two stages are involved. Pieters, in summarizing, likened the method of additive factors to a temporal factor analysis, an analogy not intended to be favorable.

Others have proposed using correlational methods in analyzing such data. One example is Kadane, Larkin, and Mayer (1981). Without going into the details of their proposal, the key idea of a correlational approach is to use Eq. 12.15 to write $\mathbf{T}_{ij} - \mathbf{T}_{ik} = \mathbf{X}_j - \mathbf{X}_k$ and then correlate this quantity with the experimental variable used to manipulate, say, stage j. Donaldson (1983) pointed out that the estimate of the correlation should not be treated as straightforward because of possible measurement error in $\mathbf{T}_{ij} - \mathbf{T}_{ik}$. He made several proposals for alternative approaches, which I do not go into.

For the fifth, I devote a separate subsection.

12.4.5 Speed-Accuracy Tradeoff

As I have already remarked, the custom in much of cognitive psychology is to use response-time measures but to ignore the speed-accuracy tradeoff function or region. (In psychophysics, the custom is to use response error and to ignore response times.) In particular, when presenting the additive factors method, Sternberg focused entirely on the times and was little concerned with errors. The usual reasoning is that the stimuli are perfectly identifiable and error-free performance is readily achieved, and so the focus is necessarily on the time taken to achieve that performance. In practice, however, some errors do occur and one of two conventions is followed: either the relative frequency of errors is reported for each experimental condition and it is noted that no systematic error pattern exists, or the trials on which errors were made are discarded from the analysis. Neither procedure is really satisfactory to those who are convinced that speed-accuracy tradeoff may well reflect a deep aspect of mental processing. For such a person, the only acceptable approach is to study the relation, both empirically and theoretically.

At a theoretical level, Ollman (1979) pointed out that when one is contemplating the method of additive factors it is important to consider the class of tradeoff models that is compatible with the method. Not all are. No completely general answer is known, but Ollman has provided two models that are sufficient.

Suppose we are dealing with a model that presupposes the existence of n additive stages, of which $n-1$ are associated with perceptual processes and one is response in nature. Each stage has some probability of introducing an error. Assume that there are no speed-accuracy tradeoffs in the perceptual stages, but that one exists in the response stage. If so, manipulations affecting the perceptual stages will alter the times but not the errors. So if the response stage is not manipulated, the error rate will be unaffected by perceptual manipulations whereas the times will be affected additively. To be more explicit, consider a two-choice situation and lump together the perceptual processes. Let $\mathbf{T}_S$ denote the latency of perceptual processing and P_S the probability that it is carried out correctly. Similarly, let $\mathbf{T}_R$ and P_R denote the latency and probability of correct response processing. Then the overall mean response time and probability of a correct response are given by

$$E(\mathbf{T}) = E(\mathbf{T}_S) + E(\mathbf{T}_R) \tag{12.23}$$

$$P = P_S P_R + (1 - P_S)(1 - P_R). \tag{12.24}$$

Suppose the speed-accuracy tradeoff of the response process is described by

$$P_R = G[E(\mathbf{T}_R)], \tag{12.25}$$

then substituting Eq. 12.25 into Eq. 12.24 and using Eq. 12.23,

$$P = (2P_S - 1)G[E(\mathbf{T}) - E(\mathbf{T}_S)] + 1 - P_S. \tag{12.26}$$

The surprising thing about this observable speed-accuracy equation is that its intercept is altered as $E(\mathbf{T}_S)$ is changed, despite the fact that it is assumed that perceptual manipulations do not entail a speed-accuracy tradeoff. Note that if $\mathbf{T}_S$ is the sum of the latencies corresponding to two or more perceptual components that can be manipulated independently, then by Eq. 12.23, the additive-factors method is appropriate.

Ollman pointed out that the fast-guess model is also appropriate to the additive-factors method. Assuming symmetry, so $P_{aA} = P_{bB} = P_S$ and setting $E(\mathbf{T}_R) = \nu_0$ and $E(\mathbf{T}_S) = \nu_1 - \nu_0$ in Eq. 7.31c, we then have as the speed-accuracy trade-off

$$P = \frac{(P_S - \frac{1}{2})}{E(\mathbf{T}_S)}[E(\mathbf{T}) - E(\mathbf{T}_R)] + \frac{1}{2}. \tag{12.27}$$

Unlike the previous model, altering the perceptual process affects not the intercept of the tradeoff, but rather its slope. But so long as the manipulation affects the sensory process in such a way that the probability of a fast guess is unaffected, there will be no speed-accuracy tradeoff and the additive factors methods is appropriate.

For other speed-accuracy tradeoff models, it is a matter to verify whether the method is appropriate. Probably one's prior bias should be against its appropriateness.

12.4.6   Critical Path Generalization of Additive-Factors Method

The only attempt of which I am aware to generalize additive factors to processing networks other than serial is due to Schweickert (1978, 1980, 1982a, b; 1983a, b). His work is both conceptually and empirically interesting; but as of now it is somewhat limited by the assumption that the processing latencies are deterministic, not random variables. It draws upon a method, called critical path analysis, originally developed in operations research and computer programming. The focus there was on calculating the time required to complete a task as a function of the flow diagram and the durations of the various stages of processing (Kelley, 1961; Modor and Phillips, 1970; Weist and Levy, 1969). In contrast to the way in which critical path methods are usually applied, when studying mental processes we do not know the processing network in advance. Rather, our task is to infer the network from the overall response times obtained under various experimental manipulations aimed at differentially affecting the latencies of the components.

We shall need some terminology. A *partial order* on a set X is a relation $<$ on X satisfying two properties:

(i) $<$ is irreflexive: for all x in X, not $x < x$.
(ii) $<$ is transitive: for all x, y, z in X, if $x < y$ and $y < z$, then $x < z$.

A relation on a set of processing stages is called a *processing network* if and only if it is a partial order for which there is a unique *starting* stage s (i.e., a stage having no antecedent element in the order) and a unique *terminating* stage t (i.e., one having no successor in the order). Two stages are called *comparable* if and only if one precedes the other in the order; otherwise, they are called *incomparable*. These two concepts generalize the primary features of, respectively, serial and parallel networks. A network is *serial* if there is a unique labeling of the elements, $x_1, x_2, \ldots, x_n$ such that $s = x_1$, $t = x_n$, and $x_i < x_j$ if and only if $i < j$. In a serial network, any two distinct stages are comparable. A network is *parallel* if for all x, y in $X - \{s, t\}$, $s < x$, $y < t$, and x and y are incomparable.

To sketch such networks one can use either of two conventions. Each stage can be represented as a node, connecting an arrow from node x to node y if and only if $x < y$, or each stage can be represented as an arrow, leading the head of stage x into the tail of stage y if and only if $x < y$. The latter seems more useful in the present context.

The first major concept in this work is that of the *slack* of a stage: the amount of delay that can be introduced into that stage before it results in an increase in the overall time to complete the network using paths through that stage. For example, in the network of Figure 12.5, where the times of the individual stages are shown, then the slack of stage x is 2. The reason is that stage w cannot be begun until z is completed, which takes 11 time units, whereas x followed by y takes only 9 units. So, the path via x and y does not slow down the entire process until it takes more than 11 units, and so x can be increased from 5 to 7 without affecting matters. Similarly, the slack for y is 2, whereas those of z and w are each 0. The latter illustrates the general fact that the slacks of stages on a *critical path*—one controlling the overall time—must all be 0. In particular, in a serial process, all stages have zero slack.

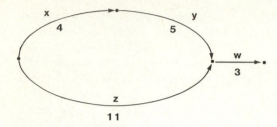

FIG. 12.5 A network of stages described in the text.

We have previously encountered slack considerations in the study of Welford's single channel hypothesis (Section 5.4). The results stated here generalize those.

Theorem 12.6 (Schweickert, 1978). *Suppose x and y are two stages of a processing network and suppose that the time of x is prolonged by Δx and that of y by Δy. Let ΔT denote the change in overall time, T, due to the prolongations shown in its argument.*

(i) *If x and y are incomparable stages, then*

$$\Delta T(\Delta x, \Delta y) = \max[\Delta T(\Delta x), \Delta T(\Delta y)]. \tag{12.28}$$

(ii) *If x and y are comparable, if x precedes y, if x and y are sufficiently large so that $\Delta T(\Delta x) > 0$, $\Delta T(\Delta y) > 0$, and if in the presence of both prolongations x and y lie on a critical path, then*

$$\Delta T(\Delta x, \Delta y) = \Delta T(\Delta x) + \Delta T(\Delta y) + K(x, y), \tag{12.29}$$

where the term $K(x, y)$, which is called the coupled slack *between x and y, depends upon x and y but not upon Δx and Δy.*

Proof. (i) Let S_x and S_y be the slacks of x and y and let $S_y(\Delta x)$ be the slack of stage y given that x has been prolonged by Δx. Introduce the notation

$$[a]^+ = \begin{cases} a & \text{if} \quad a > 0, \\ 0 & \text{if} \quad a \leq 0. \end{cases}$$

By definition of the slacks,

$$\Delta T(\Delta x, \Delta y) = T(\Delta x, \Delta y) - T$$
$$= \Delta T(\Delta x) + [\Delta y - S_y(\Delta x)]^+.$$

But clearly,

$$S_y(\Delta x) = S_y + [\Delta x - S_x]^+,$$

and so substituting and using the definition of $[a]^+$,

$$\Delta T(\Delta x, \Delta y) = \Delta T(\Delta x) + [\Delta y - S_y - [\Delta x - S_x]^+]^+$$
$$= \Delta T(\Delta x) + [\Delta T(\Delta y) - \Delta T(\Delta x)]^+$$
$$= \max[\Delta T(\Delta x), \Delta T(\Delta y)].$$

(ii) By assumption, when both Δx and Δy have been applied there is a critical path from s through x and y to t; let x_1 and x_2 denote the stages of the critical path that immediately precede and succeed, respectively, x, and let y_1 and y_2 be the similar ones for y. This path may or may not be critical when less than both prolongations have been introduced. Denote by $d(u, v)$ the duration on this path from stage u to stage v and let $d(u)$ be the duration of stage u. Thus, on this path but with no prolongations,

$$T = d(s, t) + d(s, y_1) + d(y) + d(y_2, t) + S_y.$$

Let S_{xy} denote the slack of x relative to just stage y, not to the entire process. Then,

$$d(s, y_1) = d(s, x_1) + d(x) + d(x_2, y_1) + S_{xy}.$$

Substituting,

$$T = d(s, x_1) + d(x) + d(x_2, y_1) + d(y) + d(y_2, t) + S_y + S_{xy}.$$

Since by assumption the path becomes critical when both prolongations Δx and Δy are introduced, and so all of the times simply add, we see that

$$T(\Delta x, \Delta y) = d(s, x_1) + d(x) + \Delta x + d(x_2, y_1) + d(y) + \Delta y + d(y_2, t).$$

Taking the difference,

$$\Delta T(\Delta x, \Delta y) = \Delta x - S_{xy} + \Delta y - S_y.$$

But $0 < \Delta T(\Delta x) = \Delta x - S_x$ and $0 < \Delta T(\Delta y) = \Delta y - S_y$, so Eq. 12.29 holds with

$$K(x, y) = S_x - S_{xy}. \qquad\blacksquare$$

At first glance, it appears as if the coupled slack $K(x, y)$ should be non-negative since one might anticipate that the slack of x relative to stage y is no greater than the entire slack, but that is incorrect. Consider the network shown in Figure 12.6. We see that S_{xy} is 4 because y cannot begin

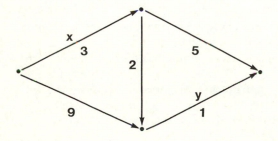

FIG. 12.6 A network of stages discussed in the text.

TABLE 12.5. Response times and changes in them from Sternberg's digit naming experiment[a]

Stimulus quality	Number of alternatives	Response transformation	Prolongation			RT	ΔRT
Intact	2	n	Baseline			328	0
Degraded	2	n	ΔQ				30
Intact	8	n		ΔN			43
Degraded	8	n	ΔQ	ΔN			97
Intact	2	$n+1$			ΔR		18
Degraded	2	$n+1$	ΔQ		ΔR		45
Intact	8	$n+1$		ΔN	ΔR		144
Degraded	8	$n+1$	ΔQ	ΔN	ΔR		197

$$K(Q, N) = \Delta RT(\Delta Q, \Delta N) - \Delta RT(\Delta Q) - \Delta RT(\Delta N)$$
$$= 97 - 30 - 43 = 24$$
$$K(N, R) = \Delta RT(\Delta N, \Delta R) - \Delta RT(\Delta N) - \Delta RT(\Delta R)$$
$$= 144 - 43 - 18 = 83$$
$$\Delta RT(\Delta Q, \Delta N, \Delta R) = \Delta RT(\Delta Q) + \Delta RT(\Delta N) + \Delta RT(\Delta R) + K(Q, N) + K(N, R)$$
$$= 30 + 43 + 18 + 24 + 83$$
$$= 198 \text{ versus } 197 \text{ observed}$$

[a] Adapted from a handout of Schweickert (1982b).

until 9 units have elapsed. But for the entire process the slack of x is only 2 because any larger value causes the upper path of $3+5=8$ to exceed 10, the total time of the originally slowest path. Thus, $K(x, y) = 2 - 4 = -2$. Schweickert (1978) has shown that a network has a negative coupled slack if and only if it includes a subnetwork of the form shown in Figure 12.6.

Part (ii) of Theorem 12.6 generalizes to three manipulations as follows:

$$\Delta T(\Delta x, \Delta y, \Delta z) = \Delta T(\Delta x, 0, 0) + \Delta T(0, \Delta y, 0) + \Delta T(0, 0, \Delta z)$$
$$+ K(x, y) + K(y, z). \tag{12.30}$$

12.4.7 An Application of the Critical Path Method

Schweickert (1982b) did a critical path analysis of Sternberg's (1971) digit-naming experiment (Section 12.4.2) in which the three manipulations were: intact or degraded stimuli, two or eight search alternatives, and respond either with the target digit or its successor. Using Q to refer to the stage(s) affected by stimulus Quality, N those affected by the Number of alternatives, and R to those affected by the Response transformation, the data are tabulated in Table 12.5. It is clear that Eq. 12.28 does not hold for any pair of the factors, so none are incomparable. Using Eq. 12.29 twice to calculate the two coupled slacks $K(Q, N)$ and $K(N, R)$ from the pairwise data, we see that Eq. 12.30 is satisfied within 1 msec. So the evidence is that we are dealing with a simple serial process with the stages either in the order $Q < N < R$ or $R < N < Q$. Rather obviously, the former is the more plausible. This conclusion is to be contrasted with Sternberg's (Section 12.4.2) that the manipulations N and Q affect at least one common stage. The reason for the different conclusion is embodied in the idea of coupled slacks. Had each manipulation been at three or more levels rather than two, one could check to see if the coupled slacks are in fact independent of the levels used, as is predicted.

Schweickert (1983a) has presented more complex analyses of other data, some of which reject network models and others yield evidence for incomparable processes that are consistent with networks more complex than the serial one of the additive-factors model.

The critical path method seems clearly a useful generalization of the additive-factors method, but its value is distinctly limited by the fact that the latencies are assumed to be fixed quantities. This does not cause great difficulties in the additive expressions such as Eqs. 12.29 and 12.30, but it surely raises problems with Eq. 12.28. Work on random variable generalizations is clearly warranted.

12.4.8 *Inferring the Processing Network from Comparability Data*

In principle, at least, Theorem 12.6 provides us with a way to decide for each pair of stages whether they are comparable or incomparable. So the next question, which Schweickert (1983b) took up in detail, is the degree to which one can uniquely infer the processing network from comparability information on all pairs of stages.

A *comparability relation* simply says for any two nodes (stages), whether or not they are comparable, which relation is obviously symmetric. Any symmetric relation C is said to be *consistent* with a partial order $<$ on the same set X of nodes if and only if for every x, y in X, xCy is equivalent to either $x < y$ or $y < x$. So the first issue is the conditions under which a comparability graph is consistent with a partial order, and the second issue is how unique is the induced partial order. To answer these two questions, we need two additional concepts.

Suppose C on X is a symmetric relation. A subset Y of X is *partitive* if and only if for all x, y in Y and all a in $X - Y$ it is true that aCx is equivalent to aCy. A subset Z of X is *stable* if and only if for all x, y in Z it is not true that xCy.

Theorem 12.7 (Shevrin and Filippov, 1970; Trotter, Moore, and Summer, 1976). *A symmetric (comparability) relation is consistent with a partial order* *if and only if every proper partitive subset is stable. In that case, the relation is consistent with exactly two partial orders, which are converses of each other.*

A proof can be found in Schweickert (1983b).

The following result attempts to make clear the meaning of partitive in those comparability relations arising from response-time experiments.

Theorem 12.8.   *A subset Y of a comparability relation arising from Theorem 12.6 is partitive if and only if for every x, y in Y and a in $X - Y$, the slack S_{ax} is defined if and only if S_{ay} is defined; when both are defined, they are equal.*

So far, the situations to which these methods have been applied are sufficiently simple, usually involving only three manipulations, that it is easy to infer the partial order and to establish its uniqueness. For more complex cases in the future, these results provide the conditions for the existence and uniqueness of the partial order. Schweickert (1983a) has provided a systematic algorithm for finding the partial order, if it exists.

12.5   CONCLUSIONS

The first conclusion of the chapter, formulated in Section 12.2.6, is that even rather complete distributional data from a single choice experiment do not permit us to infer much about the underlying organization of information processing. This was based upon a series of quite general mimicking theorems. The remaining two sections were concerned with attempts to use closely related sets of experiments to draw the desired inferences.

In Section 12.3, we examined families of related Same-Difference designs involving stimuli consisting of one or two basic elements, such as letters, which were intended to decide between serial or parallel processing and exhaustive or self-terminating searches. Results were derived that, in principle, should permit the choices to be made, but I do not find the argument entirely convincing. There were two basic problems. The least fundamental was the fact that to fit the data at all so many parameters had to be introduced that hardly any degrees of freedom were left to test the model. Presumably, that could be overcome by considering other, somewhat more complex designs. However, that would feed into my other, far more fundamental, objection: the particular search sequences postulated, which are by no means uniquely defined by the experimental situation, are not justified by any deep psychological principles. In some sense they are optimal, but there is no assurance that subjects in such an artificial experiment are performing optimally. To make the approach convincing, one really should consider all logically tenable search procedures, in which case it is doubtful if any clear inference could be drawn.

The third approach is really a historical sequence of ideas, beginning with Donders' method of pure insertion, to the serial, additive factors techniques of Sternberg and the single channel hypothesis of Welford, and ending in the critical path methods of Schweickert. All of these methods presume substantially the same experimental task, but with experimental manipulations that are believed either to eliminate a stage of processing totally (Donders) or to alter the time required of one or more stages. In different contexts, both Sternberg and Welford introduced versions of the latter idea on the assumption of a serial system. Sternberg showed how to use analysis-of-variance techniques to search for signs of nonadditivity, which within the context of a serial system, is interpreted as evidence that the manipulations affect a common stage. Schweickert, in contrast, considered any possible network of precedence relations and used various relations among the observed (and treated as deterministic) times as the manipulations are carried out singly and together. From such data, he has shown how to make reasonably detailed inferences about the underlying processing. His methods have yet to be widely used and they suffer from the fact that they have not been developed for random variables. However, they appear to hold considerable promise for clarifying the organization of processing—at least on the assumption that stages exist.

As I said at the onset, I make no attempt to draw overall conclusions, which would amount to little more than a recapitulation of the conclusions of this and the ten preceding chapters. I cannot, however, refrain from commenting that despite the fragmentary nature of the results, progress is being made. We know far more today about response times and their uses than we did a decade ago, let alone in the early 1950s when I first started to work in the area.

APPENDIXES

Appendix A: Asymptotic Results for Independent Random Variables

A.1 SERIAL MODELS: SUM OF RANDOM VARIABLES

A number of authors have suggested that perhaps the decision process, as may also be true of the residual one, is composed of a number of independent components. One way in which this might come about is for the information on several different neural fibers to be extracted sequentially. Such a notion coupled with the physiological observations that from 100 to as many as 1000 fibers are activated by, for example, a pure tone, suggests that it may be reasonable to suppose there are a relatively large number of very similar components. Of course, the possibility cannot be dismissed that before a decision is reached another component, say a computation, having quite a different distribution is added to all of them. It is not difficult to think of additional variations. I shall treat several of the best known variants in this appendix. Throughout, independence is the main assumption, and in this section I also assume that the several component times are added.

A.1.1 Identical Random Variables

The purpose of this subsection is to formulate the result that, among other things, describes how the sample mean of a random sample,

$$\bar{\mathbf{X}}_n = \frac{1}{n} \sum_{i=1}^{n} \mathbf{X}_i,$$

behaves as n becomes large. The result—that there is a unique limiting distribution and that it is Gaussian—is called the *Central Limit Theorem*. The term apparently originated with Pólya (1920) who referred to it as "the central limit theorem of probability theory," meaning "primary" or "most significant" limit theorem.

Recall that in Section 1.3.5 we argued that one should look not at $\mathbf{X}_n$ itself but the normalized random variable

$$\mathbf{X}_n^* = \frac{\bar{\mathbf{X}}_n - \mu}{\sigma/\sqrt{n}},$$

which has expected value 0 and variance 1 for every n.

Theorem A.1 (Central Limit Theorem). *Suppose $\mathbf{X}_1, \ldots, \mathbf{X}_k, \ldots$, are independent, identically distributed random variables with mean μ and variance σ^2. Then for all real a and b, $a < b$,*

$$\lim_{n \to \infty} \Pr(a < \mathbf{X}_n^* < b) = \frac{1}{(2\pi)^{1/2}} \int_a^b \exp\left[\frac{-x^2}{2}\right] dx$$
$$= \Phi(b) - \Phi(a), \qquad (A.1)$$

where Φ denotes the unit Gaussian distribution.

Proof.   Since

$$n(\overline{\mathbf{X}}_n - \mu) = \sum_{k=1}^n (\mathbf{X}_k - \mu),$$

then letting $\mathcal{M}_\mathbf{y}$ denote the mgf of $\mathbf{Y}$,

$$\mathcal{M}_{n(\overline{\mathbf{X}}_n - \mu)} = [\mathcal{M}_{(\mathbf{X} - \mu)}]^n,$$

where $\mathbf{X}$ is the generic random variable. Since

$$\mathbf{X}_n^* = \frac{\overline{\mathbf{X}}_n - \mu}{\sigma/\sqrt{n}} = \frac{1}{\sigma\sqrt{n}}[n(\overline{\mathbf{X}}_n - \mu)],$$

$$\mathcal{M}_{\mathbf{X}_n^*}(s) = \mathcal{M}_{n(\overline{\mathbf{X}}_n - \mu)}(s/\sigma\sqrt{n}) = [\mathcal{M}_{\mathbf{X} - \mu}(s/\sigma\sqrt{n})]^n.$$

Consider the Taylor's series expansion of $\mathcal{M}_{\mathbf{X} - \mu}$,

$$\mathcal{M}_{\mathbf{X} - \mu}(s) = \mathcal{M}_{\mathbf{X} - \mu}(0) + \mathcal{M}_{\mathbf{X} - \mu}^{(1)}(0)s + \mathcal{M}_{\mathbf{X} - \mu}^{(2)}(0)s^2/2!$$
$$+ \mathcal{M}_{\mathbf{X} - \mu}^{(3)}(\xi)^3/3!, \quad \text{where } 0 \le \xi \le s.$$

Let $\varepsilon(s) = s\mathcal{M}_{\mathbf{X} - \mu}^{(3)}(\xi)/3!$. Using Eq. 1.48,

$$\mathcal{M}_{\mathbf{X} - \mu}(s) = e^{-s\mu}\mathcal{M}_{\mathbf{X}}(s),$$

and so by several applications of Eq. 1.47,

$$\mathcal{M}_{\mathbf{X} - \mu}(0) = 1,$$
$$\mathcal{M}_{\mathbf{X} - \mu}^{(1)}(0) = 0,$$
$$\mathcal{M}_{\mathbf{X} - \mu}^{(2)}(0) = \sigma^2$$

Substituting into the Taylor's series expansion,

$$\mathcal{M}_{\mathbf{X} - \mu}(s) = 1 + \tfrac{1}{2}\sigma^2 s^2 + s^2 \varepsilon(s).$$

Therefore,

$$\mathcal{M}_{\mathbf{X}_n^*}(s) = \left[1 + \frac{s^2}{2n} + \frac{s^2}{\sigma^2 n}\varepsilon\left(\frac{s}{\sigma\sqrt{n}}\right)\right]^n.$$

Since $\varepsilon(s) \to 0$ as $s \to 0$, the right term is negligible relative to $s^2/2n$, and so by definition of the number *e*,

$$\lim_{n \to \infty} \mathcal{M}_{\mathbf{X}_n^*}(s) = \lim_{n \to \infty} (1 + s^2/2n)^n = \exp(s^2/2),$$

which by Eq. 1.50 is the mgf of the Gaussian with mean 0 and variance 1. ∎

Among other things, the proof establishes that a unique asymptotic distribution exists. If one is willing to assume this is so, then there is a simpler line of argument which establishes that the asymptotic distribution is Gaussian.

With no loss of generality, assume $\mu = 0$ and $\sigma = 1$. Let $\mathbf{S}_n = \sum_{k=1}^{n} \mathbf{X}_k$; clearly, $\mathbf{S}_n/\sqrt{n}$ has mean 0 and variance 1. On the assumption that an asymptotic distribution G exists, consider the very special case where all the $\mathbf{X}_k$ have that distribution, as of course so does $\mathbf{S}_n/\sqrt{n}$. Denote by $\mathcal{M}$ the moment generating function of G, then

$$\begin{aligned} \mathcal{M}(s) &= E[\exp(s\mathbf{S}_n/\sqrt{n})] \\ &= \mathcal{M}_{\mathbf{S}_n}(s/\sqrt{n}) \\ &= \mathcal{M}(s/\sqrt{n})^n, \end{aligned} \tag{A.2}$$

where we have used the fact that the mgf of a sum of independent random variables is the product of their respective mgf's. Since Eq. A.2 must hold for every positive number *s* and every integer *n*, it clearly places substantial constraints on the mgf $\mathcal{M}$. Indeed, this functional equation has a unique solution.

Theorem A.2. *If Eq. A.2 holds for* mgf $\mathcal{M}$, *then* $\mathcal{M}(s) = \exp(s^2/2)$, *which is the* mgf *of the Gaussian with mean 0 and variance 1.*

I formulate this result, even though it is implied by Theorem A.1, because it is really quite easy to prove and because the strategy involved can be generalized to other asymptotic problems. In particular, we will follow it in order to arrive at the form of the asymptotic distribution of the maximum of independent, identically distributed (abbreviated iid) random variables.

A.1.2 Distribution of Counts in a Renewal Process

Another way to view the problem of sums of independent, identically distributed random variables is in terms of the number $\mathbf{N}(t)$ of events that have occurred by time *t*. Such a counting process, in which the inter-event intervals are independent and identically distributed is called a *renewal* process. The major observation is the following equivalence of events when we look at the process both from the point of view of sums and counts:

$$\mathbf{N}(t) < n \text{ if and only if } \mathbf{S}_n > t.$$

This simple fact can be used to derive a central limit theorem for the renewal process $\{\mathbf{N}(t)\}$.

Theorem A.3. *Suppose* $\mathbf{X}_n$, $n = 1, 2, \ldots$, *are independent and identically distributed random variables with finite mean* μ *and variance* σ^2. *Let* $\mathbf{N}(t) = n$ *if and only if* $\mathbf{S}_n = \sum \mathbf{X}_i \leq t$ *and* $\mathbf{S}_{n+1} > t$. *Then*

$$\lim_{t \to \infty} \Pr\left[\frac{\mathbf{N}(t) - t/\mu}{(t\sigma^2/\mu^3)^{1/2}} < x\right] = \Phi(x),$$

where Φ *is the unit Gaussian distribution function.*

Proof. Fix x and let n and t approach ∞ so that

$$\lim_{n,t \to \infty} \frac{t - n\mu}{\sigma n^{1/2}} = -x.$$

Now, by Theorem A.1, we know that

$$\lim_{n,t \to \infty} \Pr\{\mathbf{S}_n > t\} = \lim_{n,t \to \infty} \Pr\left[\frac{\mathbf{S}_n - n\mu}{\sigma n^{1/2}} > -x\right] = 1 - \Phi(-x) = \Phi(x).$$

But,

$$\Pr\{\mathbf{S}_n > t\} = \Pr\{\mathbf{N}(t) < n\}$$
$$= \Pr\left[\frac{\mathbf{N}(t) - t/\mu}{(t\sigma^2/\mu^3)^{1/2}} < \frac{n - t/\mu}{(t\sigma^2/\mu^3)^{1/2}}\right].$$

Observe that

$$\frac{n - t/\mu}{(t\sigma^2/\mu^3)^{1/2}} = \frac{n\mu - t}{(n\sigma^2)^{1/2}}\left[\frac{\mu n}{t}\right]^{1/2}.$$

By hypothesis, as $n, t \to \infty$ the first term on the right approaches x, and we show that the second on the right approaches 1, which then establishes the assertion. To show that $\mu n/t \to 1$, consider the identity

$$\frac{t - n\mu}{(n\sigma^2)^{1/2}} = \frac{1 - \mu n/t}{\sigma n^{1/2}/t}. \tag{A.3}$$

If $\mu n/t \to \infty$ or $-\infty$, then the right term approaches $\mu n^{1/2}/\sigma$, which in turn approaches ∞. But this contradicts the assumption about the limiting process that the left term of Eq. A.3 approaches $-x$. So $\mu n/t$ must have a finite limit, say k. If $k \neq 1$, then since

$$n^{1/2}/t = (\mu n/t)(1/\mu n^{1/2}) \to k(1/\mu n^{1/2}) \to 0,$$

we see again that the right term of Eq. A.6 approaches ∞ or $-\infty$, which is impossible. Thus, $k = 1$, completing the proof. ■

Perhaps the most remarkable aspect of this result is the fact that the asymptotic variance is of the form $t\sigma^2/\mu^3$, and there is little that is intuitive about the factor μ^3 except that it leads to a dimensionless quantity, which the variance of a count must be.

A.1.3 Nearly Identical Random Variables

From the middle of the 18th century, various limit theorems were formulated and more-or-less proved, but it was not until Liapounov (1900, 1901) that the central limit theorem for iid random variables was proved rigorously and generally. During the next 40 years the problem was greatly broadened and completely solved. Basically the question became a search for conditions under which it is possible to find two sequences of numbers $\{a_n\}$ and $\{b_n\}$ such that the distribution of $a_n \mathbf{S}_n + b_n$ converges to the Gaussian distribution. Note that for the iid case, $b_n = -n^{1/2}\mu/\sigma$ and $a_n = 1/n^{1/2}\sigma$ are the normalizing sequences usually used. For those with a strong mathematical background, a full treatment can be found in Ch. VI of Loève (1963, 1977) or in Gnedenko and Kolmogorov (1954). Here we only mention a sufficient condition due to Lindeberg (1922). Suppose $\mathbf{X}_k$ are mutually independent random variables with density functions f_i for which $E(\mathbf{X}_k) = 0$ and $V(\mathbf{X}_k) = \sigma_k$. Set

$$s_n^2 = \sum_{k=1}^{n} \sigma_k^2 \qquad \text{and} \qquad \mathbf{S}_n^* = \mathbf{S}_n/s_n.$$

If for every $t > 0$,

$$\lim_{n \to \infty} \frac{1}{s_n^2} \sum_{k=1}^{n} \int_{|y| \ge +s_n} y^2 f_k(y)\, du = 0,$$

then the distribution of $\mathbf{S}_n^*$ approaches the Gaussian with 0 mean and unit variance as n approaches ∞. In particular, if there is a finite interval $[a, b]$ such that with probability 1 each of the $\mathbf{X}_k$ lies entirely in $[a, b]$, then the condition is met; however, there are many cases of unbounded variables for which it is also met.

Although great care must be exercised in invoking the central limit theorem to understand empirical phenomena—it is by no means a universal rationale for assuming that a random variable of a theory has the Gaussian distribution—certain psychophysical reaction-time situations appear to fulfill at least some of the conditions just described. For example, signals to either the eye or to the ear are known to activate relatively large numbers of anatomically parallel nerve fibers, and there is some physiological evidence to suggest that the activation of these fibers is both comparable in magnitude and independent. Thus, one might well associate with each fiber a random variable corresponding to the time it takes to extract the information on that fiber. At this point, however, it becomes less clear what one should assume. Do those times add, leading to a decision? If so, is there some additional time taken up in somehow combining the information? Or are all those times being carried out in parallel so it is the slowest that determines the total time involved in the initial extraction of information? It is clear that a variety of models are possible; some of these possibilities are treated in the remainder of the appendix.

A.1.4 Identical Gaussians

If some sort of repetition of random variables leads to an asymptotic distribution, then repeating random variables with that distribution must continue to result in it. This is the closure property of asymptotic distributions. So one anticipates that the sum of two independent Gaussian random variables must also be Gaussian. This is easily verified by a moment generating function argument. Suppose $\{X_k\}$ are independent Gaussian with means μ_k and variances σ_k^2. By Eq. 1.50, their mgf's are $\exp(\mu_k s + \frac{1}{2}\sigma_k^2 s^2)$. Thus, the mgf of the sum is

$$\prod_{k=1}^{n} \exp[\mu_k s + \tfrac{1}{2}\sigma_k^2 s^2] = \exp\left[s \sum_{k=1}^{n} \mu_k + \tfrac{1}{2}s^2 \sum_{k=1}^{n} \sigma_k^2 \right],$$

which clearly is the mgf of a Gaussian with mean $\sum_{k=1}^{n} \mu_k$ and variance $\sum_{k=1}^{n} \sigma_k^2$.

A.1.5 Identical Exponentials

Suppose the random variables X_k are independent and exponentially distributed—say, by $1 - e^{-\lambda_k x}$. By Eq. 1.49, each has the mgf $\lambda_k/(\lambda_k - s)$, and so by Eq. 1.46 the mgf of the sum S_n is $\prod_{k=1}^{n} \lambda_k/(\lambda_k - s)$. Even in the simple case where all $\lambda_k = \lambda$, it is not immediately obvious which distribution has $\lambda^n/(\lambda - s)^n$ as its mgf. One can, in fact, find it in tables (Erdelyi, Magnus, Oberhettinger, & Tricomi, 1954). However, because exponentials have nice mathematical properties, it is not very difficult to calculate the density function f_n of S_n directly by induction. Observe that $S_n = t$ occurs whenever $S_{n-1} = x$ and $X_n = t - x$. Since X_n and S_{n-1} are independent and non-negative,

$$f_n(t) = \int_0^t f_{n-1}(x)\lambda e^{-\lambda(t-x)} \, dx$$

$$= \lambda e^{-\lambda t} \int_0^t f_{n-1}(x) e^{\lambda x} \, dx.$$

(A.4)

For $n = 2$, $f_{n-1}(x) = f_1(x) = \lambda e^{-\lambda x}$, and substituting into Eq. A.4 and integrating we see $f_2(t) = \lambda^2 t e^{-\lambda t}$. Computing a few more terms suggests the induction hypothesis

$$f_n(t) = \frac{\lambda^n t^{n-1} e^{-\lambda t}}{(n-1)!}.$$

(A.5)

Substitution of Eq. A.5 into Eq. A.4 verifies the conjecture, as does computing the mgf of Eq. A.5. The density shown in Eq. A.5 is known as the *gamma*; an explicit formula, in elementary functions, for its distribution function is not possible. Obviously, being the sum of n identical exponentials, the mean is n/λ and the variance is n/λ^2. Its hazard function cannot be expressed in simple terms because the distribution function can only be expressed as an integral; however, we may use Theorem 1.1 to determine its qualitative characteristics. Observe that

$$-\ln f_n(t) = -n \ln \lambda - (n-1) \ln t + \lambda t + \ln(n-1)!,$$

and so

$$-\frac{d \ln f(t)}{dt} = -\frac{(n-1)}{t} + \lambda,$$

which for $n > 1$ is an increasing function of t. Thus, the hazard function of the gamma for $n > 1$ is increasing; for $n = 1$, it is constant.

To gain some idea of what happens when the parameters are not equal, consider the case of $n = 2$. Following McGill (1963), we may write the mgf as

$$\mathcal{M}_2(s) = \frac{\lambda_1 \lambda_2}{(\lambda_1 - s)(\lambda_2 - s)}$$

$$= \frac{\lambda_1 \lambda_2}{\lambda_2 - \lambda_1} \left[\frac{1}{\lambda_1 - s} - \frac{1}{\lambda_2 - s} \right]$$

$$= \frac{\lambda_1 \lambda_2}{\lambda_2 - \lambda_1} \int_0^\infty \left[e^{-(\lambda_1 - s)t} - e^{-(\lambda_2 - s)t} \right] dt$$

$$= \frac{\lambda_1 \lambda_2}{\lambda_2 - \lambda_1} \int_0^\infty e^{st} [e^{-\lambda_1 t} - e^{-\lambda_2 t}] dt,$$

which we see is the mgf of

$$\frac{\lambda_1 \lambda_2}{\lambda_2 - \lambda_1} [e^{-\lambda_1 t} - e^{-\lambda_2 t}]. \tag{A.6}$$

Suppose with no loss of generality that $\lambda_2 > \lambda_1$, and let $\alpha = \lambda_2 - \lambda_1$, then Eq. A.6 can be rewritten as

$$\frac{\lambda_1 \lambda_2}{\lambda_2 - \lambda_1} e^{-\lambda_1 t}(1 - e^{-\alpha t}),$$

and we see that for large t, $e^{-\alpha t}$ is negligible and the overall process is dominated by the slower process. Thus, one can estimate λ_1 by fitting $e^{-\lambda_1 t}$ to the tail of the empirical distribution, and then by deconvolving it, $\lambda_2 e^{-\lambda_2 t}$ remains. This generalizes to any number of exponentials. In principle, the slowest can be isolated and removed, then the next slowest, and so on. Clearly, however, errors accumulate, and the method has never been used in connection with response-time data.

Ashby (1982a) has established the following result, which weakens considerably the hypotheses leading to an exponential tail, but also weakens the conclusion to the point where it is not clear how to make use of the result.

Theorem A.4. *Suppose $X_1, \ldots, X_n$ are independent random variables whose hazard functions are all non-decreasing, that at least one of them is exponential, and that λ is the smallest of the exponential parameters. Then there exists a number $\eta \leq \lambda$ such that if $\lambda(t)$ is the hazard function of $\sum_{k=1}^{n} X_k$, then $\lim_{t \to \infty} \lambda(t) = \eta$.*

The result says the tail of the sum is exponential if at least one component is exponential and all others have non-decreasing hazard functions, but the trouble is that the exponential parameter of the tail need not be that of any of the components. We need to know conditions under which $\eta = \lambda$, in which case we could deconvolve the slowest exponential component.

A.2 PARALLEL MODELS: MAXIMA OF INDEPENDENT, IDENTICAL RANDOM VARIABLES

If the information from each neural fiber is extracted in parallel, not in series, then the total time required to extract that information is the maximum, not the sum, of these random variables. Suppose they are X_k and have distribution functions F_k. The only way in which the process will be completed by time t is for each of the separate ones to be completed by then. Assuming they are independent, we see that

$$\Pr[\max(X_1, X_2, \ldots, X_n) \leq x] = \prod_{k=1}^{n} F_k(x). \tag{A.7}$$

In the case where they are all identically distributed, this distribution reduces to F^n. Observe that there is some formal similarity to the additive case. There we worked with products of the mgf's, whereas here products of the distribution functions play a comparable role.

A.2.1 *Form of Asymptotic Distributions*

As we did for the sum of iid random variables, we may ask the question whether or not the distribution of the maximum converges in some sense to an asymptotic distribution that is independent of the initial distribution. And as was the case there, we may gain some initial insight into the problem by supposing that such a distribution exists and then searching for it by assuming that the components all have this distribution. So let G be that distribution, and let us suppose that X_k, $k = 1, 2, \ldots$, are independent and are distributed according to G. It follows that under some appropriate change of variable, the maximum of n of these also has the distribution G. That is, for some sequences $\{a_i\}$ and $\{b_i\}$, for all integers n, and for all real x,

$$G(a_n x + b_n) = G(x)^n. \tag{A.8}$$

The question is to find the solutions to this family of equations. The result is only slightly more complex than that for sums.

Theorem A.5. *Suppose that G is a distribution function that is differentiable and strictly increasing for $0 < G < 1$ and that $\{a_n\}$ and $\{b_n\}$ are sequences of numbers for which Eq. A.8 holds. Then there are three classes of solutions:*

(i) $G(0) \neq 0, 1$ *in which case* $a_n = 1$, $b_n = -\ln n$, *and*

$$G(x) = \exp[-e^{-\alpha(x-\beta)}], \qquad \alpha > 0. \tag{A.9}$$

(ii) $G(0) = 0$, *in which case one choice for the sequences is* $a_n = (1/n)^{1/\alpha}$, $\alpha > 0$, $b_n = 0$ *and*

$$G(x) = \begin{cases} \exp(-bx^{-\alpha}), & x > 0, \, b > 0, \\ 0, & x \leq 0. \end{cases} \tag{A.10}$$

(iii) $G(0) = 1$, *in which case one choice for the sequences is* $a_n = -n^{1/\alpha}$, $\alpha > 0$, $b_n = 0$, *and*

$$G(x) = \begin{cases} 1, & x \geq 0, \\ \exp[-b(-x)^\alpha], & x < 0, \, b > 0. \end{cases} \tag{A.11}$$

Proof. (i) $G(0) \neq 0, 1$. Since G lies in $[0, 1]$, $\ln G(x) \leq 0$, and $-\infty < \ln G(0) < 0$, and so $\psi(x) = \ln G(x)/\ln G(0)$ exists, is positive, is decreasing because $\ln G$ is non-positive and increasing, and satisfies

$$\psi(a_n x + b_n) = n\psi(x).$$

Setting $x = 0$ and noting $\psi(0) = 1$ yields $\psi(b_n) = n$, and so

$$\psi(a_n x + b_n) = \psi(b_n)\psi(x). \tag{A.12}$$

Since G is differentiable, so is ψ, whence

$$\psi'(a_n x + b_n)a_n = \psi(b_n)\psi'(x).$$

Set $x = 0$, solve for a_n, and substitute,

$$\psi'(a_n x + b_n)\psi'(0) = \psi'(b_n)\psi'(x).$$

Because ψ is decreasing, $\psi'(0) < 0$, and so we know that ψ and $-\psi'/\psi'(0)$ satisfy the same equation, whose solution we show below is unique. If so, then

$$\psi'(x) = -\alpha\psi(x),$$

whose solution is well known to be $\psi(x) = \exp(-\alpha x + b)$.

To show that the solution is unique, observe that if $a_n \neq 1$, then it is possible to select x such that $x = a_n x + b_n$, in which case it follows that $\psi(b_n) = 1$. But since we know, $\psi(b_n) = n$, this is impossible except possibly for $n = 1$. Excluding that case, we have

$$\ln \psi(x + b_n) = \ln n + \ln \psi(x), \qquad n > 1.$$

This is Abel's functional equation and it is well known that its family of possible solutions is generated from a single solution ψ_0 and a function p that is periodic with period $\ln n$ for any $n > 1$ and is of the form $\psi_0 + p(\psi_0)$. This, of course, means that p is periodic with the dense set of periods $\ln m/n$, where m and n are integers > 1. Since ψ is strictly increasing and is onto, it is continuous and so p must also be continuous. So p is periodic with every period; that is, it is a constant. Thus, $\psi = k\psi_0$, but since $\psi(0) = \psi_0(0) = 1$, the solution is unique.

Substituting $\psi = \exp(-\alpha x + b)$ into Eq. A.12 immediately yields $b_n = \ln n$ and $a_n = 1$. Solving for G yields the result.

(ii) $G(0) = 0$, whence $G(s) = 0$ for $s \leq 0$. Setting $s = 0$ in the basic equation A.8 yields $G(b_n) = 0$. Select $b_n = 0$. Assume a_n are not constant, then setting $s = 1$, we see $G(a_n) = G(1)^n$, so $G(1) \neq 0, 1$. Let $\psi(s) = \ln G(s)/\ln G(1)$; as in (i) it is decreasing and

$$\psi(a_n s) = \psi(a_n)\psi(s), \qquad \psi(a_n) = n.$$

By same uniqueness argument as used in part i, the solution is unique and it is easily verified to be $\psi(s) = s^{-\alpha}$, $\alpha > 0$, $s > 0$ and $G(s) = \exp(-bs^{-\alpha})$. From this and the basic equation, we see $a_n = (1/n)^{1/\alpha}$.

(iii) Similar to (ii).   ■

This result is due to Fisher and Tippett (1928). For more recent presentations of it and many other results, see Gumbel (1958) or, for a much more readable presentation, Galambos (1978) or Leadbetter, Lindgren, and Rootzén (1983).

These three asymptotic distributions are sometimes called the Extreme Value distributions of Type I, II, and III, respectively; in addition, the first (Eq. A.9) is often called the double exponential and the third (Eq. A.11) the Weibull. The former has recently played an important role in the work of Yellott (1977) as the distribution that in Thurstone's (1927a) discriminable dispersion model is equivalent to my (1959) choice model.

A.2.2   Conditions on Distributions Leading to Each Asymptotic Distribution

Given that we know the three possible asymptotic distributions for the maximum of iid random variables, the next natural question to ask is what properties on the underlying distribution lead to each. This is rather more difficult to formulate and answer than is the first question. I summarize the answer in the next theorem, but I do not provide a proof; one can be found in Galambos (1978).

Theorem A.6. *Suppose F is a distribution function and $\omega(F) = \sup\{x \mid F(x) < 1\}$.*
(i) *If for some a,*

$$\int_a^{\omega(F)} [1 - F(y)]\, dy < \infty$$

and

$$\lim_{x \to \infty} \frac{1 - F[x + tR(x)]}{1 - F(x)} = e^{-t},$$

where

$$R(x) = \frac{1}{1 - F(x)} \int_x^{\omega(F)} [1 - F(y)]\, dy,$$

then the asymptotic maximum is distributed as Eq. A.9 with $\alpha = 1$, $\beta = 0$, and the normalizing constants may be chosen to be $a_n = R(b_n)$ and $b_n = \inf\{x \mid 1 - F(x) \le 1/n\}$.
(ii) *If $\omega(F) = \infty$ and*

$$\lim_{x \to \infty} \frac{1 - F(xt)}{1 - F(x)} = t^{-\tau}, \quad \tau > 0, \tag{A.13}$$

then the asymptotic maximum is distributed as Eq. A.10 with $b = 1$, $\alpha = \tau$, and the normalizing constants may be chosen to be $a_n = \inf\{x \mid 1 - F(x) \le 1/n\}$ and $b_n = 0$.
(iii) *If $\omega(F) < \infty$ and if*

$$F^*(x) = F[\omega(F) - 1/x], \quad x > 0,$$

satisfies Eq. A.13, then the asymptotic maximum is distributed as Eq. A.11 with $b = 1$, $\alpha = \tau$, and the normalizing constants may be chosen to be $a_n = \omega(F) - \inf\{x \mid 1 - F(x) \le 1/n\}$ and $b_n = \omega(F)$.
(iv) *These are the only cases for which the asymptotic distribution exists.*

To get some idea of what is involved, consider two important special cases with $\omega(F) = \infty$. In the first, for large x the distribution is approximately exponential; that is,

$$F(x) \cong 1 - ke^{-\theta x}, \quad x \text{ large}.$$

It is easy to see that $R(x) = 1/\theta$, and so

$$\lim_{x \to \infty} \frac{1 - F[x + tR(x)]}{1 - F(x)} = \lim_{x \to \infty} \frac{e^{-\theta}(x + t/\theta)}{e^{-\theta x}} = e^{-t}.$$

Thus, if a distribution function is asymptotically exponential, then the asymptotic maximum is the double exponential. In the second case, suppose the distribution function is asymptotically a power function (which is a form often assumed for so-called high tailed distributions); that is,

$$F(x) \cong 1 - kx^{-\lambda}, \quad x \text{ large,}$$

then

$$\lim_{x \to \infty} \frac{1 - F(xt)}{1 - F(x)} = \lim_{x \to \infty} \frac{(xt)^{-\lambda}}{x^{-\lambda}} = t^{-\lambda}.$$

Thus, if a distribution function is asymptotically a power function, its asymptotic maximum is Eq. A.10.

Somewhat more generally, Galambos (1978, pp. 93–94) showed, first, that if a density function exists, $\omega(F) = \infty$, and

$$\lim_{x \to \infty} \frac{xf(x)}{1 - F(x)} = \tau,$$

then case (ii) holds. Basically, this condition says that for large x the hazard function is decreasing as $1/x$. And second, if a density function exists, has a derivative everywhere, $f(x) \neq 0$, and

$$\lim_{x \to \omega(F)} \frac{d}{dx} \left[\frac{1 - F(x)}{f(x)} \right] = 0,$$

then case (i) holds. This says that the reciprocal of the hazard function is flat as x approaches $\omega(F)$; if $\omega(F) = \infty$, this means that the hazard function approaches a constant; that is, the tail of the distribution is exponential.

A variety of particular cases have been studied. Galambos (1978, pp. 64–69, 99–100) included proofs that the Gaussian, log Gaussian, and gamma fall in case (i), the Cauchy $[F(x) = \frac{1}{2} + (1/\pi) \arctan x]$ and Pareto $[F(x) = 1 - x^{-\beta}]$ in (ii), and the uniform in case (iii).

From the point of view of response-time models in which the individual random variables are assumed to have to do with the time to accumulate a fixed sample of information on each nerve fiber, if the spike trains are approximately Poisson, these times are asymptotically exponential and so the maximum time over a large number of fibers is approximately the double exponential. This distribution plays a minor role (Section 9.3.4) in choice reaction times.

For particular assumptions about the underlying distributions, it is useful to know how the parameters of the asymptotic distribution relate to those of the underlying ones. The Gaussian and gamma cases have been worked out fully, and the relevant sequences are plotted in Wandell and Luce (1978).

Appendix B: Properties of Continuous Distributions for Simple Reaction Times

A general source of information about distributions is Johnson and Kotz (1970).

B.1 THEORETICALLY BASED DISTRIBUTIONS

1. *Gaussian*

$$f(t) = \frac{1}{\sqrt{2\pi}\sigma} e^{-(t-\mu)^2/2\sigma^2}, \qquad -\infty < t < \infty, \quad \sigma > 0$$

$\text{mgf} = e^{s\mu + s^2\sigma^2/2}$

$\text{mean} = \mu$

$\text{variance} = \sigma^2$

hazard function: increasing (Section 1.2.3)

$$-\frac{f'}{f} = \frac{t - \mu}{\sigma^2} \to \infty \text{ as } t \to \infty$$

Comment: limit distribution of sum of independent, nearly identically distributed random variables

Sections: 1.2.3, 1.4.3, 2.5.3, 3.2.1, 4.2.4, 4.3.1, 4.3.2, 4.3.4, 6.4.1, 6.5.1, 6.5.3, 7.1.3, 8.1.3, 8.2.4, 8.2.5, 8.4.1, 8.5.6, 9.3.1, 9.3.2, 9.3.4, 12.4.4, A.1.1–A.1.4, A.2.1

2. *Gamma*

$$f(t) = \frac{\lambda^n t^{n-1} e^{-\lambda t}}{(n-1)!}, \qquad 0 \le t < \infty, \quad \lambda > 0, \ n \text{ an integer or replace } (n-1)!$$
by $\Gamma(n)$

$\text{mgf} = 1/(1 - s/\lambda)^n$

$\text{mean} = n/\lambda$

$\text{variance} = n/\lambda^2$

hazard function: increasing (Theorem 1.4(ii), Section A.1.5)

$$-\frac{f'}{f} = \lambda - \frac{n-1}{t} \to \lambda \text{ as } t \to \infty$$

Comment: distribution of sum of n independent, identically distributed, exponential random variables

Sections: 1.2.4, 1.4.3, 2.5.3, 3.2.3, 3.2.5, 4.1.3, 4.2.2, 4.3.2, 8.2.5, 10.4.2, 11.3.3, A.1.5

3. *Double Exponential* (*Extreme Value Type* I)

$$F(t) = \exp[-e^{-\alpha(t-\beta)}], \qquad -\infty < t < \infty, \quad \alpha > 0$$

$$\text{mgf} = e^{s\beta}\Gamma(1-s/\alpha)$$

mean $= \beta - \psi(1)/\alpha$, where $\psi(1) = 0.57722$ is Euler's constant

$$\text{variance} = \frac{1}{6}\frac{\pi^2}{\alpha^2}$$

$$\text{hazard function} = \frac{F}{1-F}\alpha e^{-\alpha(t-b)}, \text{ increasing}$$

$$-\frac{f'}{f} = \alpha[1 - e^{-\alpha(t-\beta)}] \to \alpha \text{ as } t \to \infty$$

Comment: limit distribution of the maximum of independent, identically distributed random variables that are asymptotically exponential

Sections 4.3.4, A.2.1, A.2.2

4. *Extreme Value Type* II

$$F(t) = e^{-bt^{-\alpha}}, \qquad 0 < t < \infty, \quad b > 0, \quad \alpha > 0$$

mgf: No explicit formula known

mean: No explicit formula known

variance: No explicit formula known

$$\text{hazard function} = \left(\frac{F}{1-F}\right)\left(\frac{\alpha b}{t^{1+\alpha}}\right), \text{ decreasing for } t > \left(\frac{\alpha b}{1+\alpha}\right)^{1/\alpha}$$

$$-\frac{f'}{f} = \frac{1}{t}\left(1 + \alpha - \frac{\alpha b}{t^\alpha}\right) \to 0 \text{ as } t \to \infty$$

Comment: limit distribution of the maximum of independent, identically distributed random variables that are asymptotically power functions

Section A.2.1

5. *Weibull (Extreme Value Type* III)

$$F(t) = 1 - \exp\left[-\left(\frac{t-\zeta}{\alpha}\right)^k\right], \qquad t \geq \zeta, \quad k > 0$$

mgf: No explicit formula known

mean $= \alpha \Gamma(1 + 1/k) + \zeta$

variance $= \alpha^2[\Gamma(1 + 2/k) - \Gamma(1 + 1/k)]^2$

hazard function $= \dfrac{k}{\alpha}\left(\dfrac{t-\zeta}{\alpha}\right)^{k-1}$, increasing for $k > 1$, decreasing for $k < 1$

$$-\frac{f'}{f} = -\frac{k-1}{t-\zeta} + \frac{k}{\alpha}\left(\frac{t-\zeta}{\alpha}\right)^{k-1} \to \infty \text{ as } t \to \infty \text{ for } k > 1, \to 0 \text{ for } k < 1$$

Comment: limit distribution of the maximum of independent, identically distributed random variables that are bounded from above
Sections 4.3.4–4.3.5, A.2.1

6. *Wald (Inverse Gaussian)*

$$f(t) = \left(\frac{\lambda}{2\pi t^3}\right)^{1/2} \exp\left[-\frac{\lambda}{2\mu^2 t}(t-\mu)^2\right]$$

$$\text{mgf} = \exp\frac{\lambda}{\mu}\left[1 - \left(1 + \frac{2\mu^2 s}{\lambda}\right)^{1/2}\right]$$

mean $= \mu$

variance $= \mu^3/\lambda$

hazard function: peaked

$$-\frac{f'}{f} = \frac{3}{2t} + \frac{\lambda}{2\mu^2}\frac{(t-\mu)(t+\mu)}{t^2} \to \frac{\lambda}{2\mu^2} \text{ as } t \to \infty$$

Comment: arises from random walk model with one absorbing barrier
Sections: 1.2.4, 4.2.4, 4.3, 8.2.5

7. *LaPlace*

$$f(t) = \frac{\lambda}{2}e^{-\lambda|t|}, \qquad -\infty < t < \infty, \quad \lambda > 0$$

$$\text{mgf} = \frac{1}{1 - (s/\lambda)^2}$$

mean $= 0$

variance $= \dfrac{2}{\lambda^2}$

hazard function $= \begin{cases} \dfrac{\lambda e^{\lambda t}}{2 - e^{\lambda t}}, & t < 0, \text{ increasing} \\ \lambda, & t \geq 0 \end{cases}$

$-\dfrac{f'}{f} = \begin{cases} -\lambda, & t < 0 \\ \lambda, & t > 0 \end{cases}$

Section 4.2.3

B.2 AD HOC DISTRIBUTIONS

8. *Log Gaussian*

$$f(t) = \frac{1}{\sqrt{2\pi}\sigma t} e^{-(\ln t - \mu)^2/2\sigma^2}, \qquad 0 < t < \infty, \quad \sigma > 0$$

mgf: No explicit formula known

mean $= e^{\mu + \sigma^2/2}$

variance $= e^{2\mu + \sigma^2}(e^{\sigma^2} - 1)$

hazard function: increasing and then decreasing to 0

$$-\frac{f'}{f} = \frac{1}{t}\left(1 + \frac{\ln t - \mu}{\sigma^2}\right) \to 0 \text{ as } t \to \infty$$

Comment: $\log \mathbf{T}$ is Gaussian distributed
Section A.2.2; Woodworth & Schlosberg (1954) suggested it as an empirical approximation.

9. *Double Monomial*

$$f(t) = \frac{(\delta + 1)(\varepsilon - 1)}{(\delta + \varepsilon) t_0} \begin{cases} (t/t_0)^\delta, & 0 \leq y \leq t_0, \quad \delta > 0 \\ (t/t_0)^{-\varepsilon}, & t_0 < t < \infty, \quad \varepsilon > 0 \end{cases}$$

mgf: No explicit formula known

mean $= t_0 \dfrac{(\delta + 1)(\varepsilon - 1)}{(\delta + 2)(\varepsilon - 2)}$, if $\varepsilon > 2$, ∞ otherwise

variance $= t_0^2 \dfrac{(\delta + 1)(\varepsilon - 1)}{(\delta + 3)(\varepsilon - 3)} - \text{mean}^2$, if $\varepsilon > 3$, ∞ otherwise

$$\text{hazard function} = \begin{cases} \dfrac{\dfrac{1}{t_0}\left(\dfrac{t}{t_0}\right)^{\varepsilon}}{\dfrac{1}{\varepsilon-1}+\dfrac{1}{\delta+1}-\dfrac{(t/t_0)^{\delta+1}}{\delta+1}}, & 0\le t\le t_0 \\[2em] \dfrac{\varepsilon-1}{t}, & t_0 < t < \infty \end{cases}$$

$$-\frac{f'}{f} = \begin{cases} -\delta/t, & 0\le t\le t_0 \\ \varepsilon/t, & t_0 < t < \infty \to 0 \text{ as } t\to\infty \end{cases}$$

Comment: hazard function peaked
Section 4.1.2

10. *Logistic*

$$F(t) = 1/\{1+\exp[-(t-\alpha)/\beta]\}$$

$$\text{mgf} = e^{s\alpha/\beta}\pi(s/\beta)\,\text{cosec}(\pi s/\beta)$$

mean $= \alpha$

variance $= \beta^2\pi^2/3$

$$\text{hazard function} = \frac{1}{\beta}F(t), \text{ increasing}$$

$$-\frac{f'}{f} = \frac{1}{\beta}\left[1-2\frac{e^{-(t-\alpha)/\beta}}{1+e^{-(t-\alpha)/\beta}}\right]$$

11. *Ex-Gaussian*

$$f(t) = \frac{\lambda}{\sigma\sqrt{2\pi}}e^{\lambda u + \lambda^2\sigma^2/2}e^{-\lambda t}\int_{-\infty}^{(t-\mu-\lambda\sigma^2)/\sigma} e^{-y^2/2}\,dy$$

$$\text{mgf} = \frac{e^{s\mu + s^2\sigma^2/2}}{1-s/\lambda}$$

mean $= \mu + 1/\lambda$

variance $= \sigma^2 + 1/\lambda^2$

hazard function: increasing (Theorem 1.4(ii))

$$-\frac{f'}{f} = \lambda + \frac{d}{dt}\log\Phi\left(\frac{t-\mu-\lambda\sigma^2}{\sigma}\right), \text{ where } \Phi \text{ is unit Gaussian}$$

Sections 1.4.3, 3.2.1, 11.1.2, 11.3.6, 11.4.4

Appendix C: Experimental Data

For a description of the experiments, see the sections indicated.

C.1   YELLOTT (1971), EXPERIMENT 3 DATA

Section 7.6.1
Sample size: 1000 observations per condition
The nine conditions were as follows:

Condition	Deadline (msec)	$P(s_1)$
1	300	.5
2	300	.7
3	250	.5
4	250	.3
5	400	.5
6	400	.7
7	300	.1
8	250	.1
9	400	.1

| | Subject 301 | | | | | | Subject 302[a] | | | | | |
| | Prop | | MRT (msec) | | | | Prop | | MRT (msec) | | | |
Cond.	aA	bB	aA	aB	bA	bB	aA	bB	aA	aB	bA	bB
1	.86	.84	286	232	232	279	.92	.91	265	243	249	269
2	.92	.52	220	229	181	311	.97	.86	253	265	229	275
3	.77	.71	247	186	202	244	.87	.86	250	219	218	259
4	.47	.92	299	153	210	203	.57	.87	254	179	218	225
5	.70	.85	258	195	216	245	.94	.96	275	259	222	281
6	.93	.79	249	229	210	284	.98	.91	271	283	252	296
7	.18	.98	350	110	292	132	.69	.98	287	186	277	232
8	0	1.00	—	88	—	91						
9	.08	1.00	398	166	—	174						
	Subject 303						Subject 304					
1	.94	.90	259	245	258	260	.83	.89	248	199	210	238
2	.98	.85	247	263	243	268	.89	.59	200	188	158	229
3	.86	.79	239	232	229	230	.70	.63	205	166	157	201
4	.63	.93	245	195	233	218	.39	.91	214	147	168	171
5	.92	.88	254	236	250	241	.75	.82	222	181	184	217
6	.99	.91	258	272	256	271	.93	.68	218	209	185	244
7	.60	.99	259	185	268	210	.51	.98	249	163	205	188
8	.29	.99	247	163	200	174	.22	.99	253	158	201	158
9	.54	.99	254	178	231	196	.34	.99	291	172	225	179

[a] Subject 302 completed only the first seven conditions.

C.2 OLLMAN (1970), EXPERIMENT 2 DATA

Section 7.6.1

These are session-by-session data.

Observer	Number of signals		Response proportion		MRT (msec)			
	a	b	aA	bB	aA	bA	aB	bB
3	421	292	.976	.853	374	430	354	423
	407	300	.936	.883	365	403	367	419
	418	296	.950	.895	319	313	336	394
	420	292	.883	.743	292	265	317	344
		299	.908	.696	273	266	296	321
	423	293	.494	.502	226	207	230	227
	406	300	.768	.487	236	214	241	267
	418	296	.804	.382	223	206	216	264
	421	292	.898	.688	255	251	242	283
	417	342	.950	.915	310	336	325	363
	415	299	.896	.428	228	223	235	265
	416	279	.832	.480	216	208	210	257
	407	300	.934	.827	296	316	305	361
	419	289	.862	.377	220	207	202	249
	383	264	.935	.625	234	232	204	298
	415	295	.901	.563	228	224	229	276
	418	333	.974	.913	296	326	309	359
4	422	292	.991	.976	349	358	454	405
	408	301	.975	.900	283	255	274	344
	419	292	.940	.682	255	208	200	315
	415	299	.887	.645	240	200	225	270
	423	292	.868	.664	233	201	214	263
	412	302	.968	.921	286	279	322	314
	422	298	.912	.477	226	184	220	301
	420	344	.990	.980	280	275	276	317
	415	296	.508	.503	155	145	165	159
	415	296	.935	.794	233	194	124	268
	425	286	.911	.685	224	176	223	261
	408	296	.949	.696	232	184	219	276
	422	329	.995	.988	282	265	313	322

C.3 LAMING (1968), EXPERIMENT 2 DATA

Section 7.6.2
Sample size: 200 per condition-observer averaged over 24 observers for a total of 4800 per condition

Presentation probability	Response proportion		MRT (msec)			
	aA	bA	aA	bA	aB	bB
.250	.934	.009	430	381	286	373
.375	.959	.016	417	380	327	391
.500	.971	.025	414	364	351	415
.625	.981	.046	402	349	375	422
.750	.989	.069	385	329	371	433

C.4 LINK (1975) DATA

Section 7.6.2
Sample size: 700 observations per condition—observer averaged over 4 observers for a total of 2800 per condition

Presentation probability	Response proportion		MRT (msec)			
	aA	bA	aA	bA	aB	bB
.125	.559	.008	576	298	289	333
.250	.727	.044	523	377	338	395
.375	.779	.016	514	331	312	404
.500	.967	.062	442	351	339	479
.625	.985	.199	405	304	276	520
.750	.988	.250	383	314	333	544
.875	1.000	.450	334	341	—	553

C.5 CARTERETTE, FRIEDMAN, AND COSMIDES (1965) DATA

Section 7.7.2
Sample size: 1800 observations per observer—condition

Obs	Condition	Response proportion		MRT (msec)			
		aA	bA	aA	bA	aB	bB
1	.2 low	.149	.080	1652	1543	1382	1357
	.5 low	.715	.622	1527	1602	1820	1922
	.8 low	.894	.850	1329	1455	1955	1969
	.2 high	.302	.071	1744	1770	1471	1494
	.5 high	.792	.427	1421	1626	1712	1770
	.8 high	.947	.653	1478	1867	1738	1896
2	.2 low	.246	.085	3295	3025	1422	1491
	.5 low	.749	.598	1608	1789	2035	2183
	.8 low	.897	.807	1723	2064	2760	3157
	.2 high	.467	.047	4025	3577	1372	1694
	.5 high	.815	.338	1895	1956	1915	2192
	.8 high	.959	.619	1353	1364	2306	3995
3	.2 low	.333	.231	871	827	627	635
	.5 low	.660	.648	838	853	712	733
	.8 low	.900	.899	809	722	732	786
	.2 high	.271	.264	798	894	587	600
	.5 high	.754	.660	865	873	759	782
	.8 high	.912	.894	730	764	765	787

C.6 GREEN AND LUCE (1973) DATA

Section 7.7.2
Sample size: 1500 observations per observer—condition
s-deadline with (10, 10) payoff

Obs	Deadlines	Response proportion		MRT (msec)			
		aA	bA	aA	bA	aB	bB
1	2000	.994	.004	902	1029	674	1165
	1500	.993	.013	770	1266	934	1009
	1000	.972	.028	587	538	631	746
	800	.977	.045	558	595	711	726
	600	.955	.052	478	443	527	611
	500	.880	.236	382	371	424	561
	400	.870	.292	342	286	344	577
	300	.705	.565	252	188	202	348
2	2000	.997	.007	913	1020	1145	1385
	1500	.998	.002	749	839	865	998
	1000	.993	.037	599	654	690	879
	800	.994	.043	539	571	840	859
	600	.993	.109	428	480	575	730
	500	.935	.292	347	341	403	570
	400	.988	.276	338	310	565	682
	300	.896	.630	266	231	211	576
3	2000	.999	.004	965	1335	2333	1316
	1500	.997	.007	756	1315	975	1083
	1000	.992	.030	580	598	756	846
	800	.985	.062	517	532	734	772
	600	.941	.174	371	357	608	579
	500	.929	.354	322	306	435	522
	400	.929	.386	294	258	489	548
	300	.820	.693	210	196	249	361

500 msec s-deadline and varied payoffs

Obs	Payoff	Response proportion aA	bA	MRT (msec) aA	bA	aB	bB
1	(1, 20)	.618	.052	463	395	401	468
	(5, 15)	.657	.071	443	414	471	506
	(10, 10)	.859	.130	429	386	456	578
	(15, 5)	.953	.290	377	368	472	637
	(20, 1)	.978	.392	391	386	691	799
2	(1, 20)	.596	.047	431	382	372	482
	(5, 15)	.651	.065	462	458	385	528
	(10, 10)	.913	.130	413	386	448	624
	(15, 5)	.973	.334	363	362	441	647
	(20, 1)	.994	.436	344	360	562	1050
3	(1, 20)	.652	.097	368	359	596	536
	(5, 15)	.756	.159	373	412	567	575
	(10, 10)	.872	.206	362	354	672	564
	(15, 5)	.932	.300	348	334	578	616
	(20, 1)	.961	.405	338	321	519	753

sn-deadline condition with (10, 10) payoff

Obs	Deadline	Response proportion aA	bA	MRT (msec) aA	bA	aB	bB
4	2000	.935	.096	897	1020	886	933
	1500	.866	.103	717	791	722	746
	1000	.818	.130	625	665	621	634
	800	.748	.237	465	423	441	478
	600	.711	.315	398	379	379	422
	500	.643	.468	282	272	288	320
	400	.648	.480	285	265	282	296
	300	.503	.507	191	181	187	192
	250	.589	.594	140	142	140	141
5	2000	.950	.061	1044	1128	961	1093
	1500	.888	.089	769	871	792	826
	1000	.799	.115	629	716	648	654
	800	.767	.208	472	489	491	509
	600	.691	.240	427	442	424	459
	500	.629	.368	349	343	344	352
	400	.547	.458	299	290	284	311
	300	.555	.461	201	200	180	191
	250	.470	.490	179	174	174	169
	2000	.906	.103	833	980	843	837
	1500	.911	.078	804	973	823	770
	1000	.864	.113	665	736	694	679
	800	.758	.124	492	539	483	493
	600	.768	.147	468	490	478	475
	500	.648	.258	404	410	403	409
	400	.605	.402	297	276	297	326
	300	.680	.654	177	173	171	172
	250	.663	.666	125	127	130	135

600 msec *sn*-deadline and variable payoffs

		Response proportion		MRT	(msec)		
Obs	Payoff	aA	bA	aA	bA	aB	bB
4	(1, 20)	.371	.083	420	413	347	361
	(5, 15)	.549	.178	405	428	385	405
	(10, 10)	.719	.295	417	410	409	429
	(15, 5)	.803	.435	410	403	447	452
	(20, 1)	.888	.628	397	376	454	452
5	(1, 20)	.639	.165	455	469	449	464
	(5, 15)	.657	.190	434	476	425	452
	(10, 10)	.738	.222	436	455	447	464
	(15, 5)	.749	.303	426	452	454	474
	(20, 1)	.823	.363	407	418	451	471
6	(1, 20)	.582	.080	485	505	460	457
	(1, 15)	.634	.094	468	484	430	430
	(10, 10)	.755	.193	469	490	483	475
	(15, 5)	.834	.380	434	447	460	462
	(20, 1)	.879	.463	436	449	480	487

C.7   GREEN, SMITH, AND VON GIERKE (1983) DATA

Section 8.5.3

			Response proportion		MRT	(msec)		
Obs	N	P(a)	aA	bA	aA	bA	aB	bB
DS	5997	.25	.732	.006	259	232	188	186
	5800	.50	.929	.039	238	237	209	205
	5697	.75	.992	.365	202	199	233	249
CE	5999	.25	.819	.012	229	210	178	183
	5299	.50	.943	.059	206	190	193	200
	5700	.75	.984	.190	189	179	215	229
SVG	6000	.25	.743	.024	243	223	199	198
	5800	.50	.909	.091	211	211	210	214
	5699	.75	.982	.278	192	202	217	238

C.8 LAMING (1968), EXPERIMENT 6 DATA

In each case the top entry is the conditional response probability and the bottom one is the mean reaction time in msec.

Section 10.4.2

Stimulus	N	Response				
		A	B	C	D	E
A	1035	.825	.174	.001	—	—
		742	823	1340	—	—
B	2985	.013	.847	.137	.003	—
		672	837	917	1221	—
C	4121	—	.057	.862	.081	—
		—	835	794	843	—
D	4976	—	.002	.096	.891	.011
		—	913	817	734	835
E	6083	—	—	.002	.096	.902
		—	—	819	824	644
N	19200	893	2951	4453	5360	5543

References

Abeles, M. & M. H. Goldstein. Response of single units in the primary auditory cortex of the cat to tones and to tone pairs. *Brain Research*, 1972, *42*, 337–352.

Aczél, J. *Lectures on Functional Equations and their Applications.* New York: Academic Press, 1966.

Ahumada, A., Jr., R. Marken, & A. Sandusky. Time and frequency analysis of auditory signal detection. *Journal of the Acoustical Society of America*, 1975, *57*, 385–390.

Aiken, L. R., Jr. & M. Lichenstein. Interstimulus and interresponse time variables in reaction times to regularly recurring visual stimuli. *Perceptual and Motor Skills*, 1964, *19*, 339–342.

Alegria, J. Sequential effects of foreperiod duration: Some strategical factors in tasks involving time uncertainty. In P. M. A. Rabbitt and S. Dornic (eds.), *Attention and Performance V.* London: Academic Press, 1975, pp. 1–10.

Alegria, J. Sequential effects of catch-trials on choice reaction time. *Acta Psychologica*, 1978, *42*, 1–6.

Allport, D. A. Phenomenal simultaneity and the perceptual moment hypothesis. *British Journal of Psychology*, 1968, *59*, 395–406.

Anderson, J. A. Two models for memory organization using interacting traces. *Mathematical Biosciences*, 1970, *8*, 137–160.

Anderson, J. A. A simple neural network generating an interactive memory. *Mathematical Biosciences*, 1972, *14*, 197–220.

Anderson, J. A. A theory for the recognition of items from short memorized lists. *Psychological Review*, 1973, *80*, 417–438.

Anderson, J. A., J. W. Silverstein, S. Z. Ritz, & R. S. Jones. Distinctive features, catagorical perception, and probability learning: Some applications of a neural model. *Psychological Review*, 1977, *84*, 413–451.

Anderson, J. R. *Language, Memory and Thought.* Hillsdale, N.J.: Erlbaum, 1976.

Anderson, N. H. Algebraic models in perception. In E. C. Carterette & M. P. Friedman (eds.), *Handbook of Perception, II.* New York: Academic Press, 1974, pp. 215–298.

Anderson, N. H. *Foundations of Information Integration Theory.* New York: Academic Press, 1981.

Anderson, N. H. *Methods of Information Integration Theory.* New York: Academic Press, 1982.

Anderson, T. W. A modification of the sequential probability ratio test to reduce the sample size. *Annals of Mathematical Statistics*, 1960, *31*, 165–197.

Angel, A. Input-output relations in simple reaction-time experiments. *Quarterly Journal of Experimental Psychology*, 1973, *25*, 193–200.

Annett, J. Payoff and the refractory period. *Acta Psychologica*, 1969, *30*, 65–71.

Ashby, F. G. Testing the assumptions of exponential additive reaction-time models. *Memory and Cognition*, 1982a, *10*, 125–134.

Ashby, F. G. Deriving exact predictions from the cascade model. *Psychological Review*, 1982b, *89*, 599–607.

Ashby, F. G. A biased random walk model for two choice reaction times. *Journal of Mathematical Psychology*, 1983, *27*, 277–297.

Ashby, F. G. & J. T. Townsend. Decomposing the reaction time distribution: Pure insertion and selective influence revisited. *Journal of Mathematical Psychology*, 1980, *21*, 93–123.

Atkinson, R. C., J. E. Holmgren, & J. F. Juola. Processing time as influenced by the number of elements in a visual display. *Perception & Psychophysics*, 1969, *6*, 321–326.

Audley, R. J. A stochastic model for individual choice behavior. *Psychological Review*, 1960, *67*, 1–15.

Audley, R. J. & A. Mercer. The relation between decision time and the relative response frequency in a blue-green discrimination. *British Journal of Mathematical and Statistical Psychology*, 1968, *21*, 183–192.

Audley, R. J. & A. R. Pike. Some alternative stochastic models of choice. *The British Journal of Mathematical and Statistical Psychology*, 1965, *18*, 207–225.

Baddeley, A. D. & J. R. Ecob. Reaction time and short-term memory: Implications of repetition effects for the high-speed exhaustive scan hypothesis. *Quarterly Journal of Experimental Psychology*, 1973, *25*, 229–240.

Bamber, D. Reaction times and error rates for "same"–"different" judgments of multidimensional stimuli. *Perception & Psychophysics*, 1969a, *6*, 169–174.

Bamber, D. "Same"–"different" judgements of multi-dimensional stimuli: Reaction times and error rates. Unpublished doctoral dissertation. Stanford University, 1969b.

Bamber, D. Reaction times and error rates for judging nominal identity of letter strings. *Perception & Psychophysics*, 1972, *12*, 321–326.

Barlow, R. E., A. W. Marshall, & F. Proschan. Properties of probability distributions with monotone hazard rate. *Annals of Mathematical Statistics*, 1966, *37*, 1574–1592.

Barlow, R. E. & F. Proschan. *Mathematical Theory of Reliability*. New York: Wiley, 1965.

Barlow, R. E. & F. Proschan. *Statistical Theory of Reliability and Life Testing: Probability Models*. New York: Holt, Rinehart, & Winston, 1975.

Bartlett, M. S. *An Introduction to Stochastic Processes*. Cambridge, England: Cambridge University Press, 1962.

Bartlett, N. R. & S. Macleod. Effect of flash and field luminance upon human reaction time. *Journal of the Optical Society of America*, 1954, *44*, 306–311.

Bartlett, N. R. A comparison of manual reaction times as measured by three sensitive indices. *The Psychological Record*, 1963, *13*, 51–56.

Beller, H. K. Parallel and serial stages in matching. *Journal of Experimental Psychology*, 1970, *84*, 213–219.

Berliner, J. E. & N. E. Durlach. Intensity perception. IV. Resolution in roving-level discrimination. *Journal of the Acoustical Society of America*, 1973, *53*, 1270–1287.

Bertelson, P. Sequential redundancy and speed in a serial two-choice responding task. *Quarterly Journal of Psychology*, 1961, *13*, 90–102.

Bertelson, P. S-R relationships and reaction times to a new versus repeated signals in a serial task. *Journal of Experimental Psychology*, 1963, *65*, 478–484.

Bertelson, P. Serial choice reaction-time as a function of response versus signal-and-response repetition. *Nature*, 1965, *206*, 217–218.

Bertelson, P. Central intermittency twenty years later. *Quarterly Journal of Experimental Psychology*, 1966, *18*, 153–163.

Bertelson, P. The time course of preparation. *Quarterly Journal of Experimental Psychology*, 1967, *19*, 272–279.

Bertelson, P. & A. Renkin. Reaction times to new versus repeated signals in a serial task as a function of response-signal time interval. *Acta Psychologica*, 1966, *25*, 132–136.

Beyer, W. A. *Handbook of tables for probability and statistics*. Cleveland, Ohio: The Chemical Rubber Co., 1966.

Birren, J. E. & J. Botwinick. Speed of response as a function of perceptual difficulty and age. *Journal of Gerontololgy*, 1955, *10*, 433–436.

Bjork, E. L. & W. K. Estes. Detection and placement of redundant signal elements in tachistoscopic displays of letters. *Perception & Psychophysics*, 1971, *9*, 439–442.

Blackman, A. R. Test of the additive-factor method of choice reaction time analysis. *Perceptual Motor Skills*, 1975, *41*, 607–613.

Blough, D. S. Reaction times of pigeons on a wavelength discrimination task. *Journal of the Experimental Analysis of Behavior*, 1978, *30*, 163–167.

Bloxom, B. Estimating an unobserved component of a serial response-time model. *Psychometrika*, 1979, *44*, 473–484.

Bloxom, B. Some problems in estimating response time distributions. In H. Wainer & S. Messick (eds.), *Principals of Modern Psychological Measurement: A Festschrift in Honor of Frederick M. Lord*. Hillsdale, N.J.: Erlbaum, 1983, pp. 303–328.

Bloxom, B. Estimating response time hazard functions: An exposition and extension. *Journal of Mathematical Psychology*, 1984, *28*, 401–420.

Bloxom, B. A constrained spline estimator of a hazard function. *Psychometrika*, 1985, *50*, 301–321.

Blumenthal, A. L. *The Process of Cognition*. Englewood Cliffs, N.J.: Prentice-Hall, 1977.

Borger, R. The refractory period and serial choice-reactions. *Quarterly Journal of Experimental Psychology*, 1963, *15*, 1–12.

Botwinick, J., J. F. Brinley, & J. S. Robbin. The interaction effects of perceptual difficulty and stimulus exposure time on age differences in speed and accuracy of response. *Gerontologia*, 1958, *2*, 1–10.

Botwinick, J. & L. W. Thompson. Premotor and motor components of reaction time. *Journal of Experimental Psychology*, 1966, *71*, 9–15.

Bracewell, R. *The Fourier Transform and Its Applications*. New York: McGraw-Hill, 1965.

Brebner, J. M. T. & A. T. Welford. Introduction: An historical background sketch. In A. T. Welford (ed.), *Reaction Times*. New York: Academic Press, 1980, pp. 1–23.

Breitmeyer, B. G. Simple reaction time as a measure of the temporal response properties of transient and sustained channels. *Vision Research*, 1975, *15*, 1411–1412.

Briggs, G. E. The additivity principle in choice reaction time—A functionalist approach to mental processes. In R. F. Thompson & J. F. Voss (eds.), *Topics in Learning and Performance*. New York: Academic Press, 1972.

Briggs, G. E. On the predictor variable for choice reaction time. *Memory & Cognition*, 1974, *2*, 575–580.

Briggs, G. E. & J. Blaha. Memory retrieval and central comparison time in information processing. *Journal of Experimental Psychology*, 1969, *79*, 395–402.

Briggs, G. E. & A. M. Johnsen. On the nature of central processing in choice reactions. *Memory & Cognition*, 1973, *1*, 91–100.

Briggs, G. E., A. M. Johnsen, & D. Shinar. Central processing uncertainty as a determinant of choice reaction time. *Memory & Cognition*, 1974, *2*, 417–425.

Briggs, G. E., G. L. Peters, & R. P. Fisher. On the locus of the divided-attention effects. *Perception & Psychophysics*, 1972, *11*, 315–320.

Briggs, G. E. & D. Shinar. On the locus of the speed/accuracy tradeoff. *Psychonomic Science*, 1972, *28*, 326–328.

Briggs, G. E. & J. M. Swanson. Retrieval time as a function of memory ensemble size. *Quarterly Journal of Experimental Psychology*, 1969, *21*, 185–191.

Briggs, G. E. & J. M. Swanson. Encoding, decoding, and central functions in human information processing. *Journal of Experimental Psychology*, 1970, *86*, 296–308.

Briggs, G. E., S. C. Thomason, & J. D. Hagman. Stimulus classification strategies in an information reduction task. *Journal of Experimental Psychology: General*, 1978, *107*, 159–186.

Brigham, E. O. *The Fast Fourier Transform*. Englewood Cliffs, N.J.: Prentice-Hall, 1974.

Broadbent, D. E. *Perception and Communication*. London: Pergamon, 1958.

Broadbent, D. E. & M. Gregory. Vigilance considered as a statistical decision. *British Journal of Experimental Psychology*, 1963, *54*, 309–323.

Brunk, H. D. *An Introduction to Mathematical Statistics*, 3rd ed. Boston: Ginn, 1975.

Buckolz, E. & R. Rogers. The influence of catch trial frequency on simple reaction time. *Acta Psychologica*, 1980, *44*, 191–200.

Burbeck, S. L. *Change and level detectors inferred from simple reaction times*. University of California at Irvine, Ph.D. dissertation, 1979.

Burbeck, S. L. A physiologically motivated model for change detection in audition. *Journal of Mathematical Psychology*, 1985, *29*, 106–121.

Burbeck, S. L. & R. D. Luce. Evidence from auditory simple reaction times for both change and level detectors. *Perception & Psychophysics*, 1982, *32*, 117–133.

Burns, J. T. Error-induced inhibition in a serial reaction time task. *Journal of Experimental Psychology*, 1971, *90*, 141–148.

Burrows, D. Modality effects in retrieval of information from short-term memory. *Perception & Psychophysics*, 1972, *11*, 365–372.

Bush, R. R. & F. Mosteller. *Stochastic Models for Learning*. New York: Wiley, 1955.

Carterette, E. C., M. P. Friedman, & R. Cosmides. Reaction-time distributions in the detection of weak signals in noise. *Journal of the Acoustical Society of America*, 1965, *38*, 531–542.

Cattell, J. McK. The influence of the intensity of the stimulus on the length of reaction time. *Brain*, 1886a, *8*, 512–515.

Cattell, J. McK. The time taken by cerebral operations. *Mind*, 1886b, *11*, 20–242. Reprinted in A. T. Poffenberger (ed.), *James McKeen Cattell, Man of Science, Vol. I: Psychological Research*. Lancaster, PA: The Science Press, 1947.

Chocholle, R. Variations des temps de réaction auditifs en fonction de l'intensité a diverses fréquences. *L'Année Psychologique*, 1940, *41*, 65–124.

Christie, L. S. The measurement of discriminative behavior. *Psychological Review*, 1952, *59*, 443–452.

Christie, L. S., & R. D. Luce. Decision structure and time relations in simple choice behavior. *Bulletin of Mathematical Biophysics*, 1956 *18*, 89–112.

Cleland, B. G., M. W. Dubin, & W. R. Levick. Sustained and transient cells in the cat's retina and lateral geniculate nucleus. *Journal of Physiology, London*, 1971, *217*, 473–496.

Clifton, C. & Birenbaum, S. Effects of serial position and delay of probe in a memory scan task. *Journal of Experimental Psychology*, 1970, *86*, 69–76.

Cooper, W. E. (ed.). *Cognitive Aspects of Skilled Typewriting*. New York: Springer-Verlag, 1983.

Corballis, M. C. Serial order in recognition and recall. *Journal of Experimental Psychology*, 1967, *74*, 99–105.

Corbett, A. T. Retrieval dynamics for rote and visual image mnemonics. *Journal of Verbal Learning and Verbal Memory*, 1977, *16*, 233–236.

Corbett, A. T. & W. A. Wickelgren. Semantic memory retrieval: analysis by speed and accuracy tradeoff functions. *Quarterly Journal of Experimental Psychology*, 1978, *30*, 1–15.

Costa, L. D., H. G. Vaughan, & L. Gilden. Comparison of electromyographic and microswitch measures of auditory reaction time. *Perceptual and Motor Skills*, 1965, *20*, 771–772.

Cox, D. R. & W. L. Smith. *Queues*. New York: Wiley, 1961.

Craik, K. J. W. Theory of the human operator in control systems, I. The operator as an engineering system. *British Journal of Psychology*, 1947, *38*, 56–61.

Craik, K. J. W. Theory of the human operator in control systems, II. Man as an element in the control system. *British Journal of Psychology*, 1948, 142–148.

Cramér, H. *Random Variables and Probability Distributions*. Cambridge, England: Cambridge University Press, 1937.

Creamer, L. R. Event uncertainty, psychological refractory period, and human data processing. *Journal of Experimental Psychology*, 1963, *66*, 187–194.

Crossman, E. R. F. W. Entropy and choice time: The effect of frequency unbalance on choice-response. *Quarterly Journal of Experimental Psychology*, 1953, *5*, 41–52.

Crossman, E. R. F. W. The measurement of discriminability. *Quarterly Journal of Experimental Psychology*, 1955, *7*, 176–195.

Davies, D. R. & R. Parasuraman. *The Psychology of Vigilance*. London: Academic, 1982.

Davies, D. R. & G. S. Tune. *Human Vigilance Performance*. New York: American Elsevier, 1969.

Davis, R. The limits of the "psychological refractory period." *Quarterly Journal of Experimental Psychology*, 1956, *8*, 24–38.

Davis, R. The human operator as a single channel information system. *Quarterly Journal of Experimental Psychology*, 1957, *9*, 119–129.

Davis, R. The role of "attention" in the psychological refractory period. *Quarterly Journal of Experimental Psychology*, 1959, *11*, 211–220.

de Boor, C. *A Practical Guide to Splines*. New York: Springer-Verlag, 1978.

de Klerk, L. F. W. & E. Eerland. The relation between prediction outcome and choice reaction speed: Comments on the study of Geller et al., *Acta Psychologica*, 1973, *37*, 301–306.

Dixon, W. J., M. B. Brown, L. Engleman, J. W. France, M. A. Hall, R. C. Jennrich, & J. D. Toporck. *BMDP Statistical Software*. Berkeley, CA: University of California Press, 1981.

Donaldson, G. Confirmatory factor analysis models of information processing stages: An alternative to difference scores. *Psychological Bulletin*, 1983, *94*, 143–151.

Donders, F. C. Over de snelheid van psychische processen. (On the speed of mental processes.) *Onderzoekingen degaan in het physiologisch Laboratorium der Ugtrechtsche Hoogeschool*, 1868–69, Tweede reeks, *11*, 92–130. Translated by W. G. Koster, in W. G. Koster (ed.), Attention and Performance II, *Acta Psychologica*, 1969, *30*, 412–431.

Dosher, B. A. The retrieval of sentences from memory: a speed-accuracy study. *Cognitive Science*, 1976, *8*, 291–310.

Dosher, B. A. Empirical approaches to information processing: speed–accuracy tradeoff functions or reaction time—a reply. *Acta Psychologica*, 1979, *43*, 347–359.

Drazin, D. H. Effects of foreperiod, foreperiod variability, and probability of stimulus occurrence on simple reaction time. *Journal of Experimental Psychology*, 1961, *62*, 43–50.

Duncan, J. The locus of interference in the perception of simultaneous stimuli. *Psychological Review*, 1980, *87*, 272–300.

Edwards, W. Optimal strategies for seeking information: Models for statistics, choice reaction times, and human information processing. *Journal of Mathematical Psychology*, 1965, *2*, 312–329.

Efron, B. *The Jackknife, the Bootstrap and Other Resampling Plans*. Philadephia, PA: Society for Industrial and Applied Mathematics, 1982.

Egan, J. P. *Signal Detection Theory and ROC Analysis*. New York: Academic Press, 1975.

Egan, J. P., G. Z. Greenberg, & A. I. Schulman. Operating characteristics, signal detectability, and the method of free response. *Journal of the Acoustical Society of America*, 1961, *33*, 933–1007.

Egeth, H. E. Parallel versus serial processes in multidimensional stimulus discrimination. *Perception & Psychophysics*, 1966, *1*, 245–252.

Egeth, H., J. Jonides, & S. Wall. Parallel processing of multielement displays. *Cognitive Psychology*, 1972, *3*, 674–698.

Egeth, H. & E. E. Smith. On the nature of errors in a choice reaction task. *Psychonomic Science*, 1967, *8*, 345–346.

Eichelman, W. H. Stimulus and response repetition effects for naming letters at two response-stimulus intervals. *Perception & Psychophysics*, 1970, *7*, 94–96.

Elithorn, A. & C. Lawrence. Central inhibition—some refractory observations. *Quarterly Journal of Experimental Psychology*, 1955, *7*, 116–127.

Elliott, R. Simple visual and simple auditory reaction time: A comparison. *Psychonomic Science*, 1968, *10*, 335–336.

Emerson, P. L. Simple reaction time with markovian evolution of gaussian discriminal processes. *Psychometrika*, 1970, *35*, 99–109.

Emmerich, D. Receiver operating characteristics determined under several interaural conditions of listening. *Journal of the Acoustical Society of America*, 1968, *43*, 298–307.

Emmerich, D. S., J. L. Gray, C. S. Watson, & D. C. Tanis. Response latency, confidence, and ROCs in auditory signal detection. *Perception & Psychophysics*, 1972, *11*, 65–72.

Enroth-Cugell, C. & J. G. Robson. The contrast sensitivity of retinal ganglion cells of the cat. *Journal of Physiology, London*, 1966, *187*, 517–552.

Entus, A. & D. Bindra. Common features of the "repetition" and "same-different" effects in reaction time experiments. *Perception & Psychophysics*, 1970, *7*, 143–148.

Erdelyi, A., W. Magnus, F. Oberhettinger, & F. G. Tricomi. *Tables of Integral Transforms*, Vol I. New York: McGraw-Hill, 1954.

Estes, W. K. Toward a statistical theory of learning. *Psychological Review*, 1950, *57*, 94–107.

Everitt, B. & D. J. Hand. *Finite Mixture Distributions*. New York: Chapman and Hall, 1981.

Falmagne, J. C. Stochastic models for choice reaction time with applications to experimental results. *Journal of Mathematical Psychology*, 1965, *2*, 77–124.

Falmagne, J. C. Note on a simple fixed-point property of binary mixtures. *British Journal of Mathematical and Statistical Psychology*, 1968, *21*, 131–132.

Falmagne, J. C. Biscalability of error matrices and all-or-none reaction time theories. *Journal of Mathematical Psychology*, 1972, *9*, 206–224.

Falmagne, J. C., S. P. Cohen, & A. Dwivedi. Two-choice reactions as an ordered memory scanning process. In P. M. A. Rabbitt & S. Dornic (eds.), *Attention and Performance*, V. New York: Academic Press, 1975, pp. 296–344.

Falmagne, J. C. & J. Theios. On attention and memory in reaction time experiments. *Acta Psychological*, 1969, *30*, 316–323.

Feller, W. *An Introduction to Probability Theory and Its Applications*, Vols. I and II. New York: Wiley, 1957, 2nd ed., 1966.

Fernberger, S. W., E. Glass, I. Hoffman, & M. Willig. Judgment times of different psychophysical categories. *Journal of Experimental Psychology*, 1934, *17*, 286–293.

Festinger, L. Studies in decision: I. Decision time, relative frequency of judgment, and subjective confidence as related to physical stimulus difference. *Journal of Experimental Psychology*, 1943a, *32*, 291–306.

Festinger, L. Studies in decision: II. An empirical test of a quantitative theory of decision. *Journal of Experimental Psychology*, 1943b, *32*, 422–423.

Fisher, R. A. & L. H. C. Tippett. Limiting forms of the frequency distributions of the largest or smallest number of a sample. *Proceedings of the Cambridge Philosophical Society*, 24, 180–190.

Fitts, P. M. Cognitive aspects of information processing: III. Set for speed versus accuracy. *Journal of Experimental Psychology*, 1966, *71*, 849–857.

Fraisse, P. La periode refractorie psychologique. *Année Psychologique*, 1957, *57*, 315–328.

Galambos, J. *The asymptotic theory of extreme order statistics*. New York: Wiley, 1978.

Gardner, G. T. Evidence for independent parallel channels in tachistoscopic perception. *Cognitive Psychology*, 1973, *4*, 130–155.

Garrett, H. E. A study of the relation of accuracy to speed. *Archives of Psychology*, 1922, *56*, 1–105.

Geller, E. S. Prediction outcome and choice reaction time: Inhibition versus facilitation effects. *Acta Psychologica*, 1975, *39*, 69–82.

Geller, E. S. & G. F. Pitz. Effects of prediction, probability and run length on choice reaction speed. *Journal of Experimental Psychology*, 1970, *84*, 361–367.

Geller, E. S., C. P. Whitman, R. F. Wrenn, & W. G. Shipley. Expectancy and discrete reaction time in a probability reversal design. *Journal of Experimental Psychology*, 1971, *90*, 113–119.

Gerstein, G. L., R. A. Butler, & S. D. Erulkar. Excitation and inhibition in cochlear nucleus. I. Tone-burst stimulation. *Journal of Neurophysiology*, 1968, *31*, 526–536.

Gescheider, G. A., J. H. Wright, B. J. Weber, B. M. Kirchner, & E. A. Milligan. Reaction time as a function of the intensity and probability of occurrence of vibrotactile signals. *Perception & Psychophysics*, 1969, *5*, 18–20.

Ghosh, B. K. Moments of the distribution of sample size in a SPRT. *Journal of the American Statistical Association*, 1969, 64, 1560–1575.

Gihman, I. I. & A. V. Skorohod. *The Theory of Stochastic Processes*, I, II, III. New York: Springer-Verlag, 1974. (Translated from the Russian edition of 1971.)

Glaser, R. E. Bathtub and related failure rate characterizations. *Journal of the American Statistical Association*, 1980, *75*, 667–672.

Gnedenko, B. V., Yu. K. Belyayev, & A. D. Soloyev. *Mathematical Methods of Reliability Theory*. (Translated by Scripta Technica; translation edited by R. E. Barlow.) New York: Academic Press, 1969.

Gnedenko, B. V. & A. N. Kolmogorov. *Limit Distributions for Sums of Independent Random Variables*. Reading, Mass.: Addison-Wesley, 1954.

Gordon, I. E. Stimulus probability and simple reaction time. *Nature*, 1967, 875–896.

Granjon, M. & G. Reynard. Effect of length of the runs of repetitions on the simple RT-ISI relationship. *Quarterly Journal of Experimental Psychology*, 1977, *29*, 283–295.

Grayson, D. A. *The Role of the Response Stage in Stochastic Models of Simple Reaction Time*. University of Sidney, Australia, Ph.D. dissertation, 1983.

Green, D. M. Fourier analysis of reaction time data. *Behavior Research Methods & Instruments*, 1971, *3*, 121–125.

Green, D. M. & R. D. Luce. Detection of auditory signals presented at random times. *Perception & Psychophysics*, 1967, *2*, 441–449.

Green, D. M., & R. D. Luce. Detection of auditory signals presented at random times: III. *Perception & Psychophysics*, 1971, *9*, 257–268.

Green, D. M. & R. D. Luce. Speed-accuracy trade off in auditory detection. In S. Kornblum (ed.), *Attention and Performance*, IV. New York: Academic Press, 1973, pp. 547–569.

Green, D. M. & R. D. Luce. Timing and counting mechanisms in auditory discrimination and reaction time. In D. H. Krantz, R. C. Atkinson, R. D. Luce, & P. Suppes (eds.), *Contemporary Developments in Mathematical Psychology*, Vol. II. San Francisco: Freeman, 1974, pp. 372–415.

Green, D. M. & A. F. Smith. Detection of auditory signals occurring at random times: Intensity and duration. *Perception & Psychophysics*, 1982, *31*, 117–127.

Green, D. M., A. F. Smith, & S. M. von Gierke. Choice reaction time with a random foreperiod. *Perception & Psychophysics*, 1983, *34*, 195–208.

Green, D. M. & J. A. Swets. *Signal Detection Theory and Psychophysics*. New York: Wiley, 1966. Reprinted by Huntington, N.Y.: Krieger, 1974.

Greenwald, A. G. Sensory feedback mechanisms in performance control: With special reference to the ideo-motor mechanism. *Psychological Review*, 1970, *77*, 73–99.

Greenwald, A. G. On doing two things at once: Time sharing as a function of ideomotor compatibility. *Journal of Experimental Psychology*, 1972, *94*, 52–57.

Greenwald, A. G. & H. G. Shulman. On doing two things at once: II. Elimination of the psychological refractory period effect. *Journal of Experimental Psychology*, 1973, *101*, 70–76.

Gregg, L. W. & W. J. Brogden. The relation between duration and reaction time difference to fixed duration and response terminated stimuli. *Journal of Comparative and Physiological Psychology*, 1950, *43*, 329–337.

Grice, G. R. Stimulus intensity and response evocation. *Psychological Review*, 1968, *75*, 359–373.

Grice, G. R. Conditioning and a decision theory of response evocation. In G. Bower (ed.), *Psychology of Learning and Motivation*, Vol 5. New York: Academic, 1971, pp. 1–65.

Grice, G. R. Application of a variable criterion model to auditory reaction time as a function of the type of catch trial. *Perception & Psychophysics*, 1972, *12*, 103–107.

Grice, G. R., R. Nullmeyer, & J. Schnizlein. Variable criterion analysis of brightness effects in simple reaction time. *Journal of Experimental Psychology: Human Perception and Performance*, 1979, *5*, 303–314.

Grill, D. P. Variables influencing the mode of processing of complex stimuli. *Perception & Psychophysics*, 1971, *10*, 51–57.

Gross, A. J. & V. A. Clark. *Survival Distributions: Reliability Applications in the Biomedical Sciences*. New York: Wiley, 1975.

Grossberg, M. The latency of response in relation to Bloch's Law at threshold. *Perception & Psychophysics*, 1968, *4*, 229–232.

Gumbel, E. J. *The Statistics of Extremes*. New York: Columbia University Press, 1958.

Hacker, M. J. & J. V. Hinrichs. Multiple predictions in choice reaction time: A serial memory scanning interpretation. *Journal of Experimental Psychology*, 1974, *103*, 999–1005.

Hale, D. J. Sequential effects in a two-choice serial reaction task. *Quarterly Journal of Experimental Psychology*, 1967, *19*, 133–141.

Hale, D. J. Repetition and probability effects in a serial choice reaction task. *Acta Psychologica*, 1969a, *29*, 163–171.

Hale, D. J. Speed-error tradeoff in a three-choice serial reaction task. *Journal of Experimental Psychology*, 1969b, *81*, 428–435.

Hannes, M. The effect of stimulus repetitions and alternations on one-finger and two-finger responding in two-choice reaction time. *Journal of Psychology*, 1968, *69*, 161–164.

Harm, O. J. & J. S. Lappin. Probability, compatibility, speed, and accuracy. *Journal of Experimental Psychology*, 1973, *100*, 416–418.

Harwerth, R. S. & D. M. Levi. Reaction time as a measure of suprathreshold grating detection. *Vision Research*, 1978, *18*, 1579–1586.

Heath, R. A. A tandem random walk model for psychological discrimination. *British Journal of Mathematical and Statistical Psychology*, 1981, *34*, 76–92.

Hecker, M. H., K. N. Stevens, & C. E. Williams. Measurements of reaction time in intelligibility tests. *Journal of the Acoustical Society of America*, 1966, *39*, 1188–1189.

Henmon, V. A. C. The time of perception as a measure of differences in sensation. *Archives of Philosophy, Psychology and Scientific Method*, 1906, *8*, 1–75.

Henmon, V. A. The relation of the time of a judgment to its accuracy. *Psychological Review*, 1911, *18*, 186–201.

Herman, L. M. & B. H. Kantowitz. The psychological refractory period effect: Only half the double-stimulation story? *Psychological Bulletin*, 1970, *73*, 74–88.

Heuer, H. Binary choice reaction time as a criterion of motor equivalence. *Acta Psychologica*, 1981a, *50*, 35–47.

Heuer, H. Binary choice reaction time as a criterion of motor equivalence: Further evidence. *Acta Psychologica*, 1981b, *50*, 49–60.

Hick, W. E. On the rate of gain of information. *Quarterly Journal of Experimental Psychology*, 1952, *4*, 11–26.

Hinrichs, J. V. Probability and expectancy in two-choice reaction time. *Psychonomic Science*, 1970, *21*, 227–228.

Hinrichs, J. V. & J. L. Craft. Verbal expectancy and probability in two-choice reaction time. *Journal of Experimental Psychology*, 1971a, *88*, 367–371.

Hinrichs, J. V. & J. L. Craft. Stimulus and response factors in discrete choice reaction time. *Journal of Experimental Psychology*, 1971b, *91*, 305–309.

Hinrichs, J. V. & P. L. Krainz. Expectancy in choice reaction time: Stimulus or response anticipation? *Journal of Experimental Psychology*, 1970, *85*, 330–334.

Hinton, G. & J. A. Anderson (eds.). *Parallel Models of Associative Memory*. Hillsdale, N.J.: Erlbaum, 1981.

Hockley, W. E. Analysis of response time distributions in the study of cognitive processes. *Journal of Experimental Psychology: Learning, Memory, and Cognition*, 1984, *10*, 598–615.

Hohle, R. H. Inferred components of reaction times as functions of foreperiod duration. *Journal of Experimental Psychology*, 1965, *69*, 382–386.

Hopkins, G. W. Ultrastable stimulus-response latencies: Towards a model of response-stimulus synchronization. In J. Gibbon and L. Allan, *Timing and Time Perception*. New York: New York Academy of Sciences, Vol. 423, 1984, pp. 16–29.

Hopkins, G. W. & A. B. Kristofferson. Ultrastable stimulus-response latencies: Acquisition and stimulus control. *Perception & Psychophysics*, 1980, *27*, 241–250.

Hull, C. L. *Principles of Behavior*. New York: Appleton-Century 1943.

Hyman, R. Stimulus information as a determinant of reaction-time. *Journal of Experimental Psychology*, 1953, *45*, 188–196.

Isaacson, D. L. & R. W. Madsen. *Markov Chains.* New York: Wiley, 1976.

Jarvik, M. E. Probability learning and a negative recency effect in the serial anticipation of alternative symbols. *Journal of Experimental Psychology*, 1951, *41*, 291–297.

Jastrow, J. *The Time Relations of Mental Phenomena.* New York: Hodges, 1890.

Jennings, J. R., C. C. Wood, & B. E. Lawrence, Effects of graded doses of alcohol on speed-accuracy tradeoff in choice reaction time. *Perception & Psychophysics*, 1976, *19*, 85–91.

John, I. D. A statistical decision theory of simple reaction time. *Australian Journal of Psychology*, 1967, *19*, 17–34.

Johnsen, A. M. & G. E. Briggs. On the locus of display load effects in choice reactions. *Journal of Experimental Psychology*, 1973, *99*, 266–271.

Johnson, D. M. Confidence and speed in the two-category judgment. *Archives of Psychology*, 1939, *241*, 1–53.

Johnson, D. M. *The Psychology of Thought and Judgment.* New York: Harper, 1955.

Johnson, N. L. & S. Kotz. *Distributions in Statistics*, I, II, III. Boston: Houghton Mifflin Co., 1970.

Jury, E. I. *Theory and Application of the z-Transform Method.* New York: Wiley, 1964.

Kadane, J. B., J. H. Larkin, & R. H. Mayer. A moving average model for sequenced reaction-time data. *Journal of Mathematical Psychology*, 1981, *23*, 115–133.

Kahneman, D. *Attention and Effort.* Englewood Cliffs, N.J.: Prentice-Hall, 1973.

Kantowitz, B. H. Double stimulation. In B. H. Kantowitz (ed.), *Human Information Processing: Tutorials in Performance and Cognition.* Hillsdale, N.J.: Erlbaum, 1974, pp. 83–131.

Kantowitz, B. H. On the accuracy of speed-accuracy tradeoff. *Acta Psychologica*, 1978, *42*, 79–80.

Karlin, L. Reaction time as a function of foreperiod duration and variability. *Journal of Experimental Psychology*, 1959, *58*, 185–191.

Karlin, L. & R. Kestenbaum. Effects of number of alternatives on the psychological refractory period. *Quarterly Journal of Experimental Psychology*, 1968, *20*, 167–178.

Karlin, S. & H. M. Taylor. *A First Course in Stochastic Processes*, 2nd ed. New York: Academic Press, 1975.

Kay, H. & A. D. Weiss. Relationship between simple and serial reaction times. *Nature*, 1961, *191*, 790–791.

Keele, S. W. *Attention and Human Performance.* Pacific Palisades, CA: Goodyear, 1973.

Keele, S. W. & W. T. Neill. Mechanisms of attention. In E. C. Carterette & M. P. Friedman (eds.), *Handbook of Perception*, Vol. IX. London: Academic Press, 1978, pp. 3–47.

Kellas, G., A. Baumeister, & S. Wilcox. Interactive effects of preparatory intervals, stimulus intensity, and experimental design on reaction time. *Journal of Experimental Psychology*, 1969, *80*, 311–316.

Kelling, S. T. & B. P. Halpern. Taste flashes: Reaction times, intensity, and quality. *Science*, 1983, *219*, 412–414.

Kelley, J. E., Jr. Critical path planning and scheduling, mathematical basis. *Operations Research*, 1961, *9*, 296–320.

Kellogg, W. M. The time of judgment in psychometric measures. *American Journal of Psychology*, 1931, *43*, 65–86.

Kemeny, J. G. & J. L. Snell, *Finite Markov Chains.* Princeton, N.J.: Van Nostrand, 1960.

Keuss, P. J. G. Reaction time to the second of two shortly spaced auditory signals both varying in intensity. *Acta Psychologica*, 1972, *36*, 226–238.

Keuss, P. J. G. & J. F. Orlebeke. Transmarginal inhibition in a reaction time task as a function of extraversion and neuroticism. *Acta Psychologica*, 1977, *41*, 139–150.

Keuss, P. J. G. & M. W. van der Molen. Positive and negative effects of stimulus intensity in auditory reaction tasks: Further studies on immediate arousal. *Acta Psychologica*, 1982, *52*, 61–72.

Kiang, N. Y.-S., T. Watanabe, E. C. Thomas, & L. F. Clark. *Discharge Patterns of Single Fibers in the Cat's Auditory Nerve*. Cambridge, Mass.: MIT, 1965.

Kingman, J. F. C. Poisson counts for random sequences of events. *Annals of Mathematical Statistics*, 1963, *34*, 1217–1232.

Kirby, N. H. Sequential effects in serial reaction time. *Journal of Experimental Psychology*, 1972, *96*, 32–36.

Kirby, N. H. Sequential effects in an eight choice serial reaction time task. *Acta Psychologica*, 1975, *39*, 205–216.

Kirby, N. H. Sequential effects in two-choice reaction time: Automatic facilitation or subjective expectancy? *Journal of Experimental Psychology: Human Perception and Performance*, 1976, *2*, 567–577.

Kirby, N. Sequential effects in choice reaction time. In A. T. Welford (ed.), *Reaction Times*. London: Academic Press, 1980, pp. 129–172.

Klemmer, E. T. Time uncertainty in simple reaction time. *Journal of Experimental Psychology*, 1956, *51*, 179–184.

Kohfeld, D. L. Effects of the intensity of auditory and visual ready signals on simple reaction time. *Journal of Experimental Psychology*, 1969, *82*, 88–95.

Kohfeld, D. L. Simple reaction time as a function of stimulus intensity in decibels of light and sound. *Journal Experimental Psychology*, 1971, *88*, 251–257.

Kohfeld, D. L., J. L. Santee, & N. D. Wallace. Loudness and reaction time: I. *Perception & Psychophysics*, 1981a, *29*, 535–549.

Kohfeld, D. L., J. L. Santee, & N. D. Wallace. Loudness and reaction time: II. Identification of detection components at different intensities and frequencies. *Perception & Psychophysics*, 1981b, *29*, 550–562.

Kohonen, T. *Associative Memory: A System-Theoretical Approach*. Berlin: Springer-Verlag, 1977.

Koopman, B. O. The theory of search; Pt. I: Kinematic bases. *Operations Research*, 1956a, *4*, 324–346.

Koopman, B. O. The theory of search; Pt. II: Target detection, *Operations Research*, 1956b, *4*, 503–531.

Koopman, B. O. The theory of search; Pt. III: The optimum distribution of searching effort. *Operations Research*, 1957, *5*, 613–626.

Koppell, S. The latency function hypothesis and Pike's multiple-observations model for latencies in signal detection. *Psychological Review*, 1976, *83*, 308–309.

Kornblum, S. Choice reaction time for repetitions and nonrepetitions: A reexamination of the information hypothesis. *Acta Psychologica*, 1967, *27*, 178–187.

Kornblum, S. Serial-choice reaction time: Inadequacies of the information hypothesis. *Science*, 1968, *159*, 432–434.

Kornblum, S. Sequential determinants of information processing in serial and discrete choice reaction time. *Psychological Review*, 1969, *76*, 113–131.

Kornblum, S. Simple reaction time as a race between signal detection and time estimation: A paradigm and model. *Perception & Psychophysics*, 1973a, *13*, 108–112.

Kornblum, S. Sequential effects in choice reaction time. A tutorial review. In S. Kornblum (ed.), *Attention and Performance IV*, New York: Academic Press, 1973b, pp. 259–288.

Kornblum, S. An invariance in choice reaction time with varying numbers of alternatives and constant probability. In P. M. A. Rabbitt and S. Dornic. (eds.), *Attention and Performance V*. New York: Academic Press, 1975, pp. 366–382.

Kornbrot, D. E. The effect of response and speed bias on reaction time distributions in choice experiments. Paper presented to the Experimental Psychology Section, Sheffield, England, March, 1977.

Koster, W. G. & J. A. M. Bekker. Some experiments on refractoriness. *Acta Psychologica*, 1976, *27*, 64–70.

Krantz, D. H., R. D. Luce, P. Suppes, & A. Tversky. *Foundations of Measurement*, Vol. I. New York: Academic Press, 1971.

Krinchik, E. P. The probability of a signal as a determinant of reaction time. *Acta Psychologica*, 1969, *30*, 27–36.

Kristofferson, A. B. Low-variance stimulus-response latencies: Deterministic internal delays? *Perception & Psychophysics*, 1976, *20*, 89–100.

Krueger, L. E. Effect of irrelevant surrounding material on speed of same-different judgment of two adjacent letters. *Journal of Experimental Psychology*, 1973, *98*, 252–304.

Krueger, L. E. A theory of perceptual matching. *Psychological Review*, 1978, *85*, 278–304.

Krueger, L. E. & R. G. Shapiro. Repeating the target neither speeds or slows its detection: Evidence for independent channels in letter processing. *Perception & Psychophysics*, 1980, *28*, 68–76.

Kryvkov, V. I. Wald's identity and random walk models for neuron firing. *Advances in Applied Probability*, 1976, *8*, 257–277.

Kulikowski, J. J. & D. J. Tolhurst. Psychophysical evidence for sustained and transient channels in human vision. *Journal of Physiology, London*, 1973, *232*, 149–163.

LaBerge, D. A. A recruitment theory of simple behavior. *Psychometrika*, 1962, *27*, 375–396.

LaBerge, D. A. On the processing of simple visual and auditory stimuli at distinct levels. *Perception & Psychophysics*, 1971, *9*, 331–334.

Lachs, G. & M. C. Teich. A neural counting model incorporating refractoriness and spread of excitation. II. Applications to loudness estimation. *Journal of the Acoustical Society of America*, 1981, *69*, 774–782.

Laming. D. R. J. A new interpretation of the relation between choice reaction time and the number of equiprobable alternatives. *British Journal of Mathematical and Statistical Psychology*, 1966, *19*, 139–149.

Laming, D. R. J. *Information Theory of Choice-Reaction Times*. London: Academic Press, 1968.

Laming, D. R. J. Subjective probability in choice-reaction time experiments. *Journal of Mathematical Psychology*, 1969, *6*, 81–120.

Laming, D. R. J. A correction and a proof of a theorem by Duncan Luce. *British Journal of Mathematical and Statistical Psychology*, 1977a, *30*, 90–97.

Laming, D. R. J. Luce's choice axiom compared with choice-reaction data. *British Journal of Mathematical and Statistical Psychology*, 1977b, *30*, 141–153.

Laming, D. R. J. Choice reaction performance following an error. *Acta Psychologica*, 1979a, *43*, 199–224.

Laming, D. R. J. Autocorrelation of choice-reaction times. *Acta Psychologica*, 1979b, *43*, 381–412.

Laming, D. R. J. A critical comparison of two random-walk models for two-choice reaction time. *Acta Psychologica*, 1979c, *43*, 431–453.

Laming, D. R. J. *Sensory Analysis*. London: Academic Press, 1985.

Lappin, J. S. The relativity of choice behavior and the effect of prior knowledge in the speed and accuracy of recognition. In N. J. Castellan, Jr. and F. Restle (eds.), *Cognitive Theory*, Vol. 3. Hillsdale, N.J.: Erlbaum, 1978, pp. 139–168.

Lappin, J. S. & K. Disch. The latency operating characteristic: I. Effects of stimulus probability on choice reaction time. *Journal of Experimental Psychology*, 1972a, *92*, 419–427.

Lappin, J. S. & K. Disch. The latency operating characteristic: II. Effects of stimulus intensity on choice reaction time. *Journal of Experimental Psychology*, 1972b, *93*, 367–372.

Lappin, J. S. & K. Disch. Latency operating characteristic: III. Temporal Uncertainty effects. *Journal of Experimental Psychology*, 1973, *98*, 279–285.

Lazarsfeld, P. F. A conceptual introduction to latent structure analysis. In P. F. Lazarsfeld (ed.), *Mathematical Thinking in the Social Sciences*. Glencoe, Ill.: Free Press, 1954, pp. 349–387.

Leadbetter, M. R., G. Lindren, & H. Rootzén. *Extremes and Related Properties of Random Sequences and Processes*. New York: Springer-Verlag, 1983.

Lee, C. & W. K. Estes. Order and position is primary memory for letter strings. *Journal of Verbal Behavior*, 1977, *16*, 395–418.

Lee, C. & W. K. Estes. Item and order information in short-term memory: Evidence for multilevel perturbation processes. *Journal of Experimental Psychology: Human Learning and Memory*, 1981, *7*, 149–169.

Lemmon, V. W. The relation of reaction time to measures of intelligence, memory and learning. *Archives of Psychology*, 1927, *94*, 1–38.

Leonard, J. A. Tactual reactions: I. *Quarterly Journal of Experimental Psychology*, 1959, *11*, 76–83.

Leonard, J. A., R. C. Newman, & A. Carpenter. On the handling of heavy bias in a self-paced task. *Quarterly Journal of Experimental Psychology*, 1966, *18*, 130–141.

Levy, W. B., J. A. Anderson, & S. Lehmkuhle (eds.). *Synaptic Modification, Neuron Selectivity and Nervous System Organization*. Hillsdale, N.J.: Erlbaum, 1984.

Liapounov, A. M. Sur une proposition de la théorie des probabilités. *Bull. de l'Acad. Imp. des Sci. de St. Pétersbourg*, 1900, *13*, 359–386.

Liapounov, A. M. Nouvelle forms du théorème sur la limite de la probabilité. *Mém Acad. Sci. St.-Pétersbourg*, 1901, *12*, 1–24.

Lindeberg, J. W. Eine neue Herleitung des Exponentialgesetzes in der Wahrscheinlichkeits-rechnung. *Math. Zeit.*, 1922, *15*, 211–225.

Link, S. W. *A Stochastic Model for Bisensory Choice Mechanisms*. Stanford University, Ph.D. dissertation, 1968.

Link, S. W. The relative judgment theory of two-choice response time. *Journal of Mathematical Psychology*, 1975, *12*, 114–135.

Link, S. W. The relative judgment theory analysis of response time deadline experiments. In N. J. Castellan, Jr. & F. Restle (eds.), *Cognitive Theory, III*. Hillsdale, N.J.: Erlbaum Associates, 1978, pp. 117–138.

Link, S. W. Correcting response measures for guessing and partial information. *Psychological Bulletin*, 1982, *92*, 469–486.

Link, S. W. & R. A. Heath. A sequential theory of psychological discrimination. *Psychometrika*, 1975, *40*, 77–105.

Link, S. W. & A. D. Tindall. Speed and accuracy in comparative judgments of line length. *Perception & Psychophysics*, 1971, *9*, 284–288.

Loève, M. *Probability theory*, Vols. I and II. New York: Springer-Verlag, 1963, 1977.

Logan, G. D., W. B. Cowan, & K. A. Davis. On the ability to inhibit simple and choice reaction time responses: A model and a method. *Journal of Experimental Psychology: Human Perception and Performance*, 1984, *10*, 276–291.

Luce, R. D. *Individual Choice Behavior*. New York: Wiley, 1959.

Luce, R. D. Response latencies and probabilities. In K. J. Arrow, S. Karlin, & P. Suppes (eds.), *Mathematical Methods in the Social Sciences*. Stanford, CA: Stanford University Press, 1960, pp. 298–311.

Luce, R. D. Detection and recognition. In R. D. Luce, R. R. Bush, and E. Galanter (eds.), *Handbook of Mathematical Psychology*, Vol. I. New York: Wiley, 1963, pp. 103–189.

Luce, R. D. A model for detection in temporally unstructured experiments with a Poisson distribution of signal presentations. *Journal of Mathematical Psychology*, 1966, *3*, 48–64.

Luce, R. D. The choice axiom after twenty years. *Journal of Mathematical Psychology*, 1977, *3*, 215–233.

Luce, R. D. & D. M. Green. Detection of auditory signals presented at random times, II. *Perception & Psychophysics*, 1970, *7*, 1–14.

Luce, R. D. & D. M. Green. A neural timing theory for response times and the psychophysics of intensity. *Psychological Review*, 1972, *79*, 14–57.

Luce, R. D. & D. M. Green. Neural coding and psychophysical discrimination data. *Journal of the Acoustical Society of America*, 1974, *56*, 1554–1564.

Luce, R. D., R. M. Nosofsky, D. M. Green, & A. F. Smith. The bow and sequential effects in absolute identification. *Perception & Psychophysics*, 1982, *32*, 397–408.

Lupker, S. J. & J. Theios. Tests of two classes of models for choice reaction times. *Journal of Experimental Psychology: Human Perception and Performance*, 1975, *104*, 137–146.

Lupker, S. J. & J. Theios. Further tests of a two-state Markov model for choice reaction times. *Journal of Experimental Psychology: Human Perception and Performance*, 1977, *3*, 496–504.

Mackie, R. R. (ed.). *Vigilance*. New York: Plenum, 1977.

Mackworth, J. F. *Vigilance and Habituation: A Neuropsychological Approach*. Harmondsworth, England: Penguin, 1969.

Mackworth, J. F. *Vigilance and Attention*. Harmondsworth, England: Penguin, 1970.

Mackworth, N. H. *Researches in the Measurement of Human Performance*. M.R.C. Special Report 268, H.H.S.O., 1950. Reprinted in H. A. Sinaiko (ed.), *Selected Papers on Human Factors in the Design and Use of Control Systems*. New York: Dover, 1961, pp. 174–331.

MacMillan, N. A. Detection and recognition of increments and decrements in auditory intensity. *Perception & Psychophysics*, 1971, *10*, 233–238.

MacMillan, N. A. Detection and recognition of intensity changes in tone and noise: The detection-recognition disparity. *Perception & Psychophysics*, 1973, *13*, 65–75.

Maloney, L. T. & B. A. Wandell. A model of a single visual channel's response to weak test lights. *Vision Research*, 1984, *24*, 633–640.

Mansfield, R. J. W. Latency functions in human vision. *Vision Research*, 1973, *13*, 2219–2234.

Marill, T. The psychological refractory phase. *British Journal of Psychology*, 1957, *48*, 93–97.

Marrocco, R. T. Sustained and transient cells in monkey lateral geniculate nucleus: Conduction velocities and response properties. *Journal of Neurophysiology*, 1976, *39*, 340–353.

Marteniuk, R. G. & C. L. MacKenzie. Information processing in movement organization and execution. In R. S. Nickerson (ed.), *Attention and Performance VIII*. Hillsdale, N.J.: Erlbaum, 1980, pp. 29–57.

McCarthy, P. I. Approximate solutions for means and variances in a certain class of box problems. *Annals of Mathematical Statistics*, 1947, *18*, 349–383.

McClelland, J. L. On the time relations of mental processes: An examination of systems of processes in cascade. *Psychological Review*, 1979, *86*, 287–330.

McGill, W. J. Loudness and reaction time: A guided tour of the listener's private world. *Proceedings of the XVI International Congress of Psychology*, 1960. Amsterdam: North-Holland, 1960. pp. 193–199.

McGill, W. J. Random fluctuations of response rate. *Psychometrika*, 1962, *27*, 3–17.

McGill, W. J. Stochastic latency mechanisms. In R. D. Luce, R. R. Bush, & E. Galanter (eds.). *Handbook of Mathematical Psychology*, Vol. I. New York: Wiley, 1963, pp. 309–360.

McGill, W. J. Neural counting mechanisms and energy detection in audition. *Journal of Mathematical Psychology*, 1967, *4*, 351–376.

McGill, W. J. & J. P. Goldberg. Pure-tone intensity discrimination in audition. *Journal of the Acoustical Society of America*, 1968, *44*, 576–581.

Meihers, L. M. M. & E. G. J. Eijkman. The motor system in simple reaction time experiments. *Acta Psychologica*, 1974, *38*, 367–377.

Merkel, J. Die zeitlichen Verhaltnisse der Willensthatigkeit. *Philosophische Studien*, 1885, *2*, 73–127.

Miller, D. R. & N. D. Singpurwalla. Failure rate estimation using random smoothing. *National Technical Information Service*, No. AD-A040999/5ST, 1977.

Miller, J. Divided attention: Evidence for coactivation with redundant signals. *Cognitive Psychology*, 1982, *14*, 247–279.

Miller, J. & D. W. Bauer. Irrelevant differences in the "Same"–"Different" task. *Journal of Experimental Psychology: Human Perception and Performance*, 1981, 7, 196–207.

Modor, J. & C. Phillips. *Project Management with CPM and PERT*. New York: Van Nostrand, 1970, 2nd ed.

Moller, A. R. Unit responses in the cochlear nucleus of the rat to pure tones. *Acta Psychologica Scandinavia*, 1969, *75*, 530–541.

Mollon, J. D. & J. Krauskopf. Reaction time as a measure of the temporal response properties of individual color mechanisms. *Vision Research*, 1973, *13*, 27–40.

Morgan, B. B. & E. A. Alliusi. Effects of discriminability and irrelevant information on absolute judgment. *Perception & Psychophysics*, 1967, *2*, 54–58.

Morin, R. E., D. V. DeRosa, & V. Stultz. Recognition memory and reaction time. In A. F. Sanders (ed.), Attention and performance, *Acta Psychologica*, 1967, *27*, 298–305.

Morin, R. E., D. V. DeRosa, & R. Ulm. Short-term recognition memory for spatially isolated items. *Psychonomic Science*, 1967, *9*, 617–618.

Moss, S. M., S. Engel, & D. Faberman. Alternation and repetition reaction times under three schedules of event sequencing. *Psychonomic Science*, 1967, *9*, 557–558.

Moss, S. M., J. L. Myers, & T. Filmore. Short-term recognition memory of tones. *Perception & Psychophysics*, 1970, *7*, 369–373.

Mudd, S. *Briggs' Information-Processing Model of the Binary Classification Task*. Hillsdale, N.J.: Erlbaum, 1983.

Murray, H. G. & D. L. Kohfeld. Role of adaptation level in stimulus intensity dynamism. *Psychonomic Science*, 1965, *3*, 439–440.

Näätänen, R. An explanation for the longest reaction times obtained by using the shortest foreperiod of a randomized foreperiod series. *Psychological Institute Technical Report No. 4/67*, University of Helsinki, 1967.

Näätänen, R. The diminishing time-uncertainty with the lapse of time after the warning-signal in reaction-time experiments with varying foreperiods. *Acta Psychologica*, 1970, *34*, 399–419.

Näätänen, R. Non-aging foreperiod and simple reaction-time. *Acta Psychologica*, 1971, *35*, 316–327.

Näätänen, R. Time uncertainty and occurrence uncertainty of the stimulus in a simple reaction time task. *Acta Psychologica*, 1972, *36*, 492–503.

Näätänen, R. & A. Merisalo. Expectancy and preparation in simple reaction time. In S. Dornic (ed.), *Attention and Performance, VI*. Hillsdale, N.J.: Erlbaum, 1977, pp. 115–138.

Navon, D. A simple method for latency analysis in signal detection tasks. *Perception & Psychophysics*, 1975, *18*, 61–64.

Nickerson, R. S. Response times for "same"–"different" judgments. *Perceptual and Motor Skills*, 1965a, *20*, 15–18.

Nickerson, R. S. Response time to the second of two successive signals as a function of absolute and relative duration of the intersignal interval. *Perceptual and Motor Skills*, 1965b, *21*, 3–10.

Nickerson, R. S. "Same"–"different" response times: A model and a preliminary test. *Acta Psychologica*, 1969, *30*, 257–275.

Nickerson, R. S. "Same–different" response times: A further test of a "counter and clock" model. *Acta Psychologica*, 1971, *35*, 112–127.

Nickerson, R. S. Binary-classification reaction times: A review of some studies of human information-processing capabilities. *Pschychonomic Monograph Supplements*, 1972, *4*, 275–318.

Nickerson, R. S. & D. Burnham. Response times with nonaging foreperiods. *Journal of Experimental Psychology*, 1969, *79*, 452–457.

Niemi, P. Stimulus intensity effects on auditory and visual reaction processes. *Acta Psychologica*, 1979, *43*, 299–312.

Niemi, P. & E. Lehtonen. Foreperiod and visual stimulus intensity: a reappraisal. *Acta Psychologica*, 1982, *50*, 73–82.

Niemi, P. & R. Näätänen. Foreperiod and simple reaction time. *Psychological Bulletin*, 1981, *89*, 133–162.

Niemi, P. & T. Valitalo. Subjective response speed and stimulus intensity in a simple reaction time task. *Perceptual and Motor Skills*, 1980, *51*, 419–422.

Nissen, M. J. Stimulus intensity and information processing. *Perception & Psychophysics*, 1977, *22*, 338–352.

Noreen, D. L. Response probabilities and response times in psychophysical discrimination tasks: A review of three models. Unpublished monograph, 1976.

Norman, D. A. & W. Wickelgren. Strength theory and decision rules and latency in retrieval from short-term memory. *Journal of Mathematical Psychology*, 1969, *6*, 192–208.

Norman, M. F. Statistical inference with dependent observations: Extensions of classical procedures. *Journal of Mathematical Psychology*, 1971, *8*, 444–451.

Nosofsky, R. M. Shifts of attention in the identification and discrimination of intensity. *Perception & Psychophysics*, 1983, *33*, 103–112.

Ollman, R. T. Fast guesses in choice-reaction time. *Psychonomic Science*, 1966, *6*, 155–156.

Ollman, R. T. Central refractoriness in simple reaction time: The deferred processing model. *Journal of Mathematical Psychology*, 1968, *5*, 49–60.

Ollman, R. T. *A Study of the Fast Guess Model for Choice Reaction Times.* University of Pennsylvania, Ph.D. dissertation, 1970.

Ollman, R. T. Simple reactions with random countermanding of the "go" signal. In S. Kornblum (ed.), *Attention and Performance, IV.* New York: Academic Press, 1971, pp. 571–581.

Ollman, R. T. On the similarity between two types of speed/accuracy tradeoff. Unpublished manuscript, 1974.

Ollman, R. T. Discovering how display variables affect decision performances. Unpublished manuscript, 1975.

Ollman, R. T. Choice reaction time and the problem of distinguishing task effects from strategy effects. In S. Dornic (ed.), *Attention and Performance VI.* Hillsdale, N.J.: Erlbaum, 1977, pp. 99–113.

Ollman, R. T. Additive factors and the speed-accuracy tradeoff. Unpublished manuscript, 1979.

Ollman, R. T. & M. J. Billington. The deadline model for simple reaction times. *Cognitive Psychology*, 1972, *3*, 311–336.

Pachella, R. G. The interpretation of reaction time in information processing research. In B. Kantrowitz (ed.), *Human Information: Tutorials in Performance and Cognition.* Hillsdale, N.J.: Erlbaum, 1974, 41–82.

Pachella, R. G. & D. F. Fisher. Effect of stimulus degradation and similarity on the trade-off between speed and accuracy in absolute judgments. *Journal of Experimental Psychology*, 1969, *81*, 7–9.

Pachella, R. G. & D. F. Fisher. Hick's law and the speed-accuracy trade-off in absolute judgment. *Journal of Experimental Psychology*, 1972, *92*, 378–384.

Pachella, R. G., D. F. Fisher, & R. Karsh. Absolute judgments in speeded tasks: Quantification of the trade-off between speed and accuracy. *Psychonomic Science*, 1968, *12*, 225–226.

Pachella, R. G. & R. W. Pew. Speed-accuracy tradeoff in reaction time: Effect of discrete criterion times. *Journal of Experimental Psychology*, 1968, *76*, 19–24.

Pacut, A. Some properties of threshold models of reaction latency. *Biological Cybernetics*, 1977, *28*, 63–72.

Pacut, A. Stochastic model of the latency of the conditioned escape response. *Progress in Cybernetics and System Research*, Vol. 3. London: Advance Publications, 1978, pp. 633–642.

Pacut, A. Mathematical modelling of reaction latency: The structure of the models and its motivation. *Acta Neurobiologiae Experimentalis*, 1980, *40*, 199–215.

Pacut, A. Mathematical modelling of reaction latency Part II: A model of escape reaction and escape learning. *Acta Neurobiologiae Experimentalis*, 1982, *42*, 379–395.

Pacut, A. & W. Tych. Mathematical modelling of the reaction latency Part III: A model of avoidance reaction latency and avoidance learning. *Acta Neurobiologiae Experimentalis*, 1982, *42*, 397–420.

Parker, D. M. Simple reaction times to the onset, offset, and contrast reversal of sinusoidal grating stimuli. *Perception & Psychophysics*, 1980, *28*, 365–368.

Parker, D. M. & E. A. Salzen. Latency changes in the human visual evoked response to sinusoidal gratings. *Vision Research*, 1977, *17*, 1201–1204.

Parzen, E. *Modern Probability Theory and Its Applications*. New York: Wiley, 1960.

Parzen, E. *Stochastic Processes*. San Francisco: Holden-Day, 1962.

Pashler, H. Processing stages in overlapping tasks: Evidence for a central bottleneck. *Journal of Experimental Psychology: Human Perception and Performance*, 1984, *10*, 358–377.

Pearson, K. *Tables of the Incomplete Beta-Function*. London: Cambridge University Press, 1932.

Pease, V. The intensity-time relation of a stimulus in simple visual reaction time. *Psychological Record*, 1964, *14*, 157–164.

Perkel, D. H. A computer program for simulating a network of interacting neurons, I. Organization and physiological assumptions. *Computers and Biomedical Research*, 1976, *9*, 31–43.

Pew, R. W. The speed-accuracy operating characteristic. In W. G. Koster (ed.), Attention and Performance II. *Acta Psychologica*, 1969, *30*, 16–26.

Pfeiffer, R. R. Classification of response patterns of spike discharges for units in the cochlear nucleus: Tone burst stimulation. *Experimental Brain Research*, 1966, *1*, 220–235.

Pfingst, B. E., R. Hienz, J. Kimm, & J. Miller. Reaction-time procedure for measurement of hearing, I. *Journal of the Acoustical Society of America*, 1975, *57*, 421–430.

Pfingst, B. E., R. Hienz, & J. Miller. Reaction-time procedure for the measurement of hearing, II. *Journal of the Acoustical Society of America*, 1975, *57*, 431–436.

Pickett, R. M. The perception of a visual texture. *Journal of Experimental Psychology*, 1964, *68*, 13–20.

Pickett, R. M. Response latency in a pattern perception situation. In A. F. Sanders (ed.), Attention and performance, *Acta Psychologica*, 1967, *27*, 160–169.

Pickett, R. M. The visual perception of random line segment texture. Paper read at Ninth Meeting of the Psychonomic Society, 1968.

Piéron, H. Recherches sur les lois de variation des temps de latence sensorielle en fonction des intensités excitatrices. *L'Année Psychologique*, 1914, *20*, 17–96.

Piéron, H. Nouvelles recherches sur l'analyse du temps de latence sensorialle et sur la loi qui relie de temp a l'intensité d'excitation. *Année Psychologique*, 1920, *22*, 58–142.

Pierrel, R. & C. S. Murray. Some relationships between comparative judgment, confidence and decision-time in weight lifting. *American Journal of Psychology*, 1963, *76*, 28–38.

Pieters, J. P. M. Sternberg's additive factor method and underlying psychological processes: Some theoretical considerations. *Psychological Bulletin*, 1983, *93*, 411–426.

Pike, A. R. Latency and relative frequency of response in psychophysical discrimination. *British Journal of Mathematical and Statistical Psychology*, 1968, *21*, 161–182.

Pike, A. R. & L. Dalgleish. Latency-probability curves for sequential decision models: A comment on Weatherburn. *Psychological Bulletin*, 1982, *91*, 384–388.

Pike, R. Response latency models for signal detection. *Psychological Review*, 1973, *80*, 53–68.

Pike, R. & P. Ryder. Response latencies in the yes/no detection task. *Perception & Psychophysics*, 1973, *13*, 224–232.

Poffenberger, A. T. Reaction time to retinal stimulation with special reference to the time lost in conduction through nerve centers. *Archives of Psychology*, 1912, *23*, 1–73.

Pólya, G. Über den zentralin Grenzwertsatz der Wahrscheimlichkeitsrechnung und das Moment problem. *Mathematisches Zeitschriff*, 1920, *8*, 173–181.

Posner, M. I. *Chronometric Explorations of Mind*. Hillsdale, N.J.: Erlbaum, 1978.

Posner, M. I. & R. F. Mitchell. Chronometric analysis of classification. *Psychological Review*, 1967, *74*, 392–409.

Proctor, R. W. A unified theory for matching task phenomena. *Psychological Review*, 1981, *88*, 291–326.

Proctor, R. W. & K. V. Rao. On the "misguided" use of reaction-time differences: A discussion of Ratcliff and Hacker (1981). *Perception & Psychophysics*, 1982, *31*, 601–602.

Proctor, R. W. & K. V. Rao. Reinstating the original principles of Proctor's unified theory for matching-task phenomena: An evaluation of Krueger and Shapiro's reformulation. *Psychological Review*, 1983, *90*, 21–37.

Proctor, R. W., K. V. Rao, & P. W. Hurst. An examination of response bias in multiletter matching: Implications for models of the comparison process. Paper presented at the Sixteenth Annual Meeting of the Society for Mathematical Psychology, 1983.

Prucnal, P. R. & M. C. Teich. Refractory effects in neural counting processes with exponentially decaying rates. *IEEE Transactions on Systems, Man, and Cybernetics*, 1983, *13*, 1028–1033.

Purks, S. R., D. J. Callahan, L. D. Braida, & N. Durlach. I. Intensity perception. X. Effect of preceding stimulus on identification performance. *Journal of the Acoustical Society of America*, 1980, *67*, 634–636.

Raab, D. H. Effects of stimulus-duration on auditory reaction-time. *American Journal of Psychology*, 1962a, *75*, 298–301.

Raab, D. H. Magnitude estimates of the brightness of brief foveal stimuli. *Science*, 1962b, *135*, 42–43.

Raab, D. & E. Fehrer. The effect of stimulus duration and luminance on visual reaction time. *Journal of Experimental Psychology*, 1962, *64*, 326–327.

Raab, D., E. Fehrer, & M. Hershenson. Visual reaction time and the Broca-Sulzer phenomenon. *Journal of Experimental Psychology*, 1961, *61*, 193–199.

Rabbitt, P. M. A. Response facilitation on repetition of a limb movement. *British Journal of Psychology*, 1965, *56*, 303–304.

Rabbitt, P. M. A. Errors and error correction in choice-response tasks. *Journal of Experimental Psychology*, 1966, *71*, 264–272.

Rabbitt, P. M. A. Time to detect errors as a function of factors affecting choice-response time. *Acta Psychologica*, 1967, *27*, 131–142.

Rabbitt, P. M. A. Three kinds of error-signaling responses in a serial choice task. *Quarterly Journal of Experimental Psychology*, 1968a, *20*, 179–188.

Rabbitt, P. M. A. Repetition effects and signal classification strategies in social choice-response tasks. *Quarterly Journal of Experimental Psychology*, 1968b, *20*, 232–240.

Rabbitt, P. M. A. Psychological refractory delay and response-stimulus interval duration in serial, choice-response tasks. In W. G. Koster (ed.), *Attention and Performance II*. Amsterdam: North Holland, 1969, pp. 195–219.

Rabbitt, P. M. A. & B. Rogers. What does a man do after he makes an error? An analysis of response programming. *Quarterly Journal of Experimental Psychology*, 1977, *29*, 727–743.

Rabbitt, P. M. A. & S. M. Vyas. An elementary preliminary taxonomy for some errors in laboratory choice RT tasks. *Acta Psychologica*, 1977, *29*, 727–743.

Rabiner, L. R. & B. Gold. *Theory and Application of Digital Signal Processing*. Englewood Cliffs, N.J.: Prentice-Hall, 1975.

Rains, J. D. Signal luminance and position effects in human reaction time. *Vision Research*, 1963, *3*, 239–251.

Rapoport, A. A study of disjunctive reaction times. *Behavioral Science*, 1959, *4*, 299–315.

Rapoport, A., W. E. Stein, & G. J. Burkheimer. *Response Models for Detection of Change*. Dordrecht: Reidel, 1979.

Ratcliff, R. A theory of memory retrieval. *Psychological Review*, 1978, *85*, 59–108.

Ratcliff, R. A theory of order relations in perceptual matching. *Psychological Review*, 1981, *88*, 552–572.

Ratcliff, R. Theoretical interpretations of speed and accuracy of positive and negative responses. *Psychological Review*, 1985, *92*, 212–225.

Ratcliff, R. & M. J. Hacker. Speed and accuracy of same and different responses in perceptual matching. *Perception & Psychophysics*, 1981, *30*, 303–307.

Ratcliff, R. & M. J. Hacker. On the misguided use of reaction-time differences: A reply to Proctor and Rao (1982). *Perception & Psychophysics*, 1982, *31*, 603–604.

Ratcliff, R. & B. B. Murdock, Jr. Retrieval processes in recognition memory. *Psychological Review*, 1976, *86*, 190–214.

Reed, A. V. Speed accuracy trade-off in recognition memory. *Science*, 1973, *181*, 574–576.

Remington, R. J. Analysis of sequential effects in choice reaction times. *Journal of Experimental Psychology*, 1969, *82*, 250–257.

Remington, R. J. Analysis of sequential effects for a four-choice reaction time experiment. *Journal of Psychology*, 1971, 77, 17–27.

Restle, F. *Psychology of Judgment and Choice*. New York: Wiley, 1961.

Rice, J. & M. Rosenblatt. Estimation of the log survivor function and hazard function. *Sankhya* (Series A), 1976, *38*, 60–78.

Rose, J. E., J. F. Brugge, D. J. Anderson, & J. E. Hind. Phase-locked response to low-frequency tones in single auditory nerve fibers of the squirrel monkey. *Journal of Neurophysiology*, 1967, *30*, 769–793.

Ross, B. H. & J. R. Anderson. A test of parallel versus serial processing applied to memory retrieval. *Journal of Mathematical Psychology*, 1981, *24*, 183–223.

Rubinstein, L. Intersensory and intrasensory effects in simple reaction time. *Perceptual and Motor Skills*, 1964, *18*, 159–172.

Salthouse, F. A. Converging evidence for information-processing stages: A comparative-influence stage-analysis method. *Acta Psychologica*, 1981, *47*, 39–61.

Sampath, G. & S. K. Srinivasan. *Stochastic Models for Spike Trains of Single Neurons*. New York: Springer-Verlag, 1977.

Sanders, A. F. The foreperiod effect revisited. *Quarterly Journal of Experimental Psychology*, 1975, *27*, 591–598.

Sanders, A. F. Structural and functional aspects of the reaction process. In S. Dornic (ed.), *Attention and Performance VI*. Hillsdale, N.J.: Erlbaum, 1977, pp. 3–25.

Sanders, A. F. & J. E. B. Andreiessen. A suppressing effect of response selection on immediate arousal in choice reaction task. *Acta Psychologica*, 1978, *42*, 181–186.

Sanders, A. F. & W. Ter Linden. Decision making during paced arrival of probabilistic information. In A. F. Sanders (ed.), Attention and Performance, *Acta Psycholgica*, 1967, *27*, 170–177.

Sanders, A. F. & A. Wertheim. The relation between physical stimulus properties and the effect of foreperiod duration on reaction time. *Quarterly Journal of Experimental Psychology*, 1973, *25*, 201–206.

Sanders, A. F., J. L. C. Wijnen, & A. E. van Arkel. An additive factor analysis of the effects of sleep loss on reaction processes. *Acta Psychologica*, 1982, *51*, 41–59.

Santee, J. L. & H. E. Egeth. Do reaction time and accuracy measure the same aspects of letter recognition. *Journal of Experimental Psychology: Human Perception and Performance*, 1982, *8*, 489–501.

Saslow, C. A. Operant control of response latency in monkeys: Evidence for a central explanation. *Journal of the Experimental Analysis of Behavior*, 1968, *11*, 89–98.

Saslow, C. A. Behavioral definition of minimal reaction time in monkeys. *Journal of the Experimental Analysis of Behavior*, 1972, *18*, 87–106.

Scharf, B. Critical bands. In J. V. Tobias (ed.), *Foundations of Modern Auditory Theory*, Vol. I. New York: Academic, 1970, pp. 159–202.

Schmitt, J. C. & C. J. Scheiver. Empirical approaches to information processing: Speed-accuracy tradeoff function or reaction time. *Acta Psychologica*, 1977, *41*, 321–325.

Schneider, W. & R. M. Shiffrin. Controlled and automatic human information processing: I. Detection, search, and attention. *Psychological Review*, 1977, *84*, 1–66.

Schnizlein, J. M. *Psychophysics of Auditory Simple Reaction Time*. The University of New Mexico, Ph.D. dissertation, 1980.

Schouten, J. F. & J. A. M. Bekker. Reaction time and accuracy. In A. F. Sanders (ed.), Attention and Performance. *Acta Psychologica*, 1967, *27*, 143–153.

Schvaneveldt, R. W. & W. G. Chase. Sequential effects in choice reaction time. *Journal of Experimental Psychology*, 1969, *80*, 1–8.

Schweickert, R. A Critical path generalization of the additive factor method: Analysis of a Stroop task. *Journal of Mathematical Psychology*, 1978, *18*, 105–139.

Schweickert, R. Critical-path scheduling of mental processes in a dual task. *Science*, 1980, *209*, 704–706.

Schweickert, R. The bias of an estimate of coupled slack in stochastic PERT networks. *Journal of Mathematical Psychology*, 1982a, *26*, 1–12.

Schweickert, R. Scheduling decisions in critical path networks of mental processes. Presentation at the meeting of the Society for Mathematical Psychology, 1982b.

Schweickert, R. Latent network theory: Scheduling of processes in sentence verification and the Stroop effect. *Journal of Experimental Psychology: Learning, Memory and Cognition*, 1983a, *9*, 353–383.

Schweickert, R. Synthesizing partial orders given comparability information: Partitive sets and slack in critical path networks. *Journal of Mathematical Psychology*, 1983b, 27, 261–276.

Schweichert, R. The representation of mental activities in critical path networks. In J. Gibbon & L. Allan, *Timing and Time Perception*. New York: New York Academy of Sciences, Vol 423, 1984, pp. 82–95.

Shannon, C. E. A mathematical theory of communication. *Bell System Technical Journal*, 1948, *27*, 379–423 and 623–656.

Shaw, M. L. A capacity allocation model for reaction time. *Journal of Experimental Psychology: Human Perception and Performance*, 1978, *4*, 586–598.

Shaw, M. L. & P. Shaw. Optimal allocation of cognitive resources to spatial locations. *Journal of Experimental Psychology: Human Perception and Performance*, 1977, *3*, 201–211.

Shevrin, L. N. & N. D. Filippov. Partially ordered sets and their comparability graphs. *Siberian Mathematical Journal*, 1970, *11*, 497–509.

Siebert, W. M. Stimulus transformation in the peripheral auditory system. In P. A. Kolers & M. Eden (eds.), *Recognizing Patterns*. Cambridge, Mass.: MIT Press, 1968, pp. 104–133.

Siebert, W. M. Frequency discrimination in the auditory system: Place or periodicity mechanisms? *Proceedings of the IEEE*, 1970, *58*, 723–730.

Silverman, W. P. The perception of identity in simultaneously presented complex visual displays. *Memory and Cognition*, 1973, *1*, 459–466.

Silverman, W. P. & S. L. Goldberg. Further confirmation of same vs. different processing differences. *Perception & Psychophysics*, 1975, *17*, 189–193.

Simon, J. R. Sterotypic reactions in information processing. In L. E. Smith (ed.), *Psychology of Motor Learning*. Ames, Iowa: University of Iowa Press, 1969.

Simon, J. R. Effect of an auditory stimulus on the processing of a visual stimulus under single- and dual-tasks conditions. *Acta Psychologica*, 1982, *51*, 61–73.

Simon, J. R., E. Acosta, Jr., & S. P. Mewaldt. Effects of locus of a warning tone on auditory choice reaction time. *Memory and Cognition*, 1975, *3*, 167–170.

Simon, J. R., E. Acosta, Jr., S. P. Mewaldt, & C. R. Speidel. The effect of an irrelevant cue on choice reaction time: Duration of the phenomenon and its relation to stages of processing. *Perception & Psychophysics*, 1976, *19*, 16–22.

Singpurwalla, N. D. & M.-T. Wong. Estimation of the failure rate—A survey of nonparametric methods. Part I: Non-Bayesian methods. *Communications in Statistics—Theory and Methods*, 1983, *A12*, 559–588.

Skinner, B. F. Are theories of learning necessary? *Psychological Review*, 1950, *57*, 193–216.

Smith, E. E. Choice reaction time: An analysis of the major theoretical positions. *Psychological Bulletin*, 1968, *69*, 77–110.

Smith, G. A. *Studies of Compatibility and Investigations of a Model of Reaction Time*. University of Adelaide, Australia: Ph.D. dissertation, 1978.

Smith, G. A. Studies of compatibility and a new model of choice reaction time. In S. Dornic (ed.), *Attention and Performance VI*. Hillsdale, N.J.: Lawrence Erlbaum, 1977.

Smith, G. A. Models of choice reaction time. In A. T. Welford (ed.), *Reaction Times*. London: Academic Press, 1980, pp. 173–214.

Smith, M. C. Reaction time to a second stimulus as a function of the intensity of the first stimulus. *Quarterly Journal of Experimental Psychology.* 1967a, *19*, 125–132.

Smith, M. C. The psychological refractory period as a function of performance of a first response. *Quarterly Journal of Experimental Psychology.* 1967b, *19*, 350–352.

Smith, M. C. Theories of the psychological refractory period. *Psychological Bulletin*, 1967c, 67, 202–213.

Smith, M. C. The effect of varying information on the psychological refractory period. In W. G. Koster (ed.), Attention and performance, II. *Acta Psychologica*, 1969, *30*, 220–231.

Snodgrass, J. G. Foreperiod effects in simple reaction time: Anticipation or expectancy? *Journal of Experimental Psychology, Monograph*, 1969, *79*, 1–19.

Snodgrass, J. G. Reaction times for comparisons of successively presented visual patterns: Evidence for serial self-terminating search. *Perception & Psychophysics*, 1972, *12*, 364–372.

Snodgrass, J. G., R. D. Luce, & E. Galanter. Some experiments on simple and choice reaction time. *Journal of Experimental Psychology*, 1967, *75*, 1–17.

Snodgrass, J. G. & J. T. Townsend. Comparing parallel and serial models: Theory and implementation. *Journal of Experimental Psychology: Human Perception and Performance* 1980, *6*, 330–354.

Spence, K. W. The relation of response latency and speed to the intervening variables and *N* in S–R theory. *Psychological Review*, 1954, *61*, 209–216.

Sperling, G. The information available in brief visual presentations. *Psychological Monographs*, 1960, *74*.

SPSSx User's Guide. Chicago, Ill.: McGraw-Hill, 1983.

Stanovich, K. & R. Pachella. Encoding, stimulus-response compatibility and stages of processing. *Journal of Experimental Psychology: Human Perception and Performance*, 1977, *3*, 411–421.

Stanovich, K. E., R. G. Pachella, & J. E. K. Smith. An analysis of confusion errors in naming letters under speed stress. *Perception & Psychophysics*, 1977, *21*, 545–552.

Stelmach, G. E. (ed.). *Information Processing in Motor Control and Motor Learning.* New York: Academic Press, 1978.

Stelmach, G. E. & J. Requin. (eds.). *Tutorials in Motor Behavior.* Amsterdam: North-Holland, 1980.

Sternberg, S. High speed scanning in human memory. *Science*, 1966, *153*, 652–654.

Sternberg, S. Retrieval of contextual information from memory. *Psychonomic Science*, 1967a, *8*, 55–56.

Sternberg, S. Two operations in character-recognition: Some evidence from reaction-time measurements. *Perception & Psychophysics*, 1967b, *2*, 45–53.

Sternberg, S. The discovery of processing stages: Extensions of Donders' method. In W. G. Koster (ed.), Attention and performance II, *Acta Psychologica*, 1969a, *30*, 276–315.

Sternberg, S. Memory scanning: Mental processes revealed by reaction-time experiments. *American Scientist*, 1969b, *57*, 421–457. Reprinted in J. S. Antrobus (ed.), *Cognition and Affect.* Boston: Little, Brown, 1970, pp. 13–58.

Sternberg, S. Decomposing mental processes with reaction-time data. Invited address, Annual Meeting of the Midwestern Psychological Association, Detroit, May 1971.

Sternberg, S. Evidence against self-terminating memory search from properties of RT distributions. Paper presented at the Meeting of the Psychonomic Society, St. Louis, November 1973.

Sternberg, S. Memory scanning: New findings and current controversies. *Quarterly Journal of Experimental Psychology*, 1975, *17*, 1–32.

Sternberg, S., S. Monsell, R. L. Knoll, & C. E. Wright. The latency and duration of rapid movement sequences: Comparisons of speech and typewriting. In G. E. Stilmach (ed.), *Information Processing in Motor Control and Learning.* New York: Academic Press, 1978, pp. 117–152.

Sternberg, S., C. E. Wright, R. L. Knoll, & S. Monsell. Motor programs in rapid speech:

Additional evidence. In R. A. Cole (ed.), *The Perception and Production of Fluent Speech.* Hillsdale, N.J.: Erlbaum, 1980, pp. 507–534.

Stevens, J. C. & J. W. Hall. Brightness and loudness as functions of stimulus duration. *Perception & Psychophysics*, 1966, *1*, 319–327.

Stevens, S. S. *Psychophysics*. New York: Wiley, 1975.

Sticht, T. G. Effects of intensity and duration on the latency of response to brief light and dark stimuli. *Journal of Experimental Psychology*, 1969, *80*, 419–422.

Stilitz, I. Conditional probability and components of RT in the variable foreperiod experiment. *Quarterly Journal of Experimental Psychology*, 1972, *24*, 159–168.

Stone, L. D. *Theory of Optimal Search*. New York: Academic Press, 1975.

Stone, M. Models for choice-reaction time. *Psychometrika*, 1960, *25*, 251–260.

Stroh, C. M. *Vigilance: The Problem of Sustained Attention*. Oxford: Pergamon, 1971.

Stroud, J. M. The fine structure of psychological time. In H. Quastler (ed.), *Information Theory in Psychology*. Glencoe: Ill.: Free Press, 1955, pp. 174–207.

SUGI Supplemental Library User's Guide. Cary, N.C.: SAS Institute Inc., 1983.

Swanson, J. M. & G. E. Briggs. Information processing as a function of speed versus accuracy. *Journal of Experimental Psychology*, 1969, *31*, 223–229.

Swanson, J. M., A. M. Johnsen, & G. E. Briggs. Recoding in a memory search task. *Journal of Experimental Psychology*, 1972, *93*, 1–9.

Swensson, R. G. The elusive tradeoff: Speed versus accuracy in visual discrimination tasks. *Perception & Psychophysics*, 1972a, *12*, 16–32.

Swensson, R. G. Trade-off bias and efficiency effects in serial choice reactions. *Journal of Experimental Psychology*, 1972b, *95*, 397–407.

Swensson, R. G. & W. Edwards. Response strategies in a two-choice reaction task with a continuous cost for time. *Journal of Experimental Psychology*, 1971, *88*, 67–81.

Swensson, R. G. & D. M. Green. On the relations between random walk models for two-choice response times. *Journal of Mathematical Psychology*, 1977, *15*, 282–291.

Swensson, R. G. & R. E. Thomas. Fixed and optional stopping models for two-choice discrimination times. *Journal of Mathematical Psychology*, 1974, *11*, 213–236.

Swets, J. A. Signal detection applied to vigilance. In R. R. Mackie (ed.), *Vigilance*. New York: Plenum, 1977, pp. 705–718.

Taylor, D. A. Stage analysis of reaction time. *Psychological Bulletin*, 1976a, *83*, 161–191.

Taylor, D. A. Effect of identity in the multiletter matching task. *Journal of Experimental Psychology: Human Perception and Performance*, 1976b, *2*, 417–428.

Taylor, D. A., J. T. Townsend, & P. Sudevan. Analysis of intercompletion times in multielement processing. Paper presented at the Annual Meeting of the Psychonomic Society, San Antonio, November 1978.

Taylor, D. H. Latency models for reaction time distributions. *Psychometrika*, 1965, *30*, 157–163.

Taylor, D. H. Latency components in two choice responding. *Journal of Experimental Psychology*, 1966, *72*, 481–487.

Taylor, M. M., P. H. Lindsay, & S. M. Forbes. Quantification of shared capacity processing in auditory and visual discrimination. In A. F. Sanders (ed.), *Attention and Performance*, *Acta Psychologica*, 1967, *27*, 223–229.

Teich, M. C. & B. I. Cantor. Information, error, and imaging in deadtime-perturbed doubly stochastic Poisson counting processes. *IEEE Journal of Quantum Electronics*, 1978, *14*, 993–1003.

Teich, M. C. & G. Lachs. A neural counting model incorporating refractoriness and spread of excitation. I. Application to intensity discrimination. *Journal of the Acoustical Society of America*, 1979, *66*, 1738–1749.

Teich, M. C. & W. J. McGill. Neural counting and photon counting in the presence of deadtime. *Physical Review Letters*, 1976, *36*, 754–758.

Teichner, W. H. Recent studies of simple reaction time. *Psychological Bulletin*, 1954, *51*, 172–177.

Teichner, W. H. & M. J. Krebs. Laws of the simple visual reaction time. *Psychological Review,* 1972, *79,* 344–358.

Teichner, W. H. & M. J. Krebs. Laws of visual choice reaction time. *Psychological Review,* 1974, *81,* 75–98.

Telford, C. W. The refractory phase of voluntary and associative responses. *Journal of Experimental Psychology,* 1931, *14,* 1–36.

Ten Hoopen, G., S. Akerboom, & E. Raaymakers. Vibrotactual choice reaction time, tactile receptor systems and ideomotor compatibility. *Acta Psychologica,* 1982, *50,* 143–157.

Theios, J. Reaction time measurements in the study of memory processes: Theory and data. In G. H. Bower (ed.), *The Psychology of Learning and Motivation,* Vol. 7. New York: Academic Press, 1973, pp. 43–85.

Theios, J. The components of response latency in simple human information processing tasks. In P. M. A. Rabbitt and S. Dornic (eds.), *Attention and Performance V,* London: Academic Press, 1975, pp. 418–440.

Theios, J. & P. G. Smith. Can a two-state model account for two-choice reaction-time data? *Psychological Review,* 1972, *79,* 172–177.

Theios, J., P. G. Smith, S. E. Haviland, J. Traupmann, & M. C. Moy. Memory scanning as a serial self-terminating process. *Journal of Experimental Psychology,* 1973, *97,* 323–336.

Theios, J. & D. G. Walter. Stimulus and response frequency and sequential effects in memory scanning reaction times. *Journal of Experimental Psychology,* 1974, *102,* 1092–1099.

Thomas, E. A. C. Reaction time studies: The anticipation and interaction of responses. *The British Journal of Mathematical and Statistical Psychology,* 1967, *20,* 1–29.

Thomas, E. A. C. Distribution free tests for mixed probability distributions. *Biometrika,* 1969, *56,* 475–484.

Thomas, E. A. C. Sufficient conditions for monotone hazard rate and application to latency-probability curves. *Journal of Mathematical Psychology,* 1971, *8,* 303–332.

Thomas, E. A. C. On expectancy and the speed and accuracy of responses. In S. Kornblum (ed.), *Attention and Performance, IV.* New York: Academic Press, 1973, pp. 613–626.

Thomas, E. A. C. The selectivity of preparation. *Psychological Review,* 1974, *81,* 442–464.

Thomas, E. A. C. A note on the sequential probability ratio test. *Psychometrika,* 1975, *40,* 107–111.

Thomas, E. A. C. & J. L. Myers. Implications of listing data for threshold and nonthreshold models of signal detection. *Journal of Mathematical Psychology,* 1972, *9,* 253–285.

Thomas, E. A. C. & B. H. Ross. On appropriate procedures for combining probability distributions within the same family. *Journal of Mathematical Psychology,* 1980, *21,* 136–152.

Thrane, V. Sensory and preparatory factors in response latency: I. The visual intensity function. *Scandinavian Journal of Psychology,* 1960a, *1,* 82–96.

Thrane, V. Sensory and preparatory factors in response latency: II. Simple reaction or compensatory interaction? *Scandinavian Journal of Psychology,* 1960b, *1,* 169–176.

Thurstone, L. L. A law of comparative judgment. *Psychological Review,* 1927a, *34,* 273–286.

Thurstone, L. L. A mental unit of measurement. *Psychological Review,* 1927b, *34,* 415–423.

Titchmarsh, E. C. *Introduction to the Theory of Fourier Integrals.* Oxford: Oxford University Press, 1948.

Tolhurst, D. J. Reaction times in the detection of gratings by human observers: A probabilistic mechanism. *Vision Research,* 1975a, *15,* 1143–1149.

Tolhurst, D. J. Sustained and transient channels in human vision. *Vision Research,* 1975b, *15,* 1151–1155.

Townsend, J. T. Mock parallel and serial models and experimental detection of these. In *Proceedings of The Symposium on Information Processing.* Purdue University School of Electrical Engineering, 1969, 617–628.

Townsend, J. T. Some results concerning the identifiability of parallel and serial processes. *British Journal of Mathematical and Statistical Psychology,* 1972, *25,* 168–197.

Townsend, J. T. Issues and models concerning the processing of a finite number of inputs. In B.

H. Kantrowitz (ed.), *Human Information Processing: Tutorials in Performance and Cognition.* New York: Wiley, 1974, pp. 133–185.

Townsend, J. T. Serial and within-stage independent parallel model equivalence on the minimum completion time. *Journal of Mathematical Psychology,* 1976a, *14,* 219–238.

Townsend, J. T. A stochastic theory of matching processes. *Journal of Mathematical Psychology,* 1976b, *14,* 1–52.

Townsend, J. T. Paper presented at the Mathematical Psychology 9th Annual Meeting, New York University, 1976c.

Townsend, J. T. & F. G. Ashby. Methods of modeling capacity in simple processing systems. In N. J. Castellan, Jr. and F. Restle (eds.), *Cognitive Theory,* Vol. 3. Hillsdale, N.J.: Erlbaum, 1978, pp. 199–239.

Townsend, J. T. & F. G. Ashby. *Stochastic Modeling of Elementary Psychological Processes.* Cambridge: Cambridge University Press, 1983.

Townsend, J. T. & R. N. Roos. Search reaction times for single targets in multiletter stimuli with brief visual displays. *Memory and Cognition,* 1973, *1,* 319–332.

Townsend, J. T. & J. G. Snodgrass. A serial vs. parallel testing paradigm where "same" and "different" comparison rates differ. Paper presented at Psychonomic Society Meeting, Boston, 1974.

Treisman, M. A theory of criterion setting with an application to sequential dependencies. *Psychological Review,* 1985, in press.

Tretter, S. A. *Introduction to Discrete-Time Signal Processing.* New York: Wiley, 1978.

Trotter, W. T., J. I. Moore, & D. P. Sumner. The dimension of a comparability graph. *Proceedings of the American Mathematical Society,* 1976, *60,* 35–38.

Tversky, B. Pictorial and verbal encoding in a short-term memory task. *Perception & Psychophysics,* 1969, *6,* 225–233.

Uttal, W. R. & M. Krissoff. Response of the somasthetic system to patterned trains of electrical stimuli. In D. R. Krenshalo (ed.), *The Skin Senses.* Springfield, Ill.: Thomas, 1968, pp. 262–303.

van der Heijden, A. H. C. & H. W. Menckenberg. Some evidence for a self-terminating process in simple visual search tasks. *Acta Psychologica,* 1974, *38,* 169–181.

van der Molen, M. W. & P. J. G. Keuss. The relationship between reaction time and auditory intensity in discrete auditory tasks. *Quarterly Journal of Experimental Psychology,* 1979, *31,* 95–102.

van der Molen, M. W. & P. J. G. Keuss. Response selection and the processing of auditory intensity. *Quarterly Journal of Experimental Psychology,* 1981, *33,* 177–184.

van der Molen, M. W. & J. F. Orlebeke. Phasic heart rate change and the U-shaped relationship between choice reaction time and auditory intensity. *Psychophysiology,* 1980, *17,* 471–481.

Vannucci, G. & M. C. Teich. Effects of rate variation on the counting statistics of dead-time modified Poisson processes, *Optics Communications,* 1978, *25,* 267–272.

Vaughn, H. G., Jr., L. D. Costa, & L. Gilden. The functional relation of visual evoked response and reaction time to stimulus intensity. *Vision Research,* 1966, *6,* 654–656.

Vervaeck, K. R. & L. C. Boer. Sequential effects in two-choice reaction time: Subjective expectancy and automatic after-effect at short response-stimulus intervals. *Acta Psychologica,* 1980, *44,* 175–190.

Vickers, D. Evidence for an accumulator model of psychophysical discrimination. *Ergonomics,* 1970, *13,* 37–58.

Vickers, D. Discrimination. In A. T. Welford (ed.), *Reaction Times.* London: Academic Press, 1980, pp. 25–72.

Vickers, D., D. Caudrey, & R. J. Willson. Discriminating between the frequency of occurrence of two alternative events. *Acta Psychologica,* 1971, *35,* 151–172.

Vickers, D. & J. Packer. Effects of alternating set for speed or accuracy on response time, accuracy and confidence in a unidimensional task. *Acta Psychologica,* 1981, *50,* 179–197.

Vince, M. A. The intermittency of control movements and the psychological refractory period. *British Journal of Psychology*, 1948, *38*, 149–157.

Viviani, P. Choice reaction times for temporal numerosity. *Journal of Experimental Psychology: Human Perception and Performance*, 1979a, *5*, 157–167.

Viviani, P. A diffusion model for discrimination of temporal numerosity. *Journal of Mathematical Psychology*, 1979b, *19*, 108–136.

Viviani, P. & C. A. Terzuolo. On the modeling of the performance of the human brain in a two-choice task involving decoding and memorization of simple visual patterns. *Kybernetik*, 1972, *10*, 121–137.

Vorberg, D. On the equivalence of serial and parallel processing systems. Paper presented at the Mathematical Psychology 10th Annual Meeting, UCLA, 1977.

Wald, A. *Sequential Analysis*. New York: Wiley, 1947.

Wald, A. & J. Wolfowitz. Optimum character of the sequential probability ratio test. *Annals of Mathematical Statistics*, 1948, *19*, 326–339.

Wandell, B. A. Speed-accuracy tradeoff in visual detection: Applications of neural counting and timing. *Vision Research*, 1977, *17*, 217–225.

Wandell, B. A., P. Ahumada, & D. Welsh. Reaction times to weak test lights. *Vision Research*, 1984, *24*, 647–652.

Wandell, B., & R. D. Luce. Pooling peripheral information: Average versus extreme values. *Journal of Mathematical Psychology*, 1978, *17*, 220–235.

Ward, L. M. & G. R. Lockhead. Sequential effects and memory in category judgments. *Journal of Experimental Psychology*, 1970, *84*, 27–34.

Watson, C. S., M. E. Rilling, & W. T. Bourbon. Receiver-operating characteristics determined by a mechanical analog to a rating scale. *Journal of the Acoustical Society of America*, 1964, *36*, 283–288.

Weatherburn, D. Latency-probability functions as bases for evaluating competing accounts of the sensory decision process. *Psychological Bulletin*, 1978, *85*, 1344–1347.

Weatherburn, D. & D. Grayson. Latency-probability functions: A reply to Pike and Dalgleish. *Psychological Bulletin*, 1982, *91*, 389–392.

Weaver, H. R. A study of discriminative serial action: Manual response to color. *Journal of Experimental Psychology*, 1942, *31*, 177–201.

Weiss, A. D. The locus of reaction time change with set, motivation and age. *Journal of Gerontology*, 1965, *20*, 60–64.

Weist, J. D. & F. K. Levy. *A Management Guide to PERT/CPM*. Englewood Cliffs, N.J.: Prentice-Hall, 1969.

Welford, A. T. The "psychological refractory period" and the timing of high-speed performance—a review and a theory. *British Journal of Psychology*, 1952, *43*, 2–19.

Welford, A. T. Evidence of a single-channel decision mechanism limiting performance in a serial reaction task. *Quarterly Journal of Experimental Psychology*, 1959, *11*, 193–210.

Welford, A. T. Single-channel operation in the brain. *Acta Psychologica* 1967, *27*, 5–22.

Welford, A. T. (ed.). *Reaction Times*. London: Academic Press, 1980a.

Welford, A. T. Choice reaction time: Basic concepts. In A. T. Welford (ed.), *Reaction Times*. London: Academic Press, 1980b, pp. 73–128.

Welford, A. T. The single-channel hypothesis. In W. T. Welford (ed.), *Reaction Times*. London: Academic Press, 1980c, pp. 215–252.

Wells, G. R. The influence of stimulus duration on reaction time. *Psychological Monographs*, 1913, *15* (5, Whole No. 66).

Wetherill, G. B. *Sequential Methods in Statistics*. London: Chapman and Hall, 1975.

Whitman, C. P. & E. S. Geller. Prediction outcome, S-R compatibility and choice reaction time. *Journal of Experimental Psychology*, 1971a, *91*, 299–304.

Whitman, C. P. & E. S. Geller. Runs of correct and incorrect predictions as determinants of choice reaction time. *Psychonomic Science*, 1971b, *23*, 421–423.

Wickelgren, W. A. Speed-accuracy tradeoff and information processing dynamics. *Acta Psychologica*, 1977, *41*, 67–85.

Wickelgren, W. A. Wickelgren's neglect. *Acta Psychologica*, 1978, *42*, 81–82.

Wickelgren, W. A. & A. T. Corbett. Associative interference and retrieval dynamics in yes–no recall and recognition. *Journal of Experimental Psychology: Human Learning and Memory*, 1977, *3*, 189–202.

Wilding, J. M. The relation between latency and accuracy in the identification of visual stimuli. II. The effects of sequential dependencies. *Acta Psychologica*, 1971, *35*, 399–413.

Wilding, J. M. Effects of stimulus discriminability on the latency distribution of identification responses. *Acta Psychologica*, 1974, *38*, 483–500.

Williams, J. A. Sequential effects in disjunctive reaction time: Implications for decision models. *Journal of Experimental Psychology*, 1966, *71*, 665–672.

Wood, C. C. & J. R. Jennings. Speed-accuracy trade-off functions in choice reaction time: Experimental designs and computational procedures. *Perception & Psychophysics*, 1976, *9*, 93–102.

Woodrow, H. The reproduction of temporal intervals. *Journal of Experimental Psychology*, 1930, *13*, 473–499.

Woodworth, R. S. *Experimental Psychology*. New York: Holt, 1938.

Woodworth, R. S. & H. Schlosberg. *Experimental Psychology*. New York: Holt, 1954.

Yager, D. & I. Duncan. Signal-detection analysis of luminance generalization in goldfish using latency as a graded response measure. *Perception & Psychophysics*, 1971, *9*, 353–355.

Yellott, J. I., Jr. Correction for guessing in choice reaction time. *Psychonomic Science*, 1967, *8*, 321–322.

Yellott, J. I., Jr. Correction for guessing and the speed-accuracy tradeoff in choice reaction time. *Journal of Mathematical Psychology*, 1971, *8*, 159–199.

Yellott, J. I., Jr. The relationship between Luce's Choice Axiom, Thurstone's theory of comparative judgment, and the double exponential distribution. *Journal of Mathematical Psychology*, 1977, *15*, 109–144.

Author Index

Subject Index